Barcelona

"All you've got to do is decide to go
and the hardest part is over.

So go!"

TONY WHEELER, COFOUNDER – LONELY PLANET

Sally Davies, Catherine Le Nevez, Isabella Noble

Contents

Plan Your Trip   4

Welcome to Barcelona ... 4
Barcelona's Top 10 6
What's New 13
Need to Know 14
First Time Barcelona 16
Top Itineraries 18

If You Like 20
Month By Month 22
With Kids 25
Like a Local 27
For Free 29

Eating 30
Drinking & Nightlife 37
Entertainment 41
Shopping 44
LGBTI Barcelona 48

Explore Barcelona   50

**Neighbourhoods
at a Glance** 52

La Rambla &
Barri Gòtic 54

El Raval 78

La Ribera 90

Barceloneta &
the Waterfront 107

La Sagrada Família
& L'Eixample 125

Gràcia &
Park Güell 158

Camp Nou, Pedralbes
& La Zona Alta 171

Montjuïc, Poble Sec
& Sant Antoni 183

**Day Trips from
Barcelona** 200

Sleeping 212

Understand Barcelona   221

Barcelona Today 222
History 224

Catalan Culture 235
Architecture 237

Picasso, Miró & Dalí 243
Music & Dance 245

Survival Guide   249

Transport 250
Directory A–Z 255

Language 259
Index 267

Barcelona Maps   274

(left) **Tapas p32** Enjoy delicious Catalan cuisine.

(above) **Festes de la Mercè p23** One of the city's many festivals.

(right) **Basílica del Sagrat Cor de Jesús p180** Witness incredible architecture.

Gràcia &
Park Güell
(p158)

Camp Nou, Pedralbes &
La Zona Alta
(p171)

Barceloneta &
the Waterfront
(p107)

La Sagrada Família
& L'Eixample
(p125)

La Ribera
(p90)

La Rambla &
Barri Gòtic
(p54)

El Raval
(p78)

Montjuïc, Poble Sec
& Sant Antoni
(p183)

Welcome to Barcelona

Barcelona is an enchanting seaside city with boundless culture, fabled architecture and a world-class drinking and dining scene.

Architecture of the Ages

Barcelona's architectural treasures span 2000-plus years. Towering temple columns, ancient city walls and subterranean stone corridors provide a window into Roman-era Barcino. Fast forward a thousand years or so to the Middle Ages by taking a stroll through the shadowy lanes of the Gothic quarter, past tranquil plazas and soaring 14th-century cathedrals. In other parts of town bloom the sculptural masterpieces of Modernisme, a mix of ingenious and whimsical creations by Gaudí and his Catalan architectural contemporaries.

A Moveable Feast

The masters of molecular gastronomy – Albert Adrià, Carles Abellan et al – are part of the long and celebrated tradition of Catalan cooking. Simple, flavourful ingredients – seafood, *jamón* (cured ham), market-fresh produce – are transformed into remarkable delicacies. Feast on hearty, rich paella at a table overlooking the sea or step back to the 1920s at an elegant art nouveau dining room. Barcelona's wide-ranging palate adds further complexity: Basque-style tapas bars, Galician seafood taverns, avant-garde Japanese restaurants and sinful chocolate shops are all essential parts of the culinary landscape.

Under the Iberian Sun

The deep blue Mediterranean beckons. Sun-drenched beaches make a fine backdrop to a jog, bike ride or long leisurely stroll along the seaside – followed by a refreshing dip. You can also enjoy the view from out on the water while kayaking, stand-up paddleboarding or taking it easy on a sunset cruise. Looming behind the city, the rolling forest-covered Collserola hills provide a scenic setting for hiking, mountain biking or just admiring the view. Closer to the city centre, hilltop Montjuïc offers endless exploring amid botanic and sculpture gardens, an old castle and first-rate museums with panoramic views at every turn.

Twenty-Four-Hour Party People

The night holds limitless possibilities in Barcelona. Start with sunset drinks on a panoramic terrace or dig your heels in the sand at a rustic beachside *chiringuito* (bar). As darkness falls, live music transforms the city: the rapid-fire rhythms of flamenco, brassy jazz spilling out of basements, and hands-in-the-air indie-rock at vintage concert halls. Towards midnight the bars fill. Take your pick from old-school taverns adorned with 19th-century murals, plush lounges in lamp-lit medieval chambers or boisterous *cava* bars. If you're still standing at 3am, hit the clubs and explore Barcelona's unabashed wild side.

ALEXANDER SPATARI/GETTY IMAGES ©

Why I Love Barcelona

By Sally Davies, Writer

I've lived all over Spain, and there is no part that does not have something unique to offer, but when I first came to Barcelona I was charmed not only by its medieval splendour, endless beaches and spectacular architecture – all of which is amply documented – but by its countless eccentricities. By its fibreglass giants, who stroll the streets seemingly regardless of the occasion. By its fire-breathing dragons, skittering perilously through the crowds. By its peculiar language, its folk dancing, its human castles. And somehow, without ever really meaning to, I found I had made it my home.

For more about our writers, see p304

Above: Barri Gòtic laneway (p54)

Barcelona's
Top 10

1

La Sagrada Família (p127)

1 One of Barcelona's icons, this Modernista masterpiece remains a work in progress more than 90 years after the death of its creator, Antoni Gaudí. Fanciful and profound, inspired by nature and barely restrained by the Gothic style, Barcelona's quirky temple soars skyward with a playful majesty. Stepping through its sculpted portals is like walking into a fairy tale, where a forest of columns branches towards the ceiling and light shimmers through brilliant stained-glass windows. Rich with beautifully wrought detail and packed with symbolism, the basilica invites hours of contemplation.

La Sagrada Família & L'Eixample

New Catalan Cuisine (p31)

2 Barcelona's most celebrated chefs blend traditional Catalan recipes with new cooking techniques to create deliciously inventive masterpieces. Leading the way are Albert Adrià, the molecular gastronomy whizz behind a growing empire of restaurants, and Carles Abellan, who elevated the humble tapas to high art in his restaurants. The result: Barcelona has become one of the world's great culinary destinations. No matter where you go in the city, you won't be far from a memorable meal. And the critics agree: the city has more than 20 Michelin-starred restaurants.

Eating

Museu Picasso (p92)

3 For a portrait of the artist as a young man, head to the Museu Picasso, which showcases perhaps the world's best collection of the master's early work. Picasso lived in Barcelona between the ages of 15 and 23, and elements of the city undoubtedly influenced his work, from the colourful but simply painted frescoes hanging in the Museu Nacional d'Art de Catalunya to the imaginative *trencadís*-style mosaics (pre-Cubist some say) of Gaudí. The museum's setting – inside five contiguous medieval mansions – adds to the appeal.

⊙ *La Ribera*

Modernista Architecture (p150)

4 Few cities are defined by their architecture to quite the same extent as Barcelona. The weird and wonderful undulations of Antoni Gaudí's creations are echoed in countless Modernista flights of fancy across the city. You'll find shimmering mosaics, wild details (in stained glass, iron and ceramic) and sculptural elements that reference nature, mythology and medieval days. Gateway to these astonishing architectural works is L'Eixample, which was a blank canvas for some of Spain's finest buildings in the late 19th and early 20th centuries. COLÒNIA GÜELL (P189)

⊙ *Antoni Gaudí & Modernisme*

Camp Nou (p173)

5 For the sports-minded, little can compete with the spectacle of a match at FC Barcelona's massive football stadium. With a loyal fan base and an incredibly gifted team led by superstar Lionel Messi, Camp Nou always hosts a good show; even if you can't make it to a game, it's still worth visiting. The 'Camp Nou Experience' is an interactive museum and stadium tour that takes you through the locker rooms and out on to the pitch – hallowed ground for many Catalans.

🏃 *Camp Nou, Pedralbes & La Zona Alta*

Mercat de la Boqueria *(p80)*

6 This temple of temptation is one of Europe's greatest permanent produce markets. Restaurant chefs, home cooks, office workers and tourists stroll amid the endless bounty of glistening fruits and vegetables, gleaming fish counters, dangling rolls of smoked meats, pyramids of pungent cheeses, barrels of olives and marinated peppers, and chocolate truffles and other sweets. Dotted through the market are a handful of popular tapas bars serving up delectable morsels. There's almost always a queue, but it's well worth the wait.

🔒 *El Raval*

Strolling La Rambla *(p56)*

7 Sure it's the most touristy spot in town, but you can't come to Barcelona and not take the 1.2km stroll down the famous pedestrian boulevard that stretches towards the sea. It's pure sensory overload – with a parade of people amid open-air cafes, fragrant flower stands, a much-overlooked mosaic by Miró and the rather surreal human sculptures. Key venues line both sides of the street, including the elegant Gran Teatre del Liceu, the sprawling Mercat de la Boqueria and several major galleries.

👁 *La Rambla & Barri Gòtic*

La Catedral *(p60)*

8 A masterpiece of Catalan Gothic architecture, La Catedral is rightly one of the first stops on any visit to the Ciutat Vella (Old City). You can wander wide-eyed through the shadow-filled interior, with a dozen well-concealed chapels, an eerie crypt and a curious garden-style cloister that's home to 13 geese (which are deeply connected with the mythology of Barcelona's co-patron saint, Santa Eulàlia). Outside, there's always entertainment afoot, from *sardana* (Catalonia's national folk dance) on weekends to periodic processions and open-air markets, and street musicians are never far from the scene.

⦿ *La Rambla & Barri Gòtic*

Nightlife in Sant Antoni *(p196)*

9 Barcelona is a city known for reinvention, but none of its neighbourhoods has seen a regeneration as dramatic as that of the unremarkable grid of streets around the splendid old Mercat Sant Antoni. It started with the tentative opening of a couple of hip cafes on Carrer del Parlament, but over the last couple of years this has bloomed into a lively strip of bars and restaurants, with an influx of hipster pleasure-seekers and entrepreneurs, and this in turn has kick-started a slew of openings in surrounding streets. BAR CALDERS (P197)

🍷 *Montjuïc, Poble Sec & Sant Antoni*

Magical Montjuïc *(p183)*

10 When the temperature rises, head up the hill to Montjuïc for fresh air and breathtaking views over the city, best enjoyed from the dizzy heights of a cable car. At any time of year it makes for a great day out, with endless parkland, themed gardens and museums to suit every taste, whether your fire is lit by sport, art or ancient remains. If you have kids in tow, the kitsch wonderland of the Poble Espanyol is a must. CASTELL DE MONTJUÏC (P188)

👁 *Montjuïc, Poble Sec & Sant Antoni*

What's New

Food Trucks

The city's appetite for street food is apparently insatiable, and regular pop-up food markets now include Eat Street (http://eatstreet.barcelona), All Those (www.allthose.org) and Van Van (www.vanvanmarket.com).

Gaudí's Hidden Townhouse

In a quiet backstreet of Gràcia, the spectacular facade of Gaudí's Mudéjar-inspired Casa Vicens has long been an undervisited gem, but this changed at the end of 2017, when the building opened to the public for the first time. (p162)

Luxury with Pedigree

Soho House, London's famous member's club, has opened a bolt-hole in Barcelona, where regular punters can rub elbows with celebs and creative types in the stunning bar area. (p215)

Craft Makers

Hard on the heels of the gin craze, microbreweries have arrived in Barcelona, bringing an abundance of craft beer bars in their wake. You're never far from a unique IPA, no matter where you roam.

Three-Star Dining

Barcelona finally has a restaurant with three Michelin stars, in the shape of Lasarte, on the Passeig de Gràcia. For the full, no-expense-spared extravaganza, order the tasting menu. (p138)

Surfing with a Paddle

The increasingly popular sport for beach goers is gliding along on a stand-up paddleboard (SUP). Outfitters in Barceloneta hire out gear, and you can take a lesson if you've never tried.

The Meat-Free Revolution

Vegetarians and mindful eaters need not give Barcelona a pass when planning their next holiday. The city has seen an explosion of healthy animal-free eateries in recent years – and even vegan clothing shops. (p169)

Tapas Tours

Food and wine tours are a great – and leisurely – way to see the city and chat with a local at the same time. Some of the most knowledgeable guides are at Devour (www.devourbarcelonafoodtours.com), which has options for various budgets and time frames.

Poblenou Renaissance

This formerly industrial 'hood is on the make, with new galleries, colourful shops and restaurants forming the intersection for the creative tech and design folk who are increasingly moving here.

Adrià's Culinary Kingdom

Famed chef Albert Adrià now runs six celebrated restaurants all within strolling distance of one another in Sant Antoni. His latest, Enigma, opened in 2017 and is already considered one of the city's best. (p196)

For more recommendations and reviews, see **lonelyplanet.com/spain/barcelona**

Need to Know

For more information, see Survival Guide (p249)

Currency
Euro (€)

Languages
Spanish, Catalan

Visas
Generally not required for stays of up to 90 days per 180 days (visas are not required at all for members of EU or Schengen countries). Some nationalities need a Schengen visa.

Money
ATMs are widely available (La Rambla has many). Credit cards are accepted in most hotels, shops and restaurants.

Mobile Phones
Local SIM cards can be used in unlocked phones. Other phones must be set to roaming.

Time
Central European Time (GMT/ UTC plus one hour).

Tourist Information
Oficina d'Informació de Turisme de Barcelona (☑93 285 38 34; www.barcelona turisme.com; Plaça de Catalunya 17-S, underground; ☺8.30am-9pm; ⓜCatalunya) Provides maps, sights information, tours, concert and events tickets, and last-minute accommodation.

Daily Costs

Budget:
Less than €60
→ Dorm bed: €17–28
→ Set lunch: from €11
→ Bicycle hire per hour: €5

Midrange:
€60–200
→ Standard double room: €80–140
→ Two-course dinner with wine for two: €50
→ Walking and guided tours: €15–25

Top end:
More than €200
→ Double room in boutique and luxury hotels: €200 and up
→ Three-course meal at top restaurants per person: €80
→ Concert tickets to Palau de la Música Catalana: around €40

Advance Planning
Three months before Book accommodation and reserve a table at a top restaurant.

One month before Check out reviews for theatre and live music, and book tickets.

One week before Browse the latest nightlife listings, art exhibitions and other events to attend while in town. Reserve spa visits and organised tours.

A few days before Check the weather forecast.

Useful Websites
Barcelona (www.bcn.cat) Town hall's official site with plenty of links.

Barcelona Turisme (www. barcelonaturisme.com) City's official tourism website.

Lonely Planet (www.lonely planet.com/barcelona) Destination information, hotel bookings, traveller forum and more.

BCN Mes (www.bcnmes.com) Trilingual monthly mag of culture, food, art and more.

Spotted by Locals (www. spottedbylocals.com) Insider tips.

WHEN TO GO

Summer (July and August) is peak tourist season, when crowds swarm the city – and its beaches. For pleasant weather, come in late spring (May).

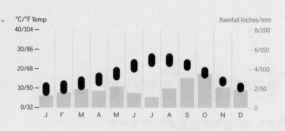

Arriving in Barcelona

El Prat airport Frequent *aerobúses* make the 35-minute run into town (€5.90) from 6am to 1am. Taxis cost around €26.

Estació Sants Long-distance trains arrive at this large station near the centre of town, which is linked by metro to other parts of the city.

Estació del Nord Barcelona's long-haul bus station is located in L'Eixample, about 1.5km northeast of Plaça de Catalunya, and is a short walk from the Arc de Triomf metro station.

Girona-Costa Brava airport The 'Barcelona Bus' operated by Sagalés (one way/return €16/25, 1½ hours) is timed with Ryanair flights and goes direct to Barcelona's Estació del Nord.

Reus airport Buses operated by Hispano-Igualadina (one way/return €16/25, 1½ hours) are timed with Ryanair flights and go direct to Barcelona's Estació Sants.

For much more on **arrival** see p250

Getting Around

Barcelona has abundant options for getting around town. The excellent metro can get you most places, with buses and trams filling in the gaps. Taxis are the best option late at night.

Metro The most convenient option. Runs 5am to midnight Sunday to Thursday, till 2am on Friday and 24 hours on Saturday. Targeta T-10 (10-ride passes; €10.20) are the best value; otherwise, it's €2.20 per ride.

Bus A hop-on, hop-off Bus Turístic (p149), from Plaça de Catalunya, is handy for those wanting to see the city's highlights in one or two days.

Taxi You can hail taxis on the street (try La Rambla, Via Laietana, Plaça de Catalunya and Passeig de Gràcia) or at taxi stands.

On foot To explore the old city, all you need is a good pair of walking shoes.

For much more on **getting around** see p251

Sleeping

Barcelona has a wide range of sleeping options, from inexpensive hostels hidden in the old quarter to luxury hotels overlooking the waterfront. The small-scale B&B-style apartment rentals scattered around the city are a good-value choice. Wherever you stay, it's wise to book ahead. If you plan to travel around holidays such as Christmas, New Year's Eve or Easter, or in summer, reserve a room a few months ahead of time.

Useful Websites

➡ **Lonely Planet** (www.lonelyplanet.com/barcelona) Neighbourhood profiles, plus extensive listings of hotels, hostels, guesthouses and apartments.

➡ **Oh Barcelona** (www.oh-barcelona.com) Hotel and apartment listings, plus tips on deciding where to stay.

➡ **Barcelona Bed and Breakfasts** (www.barcelonabedandbreakfasts.com) Listings of low-key, oft-overlooked lodging options.

For much more on **sleeping** see p212

First Time Barcelona

For more information, see Survival Guide (p249)

Checklist

➡ Check all airline flight prices before booking a ticket.

➡ Find out if you can use your phone in Spain and ask about roaming charges.

➡ Book your first night's accommodation to ensure an easy start to your stay.

➡ Check the calendar to figure out which festivals to attend or avoid.

➡ Organise travel insurance.

What to Pack

➡ Passport and/or national ID card (EU citizens)

➡ Driving licence

➡ Phrasebook

➡ Money belt

➡ Mobile phone (and charger)

➡ Earplugs for noisy weekend nights

➡ Walking shoes

➡ Bathing suit

➡ Swim towel

➡ Sunglasses

➡ Sunscreen

➡ Hat

➡ Reading material (try pageturners by Carlos Ruiz Zafón or Manuel Vázquez Montalbán)

➡ Rain jacket or umbrella

Top Tips for Your Trip

➡ Plan your visiting times to avoid the worst of the crowds. Go early in the morning or late in the day for the top Gaudí sites and the Museu Picasso.

➡ When possible, book tickets online. This will allow you to bypass the queues and is often cheaper.

➡ Be mindful of siesta time (generally 1pm to 4pm). Plan your shopping for mornings or early evenings.

➡ Travel smart; keep valuables tucked away and out of sight. Pickpocketing is a concern in busy, touristy areas.

➡ Save time and money on public transport by purchasing 10-ride passes (T-10), which can be used on the metro, buses and funicular.

➡ Take advantage of multi-course lunch specials. These are offered by many restaurants, and are often great value.

What to Wear

In Barcelona just about anything goes, and you'll rarely feel uncomfortable because of what you're wearing. That said, Catalans are fairly fashion conscious and well dressed. Most folks dress smart casual, with something perhaps a bit dressier if going somewhere special for the evening.

If you're planning on clubbing, bring something stylish (sandals or sneakers are a no-go). Meanwhile, La Catedral advertises a policy of no admittance to those in sleeveless tops and shorts. The rule isn't always enforced, but it's best not to take the risk.

Be Forewarned

➡ Violent crime is rare in Barcelona, but petty crime (bagsnatching, pickpocketing) is a major problem.

➡ You're at your most vulnerable when dragging around luggage to or from your hotel; make sure you know your route before arriving.

➡ Be mindful of your belongings, particularly in crowded areas.

➡ Avoid walking around El Raval and the southern end of La Rambla late at night.

➡ Don't wander down empty city streets at night. When in doubt, take a taxi.

➡ Take nothing of value to the beach and don't leave anything unattended.

Money

Barcelona abounds with banks, many of which have ATMs. They are in plentiful supply around Plaça de Catalunya, and along Via Laietana and La Rambla. Most ATMs allow you to use international debit or credit cards to withdraw money in euros. There is usually a charge (around 1.5% to 2%) on ATM cash withdrawals when abroad.

Major cards such as Visa, MasterCard, Maestro and Cirrus are accepted throughout the city. They can be used in many hotels, restaurants and shops, although there may be a minimum purchase requirement of €5 or €10.

When paying with a credit card, a photo ID is often required, even for chip cards where you're required to enter your PIN (for US travellers without chip cards, just indicate that you'll give a signature).

For more information, see p256.

Taxes & Refunds

Value-added tax (VAT) is a 21% sales tax levied on most goods and services. For restaurants and hotels it's 10%. Most restaurants include VAT in their prices; it's usually included in hotel room prices, too, but be sure to ask when booking.

Tipping

➡ **Restaurants** Catalans typically leave 5% or less at restaurants. Leave more for exceptionally good service.

➡ **Taxis** Optional, but most locals round up to the nearest euro.

➡ **Bars** It's rare to leave a tip in bars, though a bit of small change is always appreciated.

A bar in Gràcia

Etiquette

Barcelona is fairly relaxed with it comes to etiquette. A few basics to remember:

➡ **Greetings** Catalans, like other Spaniards, usually greet friends and strangers alike with a kiss on both cheeks, although two males rarely do this. Foreigners may be excused.

➡ **Eating and drinking** Waiters won't expect you to thank them every time they bring you something, but in more casual restaurants and bars they will expect you to keep your cutlery between courses.

➡ **Visiting churches** It is considered disrespectful to visit churches as a tourist during Mass and other worship services. Taking photos at such times is a definite no-no.

➡ **Escalators** Always stand on the right to let people pass, especially when using the metro.

Language

English is widely spoken in Barcelona. Even Catalans with only a few English words are generally happy to try them out. Learning a little Spanish before you come will greatly enhance your experience, not least in your ability to converse with locals. It's even better if you can learn some Catalan.

English signage is available at most museums (though not all). Many restaurants have English-language menus, though simpler places may have them only in Spanish and Catalan.

Top Itineraries

Day One

La Rambla & Barri Gòtic (p54)

 On day one spend the morning exploring the narrow medieval lanes of the Barri Gòtic. Have a peek inside **La Catedral** – not missing its geese-filled cloister – and stroll through the picturesque squares of **Plaça de Sant Josep Oriol** and **Plaça Reial**. Discover Barcelona's ancient roots in the fascinating **Museu d'Història de Barcelona**. Before lunch, have a wander down La Rambla to take in the passing people parade.

> ✕ **Lunch** The beautifully designed Federal (p69) whips up deliciously healthy fare.

La Ribera (p90)

 In the afternoon, wander over to La Ribera, which is packed with architectural treasures. Have a look inside the majestic **Basílica de Santa Maria del Mar**. At the **Museu Picasso**, beautifully set inside conjoined medieval mansions, you can spend a few hours taking in the early works of one of the great artists of the 20th century.

> ✕ **Dinner** Sample tapas with global accents at creative El Atril (p101).

La Ribera (p90)

☾ Before having a late dinner (as is the custom in Spain), catch a show inside the **Palau de la Música Catalana**, one of the great Modernista masterpieces of Barcelona. Afterwards, end the night with tropically infused libations at candlelit **Rubí**.

Day Two

L'Eixample (p125)

 On day two start with a morning visit to **La Sagrada Família**, Gaudí's wondrous work in progress. It's worth paying a little extra for a guided tour (or audioguide) for a deeper understanding of Barcelona's most famous sight.

> ✕ **Lunch** Celebrated Disfrutar (p138) spreads an imaginative Catalan feast.

L'Eixample (p125)

☼ After lunch, explore more of the great Modernista buildings by taking a stroll down L'Eixample's **Passeig de Gràcia**. Have a look at the three most famous buildings that make up the **Manzana de la Discòrdia**. Then visit one of Gaudí's house museums on the street – either **Casa Batlló** or **La Pedrera** further up the avenue.

> ✕ **Dinner** Enjoy excellent wines and tasty sharing plates at Viblioteca (p167).

Camp Nou, Pedralbes & La Zona Alta (p171)

☾ In the evening catch a football match at **Camp Nou**, home of the top-ranked FC Barcelona. Amid the roar of the crowds, prepare for a serious adrenaline rush, especially if Barça is playing arch-rival Real Madrid. Afterwards explore lesser-known gems in the area, like the plaza-side **El Maravillas** (great for tapas and drinks) or **Bangkok Cafe**, serving Barcelona's best Thai dishes.

Day Three

Barceloneta & the Waterfront (p107)

 On your third day in Barcelona it's time to take in the lovely Mediterranean. Start the morning with a stroll, jog or bike ride along the waterfront. Beach-facing restaurants and cafes provide refreshment along the way.

> **Lunch** Go early to snag a table at tiny La Cova Fumada (p114).

Barceloneta & the Waterfront (p107)

 Stroll through Barceloneta, stopping for a peek inside the **Mercat de la Barceloneta** and for pastries at **Baluard**. Afterwards, visit the **Museu d'Història de Catalunya** and peel back the centuries on an interactive journey into Catalan history.

> **Dinner** La Vinateria del Call (p70) has a magical setting in medieval El Call.

La Rambla & Barri Gòtic (p54)

At night catch a live band inside the Gothic quarter. **Harlem Jazz Club** and **Jamboree** are good bets for jazz and world music. If you still have energy, check out a few bars more off the beaten track, like **L'Ascensor**, a cosy drinking den with nicely mixed cocktails and a more grown-up crowd than other parts of Barri Gòtic.

Day Four

Montjuïc (p183)

 Start the day with a scenic cable-car ride up to Montjuïc, followed by a stroll past flower and sculpture gardens to the **Museu Nacional d'Art de Catalunya**. Take in the magnificent Romanesque frescos, vivid Gothic paintings and works by 17th-century Spanish masters.

> **Lunch** Pepa Tomate (p165) is a neighbourhood charmer on a peaceful square.

Gràcia (p158)

After getting a taste of Montjuïc, hop on the metro up to Gràcia and wander through its enchanting village-like streets. Cafes, bookshops and vintage shops all make for some worthwhile exploring. The bars surrounding its plazas come to life around sundown.

> **Dinner** Order the excellent-value tasting menu from La Panxa del Bisbe (p165).

El Raval (p78)

Take in the bohemian side of Barcelona in El Raval. Browse record shops and vintage stores, check out a live band at the **Jazz Sí Club**, or watch an indie feature at the **Filmoteca de Catalunya**. Finish the night over a few housemade vermouths at **La Confitería**, or at dance favourite **Moog** for something livelier.

If You Like...

Markets

Els Encants Vells Sprawling flea market with plenty of treasures and trash on the edge of Poblenou. (p122)

Mercat de la Boqueria One of Europe's largest food markets, with tempting delicacies, plus tapas bars at the back. (p80)

Mercat de Sant Antoni A massive but largely tourist-free food market that also hosts a flea market on Sunday. (p199)

Mercat de Santa Caterina La Ribera's bountiful food market, with its wavy roof and archaeological fragments from the 1400s. (p96)

Parks & Gardens

Parc de la Ciutadella Pretty landscaped grounds with dramatic fountain, curious sculptures, the Catalan parliament building and a zoo. (p96)

Park Güell Green wonderland with fine views over the city, and surreal sculptural architecture courtesy of Gaudí. (p160)

Jardí Botànic One of Montjuïc's many lush gardens, this one with Mediterranean flora and plants from similar climates. (p188)

Parc de la Creueta del Coll Near Park Güell, this is a family favourite with pool, snack bar and trails. (p175)

Jardins del Laberint d'Horta Picturesque gardens with artificial lake and waterfalls and a challenging labyrinth, outside the city centre. (p179)

The labyrinth at Jardins del Laberint d'Horta (p179)

Museums

Museu d'Història de Barcelona Stroll over Roman-era Barcino ruins, then see fine Catalan Gothic architecture inside a former royal palace. (p65)

CosmoCaixa Fun science museum that's a hit with families – especially its recreated patch of Amazonian rainforest. (p176)

Museu-Monestir de Pedralbes Peaceful old convent with a 14th-century cloister and old-world religious artwork. (p174)

Museu Blau Spacious natural history and science museum with interactive exhibits and huge animal collection – dinosaurs included. (p113)

Art & Design

Fundació Joan Miró Temple to the great artist, complete with outdoor sculpture gardens. (p185)

Fundació Antoni Tàpies Fascinating collection of a great Catalan artist set in a Modernista building. (p132)

Centre de Cultura Contemporània de Barcelona A must for art lovers, the CCCB hosts excellent cutting-edge exhibitions. (p83)

Museu d'Art Contemporani de Barcelona Packed collection of 20th-century artwork in a modern Richard Meier–designed building. (p81)

Museu Nacional d'Art de Catalunya (MNAC) Stunning collection of Romanesque art dating back 900 years. (p186)

CaixaForum Inside a modernist building designed by Puig i Cadafalch, this place hosts fantastic exhibitions. (p188)

Contemporary Architecture

Museu del Disseny de Barcelona Barcelona's design museum lies inside this geometrical edifice that's also a symbol of Poblenou's rebirth. (p112)

Torre Glòries Jean Nouvel's striking cucumber-shaped tower dominates the new high-tech zone of 22@. (p114)

Teatre Nacional de Catalunya This stately theatre is a perfect design medley of Ancient Greece with high modernism. (p122)

Edifici Fòrum Blue triangular building by Herzog & de Meuron that is both organic and weirdly futuristic. (p114)

Panoramic Views

Bunkers del Carmel Gaze 360-degrees from a scruffy hillside that was once an anti-aircraft battery. (p163)

Basílica del Sagrat Cor de Jesús It's worth the trip to the top of Tibidabo for the mesmerising view. (p180)

Teleférico del Puerto Old-fashioned cable car (with modern cables, we're told) affording sublime views from its dangling trajectory. (p252)

Mirablau Well-known Mirablau, at the foot of Tibidabo, has magnificent views out over the city. (p180)

Parc de Collserola Vast park with countless vistas (and wildlife, including roaming boars, to boot). (p180)

Staying Out Late

Guzzo Convivial drinking den in El Born with a funk-loving DJ owner. (p103)

For more top Barcelona spots, see the following:
➡ Eating (p30)
➡ Drinking & Nightlife (p37)
➡ Entertainment (p41)
➡ Shopping (p44)
➡ Gay & Lesbian Barcelona (p48)

Moog Small, fun and relatively attitude-free downtown club that's great for dancing. (p87)

Sor Rita Kitsch-filled extravaganza with a fun, festive crowd. (p72)

La Confitería A fin-de-siècle mural-covered bar that was once a confectioner's shop. (p86)

Marula Cafè Small, eclectic, dance-loving space in the Barri Gòtic with serious penchant for funk and soul. (p73)

Fashion

La Manual Alpargatera Birthplace of espadrilles, and world's best place to buy the iconic Catalan rope-soled canvas shoes. (p76)

Lady Loquita One of many hip boutiques in Gràcia selling womenswear crafted by local designers. (p169)

L'Arca Treasure chest of high-end vintage clothes dating back to the 1920s. (p76)

L'Illa Diagonal Top shopping mall for designer fashion; also a good food court on the lower level. (p182)

Adolfo Domínguez Browse for beautifully made men's and women's ready-to-wear at this elegant Passeig de Gràcia boutique. (p148)

Bagués-Masriera Beautifully crafted jewellery in the architecturally stunning Casa Amatller. (p149)

Month By Month

TOP EVENTS

Festes de Santa Eulàlia, February

Primavera Sound, May

Festival del Grec, July

Festa Major de Gràcia, August

Festes de la Mercè, September

January

Barcelonins head to the Pyrenees for action on the ski slopes, while others simply enjoy a bit of post-holiday downtime (school holidays go to around 8 January).

🎭 Reis (Reyes)

On 5 January, the day before Epifanía (Epiphany), children delight in the Cavalcada dels Reis Mags (Parade of the Three Kings), a colourful parade of floats and music, spreading bonhomie and boiled sweets in equal measure.

February

Often the coldest month in Barcelona, February sees few visitors. Nonetheless, some of the first big festivals kick off, with abundant Catalan merriment amid the wintry gloom.

🎭 Carnestoltes (Carnaval)

Celebrated in February or March, the carnival (http://lameva.barcelona.cat/carnaval) involves several days of fancy-dress balls, merrymaking and fireworks, ending on the Tuesday before Ash Wednesday. Over 30 parades happen around town on the weekend. Down in Sitges a wilder version takes place.

🎭 Festes de Santa Eulàlia

Around 12 February this big winter fest (http://lameva.barcelona.cat/santaeulalia) celebrates Barcelona's first patron saint with a week of cultural events, including parades of *gegants* (giants), open-air art installations, theatre, *correfocs* (fire runs) and *castells* (human castles).

April

Spring arrives with a flourish, complete with wildflowers blooming in the countryside, Easter revelry and school holidays, although April showers can dampen spirits. Book well ahead if coming around Easter.

🎭 Dia de Sant Jordi

Catalonia honours its patron saint, Sant Jordi (St George), on 23 April. Traditionally men and women exchange roses and books – and La Rambla and Plaça de Sant Jaume fill with book and flower stalls.

May

With sunny pleasant days and clear skies, May can be one of the best times to visit Barcelona. The city slowly gears up for summer with the opening of the *chiringuitos* (beach bars).

🎭 L'Ou Com Balla

On Corpus Christi (late May or June), L'Ou com Balla (the Dancing Egg) bobs on top of flower-festooned fountains around the city. There's also an early evening procession from La Catedral and traditional Catalan folk dancing.

🎭 Festa de Sant Ponç

To commemorate the patron saint of beekeepers and herbalists, on 11 May Carrer de l'Hospital in El Raval is taken over by a long market selling artisan honey, herbs and more.

☆ Primavera Sound

For one week in late May or early June, the open-air Parc del Fòrum stages an all-star line-up (www.primavera sound.com) of international bands and DJs. There are also associated concerts around town, including free open-air events at the Parc de la Ciutadella and the Passeig Lluís Companys.

☆ Ciutat Flamenco

One of the best occasions to see great flamenco in Barcelona, this concentrated festival (ciutatflamenco.com) is held over four days in May at the Teatre Mercat De Les Flors and other venues.

June

Tourist numbers are soaring as Barcelona plunges into summer. Live music festivals and open-air events give the month a festive air.

🎆 Festival Pedralbes

This summertime fest (www.festivalpedralbes.com) takes place in lovely gardens and stages big-name performers – many of them old-timers (Beach Boys, Sting, Blondie) from mid-June to early July.

🎆 La Revetlla de Sant Joan

On 23 June locals hit the streets or hold parties at home to celebrate the Revetlla de Sant Joan (St John's Night), which involves drinking, dancing, bonfires and fireworks. In Spanish, it's called 'Verbenas de Sant Joan'.

☆ Pride Barcelona

The Barcelona Gay Pride festival (www.pridebarcelona.

org) is a week of celebrations held late June or early July with a crammed program of culture and concerts, along with the traditional Gay Pride march on Sunday.

☆ Sónar

Usually held in mid-June, Sónar (www.sonar.es) is Barcelona's massive celebration of electronic music and technology, with concerts, DJs, exhibitions, sound labs, record fairs and urban art.

July

Prices are high and it's peak tourist season, but it's a lively time to be in the city, with sun-filled beach days, open-air dining and outdoor concerts.

☆ Festival del Grec

The major cultural event of the summer is a month-long fest (http://grec.bcn.cat) with dozens of theatre, dance and music performances held around town, including at the Teatre Grec amphitheatre on Montjuïc, from which the festival takes its name.

August

The heat index soars; barcelonins leave the city in droves for summer holidays, as huge numbers of tourists arrive. It's a great time to hit the beach.

🎆 Festa Major de Gràcia

Locals compete for the most elaborately decorated street in this popular weeklong Gràcia festival (www.festamajordegracia.org) held around 15 August. The fest also features free outdoor concerts, street fairs and other events.

🎆 Festes de Sant Roc

For four days in mid-August, Plaça Nova in the Barri Gòtic becomes the scene of parades, the *correfoc* (fire runs), a market, traditional music and magic shows for kids.

September

After a month off, barcelonins return to work, although several major festivals provide ample amusement. Temperatures stay warm through September, making for fine beach days.

🎆 Festa Major de Sants

The district of Sants hosts a five-day fest (www.festamajordesants.net) with concerts, outdoor dance parties, *correfocs* (fire runs) and elaborately decorated streets.

🎆 Diada Nacional de Catalunya

Catalonia's national day curiously commemorates Barcelona's surrender on 11 September 1714 to the Bourbon monarchy of Spain, at the conclusion of the War of the Spanish Succession.

🎆 Festes de la Mercè

Barcelona's co-patron saint is celebrated with fervour in this massive five-day fest (www.bcn.cat/merce). The city stages sporting events, free concerts, dance performances, human towers of *castellers,* parades of *gegants* and a fiery *correfoc* (fire run).

🎆 Festa Major de la Barceloneta

This big September celebration in Barcelona honours

the local patron saint, Sant Miquel, on 29 September. It lasts about a week and involves plenty of dancing and drinking, especially on the beach.

November

Cooler days and nights arrive in Barcelona, along with occasional days of rain and overcast skies. For beating the crowds (and higher summer prices), though, it's an excellent month to visit.

✲✲ Fira de Santa Llúcia

Held from late November to Christmas, this holiday market (http://en.firadesantallucia.cat) has hundreds of stalls selling all manner of Christmas decorations and gifts – including the infamous Catalan Nativity scene character, the *caganer* (the crapper).

December

As winter returns *barcelonins* gear up for Christmas, and the city is festooned with colourful decorations. Relatively few visitors arrive, at least until Christmas, when the city fills with holidaying out-of-towners.

☆ New Year's Eve

On 31 December, the fountains of Montjuïc (Font Màgica) take centre stage for the biggest celebration in town. Crowds line up along Avinguda Reina Maria Cristina to watch a theatrical procession and audiovisual performance (plus *castells*), followed by fireworks at midnight.

(Top) A *castell* at Diada Nacional de Catalunya (p23)
(Bottom) Festa Major de Gràcia (p23)

UB-FOTO/SHUTTERSTOCK ©

MARCIN D/500PX ©

With Kids

Barcelona is great for older kids and teens – the Mediterranean attitude means they are included in many seemingly adult activities, like eating late meals at bars or restaurants. Babies will love the welcoming Mediterranean culture, and toddlers will be showered with attention.

ple Espanyol (p189)

VENIAMIN KRASKOV/SHUTTERSTOCK ©

Dining Out With Kids

Barcelona – and Spain in general – is super-friendly when it comes to eating with children. Locals take their kids out all the time and don't worry too much about keeping them up late, so going out to eat or to sip a beer on a terrace on a summer evening needn't mean leaving children with minders – and they're bound to strike up a friendship or two.

Spanish kids tend to eat the Mediterranean offerings enjoyed by their parents, but many restaurants have children's menus that serve up burgers, pizzas, tomato-sauce pasta and the like. Good local – and childproof – options commonly found on tapas menus are the *tortilla de patatas* (potato omelette) or *croquetas de jamón* (croquettes with ham).

Best Kid-Friendly Eateries

La Nena
Fantastic for chocolate and all manner of sweet things, this cafe (p163) has a play area, and toys and books in a corner.

Bar del Convent
With a safe, traffic-free terrace to play in, and a raft of games and toys indoors, the Convent (p103) is a great all-weather option.

Filferro
Sit outside this tapas and snack bar (p114) and enjoy the Mediterranean breeze,

---

NEED TO KNOW

➡ **Babysitting** Get a babysitter at Tender Loving Canguros (https://tlcanguros.wordpress.com) or **5 Serveis** (✆93 412 56 76; www.5serveis.com; Carrer de Pelai 50; Ⓜ Catalunya).

➡ **Supplies** Nappies (diapers), dummies, creams and formula can be bought at any of the city's many pharmacies. Nappies are cheaper in supermarkets.

➡ **Metro** Barcelona's metro is accessible and great for families with pushchairs. Be mindful of pickpockets.

➡ **Accessibility** The narrow streets of the Ciutat Vella, with their unpredictable traffic and cobbled streets, are less buggy-friendly than the rest of Barcelona.

while junior busies about in the adjacent playground.

Pepa Tomate

With crayons provided and a tiny playground near the plaza-side tables, this fun cafe (p165) is a winner.

Granja La Pallaresa

Along a street famed for its chocolate cafes, this place (p73) is a favourite for crispy churros dipped in steaming chocolate.

Best Parks & Open Spaces

Parc de la Ciutadella

This park (p96) has a zoo, a pond and a playground that gets a bunch of fun toys out in the morning and after 4pm; it's also a great place to meet other parents.

Parc d'Atraccions

This fabulous funfair (p180) on top of Tibidabo is excellent for adrenaline-loving kids and grown-ups.

Parc de la Creueta del Coll

An excellent park (p175) for its splashing pool, swings and snack bar.

Font Màgica

The light show (p188) is guaranteed to make the little ones shout 'Again!'.

Parc de Collserola

A huge park (p180) in the hills that's attractive to families for its trails and picnicking possibilities.

Best Kid-Friendly Museums

CosmoCaixa

A fantastic science museum (p176) whose interactive displays fascinate kids of all ages.

Museu de la Xocolata

This museum (p97) is all about chocolate – need we say more? Don't miss the chocolate model-making sessions for kids.

Zoo de Barcelona

You'll find all the animals you can think of in this relatively small zoo (p97), from yawning hippos, to spluttering elephants and frowning gorillas. Big cats and monkeys are here too.

L'Aquàrium

This a fantastic aquarium (p111), one of Europe's largest, with tank after tank of glimmering, colourful fish. Seeing sharks gliding overhead is bound to be a lasting memory for all the family!

Poble Espanyol

Kids and parents can enjoy going through a mini Spain (p189) together; there are also special kid-oriented games and quests.

Best Ways to See the City

By Bike

Barcelona has tonnes of bike tours and outlets that hire out bicycles with little trolleys in the front for transporting the little ones, including Trixi (p77).

On Segway

Parents, older kids and teens can mount these futuristic-looking vehicles and scoot around town with Segway Fun (p77).

By Bus

Barcelona's bus tours (p252) are great for older kids – hop on, climb up to the open top floor and see the views.

By Cable Car

Travel to Montjuïc from Barceloneta beach through the air. The Transbordador Aeri (p252) is bound to be loved by all ages.

Best Shopping

Hibernian

Should the kids run out of reading material, this Irish-run secondhand bookshop (p168) has a good selection in English.

Papabubble

Watch candy being made the old-fashioned way at this inviting little shop (p77) in the old city.

Tintin Shop

A plethora of Tintin-related items make for gorgeous, colourful gifts in this Gràcia space (p169).

El Rei de la Màgia

A cabinet of curiosity (p104) for all budding magicians.

Like a Local

Whether you're a frequent visitor or a first-timer, taking a local approach when it comes to eating, drinking and other amusements offers a rewarding way to experience the city. You'll find Catalans much more open if you try and blend in as much as you can (and learn a few words of Catalan).

When to Dine

In Barcelona, and elsewhere in Spain, meal times run late. Most restaurants don't open for dinner until 8.30pm or 9pm and close at midnight or 1am; peak dining time is around 10pm. Locals commonly have lunch between 1pm and 4pm. This is then followed by a nice long siesta (a loll on the beach or in one of the parks is a fine choice when the weather is pleasant). Locals aren't big on breakfast – a croissant and a *cortado* (espresso with milk) is a typical way to start the day.

Water & Wine

Lunch or dinner, wine is always a fine idea, according to most *barcelonins*. Luckily, many restaurants offer *menú del día* (menu of the day, or fixed price) lunches that include a glass of red or white. If you become a regular, waiters may give you complimentary refills or even leave the bottle. Of course, you can also opt for another drink.

A word on water: no one drinks it straight from the tap (taste it and you'll know why). Order *agua mineral,* either *con gas* (sparkling) or *sin gas* (still).

Tapas

When hunger pains arrive in the afternoon or early evening, locals head out for a pre-dinner tapa. This means heading to the local favourite for a bite of anchovies, sausage, squid, wild mushrooms, roasted peppers or dozens of other tempting morsels. Wine, cava and beer all make fine accompaniments.

Many tapas spots are lively stand-around-the-bar affairs; Bormuth (p99) and Vaso de Oro (p114) are great places to start. When it's time for a change of scenery, *barcelonins* might make their way to dinner or just head to another tapas bar and skip the sit-down formality altogether.

Local Meal Spots

La Rambla is fine for a stroll, but no local would eat there. The same holds for Carrer Ferran and other tourist-packed streets in Barri Gòtic. The Gòtic does, however, have some local-favoured gems, particularly on the narrow streets of the east side – such as Onofre (p71) and Cafè de l'Acadèmia (p70). For a more authentic neighbourhood dining experience, browse the streets of El Born, Barceloneta, El Raval and Gràcia.

MATT MUNRO/LONELY PLANET ©

Quimet i Quimet (p193)

NEED TO KNOW

➡ **Miniguide** (http://miniguide.es) Culture, food, nightlife, fashion and more; published 10 times a year.

➡ **Barcelona Cultura** (http://barcelonacultura.bcn.cat) Upcoming cultural fare, including concerts, exhibitions and festivals.

➡ **Spotted by Locals** (www.spottedbylocals.com/barcelona) Reviews of favourite spots – restaurants, bars, cinemas, galleries and more, written by local residents/expats.

➡ **Barça Central** (http://barcacentral.com) The latest about FC Barcelona.

➡ **In & Out Barcelona** (www.inandoutbarcelona.net) New restaurants, bars, cafes, shops and clubs with lovely photos – in Spanish.

Weekends

Many *barcelonins* head out of town at the weekends. That could mean skiing in the Pyrenees in winter, or heading up the Costa Brava in summer. Those that stick around might check out flea markets or produce markets, head to the beach or have an outing in the park. The parks are liveliest at weekends, when local musicians, picnickers, pop-up markets and playing children add to the city's relaxed air. Culture-craving locals might hit an art opening – openings at CCCB (p83) and MACBA (p81) are good fun – see a rep film – Filmoteca de Catalunya (p88) has intriguing fare – or catch a concert, at Jazz Sí Club (p88) or Sala Apolo (p198), perhaps.

The Sunday Feast

Sunday is typically the most peaceful day for Catalans, and a fine occasion for gathering with family or friends over a big meal. Lunch is the main event, and many restaurants prepare Sunday-only specials. Lots of places close on Sunday nights too, so it's worth lingering over a long multi-course lunch. A rich paella in Barceloneta – try Barraca (p115) or Can Ros (p116) – followed by a long leisurely stroll along the waterfront is always a hit.

Festivals & Other Events

One of the best ways to join in local amusement is to come for one of the city's big festivals. During summer (June to August), Música als Parcs features 30 or so open-air concerts at a dozen parks in Barcelona, and free concerts are held at various venues around the city. Stop in at a tourist office for the latest schedule. Other great open-air concerts that goes through summer include Festival Piknic Electronik and Festival Pedralbes.

Local Listings

If you can read some Spanish (Castilian), browse the latest art openings, film screenings, concerts and other events in the *Guia del Ocio* (www.guiadelocio.com), *Time Out Barcelona* (www.timeout.cat) or daily papers like *La Vanguardia* (www.lavanguardia.com) and *El Periodico* (www.elperiodico.com). Friday papers list the weekend's events (most with pull-out supplements) and are often worth a read, even if your Spanish is limited. The council website (http://barcelonacultura.bcn.cat) also lists upcoming events.

Football

FC Barcelona plays a prominent role in the city's imagination. Heading to a match at Camp Nou (p173) from September to May is the best way to catch a bit of Barcelona fever, but watching it on screen at a tavern can be just as much fun depending on the crowd. For the most fervent fan base, head to Barceloneta, El Raval, Gràcia or Sarrià, where you'll find lively spots to catch a game. The daily journal *Marca* (www.marca.com) gives the latest on sporting news.

Tickets can be bought at www.fcbarcelona.com or FC Botiga (p77).

Sardana

The traditional Catalan folk dance *sardana* still attracts a small local following. On weekends aficionados gather in front of La Catedral for group dancing to a live 10-piece band. The action happens at 6pm on Saturday and noon on Sunday and lasts about an hour.

For Free

With planning Barcelona can be a surprisingly affordable place to travel. Many museums offer free days, and some of the best ways to experience the city don't cost a cent – hanging out on the beach, exploring fascinating neighbourhoods, and drinking in the views from hilltop heights.

Walking Tours

Numerous companies offer pay-what-you-wish walking tours. These typically take in the Barri Gòtic or the Modernista sites of L'Eixample. Recommended outfits include the following:

Discover Walks (www.discoverwalks.com)

Feel Free Tours (www.feelfreetours.com)

Orange Donut Tours (www.orangedonut tours.com)

Runner Bean Tours (p254)

Festivals & Other Events

Barcelona has loads of free festivals and events, including the **Festes de la Mercè** (www.bcn.cat/merce; ⊙Sep) and the **Festes de Santa Eulàlia** (http://lameva.barcelona. cat/santaeulalia; ⊙Feb). From June to August, the city hosts Música als Parcs (Music in the Parks), a series of open-air concerts held in different parks and green spaces around the city. Over 40 different concerts feature classical, blues and jazz groups. Popular venues include Parc de la Ciutadella (p96), Parc de Joan Miró (p190) and Parc Turó (Avenida de Pau Casals 19, Sant Gervasi). Ask at the tourist office or check online (www.bcn.cat) for a schedule.

Sights

Entry to some sights is free on occasion, most commonly on the first Sunday of the month, while quite a few attractions are free from 3pm to 8pm on Sundays. Others are always free. The following are most likely to attract your attention.

Free

➡ Centre d'Art Santa Mònica (p57)
➡ Basílica de Santa Maria del Mar (p96)
➡ Estadi Olímpic Lluís Companys (p190)
➡ Col·lecció de Carrosses Fúnebres (p191)
➡ Palau del Lloctinent (p67)
➡ Temple d'August (p62)
➡ Antic Hospital de la Santa Creu (p83)
➡ Font Màgica (p188)
➡ Jardins de Mossèn Cinto de Verdaguer (p190)
➡ Cementiri del Poblenou (p113)
➡ Universitat de Barcelona (p133)

Sometimes free

➡ Museu d'Història de Catalunya (p111)
➡ Museu Nacional d'Art de Catalunya (p186)
➡ Museu Picasso (p92)
➡ La Catedral (p60)
➡ Museu Frederic Marès (p63)
➡ Castell de Montjuïc (p188)
➡ Museu-Monestir de Pedralbes (p174)
➡ Jardins del Laberint d'Horta (p179)
➡ Museu de la Música (p113)
➡ Museu d'Història de Barcelona (p65)
➡ Museu Marítim (p109)
➡ Ajuntament (p64)

IAKOV FILIMONOV/SHUTTERSTOCK ©

Fried sardines

 **Eating**

Barcelona has a celebrated food scene fuelled by a combination of world-class chefs, imaginative recipes and magnificent ingredients fresh from farms and the sea. Catalan culinary masterminds like Ferran and Albert Adrià, and Carles Abellán have become international icons, reinventing the world of haute cuisine, while classic old-world Catalan recipes continue to earn accolades in dining rooms and tapas bars across the city.

Escalivada (p34)

New Catalan Cuisine

Avant-garde chefs have made Catalonia famous throughout the world for their food laboratories, their commitment to food as art and their crazy riffs on the themes of traditional local cooking.

Here the notion of gourmet cuisine is deconstructed as chefs transform liquids and solid foods into foams, create 'ice cream' of classic ingredients by means of liquid nitrogen, freeze-dry foods to make concentrated powders and employ spherification to create unusual and artful morsels. This alchemical cookery is known as molecular gastronomy, and invention is the keystone of this technique.

Diners may encounter olive oil 'caviar', 'snow' made of gazpacho with anchovies, jellified Parmesan turned into spaghetti, and countless other concoctions.

The dining rooms themselves also offer a reconfiguration of the five-star dining experience. Restaurateurs generally aim to create warm and buzzing spaces, with artful design flourishes, and without the stuffiness and formality typically associated with high-end dining.

Top Chefs

Albert Adrià, brother of Ferran of the late, world-class El Bulli, has brought culinary fame to Barcelona with his growing empire of restaurants. Tickets (p196) is a delectable showcase of whimsy and imagination, with deconstructed tapas dishes like liquid olives, 'air baguettes' (made with Iberian ham) and fairy-floss-covered trees with edible dark chocolate 'soil'.

NEED TO KNOW

Price Ranges

The following price ranges represent the average cost of a main course:

€ less than €12

€€ €12–€20

€€€ over €20

Opening Hours

Most restaurants open from 1pm to 4pm and from 8.30pm to midnight.

Reservations

At midrange restaurants and simpler taverns you can usually turn up without booking ahead. At high-end restaurants, especially for dinner, it is safer to make a booking. Thursday to Saturday nights are especially busy.

Tipping

A service charge is rarely included in the bill. Catalans and other Spaniards are not overwhelming tippers. If you are particularly happy, 5% on top is generally fine.

Menú de Degustación

At high-end restaurants you can occasionally opt for a *menú de degustación*, a tasting menu involving samples of different dishes. This can be a great way to get a broader view of what the restaurant does and has the advantage of coming at a fixed price.

Other great chefs continue to redefine contemporary cuisine. The Michelin-starred chef Carles Abellan, creator of Suculent (p86), Tapas 24 (p139) and other restaurants, playfully reinterprets traditional tapas with dishes like the *melón con jamón,* a millefeuille of layered caramelised Iberian ham and thinly sliced melon.

Another star of the Catalan cooking scene is Jordi Vilà, who continues to wow diners at Alkímia (p196) with reinvented Catalan classics. Other major players on the Catalan dining scene are Jordi Artal at Cinc Sentits (p139), Xavier Pellicer at Barraca (p115), and the trio of Mateu Casañas, Oriol Castro and Eduard Xatruch at Disfrutar (p138).

MENÚ DEL DIA

The *menú del día,* a full set meal with water or wine (and usually with several dish options), is a great way to cap prices at lunchtime. They start from around €11 and can go as high as €25 for more elaborate offerings.

Slightly different etiquette applies to a *menú del día,* and you will probably keep the same knife and fork throughout the meal. Once your order is taken and the first course (which could range from a simple *amanida/ensalada rusa* – Russian salad thick with potatoes and mayonnaise – to an elaborate seafood item) is in place, you may find the level of service increases disconcertingly. This especially becomes the case as you reach the end of any given course. Hovering waiters swoop like eagles to swipe your unfinished dish or lift your glass of wine, still tinged with that last sip you wanted to savour. Simply utter *'Encara no he terminat'/'Todavía no he terminado'* (I haven't finished yet) – you'll be flashed a cheerful smile and your waiter will leave you to finish in peace.

The first (ever) to win a third Michelin star for Barcelona, however, is Paolo Casagrande, at the superb Lasarte (p138), although he was followed in 2017 by Jordi Cruz at ABaC (p179).

Tapas Bars

Tapas, those bite-sized morsels of joy, are not a typical Catalan concept, but tapas bars are nonetheless found all across the city. Most open earlier than restaurants – typically around 7pm – making them a good pre-dinner (or instead-of-dinner) option. Some open from lunch and stay open without a break through late-evening closing time.

As per the 'bar' designation, these places are less formal than restaurants, and drinking is an essential component of the experience.

If you opt for *tapes*/tapas, it is handy to recognise some of the common items (as they are called in Catalan/Spanish):

➡ **bombes/bombas** large meat and potato croquettes

➡ **boquerons/boquerones** white anchovies in vinegar – delicious and tangy

➡ **carxofes/alcachofas** artichokes

➡ **gambes/gambas** prawns, either done *al all/al ajillo* (with garlic), or *a la plantxa/plancha* (grilled)

➡ **navalles/navajas** razor clams

➡ **patates braves/patatas bravas** potato chunks bathed in a slightly spicy tomato sauce, sometimes mixed with mayonnaise

➡ **pop a feira/pulpo a la gallega** tender boiled octopus with paprika

➡ **truita de patates/tortilla de patatas** potato-filled omelette; one with vegetables is a *tortilla de verduras*

➡ **xampinyons/champiñones** mushrooms

Classic Catalan Cuisine

Traditional Catalan recipes showcase the great produce of the Mediterranean: fish, prawns, cuttlefish, clams, pork, rabbit, game, first-rate olive oil, peppers and loads of garlic. Classic dishes also feature unusual pairings (seafood with meat, fruit with fowl) such as cuttlefish with chickpeas, cured ham with caviar, rabbit with prawns, or goose with pears.

Great Catalan restaurants can be found in nearly every neighbourhood around town. The settings can be a huge part of the appeal, with candlelit medieval chambers in the Ciutat Vella and Modernista design in L'Eixample setting the stage for a memorable feast. Although there are plenty of high-end places in this city, foodie-minded *barcelonins* aren't averse to eating at humbler, less elegant places – which sometimes cook up the best meals.

Seafood Restaurants

There are a wealth of restaurants specialising in seafood. Not surprisingly Barceloneta, which lies near the sea, is packed with eateries of all shapes and sizes doling out decadent paellas, cauldrons of bubbling molluscs, grilled catches of the day and other delights. Nearest the sea, you'll find pricier open-air places with Mediterranean views; plunge into the narrow lanes to find the real gems, including bustling family-run places that serve first-rate plates at great prices.

Above: Paella
Right: Restaurant 7 Portes (p116)

Market Shopping

Barcelona has some fantastic food markets. Foodies will enjoy the sounds, smells and most importantly tastes of the Mercat de la Boqueria (p80). This is probably Spain's biggest and best market, and it's conveniently located right off La Rambla. Here you can find temptations of all sorts – plump fruits and veggies, freshly squeezed juices, artisanal cheeses, smoked meats, seafood and pastries. The best feature: an array of tapas bars and food stalls where you can sample amazingly fresh ingredients cooked to perfection. Some other great market options:

➡ **Mercat de Sant Antoni** (p199)

➡ **Mercat de Santa Caterina** (p96)

➡ **Mercat del Ninot** (p148)

➡ **Mercat de la Llibertat** (p162)

➡ **Mercat de l'Abaceria Central** (p170)

Catalan Specialities

STARTERS

➡ **Calçots amb romesco** Sweet and juicy spring onions cooked up on a barbecue

➡ **Escalivada** Red pepper, aubergine and onion, grilled, cooled, peeled, sliced and served with an olive oil, salt and garlic dressing

➡ **Esqueixada** Salad of *bacallà/bacalao* (shredded salted cod) with tomatoes, red peppers, onions, white beans, olives, olive oil and vinegar

MAIN COURSES

➡ **Arròs a la cassola** Catalan paella, cooked without saffron

➡ **Arròs negre** Rice cooked in black cuttlefish ink

➡ **Bacallà a la llauna** Salted cod baked in tomato, garlic, parsley, paprika and wine

➡ **Botifarra amb mongetes** Pork sausage with fried white beans

➡ **Cargols/Caracoles** Snails, often stewed with *conill/conejo* (rabbit) and chilli

➡ **Fideuà** Similar to paella but with vermicelli noodles as the base. Often accompanied by *allioli* (pounded garlic with olive oil), which you can mix in as you wish

➡ **Fricandó** Pork and vegetable stew

➡ **Sarsuela/zarzuela** Mixed seafood cooked in *sofregit* (fried onion, tomato and garlic sauce) with seasonings

➡ **Suquet de peix** Fish and potato hotpot

DESSERTS

➡ **Crema catalana** A cream custard with a crisp burnt-sugar coating

➡ **Mel i mató** Honey and fresh cream cheese

Fish on display at Mercat de la Boqueria (p80)

Crema catalana (p34)

Lonely Planet's Top Choices

Disfrutar (p138) An avant-garde addition that has rapidly become Barcelona's most talked-about restaurant.

Kaiku (p115) Some of the most inventive and best-value paellas in town.

Tickets (p196) The celebrated restaurant of Albert Adrià, showcasing Barcelona's best *nueva cocina española*.

Tapas 24 (p139) Carles Abellan creates some of Barcelona's best tapas.

La Cova Fumada (p114) Cramped, noisy, but unmissable tapas restaurant, open at lunch only.

Restaurant 7 Portes (p116) An elegant spot that's famed for its delectable paella.

Best By Budget

€

La Cova Fumada (p114) Barceloneta hole-in-the-wall with excellent small plates.

Bormuth (p99) Tasty tapas in an old-city setting.

Can Culleretes (p70) Catalan classics in ancient dining rooms.

€€

Suculent (p86) Carles Abellan's bistro serves excellent Catalan cooking.

Casa Delfín (p101) Delicious Mediterranean fare in an atmospheric setting.

Kaiku (p115) Waterfront establishment that uses local fare.

€€€

Disfrutar (p138) Expect the unexpected – this is Catalan cooking at its most experimental.

Lasarte (p138) The ultimate eating experience, with three Michelin stars.

La Barra de Carles Abellan (p115) Seafood presented in myriad creative ways.

Best for Tapas

El 58 (p118) French-owned space on the newly hip Rambla del Poblenou.

Quimet i Quimet (p193) Mouthwatering morsels served to a standing crowd.

Palo Cortao (p193) A buzzy Poble Sec option with outstanding sharing plates.

Bar Pinotxo (p84) Pull up a bar stool at this legendary Boqueria joint.

Tapas 24 (p139) Everyone's favourite gourmet tapas bar.

Best for Catalan

Vivanda (p178) Magnificent Catalan cooking with year-round garden dining.

La Panxa del Bisbe (p165) Creative sharing plates on a quiet Gràcia street.

Cafè de l'Acadèmia (p70) High-quality dishes that never disappoint.

Can Culleretes (p70) The city's oldest restaurant, with great-value traditional dishes.

Best for Eating Like a Local

Mitja Vida (p176) Mouth-watering tapas and vermouth.

Can Lluís (p84) Loved by Catalans for its great-value daily *menú*.

Las Delicias (p163) A Sunday morning classic, well located for a walk in Park Güell.

La Cova Fumada (p114) Fight for a table at this scruffy little joint with outstanding food.

Best for Architecture

Els Quatre Gats (p72) Finely crafted interiors in a building where Picasso once supped.

El Asador de Aranda (p178) A beautiful spread of Modernista dining rooms.

Casa Calvet (p142) A stylish restaurant set in an early Gaudí building.

Enigma (p196) Dazzlingly modern in its design, if you manage to get a reservation.

Best for Vegetarians

Green Spot (p115) Designer dining room with dishes to match.

Aguaribay (p118) First-rate prix fixe lunches and a small but well-executed evening à la carte menu.

Cereria (p71) Pizzas and galettes in an old-fashioned setting.

Flax & Kale (p86) Vast, colourful salads and a truly creative approach.

Rasoterra (p71) Airy vegetarian charmer in Barri Gòtic.

Best Cafes

Bar del Convent (p103) Great terrace in a former cloister.

Café Godot (p165) Friendly and easy-going, with tasty snacks and mains.

Federal (p69) Unnervingly hip, but the food is excellent and the service friendly.

La Granja (p72) Best place in town for a hot chocolate.

La Nena (p163) Kid-friendly cafe in Gràcia.

Best for Late-Night Eating

Benedict (p69) Soul food and cocktails in a comfortable setting.

Cafè de l'Òpera (p73) Stop in for late-night snacks on La Rambla.

Elisabets (p84) Offers late-night dining (till 1am) on Fridays.

Best for Carnivores

Patagonia Beef & Wine (p142) Feast on Argentine steaks.

Bilbao (p166) A classic spot for steaks and Spanish reds.

El Asador de Aranda (p178) Roast lamb in a Modernista setting.

Best for Brunch

Federal (p192) Excellent brunches and a small roof terrace.

En Aparté (p101) French restaurant serving tasty brunch dishes.

Milk (p69) Serves brunch daily (till 4.30pm).

Benedict (p69) The clue is in the name, but there's more besides.

Copasetic (p136) Vintage-filled cafe with weekend brunch.

Best for Chocolate Lovers

Granja La Pallaresa (p73) One of many chocolate-dispensing cafes on Carrer de Petritxol.

Cacao Sampaka (p145) Chocolate decadence comes in many forms at this Eixample shop and cafe.

Museu de la Xocolata (p97) Delve into the world of chocolate, then feast in the cafe.

Best for Romantic Dining

La Vinateria del Call (p70) Flickering candles and medieval walls.

Can Recasens (p119) Romantic spot in Poblenou with market-fresh fare.

Pla (p71) Intimate setting and memorable meals.

IAKOV FILIMONOV/SHUTTERSTOCK ©

Plaça Reial (p62)

Drinking & Nightlife

Barcelona is a nightlife-lovers' town, with an enticing spread of candlelit wine bars, old-school taverns, stylish lounges and kaleidoscopic nightclubs where the party continues until daybreak. For something a little more sedate, the city's atmospheric cafes and teahouses make a fine retreat when the skies turn grey.

NEED TO KNOW

Opening Hours

➡ **Bars** Typically open around 6pm and close at 2am (3am on weekends), though many are open all day.

➡ **Clubs** Open from midnight until 6am, Thursday to Saturday.

➡ **Beach Bars** 10am to around midnight (later on weekends) from April through October.

When to Go

➡ Bars get lively around 11pm or midnight.

➡ Clubs don't start filling up until around 2am.

Getting In

Cover charges range from nothing to upwards of €20. If you go early, you'll often pay less. In most cases the admission price includes your first drink. Bouncers have the last say on dress code and your eligibility to enter. If you're in a big group, break into smaller groups.

Guides for the Latest Nightlife

➡ **Clubbingspain.com** (www.clubbingspain.com)

➡ **Barcelona Connect** (www.barcelonaconnect.com)

➡ **Miniguide** (www.miniguide.es)

➡ **Metropolitan** (www.barcelona-metropolitan.com)

➡ **enBarcelona** (www.enbarcelona.com)

Drinking Glossary

Coffee

➡ *cafe con leche* – half coffee, half milk

➡ *cafe solo* – a short black or espresso

➡ *cortado* – a short black with a little milk

Beer

➡ *cerveza* – beer

➡ *caña* – a small draught beer

➡ *tubo* – a large draught beer

➡ *jarra* – a stein of beer (sometimes a pint)

➡ *quinto* – a 200ml bottle

➡ *tercio* – a 300ml bottle

➡ *clara* – a shandy; a beer with a hefty dash of lemonade (or lemon Fanta)

Wine

➡ *vino de la casa* – house wine

Bars & Lounges

Barcelona has a dizzying assortment of bars where you can start – or end – the night. The atmosphere varies tremendously – candlelit, mural-covered chambers in the medieval quarter, antique-filled converted storefronts and buzzing Modernista spaces are all part of the scene. Of course, where to go depends as much on the crowd as it does on ambience – and whether you're in the mood to drink with the hipsters (try Sant Antoni), the bohemian crowd (El Raval) or young expats (Gràcia), you'll find a scene that suits in Barcelona.

Wherever you end up, keep in mind that eating and drinking go hand in hand in Barcelona (as in other parts of Spain), and some of the liveliest bars serve up tapas as well as alcohol.

Wine & Cava Bars

A growing number of wine bars scattered around the city provide a showcase for the great produce from Spain and beyond. Vine-minded spots such as Monvínic (p139) serve a huge selection of wines by the glass, with a particular focus on stellar new vintages. A big part of the experience is having a few bites while you drink. Expect sharing plates, platters of cheese and charcuterie, and plenty of tapas.

Cava bars tend to be more about the festive ambience than the actual drinking of *cava,* a sparkling white or rosé, most of which is produced in Catalonia's Penedès region. At the more famous *cava* bars you'll have to nudge your way through the garrulous crowds and enjoy your bubbly standing up. Two of the most famous *cava* bars are El Xampanyet (p103) in La Ribera and Can Paixano (p120) in Barceloneta.

Drinks With a View

Barcelona has a handful of rooftop bars and hillside drinking spaces that provide an enchanting view over the city. Depending on the neighbourhood, the vista may take in the rooftops of the Ciutat Vella (Old City), the curving beachfront, or the entire expanse of the city centre with the Collserola hills and Tibidabo in the distance. Most of these drinking spots are perched atop high-end hotels, but are not solely the domain of visiting foreigners. An increasing number of style-minded *barcelonins* are drawn to these spaces. Late in the evening you'll find a mostly local crowd.

Drinking by Neighbourhood

Gràcia & Park Güell
Young hipster crowd
(p166)

Camp Nou, Pedralbes & La Zona Alta
High-end clubs
(p180)

La Sagrada Família & L'Eixample
Student bars, tiny lounges, gay clubs
(p142)

La Ribera
Cava and wine bars, lounges
(p103)

Plaça de Catalunya

Port Olímpic

El Raval
Bohemian bars, small clubs
(p86)

La Rambla & Barri Gòtic
Atmospheric bars, cafes, outdoor spots, clubs
(p72)

Barceloneta & the Waterfront
Neighbourhood taverns, seaside bars, touristy clubs
(p119)

Montjuïc, Poble Sec & Sant Antoni
Art-minded bars, trendy cafes, open-air spots
(p196)

Port de Barcelona

MEDITERRANEAN SEA

Beach Bars

During summer, small wooden beach bars, known as *chiringuitos,* open up along the strand from Barceloneta all the way up to Platja de la Nova Mar Bella. Here you can dip your toes in the sand and nurse a cocktail while watching the city at play against the backdrop of the deep-blue Mediterranean. Ambient grooves add to the laid-back environment. *Chiringuitos* are also great spots for a snack – particularly the **Guingueta de la Barceloneta** (Map p286; www.carlesabellan. com; Platja de la Barceloneta; dishes €6-16; ☺9am-midnight Mar-Nov; ⓂBarceloneta) and Guingueta del Bogatell (p121) run by Michelin-starred chef Carles Abellán. The drink of choice at either is a refreshing *cava sangría.*

Clubs

Barcelona's *discotecas* (clubs) are at their best from Thursday to Saturday. Indeed, many open only on these nights. A surpris-ing variety of spots lurk in the old-town labyrinth, ranging from plush former dance halls to grungy subterranean venues that fill to capacity.

Along the waterfront it's another story. At Port Olímpic, sun-scorched crowds of visiting yachties mix it up with tourists and a few locals at noisy, back-to-back dance bars right on the waterfront.

Cafes

The cafe scene in Barcelona is incredibly vibrant and makes a great setting for an afternoon pick-me-up. You'll find charming teashops hidden on the narrow lanes of Barri Gòtic, bohemian hang-outs in the Raval, hipster haunts in L'Eixample and Modernista gems on La Rambla. While coffee, tea or perhaps *xocolata desfeta* (hot chocolate) are the main attractions, most places also serve snacks, while some serve beer, wine and cocktails.

Lonely Planet's Top Choices

Paradiso (p99) Glamorous, cavernous, speakeasy-style cocktail bar.

Guzzo (p103) Relaxed bar with great DJs and live music and tables outside on a Born square.

La Caseta del Migdia (p196) An open-air charmer, hidden high among the trees on Montjuïc.

Sor Rita (p72) Join festive crowds in a whimsical Almodovar-esque world.

El Xampanyet (p103) Sip cheap pink *cava* and munch on a bacon butty in this convivial classic.

Dry Martini (p142) This elegant drinking den serves perfect martinis and goldfish-bowl-sized gin and tonics.

Best for Wine Lovers

Viblioteca (p167) A small modern space famed for its wine (and cheese) selections.

Perikete (p119) A large and lively new wine bar in Barceloneta.

Monvínic (p139) With a staggering 3000 varieties of wines, you won't lack for options.

La Vinya del Senyor (p103) Long wine list and tables in the shadow of Basílica de Santa Maria del Mar.

Best for Beer

BlackLab (p120) Creative microbrewery near the waterfront.

La Cervecita Nuestra de Cada Día (p121) A Poblenou brew bar for beer nerds.

Napar BCN (p142) The glitzy space makes an upmarket setting for sipping beers made on site.

Cat Bar (p99) Microbrews and vegan burgers make a winning combo in El Born.

El Drapaire (p87) Atmospheric tapas and creative microbrew joint in El Raval.

Best for Cocktails

Paradiso (p99) Walk through a fridge to this glam speakeasy.

Balius (p121) Beautifully mixed elixirs in Poblenou.

Elephanta (p166) The place to linger over a creative concoction.

Dry Martini (p142) Expertly made cocktails in a classy setting.

Boadas (p73) An iconic drinking den that's been going strong since the 1930s.

Best for Old-World Ambience

Raïm (p167) Old-fashioned tavern with more than a hint of Havana.

Cafè de l'Òpera (p73) Serving opera-goers and passers-by for decades.

Bar Marsella (p87) History lives on in this 1820 watering hole.

Bar Pastís (p86) Atmospheric little bar with the warble of French cabaret tunes playing overhead.

Casa Almirall (p86) Step back into the 1860s inside this atmospheric drinking den.

Best for Dancing

Marula Cafè (p73) Barri Gòtic favourite for its lively dance floor.

Sala Apolo (p198) Gorgeous dance hall with varied programme of electro, funk and more.

Moog (p87) A small Raval club that draws a fun, dance-loving crowd.

Antilla BCN (p143) The top name in town for salsa lovers.

City Hall (p143) A legendary Eixample dance club.

Best Bohemian Hang-Outs

Gran Bodega Saltó (p198) Poble Sec icon with psychedelic decor and an eclectic crowd.

Madame George (p121) Tiny, dramatically designed space with soulful DJs.

El Rouge (p197) Bordello-esque lounge with great people-watching.

Bar Marsella (p87) Historic absinthe bar that's seen them all.

Best for Views

La Caseta del Migdia (p196) Great hillside spot for a sundowner.

Mirablau (p180) The whole city stretches out beneath you from the foot of Tibidabo.

La Terrrazza (p197) Party beneath palms in Poble Espanyol.

Martínez (p196) Drinking and dining with views on Montjuïc.

Best Beachfront Settings

Santa Marta (p120) Sit at outdoor tables and watch the passing people parade.

CDLC (p120) Come early for a beach-facing outdoor table; stay for dancing.

Guingueta del Bogatell (p121) Sit on the seafront far from the mayhem.

Entertainment

Barcelona teems with stages hosting all manner of entertainment from underground cabaret and comic opera to high drama. Dance companies are thick on the ground and popular local theatre companies, when not touring the rest of Spain, keep folks strapped to their seats.

Live Music

Almost every big international act has passed through Barcelona at some point, more often than not playing at Razzmatazz (p122), Bikini (p181), Sala Apolo (p198) or BARTS (p198), although there are a number of other decent midsize venues. There are also abundant local gigs in institutions as diverse as CaixaForum (p188), La Pedrera (p134) and L'Ateneu (p75).

Classical Music & Opera

Barcelona is blessed with a fine line-up of theatres for grand performances of classical music, opera and more. The two historic – and iconic – music venues are the Gran Teatre del Liceu (p74) and the Palau de la Música Catalana (p104), while the L'Auditori (p122) is the modern concert hall par excellence and home to the city's orchestra, the OBC.

The main season for classical and opera runs from September to June, while in high summer you might find outdoor festivals or performances around town. Check with the tourist office for details.

Dance

Some fine local contemporary dance companies, along with international visiting companies from time to time, maintain a fairly busy performance program across town. Look for leaflets at Palau de la Virreina (p57) and watch theatre listings. For ballet and other big spectacles, you need to wait for acts to arrive from abroad.

FLAMENCO

Seeing good performances of this essentially Andalucian dance and music is not easy. The few *tablaos* are touristy and often tacky. You can catch flamenco on Friday and Saturday nights at the Jazz Sí Club (p88); also watch out for big-name performers at the Palau de la Música Catalana (p104).

The Festival de Flamenco de Ciutat Vella (ciutatflamenco.com) is held in May. A series of concerts can be seen from April to July as part of the Barcelona Guitar Festival (www.guitarbcn.com).

SARDANA

In Barcelona the best chance you have of seeing people dancing the *sardana* (Catalonia's national folk dance) is either at noon on Sunday or 6pm on Saturday in front of La Catedral. It is also performed sometimes in Plaça de Sant Jaume. For more information, contact the **Agrupació Cultural Folklòrica de Barcelona** (☎93 315 14 96; www.acfbarcelona.cat).

Theatre

Most local theatre is performed in Catalan or Spanish, although physical theatre such as that performed by local group La Fura dels Baus (p42) is popular too. The monthly guide *Butxaca* can be picked up at the Palau de la Virreina (p57).

Cinemas

Outdoor cinema screens are set up in summer in the moat of the Castell de Montjuïc

NEED TO KNOW

Tickets

➡ The easiest way to get hold of tickets (*entradas*) for most venues throughout the city is through Ticketea (www.ticketea.com) or Ticketmaster (www.ticketmaster.es). Occasionally there are discounted tickets to be had on www.atrapalo.com.

Listings

➡ For exhibitions and other forms of entertainment, see www.barcelona-metropolitan.com or www.timeout.cat, and for free activities, check out www.forfree.cat.

➡ The Palau de la Virreina (p57) cultural information office has oodles of information on theatre, opera, classical music and more.

➡ Good coverage of classical music is to be found on www.classictic.com (in English).

(www.salamontjuic.org), on the beach and in the Fòrum. Foreign films with subtitles and original soundtracks are marked 'VO' (*versió original*) in movie listings.

Football

Football in Barcelona has the aura of religion and for much of the city's population, support of FC Barcelona is an article of faith. But the city has another hardy (if less illustrious) side, RCD Espanyol. FC Barcelona is traditionally associated with the Catalans and even Catalan nationalism, while Espanyol is often identified with Spanish immigrants from other parts of the country.

A match at Barça's Camp Nou (p173) can be breathtaking; the season runs from September to May, and tickets can be bought at www.fcbarcelona.com or FC Botiga. If you can't make it to see Barça play, a trip to the multimedia museum (p175) with a tour through the locker room and out on to the field is a good secondary option.

Cycling

Barcelona's long enticing seafront makes a fine setting for a ride, and the bike lane separate from traffic and pedestrians ensures you can get going at a good clip (though you'll have to move slowly at peak times, like on summer weekends).

The city itself has over 180km of bike lanes, including lanes along Passeig de Sant Joan, Carrer del Consell de Cent, Avinguda Diagonal and Ronda de Sant Pau/Carrer del Comte d'Urgell, among other major streets. Avid mountain bikers will want to make their way up to the vast Parc de Collserola (p180), where rambling trails on a wooded massif overlook the city.

Entertainment by Neighbourhood

➡ **La Rambla & Barri Gòtic** (p74) This is where you'll find the Gran Teatre de Liceu and the weekly sardana dances.

➡ **El Raval** (p88) Great for theatre, jazz and flamenco on Friday and Saturday nights at the Jazz Sí Club.

➡ **La Ribera** (p104) The eclectic and spectacular Palau de la Música Catalana is here.

➡ **Montjuïc** (p198) This is where you'll find two of the best pop and rock venues, Sala Apolo and BARTS.

LA FURA DELS BAUS

Keep your eyes peeled for any of the eccentric (if not downright crazed) performances of Barcelona's La Fura dels Baus (www.lafura.com) theatre group. It has won worldwide acclaim for its brand of startling, often acrobatic, theatre in which the audience is frequently dragged into the chaos. The company grew out of Barcelona's street-theatre culture of the late 1970s and, although it has grown in technical prowess and received great international acclaim, it has not abandoned the rough-and-ready edge of street performances.

Lonely Planet's Top Choices

Palau de la Música Catalana (p95) This glittering Modernista gem, the city's traditional home for classical and choral music, is a multi-sensory delight.

Gran Teatre del Liceu (p74) Nineteenth-century style meets cutting-edge acoustics at Barcelona's elegant opera house.

Filmoteca de Catalunya (p88) This cinema and arts centre, situated in El Raval, also includes a film archive, a bookshop and an exhibition space.

Best for Live Bands

City Hall (p145) The perfect midsize venue for up-and-coming local and international acts.

Sala Apolo (p198) Cosy booths and a warm red glow give this hugely popular venue something special.

BARTS (p198) The latest contender on the live music circuit, with superb sound and every mod con.

Bikini (p181) Hidden behind a shopping centre, Bikini still pulls in some great acts.

Best for Classical Music

Palau de la Música Catalana (p95) A Modernista fantasy, where the fabulous interior can distract from the finest musician.

Gran Teatre del Liceu (p74) One of Europe's most splendid opera houses, built to impress.

L'Auditori (p122) Fiercely modern concert venue, with a resident orchestra.

L'Ateneu (p75) This elegant old library is hard to enter if you're not a member – unless you catch one of its occasional concerts.

Best for Theatre

Teatre Nacional de Catalunya (p122) A neoclassical building hosting the best of Catalan theatre.

Teatre Romea (p88) Expect wacky (and not so wacky) versions of modern classics.

Sala Beckett (p122) With occasional shows in English, it's worth keeping an eye on the programming here.

Best for Jazz

Harlem Jazz Club (p75) Not just jazz, but also funk, blues, bossa nova and plenty more.

Jazz Sí Club (p88) Small, lively, cramped and never less than fun.

Jamboree (p75) A basement bar that's seen them all under its vaulted ceiling.

Best for Flamenco

Jazz Sí Club (p88) A tiny venue with impromptu jams and occasionally great performances.

Tablao Nervión (p104) A little bit touristy, but better than most for flamenco.

Sala Tarantos (p75) A cosy basement affair, good for up-and-coming acts.

Best for Cinema

Verdi (p168) Up-to-date releases, both commercial and less so.

Renoir Floridablanca (p198) Comfortable, modern cinema showing a good selection of recent films.

Filmoteca de Catalunya (p88) The city's premier repertory cinema, with themed cycles and rock-bottom prices.

Méliès Cinemes (p145) Now showing nondubbed foreign films, the Méliès is a useful option for recent films.

Yelmo Cines Icària (p122) Huge multiscreen affair with all the latest releases.

Vintage fashion on display in La Ribera

🛍 **Shopping**

If your doctor has prescribed an intense round of retail therapy to deal with the blues, then Barcelona is the place. Across Ciutat Vella (Barri Gòtic, El Raval and La Ribera), L'Eixample and Gràcia is spread a thick mantle of boutiques, historic shops, original one-off stores, gourmet corners, wine dens and designer labels. You name it, you'll find it here.

Design

Whether you are looking for homeware, gifts or decorations, you'll quickly realise that Barcelona is a stylish city – even the souvenirs have flair. High-end design shops are best found in L'Eixample and El Born, while arty places are scattered around El Raval, where you'll find, among other things, quirky furniture and homewares with a difference.

Boutique Barcelona

The heart of the Barri Gòtic has always been busy with small-scale merchants, but the area has come crackling to life since the mid-1990s. Some of the most curious old shops, such as purveyors of hats and candles, lurk in the narrow lanes around Plaça de Sant Jaume. The once-seedy Carrer d'Avinyó has become a minor young-fashion boulevard. Antique shops line Carrer de la Palla and Carrer dels Banys Nous.

La Ribera is nothing less than a gourmet's delight. Great old shops and some finger-licking newbies deal in speciality foodstuffs, from coffee and chocolate to roasted nuts. Amid such wonderful aromas, a crop of fashion and design stores caters to the multitude of fashionistas in the *barri* (neighbourhood).

Gràcia is also full of quirky little shops. In particular, check out Carrer de Verdi for anything from clothes to bric-a-brac.

El Raval is fantastic for unique boutiques and artists selling their own creations – fashion, prints and curios.

High-Street Chains

Everyone knows that across Europe (and further afield), Spain's chains rule the high street. This is the home of the ubiquitous Zara, Mango, Pull and Bear, Bershka, Massimo Dutti, and Zara Home (in fact, all owned by one company, Inditex) – and sure enough, you'll find all of them dotted around Barcelona. Women's underwear is stylish and affordable at Oysho and Women's Secret, while global powerhouses such as Primark, Uniqlo and Topshop also feature.

Department Stores

Spain's only surviving department store is El Corte Inglés (p146) – an enormous fortresslike main branch towers over Plaça de Catalunya. It covers all manner of things from books, music and food, to fashion, jewellery, kids' clothes and toys, technology

NEED TO KNOW

Where to Go

For high fashion, design, jewellery and department stores, the principal shopping axis starts on Plaça de Catalunya, proceeds up Passeig de Gràcia and turns left into Avinguda Diagonal, along which it extends as far as Plaça de la Reina Maria Cristina. The densely packed section between Plaça de Francesc Macià and Plaça de la Reina Maria Cristina is an especially good hunting ground.

Sale Time

The winter sales start after Reis (6 January) and, depending on the shop, can go on well into February. The summer sales start in July, with shops trying to entice locals to part with one last wad of euros before they flood out of the city on holiday in August. Some shops prolong their sales to the end of August.

Opening Hours

➡ In general, shops are open between 9am or 10am and 1.30pm or 2pm and then again from around 4pm or 4.30pm to 8pm or 8.30pm Monday to Friday. Many shops keep the same hours on Saturday, although some don't bother with the evening session.

➡ Large supermarkets, malls and department stores such as El Corte Inglés stay open all day Monday to Saturday, from about 10am to 10pm.

➡ Many fashion boutiques, design stores and the like open from about 10am to 8pm Monday to Saturday.

➡ A few shops open on Sundays and holidays, and the number increases in the run-up to key consumer holiday periods.

and homeware. There are smaller branches across town. French chain FNAC is another biggie, selling books, CDs, DVDs, computers and mobile phones.

Vintage Fashion

El Raval is best for vintage fashion. You'll discover old-time stores that are irresistible to browsers, and a colourful array of affordable, mostly secondhand clothes boutiques. The central axis here is Carrer

SHOPPING MALLS

Barcelona has no shortage of shopping malls. One of the first to arrive was **L'Illa Diagonal** (p182), designed by star Spanish architect Rafael Moneo. The **Centre Comercial Diagonal Mar** (p123), by the sea, is one of the latest additions.

The city's other emporia include Centre Comercial de les Glòries (p123), in the former Olivetti factory; **Heron City** (📞93 276 50 70; www.heroncitybarcelona.com; Avinguda de Rio de Janeiro 42; ⊙stores 9.30am-10pm Mon-Sat, cinema & restaurants 7am-1am; Ⓜ Fabra i Puig), just off Avinguda Meridiana, about 4km north of Plaça de les Glòries Catalanes; and the **Centre Comercial Gran Via 2** (📞902 30 14 44; www.granvia2.com; Gran Via de les Corts Catalanes 75; ⊙stores 9.30am-9pm Mon-Sat, restaurants & cinema 9am-1am; ℞FGC Ildefons Cerdà) in L'Hospitalet de Llobregat.

de la Riera Baixa, which plays host to '70s threads and military cast-offs. Carrer dels Tallers is also attracting a growing number of clothing and shoe shops (although CDs remain its core business). Small galleries, designer shops and arty bookshops huddle together along the streets running east of the MACBA towards La Rambla.

Designers

The heart of L'Eixample, bisected by Passeig de Gràcia, is known as the Quadrat d'Or (Golden Square) and is jammed with all sorts of glittering shops. Passeig de Gràcia is a bit of a who's who of international shopping – you'll find Spain's own high-end designers like Loewe, along with Armani, Chanel, Gucci, Stella McCartney and the rest.

El Born, particularly Carrer del Rec, is big on cool designers like Isabel Marant, Marni, Chloé and Hoss Intropia, in small, clean-line boutiques. Some Barcelona-based designs are also sold here. This is a great area if you have money to spend and hours to browse.

Markets

Barcelona's food markets are some of the best in Europe – just think of the inviting, glistening, aromatic and voluptuous offerings to be savoured in Mercat de la Boqueria (p80) or Mercat de Santa Caterina (p96). Every neighbourhood has its own central market, full of seasonal offers.

Several flea markets, like Els Encants Vells (p122), offer the opportunity to browse and enjoy the local buzz, and perhaps even find a good bargain.

Shopping Strips

Avinguda del Portal de l'Àngel This broad pedestrian avenue is lined with high-street chains, shoe shops, bookshops and more. It feeds into Carrer dels Boters and Carrer de la Portaferrissa, characterised by stores offering light-hearted costume jewellery and youth-oriented streetwear.

Avinguda Diagonal This boulevard is loaded with international fashion names and design boutiques, suitably interspersed with cafes to allow weary shoppers to take a load off.

Carrer d'Avinyó Once a fairly squalid old city street, Carrer d'Avinyó has morphed into a dynamic young fashion street.

Carrer de la Riera Baixa The place to look for a gaggle of shops flogging preloved threads.

Carrer del Consell de Cent The heart of the private art-gallery scene in Barcelona, between Passeig de Gràcia and Carrer de Muntaner.

Carrer del Petritxol Best for chocolate shops and art.

Carrer del Rec Another threads street, this one-time stream is lined with bright and cool boutiques. Check out Carrer del Bonaire and Carrer de l'Esparteria too. You'll find discount outlets and original local designers.

Carrer dels Banys Nous Along with nearby Carrer de la Palla, this is the place to look for antiques.

Passeig de Gràcia This is the premier shopping boulevard – chic with a capital 'C', and mostly given over to big-name international brands.

Lonely Planet's Top Choices

Mercat de la Boqueria (p80) Stock up on budget delicacies amid one of Europe's most vibrant food markets.

Vila Viniteca (p104) Oenophiles unite at this wonderful wine shop.

Coquette (p105) Simple and beautiful designer clothes for women.

Loisaida (p105) Men's and women's fashion, antiques and retro vinyl.

Best for Design & Craft

Drap-Art (p76) Weird and wonderful recycled art and accessories.

Arlequí Màscares (p105) Handmade masks to rival any in Venice; the perfect souvenir.

Fantastik (p89) A temple to kitsch, with kooky wonders from all around the world.

Teranyina (p89) The 'Spider's Web', so called for its intricate designs in intricate textiles.

Best for Fashion

Coquette (p105) Offbeat women's clothes that share an ethereal elegance.

Holala! Plaza (p89) Today vintage is the new designer, and nowhere has a better selection than Holala!

Bagués-Masriera (p149) Exquisite jewellery from a company with a long tradition.

Custo Barcelona (p106) Quirky, colourful clothes that are not for the shy.

Loisaida (p105) Cute, smart and somewhat retro clothing for men and women.

Best Markets

Mercat de la Boqueria (p80) The quintessential Barcelona food market.

Mercat de Santa Caterina (p96) A colourful alternative to La Boqueria, with fewer crowds and lower prices.

Els Encants Vells (p122) A sprawling flea market in a spanking new building.

El Bulevard dels Antiquaris (p148) A labyrinth of tiny antique shops that merits a morning's browsing.

Best for Souvenirs & Gifts

Born Centre de Cultura i Memòria (p97) The gift shop at this exhibition space stocks tasteful, well-made souvenirs, and books about the city.

Les Topettes (p89) Creams, oils, perfumes and soaps that look every bit as tantalising as they smell.

Sabater Hermanos (p75) Divinely fragranced shop selling handmade soaps in pretty gift boxes.

MACBA (p81) The modern art museum's gift shop has some colourful and covetable books and gifts.

Best for Food & Wine

Casa Gispert (p105) The speciality is roast nuts of every type, but you'll also find chocolate, conserves and olive oils.

Vila Viniteca (p104) A jaw-dropping cathedral of wines from Catalonia and elsewhere in Spain, tucked away in a Born side street.

Formatgeria La Seu (p75) Superb cheeses from small producers.

Caelum (p73) Deliciously wicked sweet treats made by nuns, with a little tea room downstairs.

Best for Vintage

L'Arca (p76) Ethereal gowns, often used for film sets, in the heart of the Barri Gòtic.

El Bulevard dels Antiquaris (p148) A quirky hotchpotch of antique shops.

Els Encants Vells (p122) Stunningly remodelled flea market, where you can unearth retro homeware and kitschy bric-a-brac.

Port Antic (p123) A quirky street market with finds from vintage toys to tiny oil paintings.

LGBTI Barcelona

Barcelona has a vibrant gay and lesbian scene, with a fine array of restaurants, bars and clubs in the district known as the 'Gaixample' (a portmanteau of Gay and L'Eixample), an area about five to six blocks southwest of Passeig de Gràcia around Carrer del Consell de Cent.

Local Attitudes

Despite fierce opposition from the Catholic Church, Spain legalised same-sex marriage in 2005. It became the fourth country in the world to do so. A poll just prior to the legislation passing found that over 60% of Spaniards favoured the legalisation of same-sex marriage. Gay and lesbian married couples can also adopt children.

As a rule, Barcelona is pretty tolerant and the sight of gay or lesbian couples arm in arm is generally unlikely to raise eyebrows. Transgenderism, too, is increasingly accepted.

Gay Bars

Befitting a diverse city of its size, the bar scene in Barcelona offers plenty of variety, with stylish cocktail bars, leather bars, bear bars, easygoing pubs and theme bars (with drag shows and other events) all part of the mix.

Gay Clubs

As with all clubs in town, things don't get going until well into the early morning (around 2am). The bigger and better-known clubs, like Metro (p198), one of Barcelona's pioneers in the LGBTI club scene, host top-notch DJs, multiple bars, a dark room, drag shows and other amusements. Keep in mind that most of the clubs open only from Thursday to Saturday nights.

The Lesbian Scene

The lesbian bar scene is a little sparse compared to the gay scene, with more places catering to a mixed gay-lesbian crowd (and a few straights thrown in) than an exclusively lesbian clientele. The one place that's proudly lesbian is Aire (p143), which should be a requisite stop for every nightlife-loving lesbian visiting the city. Some nominally straight bars and clubs host periodic lesbian parties. Keep an eye out for party flyers in shops and bars in the Gaixample for the latest.

Special Events

The gay and lesbian community from Barcelona and beyond takes centre stage during the annual **Pride Barcelona** (www.pride barcelona.org; ⊙late Jun-early Jul). The week-long event takes place in late June and features concerts, campy drag shows, film screenings, art shows and open-air dance parties – complete with lots and lots of foam. It culminates with a festive parade along Carrer de Sepúlveda and ends at the Plaça d'Espanya, where the big events are held.

Also of note is the LGBTI film festival, Fire! (www.cinemalambda.com), hosted by the Casal Lambda (p49) in June. Film lovers might also be able to catch a bit of the Sitges Film Festival (sitgesfilmfestival.com), which happens in early October.

Sitges: Catalonia's LGBTI Capital

Barcelona has a busy gay scene, but Spain's LGBTI capital is the saucily hedonistic Sitges, 35km southwest of Barcelona, a major destination on the international party circuit. The LGBTI community there takes a leading role in the wild Carnaval celebrations in February/March.

Lonely Planet's Top Choices

Metro (p198) The city's finest (and longest-running) gay club.

Hotel Axel (p218) Stylish gay boutique hotel in the heart of Gaixample.

Aire (p143) Barcelona's best lesbian bar, with a fab dance floor.

Best LGBTI Stays

Room Mate Pau (p218) Stylish, budget-conscious hotel on the edge of Barri Gòtic.

Hotel Axel (p218) Designer rooms, a sauna and a rooftop pool in the heart of the Gaixample.

Anakena House (p217) Not LGBT per se, but situated close to the action.

Best LGBTI Clubs

Arena Madre (p144) With striptease shows and pumping beats, it's always a fun night at Arena.

Metro (p198) One of Barcelona's top gay clubs with multiple dance floors, dark rooms and shows.

Pervert Club (p197) A fit young crowd grooves to electronic beats at this weekly party.

Best Laid-Back LGBTI

Átame (p143) Join the chatter over drinks early in the night; stay late as things heat up.

La Chapelle (p144) Casual spot for cocktails and a welcoming crowd.

Punto BCN (p144) A two-level bar with a good mix of ages and creeds.

Best Alternative Scene

New Chaps (p145) A leather bar with plenty of erotic intrigue.

Bacon Bear (p144) A man-cave retreat for burly folk and their admirers.

La Chapelle (p144) Kitschy religious symbolism is purely tongue-in-cheek at this relaxed bar.

Best Mixed Clubs

Arena Classic (p144) Fun, dance-loving crowds of all persuasions flock here.

La Terrrrazza (p197) Open-air summer dance parties up on Montjuïc.

Metro (p198) An all-inclusive door policy with a friendly mix.

Best LGBTI-Friendly Beaches

Platja de la Mar Bella (p110) A buzzing beach scene that's clothing optional at its southern tip.

Sitges (p209) Hop on a train to this LGBTI seaside mecca.

Best LGBTI-Themed Shops

Antinous (p149) Spacious bookshop with cafe in L'Eixample.

Cómplices (p76) Mix of lit and grit at this inviting bookseller.

NEED TO KNOW

Gay Organisations

Casal Lambda (Map p285; ☑93 319 55 50; www.lambda.cat; Avinguda del Marquès d'Argentera 22; ⊙5-9pm Mon-Sat; Ⓜ Barceloneta) A gay and lesbian social, cultural and information centre in La Ribera.

Useful Websites

60by80 (www.60by80. com) An excellent website for gay travellers. Click on 'Barcelona' under 'City Guides' and take it from there.

Patroc (www.patroc. com) A European gay guide, the Barcelona section of which has a useful selection of hotels, clubs and so on. Particularly good on upcoming events.

Tillate (www.tillate.es) Discover upcoming parties in this nightlife guide to regions around Spain, including Catalonia.

GaySitges (www. gaysitges.com) A specific site dedicated to this LGBTI-friendly coastal town.

PLAN YOUR TRIP LGBTI BARCELONA

Explore Barcelona

**Neighbourhoods
at a Glance** 52

**La Rambla &
Barri Gòtic**......... **54**
Top Sights 56
Sights................... 62
Eating................... 69
Drinking & Nightlife....... 72
Entertainment 74
Shopping................ 75
Sports & Activities........ 77

El Raval............. **78**
Top Sights 80
Sights................... 83
Eating................... 84
Drinking & Nightlife....... 86
Entertainment 88
Shopping................ 89
Sports & Activities........ 89

La Ribera **90**
Top Sights 92
Sights................... 96
Eating................... 99
Drinking & Nightlife......103
Entertainment 104
Shopping...............104
Sports & Activities.......106

**Barceloneta &
the Waterfront** **107**
Top Sights 109
Sights.................. 111
Eating.................. 114
Drinking & Nightlife...... 119
Entertainment 121
Shopping...............122
Sports & Activities.......124

**La Sagrada Família
& L'Eixample** **125**
Top Sights 127
Sights..................132
Eating..................136
Drinking & Nightlife......142
Entertainment 145
Shopping...............145
Sports & Activities.......149

**Gràcia &
Park Güell** **158**
Top Sights 160
Sights..................162
Eating..................162
Drinking & Nightlife......166
Entertainment 168
Shopping...............168
Sports & Activities.......170

**Camp Nou, Pedralbes
& La Zona Alta**...... **171**
Top Sights 173
Sights..................175
Eating..................176
Drinking & Nightlife......180
Entertainment 181
Shopping...............181
Sports & Activities.......182

**Montjuïc, Poble Sec
& Sant Antoni** **183**
Top Sights 185
Sights..................188
Eating..................192
Drinking & Nightlife......196
Entertainment 198
Shopping...............199
Sports & Activities.......199

**Day Trips from
Barcelona** **200**
Girona 201
Figueres............... 204
Montserrat 206
Sitges................. 208
Tarragona 210

Sleeping.......... **212**

BARCELONA'S
TOP SIGHTS

La Rambla...........................56

La Catedral 60

Museu Frederic Marès......63

Museu d'Història
de Barcelona 65

Mercat de la Boqueria 80

MACBA............................... 81

Palau Güell.........................82

Museu Picasso 92

Basílica de Santa
Maria del Mar 94

Palau de la Música
Catalana.............................95

Museu Marítim................109

El Poblenou Platges........ 110

La Sagrada Família 127

Casa Batlló.......................133

La Pedrera........................134

Park Güell.........................160

Camp Nou........................ 173

Museu-Monestir
de Pedralbes................... 174

CosmoCaixa 176

Fundació Joan Miró 185

Museu Nacional d'Art
de Catalunya 186

Neighbourhoods at a Glance

1 La Rambla & Barri Gòtic p54

La Rambla, Barcelona's most famous pedestrian strip, is a hive of activity, with buskers and peddlers, tourists and con artists mingling with the crowds strolling along the boulevard. The adjoining Barri Gòtic is packed with relics of ancient Rome, 14th-century Gothic churches and atmospheric cobblestone lanes lined with shops, bars and restaurants.

2 El Raval p78

The once down-and-out district of El Raval is still seedy in parts, though it has seen remarkable rejuvenation in recent years, with the addition of cutting-edge museums and cultural centres, including the Richard Meier–designed Museu d'Art Contemporani de Barcelona. Other highlights not to be missed include El Raval's bohemian nightlife and the sprawling culinary delights of Mercat de la Boqueria.

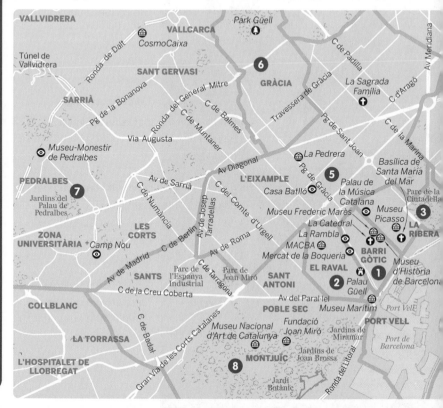

❸ La Ribera p90

This medieval quarter has a little of everything, from high-end shopping to some of Barcelona's liveliest tapas bars. Key sights include the superb Museu Picasso, the awe-inspiring Gothic Basílica de Santa Maria del Mar and the artfully sculpted Modernista concert hall of Palau de la Música Catalana. For a bit of fresh air, locals head to the leafy gardens of Parc de la Ciutadella.

❹ Barceloneta & the Waterfront p107

Since the late 20th century, Barcelona's formerly industrial waterfront has experienced a dramatic transformation, with sparkling beaches and seaside bars, elegant sculptures, a 4.5km-long boardwalk and yacht-filled marinas. The gateway is the gridlike neighbourhood of Barceloneta, a former fishing quarter full of traditional seafood restaurants.

❺ La Sagrada Família & L'Eixample p125

The elegant, if traffic-filled, district of L'Eixample (pronounced 'lay-sham-pluh') is a showcase for Modernista architecture, including Gaudí's unfinished masterpiece, La Sagrada Família. L'Eixample also has a celebrated dining scene, along with high-end boutiques and wildly diverse nightlife: university party spots, gilded cocktail lounges and the buzzing gay club scene of 'Gaixample' are all part of the mix.

❻ Gràcia & Park Güell p158

Gràcia was an independent town until the 1890s, and its narrow lanes and picturesque plazas still have a village-like feel. Well-worn cafes and bars and vintage shops make it a magnet to a young, hip crowd. On a hill to the north lies one of Gaudí's most captivating works, the outdoor Modernista storybook of Park Güell.

❼ Camp Nou, Pedralbes & La Zona Alta p171

Some of Barcelona's most sacred sights are situated within the huge expanse stretching northwest beyond L'Eixample. One is the peaceful medieval monastery of Pedralbes; another is the great shrine to Catalan football, Camp Nou. Other reasons to venture here include an amusement park and great views atop Tibidabo, the wooded trails of Parc de Collserola, and a whizz-bang, kid-friendly science museum.

❽ Montjuïc, Poble Sec & Sant Antoni p183

The hillside overlooking the port has some of the city's finest art collections: Museu Nacional d'Art de Catalunya (MNAC), Fundació Joan Miró and CaixaForum. Other galleries, gardens and an imposing castle form part of the scenery. Just below Montjuïc lie the lively tapas bars and eateries of Poble Sec, while the up-and-coming neighbourhood of Sant Antoni draws the young and hip.

La Rambla & Barri Gòtic

Neighbourhood Top Five

❶ La Rambla (p56) Taking in Barcelona's liveliest street scene, with its human statues, open-air restaurants, flower stalls and saunterers from every corner of the globe.

❷ La Catedral (p60) Exploring the spectacular cloister, shadowy chapels, nooks and crannies of this magnificent Gothic masterpiece.

❸ Museu d'Història de Barcelona (p65) Walking through the subterranean ruins of Roman-era 'Barcino'.

❹ Museu Frederic Marès (p63) Wandering through its strange and wondrous collections.

❺ Plaça Reial (p62) Enjoying an alfresco meal or a drink under the arcades of this picturesque square.

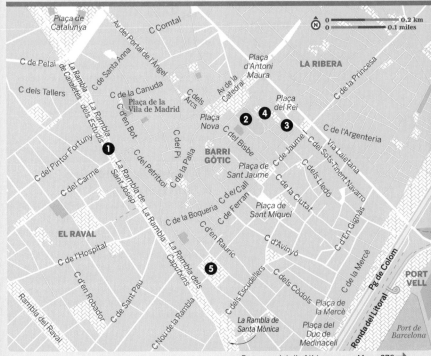

For more detail of this area see Map p276 ➡

Explore La Rambla & Barri Gòtic

La Rambla (p56) is Spain's most talked-about boulevard. It certainly packs a lot of colour into a short walk, with flower stands, historic buildings, a produce market, overpriced beers and tourist tat, and a ceaselessly changing parade of people from all corners of the globe. Once a river and sewage ditch on the edge of the medieval city, it still marks the southwest flank of the Barri Gòtic, the nucleus of old Barcelona. Come in the early morning to see it at its most peaceful, then return in the afternoon for the daily circus parade in all its colourful unruliness.

You can easily spend several days exploring the Barri Gòtic without leaving its medieval streets. In addition to major sights, the tangle of narrow lanes and tranquil plazas conceal atmospheric shops, cafes and bars. There are swarms of tourists afoot – as well as some overpriced restaurants best avoided – but Barri Gòtic has plenty of local character.

Don't miss La Catedral (p60) and the smattering of Roman ruins inside the Museu d'Història de Barcelona (p65). Another highlight is lingering over coffee or an alfresco meal at one of the Barri Gòtic's many outdoor plazas. The Plaça Reial (p62), a wide, pretty square lined with restaurants, is perhaps the best-known spot for a bite, though Plaça del Pi and tiny Plaça de Sant Just are also quite charming.

By night, Barri Gòtic transforms into a maze-like collection of bars and clubs. The streets around Plaça Reial and Plaça George Orwell (also known as Plaça del Trippy) are good places to bar-hop, though you'll find nightspots all over the neighbourhood.

Local Life

→ **Folk dancing** Although it's mostly old-timers dancing the *sardana* (Catalonia's national folk dance), a growing number of young folks are enjoying this Catalan dance. Learn a few moves and join in at 6pm on Saturday and noon on Sunday in front of La Catedral (p60).

→ **Hangouts** For cocktails and kitsch whimsy, head to Sor Rita (p72). Salterio (p73) is also a much-loved meeting spot.

→ **Bar-hopping** Plaça Reial, Plaça de George Orwell and the narrow streets between the two are lively spots to take in the local Gòtic nightlife, as are Carrer Ample and Carrer de la Mercè.

Getting There & Away

→ **Metro** Key stops near or on La Rambla include Catalunya, Liceu and Drassanes. For Barri Gòtic's east side, Jaume I and Urquinaona are handiest.

→ **Bus** Airport and night buses arrive and depart from Plaça de Catalunya.

→ **Taxi** Easiest to catch on La Rambla or Plaça de Catalunya.

Lonely Planet's Top Tip

For the best-value dining, plan to make lunch your main meal. Many restaurants in the Barri Gòtic offer three-course meals for €12 to €15, including wine.

✖ Best Places to Eat

→ La Vinateria del Call (p70)
→ Cafè de l'Acadèmia (p70)
→ Pla (p71)
→ Koy Shunka (p72)
→ Onofre (p71)
→ Rasoterra (p71)

For reviews, see p69. →

🍷 Best Places to Drink

→ Ocaña (p70)
→ Sor Rita (p72)
→ L'Ascensor (p72)
→ Polaroid (p72)

For reviews, see p72. →

👁 Best Historical Treasures

→ Temple Romà d'August (p62)
→ Via Sepulcral Romana (p69)
→ Sinagoga Major (p68)
→ Domus de Sant Honorat (p67)

TOP SIGHT
LA RAMBLA

Barcelona's most famous street is both a tourist magnet and a window into Catalan culture, with cultural centres, theatres and intriguing architecture. The middle of La Rambla is a broad pedestrian boulevard, crowded every day with a wide cross-section of society. A stroll here is pure sensory overload, with souvenir hawkers, buskers, pavement artists, mimes and living statues all part of the ever-changing street scene.

DON'T MISS

- Palau de la Virreina
- Centre d'Art Santa Mònica
- Església de Betlem
- Palau Moja
- Mosaïc de Miró

PRACTICALITIES

- Map p276, C5
- Ⓜ Catalunya, Liceu, Drassanes

History

La Rambla takes its name from a seasonal stream (*ramla* in Arabic) that once ran here. From the early Middle Ages, it was better known as the Cagalell (Stream of Shit) and lay outside the city walls until the 14th century. Monastic buildings were then built and, subsequently, mansions of the well-to-do from the 16th to the early 19th centuries. Unofficially La Rambla is divided into five sections, which explains why many know it as Las Ramblas.

La Rambla de Canaletes

The section of La Rambla north of Plaça de Catalunya is named after the **Font de Canaletes** (Map p276; La Rambla; Ⓜ Catalunya), an inconspicuous turn-of-the-20th-century drinking fountain, the water of which supposedly emerges from what were once known as the springs of Canaletes. It used to be said that a proper *barcelonin* was one who 'drank the waters of Les Canaletes'. Nowadays people claim that anyone who drinks from the fountain will return to Barcelona, which is not such a bad prospect. Delirious football fans gather here to celebrate whenever the main home side, FC Barcelona, wins a cup or the league premiership.

La Rambla dels Estudis

La Rambla dels Estudis, from Carrer de la Canuda running south to Carrer de la Portaferrissa, was formerly home to a twittering bird market, which closed in 2010 after 150 years in operation.

Església de Betlem

Just north of Carrer del Carme, this **church** (Map p276; ☑ 93 318 38 23; www.mdbetlem.net; Carrer d'en Xuclà 2; ⊙ 8.30am-1.30pm & 6-9pm; Ⓜ Liceu) was constructed in baroque style for the Jesuits in the late 17th and early 18th centuries to replace an earlier church destroyed by fire in 1671. Fire was a bit of a theme for this site: the church was once considered the most splendid of Barcelona's few baroque offerings, but leftist arsonists torched it in 1936.

Palau Moja

Looming over the eastern side of La Rambla, **Palau Moja** (Map p276; ☑ 93 316 27 40; https://palaumoja.com; Carrer de Portaferrissa 1; ⊙ 10am-9pm, cafe 9.30am-midnight Mon-Fri, 11am-midnight Sat & Sun; Ⓜ Liceu) **FREE** is a neoclassical building dating from the second half of the 18th century. Its clean, classical lines are best appreciated from across the other side of the street. It mostly houses government offices, but access is now an option thanks to a large gift shop and cafe.

La Rambla de Sant Josep

From Carrer de la Portaferrissa to Plaça de la Boqueria, what is officially called La Rambla de Sant Josep (named after a now nonexistent monastery) is lined with flower stalls, which give it the alternative name La Rambla de les Flors. This stretch also contains the bawdy Museu de l'Eròtica (p67).

Mosaïc de Miró

At Plaça de la Boqueria, where four side streets meet just north of Liceu metro station, you can walk all over a Miró – the colourful **mosaic** (Map p276; Plaça de la Boqueria; [M]Liceu) in the pavement, with one tile signed by the artist. Miró chose this site as it's near the house where he was born on the Passatge del Crèdit. The mosaic's bold colours and vivid swirling forms are instantly recognisable to Miró fans, though plenty of tourists stroll right over it without realising.

Palau de la Virreina

The **Palau de la Virreina** (Map p276; La Rambla 99; [M]Liceu) is a grand 18th-century rococo mansion (with some neoclassical elements) that now houses the **Centre de la Imatge** (Map p276; [☎]93 316 10 00; www.ajuntament.barcelona.cat/lavirreina; Palau de la Virreina; ⊙noon-8pm Tue-Sun; [M]Liceu) [FREE], which has rotating photography exhibits.

Just south of the Palau, in El Raval, is the Mercat de la Boqueria (p80), one of the best-stocked and most colourful produce markets in Europe.

La Rambla dels Caputxins

La Rambla dels Caputxins, named after a former monastery, runs from Plaça de la Boqueria to Carrer dels Escudellers. The latter street is named after the potters' guild, founded in the 13th century, the members of which lived and worked here. On the western side of La Rambla is the Gran Teatre del Liceu (p62); to the southeast is the entrance to the palm-shaded Plaça Reial (p62). Below this point La Rambla gets seedier, with the occasional strip club and peep show.

La Rambla de Santa Mònica

The final stretch of La Rambla widens out to approach the Mirador de Colom (p112) overlooking Port Vell. La Rambla here is named after the Convent de Santa Mònica, which once stood on the western flank of the street and has since been converted into the **Centre d'Art Santa Mònica** (Map p276; [☎]93 567 11 10; http://artssantamonica.gencat.cat; La Rambla 7; ⊙11am-9pm Tue-Sat, 11am-5pm Sun; [M]Drassanes) [FREE], a cultural centre that mostly exhibits modern multimedia installations.

CIVIL WAR

Many writers and journalists headed to Barcelona during the Spanish Civil War, including British author George Orwell, who vividly described La Rambla gripped by revolutionary fervour in the early days of the war in his book *Homage to Catalonia*.

ROMAN NECROPOLIS

A block east from the Rambla dels Estudis, along Carrer de la Canuda, is the Plaça de la Vila de Madrid, which has a sunken garden where Roman tombs lie exposed in what was once the Via Sepulcral Romana.

La Rambla

A TIMELINE

Look beyond the human statues and tourist-swarmed restaurants, and you'll find a fascinating piece of Barcelona history dating back many centuries.

13th century A serpentine seasonal stream (called *ramla* in Arabic) runs outside the city walls. As Barcelona grows, the stream will eventually become an open sewer until it's later paved over.

1500–1800 During this early period, La Rambla was dotted with convents and monasteries, including the baroque ❶ **Església de Betlem**, completed in the early 1700s.

1835 The city erupts in anticlericism, with riots and the burning of convents. Along La Rambla, many religious assets are destroyed or seized by the state. This paves the way for new developments, including the ❷ **Mercat de la Boqueria** in 1840, the ❸ **Gran Teatre**

Teatre Poliorama
Built in 1894 as the seat of the Royal Academy of Sciences and Arts, it later served as a cinema, and a strategic lookout for one communist faction during the Spanish Civil War.

KIEV.VICTOR/SHUTTERSTOCK ©

Església de Betlem
Dedicated to the Holy Family, this is the last standing of the many churches once lining La Rambla. Its once sumptuous interior was gutted during the Spanish Civil War.

Font de Canaletes

Via Sepulcral Romana

Plaça del Pi

Plaça de St Josep Oriol

Palau Moja

Centre de la Imatge ❶

Palau de la Virreina

❷

Mercat de la Boqueria
The official name of Barcelona's most photogenic market is El Mercat de Sant Josep, which references the convent of St Josep that once stood here.

ALE ARGENTIERI/SHUTTERSTOCK ©

Gran Teatre del Liceu
Although badly damaged by fire in 1994, this gorgeous opera house was restored and reborn in 1999, and remains one of Europe's finest theatres.

TONO BALAGUER/SHUTTERSTOCK ©

del Liceu in 1847 and ④ **Plaça Reial** in 1848.

1883 Architect Josep Vilaseca refurbishes the ⑤ **Casa Bruno Cuadros**. As Modernisme is sweeping across the city, Vilaseca creates an eclectic work using stained glass, wrought iron, Egyptian imagery and Japanese prints.

1888 Barcelona hosts the Universal Exhibition. The city sees massive urban renewal projects, with the first electric lights coming to La Rambla, and the building of the ⑥ **Mirador de Colom**.

1936–39 La Rambla becomes the site of bloody street fighting during the Spanish Civil War. British journalist and author George Orwell, who spends three days holed up in the ⑦ **Teatre Poliorama** during street battles, later describes the tumultuous days in his excellent book, *Homage to Catalonia*.

2017 A horrific terrorist attack saw a van driving into pedestrians, killing 14 and injuring scores of others.

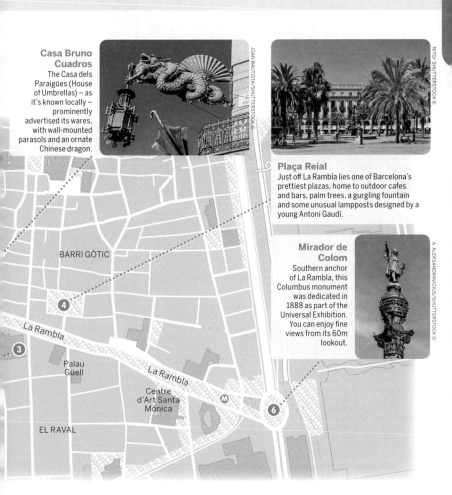

Casa Bruno Cuadros
The Casa dels Paraigües (House of Umbrellas) – as it's known locally – prominently advertised its wares, with wall-mounted parasols and an ornate Chinese dragon.

Plaça Reial
Just off La Rambla lies one of Barcelona's prettiest plazas, home to outdoor cafes and bars, palm trees, a gurgling fountain and some unusual lampposts designed by a young Antoni Gaudí.

Mirador de Colom
Southern anchor of La Rambla, this Columbus monument was dedicated in 1888 as part of the Universal Exhibition. You can enjoy fine views from its 60m lookout.

BARRI GÒTIC

La Rambla

Palau Güell

La Rambla

Centre d'Art Santa Mònica

EL RAVAL

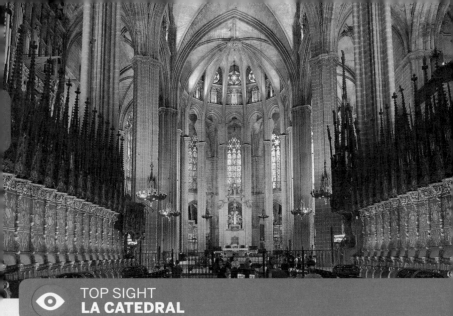

TOP SIGHT
LA CATEDRAL

Barcelona's central place of worship presents a magnificent image. The richly decorated main facade, laced with gargoyles and the stone intricacies you would expect of northern European Gothic, sets it quite apart from other churches in Barcelona. The facade was actually added in 1870, although the rest of the building was built between 1298 and 1460.

The Interior

The interior is a broad, soaring space divided into a central nave and two aisles by lines of elegant, slim pillars. The cathedral was one of the few churches in Barcelona spared by the anarchists in the civil war, so its ornamentation, never overly lavish, is intact.

Coro

In the middle of the central nave is the late-14th-century, exquisitely sculpted timber *coro* (choir stalls). The coats of arms on the stalls belong to members of the Barcelona chapter of the Order of the Golden Fleece. Emperor Carlos V presided over the order's meeting here in 1519.

Crypt

A broad staircase before the main altar leads you down to the crypt, which contains the tomb of Santa Eulàlia, one of Barcelona's two patron saints and more affectionately known as Laia. The reliefs on the alabaster sarcophagus recount some of her tortures and, along the top strip, the removal of her body to its present resting place.

DON'T MISS

➡ The *claustre* and its 13 geese
➡ Views from the roof
➡ The crypt
➡ The *coro*

PRACTICALITIES

➡ Map p276, D3
➡ ☎ 93 342 82 62
➡ www.catedralbcn.org
➡ Plaça de la Seu
➡ donation entrance €7, choir €3, roof €3
➡ ⏰ 8am-12.45pm & 5.45-7.30pm Mon-Fri, 8am-8pm Sat & Sun, entry by donation 1-5.30pm Mon,1-5pm Sat, 2-5pm Sun
➡ Ⓜ Jaume I

The Roof

For a bird's-eye view (mind the poo) of medieval Barcelona, visit the cathedral's roof and tower by taking the lift (€3) from the Capella de les Animes del Purgatori near the northeast transept.

Claustre

From the southwest transept, exit by the partly Romanesque door (one of the few remnants of the present church's predecessor) to the leafy *claustre* (cloister), with its fountains and flock of 13 geese. The geese supposedly represent the age of Santa Eulàlia at the time of her martyrdom and have, generation after generation, been squawking here since medieval days. One of the cloister chapels commemorates 930 priests, monks and nuns martyred during the civil war.

In the northwest corner of the cloister is the Capella de Santa Llúcia (p64), one of the few reminders of Romanesque Barcelona (although the interior is largely Gothic).

Casa de l'Ardiaca

Upon exiting the Capella de Santa Llúcia, wander across the lane into the 16th-century Casa de l'Ardiaca (p67), which houses the city's archives. Stroll around the supremely serene courtyard, cooled by trees and a fountain; it was renovated by Lluis Domènech i Montaner in 1902, when the building was owned by the lawyers' college. Domènech i Montaner also designed the postal slot, which is adorned with swallows and a tortoise, said to represent the swiftness of truth and the plodding pace of justice. You can get a good glimpse at some stout Roman wall in here. Upstairs, you can look down into the courtyard and across to La Catedral.

Palau Episcopal

Across Carrer del Bisbe is the 17th-century Palau Episcopal (p64). Virtually nothing remains of the original 13th-century structure. The Roman city's northwest gate was here and you can see the lower segments of the Roman towers that stood on either side of the gate at the base of the Palau Episcopal and Casa de l'Ardiaca. In fact, the lower part of the entire northwest wall of the Casa de l'Ardiaca is of Roman origin – you can also make out part of the first arch of a Roman aqueduct.

SANT CRIST DE LEPANT

In the first chapel on the right from the northwest entrance, the main Crucifixion figure above the altar is Sant Crist de Lepant. It is said Don Juan's flagship bore it into battle at Lepanto and that the figure acquired its odd stance by dodging an incoming cannonball. Left from the main entrance is the baptismal font where, according to one story, six North American Indians brought to Europe by Columbus after his first voyage of accidental discovery were bathed in holy water.

VISITING LA CATEDRAL

You may visit La Catedral in one of two ways. In the morning or afternoon, general admission is free, although you have to pay to visit the choir stalls and the roof. If you want to see more, it's worth paying the extra euro for the so-called 'donation entrance' which gives access to the cathedral floor, the cloister, the roof, the choir, the chapter hall and the Saint Christ of Lepanto's Chapel.

◉ SIGHTS

LA RAMBLA   STREET
See p56.

LA CATEDRAL   CATHEDRAL
See p60.

PLAÇA DEL REI   SQUARE
Map p276 (King's Square; Ⓜ Jaume I) Plaça del Rei is a picturesque plaza where Fernando and Isabel are thought to have received Columbus following his first New World voyage. It is the courtyard of the former Palau Reial Major. The palace today houses a superb history museum (p65), with significant Roman ruins underground.

PLAÇA REIAL   SQUARE
Map p276 (Ⓜ Liceu) One of the most photogenic squares in Barcelona, and certainly its liveliest. Numerous restaurants, bars and nightspots lie beneath the arcades of 19th-century neoclassical buildings, with a buzz of activity at all hours.

It was created on the site of a convent, one of several destroyed along La Rambla (the street was teeming with religious institutions) in the wake of the Spain-wide disentailment laws that stripped the Church of much of its property. The lamp posts by the central fountain are Antoni Gaudí's first known works in the city.

PALAU DE LA GENERALITAT HISTORIC BUILDING
Map p276 (http://presidencia.gencat.cat; Plaça de Sant Jaume; ⊘2nd & 4th weekend of month; Ⓜ Jaume I) Founded in the early 15th century, the Palau de la Generalitat is open on limited occasions only (one-hour guided tours on the second and fourth weekends of the month, plus open-door days). The most impressive of the ceremonial halls is the Saló de Sant Jordi (Hall of St George), named after the region's patron saint. To see inside, book on the website.

Marc Safont designed the original Gothic main entrance on Carrer del Bisbe. The modern main entrance on Plaça de Sant Jaume is a late-Renaissance job with neoclassical leanings. If you wander by in the evening, squint up through the windows into the Saló de Sant Jordi and you will get some idea of the sumptuousness of the interior.

Normally you will have to enter from Carrer de Sant Sever. The first rooms you pass through are characterised by low vaulted ceilings. From here you head upstairs to the raised courtyard known as the Pati dels Tarongers, a modest Gothic orangery (open about once a month for concert performances of the palace's chimes). The 16th-century Sala Daurada i de Sessions, one of the rooms leading off the patio, is a splendid meeting hall lit up by huge chandeliers. Still more imposing is the Renaissance Saló de Sant Jordi, the murals of which were added last century – many an occasion of pomp and circumstance takes place here. Finally, you descend the staircase of the Gothic Pati Central to leave by what was originally the building's main entrance.

TEMPLE D'AUGUST   RUINS
Map p276 (📞93 256 21 22; www.muhba.cat; Carrer del Paradis 10; ⊘10am-7pm Tue-Sat, to 8pm Sun, to 2pm Mon; Ⓜ Jaume I) FREE Opposite the southeast end of La Catedral, narrow Carrer del Paradis leads towards Plaça de Sant Jaume. Inside No 10, an intriguing building with Gothic and baroque touches, are four columns and the architrave of Barcelona's main Roman temple, dedicated to Caesar Augustus and built to worship his imperial highness in the 1st century AD.

You are now standing on the highest point of Roman Barcino, Mont Tàber (a grand height of 16.9m – unlikely to induce altitude sickness). You may well find the door open outside the listed hours.

GRAN TEATRE DEL LICEU   ARCHITECTURE
Map p276 (📞93 485 99 00; www.liceubarcelona. cat; La Rambla 51-59; tours adult/concession/ child under 7yr 45min €9/7.50/free, 25min €6/5/ free; ⊘45min tours hourly 2-6pm Mon-Fri, from 9.30am Sat, 25min tours 1.30pm Mon-Sat; Ⓜ Liceu) If you can't catch a night at the opera, you can still have a look around one of Europe's greatest opera houses, known to locals as the Liceu. Smaller than Milan's La Scala but bigger than Venice's La Fenice, it can seat up to 2300 people in its grand auditorium.

Built in 1847, the Liceu launched such Catalan stars as Josep (aka José) Carreras and Montserrat Caballé. Fire virtually destroyed it in 1994, but city authorities were quick to get it back into operation. Carefully reconstructing the 19th-century auditorium and installing the latest in theatre technology, technicians finalised its restoration in October 1999.

You can take a 25-minute guided tour around the main public areas of the thea-

TOP SIGHT
MUSEU FREDERIC MARÈS

One of the wildest collections of historical curios lies inside this vast medieval complex, once part of the royal palace of the counts of Barcelona. A rather worn coat of arms on the wall indicates that it was also, for a while, the seat of the Spanish Inquisition in Barcelona.

Frederic Marès i Deulovol (1893–1991) was a rich sculptor, traveller and obsessive collector. He specialised in medieval Spanish sculpture, huge quantities of which are displayed in the basement and on the ground and 1st floors – including some lovely polychrome wooden sculptures of the Crucifixion and the Virgin. Among the most eye-catching pieces is a reconstructed Romanesque doorway with four arches, taken from a 13th-century country church in the Aragonese province of Huesca.

The top two floors comprise 'the collector's cabinet', a mind-boggling array of knick-knacks: medieval weaponry, finely carved pipes, delicate ladies' fans, intricate 'floral' displays made of seashells, and 19th-century daguerreotypes and photographs. A room that once served as Marès' study and library is now crammed with sculptures.

DON'T MISS

➡ Displays from the collector's cabinet
➡ Sculptures on the 1st floor
➡ Marès' study
➡ The courtyard cafe

PRACTICALITIES

➡ Map p276, D3
➡ ✆93 256 35 00
➡ www.museumares. bcn.cat
➡ Plaça de Sant Iu 5
➡ adult/concession/ child €4.20/2.40/free, 3-8pm Sun & 1st Sun of month free
➡ ⏱10am-7pm Tue-Sat, 11am-8pm Sun
➡ Ⓜ Jaume I

---

tre or join a longer guided tour. On the 45-minute tour you are taken to the grand foyer, with its thick pillars and sumptuous chandeliers, and then up the marble staircase to the Saló dels Miralls (Hall of Mirrors). These both survived the 1994 fire and the latter was traditionally where theatregoers mingled during intermission. With mirrors, ceiling frescoes, fluted columns and high-and-mighty phrases in praise of the arts, it all exudes a typically neobaroque richness worthy of its 19th-century patrons. You are then led up to the 4th-floor stalls to admire the theatre itself.

The tour also takes in a collection of Modernista art, El Cercle del Liceu, which contains works by Ramon Casas. It is possible to book special tours: one is similar to the guided tour but also including a half-hour music recital in the Saló dels Miralls, while another penetrates the inner workings of the stage and backstage work areas.

BASÍLICA DE SANTA MARIA DEL PI CHURCH
Map p276 (✆93 318 47 43; www.basilicadelpi. com; Plaça del Pi; adult/concession/child under 7yr €4/3/free; ⏱10am-6pm; Ⓜ Liceu) This striking 14th-century church is a classic of Catalan Gothic, with an imposing facade, a wide interior and a single nave. The simple decor in the main sanctuary contrasts with the gilded chapels and exquisite stained-glass windows that bathe the interior in ethereal light. The beautiful rose window above its entrance is one of the world's largest. Occasional concerts are staged here (classical guitar, choral groups and chamber orchestras).

The third chapel on the left is dedicated to Sant Josep Oriol, who was parish priest here from 1687 to 1702. The chapel has a map showing the places in the church where he worked numerous miracles (he was canonised in 1909). According to legend, a 10th-century fisherman discovered an image of the Virgin Mary in a *pi* (pine tree) that he was intent on cutting down to build a boat. Struck by the vision, he instead built a little chapel, later to be succeeded by this Gothic church. A pine still grows in the square outside the church. There are guided tours, including of the bell towers, from Monday to Friday at noon and 1pm, and on Saturday and Sunday at noon, 1pm, 3pm and 4pm (€8.50).

PLAÇA DE SANT JAUME SQUARE

Map p276 (MLiceu, Jaume I) In the 2000 or so years since the Romans settled here, the area around this often-remodelled square, which started life as the forum, has been the focus of Barcelona's civic life. This is still the central staging area for Barcelona's traditional festivals. Facing each other across the square are the Palau de la Generalitat (p62), seat of Catalonia's regional government, on the north side and the Ajuntament to the south.

Behind the Ajuntament rise the awful town-hall offices built in the 1970s over Plaça de Sant Miquel. Opposite is a rare 15th-century gem, Palau Centelles (p65), on the corner of Baixada de Sant Miquel. You can wander into the fine Gothic-Renaissance courtyard if the gates are open.

AJUNTAMENT ARCHITECTURE

Map p276 (Casa de la Ciutat; ☑93 402 70 00; www.bcn.cat; Plaça de Sant Jaume; ☺10.30am-1.30pm Sun; MJaume I) FREE The Ajuntament, otherwise known as the Casa de la Ciutat, has been the seat of power for centuries. The Consell de Cent (the city's ruling council) first sat here in the 14th century, but the building has lamentably undergone many changes over the centuries, and only the original, now disused, entrance on Carrer de la Ciutat retains its Gothic ornament.

The main 19th-century neoclassical facade on the square is a charmless riposte to the Palau de la Generalitat opposite. Inside, the Saló de Cent is the hall in which the town council once held its plenary sessions. The broad vaulting is pure Catalan Gothic and the *artesonado* (Mudéjar wooden ceiling with interlaced beams leaving a pattern of spaces for decoration) demonstrates fine work. In fact, much of what you see is comparatively recent. The building was badly damaged in a bombardment in 1842 and has

been repaired and tampered with repeatedly. The wooden neo-Gothic seating was added at the beginning of the 20th century, as was the grand alabaster *retablo* (retable, or altarpiece) at the back. To the right you enter the small Saló de la Reina Regente, built in 1860, where the Ajuntament now sits. To the left of the Saló de Cent is the Saló de les Croniques – the murals here recount Catalan exploits in Greece and the Near East in Catalonia's empire-building days.

CAPELLA REIAL DE SANTA ÀGATA CHURCH

Map p276 (MUHBA, Plaça del Rei; ☺10am-7pm Tue-Sat, to 2pm Mon, to 8pm Sun; MJaume I) The 14th-century Capella Reial de Santa Àgata is the chapel of the Palau Reial Major (Grand Royal Palace), visited within the Museu d'Història de Barcelona (p65). Outside, a spindly bell tower rises from the northeast side of Plaça del Rei. Inside, all is bare except for the 15th-century altarpiece and the magnificent *techumbre* (decorated timber ceiling). The altarpiece is considered to be one of Jaume Huguet's finest surviving works.

HASH, MARIHUANA & HEMP MUSEUM MUSEUM

Map p276 (☑93 319 75 39; www.hashmuseum.com; Carrer Ample 35; adult/child under 13yr €9/free; ☺10am-10pm; MJaume I) The world's largest museum dedicated to all things cannabis-related opened to much fanfare in 2012 (even Virgin founder Richard Branson was at the opening). Set in the beautifully restored 16th-century Palau Mornau, exhibitions delve into the role the plant has played over the years, with 19th-century medicinal cannabis bottles, pulp film posters and consumer products made from hemp among the displays.

PALAU EPISCOPAL HISTORIC BUILDING

Map p276 (Palau del Bisbat, Bishop's Palace; Carrer del Bisbe; MJaume I) Across Carrer del Bisbe is the 17th-century Palau Episcopal. Virtually nothing remains of the original 13th-century structure. The Roman city's northwest gate stood here and you can see the lower segments of the Roman towers that stood on either side of the gate at the base of the Palau Episcopal and Casa de L'Ardiaca (p67).

CAPELLA DE SANTA LLÚCIA CHURCH

Map p276 (Plaça de la Seu; ☺8am-7.30pm Mon-Fri, to 8pm Sat & Sun; MJaume I) FREE One of the few reminders of Romanesque

---

ⓘ MANIC MONDAYS

Many attractions shut their doors on Monday, but there are plenty of exceptions, including:

Gran Teatre del Liceu (p62)

La Catedral (p60)

Museu de Cera (p69)

Museu de l'Eròtica (p67)

Sinagoga Major (p68)

TOP SIGHT
MUSEU D'HISTÒRIA DE BARCELONA

One of Barcelona's most fascinating museums takes you back through the centuries to the very foundations of Roman Barcino. You'll stroll amid extensive ruins of the town that flourished here following its founding by Emperor Augustus around 10 BC. Equally impressive is the setting inside the former Palau Reial Major (Grand Royal Palace) on Plaça del Rei (King's Sq, the former palace's courtyard), among the key locations of medieval princely power in Barcelona.

Below ground is a remarkable walk through about 4 sq km of excavated Roman and Visigothic Barcelona. After the display on the typical Roman *domus* (villa), you reach a public laundry. You pass dyeing shops, a public cold-water bath, shops dedicated to the making of *garum* (a fish sauce enjoyed across the Roman Empire), a 6th-century church and winemaking stores.

Ramparts then wind upward, past remains of the gated patio of a Roman house, the medieval Palau Episcopal (Bishops' Palace) and into two broad vaulted halls with displays on medieval Barcelona. The finale is the Saló del Tinell, the royal palace banqueting hall and a fine example of Catalan Gothic (built 1359–70). It was here that Fernando and Isabel heard Columbus' first reports of the New World.

DON'T MISS
→ Public laundry
→ Winemaking stores
→ Saló del Tinell
→ Displays on medieval Barcelona

PRACTICALITIES
→ MUHBA
→ Map p276, E3
→ ☑93 256 21 00
→ www.museuhistoria.bcn.cat
→ Plaça del Rei
→ adult/concession/child €7/5/free, 3-8pm Sun & 1st Sun of month free
→ ⊙10am-7pm Tue-Sat, to 2pm Mon, to 8pm Sun
→ Ⓜ Jaume I

Barcelona (although the interior is largely Gothic), the Capella de Santa Llúcia is located in the northwest corner of the *claustre* (cloister) in the Catedral, but originally was the chapel for the adjacent Bishop's Palace.

PALAU CENTELLES ARCHITECTURE
Map p276 (Baixada de Sant Miquel 8; Ⓜ Jaume I) A rare 15th-century gem, Palau Centelles is on the corner of Baixada de Sant Miquel. You can wander into the fine Gothic-Renaissance courtyard if the gates are open.

PLAÇA DE SANT JOSEP ORIOL SQUARE
Map p276 (Ⓜ Liceu) This small plaza flanking the majestic Basílica de Santa Maria del Pi (p63) is one of the prettiest in the Barri Gòtic. Its bars and cafes attract buskers and artists and make it a lively place to hang out. It is surrounded by quaint streets, many dotted with appealing cafes, restaurants and shops.

ESGLÉSIA DE LA MERCÈ CHURCH
Map p276 (☑93 315 27 56; www.basilicadelamerce.cat; Plaça de la Mercè 1; ⊙10am-8pm Mon, Tue, Thu, Fri & Sun, 10am-1pm & 6-8pm Wed & Sat; Ⓜ Drassanes) Raised in the 1760s on the site of its Gothic predecessor, the baroque Església de la Mercè is home to Barcelona's most celebrated patron saint. It was badly damaged during the civil war. What remains is, however, quite a curiosity. The baroque facade facing the square contrasts with the Renaissance flank along Carrer Ample. Climb the steps behind the altar for a close-up view of the Virgin Mary statue for whom the church is named; it dates from 1361.

ESGLÉSIA DE SANTS JUST I PASTOR CHURCH
Map p276 (☑93 301 74 33; www.basilicasantjust.cat; Plaça de Sant Just; ⊙11am-2pm & 5-9pm Mon & Wed-Sat, to 8pm Tue, 10am-1pm Sun; Ⓜ Jaume I) This somewhat neglected, single-nave church, with chapels on either side of the buttressing, was built in 1342 in Catalan Gothic style on what is reputedly the site of the oldest parish church in Barcelona. Inside, you can admire some fine stained-glass windows. In front of it, in a pretty little square that was used as a film set (a smelly Parisian marketplace) in 2006

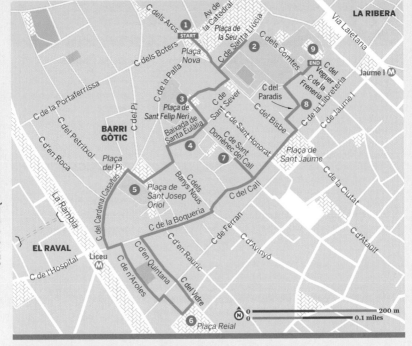

Neighbourhood Walk
Hidden Treasures in the Barri Gòtic

START LA CATEDRAL
END PLAÇA DEL REI
LENGTH 1.5KM; 1½ HOURS

This scenic walk through the Barri Gòtic will take you back in time, from the early days of Roman-era Barcino through to the medieval era.

Before entering the cathedral, have a look at ❶ **three Picasso friezes** on the building facing the square. After noting his signature style, wander through ❷ **La Catedral** (p60); don't miss the cloister with its flock of 13 geese. Leaving the cathedral, enter the former gates of the ancient fortified city and turn right into ❸ **Plaça de Sant Felip Neri**. Note the shrapnel-scarred walls of the old church, damaged by pro-Francoist bombers in 1938. A plaque commemorates the victims (mostly children) of the bombing.

Head out of the square and turn right. On this narrow lane, you'll spot a small ❹ **statue of Santa Eulàlia**, one of Barcelona's patron saints who suffered various tortures during her martyrdom. Make your way west to the looming 14th-century ❺ **Església de Sant Maria del Pi** (p63), which is famed for its magnificent rose window. Follow the curving road and zigzag down to ❻ **Plaça Reial** (p62), one of Barcelona's prettiest squares. Flanking the fountain are lamp posts designed by Antoni Gaudí.

Stroll up to Carrer de la Boqueria and turn left on Carrer de Sant Domènec del Call. This leads into the El Call district, once the heart of the medieval Jewish quarter, until the bloody pogrom of 1391. The ❼ **Sinagoga Major** (p68), one of Europe's oldest, was discovered in 1996. Head across Plaça de Sant Jaume and turn left after Carrer del Bisbe. You'll soon pass the entrance to the remnants of a ❽ **Roman Temple**, with four columns hidden in a small courtyard.

The final stop is ❾ **Plaça del Rei** (p62), a picturesque plaza where Fernando and Isabel received Columbus following his first New World voyage. The former palace today houses a superb history museum, with significant Roman ruins underground.

for *Perfume: The Story of a Murderer,* is what's claimed to be the city's oldest Gothic fountain.

On the morning of 11 September 1924, Antoni Gaudí was arrested as he attempted to enter the church from this square to attend Mass. In those days of the dictatorship of General Primo de Rivera, it took little to ruffle official feathers, and Gaudí's refusal to speak Spanish to the overbearing Guardia Civil officers who had stopped him earned him the better part of a day in the cells until a friend came to bail him out.

There are guided tours from Monday to Saturday (€5, or €10 including the bell tower).

PALAU DEL LLOCTINENT   HISTORIC SITE

Map p276 (Carrer dels Comtes; ☺10am-2pm & 4-8pm Mon-Sat; Ⓜ Jaume I) **FREE** This converted 16th-century palace has a peaceful courtyard worth wandering through. Have a look upwards from the main staircase to admire the extraordinary timber *artesonado,* a sculpted ceiling made to seem like the upturned hull of a boat. Temporary exhibitions, usually related in some way to the archives, are often held here.

Next to the Plaça del Rei, the *palau* (palace) was built in the 1550s as the residence of the Spanish *lloctinent* (viceroy) of Catalonia and later converted into a convent. From 1853 it housed the Arxiu de la Corona d'Aragón, a unique archive with documents detailing the history of the Crown of Aragón and Catalonia, starting in the 12th century and reaching to the 20th.

CASA DE L'ARDIACA   HISTORIC BUILDING

Map p276 (Arxiu Històric; Carrer de Santa Llúcia 1; ☺9am-8.45pm Mon-Fri, 10am-8pm Sat Sep-Jun, 9am-7.30pm Jul & Aug; Ⓜ Jaume I) **FREE** Across the lane from Capella de Santa Llúcia is the 16th-century Casa de l'Ardiaca (Archdeacon's House), which houses the city's archives. Step into the supremely serene courtyard, cooled by trees and a fountain; it was renovated by Lluís Domènech i Montaner in 1902, when the building was owned by the lawyers' college. Domènech i Montaner also designed the postal slot, which is adorned with swallows and a tortoise, said to represent the swiftness of truth and the plodding pace of justice.

You can get a good glimpse at some stout Roman wall in here. Upstairs, you can look down into the courtyard and across to La Catedral.

ROMAN WALLS

From Plaça del Rei it's worth taking a detour northeast to see the two best surviving stretches of Barcelona's **Roman walls** (Map p276; Ⓜ Jaume I), which once boasted 78 towers (as much a matter of prestige as of defence). One wall is on the southern side of Plaça Ramon de Berenguer Gran, with the Capella Reial de Santa Àgata (p64) atop. The square itself is dominated by a statue of count-king Ramon de Berenguer Gran done by Josep Llimona in 1880. The other wall is a little further south, by the northern end of Carrer del Sots-Tinent Navarro. The Romans built and reinforced these walls in the 3rd and 4th centuries AD, after the first attacks by Germanic tribes from the north.

DOMUS DE SANT HONORAT   ARCHAEOLOGICAL SITE

Map p276 (☏93 256 21 00; www.museuhistoria.bcn.cat; Carrer de la Fruita 2; adult/concession/child €2/1.50/free, 1st Sun of month free; ☺10am-2pm Sun; Ⓜ Jaume I) The remains of a Roman *domus* (town house) have been unearthed and opened to the public. The house (and vestiges of three small shops) lies close to the Roman forum and the owners were clearly well off. Apart from providing something of an idea of daily Roman life through these remains, the location also contains six medieval grain silos installed during the period when this was the Jewish quarter, El Call.

The whole site is housed in the mid-19th-century Casa Morell. So, in an unusual mix, one gets a glimpse of three distinct periods in history in the same spot.

MUSEU DE L'ERÒTICA   MUSEUM

Map p276 (Erotica Museum; ☏93 318 98 65; www.erotica-museum.com; La Rambla 96; €10; ☺10am-midnight; Ⓜ Liceu) Observe what naughtiness people have been getting up to since ancient times in this museum, with historical relics such as Indian bas-reliefs showing various aspects of tantric love, 18th-century wood carvings depicting Kama Sutra positions, Japanese porcelain porn and African fornication carvings. Despite the premise, overall it's a rather buttoned-up affair, and probably not worth the steep admission price (despite the free drink).

COL·LEGI DE ARQUITECTES ARCHITECTURE

Map p276 (Architectural College; MJaume I) FREE Across Plaça Nova from La Catedral your eye may be caught by childlike scribblings on the facade of the Col·legi de Arquitectes. It is, in fact, a giant contribution by Picasso from 1962. The artwork, which represents Mediterranean festivals, was much ridiculed by the local press when it was unveiled.

SINAGOGA MAJOR SYNAGOGUE

Map p276 (☎93 317 07 90; www.calldebarcelona. org; Carrer de Marlet 5; adult/child under 11yr €2.50/free; ⊙10.30am-6.30pm Mon-Fri, to 2.30pm Sat & Sun Apr-Sep, 11am-5.30pm Mon-Fri, to 3pm Sat & Sun Oct-Mar; MLiceu) When an Argentine investor bought a run-down electrician's store with an eye to converting it into central Barcelona's umpteenth bar, he could hardly have known he had stumbled onto the remains of what could be the city's main medieval synagogue (some historians cast doubt on the claim). A guide will explain what is thought to be the significance of the site in various languages.

Fragments of medieval and Roman-era walls remain in the small vaulted space that you enter from the street. Also remaining are tanners' wells installed in the 15th century. The second chamber has been spruced up for use as a synagogue. A remnant of late-Roman-era wall, given its orientation facing Jerusalem, has led some to speculate that there was a synagogue here even in Roman times. There were four synagogues in the medieval city, but after the pogroms of 1391, this one (assuming it was the Sinagoga Major) was Christianised by the placing of an effigy of St Dominic on the building.

EL CALL HISTORIC SITE

Map p276 (☎93 256 21 22; www.museuhistoria. bcn.cat; Placeta de Manuel Ribé; adult/concession/child €2.20/1.50/free, 3-7pm Sun & 1st Sun of month free; ⊙11am-2pm Mon, Wed & Fri, to 7pm Sat & Sun; MJaume I) Once a 14th-century house of the Jewish weaver Jucef Bonhiac, this small visitor centre is dedicated to the history of Barcelona's Jewish quarter, El Call. Glass sections on the ground floor allow you to inspect Mr Bonhiac's former wells and storage space. The house, also known as the Casa de l'Alquimista (Alchemist's House), hosts a modest display of Jewish artefacts, including ceramics excavated in the area of El Call, along with explanations and maps of the one-time Jewish quarter.

**MUSEU DIOCESÀ/GAUDÍ
EXHIBITION CENTER** MUSEUM

Map p276 (Casa de la Pia Almoina; ☎93 315 22 13; www.gaudiexhibitioncenter.com; Plaça de la Seu 7; adult/concession/child under 8yr €15/12/free;

EL CALL

One of our favourite places in the Ciutat Vella (Old City) to wander is **El Call** (pronounced 'kye'), which is the name of the medieval Jewish quarter that flourished here until a tragic pogrom in the 14th century. Today its narrow lanes hide some surprising sites, including an ancient synagogue unearthed in the 1990s and the fragments of a women's bathouse inside the basement of the cafe Caelum (p73). Some of the old city's most unusual shops are here, selling exquisite antiques, handmade leather products and even kosher wine. Its well-concealed dining rooms and candlelit bars and cafes make a fine destination in the evening.

El Call (which probably derives from the Hebrew word *kahal,* meaning 'community') is a tiny area, and a little tricky to find. The boundaries are roughly Carrer del Call, Carrer dels Banys Nous, Baixada de Santa Eulàlia and Carrer de Sant Honorat.

Though a handful of Jewish families remained after the bloody pogrom of 1391, the subsequent expulsion of all Jews in the country in the 15th century put an end to the Jewish presence in Barcelona. The Call Menor extended across the modern Carrer de Ferran as far as Baixada de Sant Miquel and Carrer d'en Rauric. The present Església de Sant Jaume on Carrer de Ferran was built on the site of a synagogue.

Even before the pograms of 1391, Jews in Barcelona were not exactly privileged citizens. As in many medieval centres, they were obliged to wear a special identifying mark on their garments and had trouble getting permission to expand their ghetto as El Call's population increased (as many as 4000 people were crammed into the tiny streets of the Call Major).

⊘10am-6pm Nov-Feb, to 8pm Mar-Oct; Ⓜ Jaume I) Next to the cathedral, the Diocesan Museum has a handful of exhibits on Gaudí (including a fascinating documentary on his life and philosophy) on the upper floors. There's also a sparse collection of medieval and Romanesque religious art, usually supplemented by a temporary exhibition or two.

The building itself has fragments of Barcelona's Roman wall, as well as elements from its days as an 11th-century almshouse and its later use as an ecclesiastical residence in the 15th century.

MUSEU DE CERA   MUSEUM

Map p276 (📞93 317 26 49; www.museocerabcn. com; Passatge de la Banca 7; adult/concession/ child under 5yr €15/9/free; ⊘10am-10pm Jul-Sep, 10am-1.30pm & 4-7.30pm Mon-Fri, 11am-2pm & 4.30-8.30pm Sat & Sun Oct-Jun; Ⓜ Drassanes) Inside this late-19th-century building you can wander about looking at Frankenstein, Che Guevara, Lady Diana and lots of Spanish figures you probably won't recognise. It's unintentionally funny, with a price tag that's steep for often poorly executed representations, although small children are generally enthusiastic.

VIA SEPULCRAL
ROMANA   ARCHAEOLOGICAL SITE

Map p276 (📞93 256 21 22; www.muhba.cat; Plaça de la Vila de Madrid; adult/concession/child €2/1.50/free; ⊘11am-2pm Tue & Thu, to 7pm Sat & Sun; Ⓜ Catalunya) Along Carrer de la Canuda, a block east of the top end of La Rambla, is a sunken garden where a series of Roman tombs lies exposed. A smallish display in Spanish and Catalan by the tombs explores burial and funerary rites and customs. A few bits of pottery (including a burial amphora with the skeleton of a three-year-old Roman child) accompany the display.

The burial ground stretches along either side of the road that led northwest out of Barcelona's Roman predecessor, Barcino. Roman law forbade burial within city limits and so everyone, the great and humble, were generally buried along roads leading out of cities.

✕ EATING

FEDERAL   CAFE €

Map p276 (📞93 280 81 71; www.federalcafe.es; Passatge de la Pau 11; mains €7-10; ⊘9am-11pm Mon-Thu, to 11.30pm Fri & Sat, 9am-5pm Sun; 📶;

Ⓜ Drassanes) Don't be intimidated by the industrial chic, the sea of open MacBooks or the stack of design mags – this branch of the Poble Sec Federal mothership is incredibly welcoming, with healthy, hearty and good-value food. Choose a salad and a topping (poached eggs, strips of chicken) or a yellow curry, say, and follow it up with a moist slab of carrot cake.

LA PLATA   TAPAS €

Map p276 (📞93 315 10 09; www.barlaplata.com; Carrer de la Mercè 28; tapas €2.50-5; ⊘9am-3.30pm & 6.30-11.30pm Mon-Sat; Ⓜ Jaume I) Tucked away on a narrow lane near the waterfront, La Plata is a humble but well-loved bodega that serves just three plates: *pescadito frito* (small fried fish), *butifarra* (sausage) and tomato salad. Add in the drinkable, affordable wines (per glass €1.20) and you have the makings of a fine predinner tapas spot.

MILK   INTERNATIONAL €

Map p276 (📞93 268 09 22; www.milkbarcelona. com; Carrer d'en Gignàs 21; mains €9-12; ⊘9am-2am Thu-Mon, to 3am Fri & Sat; 📶; Ⓜ Jaume I) Also known to many as an enticing cocktail spot, Irish-run Milk's key role for Barcelona night owls is providing morning-after brunches (served till 4.30pm). Avoid direct sunlight and tuck into pancakes, eggs Benedict and other hangover dishes in a cosy lounge-like setting complete with ornate wallpaper, framed prints on the wall and cushion-lined seating. The musical selection is also notable.

BENEDICT   BRUNCH €

Map p276 (📞93 250 75 11; www.benedictbcn. com; Carrer d'en Gignás 23; mains €10-11; ⊘9am-4pm Mon, 9am-4pm & 7pm-2am Tue-Fri, 9am-2.30am Sat & Sun; 📶; Ⓜ Jaume I) As the name suggests, brunch is the main event at friendly little Benedict, with eggs prepared every which way and an option for the full English fry-up. There's also a list of handmade burgers and club sandwiches, and in the evening various tapas are served, along with onion rings, deep-fried brie, chicken wings and other American favourites.

TALLER DE TAPAS   CATALAN €

Map p276 (📞93 301 80 20; www.tallerdetapas. com; Plaça de Sant Josep Oriol 9; mains €7-10; ⊘noon-1am May-Sep, noon-midnight Oct-Apr; 📶; Ⓜ Liceu) A well-placed spot with outdoor seating on Plaça de Sant Josep Oriol, with a long list of tapas and more substantial bites.

ALCOBA AZUL
MEDITERRANEAN €

Map p276 (☑93 302 81 41; Carrer de Sant Domènec del Call 14; mains €6-10; ⏰6pm-midnight; 🛜; Ⓜ Jaume I) Peel back the centuries inside this remarkably atmospheric watering hole, with medieval walls, low ceilings, wooden floors and flickering candles. Grab one of the seats at the tiny bar in front or slide into one of the table booths at the back, where you can enjoy good wines by the glass, satisfying plates of stuffed peppers, salads, *tostas* (sandwiches) and blood sausage with caramelised onions.

XURRERIA
CHURROS €

Map p276 (☑93 318 76 91; Carrer dels Banys Nous 8; cone €1.20; ⏰7am-1.30pm & 3.30-8.15pm Mon-Fri, 7am-2pm & 3.30-8.30pm Sat & Sun; Ⓜ Jaume I) It doesn't look much from the outside, but this brightly lit street joint is Barcelona's best spot for paper cones of piping-hot churros – long batter sticks fried and sprinkled with sugar and best enjoyed dunked in hot chocolate.

CERVECERÍA TALLER DE TAPAS
TAPAS, CATALAN €

Map p276 (☑93 481 62 33; www.tallerdetapas. com; Carrer Comtal 28; mains €7-10; ⏰9am-1am Mon-Fri, noon-1am Sat & Sun Mar-Sep, to midnight daily Oct-Feb; 🛜; Ⓜ Urquinaona) Amid white stone walls and a beamed ceiling, this buzzing, easy-going place serves a broad selection of tapas as well as changing daily specials like *cochinillo* (roast suckling pig). A smattering of beers from across the globe – Leffe Blonde, Guinness, Brahma (Brazil) and Sol (Mexico) – add to the appeal.

It has a few other locations around town, including a well-placed spot with outdoor seating on Plaça de Sant Josep Oriol (p69).

FORNERIA TIANA
BAKERY €

Map p276 (☑93 315 18 06; www.caltiana.cat; Carrer Ample 27; sandwiches around €3; ⏰7am-10pm; 🛜; Ⓜ Jaume I) Stop in this bright corner bakery and cafe for fresh pastries, croissants, cheese, charcuterie, quiches and other light bites. Staff whip up a decent coffee, though there's also wine and other refreshments.

★ CAFÈ DE L'ACADÈMIA
CATALAN €€

Map p276 (☑93 319 82 53; Carrer dels Lledó 1; mains €15-20; ⏰1-3.30pm & 8-11pm Mon-Fri; 🛜; Ⓜ Jaume I) Expect a mix of traditional Catalan dishes with the occasional creative twist. At lunchtime, local city hall workers pounce on the *menú del día* (€15.75). In the

evening it is rather more romantic, as low lighting emphasises the intimacy of the beamed ceiling and stone walls. On warm days you can also dine in the pretty square at the front.

★ LA VINATERIA DEL CALL
SPANISH €€

Map p276 (☑93 302 60 92; www.lavinateria delcall.com; Carrer de Sant Domènec del Call 9; raciones €7-12; ⏰7.30pm-1am; 🛜; Ⓜ Jaume I) In a magical setting in the former Jewish quarter, this tiny jewel-box of a restaurant serves up tasty Iberian dishes including Galician octopus, cider-cooked chorizo and the Catalan *escalivada* (roasted peppers, aubergine and onions) with anchovies. Portions are small and made for sharing, and there's a good and affordable selection of wines.

CAN CULLERETES
CATALAN €€

Map p276 (☑93 317 30 22; www.culleretes.com; Carrer d'en Quintana 5; mains €10-18; ⏰1.30-3.45pm & 8-10.45pm Tue-Sat, 1.30-3.45pm Sun; 🛜; Ⓜ Liceu) Founded in 1786, Barcelona's oldest restaurant is still going strong, with tourists and locals flocking here to enjoy its rambling interior, old-fashioned tile-filled decor and enormous helpings of traditional Catalan food, including fresh seafood and sticky stews. From Tuesday to Friday there is a fixed lunch menu for €14.50.

BELMONTE
TAPAS €€

Map p276 (☑93 310 76 84; Carrer de la Mercè 29; tapas €4-10, mains €13-14; ⏰8pm-midnight Tue-Fri, 1-3.30pm & 8pm-midnight Sat Jul-Oct, 7.30pm-midnight Tue-Thu, 1-3.30pm & 7.30pm-midnight Fri & Sat Oct-Jun; 🛜; Ⓜ Jaume I) This tiny tapas joint in the southern reaches of Barri Gòtic whips up beautifully prepared small plates – including an excellent *truita* (tortilla), rich *patatons a la sal* (salted new potatoes with *romesco* sauce) and tender *carpaccio de pop* (octopus carpaccio). Wash it down with the homemade *vermut* (vermouth).

OCAÑA
INTERNATIONAL €€

Map p276 (☑93 676 48 14; www.ocana.cat; Plaça Reial 13; mains €9.50-16; ⏰noon-2am Sun-Thu, to 2.30am Fri & Sat; 🛜; Ⓜ Liceu) A flamboyant but elegantly designed space of high ceilings, chandeliers and plush furnishings, Ocaña blends late-night carousing with serious eating. The Spanish and Catalan dishes are given a creative and successful twist, and are now complemented on Thursday, Friday and Saturday nights by a superb selection of Mexican dishes.

You can still have a cocktail at Moorish-inspired Apotheke downstairs, or out on the Plaça Reial terrace, but it's a shame to pass up on the culinary offering.

LEVANTE
INTERNATIONAL €€

Map p276 (☑620 470283; Placeta de Manuel Ribé 1; sharing plates €8-10; ☺9am-midnight Tue-Sat, from 11am Sun; ⓂJaume I) Opened in 2017, Levante is a small but sunny space with a 'mezze' approach to eating whereby diners can share, for example, meatballs with butternut squash or a zingy plum and fennel tart. Brunch is also served and includes superb brioche; rye bread topped with smoked mackerel and horseradish; or pita with roast tomatoes, grapes, basil and tahini.

BLACK REMEDY
CAFE €€

Map p276 (☑93 461 92 12; www.blackremedy. com; Carrer de la Ciutat 5; mains €9-14; ☺9am-7pm Mon-Sat, 11am-5.30pm Sun; ⓂJaume I) Craft beer? Check. Pulled pork sandwiches? Check. Half the clientele tapping into Mac-Books? Check. Black Remedy is the latest hipster joint in the slow transformation of the Barri Gòtic, a gallery-like space with floor-to-ceiling windows for those who like to see and be seen. Pluses include great coffee, cold-pressed juices and bottled artisanal beers, and an all-day brunch on Sundays.

OPERA SAMFAINA
CATALAN €€

Map p276 (☑93 481 78 71; www.operasamfaina. com; La Rambla 51; mains €11-15, Odissea tasting menu adult/child under 12yr €33/€20; ☺6pm-midnight Mon-Wed, to 1am Thu & Fri, 1pm-1am Sat, 1pm-midnight Sun; ⓂLiceu) A surreal sensory experience deep in the bowels of the Liceu opera house. Enter through the Vermuteria, a tenebrous tapas bar, and then either head to the Odissea – a shared table, surrounded by audiovisuals – for a tasting menu of traditional Catalan dishes; or down to the Opera Prima, a dreamlike labyrinth of wine and tapas bars and psychedelic installations.

The celebrated Roca brothers, of former Best Restaurant in the World El Celler de Can Roca, are behind the project, which takes visitors on a playful journey through Catalan mythology via the food of the region.

RASOTERRA
VEGETARIAN €€

Map p276 (☑93 318 69 26; www.rasoterra.cat; Carrer del Palau 5; platillos €6-10, lunch menu €13; ☺1-4pm & 7-11pm Tue-Sun; ☎☑; ⓂJaume I) Slow food advocates at Rasoterra cook up first-rate vegetarian dishes in a Zen-like setting with tall ceilings, low-playing jazz and fresh flowers on the tables. The creative, globally influenced menu changes regularly and might feature Vietnamese-style coconut pancakes with tofu and vegetables, beluga lentils with basmati rice, and pear and goat cheese quesadillas. Good vegan and gluten-free options.

MIRILLA
INTERNATIONAL €€

Map p276 (☑93 176 57 47; Carrer de Regomir 16; platillos €4.50-16; ☺7-11.30pm Tue-Sat; ⓂJaume I) Mirilla is a great place to stumble upon, with excellent wines by the glass and well-executed cocktails, along with a range of *platillos* (somewhere between a tapa and a main course) that includes cod ceviche, pork with wild mushrooms and mackerel teriyaki. It's a cosy little place and fills up fast. Reserve if you can.

ONOFRE
SPANISH €€

Map p276 (☑93 317 69 37; www.onofre.net; Carrer de les Magdalenes 19; mains €7-13; ☺10am-4pm & 7.30-11.30pm Mon-Fri, noon-11.30pm Sat; ☎; ⓂJaume I) Famed for its (good, affordable) wine selections, Onofre is a small, modern restaurant (and wine shop and delicatessen) that has a strong local following for its delicious dishes such as Italian greens with foie shavings, duck confit, codfish carpaccio and baked prawns. The *menú* (€10.75) is excellent value.

CERERÍA
VEGETARIAN €€

Map p276 (☑93 301 85 10; Baixada de Sant Miquel 3; mains €8-15; ☺1-11pm Tue-Sat, to 6pm Sun; ☎☑; ⓂJaume I) Black-and-white marble floors, a smattering of old wooden tables and ramshackle displays of musical instruments lend a certain bohemian charm to this small vegetarian restaurant. The pizzas are delicious and feature organic ingredients – as do the flavourful galettes, dessert crêpes and bountiful salads. Vegan options too.

PLA
FUSION €€

Map p276 (☑93 412 65 52; www.restaurantpla. cat; Carrer de la Bellafila 5; mains €17-23; ☺1.30-5.30pm & 7-11.30pm Sun-Thu, to midnight Fri & Sat; ☎; ⓂJaume I) One of Gòtic's long-standing favourites, Pla is a stylish, romantically lit medieval dining room where the cooks churn out such temptations as oxtail braised in red wine, seared tuna with oven-roasted peppers, and polenta with seasonal mushrooms.

THE SWEET LIFE

Barcelona has some irresistible temptations for those with a sweet tooth. Chocolate lovers won't want to miss Carrer del Petritxol, which is home to several famous *granjas* (milk bars) that dole out thick cups of hot chocolate, best accompanied by churros. The recommended Granja La Pallaresa (p73) always draws a crowd.

At Christmas specialist sweet stores fill with *turrón*, the traditional holiday temptation. Essentially nougat, it comes in different varieties: softer blocks are *turrón de Valencia* and a harder version is *turrón de Gijón*. You can find the treat year-round at stores such as Torrons Vicens (p75), which has been selling its signature sweets since 1775.

Other not-to-be-missed spots include Caelum (p73), and La Colmena (p76).

ALLIUM
CATALAN, FUSION €€

Map p276 (📋 93 302 30 03; www.alliumrestaurant. es; Carrer del Call 17; mains €15-18; ⏰8am-5pm Sun; 🛜; Ⓜ Liceu) This bright, modern tapas bar and restaurant serves mostly Catalan dishes with varying specials (including seafood paella for one). The menu, which changes every two or three weeks, focuses on seasonal, organic cuisine. Its kitchen is open all day, making it a good bet for those who don't want to wait until 9pm for a meal.

KOY SHUNKA
JAPANESE €€€

Map p276 (📋 93 412 79 39; www.koyshunka. com; Carrer de Copons 7; tasting menu €89-132; ⏰1.30-3pm & 8.30-11pm Tue-Sat, 1.30-3pm Sun; Ⓜ Urquinaona) Down a narrow lane north of the cathedral, Koy Shunka opens a portal to exquisite dishes from the East – mouthwatering sushi, sashimi, seared Wagyu beef and flavour-rich seaweed salads are served alongside inventive cooked fusion dishes such as steamed clams with sake or tempura of scallops and king prawns with Japanese mushrooms. Don't miss the house speciality of tender *toro* (tuna belly).

Most diners sit at the large wraparound counter, where you can watch the culinary wizardry in action. Set multicourse menus are pricey but well worth it for those seeking a truly extraordinary dining experience.

ELS QUATRE GATS
CATALAN €€€

Map p276 (📋 93 302 41 40; www.4gats.com; Carrer de Montsió 3; mains €23-29; ⏰1-4pm & 7pm-1am; Ⓜ Urquinaona) Once the lair of Barcelona's Modernista artists, Els Quatre Gats is a stunning example of the movement, inside and out, with its colourful tiles, geometric brickwork and wooden fittings. The restaurant is not quite as thrilling as its setting, though you can just have a coffee and a croissant in the cafe (open from 9am to 1am) at the front.

DRINKING & NIGHTLIFE

L'ASCENSOR
COCKTAIL BAR

Map p276 (📋 93 318 53 47; Carrer de la Bellafila 3; ⏰6pm-2.30am Mon-Thu, to 3am Fri-Sun; 🛜; Ⓜ Jaume I) Named after the lift (elevator) doors that serve as the front door, this elegant drinking den with its vaulted brick ceilings, vintage mirrors and marble-topped bar gathers a faithful crowd that comes for old-fashioned cocktails and lively conversation against a soundtrack of uptempo jazz and funk.

SOR RITA
BAR

Map p276 (📋 93 176 62 66; www.sorritabar.es; Carrer de la Mercè 27; ⏰7pm-2.30am Sun-Thu, to 3am Fri & Sat; 🛜; Ⓜ Jaume I) A lover of all things kitsch, Sor Rita is pure eye candy, from its leopard-print wallpaper to its high-heel-festooned ceiling and deliciously irreverent decorations inspired by the films of Almodóvar. It's a fun and festive scene, with special-event nights including tarot readings on Mondays, all-you-can-eat snack buffets (€7) on Tuesdays and karaoke on Thursdays.

LA GRANJA
CAFE

Map p276 (📋 93 302 69 75; Carrer dels Banys Nous 4; ⏰9am-9pm; 🛜; Ⓜ Jaume I) This long-running cafe serves up thick, rich cups of chocolate, in varying formats, but it doesn't make its own churros. Buy them a few doors down at Xurreria (p70) and bring them here for the perfect combo of churros dipped in chocolate. Also worth a look is the section of Roman wall visible at the back.

POLAROID
BAR

Map p276 (📋 93 186 66 69; www.polaroidbar.es; Carrer dels Còdols 29; ⏰7.30pm-2.30am Sun-Thu, to 3am Fri & Sat; 🛜; Ⓜ Drassanes) For a dash of 1980s nostalgia, Polaroid is a blast from the past, with its wall-mounted VHS tapes, old film posters, comic-book-covered tables, action-figure displays and other kitschy decor. Not surprisingly, it draws a fun, unpretentious crowd who come for cheap *cañas* (draught beer), mojitos and free popcorn.

MARULA CAFÉ   BAR

Map p276 (☎93 318 76 90; www.marulacafe. com; Carrer dels Escudellers 49; cover up to €10; ◷11pm-5am Mon-Thu & Sun, 11.30pm-6am Fri, 9.30pm-6am Sat; Ⓜ Liceu) A fantastic find in the heart of the Barri Gòtic, Marula will transport you to the 1970s and the best in funk and soul. James Brown fans will think they've died and gone to heaven. It's not, however, a mono-thematic place: DJs slip in other tunes, from breakbeat to house. Samba and other Brazilian dance sounds also penetrate here.

CAELUM   CAFE

Map p276 (☎93 302 69 93; Carrer de la Palla 8; ◷10am-8.30pm Mon-Fri, to 9pm Sat & Sun; ☎; Ⓜ Liceu) Centuries of heavenly gastronomic tradition from across Spain are concentrated in this exquisite medieval space in the heart of the city. The upstairs cafe is a dainty setting for decadent cakes and pastries, while descending into the underground chamber with its stone walls and flickering candles is like stepping into the Middle Ages.

Wherever you decide to sit, you'll also pass through the shop that sells sweets (such as the irresistible marzipan from Toledo) made by nuns in convents across the country.

CAFÈ DE L'ÒPERA   CAFE

Map p276 (☎93 317 75 85; www.cafeoperabcn. com; La Rambla 74; ◷8am-2am; ☎; Ⓜ Liceu) Opposite the Gran Teatre del Liceu is La Rambla's most traditional cafe. Operating since 1929 and still popular with opera-goers, it is pleasant enough for an early evening libation or, in the morning, coffee and croissants. Head upstairs for a seat overlooking the busy boulevard, and try the house speciality, the *cafè de l'Òpera* (coffee with chocolate mousse).

SALTERIO   CAFE

Map p276 (☎93 302 50 28; Carrer de Sant Domènec del Call 4; ◷noon-1am; ☎; Ⓜ Jaume I) A wonderfully photogenic candlelit spot tucked down a tiny lane in El Call, Salterio serves Turkish coffee, authentic mint teas and snacks amid stone walls, incense and ambient Middle Eastern music. If hunger strikes, try the *sardo* (grilled flat-bread covered with pesto, cheese or other toppings).

BOADAS   COCKTAIL BAR

Map p276 (☎93 318 95 92; www.boadascocktails. com; Carrer dels Tallers 1; ◷noon-2am Mon-Thu, to 3am Fri & Sat; Ⓜ Catalunya) One of the city's oldest cocktail bars, Boadas is famed for its daiquiris. Bow-tied waiters have been serving up unique, drinkable creations since Miguel Boadas opened it in 1933 – in fact Miró and Hemingway both drank here. Miguel was born in Havana, where he was the first barman at the immortal La Floridita.

GRANJA LA PALLARESA   CAFE

Map p276 (☎93 302 20 36; www.lapallaresa. com; Carrer del Petritxol 11; ◷9am-1pm & 4-9pm Mon-Sat, 9am-1pm & 5-9pm Sun; ☎; Ⓜ Liceu) An old-school cafe filled with families and specialising in cakes, churros and hot chocolate.

BOSC DE LES FADES   LOUNGE

Map p276 (☎93 317 26 49; Passatge de la Banca 5; ◷10am-1am Mon-Fri, from 11am Sat & Sun; Ⓜ Drassanes) The 'Forest of the Fairies' is touristy but offers a whimsical retreat from the busy Rambla nearby, and has a wonderfully kitsch charm. Lounge chairs and lamplit tables are scattered beneath an indoor forest complete with trickling fountain and grotto. *Bocadillos* and snacks are available.

MANCHESTER   BAR

Map p276 (☎627 733081; Carrer de Milans 5; ◷6.30pm-2.30am Sun-Thu, to 3am Fri & Sat; ☎; Ⓜ Liceu) 🚭 A drinking den that has undergone several transformations over the years now treats you to the sounds of great Manchester bands, from Joy Division to Oasis, but probably not the Hollies. It has a pleasing rough-and-tumble feel, with tables jammed in every which way. There are DJs on Thursdays.

KARMA   CLUB

Map p276 (☎93 302 56 80; www.karmadisco. com; Plaça Reial 10; ◷noon-5am Tue-Thu, to 6am Fri & Sat; Ⓜ Liceu) During the week Karma plays good, mainstream indie music, while on weekends the DJs spin anything from rock to disco. A golden oldie in Barcelona, tunnel-shaped Karma is small and becomes quite tightly packed (claustrophobic for some) with a good-natured crowd of locals and out-of-towners. The bar and terrace on the Plaça Reial open at noon, but the club opens at midnight.

LA MACARENA   CLUB

Map p276 (☎ 93 301 30 64; www.macarenaclub.com; Carrer Nou de Sant Francesc 5; cover €5-10; ⊙midnight-5am Sun-Thu, to 6am Fri & Sat; ⓂDrassanes) You won't believe this was once a tile-lined Andalucian flamenco musos' bar. Now it is a dark dance space, of the kind where it is possible to sit at the bar, meet people around you and then stand up for a bit of a shake to the DJ's electro and house offerings, all within about five square metres.

LA CLANDESTINA   CAFE

Map p276 (☎ 93 319 05 33; Baixada de Viladecols 2; ⊙10am-10pm Wed-Mon; 🅘; ⓂJaume I) Globally inspired options here include tea, Turkish coffee, mango lassi, quiche and panini, along with wine and beer. La Clandestina's white walls are enlivened with gold-painted beams and a changing display of local artwork for sale, under which sit youngish locals, often tapping away on laptops.

ČAJ CHAI   CAFE

Map p276 (☎ 93 301 95 92; www.cajchai.com; Carrer de Sant Domènec del Call 12; ⊙10.30am-10pm; ⓂJaume I) Inspired by Prague's bohemian tearooms, this bright and buzzing cafe in the heart of the old Jewish quarter is a tea connoisseur's paradise. Čaj Chai stocks around 200 teas from China, India, Korea, Japan, Nepal, Morocco and beyond. It's a much-loved local haunt.

OVISO   BAR

Map p276 (☎ 93 304 37 26; www.barnawood.com; Carrer d'Arai 5; ⊙9am-2.30am Sun-Thu, to 3am Fri & Sat; 🅘; ⓂLiceu) Oviso is a popular budget-friendly restaurant with outdoor tables on the plaza, but shows its true bohemian colours by night, with a mixed crowd, a rock-and-roll vibe and a rustic decorated two-room interior plastered with curious murals – geese taking flight, leaping dolphins and blue peacocks framing the brightly painted concrete walls.

BOULEVARD   CLUB

Map p276 (☎ 673 272480; www.boulevardculture club.es; La Rambla 27; cover up to €9; ⊙midnight-5.45am Sun-Thu, to 6.30am Fri & Sat; ⓂDrassanes) Boulevard is flanked by striptease bars (in the spirit of the lower Rambla's old days), and has undergone countless reincarnations. With three different dance spaces, one of them upstairs, it has a deliciously tacky feel, pumping out anything from 1980s hits to house music (especially on Saturdays in the main room). There's no particular dress code.

☆ ENTERTAINMENT

GRAN TEATRE DEL LICEU   THEATRE, LIVE MUSIC

Map p276 (☎ 93 485 99 00; www.liceubarcelona. cat; La Rambla 51-59; ⊙box office 9.30am-7.30pm Mon-Fri, to 5.30pm Sat & Sun; ⓂLiceu) Barcelona's grand old opera house, restored after a fire in 1994, is one of the most technologically advanced theatres in the world. To take a seat in the grand auditorium, returned to all its 19th-century glory but with the very latest in acoustics, is to be transported to another age.

Tickets can cost anything from €10 for a cheap seat behind a pillar to €200 for a well-positioned night at the opera.

EL PARAIGUA   LIVE MUSIC

Map p276 (☎ 93 302 11 31; www.elparaigua.com; Carrer del Pas de l'Ensenyança 2; ⊙noon-2am Sun-Wed, to 1am Thu, to 3am Fri & Sat; ⓂLiceu) **FREE** A tiny chocolate box of dark tinted Modernisme, the 'Umbrella' has been serving up drinks since the 1960s. The turn-of-the-20th-century decor was transferred here from a shop knocked down elsewhere in the district and cobbled back together to create this cosy locale.

Take a trip in time from Modernisme to medieval by heading downstairs to the brick and stone basement bar area. Amid 11th-century walls, live bands – funk, soul, rock, blues – hold court on Fridays and Saturdays (from 11.30pm).

BEST CAFES

Some of Barcelona's most atmospheric cafes lie hidden in the old cobbled lanes of Barri Gòtic. Our favourite spots for a pick-me-up include:

Salterio (p73)

Čaj Chai

La Clandestina

Caelum (p73)

Cafè de l'Òpera (p73)

La Granja (p72)

HARLEM JAZZ CLUB JAZZ

Map p276 (☎93 310 07 55; www.harlemjazzclub.
es; Carrer de la Comtessa de Sobradiel 8; tickets
€7-10; ☺8pm-3am Sun & Tue-Thu, to 5am Fri &
Sat; MLiceu) This narrow, old-city dive is one
of the best spots in town for jazz, as well as
funk, Latin, blues and gypsy jazz. It attracts
a mixed crowd that maintains a respectful
silence during the acts. Most concerts start
around 10pm. Get in early if you want a seat
in front of the stage.

SIDECAR FACTORY CLUB LIVE MUSIC

Map p276 (☎93 302 15 86; www.sidecarfactory
club.com; Plaça Reial 7; ☺7pm-5am Mon-Thu, to
6am Fri & Sat; MLiceu) Descend into the red-
tinged, brick-vaulted bowels for live music
most nights. Just about anything goes here,
from UK indie through to country punk, but
rock and pop lead the way. Most shows start
around 10pm and DJs take over at 12.30am.
Upstairs at ground level you can get food
(until midnight) or a few drinks (until 3am).

JAMBOREE LIVE MUSIC

Map p276 (☎93 319 17 89; www.masimas.com/
jamboree; Plaça Reial 17; tickets €5-20; ☺8pm-
6am; MLiceu) For over half a century, Jamboree has been bringing joy to the jivers of
Barcelona, with high-calibre acts featuring
jazz trios, blues, Afrobeats, Latin and big-
band sounds. Two concerts are held most
nights (at 8pm and 10pm), after which Jamboree morphs into a DJ-spinning club at
midnight. WTF jam sessions are held Mondays (entrance a mere €5).

Buy tickets online to save a few euros.

L'ATENEU CLASSICAL MUSIC

Map p276 (☎93 343 61 21; www.ateneubcn.org;
Carrer de la Canuda 6; tickets €0-10; MCatalunya)
This historic private library and cultural
centre (dating back 150 years) hosts a range
of high-brow fare, from classical recitals to
film screenings and literary readings.

SALA TARANTOS FLAMENCO

Map p276 (☎93 304 12 10; www.masimas.com/
tarantos; Plaça Reial 17; tickets €15; ☺shows
7.30pm, 8.30pm & 9.30pm Oct-Jun, plus 10.30pm
Jul-Sep; MLiceu) Since 1963, this basement
locale has been the stage for up-and-coming flamenco groups performing in Barcelona. These days Tarantos has become a
mostly tourist-centric affair, with half-hour
shows held three times a night. Still, it's a
good introduction to flamenco, and not a
bad setting for a drink.

 SHOPPING

**A handful of shops dots La Rambla, but
the real fun starts inside the labyrinth.
Young fashion on Carrer d'Avinyó, a
mixed bag on Avinguda del Portal de
l'Àngel, some cute old shops on Carrer
de la Dagueria and lots of exploring in
narrow little streets awaits.**

TORRONS VICENS FOOD

Map p276 (☎93 304 37 36; www.vicens.com;
Carrer del Petritxol 15; ☺10am-8.30pm Mon-Sat,
11am-8pm Sun; MLiceu) You can find the *turrón* (nougat) treat year-round at Torrons
Vicens, which has been selling its signature
sweets since 1775.

SABATER HERMANOS COSMETICS

Map p276 (☎93 301 98 32; www.sabater
hermanos.es; Plaça de Sant Felip Neri 1;
☺10.30am-9pm; MJaume I) This fragrant little shop sells handcrafted soaps of all sizes.
Varieties such as fig, cinnamon, grapefruit
and chocolate smell good enough to eat,
while sandalwood, magnolia, mint, ce-
dar and jasmine add spice to any sink or
bathtub.

FORMATGERIA LA SEU FOOD

Map p276 (☎93 412 65 48; www.formatgerialaseu.
com; Carrer de la Dagueria 16; ☺10am-2pm
& 5-8pm Tue-Sat Sep-Jul; MJaume I) Dedicated to artisan cheeses from all across
Spain, this small shop is run by the oh-so-
knowledgeable Katherine McLaughlin and
is the antithesis of mass production – it
sells only the best from small-scale farmers
and the stock changes regularly. Wine and
cheese tastings in the cosy room at the back
are fun.

ESCRIBÀ FOOD & DRINKS

Map p276 (☎93 301 60 27; www.escriba.es; La
Rambla 83; ☺9am-9.30pm; ☎; MLiceu) Chocolates, dainty pastries and mouth-watering
cakes can be nibbled behind the Modernista mosaic facade here or taken away for
private, guilt-ridden consumption. This
Barcelona favourite is owned by the Escribà
family, a name synonymous with sinfully
good sweet things. More than that, it adds
a touch of authenticity to La Rambla.

EL CORTE INGLÉS DEPARTMENT STORE

Map p276 (☎93 306 38 00; www.elcorteingles.
es; Av del Portal de l'Àngel 19-21; ☺9.30am-9pm
Mon-Sat Oct-May, 9.30am-10.15pm Jun-Sep;

Ⓜ Catalunya) A secondary branch of Spain's only remaining department store, selling electronics, fashion, stationery and sports gear.

L'ARCA
VINTAGE, CLOTHING

Map p276 (☑93 302 15 98; www.larca.es; Carrer dels Banys Nous 20; ⊙11am-2pm & 4.30-8.30pm Mon-Sat; Ⓜ Liceu) Step inside this enchanting shop for a glimpse of beautifully crafted apparel from the past, including 18th-century embroidered silk vests, elaborate silk kimonos, and wedding dresses and shawls from the 1920s. Thanks to its incredible collection, it has provided clothing for films including *Titanic, Talk to Her* and *Perfume: The Story of a Murderer*.

HERBORISTERIA DEL REI
COSMETICS

Map p276 (☑93 318 05 12; www.herboristeria delrei.com; Carrer del Vidre 1; ⊙2.30-8.30pm Tue-Thu, 10.30am-8.30pm Fri & Sat; Ⓜ Liceu) Once patronised by Queen Isabel II, this timeless corner store flogs all sorts of weird and wonderful herbs, spices and medicinal plants. It's been doing so since 1823 and the decor has barely changed since the 1860s – some of the products have, however, and nowadays you'll find anything from fragrant soaps to massage oil.

Film director Tom Tykwer shot scenes from *Perfume: The Story of a Murderer* here.

CERERIA SUBIRÀ
HOMEWARES

Map p276 (☑93 315 26 06; http://cereriasubira. net; Calle de la Llibreteria 7; ⊙9.30am-1.30pm & 4-8pm Mon-Thu, 9.30am-8pm Fri, 10am-8pm Sat; Ⓜ Jaume I) Even if you're not interested in myriad mounds of colourful wax, pop in just so you've been to the oldest shop in Barcelona. Cereria Subirà has been churning out candles since 1761 and at this address since the 19th century; the interior has a beautifully baroque quality, with a picturesque *Gone With the Wind*–style staircase.

ARTESANIA CATALUNYA
ARTS & CRAFTS

Map p276 (☑93 467 46 60; www.bcncrafts.com; Carrer dels Banys Nous 11; ⊙10am-8pm Mon-Sat, to 2pm Sun; Ⓜ Liceu) A celebration of Catalan products, this nicely designed store is a great place to browse for unique gifts. You'll find jewellery with designs inspired by Roman iconography (as well as works that reference Gaudí and Barcelona's Gothic era), plus pottery, wooden toys, silk scarves, notebooks, housewares and more.

DRAP-ART
ARTS & CRAFTS

Map p276 (☑93 268 48 89; www.drapart.org; Carrer Groc 1; ⊙11am-2pm & 5-8pm Tue-Fri, 6-9pm Sat; Ⓜ Jaume I) A non-profit arts organisation runs this small store and gallery space, which exhibits wild designs made from recycled products. Works change regularly, but you might find sculptures, jewellery, handbags and other accessories from artists near and far, as well as mixed-media installations.

LA COLMENA
FOOD

Map p276 (☑93 315 13 56; www.pastisseria lacolmena.com; Plaça de l'Angel 12; ⊙9am-9pm; Ⓜ Jaume I) A pastry shop selling many delicacies including pine-nut-encrusted *panellets* (sweet almond cakes), flavoured meringues and feather-light *ensaïmadas* (soft, sweet buns topped with powdered sugar) from Mallorca.

COIN & STAMP MARKET
MARKET

Map p276 (Mercat de Numismàtica i Filatèlia; Plaça Reial; ⊙9am-2.30pm Sun; Ⓜ Liceu) A relic of bygone Barcelona, in the shape of a dusty philatelic and coin market.

TALLER DE MARIONETAS TRAVI
MARIONETTES

Map p276 (☑93 412 66 92; www.marionetastravi. com; Carrer de n'Amargós 4; ⊙noon-9pm Mon-Sat; Ⓜ Urquinaona) Opened in the 1970s, this atmospheric shop sells beautifully hand-crafted marionettes. Don Quixote, Sancho Panza and other iconic Spanish figures are on hand, as well as unusual works from other parts of the world – including rare Sicilian puppets and pieces from Myanmar (Burma), Indonesia and elsewhere.

CÓMPLICES
BOOKS

Map p276 (☑93 412 72 83; www.libreriacomplices. com; Carrer de Cervantes 4; ⊙10.30am-8pm Mon-Fri, from noon Sat; Ⓜ Jaume I) One of the most extensive gay and lesbian bookstores in the city has a mix of erotica in the form of DVDs and comics as well as books. It's a welcoming place for all ages and orientations.

LA MANUAL ALPARGATERA
SHOES

Map p276 (☑93 301 01 72; www.lamanualal pargatera.es; Carrer d'Avinyó 7; ⊙9.30am-1.30pm & 4.30-8pm Mon-Fri, from 10am Sat; Ⓜ Liceu) Clients from Salvador Dalí to Jean Paul Gaultier have ordered a pair of *espadrilles* (rope-soled canvas shoes) from this famous store. The shop was founded just after the Spanish Civil War, though the roots of the simple shoe design date back hundreds of years and originated in the Catalan Pyrenees.

SALA PARÉS
ARTS & CRAFTS

Map p276 (📞93 318 70 20; www.salapares.com; Carrer del Petritxol 5; ⏰10.30am-2pm & 4-8pm Tue-Thu, to 8.30pm Fri & Sat Jun-Sep, plus 11.30am-2pm Sun Oct-May; MLiceu) In business since 1877, this gallery has maintained its position as one of the city's leading purveyors of Catalan art, with works from the 19th century to the present. Increasingly it stocks more work from elsewhere in Spain and Europe.

FC BOTIGA
GIFTS & SOUVENIRS

Map p276 (📞93 269 15 32; Carrer de Jaume I 18; ⏰10am-9pm; MJaume I) Need a Lionel Messi football jersey, a blue and burgundy ball, or any other football paraphernalia pertaining to what many locals consider the greatest team in the world? This is a convenient spot to load up without traipsing to the stadium.

PAPABUBBLE
FOOD

Map p276 (📞93 268 86 25; www.papabubble.com; Carrer Ample 28; ⏰10am-2pm & 4-8.30pm Mon-Fri, 10am-8.30pm Sat; MJaume I) It feels like a step into another era in this sweet shop, which makes up pots of rainbow-coloured boiled lollies, just like some of us remember from corner-store days as kids. Watch the sticky sweets being made before your eyes.

PETRITXOL XOCOA
FOOD

Map p276 (📞93 301 82 91; www.xocoa-bcn.com; Carrer del Petritxol 11-13; ⏰9.30am-9pm; MLiceu) Tucked along 'chocolate street' Carrer del Petritxol, this den of dental devilry displays ranks and ranks of original bars in stunning designs, chocolates stuffed with sweet stuff, gooey pastries and more. It has various other branches scattered about town.

OBACH
FASHION & ACCESSORIES

Map p276 (📞93 318 40 94; Carrer del Call 2; ⏰10am-2pm & 4-8pm Mon-Sat Oct-Jul, 10am-2pm Mon-Sat Aug-Sep; MJaume I) Since 1924 this store has been purveying all manner of headgear. You'll find Kangol mohair berets, hipsterish short-brimmed hats, fedoras, elegant straw sun hats and a full-colour spectrum of *barrets* (berets).

LA BASILICA GALERIA
JEWELLERY

Map p276 (📞93 304 20 47; www.labasilicagaleria. com; Carrer Sant Sever 7; ⏰noon-9pm Mon-Sat; 📶; MJaume I) A pure wonderland for the senses, La Basilica Galeria is a whimsical jewellery store with artful displays set among crystal- and flower-covered mannequins. In addition to eye-catching necklaces, delicate rings and fairy-tale pendants, there are a few original paintings for sale, though there's more artwork a few doors down in Basilica's gallery and perfume shop.

FIRA ALIMENTACIÓ
MARKET

Map p276 (Plaça del Pi; ⏰11am-9pm Fri-Sun, 1st & 3rd week of month; MLiceu) Once a fortnight, gourmands can poke about the homemade honeys, sweets, cheeses and other edible delights at the Fira Alimentació from Friday to Sunday.

ART & CRAFTS MARKET
MARKET

Map p276 (Mostra d'Art; Plaça de Sant Josep Oriol; ⏰11am-8pm Sat, to 2pm Sun; MLiceu) The Barri Gòtic is enlivened by an art and crafts market on Saturdays and Sundays.

🏃 SPORTS & ACTIVITIES

BARCELONA BIKING
CYCLING

Map p276 (📞656 356300; www.barcelonabiking. com; Baixada de Sant Miquel 6; bike hire per 1/24hr €5/15, tour €21; ⏰10am-8pm, tour 11am; MJaume I, Liceu) Hires city, road and mountain bikes. Also offers a 3.5-hour tour.

FAT TIRE BIKE TOURS
CYCLING

Map p276 (📞93 342 92 75; http://barcelona. fattirebiketours.com; Carrer de Marlet 7; adult/concession/child from €26/24/21; ⏰tours 11am & 4pm; MJaume I, Liceu) Various guided bicycle tours are offered, but be warned that groups can be quite large.

BARCELONA SEGWAY FUN
TOURS

Map p276 (📞93 550 48 90; www.barcelona segwayfun.com; Carrer del Sots-Tinent Navarro 26; tours €45-55; MJaume I) Guided tours of the old city by Segway, in small groups.

TRIXI
CYCLING

Map p276 (📞93 310 13 79; www.trixi.com/barcelona; Plaça dels Traginers 4; tours per half/1/2hr €15/25/50; ⏰9am-8pm Mar-Nov; MJaume I) Hires out bicycles, kickbikes and 'trixi-kids', tricycles with a kind of front-end trolley for transporting young children. It also offers tours using three-wheeled cycle taxis, which operate around the old town, the waterfront and much of the centre.

El Raval

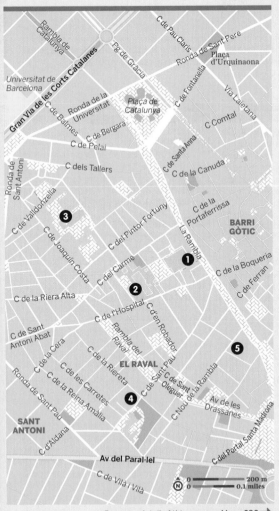

Neighbourhood Top Five

1 **Mercat de la Boqueria** (p80) Shopping and browsing at this buzzing and beautiful market, and tucking into some tapas at one of the lively bars.

2 **Antic Hospital de la Santa Creu** (p83) Exploring the historic building and relaxing under the trees in its elegant courtyard.

3 **MACBA** (p81) Getting to grips with the occasionally challenging art collection and watching the skaters performing their tricks in the space at the front.

4 Historical bars (p87) Partaking in a glass of cloudy absinthe while admiring some lesser-known works of Modernisme.

5 **Palau Güell** (p82) Walking around the artfully restored palace, designed by Gaudí, and snapping its colourful rooftop chimneys.

For more detail of this area see Map p280 ➡

Explore El Raval

Long one of the most rough-and-tumble parts of Barcelona, El Raval is now so hip – in a grungy, inner-city way – that *barcelonins* have even invented a verb for rambling around El Raval: *ravalejar*.

The northern half of El Raval is the best place to start your stroll – this part of the *barri* (neighbourhood) has an almost respectable air about it. Spend a day wandering around the art shops on the streets around Carrer del Pintor Fortuny, lunching in the colourful Mercat de la Boqueria (p80) and dedicating a few hours to the fascinating MACBA (p81).

Night-time is El Raval's forte, and not only because of all the illicit activities taking place under the shroud of darkness. This is where you will find some of Barcelona's more eccentric, trendy and downright ancient bars and clubs.

The area between Carrer de l'Hospital and the waterfront – also known as Barri Xino – is where El Raval retains its dodgy flavour of yore, and you should keep a reasonable eye on your belongings here. The national cinema and film archive, Filmoteca de Catalunya (p88), has been relocated to just off the Rambla de Raval in an attempt to change the face of this area of town. Despite its slight edginess, you shouldn't miss this part of El Raval – several fine old bars have stood the test of time in these streets.

If you're curious about the fabric of life in multicultural Raval, take a stroll along Carrer de l'Hospital, home to the local mosque and numerous halal butchers' shops, cafes and barber shops.

Local Life

→ **Market lunch** Don't miss the food at the Mercat de la Boqueria (p80) – either queue up and buy some fresh produce to cook yourself, or sit down at a stall and let the local chefs shower you with Catalan delicacies.

→ **Vintage shops** El Raval is the epicentre of Barcelona's fascination with all things vintage – you'll find plenty of secondhand shops along the pedestrian Carrer de la Riera Baixa, particularly.

→ **Sugar rush** Locals swear that the best chocolate in town is to be had at Granja M Viader (p87).

Getting There & Away

→ **Metro** El Raval is encircled by three metro lines. Línies 1, 2 and 3 stop at strategic points around the district, so nothing is far from a metro stop. The Línia 3 stop at Liceu is a convenient exit point.

Lonely Planet's Top Tip

For a spot of peace away from the noisy El Raval streets, head for the garden at the Antic Hospital de la Santa Creu (p83), where you'll find a giant chessboard.

EL RAVAL

 Best Places to Eat

→ Bar Pinotxo (p84)
→ Caravelle (p84)
→ Suculent (p86)
→ Elisabets (p84)

For reviews, see p69. →

 Best Places to Drink

→ Bar La Concha (p87)
→ Casa Almirall (p86)
→ La Confitería (p86)
→ Negroni (p87)

For reviews, see p72. →

◉ **Best Gift Shops**

→ Les Topettes (p89)
→ Fantastik (p89)
→ Teranyina (p89)

For reviews, see p75. →

TOP SIGHT
MERCAT DE LA BOQUERIA

Barcelona's most central produce market, the Mercat de la Boqueria, provides one of the greatest sound, smell and colour sensations in Europe, and is housed in a building every bit as impressive. It spills over with the rich and varied colours of plentiful fruit and vegetable stands, and seemingly limitless varieties of sea critters, cheeses and meats.

It is believed that there has been a market in this location since 1217, and, as much as it has become a modern-day attraction, it has always been the place where locals have come to shop. What is now known as La Boqueria didn't come to exist until the 19th century, and the iron Modernista gate was constructed in 1914.

While stalls aimed at tourists make tentative inroads, the fish market in La Boqueria's geographical centre is the guardian of tradition. Razor clams and red prawns, salmon, sea bass and swordfish, all almost as fresh as when it was caught; so much so that there's scarcely a fishy aroma to inhale. Barcelona's love affair with fish and seafood starts here.

La Boqueria has a handful of unassuming places to eat – and eat well – although many of them open only at lunchtime. Try the wonderful tortillas at El Quim (p84) or any dish at Bar Pinotxo (p84).

It's worth picking up some of Catalonia's gastronomic specialities, such as *bacallà salat* (dried salt cod), *calçots* (spring onions) when in season, *cargols* (snails), *peus de porc* (pig's trotters) and *percebes* (goose-necked barnacles).

Many of Barcelona's top restaurateurs buy their produce here, although nowadays it's no easy task getting past the seething crowds of tourists to snare a slippery slab of sole or tempting piece of goat cheese.

DON'T MISS

➜ The sparkling fish market

➜ Tucking in at the market bars

➜ Picking up cheese and ham for a picnic lunch

PRACTICALITIES

➜ Map p280, E4

➜ ☏93 318 20 17

➜ www.boqueria.info

➜ La Rambla 91

➜ ⊗8am-8.30pm Mon-Sat

➜ Ⓜ Liceu

TOP SIGHT
MACBA

Designed by Richard Meier and opened in 1995, MACBA has become the city's foremost contemporary art centre. The permanent collection, displayed on the ground and first floors, features some 3000 pieces centred on three periods: post-WWII; circa 1968; and the years since the 1989 fall of the Berlin Wall, right up until the present day. The emphasis is on Spanish and Catalan art from the second half of the 20th century, with works by Antoni Tàpies, Joan Brossa and Miquel Barceló, among others, though international artists, such as Paul Klee, Bruce Nauman and John Cage, are also represented.

The temporary visiting exhibitions are almost always challenging and intriguing. MACBA's philosophy is to do away with the old model of a museum where an artwork is a spectacle and to create a space where art can be viewed critically, so the exhibitions are usually tied in with talks and events. This is food for the brain as well as the eyes.

The library and auditorium stage regular concerts, talks and events, all of which are either reasonably priced or free.

DON'T MISS

➡ The permanent collection of 20th-century Spanish and Catalan art

➡ The fascinating temporary exhibitions

➡ Richard Meier's extraordinary building

PRACTICALITIES

➡ Museu d'Art Contemporani de Barcelona

➡ Map p280, B3

➡ ☑93 412 08 10

➡ www.macba.cat

➡ Plaça dels Àngels 1

➡ adult/concession/child under 14yr €10/8/free

➡ ⊙11am-7.30pm Mon & Wed-Fri, 10am-9pm Sat, 10am-3pm Sun & holidays

➡ Ⓜ Universitat

TOP SIGHT
PALAU GÜELL

Palau Güell is a magnificent example of the early days of Antoni Gaudí's fevered architectural imagination. The extraordinary neo-Gothic mansion, one of the few major buildings of that era raised in Ciutat Vella, gives an insight into its maker's prodigious genius.

Gaudí built this palace off La Rambla in the late 1880s for his wealthy patron, the industrialist Eusebi Güell. Although sombre compared with some of his later whimsy, the Palau is still a characteristic riot of materials and styles (Gothic, Islamic, art nouveau). After the civil war the police tortured political prisoners in the basement, but the building was then abandoned, leading to its long-term disrepair. It was finally reopened in 2012 after several years of refurbishment.

Central to the structure of the building is the magnificent music room, with a rebuilt organ that is played during opening hours. The hall is a parabolic pyramid – each wall an arch stretching up three floors and coming together to form a dome, giving a magnificent sense of space in what is a surprisingly narrow building, constructed on a site of just 500 sq metres.

The attic now holds a detailed exhibition on the history of the building, and the roof is a tumult of tiled mosaics and fanciful design. The audioguide is worth listening to for the detailed descriptions of the architecture, as well as the music and the illustrations of the Güell family's life.

DON'T MISS

➡ The music room
➡ The basement stables
➡ The tiled chimney pots

PRACTICALITIES

➡ Map p280, G6
➡ ☏93 472 57 71
➡ www.palauguell.cat
➡ Carrer Nou de la Rambla 3-5
➡ adult/concession/child under 10yr incl audioguide €12/9/free, 1st Sun of month free
➡ ⏰10am-8pm Tue-Sun Apr-Oct, to 5.30pm Nov-Mar
➡ Ⓜ Drassanes

 SIGHTS

MERCAT DE LA BOQUERIA MARKET
See p80.

MACBA ARTS CENTRE
See p81.

PALAU GÜELL PALACE
See p82.

**CENTRE DE CULTURA
CONTEMPORÀNIA DE BARCELONA** GALLERY
Map p280 (CCCB; ☎93 306 41 00; www.cccb.
org; Carrer de Montalegre 5; adult/concession/
child under 12yr for 1 exhibition €6/4/free, 2 exhibitions €8/6/free, Sun 3-8pm free; ⊙11am-8pm
Tue-Sun; MUniversitat) A complex of auditoriums, exhibition spaces and conference halls
opened here in 1994 in what had been an
18th-century hospice, the Casa de la Caritat. The courtyard, with a vast glass wall
on one side, is spectacular. With 4500 sq
metres of exhibition space in four separate
areas, the centre hosts a constantly changing program of exhibitions, film cycles and
other events.

**ESGLÉSIA DE SANT
PAU DEL CAMP** CHURCH
Map p280 (☎93 441 00 01; Carrer de Sant Pau 101;
adult/concession/child under 14yr €3/2/free;
⊙10am-1.30pm & 4-7.30pm Mon-Sat; MParal·lel)
The best example of Romanesque architecture in the city is the dainty little cloister of
this church. Set in a somewhat dusty garden, the 12th-century church also boasts
some Visigothic sculptural detail on the
main entrance.

**ANTIC HOSPITAL DE LA
SANTA CREU** HISTORIC BUILDING
Map p280 (Former Hospital of the Holy Cross;
www.barcelonaturisme.com; Carrer de l'Hospital
56; ⊙9am-10pm; MLiceu) **FREE** Behind La
Boqueria stands the Antic Hospital de la
Santa Creu, which was once the city's main
hospital. Founded in 1401, it functioned until the 1930s, and was considered one of the
best in Europe in its medieval heyday – it
is famously the place where Antoni Gaudí
died in 1926. Today it houses the **Biblioteca
de Catalunya** and the Institut d'Estudis
Catalans. The hospital's 15th-century former chapel, La Capella, shows temporary
exhibitions.

Entering from Carrer de l'Hospital,
you find yourself in a peaceful **courtyard**

ARTICKET

Barcelona's best bargain for art lovers
is the **Articket BCN** (www.articket
bcn.org; €30), which gives you
entry to six museums for a fraction of what you'd pay if you bought
individual tickets. The museums are
the MACBA (p81), **CCCB**, Fundació
Antoni Tàpies (p132), Fundació Joan
Miró (p188), MNAC (p186) and Museu
Picasso (p92).

garden. Up a sweep of stone steps is the
members-only Catalan national library.
Approaching the complex from Carrer del
Carme or down a narrow lane from Jardins
del Doctor Fleming (the little playground),
you arrive at the entrance to the institute,
which was once the 17th-century Casa de
Convalescència de Sant Pau. The public can
visit the patio, in the centre of which you'll
find a statue of St Paul. The building (especially the entrance vestibule) is richly decorated with ceramic tiles. Situated up on the
1st floor at the far end is what was once an
orange garden, now named after the Catalan novelist Mercè Rodoreda.

INSTITUT D'ESTUDIS CATALANS COLLEGE
Map p280 (Institute for Catalan Studies; ☎93 270
16 20; www.iec.cat; Carrer del Carme 47; ⊙8am-
8pm Mon-Fri Sep-Jul; MLiceu) The Institute
for Catalan Studies sits in the 17th-century
Casa de Convalescència, once part of the
hospital that formed this complex.

RAMBLA DEL RAVAL STREET
Map p280 (MLiceu) This broad boulevard was
laid out in 2000 as part of the city's plan
to open up this formerly sleazy neighbourhood, with some success. Now lined with
palm trees and terrace cafes, it hosts a craft
market every weekend and is presided over
by a glossy four-star hotel. Fernando Botero's huge sculpture of a plump cat, which
stands near the bottom of the Rambla, never fails to delight children.

LA CAPELLA GALLERY
Map p280 (☎93 256 20 44; www.bcn.cat/
lacapella; Carrer de l'Hospital 56; ⊙noon-8pm
Tue-Sat, 11am-2pm Sun & holidays; MLiceu)
FREE The Antic Hospital de la Santa Creu's
15th-century former chapel is now an exhibition space, with frequent temporary
exhibitions.

# EATING

SÉSAMO
VEGETARIAN €

Map p280 (📞93 441 64 11; Carrer de Sant Antoni Abat 52; mains €9-13; ⏱7pm-midnight Tue-Sun; 📶🍴; Ⓜ Sant Antoni) Widely held to be the best veggie restaurant in the city (admittedly not as great an accolade as it might be elsewhere), Sésamo is a cosy, fun place. The menu is mainly tapas, and most people go for the seven-course tapas menu (€25, wine included), but there are a few more substantial dishes. Nice touches include the home-baked bread and cakes.

CARAVELLE
INTERNATIONAL €

Map p280 (📞93 317 98 92; www.caravelle.es; Carrer del Pintor Fortuny 31; mains €10-13; ⏱9.30am-5pm Mon, 9.30am-midnight Tue-Thu, 10am-1am Fri & Sat, 10am-5pm Sun; Ⓜ Liceu) A bright little joint, beloved of the hipster element of El Raval and anyone with a discerning palate. It dishes up tacos as you've never tasted them (cod, lime aioli and radish, and pulled pork with roast corn and avocado), a superior steak sandwich on homemade brioche with pickled celeriac, and all manner of soul food.

Drinks are every bit as inventive – try the homemade ginger beer or grapefruit soda.

BAR MUY BUENAS
CATALAN €

Map p280 (📞93 807 28 57; Carrer del Carme 63; mains €9-13; ⏱1-3.30pm & 8-11pm Sun-Thu, 1-4pm & 8-11.30pm Fri & Sat; Ⓜ Liceu) After a couple of years in the doldrums, the Modernista classic Muy Buenas, which has been a bar since 1924, is back on its feet and under new ownership. Its stunning and sinuous century-old woodwork has been meticulously restored, as have its etched-glass windows and marble bar. These days it's more restaurant than bar, though the cocktails are impressive.

Though the kitchen (which turns out traditional Catalan dishes) is only open during the listed hours, Muy Buenas is open all day, until 2am (later on Friday and Saturday nights). From Monday to Friday it offers a two-course *menú del día* for €13.

BAR KASPARO
CAFE €

Map p280 (📞93 302 20 72; www.kasparo.es; Plaça de Vicenç Martorell 4; mains €7-11; ⏱9am-11pm Tue-Sat, to midnight Jun-Sep; 📶; Ⓜ Catalunya) This friendly outdoor cafe, which overlooks a traffic-free square with a playground, is a favourite with the neighbourhood parents and serves juices, tapas and salads, as well as more substantial dishes from around the globe.

ELISABETS
CATALAN €

Map p280 (📞93 317 58 26; Carrer d'Elisabets 2-4; mains €8-10; ⏱7.30am-11.30pm Mon-Thu & Sat, to 1.30am Fri Sep-Jul; Ⓜ Catalunya) A great old neighbourhood restaurant, its walls dotted with old radio sets, Elisabets is known for its unpretentious, good-value cooking. The *menú del día* (€12) changes daily, but if you prefer *a la carta*, try the *ragú de jabalí* (wild boar stew) and finish with *mel i mató* (Catalan dessert made from cheese and honey).

EL COLECTIVO
CAFE €

Map p280 (📞93 318 63 80; Carrer del Pintor Fortuny 22; bocadillos from €4; ⏱9am-8.30pm Mon-Sat, 9am-4pm Sun; 📶; Ⓜ Catalunya) A relaxed little cafe on a quiet Raval street, El Colectivo makes excellent cake (carrot, pineapple and many more), creative *bocadillos* (filled rolls) and excellent coffee. It's minimal, with a single row of wooden tables, and the shop-window seating is perfect for street watching, with some good jazz playing in the background. Tapas are served on Thursdays and Fridays.

★ BAR PINOTXO
TAPAS €€

Map p280 (📞93 317 17 31; www.pinotxobar.com; Mercat de la Boqueria; mains €9-17; ⏱7am-4pm Mon-Sat; Ⓜ Liceu) Bar Pinotxo is arguably La Boqueria's, and even Barcelona's, best tapas bar. The ever-charming owner, Juanito, might serve up chickpeas with pine nuts and raisins, a soft mix of potato and spinach sprinkled with salt, soft baby squid with cannellini beans, or a quivering cube of caramel-sweet pork belly.

EL QUIM
TAPAS €€

Map p280 (📞93 301 98 10; www.elquimdela boqueria.com; Mercat de la Boqueria; mains €16-21; ⏱noon-4pm Mon, 7am-4pm Tue-Thu, 7am-5pm Fri & Sat; Ⓜ Liceu) This classic counter bar in the Mercat de la Boqueria is ideal for trying traditional Catalan dishes such as fried eggs with baby squid (the house speciality) or *escalivada* (smoky grilled vegetables). Daily specials are prepared using whatever is in season, and might include artichoke chips or sautéed wild mushrooms.

CAN LLUÍS
CATALAN €€

Map p280 (📞93 441 11 87; www.restaurantcanlluis.cat; Carrer de la Cera 49; mains €14-16; ⏱1.30-4pm & 8.30-11.30pm Mon-Sat; Ⓜ Sant Antoni) Three generations have kept this spick-and-span old-time classic in business since 1929. Beneath the olive-green beams in the back dining room you can see the spot where an

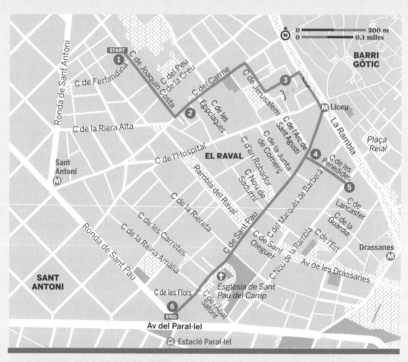

Neighbourhood Walk
Modernista Wining & Dining in El Raval

START CASA ALMIRALL
END LA CONFITERÍA
LENGTH 2KM; ONE HOUR

Long run by the Almirall family that opened it in the mid-19th century, the corner tavern **1** **Casa Almirall** (p86) on Carrer de Joaquín Costa preserves much of its Modernista decor, especially in the picture windows opening on to the street, and the counter and display cabinet.

You'll recognise similarly sinuous curves as you enter the **2** **Bar Muy Buenas** (p84) on Carrer del Carme. Opened as a milk bar in the late 19th century, it retains much of its original decoration. It's a welcoming, cosy place for lunch or a drink.

The **3** **Mercat de la Boqueria** (p80), with half a dozen or so unassuming places to eat, dates back to the 13th century, but it wasn't until 1840 that it was officially inaugurated on this site. In 1914 it was capped with a metal roof and given its charming, wrought-iron, Modernista entrance sign, which is inset with colourful stained glass.

The **4** **Hotel España** (p216) is known above all for its dining rooms, part of the 1903 design by Domènech i Montaner. The Sala Arnau (Arnau Room) features a magnificent alabaster fireplace designed by Eusebi Arnau. Moderately priced traditional Catalan fare is served.

While wandering around El Raval you should not miss **5** **Palau Güell** (p82), one of Gaudí's earlier big commissions. Not designed in his conventional Modernista style, it nonetheless has unmistakeable Gaudí touches, such as the smashed tile chimneys on the rooftop terrace. If passing by at night while doing a round of the bars, make a note to return here by day.

On Carrer de Sant Pau, walk south past the Romanesque church to **6** **La Confitería** (p86), once a barber's shop and then a long-time confectioner's. It was lovingly restored for its reconversion into a bar in 1998. Most of the elements in the front section, including facade, bar counter and cabinets, are the real deal. The back room has been completely renovated more recently, but the style is sympathetic.

anarchist's bomb went off in 1946, killing the then owner. The restaurant is still going strong, however, with excellent seafood dishes and a good *menú del día* for €10.90.

GATS
FUSION €€

Map p280 (☑93 144 00 44; www.encompania delobos.com; Carrer d'en Xuclà 7; mains €9-19; ☺noon-midnight; 🛜; ⓂLiceu) A relatively recent addition to the *barri,* Gats has been an instant hit, and its terrace is constantly full. A deliciously fresh spread of dishes ranges from baba ganoush to Thai green curry, but there's plenty here that's local – try the 'mountain paella' with sausage, or the smoked sardines with honey and truffle. The kitchen is open all day.

FLAX & KALE
VEGETARIAN €€

Map p280 (☑93 317 56 64; www.teresacarles. com; Carrer dels Tallers 74; mains €13-18; ☺9.30am-11.30pm Mon-Fri, from 10am Sat & Sun; 🛜☑; ⓂUniversitat) A far cry from the veggie restaurants of old, Flax & Kale marks a new approach (for Barcelona, at least) that declares that going meat-free does not mean giving up on choice, creativity or style. There are gluten-free and vegan options, and dishes include tacos with guacamole, aubergine and sour cashew cream, or Penang red curry.

BAR CAÑETE
TAPAS €€

Map p280 (☑93 270 34 58; www.barcanete.com; Carrer de la Uniò 17; tapas from €4.50; ☺1pm-midnight Mon-Sat; 🛜; ⓂLiceu) Part of a trend in creating upmarket versions of traditional bars with food to match. A long, narrow dining room holds an open kitchen along which runs a wooden bar, where diners sit – from here, they can point at what they want or order from a long list of classic tapas and *platillos* (plates for sharing).

Many of the choices (such as the mussels with a citric dressing) have a modern twist.

EN VILLE
FRENCH €€

Map p280 (☑93 302 84 67; www.envillebarcelona. es; Carrer del Doctor Dou 14; mains €14-18; ☺1-4pm & 8-11.30pm Tue-Sat, 1-4pm Sun & Mon; ⓂUniversitat) You'll want to come here for the divine decor – the dramatic bouquets, the oil paintings and the antique details all around – as much as the food, which is mostly, but not always, Spanish, and is entirely gluten-free. Turn up early for lunch to beat the queues.

RESTAURANT EL CAFETÍ
CATALAN €€

Map p280 (☑93 329 24 19; www.elcafeti.com; Carrer de Sant Rafael 18; mains €12-18; ☺1.30-4pm & 8-11pm Tue-Sat, 1.30-4pm Sun; 🛜; ⓂLiceu) This diminutive and atmospheric little place is filled with antique furniture and offers traditional local cooking, with one or two unorthodox variations. A more recent addition is tapas, but paella and other rice dishes dominate, and there is a good *menú del día* (€11). The entrance is down the narrow alleyway of Passatge de Bernardí Martorell.

SUCULENT
CATALAN €€€

Map p280 (☑93 443 65 79; www.suculent.com; Rambla del Raval 43; tasting menus €45-75; ☺1-4pm & 8-11.30pm Wed-Sun; 🛜; ⓂLiceu) Celebrity chef Carles Abellan adds to his stable with this old-style bistro, which showcases the best of Catalan cuisine. From the cod brandade to the oxtail stew with truffled sweet potato, only the best ingredients are used. There is no à la carte, just four different tasting menus to choose from.

The Taverna del Suculent next door is nowadays more of a cocktail bar, but still offers updated versions of traditional tapas.

DRINKING & NIGHTLIFE

★LA CONFITERÍA
BAR

Map p280 (☑93 140 54 35; Carrer de Sant Pau 128; ☺7pm-2.30am Mon-Thu, 6pm-3am Fri & Sat, 5pm-2.30am Sun; 🛜; ⓂParal·lel) This is a trip into the 19th century. Until the 1980s it was a confectioner's shop, and although the original cabinets are now lined with booze, the look of the place barely changed with its conversion. A recent refurb of the back room is similarly sympathetic, and the vibe these days is lively cocktail bar.

Later in the evening, it fills with those falling out of the nearby BARTS (p198) and Sala Apolo (p198) concert halls.

CASA ALMIRALL
BAR

Map p280 (☑93 318 95 92; www.casaalmirall.com; Carrer de Joaquín Costa 33; ☺5.30pm-2am Mon-Wed, noon-2.30am Thu-Sat, noon-12.30am Sun; 🛜; ⓂUniversitat) In business since the 1860s, this unchanged corner bar is dark and intriguing, with Modernista decor and a mixed clientele. There are some great original pieces in here, such as the marble counter, and the cast-iron statue of the muse of the Universal Exposition, held in Barcelona in 1888.

BAR PASTÍS
BAR

Map p280 (www.barpastis.es; Carrer de Santa Mònica 4; ☺8pm-2am Tue-Thu & Sun, to 3am Fri & Sat; 🛜; ⓂDrassanes) A French cabaret theme (with lots of Piaf on the stereo) pervades this tiny, cluttered classic, which has been going, on and off, since the end of WWII. You'll need to be in before 9pm to have any hope of sitting or getting near the bar. On some nights it features live acts, usually performing French *chanson*.

BAR MARSELLA
BAR

Map p280 (⌨93 442 72 63; Carrer de Sant Pau 65; ☺10pm-2.30am Mon-Thu, to 3am Fri & Sat; ⓜLiceu) Bar Marsella has been in business since 1820, and has served the likes of Hemingway, who was known to slump here over an *absenta* (absinthe). The bar still specialises in absinthe, a drink to be treated with respect.

Your absinthe glass comes with a lump of sugar, a fork and a little bottle of mineral water. Hold the sugar on the fork, over your glass, and drip the water onto the sugar so that it dissolves into the absinthe, which turns yellow. The result should give you a warm glow.

GRANJA M VIADER
CAFE

Map p280 (⌨93 318 34 86; www.granjaviader. cat; Carrer d'en Xuclà 6; ☺9am-1pm & 5-9pm Mon-Sat; ⓜLiceu) For more than a century, people have been coming here for hot chocolate with whipped cream (ask for a *suís*) ladled out in this classically Catalan milk bar. In 1931, the Viader clan invented Cacaolat, a bottled chocolate milk drink, with iconic label design. The interior here is delightfully old-fashioned and the atmosphere always lively.

EL DRAPAIRE
BAR

Map p280 (⌨607 466446; www.drapaire.com; Carrer de les Sitges 11; ☺6pm-2am Sun-Thu, 3pm-3am Fri & Sat; 🛜; ⓜCatalunya) Part of the recent explosion in the craft-beer scene, this cosy, beamed tavern has been given a new lease on life and now has 13 taps, featuring Spanish and international beers of all styles. There are tapas and platters of cheese and charcuterie to share. Live music on Fridays.

33|45
BAR

Map p280 (⌨93 187 41 38; www.3345.struments. com; Carrer de Joaquín Costa 4; ☺1pm-2am Sun-Mon, to 3am Fri & Sat; 🛜; ⓜUniversitat) A super-trendy bar on a street that's not short of them, this place has excellent mojitos, a fashionable crowd and a frequently changing exhibition of art on the walls. There are DJs most nights, along with plenty of sofas and armchairs for a post-dancing slump.

> ### HISTORICAL RAVAL BARS
> ➡ **Bar Marsella**
> ➡ **La Confitería** (p86)
> ➡ **Casa Almirall** (p86)

MOOG
CLUB

Map p280 (⌨93 319 17 89; www.masimas.com/ moog; Carrer de l'Arc del Teatre 3; entry €5-10; ☺midnight-5am Sun-Thu, to 6am Fri & Sat; ⓜDrassanes) This fun and minuscule club is a standing favourite with the downtown crowd. In the main dance area DJs dish out house, techno and electro, while upstairs you can groove to a nice blend of indie and occasional classic-pop throwbacks.

NEGRONI
COCKTAIL BAR

Map p280 (www.negronicocktailbar.com; Carrer de Joaquín Costa 46; ☺7pm-2.30am Sun-Thu, to 3am Fri & Sat; ⓜUniversitat) Good things come in small packages and this dark, teeny cocktail bar confirms the rule. The mostly black decor lures in a largely student set to try out the cocktails, among them, of course, the celebrated Negroni, a Florentine invention with one part Campari, one part gin and one part sweet vermouth.

MARMALADE
BAR

Map p280 (⌨93 442 39 66; www.marmalade barcelona.com; Carrer de la Riera Alta 4-6; ☺6.30pm-2am Mon-Thu, 10am-3am Fri-Sun; 🛜; ⓜSant Antoni) The golden hues of this backlit bar and restaurant beckon seductively through the glass facade. There are various distinct spaces, decorated in different but equally sumptuous styles, and a pool table next to the bar. Cocktails are big business here, and a selection of them are €5 all night.

BAR LA CONCHA
BAR, GAY

Map p280 (www.laconchadelraval.com; Carrer de la Guàrdia 14; ☺5pm-2.30am Sun-Thu, to 3am Fri & Sat; 🛜; ⓜDrassanes) This place is dedicated to the actress Sara Montiel: the walls groan with more than 250 photos of the sultry star, now surrounding an incongruous large-screen TV. La Concha used to be a largely gay and transvestite haunt, but anyone is welcome and bound to have fun – especially when the drag queens come out to play.

Born in 1928, Sara Montiel bared all on the silver screen in an era that condemned nudity to shameful brazenness – hence 'la concha' (a word commonly used in Spanish slang) can be read as a sly salute to the female genitalia.

BETTY FORD'S   BAR

Map p280 (☑93 304 13 68; Carrer de Joaquín Costa 56; ☺1pm-2.30am Tue-Sat, from 5pm Sun & Mon; ☎; MUniversitat) This enticing corner bar is one of several good stops along the student-jammed run of Carrer de Joaquín Costa. It puts together some nice cocktails and the place fills with an even mix of locals and foreigners, generally aged not much over 30. There's a decent line in burgers and soups, too.

KENTUCKY   BAR

Map p280 (Carrer de l'Arc del Teatre 11; ☺10pm-4am Wed-Sat; MDrassanes) Once a haunt of visiting US Navy boys, this exercise in Americana kitsch is the perfect way to finish an evening – if you can squeeze in. All sorts of odd bods from the *barri* and beyond gather here. An institution in the wee hours, Kentucky often stays open (unofficially) until dawn.

☆ ENTERTAINMENT

★FILMOTECA DE CATALUNYA   CINEMA

Map p280 (☑93 567 10 70; www.filmoteca.cat; Plaça de Salvador Seguí 1-9; adult/concession €4/3; ☺screenings 5-10pm, ticket office 10am-3pm & 4-9.30pm Tue-Sun; MLiceu) The Filmoteca de Catalunya – Catalonia's national cinema – sits in a modern 6000-sq-metre building in the midst of the most louche part of El Raval. The films shown are a superior mix of classics and more recent

REVIVING EL RAVAL

The relocation of the **Filmoteca de Catalunya** to El Raval from the neighbourhood of Sarrià is part of the 'Raval Cultural', an ongoing project to set up the neighbourhood as one of Spain's most influential cultural centres. As part of the project, representatives from the MACBA, Gran Teatre del Liceu, Centre de Cultura Contemporània de Barcelona, Biblioteca de Catalunya, Arts Santa Mònica, Virreina Centre de la Imatge, Institut d'Estudis Catalans and Filmoteca de Catalunya work together to sustain a cultural network with El Raval as its nucleus. The project includes complementary exhibitions, cultural events, tours and collaboration in educational projects.

releases, with frequent themed cycles. A 10-session pass is an amazingly cheap €20.

In addition to two cinemas totalling 555 seats, the Filmoteca comprises a film library, a bookshop, a cafe, offices and a dedicated space for exhibitions.

23 ROBADORS   LIVE MUSIC

Map p280 (www.23robadors.wordpress.com; Carrer d'en Robador 23; ☺8pm-2.30am; MLiceu) On what remains a sleazy Raval street, where streetwalkers, junkies and other misfits hang out in spite of all the work being done to gentrify the area, this narrow little bar has made a name for itself with its shows and live music. Jazz is the name of the game, but you'll also find live poetry, flamenco and plenty more.

JAZZ SÍ CLUB   LIVE MUSIC

Map p280 (☑93 329 00 20; www.tallerdemusics.com/en/jazzsi-club; Carrer de Requesens 2; entry incl drink €6-10; ☺8.30-11pm Tue-Sat, 6.30-10pm Sun; MSant Antoni) A cramped little bar run by the Taller de Músics (Musicians' Workshop) serves as the stage for a varied program of jazz jams through to some good flamenco (Friday and Saturday nights). Thursday night is Cuban night, Tuesday and Sunday are rock, and the rest are devoted to jazz and/or blues sessions. Concerts start around 9pm but the jam sessions can get going earlier.

TEATRE LLANTIOL   THEATRE

Map p280 (☑93 329 90 09; www.llantiol.com; Carrer de la Riereta 7; MSant Antoni) At this small, charming cafe-theatre, which has a certain scuffed elegance, all sorts of odd stuff, from concerts and theatre to magic shows, is staged. The speciality, though, is stand-up comedy, which is occasionally in English (Eddie Izzard did his recent Barcelona run of gigs here). Check the website for details.

TEATRE ROMEA   THEATRE

Map p280 (☑93 309 70 04; www.teatreromea.com; Carrer de l'Hospital 51; ☺box office 5.30pm to start of show Tue-Fri, from 4.30pm Sat & Sun; MLiceu) Just off La Rambla, this 19th-century theatre was resurrected at the end of the 1990s and is one of the city's key stages for quality drama. It usually fills up for a broad range of interesting plays, often classics with a contemporary flavour, in Catalan and Spanish.

EL CANGREJO   GAY

Map p280 (☑93 301 29 78; Carrer de Montserrat 9; ☺11pm-3am Fri & Sat; MDrassanes) This altar to kitsch is a dingy dance hall that has transgressed since the 1920s, and for years starred the luminous underground cabaret figure of Carmen Mairena. It exudes a gorgeously tacky feel, especially with the midnight drag shows. Due to its popularity with tourists, getting in is all but impossible unless you turn up early.

🛍 SHOPPING

★LES TOPETTES
COSMETICS

Map p280 (☏93 500 55 64; www.lestopettes. com; Carrer de Joaquín Costa 33; ☺11am-2pm & 4-9pm Tue-Sat, 4-9pm Mon; ⓜUniversitat) It's a sign of the times that such a chic little temple to soap and perfume can exist in El Raval. The items in Les Topettes' collection have been picked for their designs as much as for the products themselves, and you'll find gorgeously packaged scents, candles and unguents from Diptyque, Cowshed and L'Artisan Parfumeur, among others.

JOAN LA LLAR DEL PERNIL
FOOD

Map p280 (☏93 317 95 29; www.joanllardel pernil.com; Stalls 667-671, Mercat de la Boqueria; ☺8am-3pm Mon-Thu, to 8pm Fri & Sat; ⓜLiceu) This stall in the Mercat de la Boqueria sells some of the best ham and charcuterie in the city, much of which is sliced and presented in little cones as a snack.

FANTASTIK
ARTS & CRAFTS

Map p280 (☏93 301 30 68; www.fantastik. es; Carrer de Joaquín Costa 62; ☺11am-2pm & 4-8.30pm Mon-Fri, 11am-3pm & 4-9pm Sat; ⓜUniversitat) Over 400 products, including a Mexican skull rattle, robot moon explorer from China and recycled plastic zebras from South Africa, are to be found in this colourful shop, which sources its items from Mexico, India, Bulgaria, Russia, Senegal and 20 other countries. It's a perfect place to buy all the things you don't need but can't live without.

HOLALA! PLAZA
FASHION & ACCESSORIES

Map p280 (www.holala-ibiza.com; Plaça de Castella 2; ☺11am-9pm Mon-Sat; ⓜUniversitat) Backing on to Carrer de Valldonzella, where it boasts an exhibition space (Gallery) for temporary art displays, this Ibiza import is inspired by that island's long-established (and somewhat commercialised) hippie tradition. Vintage clothes are the name of the game, along with an eclectic program of exhibitions and activities.

CHÖK
FOOD

Map p280 (☏93 304 23 60; www.chokbarcelona. com; Carrer del Carme 3; ☺9am-9pm; ⓜLiceu) Set inside an old chocolate-maker's, with original wooden shelving and stained glass, Chök now specialises in all things sweet, but especially doughnuts. These come in a huge array of colours and flavours, but there are also cookies, macarons, marshmallows and, of course, the ubiquitous cronut. There's a tiny space where you can order and drink coffee.

TERANYINA
ARTS & CRAFTS

Map p280 (☏93 317 94 36; www.textilteranyina. com; Carrer del Notariat 10; ☺11am-2pm & 5-8pm Mon-Fri; ⓜCatalunya) Artist Teresa Rosa Aguayo runs this textile workshop in the heart of the artsy bit of El Raval. You can join courses at the loom, admire some of the rugs and other works that Teresa has created, and, of course, buy them.

LA PORTORRIQUEÑA
COFFEE

Map p280 (☏93 317 34 38; Carrer d'en Xuclà 25; ☺9am-2pm & 5-8pm Mon-Fri, 9am-2pm Sat; ⓜCatalunya) Coffee beans from around the world, freshly ground before your eyes, have been the winning formula in this store since 1902. It also offers all sorts of chocolate goodies. The street it's on is good for little old-fashioned food boutiques.

🏃 SPORTS & ACTIVITIES

CICLOTOUR
CYCLING

Map p280 (☏93 317 19 70; www.barcelonaciclo tour.com; Carrer dels Tallers 45; tours €22; ☺11am, 2pm & 4.30pm daily May-Oct, 11am Mon-Fri, 11am & 4.30pm Sat & Sun Nov, plus 7.30pm Thu-Sun Jun-Sep; ⓜUniversitat) Daily bike tours around the city's main sights. The evening tour also includes a visit to the Font Màgica.

EL RAVAL SHOPPING

La Ribera

Neighbourhood Top Five

1 **Basílica de Santa Maria del Mar** (p94) Admiring the simplicity and beauty of this fine example of Catalan Gothic.

2 **Museu Picasso** (p92) Being introduced to the origins of Picasso's genius at this fascinating museum, set in a series of interconnected palazzos.

3 **Palau de la Música Catalana** (p95) Experiencing a show or just taking a tour of the Modernista interior of this concert hall.

4 **Parc de la Ciutadella** (p96) Enjoying a stroll, having a picnic, taking a boat out on the lake and spotting the art works.

5 **Bormuth** (p99) Tucking into old-school tapas in a lively atmosphere, and making the most of the excellent lunch deal.

For more detail of this area see Map p284 ➡

Explore La Ribera

La Ribera is widely used to refer to the area covered by the city council's rather long-winded appellation of Sant Pere, Santa Caterina i la Ribera. Carrer de la Princesa, ramrod straight between the traffic-choked Via Laietana and Parc de la Ciutadella, cuts La Ribera in half. The gentrified southern half is generally known as El Born, after Passeig del Born, Barcelona's main drag from the 13th to the 18th centuries, now lined with bars and cafes. Capped at one end by the magnificent Gothic Basílica de Santa Maria del Mar (p94) and along to the Born Centre de Cultura i Memòria (p97), in what used to be the neighbourhood's market building. This area should be your first port of call, specifically a stroll down the Carrer de Montcada, a street rich in Gothic and baroque mansions as well as the location of one of the city's major museums, the Museu Picasso (p92).

Northwest of Carrer de la Princesa, a mess of narrow streets wiggles northward around the striking modern reincarnation of the Mercat de Santa Caterina (p96) and on toward the Modernista Palau de la Música Catalana (p95). Some good eating and drinking options have opened up in these narrow streets.

Via Laietana marks the southwest side of La Ribera, while the Parc de la Ciutadella (p96) closes off its northeastern flank. The park is a rare green space in central Barcelona, where you can lounge on its stretches of grass, sit by the water at the grand fountain, visit the zoo and, if accompanied by small children, take advantage of its playgrounds.

Local Life

→ **Market secrets** Locals get their eggs at the Mercat de Santa Caterina (p96), where, in season, stand holders 'flavour' their eggs by stacking them up and placing truffles among them. Soft-boiled, they are divine.

→ **Catching the rays** Local favourite strip Passeig del Born is perfect for lazy Sunday morning sunbathing on the cafe terraces, as you enjoy a leisurely brunch.

→ **A slice of culture** Join the largely local clientele for a weekend lunchtime classical concert at the Palau de la Música Catalana (p95) and take advantage of the natural daylight to see the beautiful interior of the main auditorium.

→ **Barcelona style** Join the *barcelonins* and shop in some of the city's quirkiest fashion boutiques.

Getting There & Away

→ **Metro** Línia 4 coasts down the southwest flank of La Ribera, stopping at Urquinaona, Jaume I and Barceloneta. Línia 1 also stops nearby, at Urquinaona and Arc de Triomf (the nearest stop for the Parc de la Ciutadella).

Lonely Planet's Top Tip

Getting around all of Barcelona's museums can be anything but cheap, so take advantage of free Sunday afternoons, when entry into many of the city's museums will cost you zilch!

 Best Places to Eat

→ Casa Delfín (p101)
→ El Atril (p101)
→ Nakashita (p102)
→ Bormuth (p99)
→ En Aparté (p101)

For reviews, see p99.➡

 Best Places to Drink

→ Mudanzas (p104)
→ La Vinya del Senyor (p103)
→ Rubí (p103)
→ Miramelindo (p103)

For reviews, see p103.➡

 Best Architecture

→ Basílica de Santa Maria del Mar (p94)
→ Palau de la Música Catalana (p95)
→ Carrer de Montcada (p96)

LA RIBERA

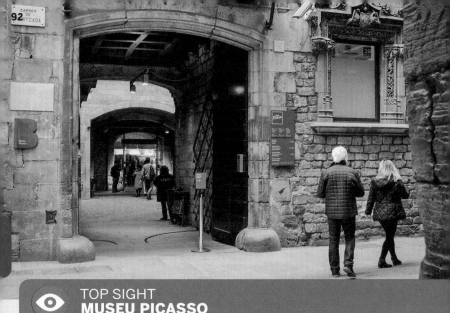

TOP SIGHT
MUSEU PICASSO

The setting alone, in five contiguous medieval stone mansions, makes the Museu Picasso unique. The permanent collection is housed in Palau Aguilar, Palau del Baró de Castellet and Palau Meca, all dating from the 14th century. The 18th-century Casa Mauri, built over medieval remains (even some Roman leftovers have been identified), and the adjacent 14th-century Palau Finestres accommodate temporary exhibitions.

History of the Museum

Allegedly it was Picasso himself who proposed the museum's creation to his friend and personal secretary Jaume Sabartés, a Barcelona native, in 1960. Three years later, the 'Sabartés Collection' was opened, since a museum bearing Picasso's name would have been met with censorship – Picasso's opposition to the Franco regime was well known. The Museu Picasso we see today opened in 1983. It originally held only Sabartés' personal collection of Picasso's art and a handful of works hanging at the Barcelona Museum of Art, but the collection gradually expanded with donations from Salvador Dalí and Sebastià Junyer i Vidal, among others, though most artworks were bequeathed by Picasso himself. His widow, Jacqueline Roque, also donated 41 ceramic pieces and the *Woman with Bonnet* painting after Picasso's death.

Sabartés' contribution and years of service are honoured with an entire room devoted to him, including Picasso's famous Blue Period portrait of him wearing a ruff.

DON'T MISS

- ➡ *Retrato de la tía Pepa* (Portrait of Aunt Pepa)
- ➡ *Ciència i caritat* (Science and Charity)
- ➡ *Terrats de Barcelona* (Roofs of Barcelona)
- ➡ *El foll* (The Madman)
- ➡ *Las meninas* (The Ladies-in-Waiting)

PRACTICALITIES

- ➡ Map p284, D5
- ➡ ☎93 256 30 00
- ➡ www.museupicasso.bcn.cat
- ➡ Carrer de Montcada 15-23
- ➡ adult/concession/child under 16yr all collections €14/7.50/free, permanent collection €11/7/free, temporary exhibitions varies, 6-9.30pm Thu & 1st Sun of month free
- ➡ ⏰9am-7pm Tue-Sun, to 9.30pm Thu
- ➡ Ⓜ Jaume I

The Collection

The collection concentrates on the artist's formative years in Barcelona and elsewhere in Spain, yet there is enough material from subsequent periods to give you a thorough impression of the man's versatility and genius. Above all, you come away feeling that Picasso was the true original, always one step ahead of himself (let alone anyone else) in his search for new forms of expression. The collection includes more than 3500 artworks, largely pre-1904, which is apt considering the artist spent his formative creative years in Barcelona.

It is important, however, not to expect a parade of his well-known works, or even works representative of his best-known periods. What makes this collection truly impressive – and unique among the many Picasso museums around the world – is the way in which it displays his extraordinary talent at such a young age. Faced with the technical virtuosity of a painting such as *Ciència i caritat* (Science and Charity), for example, it is almost inconceivable that such a work could have been created by the hands of a 15-year-old. Some of his self-portraits and the portraits of his parents, which date from 1896, are also evidence of his precocious talent.

Las Meninas Through the Prism of Picasso

From 1954 to 1962 Picasso was obsessed with the idea of researching and 'rediscovering' the greats, in particular Velázquez. In 1957 he created a series of renditions of the Velázquez masterpiece *Las meninas* (The Ladies-in-Waiting), now displayed in rooms 12–14. It is as though Picasso has looked at the original Velázquez painting through a prism reflecting all the styles he had worked through until then, creating his own masterpiece in the process. This is a wonderful opportunity to see *Las meninas* in its entirety in this beautiful space.

Ceramics

What is also special about the Museu Picasso is its showcasing of his work in lesser-known media. The last rooms contain engravings and some 40 ceramic pieces completed throughout the latter years of his unceasingly creative life. You'll see plates and bowls decorated with simple, single-line drawings of fish, owls and other animal shapes, typical of Picasso's daubing on clay.

GETTING AROUND THE COLLECTION

The permanent collection is housed in Palau Aguilar, Palau del Baró de Castellet and Palau Meca. Casa Mauri and the adjacent 14th-century Palau Finestres accommodate temporary exhibitions.

TOP TIPS

➡ At €15, the Carnet del Museu Picasso annual pass is barely more expensive than a day pass, and allows multiple entries. There is a special desk for this, separate from the general ticket desk.

➡ Avoid queues by booking tickets online and choosing a time slot.

LA RIBERA MUSEU PICASSO

TOP SIGHT
BASÍLICA DE SANTA MARIA DEL MAR

At one end of Passeig del Born stands the apse of Barcelona's finest Catalan Gothic church, Santa Maria del Mar (Our Lady of the Sea). Its construction started in 1329, with Berenguer de Montagut and Ramon Despuig as the architects. Famously the parishioners themselves gave up their time to help construct the church, particularly the stevedores from the nearby port.

The pleasing unity of form and symmetry of the church's central nave and two flanking aisles owed much to the rapidity with which the church was built – a mere 54 years, which must be a record for a major European house of worship. The slender, octagonal pillars create an enormous sense of lateral space bathed in the light of stained glass.

Even before anarchists gutted the church in 1909 and again in 1936, Santa Maria always lacked superfluous decoration. Gone are the gilded chapels that weigh heavily over so many Spanish churches, while the splashes of colour high above the nave are subtle – unusually and beautifully so. It all serves to highlight the church's fine proportions, purity of line and sense of space.

DON'T MISS
➡ The church's builders portrayed in memorial stone relief
➡ A live-music performance
➡ El Fossar de les Moreres

PRACTICALITIES
➡ Map p284, E6
➡ ☎ 93 310 23 90
➡ www.santamariadel marbarcelona.org
➡ Plaça de Santa Maria del Mar
➡ €8 1-5pm, incl guided tour
➡ ⏱ 9am-8.30pm Mon-Sat, 10am-8pm Sun
➡ Ⓜ Jaume I

TOP SIGHT
PALAU DE LA MÚSICA CATALANA

This concert hall is a high point of Barcelona's Modernista architecture, a symphony in tile, brick, sculpted stone and stained glass. Built by Domènech i Montaner between 1905 and 1908 for the Orfeó Català musical society, it was conceived as a temple for the Catalan Renaixença (Renaissance). The *palau* (palace) was built with the help of some of the best Catalan artisans of the time, and since 1990 it has undergone several major changes.

The *palau*, like a peacock, shows off much of its splendour on the outside. Take in the principal facade with its mosaics, floral capitals and the sculpture cluster representing Catalan popular music; wander inside the foyer and restaurant areas to admire the spangled, tiled pillars. Best of all, however, is the richly colourful auditorium upstairs, with its ceiling of blue-and-gold stained glass and shimmering skylight that looks like a giant, crystalline, downward-thrusting nipple. Above a bust of Beethoven on the stage towers a wind-blown sculpture of Wagner's Valkyries (Wagner was top of the Barcelona charts at the time it was created).

DON'T MISS

➡ The principal facade's mosaics and columns

➡ The foyer and pillars in the restaurant

➡ The main auditorium

➡ A performance – day or night

PRACTICALITIES

➡ Map p284, A3

➡ ☏93 295 72 00

➡ www.palaumusica.cat

➡ Carrer de Palau de la Música 4-6

➡ adult/concession/child under 10yr €18/15/free

➡ ⊘guided tours 10am-3.30pm, to 6pm Easter, Jul & Aug

➡ ⓂUrquinaona

◉ SIGHTS

MUSEU PICASSO   MUSEUM
See p92.

**BASÍLICA DE SANTA
MARIA DEL MAR**   CHURCH
See p94.

**PALAU DE LA MÚSICA
CATALANA**   ARCHITECTURE
See p95.

PARC DE LA CIUTADELLA   PARK
Map p284 (Passeig de Picasso; ⊘8am-9pm May-
Sep, to 7pm Oct-Apr; 🚹; ⓜArc de Triomf) Come
for a stroll, a picnic, a boat ride on the lake
or to inspect Catalonia's parliament, but
don't miss a visit to this, the most central
green lung in the city. Parc de la Ciutadella
is perfect for winding down.

After the War of the Spanish Succession,
Felipe V razed a swath of La Ribera to build
a huge fortress (La Ciutadella), designed to
keep watch over Barcelona. It became a symbol of everything Catalans hated about Madrid and the Bourbon kings, and was later
used as a political prison. Only in 1869 did
the central government allow its demolition,
after which the site was turned into a park
and used for the Universal Exhibition of 1888.

The monumental **cascada** (waterfall)
near the Passeig de Pujades park entrance,
created between 1875 and 1881 by Josep
Fontserè with the help of an enthusiastic
young Gaudí, is a dramatic combination of
statuary, rugged rocks, greenery and thundering water – all of it perfectly artificial.
Nearby you can hire a rowing boat to pad-
dle about in the small lake.

To the southeast, in what might be seen
as an exercise in black humour, the fort's
former arsenal now houses the **Parlament
de Catalunya** (Map p284; ☑93 304 65 00;
www.parlament.cat; ⊘guided tours 10am-1pm
Sat, Sun & holidays) FREE. You can join free
guided tours, in Catalan and Spanish only,
on Saturdays and Sundays. The building
is only open for independent visiting on 11
September from 10am to 7pm. On show to
the public are the sweeping Escala d'Honor
(Stairway of Honour) and the several sol-
emn halls that lead to the Saló de Sessions,
the semicircular auditorium where parliament sits. In the lily pond at the centre of
the garden in front of the building is a statue of a seemingly heartbroken woman, *Des-
consol* (Distress; 1907), by Josep Llimona.

The Passeig de Picasso side of the park
is lined with several buildings constructed
for, or just before, the Universal Exhibition.
The medieval-looking caprice at the top end
is the most engaging. Known as the **Castell dels Tres Dragons** (Castle of the Three
Dragons), it long housed the Museu de Zoo-
logia, which has since moved to the Fòrum
area and is now known as the Museu Blau.
Domènech i Montaner put the 'castle's'
trimmings on a pioneering steel frame.
The coats of arms are all invented and the
whole building exudes a teasing, playful air.
It was used as a cafe-restaurant during the
Universal Exhibition.

To the south is L'Hivernacle, an elaborate greenhouse. Next come the former
Museu de Geologia and L'Umbracle, a palm
house. On Passeig de Picasso itself is Antoni
Tàpies' typically impenetrable **Homenatge
a Picasso**. Water runs down the panes of
a glass box full of bits of old furniture and
steel girders.

Northwest of the park, Passeig de Lluís
Companys is capped by the Modernista
Arc de Triomf, designed by Josep Vilaseca
as the principal exhibition entrance, with
unusual, Mudéjar-style brickwork. Josep
Llimona did the main reliefs. Just what the
triumph was eludes us, especially since the
exhibition itself was a commercial failure. It
is perhaps best thought of as a bricks-and-
mortar embodiment of the city's general fin
de siècle feel-good factor.

CARRER DE MONTCADA   STREET
Map p284 (ⓜJaume I) An early example of
town planning, this medieval high street
was driven towards the sea from the
road that in the 12th century led northeast from the city walls. It was the city's
most coveted address for the merchant
classes. The great mansions that remain
today mostly date from the 14th and 15th
centuries.

MERCAT DE SANTA CATERINA   MARKET
Map p284 (☑93 319 57 40; www.mercatsanta
caterina.com; Avinguda de Francesc Cambó 16;
⊘7.30am-3.30pm Mon, Wed & Sat, to 8.30pm
Tue, Thu & Fri, closed afternoons Jul & Aug;
ⓜJaume I) Come shopping for your tomatoes at this extraordinary-looking produce
market, designed by Enric Miralles and
Benedetta Tagliabue to replace its 19th-
century predecessor. Finished in 2005, it
is distinguished by its kaleidoscopic and
undulating roof, held up above the bustling

produce stands, restaurants, cafes and bars by twisting slender branches of what look like grey steel trees.

The multicoloured ceramic roof (with a ceiling made of warm, light wood) recalls the Modernista tradition of *trencadís* decoration (a type of mosaic, such as that in Park Güell). Indeed, its curvy design, like a series of Mediterranean rollers, seems to plunge back into an era when Barcelona's architects were limited only by their (vivid) imaginations. The market roof bears an uncanny resemblance to that of the Escoles de Gaudí at La Sagrada Família.

BORN CENTRE DE CULTURA I MEMÒRIA
HISTORIC BUILDING

Map p284 (☑93 256 68 51; http://elborncultura imemoria.barcelona.cat; Plaça Comercial 12; centre free, exhibition spaces adult/concession/child under 16yr €4.40/3/free; ☉10am-8pm Tue-Sun Mar-Oct, 10am-7pm Tue-Sat, to 8pm Sun Nov-Feb; ⓂJaume I) Launched in 2013, as part of the events held for the tercentenary of the Catalan defeat in the War of the Spanish Succession, this cultural space is housed in the **former Mercat del Born**, a handsome 19th-century structure of slatted iron and brick. Excavation in 2001 unearthed remains of whole streets flattened to make way for the much-hated *ciutadella* (citadel) – these are now on show on the exposed subterranean level.

On the ground floor there are panels giving information about the ruins, along with an exhibition space showing items from the period and explaining in greater depth the events surrounding the destruction of the area. There is also a stark and lofty restaurant serving Catalan cuisine, and a gift shop selling upmarket and high-design souvenirs, along with books about the region.

MUSEU DE LA XOCOLATA
MUSEUM

Map p284 (☑93 268 78 78; www.museuxocolata. cat; Carrer del Comerç 36; adult/concession/child under 7yr €6/5/free; ☉10am-7pm Mon-Sat, 10am-3pm Sun; ⓘ; ⓂArc de Triomf) Chocoholics have a hard time containing themselves in this museum dedicated to the fundamental foodstuff – particularly when faced with tempting displays of cocoa-based treats in the cafe at the exit. The displays trace the origins of chocolate, its arrival in Europe, and the many myths and images associated with it. Among the informative stuff and machinery used in the production of chocolate are large chocolate models of emblem-

PALAU DE LA MÚSICA CATALANA THROUGH THE AGES

The original Modernista creation (p95), now a World Heritage site, did not meet with universal approval in its day. The doyen of Catalan literature, Josep Pla, did not hesitate to condemn it as 'horrible', but few share his sentiments today. Domènech i Montaner himself was also in a huff. He failed to attend the opening ceremony in response to unsettled bills.

The *palau* (palace) was at the centre of a fraud scandal from 2009 to 2012, as its president, Felix Millet, who subsequently resigned, admitted to having siphoned off millions of euros of funds. He and his partner were ordered to repay the embezzled money to the *palau* in March 2012.

atic buildings such as La Sagrada Família, along with various characters, local and international.

MONESTIR DE SANT PERE DE LES PUELLES
CHURCH

Map p284 (☑93 268 07 42; www.parroquiasant pere.org; Carrer de Lluís el Piadós 1; ☉9am-1pm & 5-7.45pm Mon-Fri, 9am-1pm & 4.30-6.45pm Sat, 11am-1.15pm Sun; ⓂArc de Triomf) **FREE** It was around this church that settlement began in La Ribera. In AD 985 a Muslim raiding force under Al-Mansur attacked Barcelona and largely destroyed what was then a convent, killing or capturing the nuns. It was rebuilt in early medieval times, but not a great deal remains. The church's pre-Romanesque Greek-cross floor plan survives, as do some Corinthian columns, beneath the 12th-century dome, and a much-damaged Renaissance vault leading into a side chapel.

ZOO DE BARCELONA
ZOO

Map p284 (☑902 457545; www.zoobarcelona. cat; Parc de la Ciutadella; adult/concession/child under 3yr €20/12/free; ☉10am-5.30pm Nov-Mar, 10am-7pm Apr, May, Sep & Oct, 10am-8pm Jun-Aug; ⓘ; ⓂBarceloneta) The zoo is a great day out for kids, with 7500 critters that range from geckos to gorillas, lions and elephants – there are more than 400 species, plus picnic areas dotted all around and a

LA RIBERA SIGHTS

SQUARING UP TO THE PAST

Antonio López y López was an entrepreneur and philanthropist, whose generosity funded the construction of most of the buildings at the port-end of the Via Laietana, where a square now bears his name (and a large statue). In recent years, it's emerged that some of his money was made from the slave trade, and there is a move to rename the square after Nelson Mandela, among other proposals.

The council is dragging its heels, however, so in the meantime, activists have covered the street sign with a plaque reading 'Plaça de Idrissa Diallo', named for a young Guinean immigrant who died in a local detention centre in 2012.

wonderful adventure playground. There are pony rides, a petting zoo and a mini-train meandering through the grounds. Thanks to recent advances in legislation prohibiting the use of animals for performances (including circuses and bullfighting) the zoo called time on its dolphin shows in late 2015.

There is a 20% discount if you book online.

MUSEU DE CULTURES DEL MÓN
MUSEUM

Map p284 (☑93 256 23 00; http://museucultures mon.bcn.cat; Carrer de Montcada 12; adult/concession/under 16yr €5/3.50/free, temporary exhibition €2.20/1.50/free, 3-8pm Sun & 1st Sun of month free; ⊙10am-7pm Tue-Sat, to 8pm Sun; Ⓜ Jaume I) The Palau Nadal and the Palau Marquès de Lliò, which once housed the Museu Barbier-Mueller and the Museu Tèxtil respectively, reopened in 2015 to the public as the site of the new Museum of World Cultures. Exhibits from private and public collections, including many from the Museu Etnològic on Montjuïc, take the visitor on a trip through the ancient cultures of Africa, Asia, the Americas and Oceania. There's a combined ticket with the Museu Egipci (p135) and Museu Etnològic (p190) for €12.

FUNDACIÓ FOTO COLECTANIA
GALLERY

Map p284 (☑93 217 16 26; www.colectania.es; Passeig de Picasso 14; adult/concession/child under 14yr €4/3/free, free 1st Sun of month; ⊙11am-8pm Mon-Sat, 11am-3pm Sun; Ⓜ Arc de Triomf, Jaume I) Photography lovers should swing by here to see the latest exhibition from this nonprofit foundation, which showcases thought-provoking works from across the globe. In 2016 the foundation moved from its base in Gràcia to this 500-sq-metre space in El Born. The exhibits may come from the foundation's extensive 3000-piece collection of Spanish and Portuguese photographers from the 1950s onwards, but more likely will be temporary exhibitions.

CASA DE LA SEDA
HISTORIC BUILDING

Map p284 (☑93 310 77 78; www.casadelaseda. com; Carrer de Sant Pere més Alt 1; adult/concession/child under 11yr €10/8/free; ⊙11am Sat guided tour in English/Spanish/Catalan; Ⓜ Urquinaona) The former headquarters of the Silk Sailmakers' Guild, a handsome 18th-century mansion covered in caryatid sgraffiti that sits on the Via Laietana, is now open to the public. Obligatory guided tours are in English, Spanish and Catalan, last 45 minutes and take in rooms including the luxuriously appointed guild hall, meeting rooms and library.

EL FOSSAR DE LES MORERES
SQUARE

Map p284 (Ⓜ Jaume I) Opposite Basílica de Santa Maria del Mar's eastern flank, an eternal flame burns brightly over an apparently anonymous sunken square. This is El Fossar de les Moreres (Mulberry Cemetery), the site of a Roman cemetery. It's also where Catalan resistance fighters were buried after the siege of Barcelona ended in defeat in September 1714, and for whom the flame burns.

MUSEU EUROPEU D'ART MODERN
MUSEUM

Map p284 (MEAM; ☑93 319 56 93; www.meam. es; Carrer Barra de Ferro 5; adult/concession/child under 10yr €9/7/free; ⊙10am-8pm Tue-Sun; Ⓜ Jaume I) The European Museum of Modern Art opened in the summer of 2011 in the Palau Gomis, a handsome 18th-century mansion around the corner from the Museu Picasso. The art within is strictly representational (the 'Modern' of the name simply means 'contemporary') and is mostly from young Spanish artists, though there are some works from elsewhere in Europe.

ARXIU FOTOGRÀFIC DE BARCELONA
GALLERY

Map p284 (☑93 256 34 20; http://arxiufoto grafic.bcn.cat; Plaça de Pons i Clerch 2, 2A; ⊙10am-7pm Mon-Sat; Ⓜ Arc de Triomf) FREE On the 2nd floor of the former Convent de

Sant Agustí is the modest exhibition space of this photo archive. Photos on show are generally related to the city, as the photo collection is principally devoted to that theme, from the late 19th century until the late 20th century.

CASA LLOTJA DE MAR
ARCHITECTURE

Map p284 (La Llotja; ☑93 547 88 49; www.casa llotja.com; Passeig d'Isabel II 1; ☺10am-2pm Mon-Fri; ⓜBarceloneta) FREE The centrepiece of the city's medieval stock exchange (more affectionately known as La Llotja) is the fine Gothic Saló de Contractacions (Transaction Hall), built in the 14th century. Pablo Picasso and Joan Miró attended the art school that was housed in the Saló dels Cònsols from 1849.

 **EATING**

PARADISO/ PASTRAMI BAR
SMOKERY, COCKTAIL BAR €

Map p284 (☑639 310671; www.rooftopsmoke house.com; Carrer de Rera Palau 4; mains €7-9; ☺7pm-2am Mon-Thu, to 3am Fri & Sat; ☎; ⓜBarceloneta) A kind of Narnia-in-reverse, Paradiso is fronted with a snowy-white space, not much bigger than a wardrobe, with pastrami sandwiches, pulled pork and other home-cured delights. But this is only the portal – pull open the huge wooden fridge door, and step through into a glam, sexy speakeasy of a cocktail bar guaranteed to raise the most world-weary of eyebrows.

EUSKAL ETXEA
TAPAS €

Map p284 (☑93 310 21 85; www.euskaletxea taberna.com; Placeta de Montcada 1; tapas €2.10; ☺10am-12.30am Sun-Thu, to 1am Fri & Sat; ☎; ⓜJaume I) Barcelona has plenty of Basque and pseudo-Basque tapas bars, but this is the real deal. It captures the feel of San Sebastián better than many of its newer competitors. Choose your *pintxos* (Basque tapas piled on slices of bread), sip *txakoli* (Basque white wine), and keep the toothpicks so the staff can count them up and work out your bill.

BORMUTH
TAPAS €

Map p284 (☑93 310 21 86; Carrer del Rec 31; tapas €4-10; ☺noon-1.30am Sun-Thu, to 2.30am Fri & Sat; ☎; ⓜJaume I) Bormuth has tapped into the vogue for old-school tapas with modern-day service and decor, and serves all the old favourites – *patatas bravas* (potatoes in a spicy tomato sauce), *ensaladilla* (Russian salad) and tortilla – along with some less predictable and superbly prepared numbers (try the chargrilled red pepper with black pudding).

KOKU KITCHEN BUNS
ASIAN €

Map p284 (☑93 269 65 36; www.kokukitchen. es; Carrer del Comerç 29; mains €9-11; ☺1-4pm & 7.30-11.30pm; ☎; ⓜBarceloneta) Steamed buns stuffed with beef or pork with coriander, peanuts, pickled fennel and a sake sauce are the big draw here, but the starters, sides and even the excellent homemade lemonade are also worthy of note, as is the list of inventive cocktails. A great-value lunch *menú del día* is €13.

EL CASAL
MODERN FRENCH €

Map p284 (☑93 268 40 04; www.elcasalcafe. com; Plaça Victor Balaguer 5; menú del día €12, sandwiches €3.50-4.50; ☺7am-5pm Mon-Wed, 6pm-midnight Thu-Sat; ⓜJaume I) A French-run cafe serving excellent food for a great price in noisy but welcoming surroundings, adorned with *objets* from the motherland. The fixed lunch changes daily, but look out for the superior cauliflower cheese and an authentic tarte Tatin. Breakfast is available until 1pm, and tapas and sandwiches are available throughout the day. Arrive early for a terrace table.

ROCKATA
ARGENTINE €

Map p284 (☑93 181 90 42; www.rockata barcelona.com; Carrer del Comerç 20; mains €8-€9; ☺11.30am-11.30pm; ☎; ⓜArc de Triomf) Not much more than a corridor with a kitchen, Rockata is the 2017 incarnation of a laksa bar, and has maintained a bowl of it (prawn, since you ask) on the menu, but otherwise the Argentine running the joint has returned to his roots – expect lots of grilled meats and burgers, and a long list of hearty sandwiches.

CAT BAR
VEGAN €

Map p284 (www.catbarcat.com; Carrer de la Bòria 17; mains €6-9; ☺1-10pm Thu-Mon; ☎☑; ⓜJaume I) This tiny little joint squeezes in a vegan kitchen, a great selection of local artisanal beers and a smattering of live music. The food mostly centres on a list of different burgers, plus a gluten-free dish of the day, tapas and hummus. The beers change regularly, but there is always one wheat, one porter, one gluten-free and an IPA.

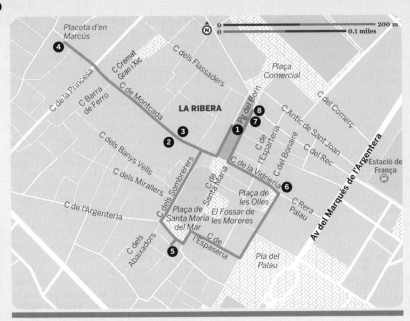

Local Life
Tapas & Bar-Hopping in El Born

If there's one place that distils Barcelona's enduring cool and provides a snapshot of all that's irresistible about this city, it has to be El Born, the tangle of streets surrounding the Basílica de Santa Maria del Mar. Its secret is simple: this is where locals go for an authentic Barcelona night out.

❶ Passeig del Born

Most nights in El Born begin along the Passeig del Born, one of the prettiest little boulevards in Europe. It's a place to sit as much as to promenade, and it's the graceful setting beneath the trees from which El Born's essential appeal is obvious – thronging people, brilliant bars and architecture from a medieval film set.

❷ Catalan Tapas

Push through the crowd to order a *cava* (sparkling wine) and an assortment of tapas at El Xampanyet (p103), one of the city's best-known *cava* bars, in business since 1929. Star dishes include tangy *boquerones en vinagre* (white anchovies in vinegar) and there's high-quality seafood served from a can in the Catalan way.

❸ Best of Basque

Having taken your first lesson in Barcelona-style tapas it's time to compare it with the

pintxos (Basque tapas of food morsels perched atop pieces of bread) lined up along the bar at Euskal Etxea (p99).

❹ Spain with a Twist

The detour to Bar del Pla (p102) on the northern limits of El Born is worth the walk. The tapas may look traditionally Spanish but a confident hand in the kitchen bestows deft touches of originality.

❺ Tapas with a View

Back in the heart of El Born, in the shadow of the Basílica de Santa Maria del Mar, pastry chef Carles Mampel operates **Bubó** (Map p284; ☑93 268 72 24; www.bubo. es; Carrer de les Caputxes 6 & 10; tapas from €4; ⊙10am-9pm Mon-Thu, to 11pm Fri & Sat, 10am-10pm Sun; Ⓜ Barceloneta). If you're not already sated, try the salted-cod croquettes at one of the outdoor tables inching onto the lovely square.

Seafood at Cal Pep (p102)

❻ Cal Pep

Boisterous Cal Pep (p102) is one of Barcelona's enduring stars. It can be difficult to snaffle a bar stool from which to order gourmet bar snacks such as *cloïsses amb pernil* (clams with ham); so if it's full, order a drink and wait.

❼ El Born's Favourite Bar

El Born Bar (p103) effortlessly attracts everyone from cool thirty-somethings from all over town to locals who pass judgment on Passeig del Born's passing parade. Its staying power depends on a good selection of beers, spirits, and *empanadas* and other snacks.

❽ The Last Mojito

So many Barcelona nights end with a mojito, and El Born's biggest and best are to be found at Cactus Bar (p104). The outdoor tables next to Passeig del Born are the perfect way to wind down the night.

EN APARTÉ   FRENCH €

Map p284 (☑93 269 13 35; www.enaparte.es; Carrer de Lluís el Piadós 2; mains €8-13; ☺10am-1am Mon-Thu, to 2am Fri & Sat, to 12.30am Sun; 🤏; ⓜArc de Triomf) A great low-key place to eat good-quality French food, just off the quiet Plaça de Sant Pere. The restaurant is small but spacious, with sewing-machine tables and vintage details, and floor-to-ceiling windows that bring in some wonderful early-afternoon sunlight.

TANTARANTANA   MEDITERRANEAN €

Map p284 (☑93 268 24 10; www.gruposantelmo. com; Carrer d'en Tantarantana 24; mains €9-12; ☺1pm-midnight; 🤏; ⓜJaume I) There is something comforting about the old-style marble-top tables, upon which you can try simple but well-prepared dishes such as wild-mushroom risotto or cod with ratatouille. There's also a long list of tapas. Tantarantana attracts a thirty-something crowd who make the most of the outdoor seating in warmer months.

LA LLAVOR DELS ORÍGENS   CATALAN €

Map p284 (☑93 310 75 31; www.lallavordels origens.com; Carrer de la Vidrieria 6-8; mains €9-15; ☺1-5pm & 7pm-midnight Mon-Thu, 1pm-midnight Fri & Sat; 🤏; ⓜJaume I) In this treasure chest of Catalan regional products, the shop shelves groan under the weight of bottles. It also has a long menu of small-ish dishes, such as *sopa de carbassa i castanyes* (pumpkin and chestnut soup) or *mandonguilles amb alberginies* (rissoles with aubergine), which you can mix and match over wine by the glass.

★EL ATRIL   INTERNATIONAL €€

Map p284 (☑93 310 12 20; www.elatrilbarcelona. es; Carrer dels Carders 23; mains €11-18; ☺11am-11.30pm Sun-Thu, to midnight Fri & Sat; 🤏; ⓜJaume I) El Atril is influenced by culinary flavours from all over the globe, so while you'll see plenty of tapas (the *patatas bravas* are recommended), you'll also find kangaroo fillet, *moules-frites* (mussels and fries), duck cannelloni, and a good selection of substantial salads. There's also a mix of meats you can cook yourself on a salt block (€19, minimum two people).

★CASA DELFÍN   CATALAN €€

Map p284 (☑93 319 50 88; www.facebook.com/ Casa-Delfin-326525620764565/; Passeig del Born 36; mains €10-17; ☺8am-midnight Sun-Thu, to 1am Fri & Sat; 🤏; ⓜJaume I) One of

Barcelona's culinary delights, Casa Delfín is everything you dream of when you think of Catalan (and Mediterranean) cooking. Start with the tangy and sweet *calçots* (spring onions; February and March only) or salt-strewn *Padrón* peppers, moving on to grilled sardines speckled with parsley, then tackle the meaty monkfish roasted in white wine and garlic.

NAKASHITA   JAPANESE €€

Map p284 (☑93 295 53 78; www.nakashitabcn. com; Carrer del Rec Comtal 15; mains €12-22; ⏱1.30-4pm & 8.30pm-midnight Mon-Sun; 🛜; Ⓜ Arc de Triomf) Brazil's particular immigration story means it has a tradition of superb Japanese food, and the Brazilian chef at Nakashita is no slouch, turning out excellent sashimi, maki rolls, softshell crab and *kakiage* (a mix of tempura). One of the best Japanese restaurants in the city, with just a handful of tables – book if you can.

BAR DEL PLA   TAPAS €€

Map p284 (☑93 268 30 03; www.bardelpla.cat; Carrer de Montcada 2; mains €12-16; ⏱noon-11pm Mon-Thu, to midnight Fri & Sat; 🛜; Ⓜ Jaume I) A bright and occasionally rowdy place, with glorious Catalan tiling, a vaulted ceiling and bottles of wine lining the walls. At first glance, the tapas at informal Bar del Pla are traditionally Spanish, but the riffs on a theme display an assured touch. Try the ham croquettes, Wagyu burger, T-bone steak or marinated salmon, yoghurt and mustard.

CAL PEP   TAPAS €€

Map p284 (☑93 310 79 61; www.calpep.com; Plaça de les Olles 8; mains €13-20; ⏱7.30-11.30pm Mon, 1-3.45pm & 7.30-11.30pm Tue-Sat, closed last 3 weeks Aug; Ⓜ Barceloneta) It's getting a foot in the door of this legendary fish restaurant that's the problem – there can be queues out into the square. And if you want one of the five tables out the back, you'll need to call ahead. Most people are happy elbowing their way to the bar for some of the tastiest seafood tapas in town.

GINETTE   FRENCH €€

Map p284 (☑93 280 95 03; www.ginette.es; Carrer del Rec Comtal 12; mains €16-18; ⏱8.30am-2am Tue-Sun Sep-Jun, 6pm-2am Mon-Sat Jul & Aug; Ⓜ Arc de Triomf) Opened in 2017, with a Parisian chef at the helm, Ginette blends Scandinavian and Barcelona chic in its decor, but the menu has an overwhelm-

ingly Gallic feel, with dishes such as cod *meunière* with hazelnuts or duck *magret* with orange. There are also tapas – and even these include a *croque monsieur* with Comté cheese.

EL CHIGRE   TAPAS €€

Map p284 (☑93 782 63 30; http://elchigre1769. com; Carrer dels Sombrerers 7; mains €10-17; ⏱noon-11.45pm, from 1pm Mon-Fri Nov-Mar; Ⓜ Jaume I) Styling itself as part Asturian cider house and part Catalan *vermuteria* (bar specialising in vermouth, served on ice with a slice of orange and a green olive), El Chigre brings sophisticated versions of classic dishes from both regions to its menu. Try the superb tomato and tuna salad with tomato *gelée*, or the puffed corn *tortos* with lamb stew.

LE CUCINE MANDAROSSO   ITALIAN €€

Map p284 (☑93 269 07 80; www.lecucine mandarosso.com; Carrer de Verdaguer i Callís 4; mains €12-14, menú del día €12; ⏱1.30-4pm & 9pm-midnight Tue-Sun; Ⓜ Urquinaona) This is comfort food done to perfection – the menu changes daily, with only a handful of mains to choose from, most of which are pasta, with one or two fish or meat. The antipasti can be vegetables, or fresh cheese, such as the wonderfully creamy *burrata* (made from mozzarella and cream), buffalo-milk mozzarella, or smoked *scamorza* and *provola* cheese.

FARIGOLA   MEDITERRANEAN €€

Map p284 (☑93 488 55 83; Carrer del Davant del Portal Nou 3; mains €6-8; ⏱11am-1am; Ⓜ Arc de Triomf) Farigola is a bit of a gem, hidden on a quiet backstreet and known only to locals. Its small terrace and cosy dining room/bar are rarely full, but its lunch deal (two dishes for €12) is good. Dishes might include roast beef with rosemary potatoes, or beetroot couscous with ricotta, or otherwise sandwiches (the pastrami is superb) are available all day.

SANTAGUSTINA   TAPAS €€

Map p284 (☑93 315 79 04; www.santagustina. com; Plaça Sant Agustí Vell 9; mains €9-14; ⏱noon-1am Sun-Thu, to 3am Fri & Sat; 🛜; Ⓜ Arc de Triomf) This tapas bar–restaurant has tables outside on a charming little plaza. Invoking a slightly wicked ecclesiastical theme, with menus sectioned into 'Blessed Tapas', 'Divine Tapas', 'Immaculate Tapas' and 'Temptations', it serves up well-executed Spanish and Catalan food – oxtail stew, 'Granny's meatballs', grilled octopus etc – in small portions designed for sharing. Service could be a little more attentive.

EL FORO
ARGENTINE €€

Map p284 (☑93 310 10 20; www.restaurante elforo.com; Carrer de la Princesa 53; mains €9-16; ⏰11.30am-11.30pm Tue-Thu & Sun, to 12.30am Fri & Sat; 🛜🍽; Ⓜ Jaume I) Friendly El Foro does everything you'd expect an Argentine restaurant to do – huge slabs of red meat in a variety of cuts, *empanadas* (small pasties with various fillings) and the inevitable Italian element in the shape of pizzas and pasta dishes. Less predictable is the list of vegetarian dishes (such as vegetable curry with quinoa and coconut milk) and the range of salads.

CUINES DE SANTA CATERINA
MEDITERRANEAN, ASIAN €€

Map p284 (☑93 268 99 18; www.grupotragaluz. com; Mercat de Santa Caterina; mains €12-16; ⏰1-4pm & 7.30-11pm Sun-Thu, to 11.30pm Fri & Sat; 🛜; Ⓜ Jaume I) With a contemporary feel and open kitchens, this multifaceted restaurant inside the Mercat de Santa Caterina offers all sorts of food. Peck at the sushi bar, tuck into classic rice dishes or chargrilled meat, or go vegetarian. It does some things better than others (skip the hummus and tarte Tatin). Reservations aren't taken, so you may have to queue.

🍷 DRINKING & NIGHTLIFE

GUZZO
COCKTAIL BAR

Map p284 (☑93 667 00 36; www.guzzoclub.es; Plaça Comercial 10; ⏰6pm-2.30am Mon-Thu, to 3am Fri & Sat, noon-3am Sun; 🛜; Ⓜ Jaume I) This swish but relaxed cocktail bar is run by much-loved Barcelona DJ Fred Guzzo, who is often to be found at the decks, spinning his delicious selection of funk, soul and rare groove. You'll also find frequent live-music acts of consistently decent quality, and a funky atmosphere at almost any time of day.

LA VINYA DEL SENYOR
WINE BAR

Map p284 (☑93 310 33 79; Plaça de Santa Maria del Mar 5; ⏰noon-1am Mon-Thu, to 2am Fri & Sat, to midnight Sun; 🛜; Ⓜ Jaume I) Relax on the *terraza*, which lies in the shadow of the Basílica de Santa Maria del Mar, or crowd

inside at the tiny bar. The wine list is as long as *War and Peace* and there's a table upstairs for those who opt to sample the wine away from the madding crowd.

BAR DEL CONVENT
CAFE

Map p284 (☑93 256 50 17; www.bardelconvent. com; Plaça de l'Acadèmia; ⏰10am-9pm Tue-Sat; ♿; Ⓜ Arc de Triomf) Alongside the Gothic arches of what remains of the Sant Agusti convent's cloister is this pleasant cafe-bar – particularly good for people with children. Kids often play football in the cloister grounds, and there are children's books and toys in the cafe itself. You can also enter at Carrer del Comerç 36 through James Turrell's light sculpture.

RUBÍ
BAR

Map p284 (☑647 737707; Carrer dels Banys Vells 6; ⏰7.30pm-2.30am Sun-Thu, to 3am Fri & Sat; 🛜; Ⓜ Jaume I) With its boudoir lighting and cheap mojitos, Rubí is where the Born's cognoscenti head for a nightcap – or several. It's a narrow, cosy space – push through to the back where you might just get one of the coveted tables, with superior bar food, from Vietnamese rolls to more traditional selections of cheese and ham.

EL BORN BAR
BAR

Map p284 (☑93 319 53 33; www.elbornbar.com; Passeig del Born 26; ⏰10am-2am Mon-Thu, to 3am Fri & Sat, noon-2.30am Sun; 🛜; Ⓜ Jaume I) Moss-green paintwork, marble tables and a chequered black-and-white tiled floor create a timeless look for this popular little cafe-bar. A spiral wrought-iron staircase leads to a quieter room upstairs (the twisting steps mean that there is no table service and hot drinks can't be carried upstairs).

EL XAMPANYET
WINE BAR

Map p284 (☑93 319 70 03; Carrer de Montcada 22; ⏰noon-3.30pm & 7-11.15pm Tue-Sat, noon-3.30pm Sun; 🛜; Ⓜ Jaume I) Nothing has changed for decades in this, one of the city's best-known *cava* (wine) bars. Plant yourself at the bar or seek out a table against the decoratively tiled walls for a glass or three of the cheap house *cava* and an assortment of tapas, such as the tangy *boquerones en vinagre* (fresh anchovies in vinegar).

MIRAMELINDO
BAR

Map p284 (☑93 310 37 27; www.barmiramelindo bcn.com; Passeig del Born 15; ⏰8pm-2.30am Mon-Thu, to 3.30am Fri & Sat, 7pm-2.30am Sun;

🔊; Ⓜ Jaume I) A spacious tavern in a Gothic building, this remains a classic on Passeig del Born for mixed drinks, while soft jazz and soul sounds float overhead. Try for a comfy seat at a table towards the back before it fills to bursting. A couple of similarly barn-sized places sit on this side of the *passeig.*

MUDANZAS   BAR

Map p284 (📞 93 319 11 37; Carrer de la Vidrieria 15; ⊙8am-2.30am Mon-Fri, 10am-2.30am Sat & Sun; 🔊; Ⓜ Jaume I) This was one of the first bars to get things into gear in El Born and it still attracts a faithful crowd. With its chequered floor and marble-topped tables, it's an attractive, lively place for a beer and perhaps a sandwich or a tapa. It also has a nice line in rum and malt whisky.

MAGIC   CLUB

Map p284 (📞 93 310 72 67; www.magic-club.net; Passeig de Picasso 40; ⊙11pm-6am Thu-Sat; Ⓜ Barceloneta) Although it sometimes hosts live acts in its sweaty basement, Magic is basically a straightforward, subterranean nightclub offering rock, mainstream dance faves and Spanish pop. It's an established favourite on the scene, and queues can be long.

CACTUS BAR   BAR

Map p284 (📞 93 247 92 90; Passeig del Born 30; ⊙3pm-3am; Ⓜ Jaume I) A lively bar that hops until late into the night, often thanks to visiting DJs. The bar itself is tiny, but the terrace outside is a good spot, and overlooks the pretty Passeig del Born.

A MEDIEVAL CONCERT HALL

You can sip wine or cocktails (both rather expensive) inside the baroque courtyard and theatrical interior of the originally medieval **Palau de Dalmases** (Map p284; 📞 93 310 06 73; www.palaudalmases.com; Carrer de Montcada 20; ⊙6pm-2am Tue-Sat, 6-10pm Sun; Ⓜ Jaume I). There are flamenco shows at 6pm, 7.30pm and 9.30pm (€25 including one drink). On Wednesdays there is a free jazz concert at 11pm, and on Thursdays opera (€20).

 # ENTERTAINMENT

★ PALAU DE LA
MÚSICA CATALANA   CLASSICAL MUSIC

Map p284 (📞 93 295 72 00; www.palaumusica. cat; Carrer de Palau de la Música 4-6; tickets from €18; ⊙box office 9.30am-9pm Mon-Sat, 10am-3pm Sun; Ⓜ Urquinaona) A feast for the eyes, this Modernista confection is also the city's most traditional venue for classical and choral music, although it has a wide-ranging program, including flamenco, pop and – particularly – jazz. Just being here for a performance is an experience. In the foyer, its tiled pillars all a-glitter, you can sip a pre-concert tipple.

Head up the grand stairway to the main auditorium, a whirlpool of Modernista whimsy.

TABLAO NERVIÓN   DANCE

Map p284 (📞 93 315 21 03; www.restaurant enervion.com; Carrer de la Princesa 2; show incl 1 drink €18, show & set dinner €30; ⊙shows 8-10pm Wed-Sun; Ⓜ Jaume I) For admittedly tourist-oriented flamenco, this unassuming bar (shows take place in the basement) is cheaper than most, and has good offerings. Check the website for further details.

🛍 SHOPPING

EL REI DE LA MÀGIA   MAGIC

Map p284 (📞 93 319 39 20; www.elreydela magia.com; Carrer de la Princesa 11; ⊙10.30am-2pm & 4-7.30pm Mon-Sat; Ⓜ Jaume I) For more than 100 years, the owners have been keeping locals both astounded and amused. Should you decide to stay in Barcelona and make a living as a magician, this is the place to buy levitation brooms, glasses of disappearing milk and decks of magic cards.

VILA VINITECA   WINE

Map p284 (📞 93 777 70 17; www.vilaviniteca.es; Carrer dels Agullers 7; ⊙8.30am-8.30pm Mon-Sat; Ⓜ Jaume I) One of the best wine stores in Barcelona (and there are a few...), Vila Viniteca has been searching out the best local and imported wines since 1932. On a couple of November evenings it organises what has become an almost riotous wine-tasting event in Carrer dels Agullers and surrounding lanes, at which cellars from around Spain present their young new wines.

CASA GISPERT
FOOD

Map p284 (☏93 319 75 35; www.casagispert. com; Carrer dels Sombrerers 23; ☺10am-8.30pm Mon-Sat; MJaume I) The wonderful, atmospheric and wood-fronted Casa Gispert has been toasting nuts and selling all manner of dried fruit since 1851. Pots and jars piled high on the shelves contain an unending variety of crunchy titbits: some roasted, some honeyed, all of them moreish. Your order is shouted over to the till, along with the price, in a display of old-world accounting.

EL MAGNÍFICO
COFFEE

Map p284 (☏93 319 60 81; www.cafeselmagnifico. com; Carrer de l'Argenteria 64; ☺9.30am-8pm Mon-Sat; MJaume I) All sorts of coffee has been roasted here since the early 20th century. The variety of coffee (and tea) available is remarkable – and the aromas hit you as you walk in. Across the road, the same people run the exquisite tea shop **Sans i Sans** (Map p284; ☏93 310 25 18; www. sansisans.com; Carrer de l'Argenteria 59; ☺10am-8pm Mon-Sat).

MI.VINTAGE
VINTAGE

Map p284 (www.mivintagelabel.com; Carrer dels Consellers 2; ☺10am-8pm Mon-Sat; MBarceloneta) Opened in 2017, this breathtakingly hip vintage store stocks a mix of secondhand and revamped clothes – treated, repaired, improved or, as the owner says, made 'street-ready'. Expect silk bomber jackets aplenty, colourful leather blazers, Hawaiian shirts and Emian sunglasses, along with Taschen books, Casio digital watches and funky PVC jewellery.

OGGETTO
DESIGN

Map p284 (☏93 515 31 11; www.oggettobcn.com; Carrer dels Canvis Nous 4; ☺4.30pm-8.30pm Mon, 12.30pm-8.30pm Tue-Sat, from 4.30pm Tue-Sat Jul, closed Aug; MBarceloneta) A gorgeous little showcase for designer homeware. The cushions are made locally and based on the typical 'mosaic' Barcelona floor tiles, but look out too for the Scandi tea sets, stunning hand-blown glassware from France and colourful wire baskets made in Milan.

MARSALADA
GIFTS & SOUVENIRS

Map p284 (☏609 285953; www.marsalada design.com; Carrer de Sant Jacint 6; ☺10am-2pm & 4-8pm Mon-Sat; MJaume I) For souvenirs with a difference, Marsalada has hand-printed tote bags in unbleached cotton, engravings and T-shirts. Each of these is emblazoned with a well-known Barcelona attraction, sketched in pen and ink and adorned with abstract colour mosaics.

LOISAIDA
CLOTHING, ANTIQUES

Map p284 (☏93 295 54 92; www.loisaidabcn.com; Carrer dels Flassaders 42; ☺11am-9pm Mon-Sat, 11am-2pm & 4-8pm Sun; MJaume I) A sight in its own right, housed in the former coach house and stables for the Royal Mint, Loisaida (from the Spanglish for 'Lower East Side') is a deceptively large emporium of colourful, retro and somewhat preppy clothing for men and women, costume jewellery, music from the 1940s and '50s and some covetable antiques. One space is devoted entirely to denim.

ARLEQUÍ MÀSCARES
ARTS & CRAFTS

Map p284 (☏93 268 27 52; www.arlequimask. com; Carrer de la Princesa 7; ☺11.30am-8pm Mon, 10.30am-8pm Tue-Fri, 11am-8pm Sat, 11.30am-7pm Sun; MJaume I) A wonderful little oasis of originality, this shop specialises in masks for costume and decoration. Some of the pieces are superb, while stock also includes a beautiful range of decorative boxes in Catalan themes, and some old-style marionettes.

COQUETTE
FASHION & ACCESSORIES

Map p284 (☏93 319 29 76; www.coquettebcn. com; Carrer del Rec 65; ☺11am-3pm & 5-9pm Mon-Fri, 11.30am-9pm Sat; MBarceloneta) With its spare, cut-back and designer look, this friendly fashion store is attractive in its own right. Women can browse through casual, feminine wear by such designers as Humanoid, Vanessa Bruno, UKE and Hoss Intropia and others, with a further collection nearby at **Carrer de Bonaire 5** (Map p284; ☏93 310 35 35).

HOFMANN PASTISSERIA
FOOD

Map p284 (☏93 268 82 21; www.hofmann-bcn. com; Carrer dels Flassaders 44; ☺9am-2pm & 3.30-8pm Mon-Sat, 9am-2.30pm Sun; MBarceloneta) With its painted wooden cabinets, this bite-sized gourmet patisserie, linked to the prestigious Hofmann cooking school, has an air of timelessness. Choose between jars of delicious chocolates, the renowned croissants (in various flavours) and more dangerous pastries, or an array of cakes and other sweet treats.

NU SABATES
SHOES

Map p284 (☑93 268 03 83; www.nusabates.com; Carrer dels Cotoners 14; ☺11am-8pm Mon-Sat; Ⓜ Jaume I) A modern-day Catalan cobbler has put together some original handmade leather shoes for men and women (and a handful of bags and other leather items) in their friendly and stylish locale, which is enlivened by some inspired musical selections.

OLISOLIVA
FOOD

Map p284 (☑93 268 14 72; www.olisoliva.com; Mercat de Santa Caterina; ☺9.30am-3.30pm Mon, Wed & Sat, to 7pm Tue, to 8pm Thu-Fri; Ⓜ Jaume I) Inside the Mercat de Santa Caterina, this simple, glassed-in store is stacked with olive oils and vinegars from all over Spain. Taste some of the products before deciding. Some of the best olive oils come from southern Spain. The range of vinegars is astounding, too.

CUSTO BARCELONA
FASHION & ACCESSORIES

Map p284 (☑93 268 78 93; www.custo.com; Plaça de les Olles 7; ☺noon-8.30pm Mon-Sat; Ⓜ Barceloneta) The psychedelic decor and casual atmosphere lend this avant-garde Barcelona fashion store a youthful edge. Custo presents daring new women's and men's collections each year on the New York catwalks. The dazzling colours and cut of everything from dinner jackets to hot pants are for the uninhibited. It has three other stores around town.

 # SPORTS & ACTIVITIES

BIKE TOURS BARCELONA
CYCLING

Map p284 (☑93 268 21 05; www.biketoursbarcelona.com; Carrer de l'Esparteria 3; per person €25; ☺10am-7pm; Ⓜ Jaume I) One of numerous operators offering daily three-hour tours of the Barri Gòtic, waterfront, La Sagrada Família and other Gaudí landmarks. Tours depart from the tourist office on Plaça de Sant Jaume; check the website for departure times, and for details of vineyard tours. Bike rental is also available, from €5 per hour.

AIRE DE BARCELONA
SPA

Map p284 (☑93 295 57 43; www.airedebarcelona.com; Passeig de Picasso 22; thermal baths & aromatherapy Mon-Thu €36, Fri-Sun €39; ☺9am-11pm Sun-Thu, to midnight Fri & Sat; Ⓜ Arc de Triomf) With low lighting and relaxing perfumes wafting around you, this basement spa could be the perfect way to end a day. Hot, warm and cold baths, steam baths and options for various massages, including on a slab of hot marble, make for a delicious hour or so. Book ahead and bring a swimming costume.

Barceloneta & the Waterfront

PORT VELL | BARCELONETA | PORT OLÍMPIC | POBLENOU | EL FÒRUM

Neighbourhood Top Five

1 **Museu d'Història de Catalunya** (p111) Learning about Romans, Muslims, feudal lords and civil war freedom fighters, followed by drinks in the museum's rooftop restaurant.

2 **Museu Marítim** (p109) Stepping back in time in this fascinating Gothic shipyard and exploring Barcelona's rich maritime past.

3 **Museu Can Framis** (p112) Studying avant-garde paintings by contemporary Catalan artists in the up-and-coming, formerly industrial neighbourhood of Poblenou.

4 **Platja de la Nova Mar Bella** (p110) Basking on this sun-kissed sandy beach, before an invigorating dip in the glittering Mediterranean.

5 **Teleférico del Puerto** (p111) Gazing out over the city on a scenic 10-minute cable-car ride from the Barceloneta seaside to hilltop Montjuïc.

For more detail of this area see Map p286 and p288 ➡

Lonely Planet's Top Tip

If you'd like to explore the sea and the mountains on the same day, take advantage of the Teleférico del Puerto (p111) cable car, which whisks passengers from Barceloneta's Torre de Sant Sebastià up to Montjuïc.

Best Places to Eat

➜ La Barra de Carles Abellán (p115)

➜ Can Solé (p116)

➜ Minyam (p119)

➜ Oaxaca (p116)

➜ Can Recasens (p119)

For reviews, see p114.

Best Places to Drink

➜ Perikete (p119)

➜ BlackLab (p120)

➜ Can Paixano (p120)

➜ Bodega Vidrios y Cristales (p119)

➜ Absenta (p120)

For reviews, see p119. ➜

Best Places to Shop

➜ Els Encants Vells (p122)

➜ La Bazart (p123)

➜ Bestiari (p123)

➜ System Action (p122)

➜ Vernita (p122)

For reviews, see p122. ➜

Explore Barceloneta & the Waterfront

Barcelona's long, sun-drenched waterfront provides a pleasant escape when you need a break from Gothic lanes and Modernisme. Heading northeast from the old city, you'll soon find yourself amid tempting seafood restaurants and waterfront bars, with a palm-lined promenade taking cyclists, joggers and strollers out to the beaches running some 4km up to Parc del Fòrum in the modern El Fòrum (p114) precinct.

At the foot of La Rambla, Port Vell is where many visitors first lay eyes on Barcelona's slice of the Mediterranean. This transformed area, once an industrial wasteland, draws locals and tourists alike who come to stroll the peaceful pedestrian bridge of Rambla de Mar, which leads out to the shops and restaurants in Maremàgnum (p123) mall and the aquarium (p111) next door.

Northeast of here, upmarket, open-air restaurants overlook a marina and one of the city's best museums for learning about the Catalan experience, the Museu d'Història de Catalunya (p111). Nearby is Barceloneta, an old fishing quarter laid out in the mid-18th century with narrow gridlike lanes criss-crossed with laundry in the breeze. The few visitors venturing here stick mostly to the outdoor restaurants lining Passeig de Joan de Borbo. For something more atmospheric, delve into the narrow lanes, which are dotted with festive tapas spots, old-fashioned seafood joints and bohemian bars.

Where Barceloneta abuts the water, you'll find open-air restaurants looking out over the promenade and the beaches beyond. Inland from these modern artificial beaches is the design and high-tech zone of El Poblenou with a growing number of cafes, shops and restaurants.

Local Life

➜ **Hang-outs** There are many great local haunts full of flowing *cava,* beer and flavourful tapas: Vaso de Oro (p114) and Can Paixano (p120) are long-time favourites, while Perikete (p119) is a popular newcomer.

➜ **Markets** Port Vell hosts Port Antic (p123), a small weekend antiques market; near the marina is the craft market of Feria d'Artesanía del Palau de Mar (p123).

➜ **Beach action** From June to September informal rustic bars known as *chiringuitos* dot the sands, doling out cold drinks and festive ambience.

Getting There & Away

➜ **Foot** From the old city, La Rambla and Via Laietana are the main pedestrian access points across busy Ronda del Litoral.

➜ **Metro** Go to Drassanes (Línia 3) to reach Port Vell; Barceloneta (Línia 4) has its own stop for the neighbourhood. Línia 4 continues out to Ciutadella Vila Olímpica (the best stop for Port Olímpic), the city's northern beaches El Poblenou Platges, and El Maresme Fòrum.

TOP SIGHT
MUSEU MARÍTIM

The mighty Reials Drassanes (Royal Shipyards) are an extraordinary piece of civilian architecture. From here, Don Juan of Austria's flagship galley was launched to lead a joint Spanish-Venetian fleet into the momentous Battle of Lepanto against the Turks in 1571. Today the broad arches shelter the Museu Marítim, the city's seafaring-history museum and one of Barcelona's most intriguing museums.

DON'T MISS

➡ The replica of Don Juan of Austria's flagship
➡ Temporary exhibitions
➡ *Ictíneo I*
➡ The courtyard cafe

PRACTICALITIES

➡ Map p286, A4
➡ ☑ 93 342 99 20
➡ www.mmb.cat
➡ Avinguda de les Drassanes
➡ adult/child €10/5, free from 3pm Sun
➡ ⏱ 10am-8pm
➡ Ⓜ Drassanes

Royal Shipyards

The shipyards were, in their heyday, among the greatest in Europe. Begun in the 13th century and completed by 1378, the long, arched bays (the highest arches reach 13m) once sloped off as slipways directly into the water, which lapped the seaward side of the Drassanes until at least the end of the 18th century. Shipbuilding was later moved to southern Spain, and the Drassanes became a barracks for artillery.

Replica of Don Juan of Austria's Flagship

The centre of the shipyards is dominated by a full-scale replica (made in the 1970s) of Don Juan of Austria's flagship. A clever audiovisual display aboard the vessel brings to life the ghastly existence of the slaves, prisoners and volunteers (!) who, at full steam, could haul this vessel along at 9 knots. They remained chained to their seats, four to an oar, at all times. Here they worked, drank (fresh water was stored below decks, where the infirmary was also located), ate, slept and went to the loo. You could smell a galley like this from miles away.

Exhibitions

Fishing vessels, old navigation charts, models and dioramas of the Barcelona waterfront make up the rest of this engaging museum. Temporary exhibitions are also held (an intriguing show on the history of explorations in Antarctica was held here in 2014). Following major renovations completed in 2017, it has a greatly expanded collection with multimedia exhibits evoking more of Spain's epic history on the high seas.

Ictíneo

In the courtyard, you can have a look at a life-size replica of the *Ictíneo I,* one of the world's first submarines. It was invented and built in 1858 by Catalan polymath Narcis Monturiol, and was operated by hand-cranked propellers turned by friends of Monturiol who accompanied him on dozens of successful short dives (two hours maximum) in the harbour. He later developed an even larger submarine *(Ictíneo II)* powered by a combustion engine that allowed it to dive to 30m and remain submerged for seven hours. Despite impressive demonstrations to awestruck crowds he never attracted the interest of the navy, and remains largely forgotten today.

TOP SIGHT
EL POBLENOU PLATGES

From the Port Olímpic marina, gold-sand beaches stretch northeast. Although the beaches are largely artificial, it doesn't stop millions of swimmers and sunbathers flocking here each year.

The busiest of El Poblenou's beaches is the southernmost, **Platja de la Nova Icària**. Across the Avinguda del Litoral highway behind the beach is the Plaça dels Campions, site of the rusting three-tiered platform used to honour medallists in the sailing events of the 1992 Olympic Games.

Heading north, the next beach is **Platja de Bogatell**. Just inland, the 1773-created Cementiri del Poblenou (p113) contains bombastic family memorials. An altogether disquieting touch is the sculpture *El petó de la mort* (The Kiss of Death), in which a winged skeleton kisses a young kneeling lifeless body.

At **Platja de la Mar Bella**, there's a brief nudist strip. **Platja de la Nova Mar Bella** follows, leading into the contemporary residential and commercial waterfront strip, the Front Marítim, part of the Diagonal Mar project in the modern El Fòrum (p114) district. Fronting it is the last of these artificial beaches to be created, **Platja del Llevant**.

DON'T MISS

➡ The vibrant bustle of Platja de la Nova Icària

➡ The poignant *El petó de la mort* sculpture in Cementiri del Poblenou

PRACTICALITIES

➡ Map p288, E3

➡ http://lameva.barcelona.cat

➡ Ⓜ Ciutadella Vila Olímpica, Llacuna, Poblenou, Selva de Mar

SIGHTS

Port Vell & Barceloneta

MUSEU MARÍTIM
MUSEUM
See p109.

L'AQUÀRIUM
AQUARIUM
Map p286 (☏93 221 74 74; www.aquariumbcn. com; Moll d'Espanya; adult/child €20/15, dive €300, Sleeping with Sharks €90; ☺10am-9.30pm Jul & Aug, shorter hours Sep-Jun; Ⓜ Drassanes) It's hard not to shudder at the sight of a shark gliding above you, displaying its toothy, wide-mouthed grin. But this, the 80m shark tunnel, is the highlight of one of Europe's largest aquariums. It has the world's best Mediterranean collection and plenty of colourful fish from as far off as the Red Sea, the Caribbean and the Great Barrier Reef. All up, some 11,000 creatures (including a dozen sharks) of 450 species reside here. Tickets are €2 cheaper online.

Back in the shark tunnel, which you reach after passing a series of themed fish tanks with everything from bream to sea horses, various species of shark (white tip, sand tiger, bonnethead, black tip, nurse and sandbar) flit around you, along with a host of other critters, from flapping rays to bloated sunfish. An interactive zone, Planeta Aqua, is host to a family of Antarctic penguins and a tank of rays that you watch close up. Explora is a dedicated children's area with activities spread over three themed environments.

Those with a valid dive certificate may dive in the main tank with the sharks.

Children aged eight to 12 can stay overnight on a Sleeping with Sharks program (including supper and breakfast). Check dates online and reserve by phone at least one week in advance. Kids should bring a sleeping bag and torch.

MUSEU D'HISTÒRIA DE CATALUNYA
MUSEUM
Map p286 (Museum of the History of Catalonia; ☏93 225 47 00; www.mhcat.cat; Plaça de Pau Vila 3; adult/child €4.50/3.50, last Tue of the month Oct-Jun free; ☺10am-7pm Tue & Thu-Sat, to 8pm Wed, to 2.30pm Sun; Ⓜ Barceloneta) Inside the **Palau de Mar**, this worthwhile museum takes you from the Stone Age through to the early 1980s. It's a busy hotchpotch of dioramas, artefacts, videos, models, documents and interactive bits: all up, an entertaining exploration of 2000 years of Catalan history. Signage is in Catalan and Spanish.

You'll see how the Romans lived, listen to Arab poetry from the time of the Muslim occupation of the city, peer into the dwelling of a medieval family in the Pyrenees, and try to mount a knight's horse or lift a suit of armour.

Afterwards, descend into a civil-war air-raid shelter, watch a video in Catalan on post-Franco Catalonia, or head upstairs to the first-rate rooftop restaurant and cafe, 1881 (p116). The temporary exhibitions are often as interesting as the permanent display. Its shop, Bestiari (p123), stocks nifty Catalan gifts.

Outside the museum, you'll find a string of elegant open-air restaurants with harbourfront views serving classic seafood dishes.

TELEFÉRICO DEL PUERTO
CABLE CAR
Map p286 (www.telefericodebarcelona.com; Passeig de Joan de Borbó; one way/return €11/16.50; ☺10.30am-8pm Jun-early Sep, shorter hours early Sep-May; ☐V15, 39, Ⓜ Barceloneta) First built for the 1929 Expo, this cable car strung across the harbour to Montjuïc provides an eagle-eye view of the city. The cabins float between the Torre de Sant Sebastià (Barceloneta) – topped by a panoramic restaurant, **Torre d'Alta Mar** (Map p286; ☏93 221 00 07;

BEACH LIBRARIES

In July and August (typically 10am to 5pm Tuesday to Sunday), the city sets up *biblioplatges* ('beach libraries') underneath the boardwalk at the northern end of **Platja de la Barceloneta** (Map p286; http://lameva.barcelona. cat; Ⓜ Barceloneta) – technically called Platja de Somorrostro – and at Platja de la Mar Bella (p110) at the Espigó de Bac de Roda. You'll find magazines, newspapers and a small foreign-language selection among the Spanish titles.

At the same locations, you can also hire out frisbees, volleyballs and nets, beach rackets, balls and *petanque* games; for the kiddies, you'll find buckets, spades and watering cans. They're free to use; all you need to hire out books or gear is your ID.

LOCAL KNOWLEDGE

MEET YOU AT THE CUBES

German artist Rebecca Horn's elegant **Homenatge a la Barceloneta** (*Homage to Barceloneta;* Map p286; Passeig Marítim; Ⓜ Barceloneta) sculpture was commissioned for the 1992 Olympics and commemorates the old-fashioned shacks that once lined the beach.

Popularly known as 'The Cubes', it's a time-honoured seaside meeting place.

www.torredealtamar.com; Torre de Sant Sebastià, Passeig de Joan de Borbó 88; mains €34.50-44, seven-/nine-course menus €80/96, €112/135 with wine; ⊙1-3.30pm Tue-Thu, 1-3.30pm & 7.30-11pm Fri & Sat) – and Miramar (Montjuïc). The total 1292m journey takes around 10 minutes. Be aware the cable car doesn't run in windy conditions.

EDGE BREWING   BREWERY

Map p288 (www.edgebrewing.com; Carrer de Llull 62; tours incl beer tastings €20; ⊙tours by appointment; Ⓜ Bogatell) Founded by two Americans in 2013, Edge Brewing has racked up some impressive awards for its craft beers (among other accolades, RateBeer.com named it the top new brewer in the world the year after it opened). Two-hour English-language brewery tours take you behind the scenes and offer the chance to taste classic brews and seasonal varieties, like the Hoptimista, an award-winning 6.6% IPA, and the passionfruit sour ale Apassionada.

BARCELONA HEAD   SCULPTURE

Map p286 (Passeig de Colom; Ⓜ Barceloneta) An icon by the waterfront, this eye-catching 15m-high primary-coloured sculpture was designed by famous American pop artist Roy Lichtenstein for the 1992 Olympics.

MIRADOR DE COLOM   VIEWPOINT

Map p286 (Columbus Monument; ☑93 285 38 32; www.barcelonaturisme.com; Plaça del Portal de la Pau; adult/child €6/4; ⊙8.30am-8.30pm; Ⓜ Drassanes) High above the swirl of traffic on the roundabout below, Columbus keeps permanent watch, pointing vaguely out to the Mediterranean from this Corinthian-style iron column built for the 1888 Universal Exhibition. Zip up 60m in a lift for bird's-eye views back up La Rambla and across Barcelona's ports.

It was in Barcelona that Columbus allegedly gave the delighted Catholic monarchs a report of his first explorations in the Americas after his voyage in 1492. In the 19th century, it was popularly believed here that Columbus was one of Barcelona's most illustrious sons. Some historians still make that claim.

HOMENATGE A LA NATACIÓ   SCULPTURE

Map p286 (Homage to the Swimmers; Plaça del Mar; Ⓜ Barceloneta) Designed by Alfredo Lanz in 2004, this steel sculpture depicts various graceful if abstract poses of swimmers taking to the sea.

◉ Port Olímpic, Poblenou & El Fòrum

EL POBLENOU PLATGES   BEACH
See p110.

MUSEU CAN FRAMIS   MUSEUM

Map p288 (☑93 320 87 36; www.fundaciovila casas.com; Carrer de Roc Boronat 116-126; adult/child €5/2; ⊙11am-6pm Tue-Sat, to 2pm Sun; Ⓜ Glòries, Llacuna) Set in an 18th-century former textile factory, this contemporary museum is a showcase for Catalan painting from the 1960s onwards. The galleries display some 300 works, arranged in thought-provoking ways – with evocative paintings by different artists (sometimes working in different time periods) creating fascinating intersections and collisions.

Highlights include the intricate, tapestry-style paintings of Victor Pérez-Porro, desolate black-and-white scenes of Gregori Iglesias, dreamlike sequences of Perejaume, photographic portraits by Pedro Madueño, Agustí Puig's ethereal *Menines* (whose point of departure is Velázquez' iconic *Las meninas* created three centuries earlier) and the luminous works by self-taught painter Xevi Vilaro.

MUSEU DEL DISSENY DE BARCELONA   MUSEUM

Map p288 (☑93 256 68 00; www.museudel disseny.cat; Plaça de les Glòries Catalanes 37; permanent/temporary exhibition adult €6/4.50, child €4/3, combination ticket adult/child €8/5.50, free from 3pm Sun & 1st Sun of the month; ⊙10am-8pm Tue-Sun; Ⓜ Glòries) Barcelona's design museum lies inside a monolithic contemporary building with geometric facades and a rather brutalist appearance that's nicknamed *la grapadora* (the stapler) by locals. Inside, it houses a dazzling collection of ceramics, decorative arts and textiles, and is a must for anyone interested in the design world.

Start at the top and work your way down. On the 4th floor, you'll enter the terrain of the graphic arts, specifically posters from Catalan design firms dating from the post-WWII years to the present. On the floor below, the museum provides a highly condensed overview of fashion from the 1500s onward. Among other things, you'll find a dramatically lit room with 19th-century crinolines (cage-like frames worn as an undergarment to hold up flouncy dresses), displayed like rare sea creatures inside giant glass tubes.

The 2nd floor is devoted to the decorative arts, with a wildly varied collection that includes 3rd-century Coptic works, an elaborate 16th-century Brussels tapestry, antique jewel-crusted pocket watches, and sculptural works by Picasso and Miró. Don't miss the glittering stained-glass panel created for the 1888 Expo. The 1st floor houses Catalan product design from the 20th century – worth a quick peek for the furniture.

Temporary exhibitions run the gamut from 17th-century Turkish ceramics to contemporary fashion photography.

CEMENTIRI DEL POBLENOU   CEMETERY

Map p288 (Poblenou Cemetery; ☑93 225 16 61; www.cbsa.cat; Av d'Icària; ⊘8am-6pm; ⓂLlacuna) FREE Located just inland from Platja de Bogatell near Carrer del Taulat, this cemetery dates from 1773. The cemetery was positioned outside the then city limits for health reasons; its central monument commemorates the victims of a yellow-fever epidemic that swept across Barcelona in 1821. It is full of bombastic family memorials, but an altogether disquieting touch is the sculpture *El petó de la mort* (The Kiss of Death), in which a winged skeleton kisses a young kneeling lifeless body.

PARC DEL CENTRE DEL POBLENOU   PARK

Map p288 (Avinguda Diagonal; ⊘10am-sunset; ⓂPoblenou) Barcelona is sprinkled with parks whose principal element is concrete, and Jean Nouvel's 5-hectare Parc del Centre del Poblenou, with its statuary and stylised metal seats, is no exception. However, the park's Gaudí-inspired walls are increasingly covered by rambling bougainvillea

and, inside, some 1000 mostly Mediterranean trees, including 35 palm species, are complemented by thousands of aromatic bushes and plants. Nouvel's idea is that the trees, sustained by local ground water, will eventually form a natural canopy over the park.

MUSEU DE LA MÚSICA   MUSEUM

Map p288 (☑93 256 36 50; www.museumusica. bcn.cat; Carrer de Lepant 150; adult/child €6/4.50, free from 3pm Sun; ⊘10am-6pm Tue, Wed & Fri, to 9pm Thu, to 7pm Sat & Sun; ⓂMonumental) Some 500 instruments (less than a third of those held) are on show in this museum, housed on the 2nd floor of the administration building in L'Auditori (p122), the city's main classical-music concert hall.

Instruments range from a 17th-century baroque guitar through to lutes (look out for the many-stringed 1641 archilute from Venice), violins, Japanese kotos, sitars from India, eight organs (some dating from the 18th century), pianos and a varied collection of drums and other percussion instruments from across Spain and beyond, along with all sorts of phonographs and gramophones. There are some odd pieces indeed, like the *buccèn*, a snake-head-adorned brass instrument. Much of the documentary and sound material can be enjoyed through audiovisual displays as you proceed.

The museum periodically hosts daytime concerts, in which musicians perform on rare instruments held in the collection.

EL FÒRUM   AREA

Map p288 (ⓂEl Maresme Fòrum) Once an urban wasteland, this area has seen dramatic changes since the turn of the millennium, with sparkling buildings, open plazas and

> ### REMEMBERING THE VICTIMS OF FRANCO
>
> Buried beneath the concrete expanses, bathing zone and marina created in El Fòrum lies the memory of more than 2000 people executed in the fields of Camp de la Bota between 1936 and 1952, most of them under Franco from 1939 onward. A commemorative, *Fraternitat* (Brotherhood), by Miquel Navarro, stands on Rambla de Prim.

waterfront recreation areas. The most striking element is the eerily blue, triangular *2001: A Space Odyssey*–style **Edifici Fòrum** building by Swiss architects Herzog & de Meuron, which houses the Museu Blau (p113).

MUSEU BLAU
MUSEUM

Map p288 (Blue Museum; ☑93 256 60 02; www.museuciencies.cat; Edifici Fòrum, Parc del Fòrum; adult/child €6/free, free from 3pm Sun & 1st Sun of month; ☺10am-7pm Tue-Sat, to 8pm Sun Mar-Sep, to 6pm Tue-Fri, to 7pm Sat, to 8pm Sun Oct-Feb; Ⓜ El Maresme Fòrum) Set inside the futuristic Edifici Fòrum (p113), the Museu Blau takes visitors on a journey across the natural world. Multimedia and interactive exhibits explore topics like the history of evolution, the earth's formation and the great scientists who have helped shaped human knowledge. There are also specimens from the animal, plant and mineral kingdoms – plus dinosaur skeletons – all rather dramatically set amid the sprawling 9000 sq metres of exhibition space.

TORRE GLÒRIES
ARCHITECTURE

Map p288 (Avinguda Diagonal 225; Ⓜ Glòries) Barcelona's cucumber-shaped tower, Jean Nouvel's luminous Torre Glòries (formerly Torre Agbar) is among the most daring additions to the skyline since the first towers of La Sagrada Família went up. Completed in 2005, the 38-storey structure shimmers at night in shades of midnight blue and lipstick red. The interior is home to offices and is closed to the public.

EATING

✗ Port Vell & Barceloneta

VASO DE ORO
TAPAS €

Map p286 (☑93 319 30 98; www.vasodeoro.com; Carrer de Balboa 6; tapas €4-12; ☺11am-midnight; Ⓜ Barceloneta) Always packed, this narrow bar gathers a high-spirited crowd who come for fantastic tapas. Wisecracking, white-jacketed waiters serve plates of grilled *gambes* (prawns), *foie a la plancha* (grilled liver pâté) or *solomillo* (sirloin) chunks. Want something a little different to drink? Ask for a *flauta cincuenta* – half lager and half dark beer.

LA COVA FUMADA
TAPAS €

Map p286 (☑93 221 40 61; Carrer del Baluard 56; tapas €4-12; ☺9am-3.15pm Mon-Wed, 9am-3.15pm & 6-8.15pm Thu & Fri, 9am-1pm Sat; Ⓜ Barceloneta) There's no sign and the setting is decidedly downmarket, but this tiny, buzzing family-run tapas spot always packs in a crowd. The secret? Mouthwatering *pulpo* (octopus), calamari, sardines, *bombas* (meat and potato croquettes served with aioli) and grilled *carxofes* (artichokes) cooked in the open kitchen. Everything is amazingly fresh.

CAN MAÑO
SEAFOOD €

Map p286 (Carrer del Baluard 12; mains €7-15; ☺8-11pm Mon, 8.30am-4pm & 8-11pm Tue-Fri, 8.30am-4pm Sat; Ⓜ Barceloneta) It may look like a dive, but you'll need to be prepared to wait before being squeezed in at a packed table for a raucous night of *raciones* (full-plate-size tapas serving) over a bottle of cloudy white *turbio* (Galician wine) at this family-run stalwart. The seafood is abundant, with first-rate squid, prawns and fish served at rock-bottom prices.

LA BODEGA LA PENINSULAR
TAPAS €

Map p286 (☑93 221 40 89; www.tabernaycafetin.es; Carrer del Mar 29; tapas €3.50-9; ☺11.30am-midnight; Ⓜ Barceloneta) ✿ Wine barrels double as tables at this traditional bodega, where over three dozen different tapas dishes pair with Catalan vintages and house-made vermouth. Adhering to the Slow Food ethos, ingredients are organic, seasonal and locally sourced; try the *mojama* (salt-cured, air-dried tuna) or renowned spicy *bombas* (meat and potato croquettes) topped with tangy aioli. It's standing room only most nights.

NAP MAR
PIZZA €

Map p286 (☑93 007 36 39; www.facebook.com/nap; Carrer del Baluard 69; pizzas €5-10; ☺1.30-4.30pm & 8pm-midnight Mon-Fri, 1.30pm-midnight Sat & Sun; ☏✑; Ⓜ Barceloneta) NAP (Neapolitan Authentic Pizza) has an elegant dining room but its location footsteps from Platja de Sant Miquel makes it perfect for picking up a pizza to take to the beach. Fired in an Italian Stefano Ferrara wood-burning oven, pizzas come with toppings such as speck, truffle cream and ruccola, with plenty of veggie varieties available.

FILFERRO
TAPAS €

Map p286 ([📋]93 221 98 36; Carrer de Sant Carles 29; tapas €5-8, mains €7-12; ☉10am-1am; 🛜🍴; MⒷarceloneta) One of the few spots in Barceloneta where the focus isn't on seafood, Filferro has a loyal following for its good-value tapas, *bocadillos* (filled rolls), salads and pasta. It has a warmly lit and eclectically furnished interior, or you can dine at an outdoor table on the square (popular with families, with a playground just a few steps away).

BALUARD BARCELONETA
BAKERY €

Map p286 (Carrer del Baluard 38; items €1-3.50; ☉8am-9pm Mon-Sat; MⒷarceloneta) Baluard has one of the best ranges of freshly baked breads in the city, along with filled baguettes that are perfect for beach picnics. It also bakes a range of tempting pastries, such as *xuixixo* (deep-fried custard-filled pastries from Girona) and *bunyols* (doughnut-shaped pastries stuffed with cheese or jam), and tarts such as fig or wild berries.

MAIANS
TAPAS €

Map p286 ([📋]93 221 10 20; Carrer de Sant Carles 28; tapas €4-8, mains €8-22; ☉1-4pm & 8-11pm Tue-Sat; MⒷarceloneta) This tiny jovial bar serves excellent tapas to a hip, largely neighbourhood crowd. Highlights include the not-to-be-missed *cazón en adobo* (marinated fried dogfish) and *mejillones a la marinera* (mussels in a rich tomato broth) followed by hearty *arroz negra* (paella with cuttlefish and squid ink).

BITÁCORA
TAPAS €

Map p286 ([📋]93 319 11 10; Carrer de Balboa 1; tapas €4-12.50; ☉9am-2.30am Mon-Fri, from 10am Sat & Sun; MⒷarceloneta) Bitácora is a neighbourhood favourite for its simple but congenial ambience and well-priced tapas plates, which come in ample portions. There's also a small hidden terrace at the back. Top picks: *ceviche de pescado* (fish ceviche), *chipirones* (baby squid) and *gambas a la plancha* (grilled prawns). Cash only, no cards.

KAIKU
SEAFOOD €€

Map p286 ([📋]93 221 90 82; www.restaurantkaiku.cat; Plaça del Mar 1; mains €13-19; ☉1-3.30pm & 7-10.30pm Tue-Sat, 1-3.30pm Sun; MⒷarceloneta) Overlooking the waterfront at the south end of Barceloneta, Kaiku incorporates ingredients from the nearby fish market in

dishes such as crayfish with mint, swordfish carpaccio with avocado and sun-dried tomatoes, chilli-smeared tuna with green apples and mushrooms, and rice dishes for two.

GREEN SPOT
VEGETARIAN €€

Map p286 ([📋]93 802 55 65; www.encompania delobos.com/en/the-green-spot; Carrer de la Reina Cristina 12; mains €10-15; ☉12.30pm-midnight Mon-Fri, from 1pm Sat & Sun; 🍴; MⒷarceloneta) Purple carrot salad with papaya and feta, aubergine and courgette tacos, buckwheat and spinach *spätzle* (hand-rolled egg noodles), sweet potato gnocchi with black truffle, and hemp pizza with cashew cheese and asparagus are among the inventive vegetarian, vegan and gluten-free dishes presented in a stylish, minimalist dining room with vaulted ceilings. Live flamenco plays on Tuesday evenings.

BARRACA
SEAFOOD €€

Map p286 ([📋]93 224 12 53; www.tribuwoki.com; Passeig Marítim de la Barceloneta 1; mains €16-22; ☉12.30-11pm; 🍴; MⒷarceloneta) 🍃 Opening to an elevated terrace, this buzzing space has mesmerising views over the Mediterranean – a key reference point in the all-organic dishes served here. Start off with a cauldron of chilli-infused clams, cockles and mussels before moving on to the lavish rice dishes. Vegetarian options are plentiful and it's one of the few places in Barcelona serving a vegan paella.

L'ÒSTIA
TAPAS €€

Map p286 ([📋]93 221 47 58; www.facebook.com/barcelonadeta; Plaça de la Barceloneta 1; tapas €2.50-8, mains €11-19; ☉10am-11.45pm; 🛜; MⒷarceloneta) On a charming hidden square, this neighbourhood bar opens to a terrace facing Barceloneta's beautiful baroque church Església de Sant Miquel del Port. Tapas reflect the area's heritage but also come with fusion twists like Szechuan pepper-dusted sardines or Spanish omelette with duck and truffles. Wines are primarily Catalan; the sangría is some of the best around.

★LA BARRA DE CARLES ABELLÁN
SEAFOOD €€€

Map p286 ([📋]93 760 51 29; www.carlesabellan.com/mis-restaurantes/la-barra; Passeig Joan de Borbó 19; tapas €5-8.50, mains €24-36; ☉1.30-4pm & 8-11pm; MⒷarceloneta) Catalan chef

Carles Abellán's stunning glass-encased, glossy-tiled restaurant celebrates seafood in tapas such as pickled octopus, mini anchovy omelettes and fried oyster with salmon roe. Even more show-stopping are the mains: grilled razor clams with *ponzu* citrus sauce, squid filled with spicy poached egg yolk, stir-fried sea cucumber, and lush lobster paella with smoked prawns.

★OAXACA   MEXICAN €€€
Map p286 (⍇93 018 06 59; www.oaxacacuina mexicana.com; Pla de Palau 19; mains €22-32; ◔1-4pm & 8pm-midnight; ⯑; ⓜBarceloneta) Chef Joan Bagur trained in Mexico for a decade under traditional cooks, and has his own garden of Mexican plants, which supplies ingredients for culinary creations like *coyoacán* (roast corn with chilli ash) and *cochinita pibil* (slow-roasted pork tacos). Hefty tables are made from Mexican hardwoods and original Mexican art lines the walls; there's alfresco seating under the cloisters.

★CAN SOLÉ   SEAFOOD €€€
Map p286 (⍇93 221 50 12; http://restaurant cansole.com; Carrer de Sant Carles 4; mains €17-39; ◔1-4pm & 8-11pm Tue-Thu, 1-4pm & 8.30-11pm Fri & Sat, 1-4pm Sun; ⓜBarceloneta) Behind imposing wooden doors, this elegant restaurant with white-clothed tables and white-jacketed waiters has been serving seafood since 1903, and is now run by the fourth generation of owners. Freshly landed seafood stars in traditional dishes such as *arròs caldòs* (rice broth with squid and langoustines) and *zarzuela* (casserole with ground almonds, saffron, garlic, tomatoes, mussels, fish and white wine).

RESTAURANT 7 PORTES   SEAFOOD €€€
Map p286 (⍇93 319 30 33; www.7portes.com; Passeig d'Isabel II 14; mains €19-32; ◔1pm-1am; ⯑; ⓜBarceloneta) Founded in 1836 as a cafe and converted into a restaurant in 1929, 7 Portes has a grand setting beneath the cloisters, and exudes an old-world atmosphere with its wood panelling, tiles, mirrors and plaques naming luminaries – such as Orson Welles – who have passed through. Paella is the speciality, or try the *gran plat de marisc* ('big plate of seafood').

CAN MAJÓ   SEAFOOD €€€
Map p286 (⍇93 221 54 55; www.canmajo. es; Carrer del Almirall Aixada 23; mains €15-36; ◔1-4pm & 8-11.30pm Tue-Sat, 1-4pm Sun; ⓜBarceloneta) On a square across from the beachside promenade, with outdoor tables and heat lamps in winter, Can Majó has a long and steady reputation for fine seafood, particularly its rice dishes and bountiful *suquets* (fish stews). The bouillabaisse of fish and seafood is succulent.

SUQUET DE L'ALMIRALL   SEAFOOD €€€
Map p286 (⍇93 221 62 33; www.suquetde lalmirall.com; Passeig de Joan de Borbó 65; mains €16-28; ◔1-11pm Tue-Sat; ⓜBarceloneta) A family business, Suquet De L'Almirall does a short but stellar updated take on top-class seafood. The house speciality is its 'paella Catalan', with 12 different types of seafood; other dishes include wild Avilés turbot, salt-baked sea bass, and baby squid stuffed with anchovies and black rice. Arrive early to nab one of the few outdoor tables.

LA GAVINA   SEAFOOD €€€
Map p286 (⍇93 221 05 95; www.grupgavina.es; Plaça Pau Vila 1; mains €18-44; ◔noon-11.30pm; ⓜBarceloneta) The pick of the promenade-facing restaurants in the 19th-century edifice Palau de Mar (p111) is this swish white-tableclothed seafood specialist, whose interior is dominated by neon-lit glass-fronted wine cabinets containing over 300 Spanish and Catalan varieties. Swordfish marinated in garlic and white wine, squid-ink shell-off paella, and spectacular seafood platters on beds of shaved ice are highlights.

1881   BASQUE €€€
Map p286 (⍇93 221 00 50; www.gruposagardi. com/restaurante/1881-per-sagardi; Plaça de Pau Vila 3; mains €19-29; ◔kitchen 10am-midnight Sun-Thu, to 1am Fri & Sat, bar to 1am Sun-Thu, to 3am Fri & Sat; ⯑; ⓜBarceloneta) On the top floor of the Museu d'Història de Catalunya (p111), 1881 has dazzling views over the waterfront. *Txuletón* (aged Basque beef) is a speciality, complemented by Basque wines. It's a great stop for cocktails (particularly around sunset); the terrace transitions into a festive party space later on weekend nights.

CAN ROS   SEAFOOD €€€
Map p286 (⍇93 221 45 79; www.canros.cat; Carrer del Almirall Aixada 7; mains €15-29; ◔1-4pm & 7-11pm Tue-Sun; ⓜBarceloneta) The fifth generation is now at the controls of this immutable seafood favourite, which

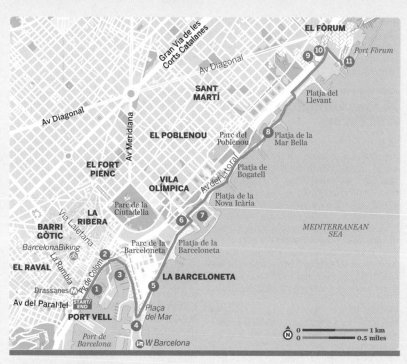

Cycling Tour
Barcelona's Waterfront

START PORT VELL
END PORT VELL
LENGTH 12KM RETURN, 1½ HOURS

This bike tour takes in boardwalks, beaches, sculpture and architecture along Barcelona's ever-changing waterfront. It's a flat and safe ride along a dedicated bike path separate from traffic – though watch out for pedestrians. There are several convenient places to hire bikes nearby, including Barcelona Biking (www.barcelonabiking.com) in the Barri Gòtic.

With Columbus at your back, make your way northeast along the waterfront. Keep an eye out for the three-mast schooner, **1 Pailebot de Santa Eulàlia**, built in 1918. You can see it perfectly well without going aboard; there's not an awful lot to behold below deck. Another 400m up the road, you'll pass the colourful **2 Barcelona Head** (p112) sculpture. Soaring 15m high, it was created by American pop artist Roy Lichtenstein for the 1992 Olympics.

As you make your way along the **3 marina**, you may have to dismount

amid the throng of strollers and open-air restaurants. Hop back on and pedal to the Plaça del Mar, which sports an elegant sculpture entitled **4 Homenatge a la Natació** (p112). The abstract work was designed by Alfredo Lanz in 2004.

Follow the crowds north, past another well-known sculpture, the **5 Homenatge a la Barceloneta** (p112), installed by German artist Rebecca Horn. Cycle another kilometre and you'll pass beneath the copper-hued **6 Peix sculpture**, designed by Frank Gehry. Next up is **7 Port Olímpic**, which is lined with restaurants and bars. From here you'll pass more **8 beaches** (p110), which fill with sunseekers in summer.

At the end, you'll find the **9 El Fòrum** (p114) precinct. Dominating its empty Parc del Fòrum plaza is the rather harsh-looking sculpture **10 Fraternitat** (p113), dedicated to the hundreds executed here during the Franco years.

The protected bathing area **11 Zona de Banys** is a popular summer attraction for families. Just behind it looms the giant solar panel that powers the area. From here, you can retrace your journey back to Port Vell.

first opened in 1908. In a restaurant where the decor is a reminder of simpler times, there's a straightforward guiding principle: juicy fresh fish cooked with a light touch.

✕ Port Olímpic, Poblenou & El Fòrum

EL 58 TAPAS €

Map p288 (Le cinquante huit; Rambla del Poblenou 58; tapas €3.50-12; ⊙1.30-11pm Tue-Sat, to 4pm Sun; ⓂLlacuna) This French-Catalan place serves imaginative, beautifully prepared tapas dishes: codfish balls with romesco sauce, scallop ceviche, *tartiflette* (cheese, ham and potato casserole), salmon tartare. Solo diners can take a seat at the marble-topped front bar. The back dining room with its exposed brick walls, industrial light fixtures and local artworks is a lively place to linger over a long meal.

EL TÍO CHÉ CAFE €

Map p288 (www.eltioche.es; Rambla del Poblenou 44; dishes €2-6; ⊙10am-10pm Sun-Thu, to 1am Fri & Sat; ⓂPoblenou) First opened back in 1912 (in El Born), this local icon is famed for its *horchata,* a sweet and refreshing if mildly grainy drink made of tigernut milk. Some love it, others less so, though you can also opt for other home-made beverages along with sandwiches and ice cream.

TIMESBURG POBLENOU BURGERS €

Map p288 (www.timesburg.com; Carrer de Pujades 168; burgers €6-13; ⊙1-4.30pm & 8.30pm-midnight; 🛜; ⓂPoblenou) Barcelona success story Timesburg has several locations including this cavernous mezzanine space in El Poblenou. Burger buns are stamped with its logo; its 16 different varieties include La Massimo (beef, parmesan, sun-dried tomato, sunflower seeds and red onion) and Balear (Mallorca sausage, Mahón cheese, capers and honey mayo). Hand-cut fries are twice-fried in olive oil.

MÉS DE VI TAPAS €

Map p288 (☑93 007 91 51; www.mesdvi.cat; Carrer de Marià Aguiló 123; tapas €8-13; ⊙7-11pm Mon, 1-4pm & 7-11pm Tue-Sat; ⓂPoblenou) At this buzzing wine bar, Catalan wines are accompanied by tapas dishes that are inventive and delicious: courgette pesto and burrata salad, red tuna pickled with Peruvi-

an yellow chilli, smoked mackerel with aubergine caviar and lamb neck with mashed baked turnip. Brick walls, hardwood floors, timber tables and studded Chesterfield sofas give it a cosy ambience.

CAL CUC ASIAN €

Map p288 (☑93 000 28 37; www.mosquitotapas.com/calcuc; Carrer del Taulat 109; tapas €4-8; ⊙6pm-midnight Mon-Thu, 1pm-1am Fri-Sun; 🖋; ⓂPoblenou) At this sleek spot, Asian street-food-inspired tapas such as Chinese-inspired bang bang aubergine (in spicy sauce), *gyoza* (Japanese pan-fried dumplings), kimchi (Korean fermented cabbage), tofu *larb* (Laotian marinated tofu) and *takoyaki* (Japanese battered octopus) pair with craft beers from local brewers including BeerCat, Guineu and Les Clandestines.

L'ATELIER BY AMIS CAFE €

Map p288 (☑662 370229; www.atelierpoblenou.com; Carrer del Joncar 29; dishes €2-9; ⊙9.30am-1.30pm & 4-8.30pm Mon-Sat, 10am-2pm Sun; ⓂPoblenou) Behind a blond-wood facade, this sweet little cafe has bare boards, fresh flowers and a great array of home-baked cakes, cupcakes, pancakes, sweet and savoury scones, and gourmet bagels such as smoked salmon with beetroot slaw and lemon aioli.

CAN DENDÊ AMERICAN €

Map p288 (☑646 325551; www.candende.com; Carrer de la Ciutat de Granada 44; dishes €5-13; ⊙9am-4pm Mon-Thu, to 4.30pm Fri, 10am-4.30pm Sat & Sun; ⓂLlacuna) An eclectic crowd gathers at this bohemian Brazilian-run spot in El Poblenou. All-day brunch is the culinary star here: you can tuck into eggs Benedict with smoked salmon, fluffy pancakes or pulled pork sandwiches, accompanied by a bloody Mary or home-made pink lemonade by the jug while watching the cooks in action and listening to Latin tropicalia and American grooves.

AGUARIBAY VEGETARIAN €

Map p288 (☑93 300 37 90; www.aguaribay -bcn.com; Carrer del Taulat 95; mains €7-13; ⊙1-4pm Mon-Wed, 1-4pm & 8.30-11pm Thu-Sat, 1-4.30pm Sun; 🖋; ⓂLlacuna) ⊘ Polished Aguaribay serves a small well-executed à la carte menu by night: miso and smoked tofu meatballs, soba noodles with shiitake mushrooms, and seasonal vegetables with rich black rice, along with craft beers and biodynamic wines. At lunchtime, stop in for the prix-fixe lunch specials, which change daily. All ingredients are organic; vegan and gluten-free options abound.

★ **MINYAM** — SEAFOOD €€

Map p288 (93 348 36 18; www.facebook.com/minyamcisco; Carrer de Pujades 187; tapas €2-10, mains €15-25; 12.30pm-midnight Tue-Thu, to 2am Fri & Sat, to 5pm Sun; Poblenou) Billowing with smoke beneath a tajine-like metal lid, smouldering herbs infuse the rice of Minyam's signature Vulcanus (smoked seafood paella with squid ink). Tapas dishes at this stylish, contemporary El Poblenou restaurant are equally inventive and include asparagus fritters, oysters with sea urchin and lemon, fried anchovies, and prawn tortillas. Crayons and paper are provided for kids.

★ **CAN RECASENS** — CATALAN €€

Map p288 (93 300 81 23; www.facebook.com/canrecasens; Rambla del Poblenou 102; mains €8-21; 8.30am-1.30pm & 5-11.45pm Mon, to 1am Tue-Thu, to 3am Fri, 9am-1pm & 9pm-3am Sat, 9pm-1am Sun; Poblenou) One of El Poblenou's most romantic settings, Can Recasens hides a warren of warmly lit rooms full of oil paintings, flickering candles, fairy lights and baskets of fruit. The food is outstanding, with a mix of salads, smoked meats, fondues, and open sandwiches topped with delicacies like wild mushrooms and Brie, *escalivada* (grilled vegetables) and Gruyère, and spicy chorizo.

EL CALIU DEL POBLENOU — CATALAN €€

Map p288 (630 222488; http://caliupoblenou.eltenedor.rest; Rambla del Poblenou 78; mains €11-22; noon-11.45pm Tue-Sun; Poblenou) Right on the Rambla del Poblenou, this narrow-fronted restaurant opens to a rustic, elongated interior with exposed stone walls and dark timber tables. Paella comes in seafood, meat and vegetable varieties, but most locals head here for chargrilled meats (lamb, beef, Iberian pork and Catalan sausage) and poultry (including duck).

ELS PESCADORS — SEAFOOD €€€

Map p288 (93 225 20 18; www.elspescadors.com; Plaça de Prim 1; mains €18-42; 1-3.45pm & 8-11.30pm; Poblenou) On a picturesque square lined with low houses and long-established South American *bella ombre* trees, this quaint family restaurant contin-

ues to serve some of the city's best grilled fish and seafood-and-rice dishes. There are three dining areas inside: two are quite modern, while the main room preserves its old tavern flavour. On warm nights, try for a table outside.

XIRINGUITO ESCRIBÀ — SEAFOOD €€€

Map p288 (93 221 07 29; www.xiringuitoescriba.com; Avinguda del Litoral 62; mains €15-27; 1-5pm & 7-10.30pm Mon-Fri, 1-10.30pm Sat & Sun; Llacuna) The clan behind 1906-established Escribà's sweets and pastries also operates one of Barcelona's most popular waterfront seafood restaurants. This is one of the few places where one person can order paella or Catalan *fideuà* with vermicelli noodles (most restaurants require a minimum of two diners for these). Finish off with Escribà pastries for dessert.

DRINKING & NIGHTLIFE

Port Vell & Barceloneta

★ **PERIKETE** — WINE BAR

Map p286 (www.gruporeini.net/perikete; Carrer de Llauder 6; 11am-1am; Barceloneta) Since opening in 2017, this fabulous wine bar has been jam-packed with locals. Hams hang from the ceilings, barrels of vermouth sit above the bar and wine bottles cram every available shelf space – over 200 varieties are available by the glass or bottle, accompanied by 50-plus tapas dishes. In the evening, the action spills into the street.

BODEGA VIDRIOS Y CRISTALES — WINE BAR

Map p286 (www.gruposagardi.com/restaurante/bodega-vidrios-y-cristales; Passeig d'Isabel II 6; noon-midnight Sun-Thu, to 1am Fri & Sat; Barceloneta) In a history-steeped, stone-floored building dating from 1840, this atmospheric little jewel recreates a neighbourhood bodega with tins of sardines, anchovies and other delicacies lining the shelves (used in exquisite tapas dishes), house-made vermouth, and a wonderful array of wines. Be prepared to stand as there are no seats (a handful of upturned wine barrels let you rest your glass).

BARCELONETA & THE WATERFRONT DRINKING & NIGHTLIFE

BLACKLAB
MICROBREWERY

Map p286 (☑93 221 83 60; www.blacklab.es; Plaça de Pau Vila 1; ⊗noon-1.30am; MBarceloneta) Barcelona's first brewhouse opened back in 2014 inside the historic Palau de Mar (p111). Its taps feature 18 house-made brews, including saisons, double IPAs and dry stouts, and the brewmasters constantly experiment with new flavours, such as a sour Berliner Weisse with fiery jalapeño. One-hour tours (5pm Sundays; €12) offer a behind-the-scenes look at the brewers in action plus four samples.

The kitchen sizzles up burgers, barbecued pulled pork sandwiches and marinated ribs; other dishes include poké bowls.

ABSENTA
BAR

Map p286 (☑93 221 36 38; www.absenta.bar; Carrer de Sant Carles 36; ⊗6pm-2am Mon-Thu, 11am-3am Fri & Sat, 6pm-1am Sun; MBarceloneta) Decorated with old paintings, vintage lamps and curious sculptures (including a dangling butterfly woman), this whimsical drinking den specialises in absinthe, with over 20 varieties available. (Go easy, though: an alcohol content of 50% to 90% provides a kick!) It also has a house-made vermouth, if you're not a fan of the green fairy.

CAN PAIXANO
WINE BAR

Map p286 (☑93 310 08 39; www.canpaixano.com; Carrer de la Reina Cristina 7; ⊗9am-10.30pm Mon-Sat; MBarceloneta) This lofty *cava* bar (also called La Xampanyeria) has long been run on a winning formula. The standard tipple is bubbly rosé in elegant little glasses, combined with bite-sized *bocadillos* (filled rolls) and tapas. Note that this place is usually packed to the rafters, and elbowing your way to the bar can be a titanic struggle.

LA DELICIOSA
BAR

Map p286 (www.ladeliciosabeachbar.com; Passeig Marítim de la Barceloneta; ⊗10am-10pm Mar-Oct; 🛜; MBarceloneta) Surfboards frame this beach bar on the sand at Platja de la Barceloneta – an idyllic spot for fresh juices, regional wines and cocktails such as Basil Instinct (vodka, pineapple juice, lemon, ginger, raspberries and basil) or Passion Smash (Jack Daniels, passionfruit pulp and mint). Soak them up with gourmet sandwiches, organic burgers, black-bean nachos and bite-size tapas.

THE MINT
COCKTAIL BAR

Map p286 (☑647 737707; www.facebook.com/themintbarcelona; Passeig d'Isabel II 4; ⊗7.30pm-2.30am Sun-Thu, to 3am Fri & Sat; MBarceloneta) Named after the prized cocktail ingredient, this mojito-loving spot has an upstairs bar where you can peruse the first-rate house-infused gins (over 20 on hand, including creative blends like lemon grass and Jamaican pepper). Downstairs in the brick-vaulted cellars, red lights and driving beats create a more celebratory vibe.

BAR LEO
BAR

Map p286 (Carrer de Sant Carles 34; ⊗noon-9.30pm; MBarceloneta) An almost entirely *barcelonin* crowd spills out into the street from Bar Leo, a hole-in-the-wall drinking spot plastered with images of late Andalucian singer and heart-throb Bambino, and a jukebox mostly dedicated to flamenco. It's at its liveliest on weekends.

SANTA MARTA
BAR

Map p286 (www.santamartabarcelona.com; Carrer de Grau i Torras 59; ⊗10am-midnight; MBarceloneta) Just back from the beach, this laid-back bar attracts a garrulous mix of locals and expats, who come for prime people-watching at one of the outdoor tables near the boardwalk. Alongside classic cocktails, craft creations include Santa Delicious (tequila, Campari, pink grapefruit and mint). Over 15 varieties of thin-crust pizzas are also available.

CDLC
LOUNGE

Map p288 (Carpe Diem Lounge Club; ☑93 224 04 70; www.cdlcbarcelona.com; Passeig Marítim de la Barceloneta 32; ⊗noon-5am; MCiutadella Vila Olímpica) Ideal for a slow warm-up before heading to the nearby clubs, Carpe Diem Lounge Club has Asian-inspired decor and opens onto the beach. Its Asian-fusion food (sushi et al) is quite good, but pricey; alternatively wait until about midnight, when the tables are rolled up and the DJs and dancers take full control.

CATWALK
CLUB

Map p288 (☑93 224 07 40; www.clubcatwalk.net; Carrer de Ramon Trias Fargas 2-4; cover €15-20; ⊗11.30pm-6am; MCiutadella Vila Olímpica) One of the largest nightclubs in the Port Olímpic area, beachside Catwalk has a capacity of 1000 over two floors. A well-dressed crowd piles in for good house music, occasionally mellowed down with electro, R&B, hip-hop and funk. The chill-out zone, with comfy lounges, is upstairs from the dance floor. Entry is usually free before 1am. Check the schedule online.

OPIUM — CLUB

Map p288 (📞93 225 91 00; www.opiumbarcelona.com; Passeig Marítim de la Barceloneta 34; cover €10-20; ⏱club 10pm-5am Sun-Thu, to 6am Fri & Sat, restaurant from noon; MCiutadella Vila Olímpica) This seaside dance place has a spacious dance floor that only begins to fill from about 3am and is best in summer, when you can spill onto a terrace overlooking the beach. The beachside outdoor section works as a chilled restaurant-cafe.

⚑ Port Olímpic, Poblenou & El Fòrum

BALIUS — COCKTAIL BAR

Map p288 (📞93 315 86 50; www.baliusbar.com; Carrer de Pujades 196; ⏱6pm-2am Tue & Wed, 5pm-3am Thu-Sat, to 1am Sun; MPoblenou) There's an old-fashioned jauntiness to this vintage cocktail den in El Poblenou. Staff pour a mix of classic libations as well as vermouths, and there's a small tapas menu until 10.30pm. Stop by on Sundays to catch live jazz, starting around 7.30pm.

LA CERVECITA NUESTRA DE CADA DÍA — BAR

Map p288 (Carrer de Llull 184; ⏱11.30am-2pm & 5.30-9.30pm Tue-Sat, 5.30-9.30pm Sun & Mon; MLlacuna) Equal parts beer shop and craft brew bar, La Cervecita has a changing selection of unique beers from around Europe and the USA. You might stumble across a Catalan sour fruit beer, a rare English stout, a potent Belgian triple ale or half a dozen other draughts on hand – plus many more varieties by the bottle.

ESPAI JOLIU — CAFE

Map p288 (Carrer Badajoz 95; ⏱3-7pm Mon, 9am-7pm Tue-Fri, 10am-3pm Sat; 🛜; MLlacuna) Inspired by its owner's time in Berlin, this is a charming little post-industrial space with pockmarked walls, concrete floors and exposed bulbs. Potted plants, art prints and ceramics are sold up the front. Tucked up the steps at the back, its peaceful cafe has recycled timber furniture and serves Barcelona-roasted Nømad coffee and organic cakes to a melodic indie soundtrack.

MADAME GEORGE — LOUNGE

Map p288 (www.madamegeorgebar.com; Carrer de Pujades 179; ⏱6pm-2am Mon-Thu, to 3am Fri & Sat, to 12.30am Sun; MPoblenou) A theatrical (veering towards campy) elegance marks the interior of this small, chandelier-lit lounge just off the Rambla del Poblenou. Deft bartenders stir well-balanced cocktails like a Lychee-tini (vanilla-infused vodka, fresh lychees, lychee liqueur and lemon juice) in vintage glassware, while a DJ spins vinyl (mainly soul and funk) in the corner.

D9 AL POBLENOU — SPORTS BAR

Map p288 (📞93 309 92 02; www.denou.bar; Carrer de Pallars 122; ⏱6pm-2.30am Sun-Thu, to 3am Fri & Sat; MBogatell) Eye-catching D9 draws a sports-minded crowd, with a long, colourfully lit bar, table football, outdoor seating and a big screen showing key football matches. The drinks menu includes 25 house-creation shots, as well as tropical cocktails and local wines.

GUINGUETA DEL BOGATELL — BAR

Map p288 (Platja del Bogatell; ⏱9am-10.30pm May-Sep; MLlacuna) At this summertime spot, you can dig your feet in the sand and enjoy a cold brew, cocktail or fruity glass of sangría while watching the lapping waves.

BHARMA — BAR

Map p288 (www.bharma.com; Carrer de Pere IV 93; ⏱7am-11pm Mon-Thu, to 3am Fri, 10pm-3am Sat, closed Aug; MLlacuna) Wildly configured, this El Poblenou bar pays homage to the famously addictive American TV series, *Lost*. Its stone-lined interior is reminiscent of the bunker-like 'hatch', save for the tail end of a plane wreck embedded in one wall. The drink of choice is Bharma Initiative beer, an (almost) exact duplication of the show's Dharma logo.

☆ ENTERTAINMENT

SALA MONASTERIO — LIVE MUSIC

Map p288 (📞616 287197; www.facebook.com/sala.monasterio; Moll de Mestral 30; tickets vary; ⏱10pm-5am Sun-Thu, to 6am Fri & Sat; MCiutadella Vila Olímpica) Overlooking the bobbing masts and slender palm trees of Port Olímpic, this pocket-sized music spot stages an eclectic line-up of live bands, including jazz, *forró* (music from northeastern Brazil), blues jams and rock.

RAZZMATAZZ
LIVE MUSIC

Map p288 (☑93 320 82 00; www.salarazzmatazz.com; Carrer de Pamplona 88; tickets from €17; ◷9pm-4am; ⓂBogatell) Bands from far and wide occasionally create scenes of near hysteria in this, one of the city's classic live-music and clubbing venues. Bands can appear throughout the week (check the website), with different start times. On weekends live music later gives way to club sounds.

Five different clubs in one huge post-industrial space attract people of all dance persuasions and ages. The main space, the **Razz Club**, is a haven for the latest international rock and indie acts. **The Loft** does house and electro, while the **Pop Bar** offers anything from garage to soul. **The Lolita Room** is the land of house, hip-hop and dubstep, and upstairs in the **Rex Room** club-goers sweat it out to experimental sounds. You can save a few euros by purchasing tickets to concerts in advance online.

L'AUDITORI
CLASSICAL MUSIC

Map p288 (☑93 247 93 00; www.auditori.cat; Carrer de Lepant 150; tickets free-€59; ◷box office 5-9pm Tue-Fri, 10am-1pm & 5-9pm Sat; ⓂMarina) Barcelona's modern home for the Orquestra Simfònica de Barcelona i Nacional de Catalunya, L'Auditori puts on plenty of orchestral, chamber, religious and other music. Designed by Rafael Moneo and opened in 1999, the main auditorium can accommodate over 2000 concertgoers. The Museu de la Música (p113) is located in the same building.

TEATRE NACIONAL DE CATALUNYA
PERFORMING ARTS

Map p288 (☑93 306 57 00; www.tnc.cat; Plaça de les Arts 1; tickets free-€28; ◷box office 3-7pm Wed, 4-8pm Thu-Sat, 4-6pm Sun; ⓂGlòries) The National Theatre of Catalonia hosts a wide range of performances, including dramas, comedies, musicals and dance in this ultra-neoclassical theatre designed by Barcelona architect Ricardo Bofill, which opened in 1996. Performances are in Catalan.

YELMO CINES ICÀRIA
CINEMA

Map p288 (☑902 220922; www.yelmocines.es; Carrer de Salvador Espriu 61; tickets adult/child €9.90/7.30; ⓂCiutadella Vila Olímpica) This vast cinema complex shows films in the original language on 15 screens, making for plenty of choice. Aside from the screens,

you'll find several cheerful places to eat, bars and the like to keep you occupied before and after the movies.

SALA BECKETT
THEATRE

Map p288 (☑93 284 53 12; www.salabeckett.cat; Carrer de Pere IV 228-232; tickets from €3; ⓂPoblenou) One of the city's principal alternative theatres, the Sala Beckett doesn't shy away from challenging theatre, and stages an eclectic mix of productions. Performances are primarily in Catalan. Formerly based in Gràcia, the theatre moved in 2016 to this lovely space in a historic 1920s building.

 # SHOPPING

ELS ENCANTS VELLS
MARKET

Map p288 (Fira de Bellcaire; ☑93 246 30 30; www.encantsbcn.com; Plaça de les Glòries Catalanes; ◷9am-8pm Mon, Wed, Fri & Sat; ⓂGlòries) In a gleaming open-sided complex near Plaça de les Glòries Catalanes, the 'Old Charms' flea market is the biggest of its kind in Barcelona. Over 500 vendors ply their wares beneath massive mirror-like panels. It's all here, from antique furniture through to secondhand clothes. There's a lot of junk, but you'll occasionally stumble across a *ganga* (bargain).

Catch some behind-the-scenes action from 7am to 9am on Monday, Wednesday and Friday, when the *subastas* (auctions) take place.

VERNITA
CHILDREN'S CLOTHING

(☑625 092341; www.facebook/vernitastudioshop; Carrer del Joncar 27; ◷10am-1.30pm & 5-8pm Tue-Fri, 10am-2pm & 5-8pm Sat; ⓂPoblenou) Three mothers, Neli, Laura and Nacha, design and hand-stitch children's clothing and accessories such as animal-print cushions, bags, kids' jewellery, bow ties, towels (including adorable dinosaur designs) and washable nappies as well as soft cuddly toys at this light, bright studio-boutique. During the evenings, they also offer sewing lessons and origami workshops for kids (English available).

SYSTEM ACTION
CLOTHING

Map p288 (☑93 463 85 82; www.systemaction.es; Carrer de Pere IV 122; ◷10am-7pm Fri & Sat; ⓂLlacuna) If you like discovering local producers, track down this outlet store on Carrer de Pere IV. Though System Action has stores across Catalonia (and in Madrid), its design headquarters are a few blocks south in a former Poblenou ice factory. Fashions are feminine but rugged, and you'll find good basics here including very wearable sweaters, skirts, scarves and shoes.

ULTRA-LOCAL RECORDS   MUSIC
Map p288 (☑661 017638; www.ultralocalrecords. com; Carrer de Pujades 113; ☺4-8.30pm Mon-Fri, 11am-8.30pm Sat; MLlacuna) Along a fairly empty stretch of El Poblenou, this small, well-curated shop sells mostly used records (plus some re-releases and albums by current indie rock darlings) from Catalan, Spanish, French, American and British artists. Vinyl aside, you'll find a smaller CD selection, plus zines and a few other curiosities. There's a €1 bargain bin in front of the store.

LA BAZART   FASHION & ACCESSORIES
Map p288 (☑633 455378; www.labazart.com; Carrer de la Ciutat de Granada 44; ☺10.30am-6pm Mon, Tue, Thu & Fri, to 2.30pm Sat; MLlacuna) If you can't make it to a handicrafts market in South America, La Bazart may be your next best bet. This colourfully decorated shop stocks handcrafted goods from across the Andes. There are lots of great gift ideas, including silver jewellery from Ecuador, woven pillowcases from Bolivia, and alpaca gloves, scarves and blankets from the owner's native Chile.

BESTIARI   BOOKS, HANDICRAFTS
Map p286 (www.bestiari.net; Plaça de Pau Vila 3; ☺10am-7pm Tue & Thu-Sat, to 8pm Wed, to 2.30pm Sun; MBarceloneta) On the ground floor of the Museu d'Història de Catalunya (p111), this well-stocked shop sells books in English, Catalan and Spanish for all ages, along with Catalan-themed gift ideas: CDs, T-shirts, umbrellas, messenger bags, chess sets, mugs and toys (along the lines of the build-your-own Gothic or Gaudí structures).

MERCAT DE LA BARCELONETA   MARKET
Map p286 (☑93 221 64 71; www.mercatdela barceloneta.com; Plaça de la Font 1; ☺7am-2pm Mon-Thu & Sat, to 8pm Fri, to 3pm Sun; MBarceloneta) Set in a modern glass and steel building fronting a long plaza in the heart of Barceloneta, this airy market has seasonal produce and seafood stalls, as well as several places where you can enjoy a sit-down meal. **El Guindilla** (Map p286; ☑93 221 54 58; Plaça del Poeta Boscà 2; tapas €5-11,

mains €10-16; ☺9.30am-1am Sun-Thu, to 2am Fri & Sat) deserves special mention for its good-value lunch specials and outdoor seating on the plaza.

MAREMÀGNUM   MALL
Map p286 (☑93 225 81 00; www.maremagnum. es; Moll d'Espanya 5; ☺10am-10pm; MDrassanes) Created out of largely abandoned docks, this buzzing shopping centre, with its 19 places to eat, bars and cinemas, is home to 59 shops including youthful Spanish chain Mango, and eye-catching fashions from Barcelona-based Desigual. Football fans will be drawn to the paraphernalia at FC Botiga. It's particularly popular on Sundays when most other stores in the city remain shuttered.

CENTRE COMERCIAL
DE LES GLÒRIES   MALL
Map p288 (www.lesglories.com; Avinguda Diagonal 208; ☺9am-9pm Mon, Tue, Thu & Fri, to 10pm Wed, to 9.30pm Sat; MGlòries) A huge supermarket is among this mall's 77 shops. Also here are 27 places to eat and a cinema complex.

CENTRE COMERCIAL
DIAGONAL MAR   MALL
Map p288 (☑93 567 76 37; www.diagonalmar centre.es; Avinguda Diagonal 3; ☺9.30am-10pm Mon-Sat Jun-Sep, 9am-9pm Mon-Sat Oct-May;

Ⓜ El Maresme Fòrum) This massive shopping centre has some 200 stores, plus restaurants and cinemas.

SPORTS & ACTIVITIES

MOLOKAI SUP CENTER WATER SPORTS
Map p286 (✆93 221 48 68; www.molokaisup center.com; Carrer de Meer 39; 2hr private lesson €60, SUP rental per hour €15; ⓂBarceloneta) This respected outfit will give you a crash course in stand-up paddleboarding (SUP). In addition to the two-hour beginner's class, Molokai can help you improve your technique (in intermediate and advanced lessons – all in two-hour blocks); gear and wetsuits are included. If you'd rather just hire a SUP board, staff can get you out on the sea in no time.

BARCELONA BY BIKE CYCLING
Map p288 (✆671 307 325; www.barcelonabybike. com; Carrer de la Marina 13; tours from €24; ⓂCiutadella Vila Olímpica) This outfit offers various tours by bicycle, including 'The Original', a three-hour pedal that takes in a bit of Gothic Barcelona, L'Eixample (including La Sagrada Família) and the Barceloneta beachfront.

ORSOM CRUISE
Map p286 (✆93 441 05 37; www.barcelona -orsom.com; Moll de les Drassanes; adult/child €15.50/13.50; ◷May-early Oct; ⓂDrassanes) Orsom's large sailing catamaran makes the 90-minute journey to Port Olímpic and back. There are up to four departures per day; the last of the day is a jazz cruise.

BASE NAUTICA MUNICIPAL WATER SPORTS
Map p288 (✆93 221 04 32; www.basenautica. org; Avinguda de Litoral; 2hr lessons from €40, equipment hire per hour from €20, wetsuit hire per day €10; ◷10am-7pm; ⓂPoblenou) Just back from Platja de la Mar Bella, at Base Nautica Municipal you can learn the basics of kayaking, windsurfing, catamaran sailing or stand-up paddleboarding. You can also hire equipment here. Prices for lessons are cheaper in groups of two or more. Longer courses, running from eight to 12 hours over several days, are also available.

LAS GOLONDRINAS CRUISE
Map p286 (✆93 442 31 06; www.lasgolondrinas. com; Moll de las Drassanes; adult/child port tour €7.50/2.80, catamaran tour €15/5.50; ⓂDrassanes) Las Golondrinas offers popular cruises from its dock in front of Mirador de Colom. The 90-minute catamaran tour takes you out past Barceloneta and the beaches to the Fòrum and back. For a quick overview of the port area, take a 40-minute excursion to the breakwater and back. Both trips depart regularly throughout the day.

CLUB NATACIÓ ATLÈTIC-BARCELONA SWIMMING
Map p286 (✆93 221 00 10; www.cnab.cat; Plaça del Mar; day pass adult/child €12.55/7.15; ◷7am-11pm Mon-Fri, to 10pm Sat, to 8pm Sun; ☒V15, 39, 59, 64, ⓂBarceloneta) Operating since 1907, this athletic club has one indoor and two outdoor pools. Of the latter, one is heated for lap swimming in winter. Admission includes use of the gym, spa and private beach access.

La Sagrada Família & L'Eixample

L'ESQUERRA DE L'EIXAMPLE | LA DRETA DE L'EIXAMPLE

Neighbourhood Top Five

1 **La Sagrada Família** (p127) Seeing history being made at Spain's most visited monument and Gaudí's greatest legacy, the soaring Catholic church, begun in 1882 and still under construction to this day.

2 **La Pedrera** (p134) Wandering through the superbly preserved early 20th-century apartment inside this wavy Gaudí edifice.

3 **Casa Batlló** (p133) Marvelling at the swirling, almost-alive facade of this Gaudí-designed apartment building with its wave-shaped window frames and balconies.

4 **Fundació Antoni Tàpies** (p132) Deciphering the fasci-nating contemporary art of leading 20th-century Catalan artist Antoni Tàpies.

5 **Recinte Modernista de Sant Pau** (p134) Admiring this lesser-known master-piece of Modernisme, a Unesco-listed former hospital designed by Domènech i Montaner.

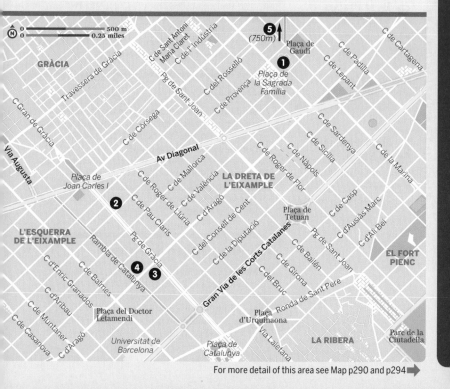

For more detail of this area see Map p290 and p294 ➡

Lonely Planet's Top Tip

Travellers interested in running the gamut of L'Eixample's Modernista gems should consider the Ruta del Modernisme pack (€12; www.rutadelmodernisme.com). It includes a guide (in various languages) and discounted entry prices to the city's major Modernista sights.

Best Places to Eat

➡ Lasarte (p138)

➡ Disfrutar (p138)

➡ Mont Bar (p138)

➡ Auto Rosellon (p137)

➡ Tapas 24 (p139)

For reviews, see p136. ➡

Best Places to Drink

➡ Napar BCN (p142)

➡ Monvínic (p142)

➡ Milano (p142)

➡ Les Gens Que J'Aime (p144)

For reviews, see p142. ➡

Best Places to Shop

➡ Joan Múrria (p145)

➡ Flores Navarro (p145)

➡ Cacao Sampaka (p145)

For reviews, see p145. ➡

LA SAGRADA FAMÍLIA & L'EIXAMPLE

Explore La Sagrada Família & L'Eixample

In the 1820s rows of trees were planted on either side of the road linking Barcelona and the town of Gràcia. The resulting Passeig de Gràcia is a strollers' boulevard that is now home to many of the city's most expensive shops and a diverse range of restaurants. This is the street to head to for Modernista architecture, the best of which – apart from La Sagrada Família – is clustered on or near it. Eating is at the high end (though set-lunch options are available for lower budgets), and the emphasis is on designer fashion, though there are some notable exceptions. Drinking and nightlife in the area tend to be student- and gay-oriented – part of the area is dubbed 'Gaixample'.

La Dreta (the Right) de L'Eixample, stretching from Passeig de Gràcia to Passeig de Sant Joan, contains much sought-after real estate. Beyond it takes on a dowdy feel, even around La Sagrada Família (p127). L'Esquerra (the Left) de L'Eixample, running southwest from Passeig de Gràcia, changes character several times. The whole area between Carrer d'Aribau, Passeig de Sant Joan, Avinguda Diagonal and the Ronda de Sant Pere has been known since the early 20th century as the Quadrat d'Or (Golden Square) thanks to its extravagant architecture and grand houses; it's now the domain of high-end shops.

The Modernista stars include Gaudí's La Pedrera (p134) and the Illa de la Discòrdia, which comprises three gems – Casa Batlló (p133), Casa Amatller (p132) and Casa Lleó Morera (p132) – by the three top architects of the period. As you wander, be sure to always look up.

Local Life

➡ **Student life** Join students from the Universitat de Barcelona (p133) at the string of unpretentious hangouts nearby on the Carrer d'Enric Granados.

➡ **Coffee with a view** Take a lift to the very top of El Corte Inglés (p146) for a restaurant with a great view across the neighbourhood and beyond.

➡ **Say it with flowers** Walking around the Flores Navarro (p145), a cathedral to colourful plant life, is quite a trip at 4am.

Getting There & Away

➡ **Metro** Four metro lines criss-cross L'Eixample, three stopping at Passeig de Gràcia for the Illa de la Discòrdia. Línia 3 stops at Diagonal for La Pedrera, while Línies 2 and 5 stop at Sagrada Família.

➡ **Train** FGC lines from Plaça de Catalunya take you one stop to Provença, in the heart of L'Eixample.

⊙ TOP SIGHT
LA SAGRADA FAMÍLIA

If you have time for only one sightseeing outing, this should be it. La Sagrada Família inspires awe by its sheer verticality, and, in the manner of the medieval cathedrals it emulates, it's still under construction: work began in 1882 and is hoped (although by no means expected) to be finished in 2026, a century after the architect's death.

A Holy Mission

The Temple Expiatori de la Sagrada Família (Expiatory Temple of the Holy Family) was Antoni Gaudí's all-consuming obsession. Given the commission by a conservative society that wished to build a temple as atonement for the city's sins of modernity, Gaudí saw its completion as his holy mission. As funds dried up, he contributed his own, and in the last years of his life he was never shy of pleading with anyone he thought a likely donor.

Gaudí devised a temple 95m long and 60m wide, able to seat 13,000 people, with a central tower 170m high above the transept (representing Christ) and another 17 of 100m or more. The 12 along the three facades represent the Apostles, while the remaining five represent the Virgin Mary and the four evangelists. With his characteristic dislike for straight lines (there were none in nature, he said), Gaudí gave his towers swelling outlines inspired by the weird peaks of the holy mountain Montserrat outside Barcelona, and encrusted them with a tangle of sculpture that seems an outgrowth of the stone.

At Gaudí's death, only the crypt, the apse walls, one portal and one tower had been finished. Three more towers were added by 1930, completing the northeast (Nativity) facade. In 1936 anarchists burned and smashed the interior, including workshops, plans and models. Work began again in 1952, but controversy has always clouded progress. Opponents of

DON'T MISS

→ The apse, the extraordinary pillars and stained glass
→ Nativity Facade
→ Passion Facade
→ Museu Gaudí

PRACTICALITIES

→ Map p294, E1
→ ☑93 208 04 14
→ www.sagradafamilia.org
→ Carrer de Mallorca 401
→ adult/child €15/free
→ ⊙9am-8pm Apr-Sep, to 7pm Mar & Oct, to 6pm Nov-Feb
→ Ⓜ Sagrada Família

A HIDDEN PORTRAIT

Careful observation of the Passion Facade will reveal a special tribute from sculptor Josep Subirachs to Gaudí. The central sculptural group (below Christ crucified) shows, from right to left, Christ bearing his cross, Veronica displaying the cloth with Christ's bloody image, a pair of soldiers and, watching it all, a man called the evangelist. Subirachs used a rare photo of Gaudí, taken a couple of years before his death, as the model for the evangelist's face.

VISITORS

Unfinished it may be, but La Sagrada Família attracts over 4.5 million visitors a year and is the most visited monument in Spain. Pope Benedict XVI consecrated it as a minor basilica in a huge ceremony in November 2010.

the continuation of the project claim that the computer models based on what little of Gaudí's plans survived the anarchists' ire have led to the creation of a monster that has little to do with Gaudí's plans and style. It is a debate that appears to have little hope of resolution. Like or hate what is being done, the fascination it awakens is undeniable.

Even before reaching completion, some of the oldest parts of the church, especially the apse, have required restoration work.

The Interior & the Apse

Inside, work on roofing over the church was completed in 2010. The roof is held up by a forest of extraordinary angled pillars. As the pillars soar towards the ceiling, they sprout a web of supporting branches, creating the effect of a forest canopy. The tree image is in no way fortuitous – Gaudí envisaged such an effect. Everything was thought through, including the shape and placement of windows to create the mottled effect one would see with sunlight pouring through the branches of a thick forest. The pillars are of four different types of stone. They vary in colour and load-bearing strength, from the soft Montjuïc stone pillars along the lateral aisles through to granite, dark grey basalt and finally burgundy-tinged Iranian porphyry for the key columns at the intersection of the nave and transept. The stained glass, divided in shades of red, blue, green and ochre, creates a hypnotic, magical atmosphere when the sun hits the windows. Tribunes built high above the aisles can host two choirs: the main tribune up to 1300 people and the children's tribune up to 300.

Nativity Facade

The Nativity Facade is the artistic pinnacle of the building, mostly created under Gaudí's personal supervision. You can climb high up inside some of the four towers by a combination of lifts and narrow spiral staircases – a vertiginous experience. Do not climb the stairs if you have cardiac or respiratory problems. The towers are destined to hold tubular bells capable of playing complex music at great volume. Their upper parts are decorated with mosaics spelling out *'Sanctus, Sanctus, Sanctus, Hosanna in Excelsis, Amen, Alleluia'*. Asked why he lavished so much care on the tops of the spires, which no one would see from close up, Gaudí answered: 'The angels will see them.'

Three sections of the portal represent, from left to right, Hope, Charity and Faith. Among the forest of sculpture on the Charity portal you can see, low down, the manger surrounded by an ox, an ass, the shepherds and kings, and angel musicians. Some 30 different species of plant from around Catalonia are reproduced here, and the faces of the many figures are taken from plaster casts done of local people and the occasional one made from corpses in the local morgue.

Directly above the blue stained-glass window is the archangel Gabriel's Annunciation to Mary. At the top is a green cypress tree, a refuge in a storm for the white doves of peace dotted over it. The mosaic work at the pinnacle of the towers is made from Murano glass from Venice.

To the right of the facade is the curious Claustre del Roser, a Gothic-style mini-cloister tacked on to the outside of the church (rather than the classic square enclosure of the great Gothic church monasteries). Once inside, look back to the intricately decorated entrance. On the lower right-hand side you'll notice the sculpture of a reptilian devil handing a terrorist a bomb. Barcelona was regularly rocked by political violence, and bombings were frequent in the decades prior to the civil war. The sculpture is one of several on the 'temptations of men and women'.

Passion Facade

The southwest Passion Facade, on the theme of Christ's last days and death, was built between 1954 and 1978 based on surviving drawings by Gaudí, with four towers and a large, sculpture-bedecked portal. The sculptor, Josep Subirachs, worked on its decoration from 1986 to 2006. He did not attempt to imitate Gaudí, instead producing angular, controversial images of his own. The main series of sculptures, on three levels, are in an S-shaped sequence, starting with the Last Supper at the bottom left and ending with Christ's burial at the top right.

To the right, in front of the Passion Facade, the Escoles de Gaudí is one of his simpler gems. Gaudí built this as a children's school, creating an original, undulating roof of brick that continues to charm architects to this day. Inside is a re-creation of Gaudí's modest office as it was when he died, and explanations of the geometric patterns and plans at the heart of his building techniques.

Glory Facade

The Glory Facade will, like the others, be crowned by four towers – the total of 12 representing the Twelve Apostles. Gaudí wanted it to be the most magnificent facade of the church. Inside will be the narthex, a kind of foyer made up of 16 'lanterns', a series of hyperboloid forms topped by cones. Further decoration will make the whole building a microcosmic symbol of the Christian church, with Christ represented by a massive 170m central tower above the transept, and the five remaining planned towers symbolising the Virgin Mary and the four evangelists.

Museu Gaudí

Open at the same times as the church, the Museu Gaudí, below ground level, includes interesting material on Gaudí's life and other works, as well as models and photos of La Sagrada Família. You can see a good example of his plumbline models that showed him the stresses and strains he could get away with in construction. A side hall towards the eastern end of the museum leads to a viewing point above the simple crypt in which the genius is buried. The crypt, where Masses are now held, can also be visited from the Carrer de Mallorca side of the church.

La Sagrada Família

A TIMELINE

1882 Construction begins on a neo-Gothic church designed by Francisco de Paula del Villar y Lozano.

1883 Antoni Gaudí takes over as chief architect and plans a far more ambitious church to hold 13,000 faithful.

1926 Gaudí dies; work continues under Domènec Sugrañes i Gras. Much of the **apse ❶** and **Nativity Facade ❷** is complete.

1930 Bell towers ❸ of the Nativity Facade completed.

1936 Construction interrupted by Spanish Civil War; anarchists destroy Gaudí's plans.

1939–40 Architect Francesc de Paula Quintana i Vidal restores the crypt and meticulously reassembles many of Gaudí's lost models, some of which can be seen in the **museum ❹**.

1976 Passion Facade ❺ completed.

1986–2006 Sculptor Josep Subirachs adds sculptural details to the Passion Facade including the panels telling the story of Christ's last days, amid much criticism for employing a style far removed from what was thought typical of Gaudí.

2000 Central nave vault ❻ completed.

2010 Church completely roofed over; Pope Benedict XVI consecrates the church; work begins on a high-speed rail tunnel that will pass beneath the church's **Glory Facade ❼**.

2020s–40s Projected completion date.

TOP TIPS

➡ The best light through the stained-glass windows of the Passion Facade bursts into the heart of the church in the late afternoon.

➡ Visit at opening time on weekdays to avoid the worst of the crowds.

➡ Head up the Nativity Facade bell towers for the views, as long queues generally await at the Passion Facade towers.

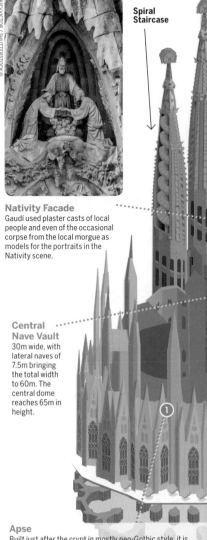

KIEV.VICTOR / SHUTTERSTOCK ©

Spiral Staircase

Nativity Facade
Gaudí used plaster casts of local people and even of the occasional corpse from the local morgue as models for the portraits in the Nativity scene.

Central Nave Vault
30m wide, with lateral naves of 7.5m bringing the total width to 60m. The central dome reaches 65m in height.

Apse
Built just after the crypt in mostly neo-Gothic style, it is capped by pinnacles that show a hint of the genius that Gaudí would later deploy in the rest of the church.

STEFAN CIOATA / GETTY IMAGES ©

Bell Towers
The towers of the three facades will represent the Twelve Apostles. Eight are completed. Lifts whisk visitors up one tower of the Nativity and Passion Facades (the latter gets longer queues) for fine views.

NIKADA / GETTY IMAGES ©

Completed Church
Along with the Glory Facade and its four towers, six other towers remain to be completed. They will represent the four evangelists, the Virgin Mary and, soaring above them all over the transept, a 170m colossus symbolising Christ.

Glory Facade
This will be the most fanciful facade of all, with a narthex boasting 16 hyperboloid lanterns topped by cones that will look something like an organ made of melting ice cream.

Museu Gaudí
Jammed with old photos, drawings and restored plaster models that bring Gaudí's ambitions to life, the museum also houses an extraordinarily complex plumb-line device he used to calculate his constructions.

Escoles de Gaudí

Crypt
The first completed part of the church, the crypt is in largely neo-Gothic style and lies under the transept. Gaudí's burial place here can be seen from the Museu Gaudí.

FOTOKON / SHUTTERSTOCK ©

Passion Facade
See the story of Christ's last days from Last Supper to burial in an S-shaped sequence from bottom to top of the facade. Check out the cryptogram in which the numbers always add up to 33, Christ's age at his death.

YURY DMITRIENKO / SHUTTERSTOCK ©

◎ SIGHTS

◎ L'Esquerra de L'Eixample

CASA AMATLLER   ARCHITECTURE

Map p290 (☑93 461 74 60; www.amatller.org; Passeig de Gràcia 41; adult/child 1hr guided tour €17/8.50, 40min multimedia tour €14/7, with 20min chocolate tasting €17/10; ◎11am-6pm; ⓂPasseig de Gràcia) One of Puig i Cadafalch's most striking flights of Modernista fantasy, Casa Amatller combines Gothic window frames with a stepped gable borrowed from Dutch urban architecture. But the busts and reliefs of dragons, knights and other characters dripping off the main facade are pure caprice.

The pillared foyer and staircase lit by stained glass are like the inside of some romantic castle. The building was renovated in 1900 for the chocolate baron and philanthropist Antoni Amatller (1851–1910).

The 1st (main) floor has been converted into a museum, with period pieces and original furniture and decor, which you can visit by guided tour. Amatller was a keen traveller and photographer (his absorbing shots of turn-of-the-20th-century Morocco are occasionally on show).

There is a one-hour guided visit in English at 11am; 40-minute express tours run throughout the day and include a multimedia tablet. You can also take a 40-minute multimedia tour that includes a taste of Amatller chocolate in the original kitchen. It's free to wander into the foyer and admire the staircase and lift.

FUNDACIÓ ANTONI TÀPIES   GALLERY

Map p290 (☑93 487 03 15; www.fundaciotapies. org; Carrer d'Aragó 255; adult/child €7/5.60; ◎10am-7pm Tue-Sun; ⓂPasseig de Gràcia) The Fundació Antoni Tàpies is both a pioneering Modernista building (completed in 1885) and the major collection of leading 20th-century Catalan artist Antoni Tàpies. Tàpies died in February 2012, aged 88; known for his esoteric work, he left behind a powerful range of paintings and a foundation intended to promote contemporary artists. Admission includes an audioguide.

The building, designed by Domènech i Montaner for the publishing house Editorial Montaner i Simón (run by a cousin of the architect), combines a brick-covered iron frame with Islamic-inspired decoration. Tàpies crowned it with the meandering of his own mind, a work called *Núvol i cadira* (Cloud and Chair) that spirals above the building like a storm.

Although it's difficult to understand the art of Antoni Tàpies, it's worth seeing the one-hour documentary on his life, on the top floor, to learn about his influences and method, and the course of his interesting life. In his work, Tàpies expressed a number of themes, such as left-wing politics and humanitarianism; the practices of Zen meditation and its relationship between nature and insight; incarnation as seen in Christian faith; and art as alchemy or magic.

He launched the Fundació in 1984 to promote contemporary art, donating a large part of his own work. The collection spans the arc of Tàpies' creations (with more than 800 works) and contributions from other contemporary artists. In the main exhibition area (level 1, upstairs) you can see an ever-changing selection of around 20 of Tàpies' works, from early self-portraits of the 1940s to grand items like *Jersei negre* (Black Jumper; 2008). Level 2 hosts a small space for temporary exhibitions. Rotating exhibitions take place in the basement levels.

SALA FUNDACIÓN MAPFRE   GALLERY

Map p290 (☑93 401 26 03; www.fundacion mapfre.org; Carrer de la Diputació 250; adult/child €3/free, Mon free; ◎2-8pm Mon, 10am-8pm Tue-Sat, 11am-7pm Sun; ⓂPasseig de Gràcia) Formerly the Fundación Francisco Godia, this stunning, carefully restored Modernista residence was taken over in late 2015 by the charitable cultural arm of Spanish insurance giants MAPFRE as a space for art and photography exhibitions. Housed in the Casa Garriga i Nogués, it is a stunning, carefully restored Modernista residence originally built for a rich banking family by Enric Sagnier in 1902–05.

Exhibitions are shown on the ground floor and in a number of small rooms up the curvaceous marble stairway. Look out for the fine Modernista stained-glass windows in room 8. An audioguide costs €3.50.

CASA LLEÓ MORERA   ARCHITECTURE

Map p290 (Passeig de Gràcia 35; ⓂPasseig de Gràcia) Domènech i Montaner's 1905 contribution to the Illa de la Discòrdia, with Modernista carving outside and a bright, tiled lobby in which floral motifs predominate, is perhaps the least odd-looking of the three main buildings on the block. Luxury fashion store Loewe (p148) is located here.

TOP SIGHT
CASA BATLLÓ

Casa Batlló is one of the most extraordinary structures to emerge from Gaudí's fantastical imagination. To Salvador Dalí it resembled 'twilight clouds in water'. Others see a more-than-passing resemblance to the impressionist masterpiece *Water Lilies* by Claude Monet. A Rorschach blot for the imagination, Casa Batlló's facade is exquisite and whimsical, sprinkled with fragments of blue, mauve and green tiles, and studded with wave-shaped window frames and mask-like balconies.

Casa Batlló's roof, with the twisting chimney pots so characteristic of Gaudí's structures, is the building's grand crescendo. The eastern end represents Sant Jordi (St George) and the Dragon; one local name for Casa Batlló is the *casa del drac* (house of the dragon). The ceaseless curves of coloured tiles have the effect of making the building seem like a living being.

The staircase wafts you to the 1st floor, where everything swirls in the main salon: the ceiling twists into a whirlpool-like vortex around its sun-like lamp; the doors, window and skylights are dreamy waves of wood and coloured glass in mollusc-like shapes. The sense of light and space here is extraordinary thanks to the wall-length window onto Passeig de Gràcia.

DON'T MISS

➡ The facade and balconies
➡ The swirling interior
➡ The dragon-back roof

PRACTICALITIES

➡ Map p290, G3
➡ ☎93 216 03 06
➡ www.casabatllo.es
➡ Passeig de Gràcia 43
➡ adult/child €28/free
➡ ◷9am-9pm, last admission 8pm
➡ Ⓜ Passeig de Gràcia

MUSEU DEL MODERNISME BARCELONA

MUSEUM

Map p290 (☎93 272 28 96; www.mmbcn.cat; Carrer de Balmes 48; adult/child €10/5; ◷10.30am-7pm Tue-Sat, to 2pm Sun; Ⓜ Passeig de Gràcia) Housed in a Modernista building, this museum's ground floor seems like a big Modernista furniture showroom. Several items by Antoni Gaudí, including chairs from Casa Batlló and a mirror from Casa Calvet, are supplemented by a host of items by his lesser-known contemporaries, including some typically whimsical, mock medieval pieces by Puig i Cadafalch.

The basement, which has mosaic-coated pillars, bare-brick vaults and metal columns, is lined with Modernista art, including paintings by Ramon Casas and Santiago Rusiñol, and statues by Josep Llimona and Eusebi Arnau.

PALAU ROBERT

GALLERY

Map p290 (☎93 238 80 91; http://palaurobert.gencat.cat; Passeig de Gràcia 107; ◷9am-8pm Mon-Sat, to 2.30pm Sun; Ⓜ Diagonal) FREE Catalonia's regional tourist office also serves as an exhibition space, mostly for shows with Catalan themes. In summer, concerts are occasionally held in the peaceful gardens at the back of the 1903-completed building, or in its main hall.

CASA GOLFERICHS

CULTURAL CENTRE

Map p290 (☎93 323 77 90; www.golferichs.org; Gran Via de les Corts Catalanes 491; ◷10am-10pm Mon-Fri, to 2pm Sat; Ⓜ Rocafort) This quirky mansion is an oddity of another era on one of the city's busiest boulevards, a Modernista villa owned by businessman Macari Golferichs. Brick, ceramics and wood are the main building elements of the house, which displays a distinctly Gothic flavour. It came close to demolition in the 1970s but was saved by the town hall and converted into a cultural centre. Opening times and prices can vary depending on temporary exhibitions, concerts and other activities.

UNIVERSITAT DE BARCELONA

ARCHITECTURE

Map p290 (☎93 402 11 00; www.ub.edu; Gran Via de les Corts Catalanes 585; ◷8am-8pm Mon-Fri; Ⓜ Universitat) Although a university was first set up on what is now La Rambla in the 16th century, the present, glorious mix of (neo) Romanesque, Gothic, Islamic and

LA SAGRADA FAMÍLIA & L'EIXAMPLE SIGHTS

TOP SIGHT
LA PEDRERA

This madcap Gaudí masterpiece was built in 1905–10 as a combined apartment and office block. Formally called Casa Milà, after the businessman who commissioned it, it is better known as La Pedrera (the Quarry) because of its uneven grey stone facade, which ripples around the corner of Carrer de Provença.

Pere Milà had married the older and far richer Roser Guardiola, the widow of Josep Guardiola, and clearly knew how to spend his new wife's money. Milà was one of the city's first car owners and Gaudí built parking space into this building, itself a first.

The roof is the most extraordinary element, with its giant chimney pots looking like multicoloured medieval knights. Short concerts are often staged up here in summer. Gaudí wanted to put a tall statue of the Virgin up here too: when the Milà family said no, fearing it might make the building a target for anarchists, Gaudí resigned from the project in disgust.

Two floors down is the apartment (El Pis de la Pedrera). It is fascinating to wander around this elegantly furnished home, done up in the style a well-to-do family might have enjoyed in the early 20th century. There are sensuous curves and unexpected touches in everything from light fittings to bedsteads, from door handles to balconies.

DON'T MISS

➡ The marvellous roof
➡ The apartment
➡ The stone facade

PRACTICALITIES

➡ Casa Milà
➡ Map p290, A4
➡ ☏902 202138
➡ www.lapedrera.com
➡ Passeig de Gràcia 92
➡ adult/child €25/15
➡ ⊙9am-8.30pm Mar-Oct, 9am-6.30pm Nov-Feb
➡ Ⓜ Diagonal

Mudéjar architecture is a caprice of the 19th century (built 1863–82). Wander into the main hall, up the grand staircase and around the various leafy cloisters, or take a stroll in the rear gardens.

MUSEU DEL PERFUM   MUSEUM
Map p290 (☏93 216 01 21; www.museudelperfum.com; Passeig de Gràcia 39; adult/child €5/free; ⊙10.30am-8pm Mon-Fri, 11am-2pm Sat; Ⓜ Passeig de Gràcia) At the back of the Regia perfume store (p148), this museum contains oddities from ancient Egyptian and Roman scent receptacles (the latter mostly from the 1st to 3rd centuries AD) to classic eau de cologne bottles – all in all, some 5000 bottles of infinite shapes, sizes and histories. Other items include ancient bronze Etruscan tweezers and little early-19th-century potpourri bowls made of fine Sèvres porcelain. Also on show are old catalogues and advertising posters.

PLAÇA DE CATALUNYA   SQUARE
Map p290 (Ⓜ Catalunya) At the intersection of the old city and L'Eixample, Plaça de Catalunya is the city's central transport hub, both for buses and trains, and a convenient meeting point. A large square with some impressive fountains and elegant statuary, it is ringed with four lanes of traffic and thus is not really a place to linger.

⊙ La Dreta de L'Eixample

LA SAGRADA FAMÍLIA   CHURCH
See p127.

RECINTE MODERNISTA DE SANT PAU   ARCHITECTURE
(☏93 553 78 01; www.santpaubarcelona.org; Carrer de Sant Antoni Maria Claret 167; adult/child €13/free; ⊙9.30am-6.30pm Mon-Sat, to 2.30pm Sun Apr-Oct, 9.30am-4.30pm Mon-Sat, to 2.30pm Sun Nov-Mar; Ⓜ Sant Pau/Dos de Maig) Domènech i Montaner outdid himself as architect and philanthropist with the Modernista Hospital de la Santa Creu i de Sant Pau, renamed the 'Recinte Modernista' in 2014. It was long considered one of the city's most important hospitals but was repurposed, its various spaces becoming cultural centres, offices and something of a monument. The complex, including 16 pavilions – together with the Palau de la Música Catalana (p95),

a joint Unesco World Heritage Site – is lavishly decorated and each pavilion is unique.

Domènech i Montaner wanted to create an environment that would also cheer up patients. Among artists who contributed statuary, ceramics and artwork was the prolific Eusebi Arnau.

Guided tours (adult/child €19/free) lasting 90 minutes are available in a variety of languages; English tours depart at 10.30am.

MUSEU EGIPCI — MUSEUM

Map p294 (☎93 488 01 88; www.museuegipci.com; Carrer de València 284; adult/child €11/5; ⏱10am-8pm Mon-Sat, to 2pm Sun mid-Jun–early Oct & Dec, 10am-2pm & 4-8pm Mon-Fri, 10am-8pm Sat, 10am-2pm Sun Jan–mid-Jun & early Oct-Nov; Ⓜ Passeig de Gràcia) Hotel magnate Jordi Clos has spent much of his life collecting ancient Egyptian artefacts, brought together in this private museum. It's divided into different thematic areas (the pharaoh, religion, funerary practices, mummification, crafts etc) and boasts an interesting variety of exhibits.

There are funereal implements and containers, statuary, jewellery (including a fabulous golden ring from around the 7th century BC), ceramics, and even a bed made of wood and leather. In the basement is an exhibition area and library, displaying volumes including original editions of works by Carter, the Egyptologist who led the Tutankhamun excavations. The rooftop terrace has a cafe.

A combined ticket with the Museu de Cultures del Món (p98) costs €12.

CASA DE LES PUNXES — ARCHITECTURE

Map p294 (Casa Terrades; ☎93 016 01 28; www.casadelespunxes.com; Avinguda Diagonal 420; adult/child audiogude tour €12.50/11.25, guided tour €20/17; ⏱9am-8pm; Ⓜ Diagonal) Puig i Cadafalch's Casa Terrades, completed in 1905, is better known as the Casa de les Punxes (House of Spikes) because of its pointed turrets. Resembling a medieval castle, the former apartment block is the only fully detached building in L'Eixample, and was declared a national monument in 1976. Since 2017 it has been open to the public. Visits take in its stained-glass bay windows, handsome iron staircase, and rooftop. Guided tours in English lasting one hour depart at 4pm.

Various other tour options include a night-time tour with a glass of *cava* (€23).

PALAU DEL BARÓ QUADRAS — ARCHITECTURE

Map p294 (☎93 467 80 00; www.llull.cat; Avinguda Diagonal 373; tour adult/child €10/free; ⏱11am-1pm Wed; Ⓜ Diagonal) Puig i Cadafalch designed Palau del Baró Quadras (built 1902–06) in an exuberant Gothic-inspired style. The main facade is its most intriguing, with a soaring, glassed-in gallery. Take a closer look at the gargoyles and reliefs – the pair of toothy fish and the sword-wielding knight clearly have the same artistic signature as the architect behind Casa Amatller. The only way to visit the interior is on a 45-minute tour; English tours depart on Wednesday at 11am.

Decor inside is eclectic, but dominated by Middle Eastern and East Asian themes.

ESGLÉSIA DE LA PURÍSSIMA CONCEPCIÓ I ASSUMPCIÓ DE NOSTRA SENYORA — CHURCH

Map p294 (☎93 457 65 52; www.parroquiaconcepciobcn.org; Carrer de Roger de Llúria 70; ⏱7.30am-1pm & 5-9pm Mon-Sat, 7.30am-2pm & 5-9pm Sun; Ⓜ Passeig de Gràcia) One hardly expects to run into a medieval church on the grid-pattern streets of the late-19th-century city extension, yet that is just what this is. Transferred stone by stone from the old centre in 1871–88, this 14th-century church has a pretty 16th-century cloister with a peaceful garden.

Behind is a Romanesque-Gothic bell tower (11th to 16th century), moved from another old town church that didn't survive, Església de Sant Miquel. This is one of a handful of such old churches shifted willy-nilly from their original locations to L'Eixample.

FUNDACIÓ SUÑOL — GALLERY

Map p294 (☎93 496 10 32; www.fundaciosunol.org; Passeig de Gràcia 98; adult/child €4/free; ⏱11am-2pm & 4-8pm Mon-Fri, 4-8pm Sat; Ⓜ Diagonal) Rotating exhibitions of portions of this private collection of mostly 20th-century art (some 1200 works in total) offer anything from Man Ray's photography to sculptures by Alberto Giacometti. Over two floors, you are most likely to run into Spanish artists – anyone from Picasso to Jaume Plensa – along with a sprinkling of international artists.

It makes a refreshing pause between the crush of crowded Modernista monuments on this boulevard. Indeed, you get an interesting side view of one of them, La Pedrera (p134), from out the back.

LOCAL KNOWLEDGE

PLATJA DE L'EIXAMPLE

In a hidden garden inside a typical Eixample block is an old water tower and an urban 'beach', the **Platja de l'Eixample** (Map p294; ☑93 423 43 50; Carrer de Roger de Llúria 56; €1.55; ☺10am-8pm late Jun–Sep; MGirona). In reality, this is a knee-height swimming pool (60cm at its deepest) surrounded by sand. It's perfect for little ones, with lifeguards on hand.

ESGLÉSIA DE LES SALESES   CHURCH

Map p294 (☑93 458 76 67; www.parroquia concepciobcn.org; Passeig de Sant Joan 90; ☺10am-1pm & 5-7pm Mon-Sat, 10am-2pm Sun; MVerdaguer) A singular neo-Gothic effort, this church is interesting because it was designed by Joan Martorell i Montells (1833–1906), Gaudí's architecture professor. Raised in 1878–85 with an adjacent convent (badly damaged in the civil war and now a school), it offers hints of what was to come with Modernisme, with his use of brick, mosaics and stained glass.

PALAU MONTANER   ARCHITECTURE

Map p294 (☑93 317 76 52; www.fundaciotapies. org; Carrer de Mallorca 278; adult/child €7/ free; ☺by reservation; MPasseig de Gràcia) Interesting on the outside and made all the more enticing by its gardens, this creation by Domènech i Montaner is spectacular on the inside. Completed in 1893, its central feature is a grand staircase beneath a broad, ornamental skylight. The interior is laden with sculptures (some by Eusebi Arnau), mosaics and fine woodwork. It is only open by two-hour guided tour, organised by the Fundació Tàpies (in English by prior request).

✖ EATING

✖ L'Esquerra de L'Eixample

COPASETIC   CAFE €

Map p290 (☑93 532 76 66; www.copasetic barcelona.com; Carrer de la Diputació 55; mains €6-13.50; ☺10.30am-midnight Tue & Wed, to 1am Thu, to 2am Fri & Sat, to 5.30pm Sun; ☜☑; MRocafort) Decked out with retro furniture,

Copasetic has a fun, friendly vibe. The menu holds plenty for everyone, whether your thing is eggs Benedict, wild-berry tartlets or a fat, juicy burger. There are lots of vegetarian, gluten-free and organic options, and superb (and reasonably priced) weekend brunches. Lunch *menús* (Tuesday to Friday) cost between €9.50 and €12.

CREMERIA TOSCANA   GELATO €

Map p290 (☑93 539 38 25; www.cremeriatoscana. es; Carrer de Muntaner 161; ice cream €2.80-5.40; ☺1pm-midnight Mon-Thu, to 1am Fri & Sat, noon-midnight Sun Apr-Oct, 1-9pm Tue-Thu, to 11pm Fri & Sat, noon-11pm Sun Nov-Mar; MHospital Clínic) At the most authentic gelato outlet in town, all flavours are natural and most are gluten-free. Along with classic Italian choices such as creamy *stracciatella* and wavy hazelnut *nocciola* are more unusual offerings such as goat cheese and caramelised fig, pear and chocolate or plum and pink grapefruit. Buy a cone or a tub.

KOYUKI   JAPANESE €

Map p290 (☑93 237 84 90; http://koyuki.elte nedor.rest; Carrer de Còrsega 242; mains €8-12; ☺1-3.30pm & 8-11pm Tue-Sun; ⓇFGC Provença) This unassuming basement Japanese diner is one of those rough-edged diamonds. Order from the menu complete with pictures courtesy of the Japanese owner – you won't be disappointed. The variety of *sashimi moriawase* is generous and constantly fresh. The tempura udon is a particularly hearty noodle option with breaded shrimp.

Wash it all down with Sapporo beer.

CHARLOT CAFÈ   CAFE €

Map p290 (☑93 451 15 65; Carrer d'Aribau 67; dishes €6.50-13.50; ☺kitchen 8.30am-10pm Mon-Fri, 7am-10pm Sat, bar to 3am Fri & Sat; ☜☑; ⓇFGC Provença) Movie stills and posters, from *Breakfast at Tiffany's* to *Pulp Fiction,* line the walls at Charlot. Get a morning kick-start with a truffled *tortilla española* (Spanish omelette) or eggs baked in Iberian ham, or drop by for lunch (sautéed quinoa salad; burgers with hand-cut fries) or dinner (duck with blackberry sauce). Craft beers and cocktails are all-day-long options.

Twists on classics include a burnt pineapple caipirinha, smoked red pepper Bloody Mary, or white chocolate and cardamom mudslide.

MAURI
BAKERY €

Map p290 (☎93 215 10 20; www.pastelerias mauri.com; Rambla de Catalunya 102; pastries €3.50-6.50; ⊗8am-midnight Mon-Fri, 9am-10pm Sat, 9am-4.30pm Sun; ⋈Diagonal) Ever since it opened in 1929, this grand old pastry shop and teahouse has dazzled its regular customers with its spectacular sweets, chocolate croissants and gourmet delicatessen items. Dining on the terrace incurs a surcharge of €2 per dish.

CRUSTO
BAKERY €

Map p290 (☎93 487 05 51; www.crusto.es; Carrer de València 246; pastries €3-5.50; ⊗7.30am-9pm Mon-Fri, 8.30am-9pm Sat, 9am-3pm Sun; ☎; ⋈Passeig de Gràcia) A French-inspired bakery and pastry shop, Crusto's aromas of freshly baked bread, baguettes, croissants and countless pastries will be enough to convince you that it's worth pulling up a stool here for breakfast or weekend brunch.

CAFÉ SAN TELMO
CAFE €

Map p290 (☎93 439 17 09; www.gruposantelmo. com; Carrer de Buenos Aires 60; mains €8-13.50; ⊗8.30am-2am Mon-Wed, 8.30am-3am Thu-Sat, 9am-1am Sun; ☎; ⋈Hospital Clínic) Framed by big windows, this stylish corner cafe serves hearty breakfasts, sandwiches (such as Spanish roast beef and mustard or Milanese chicken with tomato and Brie), 'eco-burgers' (like the Palermo, with beef, mozzarella, pesto and herb mayo), salads and the like, along with a great list of gin and tonics.

EL RINCÓN MAYA
MEXICAN €

Map p290 (☎93 451 39 46; Carrer de València 183; mains €6-10; ⊗9pm-midnight Mon, 1.30-4pm & 8.30pm-midnight Tue-Sat; ☎; ⋈Universitat) Getting a seat in this modest, warm and simple Mexican eatery can be a trial but it's worth it. Pocket-sized serves of nachos, guacamole and fajitas all burst with flavour, as do the *tacos de pibil* (pork tacos). The owner-chef spent much of his life in the restaurant business in Mexico City.

AMALTEA
VEGETARIAN €

Map p290 (☎93 454 86 13; www.restaurante amaltea.com; Carrer de la Diputació 164; set menus day €8.90-10.90, evening €15.90; ⊗1-4pm & 8-11pm Mon-Thu, 1-4pm & 8-11.45pm Fri & Sat; ☎⌨; ⋈Urgell) Framed by a fresco of blue sky, this vegetarian eatery serves simple *menús del día* (daily set menus) and two-course evening meals. Most mains (curries, stews, roast veggies) are accompanied by rice.

★AUTO ROSELLON
INTERNATIONAL €€

Map p290 (☎93 853 93 20; www.autorosellon. com; Carrer de Rosselló 182; mains €12-18; ⊗8am-1am Mon-Wed, 8am-2am Thu & Fri, 9am-2am Sat, 9am-midnight Sun; ☎⌨; ⋈FGC Provença) ✍ With cornflower-blue paintwork and all its fresh produce on display, Auto Rosellon utilises mostly organic ingredients sourced from small producers and its own garden in dishes like eggs Benedict, salmon tartare with avocado, ricotta gnocchi with confit tomatoes and thyme, and slow-roasted pork tacos. Homemade juices and rose lemonade are exceptional; there are also great cocktails and craft beers.

PARKING PIZZA
PIZZA €€

Map p290 (☎93 633 96 45; www.parkingpizza. com; Carrer de Londres 98; pizza €9.50-14.50; ⊗1-4pm & 8-11pm Mon-Sat, 1-4pm Sun; ⋈FGC Provença) In this garage-style space, you might well have to share a long unvarnished wooden table, squeezed in on a cardboard box stool. The wood-fired pizzas more than make up for any forced intimacy, however, as do the starters, which include a creamy burrata *stracciatella* and a superb red quinoa salad with guacamole and a poached egg.

LA BODEGUETA PROVENÇA
TAPAS €€

Map p290 (☎93 215 17 25; www.provenca. labodegueta.cat; Carrer de Provença 233; tapas €6-15, mains €9.50-16; ⊗7am-1.45am Mon-Fri, 8am-1.45am Sat, 1pm-12.45am Sun; ☎; ⋈FGC Provença) The 'Little Wine Cellar' offers classic tapas presented with a touch of class, from *calamares a la andaluza* (lightly battered squid rings) to *cecina* (dried cured veal meat). The house speciality is *ous estrellats* (literally 'smashed eggs') – a mix of scrambled egg white, egg yolk, potato and ingredients ranging from foie gras to *morcilla* (black pudding).

Pair it with a good Ribera del Duero or *caña* (little glass) of beer. A lunchtime *menú* is €15.

CERVESERIA CATALANA
TAPAS €€

Map p290 (☎93 216 03 68; Carrer de Mallorca 236; tapas €3-14; ⊗9am-1.30am; ⋈FGC Provença) The 'Catalan Brewery' is perfect at all hours: for a morning coffee and croissant, or sangria, *montaditos* (canapés) and tapas at lunch or dinner. You can sit at the bar, on the pavement terrace or in the restaurant at the back. The variety of hot tapas, salads and other snacks draws a well-dressed crowd. No reservations.

CERVESERIA BRASSERIA GALLEGA

SEAFOOD €€

Map p290 (☑93 177 07 29; Carrer de Casanova 238; mains €9.50-19.50; ☺1.30-4pm & 9pm-midnight Mon-Sat, closed Aug; ☜; ⓜHospital Clínic) You could walk right by this modest establishment without giving it a second glance. If you did, you'd notice it was chock-full of locals immersed in animated banter and surrounded by plates of abundant Galician classics. The fresh *pulpo a la gallega* (spicy octopus chunks with potatoes) as a starter marks this place as a cut above the competition.

The setting is simple, the meat dishes succulent and the *fideuà* (Catalan-style paella with vermicelli noodles as the base) full of seafood flavour.

EL VELÓDROMO

TAPAS, MEDITERRANEAN €€

Map p290 (☑93 430 60 22; www.moritz.com; Carrer de Muntaner 213; tapas €2.50-10.50, mains €9.50-24; ☺kitchen 1pm-1am, bar 24hr; ☜; ⓜHospital Clínic) The restoration of this history-steeped literary tavern by Barcelona brewer Moritz brought back a wonderfully atmospheric establishment. Stop in for an aperitif and tapas or more substantial dishes such as salmon with caramelised cabbage or veal meatballs with fresh tomato and mozzarella. The spectacular high-ceilinged space retains many of its original art deco fittings.

SHIBUI

JAPANESE €€

Map p290 (☑93 321 90 04; www.shibui restaurantes.com; Carrer del Comte d'Urgell 272; mains €13-28; ☺1-3.45pm & 8.30-11pm; ☜; ⓜHospital Clínic) Shibui is where discerning sushi-loving locals come to dine on quality Japanese food. Go for the sushi and sashimi 'platters', which are served in wicker boats, Japanese style.

CU-CUT!

SPANISH €€

Map p290 (☑93 667 79 69; www.cu-cut.cat; Carrer d'Enric Granados 68; mains €9-13; ☺10am-2am; ⓡFGC Provença) Named after a popular Catalan satirical magazine from the early 19th century, Cu-Cut! is a beautiful beamed tavern with a large covered porch out front, a timber bar and a long, romantically lit dining room. There are dishes from all over Spain and further afield, including octopus *a feira* (with paprika), roast Iberian pork and hake ceviche.

TAKTIKA BERRI

PINTXOS €€

Map p290 (☑93 453 47 59; Carrer de València 169; pintxos €4-15.50, mains €12-28; ☺1-4pm & 8.30-11pm Mon-Fri, 1-4pm Sat, closed early-late Aug; ☜; ⓜHospital Clínic) Reservations are essential at Taktika Berri, which teems with diners here for some of the best *pintxos* (Basque tapas) in town. Morsels like blood sausage or *bacalao* (salt cod) with potato gratin are snapped up as soon as they arrive from the kitchen, so keep your eyes peeled.

★LASARTE

MODERN EUROPEAN €€€

Map p290 (☑93 445 32 42; www.restaurant lasarte.com; Carrer de Mallorca 259; mains €52-58; ☺1.30-3.30pm & 8.30-10.30pm Tue-Sat, closed 1st 3 weeks Aug; ⓜDiagonal) One of the preeminent restaurants in Barcelona – and the city's first to gain three Michelin stars – Lasarte is overseen by lauded chef Martín Berasategui. From Duroc pig's trotters with quince to squid tartare with kaffir consommé, this is seriously sophisticated stuff, served in an ultra-contemporary dining room by waiting staff who could put the most overawed diners at ease.

For an all-out dining extravaganza, order the 12-course tasting menu (€210).

★DISFRUTAR

MODERN EUROPEAN €€€

Map p290 (☑93 348 68 96; www.en.disfrutar barcelona.com; Carrer de Villarroel 163; tasting menus €120-185; ☺1-2.45pm & 8-9.45pm Tue-Sat; ⓜHospital Clínic) Disfrutar ('Enjoy' in Catalan) is among the city's finest restaurants, with two Michelin stars. Run by alumni of Ferran Adrià's game-changing (now closed) El Bulli restaurant, nothing is as it seems, such as black and green olives that are actually chocolate ganache with orange-blossom water.

The decor is fabulously on point, with latticed brickwork and trademark geometric ceramics from Catalan design team Equipo Creativo, and the service is faultless.

★MONT BAR

BISTRO €€€

Map p290 (☑93 323 95 90; www.montbar.com; Carrer de la Diputació 220; tapas €2-13, mains €12.50-26.50; ☺noon-3.30pm & 7pm-midnight; ⓜUniversitat) Named for the owner's Val d'Aran hometown, this stylish wine-bar-style space with black-and-white floors, forest-green banquette and bottle-lined walls offers next-level cooking. Exquisite tapas (pig's trotters with baby shrimp; plankton meringue with sea anemone and

Mascarpone) precede 'small plate' mains (tuna belly with pine-nut emulsion) and showstopping desserts (sheep's milk ice cream with blackcurrant liqueur sauce). Reservations essential.

Stunning wines (over 250 varieties) span all price points.

CINC SENTITS INTERNATIONAL €€€
Map p290 (📞93 323 94 90; www.cincsentits. com; Carrer d'Aribau 58; tasting menus €100-120; ⊙1.30-2.30pm & 8.30-9.30pm Tue-Sat; Ⓜ Passeig de Gràcia) Enter the realm of the 'Five Senses' to indulge in a jaw-dropping tasting menu consisting of a series of small, experimental dishes (there is no à la carte, although dishes can be tweaked to suit diners' requests). The use of fresh local produce, such as Costa Brava line-caught fish and top-quality Extremadura suckling pig, is key.

Also key is the kind of creative genius that has earned chef Jordi Artal a Michelin star. A lunch *menú* is available for €55.

SPEAKEASY INTERNATIONAL €€€
Map p290 (📞93 217 50 80; www.drymartiniorg. com; Carrer d'Aribau 162; mains €18.50-28; ⊙8-11pm Mon-Sat; 🚉FGC Provença) This clandestine restaurant lurks behind the Dry Martini bar (p142). You will be shown a door through the open kitchen area to the 'storeroom', lined with hundreds of bottles of backlit, quality tipples. Tempting menu options might include prawn ravioli with Parmesan crème or venison with braised celery.

Dark decor, a few works of art, low lighting and light jazz complement the smooth service.

MONVÍNIC SPANISH €€€
Map p290 (📞93 272 61 87; www.monvinic.com; Carrer de la Diputació 249; mains €17-36; ⊙1.30-3.30pm & 8-10.30pm Tue-Fri, 8-10.30pm Mon & Sat; Ⓜ Passeig de Gracia) 🌿 Opening to a leafy, table-filled garden, this is the *'espacio culinario'* of world-famous wine emporium Monvínic (p142). The menu offers elaborate confections such as sea urchin and lobster consommé, chargrilled duck with red-wine-poached pears or langoustine ravioli. Its ingredients, wine and building materials are all sourced from Catalonia.

Designed by Alfons Tost, the sustainable space has air-purifying plants, energy-efficient LED lighting, and a water and food recycling system.

🍴 La Dreta de L'Eixample

★TAPAS 24 TAPAS €
Map p294 (📞93 488 09 77; www.carlesabellan. com; Carrer de la Diputació 269; tapas €2.20-12; ⊙9am-midnight; 📶; Ⓜ Passeig de Gràcia) Hotshot chef Carles Abellán runs this basement tapas haven known for its gourmet versions of old faves. Highlights include the *bikini* (toasted ham and cheese sandwich – here the ham is cured and the truffle makes all the difference) and zesty *boquerones al limón* (lemon-marinated anchovies). You can't book but it's worth the wait.

For dessert, choose *xocolata amb pa, sal i oli* (delicious balls of chocolate in olive oil with a touch of salt and wafer).

HAWKER 45 ASIAN €
Map p294 (📞93 763 83 15; Carrer de Casp 45; mains €8.50-16; ⊙1-4pm & 8-11pm Mon-Fri, 12.30-4pm & 8-11.30pm Sat, 12.30-4pm Sun; Ⓜ Tetuan) Taking its cues from an Asian hawkers market, this aromatic spot sizzles up street-food dishes such as spicy Malaysian squid laksa, Indonesian lamb satay, Korean Kalbi pork ribs with rice cakes, Thai crying tiger beef salad and Singaporean green mango sambal with steamed crab. Its six-course tasting menu (€35) is best paired with craft beers (€42) or Asian-inspired cocktails (€60).

Dine at the long, red bar overlooking the open kitchen or head out the back to the cavernous postindustrial dining space with bare beams and ventilation pipes.

GRANJA PETITBO MEDITERRANEAN €
Map p294 (📞93 265 65 03; www.granjapetitbo. com; Passeig de Sant Joan 82; sandwiches €4-8, mains €8-12; ⊙9am-11pm Mon-Wed, 9am-11.30pm Thu & Fri, 10am-11.30pm Sat, 10am-5pm Sun; 📶; Ⓜ Girona) High ceilings, battered leather armchairs and dramatic flower arrangements set the tone in this sunny little corner cafe, beloved of local hipsters and young families. As well as an all-day parade of homemade cakes, freshly squeezed juices and superior coffee, there are burgers, salads and pastas, along with a brunch menu on weekends.

CANTINA MEXICANA MEXICAN €
Map p294 (📞93 667 66 68; www.cantinala mexicana.es; Carrer de València 427; mains €7-13; ⊙1pm-midnight; 🖉; Ⓜ Sagrada Família) Just far enough from La Sagrada Família to dodge

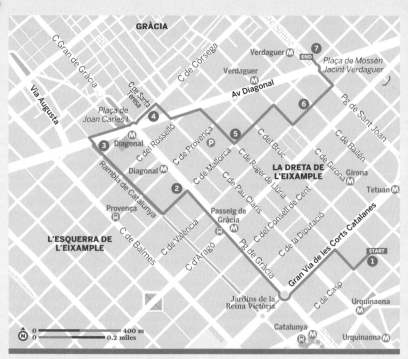

Neighbourhood Walk
More Modernisme in L'Eixample

START CASA CALVET
END CASA MACAYA
LENGTH 4KM; ONE HOUR

Gaudí's most conventional contribution to L'Eixample is **①Casa Calvet**, built in 1900. Inspired by baroque, the noble ashlar facade is broken up by protruding wrought-iron balconies. Inside, the main attraction is the staircase, which you can admire if you eat in the swanky restaurant.

②Casa Enric Batlló was completed in 1896 by Josep Vilaseca (1848–1910), part of the Comtes de Barcelona hotel. The brickwork facade is especially graceful when lit up at night.

Puig i Cadafalch let his imagination loose on **③Casa Serra** (1903–08), a neo-Gothic whimsy that is today home to government offices. With its central tower topped by a conical roof, grandly decorated upper-floor windows and tiled roof, you'll find yourself pondering what a strange house it must have been to live in for its former residents.

④Casa Comalatis, built in 1911 by Salvador Valeri (1873–1954), is similarly strik-ing. Note Gaudí's obvious influence on the main facade, with its wavy roof and bulging balconies. Head around the back to Carrer de Còrsega to see a more playful facade, with its windows stacked like cards.

Completed in 1912, **⑤Casa Thomas** was one of Domènech i Montaner's ear-lier efforts – the floral motifs and reptile figurines are trademarks and the massive ground-level wrought-iron decoration (and protection?) is magnificent. Wander inside to the Cubiña design store to admire his interior work including brick columns.

⑥Casa Llopis i Bofill is an interesting block of flats designed by Antoni Gallissà (1861–1903) in 1902. The graffiti-covered facade is particularly striking to the visitor's eye. The use of elaborate parabolic arches on the ground floor is a clear Modernista touch, as are the wrought-iron balconies.

Puig i Cadafalch's **⑦Casa Macaya** (1901) has a wonderful courtyard and features the typical playful, pseudo-Gothic decoration that characterises many of the architect's projects. It belongs to La Caixa bank and is occasionally used for temporary exhibitions, when visitors are permitted to enter.

the crowds, this simply decorated spot serves authentic Mexican fare, including over 20 different corn or flour tacos (such as sautéed shrimp and beans), *cochinita pibil* (traditional slow-roasted pork seasoned with annatto seeds) and four styles of ceviche. Vegetarian options include a delicious pumpkin-flower quesadilla.

MR KAO   DIM SUM €€

Map p294 (☑93 445 25 88; www.misterkao.com; Carrer de València 271; dim sum €2.80-4, mains €11-28; ⊙12.30-3.30pm & 8.30-11.30pm Tue-Sat, 12.30-3.30pm Sun; MPasseig de Gràcia) Within the grand Hotel Claris, this elegant Shanghai-style dim sum restaurant serves top-flight dumplings. They're not cheap, but every bite is a joy; the *jiao zi* with pig's trotters are especially good, as are the *siu mai* with langoustines and trout roe. More substantial dishes include Peking duck and noodles with wild mushrooms, poached egg and truffles.

ENTREPANES DÍAZ   SANDWICHES €€

Map p294 (☑93 415 75 82; Carrer de Pau Claris 189; sandwiches €6-10, tapas €3-10; ⊙1pm-midnight; MDiagonal) Gourmet sandwiches, from roast beef to suckling pig or crispy squid with squid-ink aioli, are the highlight at this sparkling old-style bar, along with sharing plates of Spanish specialities such as sea urchins and prawn fritters or blood-sausage croquettes. The policy of only hiring experienced waiters over 50 lends a certain gravitas to the operation and some especially charming service.

Black-and-white photos of Barcelona line the walls.

CHICHA LIMONÁ   MEDITERRANEAN €€

Map p294 (☑93 277 64 03; www.chichalimona.com; Passeig de Sant Joan 80; mains €12-17; ⊙9.30am-1am Tue-Thu, to 2am Fri & Sat, to 5pm Sun; ☎; MTetuan) Passeig de Sant Joan is a hipster hot spot, and bright, bustling Chicha Limoná has provided them with somewhere great to eat. Steak tartare with yuzu dressing, rabbit tacos, yoghurt-marinated salmon and tequila, mango and chilli sorbet are among the oft-changing dishes (set menu €13.90), along with steaming pizza.

CAN KENJI   JAPANESE €€

Map p294 (☑93 476 18 23; www.cankenji.com; Carrer del Rosselló 325; mains €10-14; ⊙1-3.30pm & 8.30-11pm; MVerdaguer) The chef of this understated little *izakaya* (the Japanese version of a tavern) gets his ingredients fresh from the city's markets, with traditional Japanese recipes receiving a Mediterranean touch. Choices include sardine tempura with an aubergine, miso and anchovy purée, or *tataki* (lightly grilled meat) of *bonito* (tuna) with *salmorejo* (a Cordoban cold tomato and bread soup).

CASA ALFONSO   SPANISH €€

Map p294 (☑93 301 97 83; www.casaalfonso.com; Carrer de Roger de Llúria 6; tapas & sandwiches €4-15, mains €13-23; ⊙8am-1am Mon-Fri, 1pm-1am Sat; ☎; MUrquinaona) In business since 1934, Casa Alfonso is perfect for a morning coffee or a tapas stop at the long marble bar. Wood-panelled and festooned with old photos, posters and swinging hams, it attracts a faithful local clientele at all hours for its *flautas* (thin baguettes with a choice of fillings), hams, cheeses, hot dishes and homemade desserts.

There are also more substantial dishes, mostly involving grilled meat. Consider rounding off with an *alfonsito* (miniature Irish coffee).

CASA AMALIA   CATALAN €€

Map p294 (☑93 458 94 58; www.casamaliabcn.com; Passatge del Mercat 4-6; mains €9-20; ⊙1-3.30pm & 9-10.30pm Tue-Sat, 1-3.30pm Sun; MGirona) This very local split-level restaurant is popular for its hearty Catalan cooking that uses fresh produce from the busy market next door. On Thursdays during winter it offers the mountain classic, *escudella* (Catalan stew). Otherwise, try light variations on local cuisine like the *bacallà al allioli de poma* (cod in apple-based aioli sauce). The three-course *menú del día* is a bargain at €15.50.

CAFE EMMA   BISTRO €€

Map p294 (☑93 215 12 16; www.cafe-emma.com; Carrer de Pau Claris 142; mains €14-25.50; ⊙8am-10.30pm Mon-Fri, 9am-10.30pm Sat & Sun; ☎; MPasseig de Grácia) French-inspired Cafe Emma combines local and international influences, though wines are sourced solely from France. It's a superb bet for all-day dining on its terrace, in its dining room or at its bar. Tartines (open sandwiches), such as goat cheese, beetroot and roast beef, are excellent. Don't miss the freshly shucked oysters with a crisp glass of white in season.

EMBAT   MEDITERRANEAN €€

Map p294 (☑93 458 08 55; Carrer de Mallorca 304; mains €10.50-21; ⊙1-3.45pm Mon-Wed, 1-3.45pm & 8.30-11pm Thu-Sat; ☎; MVerdaguer)

LA SAGRADA FAMÍLIA & L'EIXAMPLE EATING

Enthusiastic young chefs turn out beautifully presented dishes in this bright, Scandinavian-style setting. Indulge perhaps in *raviolis de pollo amb bacon i calabassó* (chicken ravioli in a sauce of finely chopped bacon, courgette and other vegetables) followed by melt-in-the-mouth *lluç amb pa amb tomàquet, carxofes i maionesa de peres* (thick-cut hake on tomato-drenched bread, with artichoke slices and pear mayonnaise).

DE TAPA MADRE
CATALAN €€

Map p294 (☏93 459 31 34; www.detapamadre. com; Carrer de Mallorca 301; tapas €4-7.50, mains €14-25.50; ⏱11.30am-midnight; MVerdaguer) A lively atmosphere greets you from the moment you swing open the door. A few tiny tables line the window (there's also terrace seating out front), but head upstairs for more space in the gallery, which hovers above the array of tapas on the bar below. The *arròs amb llamàntol* (a hearty rice dish with lobster) is delicious.

CASA CALVET
CATALAN €€€

Map p294 (☏93 412 40 12; www.casacalvet.es; Carrer de Casp 48; mains €27-35; ⏱1-3.30pm & 8-10.30pm Mon-Sat; MUrquinaona) An early Gaudí masterpiece loaded with his trademark curvy features houses a swish restaurant (just to the right of the building's main entrance). Dress up and ask for an intimate *taula cabina* (wooden booth). You could opt for scallop- and prawn-stuffed artichokes, partridge and chestnut casserole or veal with duck-liver sauce.

A four-course lunch menu costs €38, while a five-course dinner menu is €59.

PATAGONIA BEEF & WINE
SOUTH AMERICAN €€€

Map p294 (☏93 304 37 35; www.patagoniabw. com; Gran Via de les Corts Catalanes 660; mains €20-38; ⏱1.30-3.30pm & 7-11pm Mon-Thu, to 11.30pm Fri & Sat, to 10.30pm Sun; 🕾; MPasseig de Gràcia) This stylish restaurant delivers on its promise of an Argentinian meatfest. Start with *empanadas* (small pastries with various meat fillings), then head for a hearty main, such as a juicy beef *medallón con salsa de colmenillas* (a medallion in a morel sauce) or such classics as the *bife de chorizo* (sirloin strip) or Brazilian *picanha* (rump).

You can choose from one of five side dishes to accompany your pound of flesh.

🍷 DRINKING & NIGHTLIFE

🍷 L'Esquerra de L'Eixample

DRY MARTINI
BAR

Map p290 (☏93 217 50 80; www.drymartiniorg. com; Carrer d'Aribau 162-166; ⏱1pm-2.30am Mon-Fri, 6.30pm-2.30am Sat & Sun; ☒FGC Provença) Waiters make expert cocktail suggestions, but the house drink, taken at the bar or on one of the plush green banquettes, is always a good bet. The gin and tonic comes in an enormous mug-sized glass – one will take you most of the night.

Out the back hides a superb restaurant, Speakeasy (p139).

★MILANO
COCKTAIL BAR

Map p290 (☏93 112 71 50; www.camparimilano. com; Ronda de la Universitat 35; ⏱noon-3am; MCatalunya) Completely invisible from street level, this gem of hidden Barcelona nightlife is a subterranean old-school cocktail bar with velvet banquettes and glass-fronted cabinets, presided over by white-jacketed waiters. Live music (Cuban, jazz, blues, flamenco and swing) plays nightly; a DJ takes over after 11pm. Fantastic cocktails include the Picasso (tequila, honey, absinthe and lemon) and six different Bloody Marys.

★MONVÍNIC
WINE BAR

Map p290 (☏93 272 61 87; www.monvinic.com; Carrer de la Diputació 249; ⏱1-11pm Tue-Fri, 7-11pm Mon & Sat; MPasseig de Gràcia) 🍷 At this rhapsody to wine, the digital wine list details more than 3000 international varieties searchable by origin, year or grape. Some 50 selections are available by the glass; you can, of course, order by the bottle too. There is an emphasis on affordability, but if you want to splash out, there are fantastic vintage options.

★NAPAR BCN
BREWERY

Map p290 (☏93 408 91 62; www.naparbcn.com; Carrer de la Diputació 223; ⏱5pm-midnight Tue & Wed, to 1am Thu, to 2am Fri & Sat; 🕾; MUniversitat) A standout on Barcelona's burgeoning craft-beer scene, Napar has 14 beers on tap, six of which are brewed on-site, including IPA, pale ale and stout. There's also an accomplished list of bottled beers.

It's a stunning space, with a gleaming steampunk aesthetic and a great rock and indie soundtrack. Creative food changes seasonally.

GARAGE BEER CO   CRAFT BEER

Map p290 (☑93 528 59 89; www.garagebeer.co; Carrer del Consell de Cent 261; ☺5pm-midnight Mon-Thu, 5pm-2.30am Fri, noon-3am Sat, 2pm-midnight Sun; ⓂUniversitat) One of the first of the slew of craft-beer bars to pop up in Barcelona, Garage brews its own in a space at the bar, and offers around 10 different styles at a time. The eponymous Garage (a delicate session IPA) and Slinger (a more robust IPA) are always present on the board.

Other favourites include Imperial Chocolate (stout) and Culture Trip (raspberry Berliner Weisse).

BIERCAB   CRAFT BEER

Map p290 (☑644 689045; www.biercab.com; Carrer de Muntaner 55; ☺bar noon-midnight Mon-Thu, noon-2am Fri & Sat, 5pm-midnight Sun, shop 3.30pm-10pm Mon-Sat; 🐾; ⓂUniversitat) Beneath an artistic ceiling installation resembling a forest of giant matchsticks, this brilliant craft-beer bar has 30 brews from around the world rotating on its taps. Burgers to accompany them are made from Wagyu beef and named for Barcelona neighbourhoods. Pop into its adjacent shop for another 500 bottled varieties kept cold in fridges.

MONKEY FACTORY   COCKTAIL BAR

Map p290 (☑93 681 78 93; Carrer de Còrsega 234; ☺6.30pm-2am Tue & Wed, to 3am Thu-Sat; ⓇFGC Provença) DJs spin on weekends at this high-spirited venue but it's positively hopping from early on most nights. 'Funky monkey' (triple sec, gin, lime and egg white), 'chimpa sour' (cardamom-infused pisco sour) and 'chita' (passionfruit purée, vodka, cinnamon syrup and ginger) are among the inventive cocktails mixed up behind the neon-green-lit bar.

ANTILLA BCN   CLUB

Map p290 (☑93 451 45 64; www.antillasalsa.com; Carrer d'Aragó 141; cover Fri & Sat €10; ☺10pm-4am Wed, 11pm-4am Thu, 11pm-6am Fri & Sat, 7pm-2am Sun; ⓂUrgell) *The* salsateca in town, this is the place to come for Cuban *son*, merengue, salsa and a whole lot more.

CITY HALL   CLUB

Map p290 (☑93 238 07 22; www.cityhallbarcelona.com; Rambla de Catalunya 2-4; cover from €10; ☺10pm-6am Mon, 12.30am-6am Tue-Sun; ⓂCatalunya) A long corridor leads to the dance floor of this venerable and popular club, located in a former theatre. Music styles, from house and other electric sounds to funk, change nightly; check the agenda online. The cover charge includes a drink.

It's also a live music venue (p145).

ÁTAME   GAY

Map p290 (☑93 421 41 33; Carrer del Consell de Cent 257; ☺7.30pm-2.30am Tue, 8.30pm-2.30am Wed, Thu & Sun, 8.30pm-3am Fri & Sat; ⓂUniversitat) Cool for a coffee earlier on, Átame (Tie Me Up) heats up later in the night when the gay crowd comes out to play. There is usually a raunchy show on Friday nights.

AIRE   LESBIAN

Map p290 (Sala Diana; ☑93 487 83 42; www.grupoarena.com; Carrer de la Diputació 233; cover Fri/Sat €5/6; ☺11pm-2.30am Thu-Sat; ⓂPasseig de Gràcia) At this popular lesbian hang-out, the dance floor is spacious and there's usually a DJ in command of the tunes, which veer from hits of the '80s and '90s to Latin and techno. As a rule, only male friends of the girls are allowed entry, although in practice the crowd tends to be fairly mixed.

PLATA BAR   GAY

Map p290 (☑93 452 46 36; www.platabar.com; Carrer del Consell de Cent 233; ☺8pm-1.30am Wed & Thu, to 3am Fri & Sat; ⓂUniversitat) Summer seats on the corner terrace of this wide-open bar attract a lot of lads hopping between the area's gay bars. Inside, metallic horse-saddle stools are lined up at the bar and high tables, the music is a mix of dance and trance, and bartenders whip up eye-popping cocktails.

COSMO   CAFE

Map p290 (☑93 105 79 92; www.galeriacosmo.com; Carrer d'Enric Granados 3; ☺10am-10pm; ⓂUniversitat) Set on a pedestrian strip just behind the university, this groovy cafe-gallery has a bicycle hanging from the high, white walls, bright splashy murals and gaily painted ventilation pipes, and even makes a feature of its fire hose. Along with fresh juices, hot chocolate, teas, pastries and snacks, it serves beer and wine.

LA SAGRADA FAMÍLIA & L'EIXAMPLE DRINKING & NIGHTLIFE

THE GAIXAMPLE

The area just above Gran Via de les Corts Catalanes and to the left of Rambla de Catalunya is popularly known as the 'Gaixample', for its proliferation of gay bars and restaurants. Some of the best include **Átame** (p143), **Arena Classic** and **Aire** (p143; this last one's for the ladies), but note that some old favourites are also to be found in adjoining neighbourhoods, such as **Metro** (p198) in Sant Antoni.

QUILOMBO   BAR

Map p290 (☑606 144272; Carrer d'Aribau 149; ☺9pm-2.30am Mon-Thu, 8.30pm-3am Fri & Sat; ☒FGC Provença) Some formulas just work, and this place has been working since the 1970s. Set up some guitars in the table-packed back room, add some cheapish pre-prepared mojitos and plastic tubs of nuts, and let the punters do the rest. They pour in, creating plenty of *quilombo* (fuss). Live music plays most nights from 11pm and impromptu parties are common.

LA FIRA   BAR

Map p290 (☑682 323714; Carrer de Provença 171; cover €14; ☺11pm-5am Thu, to 6am Fri & Sat; ☒FGC Provença) Wander in past crazy mirrors, penny slot machines and other ancient fairground attractions from Germany as well as futuristic furniture like glowing cuboid stools. The music swings wildly from house through '90s hits to Spanish pop classics. Admission includes two drinks. With 150 spirits on hand, it claims to have 500 varieties of shots.

PUNTO BCN   GAY

Map p290 (☑93 451 91 52; www.grupoarena. com; Carrer de Muntaner 65; ☺6pm-2.30am Sun-Thu, to 3am Fri & Sat; ☒Universitat) It's an oldie but a goody. A big bar over two levels with a slightly older crowd, this place fills to bursting on Friday and Saturday nights with its blend of Spanish pop and dance. It's a friendly early stop on a gay night out, and you can shoot a round of pool here.

LA CHAPELLE   GAY

Map p290 (☑93 453 30 76; Carrer de Muntaner 67; ☺4pm-2am Sun-Thu, to 2.30am Fri & Sat; ☒Universitat) A typical long, narrow Eixample bar with white-tiled walls, La Chapelle houses a plethora of crucifixes and niches that far outdo what you'd find in any other 'chapel'. No need for six-pack abs here: this is a relaxed gay meeting place that welcomes all types.

BACON BEAR   GAY

Map p290 (☑93 431 00 00; Carrer de Casanova 64; ☺6pm-2.30am Mon-Thu, to 3am Fri & Sat, to 2.30am Sun; ☒Urgell) Every bear needs a cave to go to, and this is a rather friendly one. It's really just a big bar for burly gay folk. The music cranks up on weekends.

ARENA MADRE   GAY

Map p290 (☑93 487 83 42; www.grupoarena. com; Carrer de Balmes 32; cover Sun-Fri €6, Sat €12; ☺12.30-5.45am Sun-Thu, to 6.45am Fri & Sat; ☒Passeig de Gràcia) Popular with a hot young crowd, Arena Madre is one of the top clubs in town for boys seeking boys. Mainly electronic and house, with a striptease show on Monday, techno on Thursday, and live shows throughout the week. Heteros are welcome but a minority.

ARENA CLASSIC   GAY

Map p290 (☑93 487 83 42; www.grupoarena. com; Carrer de la Diputació 233; cover Fri/Sat €6/12; ☺2.30am-6am Fri & Sat; ☒Passeig de Gràcia) Spinning mostly techno, Arena Classic attracts an upbeat, energetic gay crowd. Entry includes a drink.

🍺 La Dreta de L'Eixample

★LES GENS QUE J'AIME   BAR

Map p294 (☑93 215 68 79; www.lesgensque jaime.com; Carrer de València 286; ☺6pm-2.30am Sun-Thu, 7pm-3am Fri & Sat; ☒Passeig de Gràcia) Atmospheric and intimate, this basement relic of the 1960s follows a deceptively simple formula: chilled jazz music in the background, minimal lighting from an assortment of flea-market lamps and a cosy, cramped scattering of red-velvet-backed lounges around tiny dark tables.

EL VITI   BAR

Map p294 (☑93 633 83 36; www.elviti.com; Passeig de Sant Joan 62; ☺noon-midnight Sun-Thu, to 1am Fri & Sat; ☎; ☒Tetuan) Along the hip Passeig de Sant Joan, El Viti checks all the boxes – high ceilings, brick walls both bare and glazed, black-clad staff and a barrel of artisanal vermouth on the bar. It also serves a good line in tapas.

CAFÈ DEL CENTRE
CAFE

Map p294 (☑93 488 11 01; Carrer de Girona 69; ⊙9am-11pm Mon-Fri, 11am-11pm Sat; ☎; MGirona) Step back into the 19th century in this cafe that's been in business since 1873. The mahogany bar extends down the right side as you enter, fronted by marble-topped tables and wooden chairs. It exudes an almost melancholy air by day but gets busy at night, when live jazz piano plays. It stocks 50 beers and 15 loose-leaf teas.

MICHAEL COLLINS PUB
IRISH PUB

Map p294 (☑93 459 19 64; www.michaelcollins pubs.com; Plaça de la Sagrada Família 4; ⊙1pm-2.30am Sun-Thu, to 3am Fri & Sat; ☎; MSagrada Família) To be sure of a little Catalan-Irish *craic,* this barn-sized, storming pub beloved by locals and expats is just the ticket. Traditional Irish music sessions strike up on Mondays; live music also plays most weekends.

It's ideal for football fans wanting big-screen action over their pints, too.

NEW CHAPS
GAY

Map p294 (☑93 215 53 65; www.newchaps.com; Avinguda Diagonal 365; ⊙9pm-3am Sun-Thu, to 3.30am Fri & Sat; MDiagonal) Leather lovers get in some close-quarters inspection on the dance floor and especially in the dark room, downstairs past the fairly dark loos in the vaulted cellars. It's a classic handlebar-moustache gay porn kinda place that attracts an older crowd.

⭐ ENTERTAINMENT

CITY HALL
LIVE MUSIC

Map p290 (☑93 238 07 22; www.cityhallbarcelona. com; Rambla de Catalunya 2-4; MCatalunya) Also home to a nightclub (p143), this former theatre is also the perfect size and shape for live music, holding a crowd of around 500. The acoustics are great and the layout means everyone gets a good view of the stage.

MEDITERRÁNEO
LIVE MUSIC

Map p290 (www.elmedi.net; Carrer de Balmes 129; ⊙10.30pm-3am; ℞FGC Provença) Free live music plays nightly at this student favourite. Order a beer and enjoy the free nuts at one of the tiny tables while waiting for the next act to tune up at the back. Often the young performers are surprisingly good.

MÉLIÈS CINEMES
CINEMA

Map p290 (☑93 451 00 51; www.meliescinemes. com; Carrer de Villarroel 102; tickets €4-7; MUrgell) A cosy cinema with two screens, the Méliès specialises in the best of recent releases from Hollywood and Europe.

TEATRE TÍVOLI
THEATRE

Map p294 (☑93 412 20 63; www.grupbalana. com; Carrer de Casp 8; ticket prices vary; ⊙box office 5-8pm & 90min before shows; MCatalunya) Dating from 1919, this grand theatre has three storeys of boxes and a generous stage. There's a fairly rapid turnover of drama and musicals, with pieces often not staying on for more than a couple of weeks. Concerts (such as Bruce Springsteen, Elvis Costello and Radiohead) also take place here.

 ## SHOPPING

⭐JOAN MÚRRIA
FOOD & DRINKS

Map p294 (☑93 215 57 89; www.murria.cat; Carrer de Roger de Llúria 85; ⊙10am-8.30pm Tue-Fri, 10am-2pm & 5-8.30pm Sat; MGirona) Ramon Casas designed the 1898 Modernista shopfront advertisements featured at this culinary temple of speciality food goods from around Catalonia and beyond. Artisan cheeses, Iberian hams, caviar, canned delicacies, smoked fish, *cavas* and wines, coffee and loose-leaf teas are among the treats in store.

⭐FLORES NAVARRO
FLOWERS

Map p294 (☑93 457 40 99; www.floristerias navarro.com; Carrer de València 320; ⊙24hr; MGirona) You never know when you might need flowers, and this florist never closes. Established in 1960, it's a vast space (or couple of spaces, in fact), and worth a visit just for the bank of colour and wonderful fragrance.

CACAO SAMPAKA
FOOD

Map p290 (☑93 272 08 33; www.cacaosampaka. com; Carrer del Consell de Cent 292; ⊙9am-9pm Mon-Sat; MPasseig de Gràcia) Chocoholics will be convinced they have died and passed on to a better place. Load up in the shop or head for the bar out the back where you can have a classic *xocolata* (hot chocolate) and munch on exquisite chocolate cakes, tarts, ice cream, sweets and sandwiches. The bonbons make particularly good presents.

ALTAÏR
BOOKS

Map p290 (🖉93 342 71 71; www.altair.es; Gran Via de les Corts Catalanes 616; ⊙10am-8.30pm Mon-Sat; 🕾; Ⓜ Catalunya) Enter a wonderland of travel in this extensive bookshop, which has enough guidebooks, maps, travel literature and other books to induce a severe case of itchy feet. It has a travellers noticeboard and, downstairs, a cafe.

DR BLOOM
FASHION & ACCESSORIES

Map p290 (🖉93 292 23 27; www.drbloom.es; Rambla de Catalunya 30; ⊙10am-9pm Mon-Sat; Ⓜ Passeig de Gràcia) A new collection comes out every month at Dr Bloom, so the stock is constantly rotating. Designed and made in Barcelona, the label's dresses, tops, shawls and more have an emphasis on bright colours and bold prints no matter the season.

SERGIO ARANDA
JEWELLERY

Map p294 (🖉648 796029; www.sergioaranda.shop; Carrer Roger de Llúria 93; ⊙10am-2pm & 5-8pm Mon-Fri, noon-2.30pm Sat; Ⓜ Passeig de Gràcia) Swiss-born jeweller Sergio Aranda has worked throughout Europe for some of the world's most prestigious names, and now creates unique pieces incorporating materials such as coins and cultured pearls. Exquisite items in his collections span all budgets.

LURDES BERGADA
FASHION & ACCESSORIES

Map p290 (🖉93 218 48 51; www.lurdesbergada.es; Rambla de Catalunya 112; ⊙10.30am-8.30pm Mon-Sat; Ⓜ Diagonal) Mother-and-son design team Lurdes Bergada and Syngman Cucala's classy men's and women's fashions are made from natural fibres and have attracted a cult following.

EL CORTE INGLÉS
DEPARTMENT STORE

Map p294 (🖉93 306 38 00; www.elcorteingles.es; Plaça de Catalunya 23; ⊙9.30am-9pm Mon-Sat; Ⓜ Catalunya) Spain's only remaining department-store chain stocks everything you'd expect, from computers to cushions and high fashion to homewares. Fabulous city views extend from the top-floor restaurant. Nearby branches include one at **Avinguda Diagonal 471-473** (Map p290; 🖉93 493 48 00; Ⓜ Hospital Clínic).

PURIFICACIÓN GARCÍA
FASHION & ACCESSORIES

Map p290 (🖉934961336; www.purificaciongarcia.com; Carrer de Provença 292; ⊙10am-8.30pm Mon-Sat; Ⓜ Diagonal) Spanish designer Purificación García's collections are breathtaking

LA SAGRADA FAMÍLIA & L'EIXAMPLE SHOPPING

🏃 Local Life
Shopping in the Quadrat d'Or

While visitors to L'Eixample do the sights, locals go shopping in the Quadrat d'Or, the grid of streets either side of Passeig de Gràcia. This is Barcelona at its most fashion- and design-conscious, which also describes a large proportion of L'Eixample's residents. All the big names are here, alongside boutiques of local designers who capture the essence of Barcelona cool.

❶ The New Wave

You could spend an entire day just along Passeig de Gràcia but detour for a moment to Lurdes Bergada, a boutique run by mother-and-son designer team Lurdes Bergada and Syngman Cucala. Their classy men's and women's fashions using natural fibres have attracted a cult following.

❷ A Pastry Stop

Time for a refuelling stop. Few pastry shops have such a long-established pedigree as Mauri (p137). The plush interior is capped by an ornate fresco dating back to Mauri's first days in 1929. Its croissants and feather-light *ensaïmadas* (sweet buns) are near perfect.

❸ Modernista Jewellery

This is more than just any old jewellery store. The boys from Bagués-Masriera (p149) have been chipping away at precious stones and moulding metal since the 19th century, and many of the classic pieces here have a flighty, Modernista influence. Bagués backs it up with service that owes much to old-school courtesies.

Above: El Corte Inglés (p146)

④ Luxury Luggage

While bags and suitcases in every conceivable colour of butter-soft leather are the mainstay at 1846-founded Loewe (p148), there is also a range of clothing for men and women, along with some stunning – and stunningly priced – accessories. The luxurious shop is fittingly housed in the Casa Lleó Morera (p132), with some interior details by Domènech i Montaner.

⑤ Say It with Chocolate

A sleek and modern temple to chocolate, Cacao Sampaka (p145) is both a cafe and shop, and is the perfect place to stock up with gifts to take back home. Select from every conceivable flavour (rosemary, perhaps, or curry?), either in bar form or as individual choccies to fill your own elegant little gift box.

⑥ Fine Wines

For superior souvenirs in liquid form, head to the state-of-the-art Monvínic (p142), a veritable temple of wine with more than 3000 wines in its cellar, including some extremely rare finds. Try before you buy in the wine bar (or over a meal at its restaurant).

⑦ Chill Down

Cosmo (p143) is a bright, white cavernous space, dotted with colour from the exhibitions that adorn its high walls. It has a nice selection of teas, cakes and snacks. Set on a pedestrian strip, it's perfect for an evening tipple inside the groovy interior or out on the terrace.

LA SAGRADA FAMÍLIA & L'EIXAMPLE SHOPPING

AN OUTLET OUTING

For the ultimate discount-fashion overdose, head out of town for some outlet shopping at **La Roca Village** (☑93 842 39 39; www.larocavillage.com; Santa Agnès de Malayanes; ☺10am-9pm Mon-Fri, to 10pm Sat & Sun). Here, a village has been given over to consumer madness. At a long line of Spanish and international fashion boutiques you'll find clothes, shoes, accessories and designer homewares at (they claim) up to 60% off normal retail prices.

To get here, follow the AP-7 tollway north from Barcelona, take exit 12 (marked Cardedeu) and follow the signs for 'Centre Comercial'. The Sagalés Bus Company organises the Shopping Express from Passeig de Gràcia and the World Trade Center – see www.sagales.com for details. Alternatively, take a slower bus from the same company from Fabra i Puig metro station (four departures Monday to Friday, three in August) or a *rodalies* train to Granollers and pick up the shuttle (Monday to Friday only) or a taxi there.

as much for their breadth as anything else. You'll find all kinds of clothing over this shop's two floors, from women's cardigans to men's ties, as well as light summer dresses and jeans.

REGIA COSMETICS
Map p290 (☑93 216 01 21; www.regia.es; Passeig de Gràcia 39; ☺9.30am-8.30pm Mon-Fri, 10.30am-8.30pm Sat; Ⓜ Passeig de Gràcia) In business since 1928, Regia stocks all the name brands and also has a private perfume museum (p134) out the back. Fragrances aside, it carries a range of cosmetics and has its own line of bath products.

MERCAT DEL NINOT MARKET
Map p290 (☑93 323 49 09; www.mercatdelninot. com; Carrer de Mallorca 133; ☺9am-8pm Mon-Fri, to 2pm Sat; ☞; Ⓜ Hospital Clínic) A gleaming, modern neighbourhood food market, selling mostly meat and fish, Mercat del Ninot also has a couple of stalls where you can grab a bite to eat.

MERCAT DE LA CONCEPCIÓ MARKET
Map p294 (☑675 693616; www.laconcepcio. cat; Carrer d'Aragó 313-317; ☺8am-8pm Tue-Fri, to 3pm Mon & Sat; Ⓜ Girona) Mercat de la Concepció has 54 stalls selling food, flowers, wine and more, including several on-site bars.

EL BULEVARD DELS ANTIQUARIS ANTIQUES
Map p290 (☑93 215 44 99; www.bulevarddels antiquaris.com; Passeig de Gràcia 55-57; ☺10.30am-8.30pm Mon-Sat; Ⓜ Passeig de Gràcia) More than 70 stores (be warned most close for lunch) are gathered under one roof

to offer the most varied selection of collector's pieces. These range from old porcelain dolls through to fine crystal, from Asian antique furniture to old French goods, and from African and other ethnic art to jewellery.

It's on the floor above the more general Bulevard Rosa (p149) arcade.

ADOLFO DOMÍNGUEZ FASHION & ACCESSORIES
Map p294 (☑93 487 41 70; www.adolfodominguez. com; Passeig de Gràcia 32; ☺10am-9pm Mon-Sat; Ⓜ Passeig de Gràcia) One of the stars of Spanish prêt-à-porter, this label produces classic men's and women's garments from quality materials. Encompassing anything from regal party gowns to kids' outfits (that might have you thinking of British aristocracy), the broad range generally has a conservative air, with elegant cuts that make no concessions to rebellious urban ideals.

LOEWE FASHION & ACCESSORIES
Map p290 (☑93 216 04 00; www.loewe.com; Passeig de Gràcia 35; ☺10am-8.30pm Mon-Sat; Ⓜ Passeig de Gràcia) Loewe is one of Spain's leading and oldest fashion stores, founded in 1846. It specialises in luxury leather (shoes, accessories and travel bags), and also has lines in perfume, sunglasses, cuff links, silk scarves and jewellery. This branch opened in 1943 in the Modernista Casa Lleó Morera (p132).

LAIE BOOKS
Map p294 (☑93 318 17 39; www.laie.es; Carrer de Pau Claris 85; ☺9am-9pm Mon-Fri, 10am-9pm Sat; Ⓜ Urquinaona) Laie has novels and books on architecture, art and film in English,

French, Spanish and Catalan. It also has a great upstairs cafe where you can examine your latest purchases or browse through the newspapers provided for customers in Central European style.

BAGUÉS-MASRIERA   JEWELLERY

Map p290 (☑93 216 01 74; www.bagues-masriera. com; Passeig de Gràcia 41; ⊙10am-8.30pm Mon-Fri, 11am-8pm Sat; ⓂPasseig de Gràcia) This jewellery store, in business since the 19th century, is in thematic harmony with its location in the Modernista Casa Amatller. Some of the classic pieces to come out of the Bagués clan's workshops have an equally playful, Modernista bent.

NORMA COMICS   BOOKS

Map p294 (☑93 244 84 23; www.normacomics. com; Passeig de Sant Joan 7-9; ⊙10.30am-8.30pm Mon-Sat; ⓂArc de Triomf) Norma stocks a huge range of comics, both Spanish and international – everything from Tintin to out-there sci-fi comics can be found here, along with figurines, clothing, mugs and other merchandise.

BULEVARD ROSA   SHOPPING CENTRE

Map p290 (☑93 215 83 31; www.bulevardrosa. com; Passeig de Gràcia 55-57; ⊙10.30am-9pm Mon-Sat; ⓂPasseig de Gràcia) Bulevard Rosa is a small shopping arcade with a clutch of up-market boutiques selling handbags, shoes, fashion and the like.

CASA DEL LLIBRE   BOOKS

Map p294 (☑902 026407; www.casadellibro. com; Passeig de Gràcia 62; ⊙9am-9.30pm Mon-Sat, 11am-9.30pm Sun; ⓂPasseig de Gràcia) With branches throughout Spain, the 'Home of the Book' is a well-stocked general bookshop with sections devoted to literature in English, French and other languages, as well as a good number of guidebooks.

FNAC   ELECTRONICS, BOOKS

Map p290 (☑902 100632; www.fnac.es; El Triangle, Plaça de Catalunya 4; ⊙9.30am-9pm Mon-Sat; ⓂCatalunya) FNAC, the French electronics, book and music emporium, has a couple of branches around town, but this is the biggest.

ANTINOUS   BOOKS

Map p290 (☑93 301 90 70; www.antinous libros.com; Carrer de Casanova 72; ⊙11am-2pm & 5-8pm Mon-Sat; ⓂUniversitat) LGBT travellers may want to browse in this spacious and relaxed gay bookshop in the Gaixample.

 SPORTS & ACTIVITIES

CATALUNYA BUS TURÍSTIC   BUS

Map p294 (☑932 85 38 32; www.catalunyabus turistic.cat; Plaça de Catalunya; adult/child 1-day ticket €29/16, 2-day ticket €39/20; ⊙9am-8pm Jun-Sep, to 7pm Oct-May; ⓂCatalunya) Open-topped buses run three different hop-on, hop-off circuits around Barcelona's main sights. One- and two-day passes are valid on all three routes. There are up to two services per hour. Tickets are cheaper online.

ESPAI BOISÀ   COOKING

Map p290 (☑93 192 60 21; www.espaiboisa.com; Passatge Lluís Pellicer 8; 2½-hour course from €45; ⓂHospital Clínic) ✔ Run by a young, multilingual Venezuelan-Catalan couple, this first-rate outfit offers various themed cooking courses. They emphasise organic, seasonal ingredients from local producers outside of Barcelona – put to good use in dishes including paella, a range of tapas dishes and *crema catalana* (a Catalan version of crème brûlée).

The best part is feasting on your creations, accompanied by generous glasses of organic Catalan wine or sangria.

TERRA BIKETOURS   CYCLING

Map p294 (☑93 416 08 05; www.terrabiketours. com; Carrer de València 337; self-guided tour from €29, 1-day guided tour from €57; ⓂVerdaguer) This outfit offers a wide range of cycling tours from one day to one week. Options include mountain biking in the Parc de Collserola or outside of Barcelona in the Pyrenees, and a road-biking tour on Barcelona's north coast and beyond. Self-guided trips (including preloaded GPS routes and gear) are also available.

Antoni Gaudí & Modernisme

Barcelona's architectural gift to the world was Modernisme, a flamboyant Catalan creation that erupted in the late 19th century. Modernisme was personified by the visionary work of Antoni Gaudí, a giant in the world of architecture. Imaginative creations by Gaudí and his contemporaries have filled Barcelona with dozens of masterpieces.

A Blank Canvas

In the 1850s a rapidly growing city fuelled by industrialisation meant notoriously crowded conditions in the narrow streets of the *ciutat vella*, Barcelona's old quarter. It was time to break down the medieval walls and dramatically expand the city. In 1869 the architect Ildefons Cerdà was chosen to design a new district, which would be called L'Eixample (the Enlargement).

He drew wide boulevards on a gridlike layout, and envisioned neighbourhoods with plenty of green space – an objective that city planners unfortunately overruled amid the rampant land speculation of the day. With a blank slate before them, and abundant interest from upper-class residents eager to custom design a new home, architects were much in demand. What developers could not have predicted was the calibre of those architects.

Antoni Gaudí

Leading the way was Antoni Gaudí. Born in Reus to a long line of coppersmiths, Gaudí was initially trained in metalwork. In childhood he suffered from poor health, including rheumatism, and became an early adopter of a vegetarian diet. He was not a promising student. In 1878, when he obtained his architecture degree, the school's headmaster is reputed to have said, 'Who knows if we have given a diploma to a nutcase or a genius. Time will tell.'

The Book of Nature

As a young man, what most delighted Gaudí was being outdoors, and he became fascinated by the plants, animals and geology beyond his door. This admiration for the natural world would heavily influence his designs. 'This tree is my teacher,' he once said. 'Everything comes from the book of nature.' Throughout his work, he sought to emulate the harmony he observed in the natural world, eschewing the straight line and favouring curvaceous forms and more organic shapes.

The spiral of a nautilus shell can be seen in staircases and ceiling details, tight buds of flowers in chimney pots and roof ornamentation, while undulating arches

....
1. Interior of the Palau de la Música Catalana (p95)
2. Casa Batlló (p133)

GAUDÍ OFF THE BEATEN TRACK

Gaudí, like any freelancer, was busy all over town. While his main patron was Eusebi Güell and his big projects were bankrolled by the wealthy bourgeoisie, he also took on smaller jobs. One example is the Casa Vicens, a remarkable home with Moorish and Eastern motifs. Another is the Col·legi de les Teresianes, for which he created an unusual brick facade, topped with castle-like merlons. Gaudí fanatics might also want to reach Bellesguard, whose castle-like appearance is reinforced by heavy stonework, generous wrought iron and a tall spire.

evoke a cavern, overlapping roof tiles mimic the scales of an armadillo and flowing walls resemble waves on the sea. Tree branches, spider webs, stalactites, honeycombs, starfish, mushrooms, shimmering beetle wings and many other elements from nature – all were part of the Gaudían vernacular.

Gaudí's Creations

The architect's work is an earthy appeal to sinewy movement, but often with a dreamlike or surreal quality. The private apartment house Casa Batlló is a fine example in which all appears a riot of the unnaturally natural – or the naturally unnatural. Not only are straight lines eliminated, but the lines between real and unreal, sober and dream-drunk, good sense and play are all blurred. Depending on how you look at the facade, you might see St George (one of Barcelona's patron saints) defeating a dragon, a magnificent and shimmering fish (a symbol of Mediterranean peoples) or elements of an effusive Carnaval parade.

Gaudí seems to have particularly enjoyed himself with rooftops. At Palau Güell he created all sorts of fantastical, multicoloured tile figures, like chimney pots resembling oversized budlike trees that seem straight out of *Alice in Wonderland* – or perhaps Dr Seuss.

1. Park Güell (p160) 2. La Sagrada Família (p127)

La Sagrada Família

Gaudí's masterpiece was La Sagrada Família (begun in 1882), and in it you can see the culminating vision of many ideas developed over the years. Its massive scale evokes the grandeur of Catalonia's Gothic cathedrals, while organic elements foreground its harmony with nature.

The church is rife with symbols that tangibly express Gaudí's Catholic faith through architecture: 18 bell towers symbolise Jesus, the Virgin Mary, the four evangelists and the 12 apostles. Three facades cover Jesus' life, death and resurrection. Even its location: the Nativity Facade faces east where the sun rises; the Passion Facade depicting Christ's death faces west where the sun sets.

Gaudí: A Catholic & a Catalan

Gaudí was a devout Catholic and a Catalan nationalist. In addition to nature, Catalonia's great medieval churches were a source of inspiration to him. He took pride in utilising the building materials of the countryside: clay, stone and timber.

In contrast to his architecture, Gaudí's life was simple; he was not averse to knocking on doors, literally begging for money to help fund construction of the cathedral. As Gaudí became more adventurous he appeared as a lone wolf. With age he became almost exclusively motivated by stark religious conviction, and he devoted much of the latter part of his life to what remains Barcelona's call sign – the unfinished La Sagrada Família. He died in 1926, struck down by a streetcar while walking to the Sant Felip Neri church. Wearing ragged clothes with empty pockets – save for some orange peel – Gaudí was initially taken for a beggar and taken to a nearby hospital where he was left in a pauper's ward; he died two days later. Thousands attended his funeral, forming a half-mile procession to La Sagrada Família, where he was buried in the crypt.

Much like his work in progress, La Sagrada Família, Gaudí's story is far from over. In March 2000 the Vatican decided to proceed with the case for canonising him, and pilgrims already stop by the crypt to pay him homage. One of the key sculptors at work on the church, the Japanese Etsuro

Sotoo, converted to Catholicism because of his passion for Gaudí.

Domènech i Montaner

Although overshadowed by Gaudí, Lluís Domènech i Montaner (1850–1923) was one of the great masters of Modernisme. He was a widely travelled man of prodigious intellect, with knowledge of everything from mineralogy to medieval heraldry, and he was an architectural professor, a prolific writer and a nationalist politician. The question of Catalan identity and how to create a national architecture consumed Domènech i Montaner, who designed more than a dozen large-scale works in his lifetime.

The exuberant, steel-framed Palau de la Música Catalana is one of his masterpieces. Adorning the facade are elaborate Gothic-style windows, floral designs (Domènech i Montaner also studied botany) and sculptures depicting characters from Catalan folklore and the music world as well as everyday citizens of Barcelona. Inside, the hall leaves visitors dazzled with delicate floral-covered colonnades, radiant stained-glass walls and ceiling, and a rolling, sculpture-packed proscenium referencing the epics of musical lore.

His other great masterpiece is the Hospital de la Santa Creu i de Sant Pau, with sparkling mosaics on the facade and a stained-glass skylight that fills the vestibule with golden light (like Matisse, Domènech i Montaner believed in the therapeutic powers of colour).

Puig i Cadafalch

Like Domènech i Montaner, Josep Puig i Cadafalch (1867–1956) was a polymath; he was an archaeologist, an expert in Romanesque art and one of Catalonia's most prolific architects. As a politician – and later president of the Mancomunitat de Catalunya (Commonwealth of Catalonia) – he was instrumental in shaping the Catalan nationalist movement.

One of his many Modernista gems is the Casa Amatller, a rather dramatic contrast to Gaudí's Casa Batlló next door. Here the straight line is very much in evidence, as is the foreign influence (the gables are borrowed from the Dutch). Blended with playful Gothic-style sculpture, Puig i Cadafalch has designed a house of startling beauty and invention.

Another pivotal work by Puig i Cadafalch was the Casa Martí (better known as Els Quatre Gats), which was one of Barcelona's first Modernista-style buildings (from 1896).

Materials & Decorations

Modernista architects relied on artisan skills that have now been all but relegated to history. There were no concrete pours (contrary to what is being done at La Sagrada Família today). Stone, unclad brick, exposed iron and steel frames, and the copious use of stained glass and ceramics in decoration were all features of the new style – and indeed it is often in the decor that Modernisme is at its most flamboyant.

The craftspeople required for these tasks were the heirs of the guild masters and had absorbed centuries of know-how about just what could and could not be done with these materials. Forged iron and steel were newcomers to the scene, but the approach to learning how they could be used was not dissimilar to that adopted for more traditional materials. Gaudí, in particular, relied on these old skills and even ran schools in La Sagrada Família workshops to keep them alive.

1. La Pedrera (p134) 2. Tiled benches in Park Güell (p160)

Exploring Modernisme

Barcelona is home to dozens of Modernista masterpieces, making for some tough decisions when it comes to deciding what to see. The following are two suggested half-day itineraries of the major highlights, though the very ambitious could combine these for a packed day of architectural gazing.

A MORNING OF MODERNISME

Start the day off with pastries and coffee at the Modernista gem **❶ Escribà**. From there walk a few blocks south and down Carrer Nou de Rambla to visit the **❷ Palau Güell**, one of Gaudí's early masterpieces. Afterwards take the metro up to Passeig de Gràcia and have a look at the so-called Manzana de la Discordia – **❸ Casa Batlló, Casa Amatller** and Casa Lleó Morera – deciding for yourself who among Gaudí, Puig i Cadafalch and Domènech i Montaner has created the most successful work of art. Afterwards, stroll up Passeig de Gràcia, a true architectural showcase, and end your tour at Gaudí's **❹ La Pedrera** (Casa Milà). Don't miss the sentinel-like chimney pots on the roof – and the great view over the city.

La Sagrada Família
Still probably a decade from completion, the magnificent basilica is an ever-changing work in progress. The beautifully sculpted Nativity Facade, with its rich symbolism, is a masterpiece unto itself.

GRÀCIA

SANT GERVASI

Park Güell
Gaudí's imagination runs wild here, with fairy-tale-like gatehouses, tilting tree-like columns, organic rock-strewn passageways and one much photographed lizard.

La Pedrera
Full of curving walls, La Pedrera presented challenges to one tenant, who complained there was no obvious place to put her piano. Gaudí's response: 'Madam, I suggest you take up the flute.'

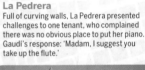

AN AFTERNOON OF MODERNISME

Start the tour at ❺ **La Sagrada Família** where you can gaze upon one of the world's most dynamic ecclesiastical designs. Afterwards, make your way up to ❻ **Park Güell** for an afternoon stroll through the eye-catching park. If time allows, pay a visit to the Casa-Museu Gaudí in the park. Next head back down to the Ciutat Vella for a guided tour (or perhaps attend a concert) inside the luminescent ❼ **Palau de la Música Catalana**. Afterwards, stroll over to ❽ **Els Quatre Gats** for a drink (or a meal) inside a whimsical building designed by Puig i Cadafalch.

TOP TIPS

➡ Go first thing in the morning or late in the day to beat the crowds at Gaudí sites.

➡ Buy La Sagrada Família tickets online to avoid long queues.

➡ La Pedrera also hosts rooftop evening concerts in the summer.

Palau de la Música Catalana
The sculptural facade is packed with folk symbols, with an open-armed nymph, a peasant, a fisherman, and other types gathered below a sword-bearing St George.

Escribà
This magnificent pastry shop has a stunning art nouveau exterior. Note the swirling mosaics and stained glass, key elements of Modernista design.

LA RIBERA

L'EIXAMPLE

❼

❽

BARRI GÒTIC

Passeig de Gràcia

❸

La Rambla

❶

❷

Palau Güell
There are many unusual features in this early work by Antoni Gaudí, including the massive entry doors, which allowed carriages to be driven right into the house.

Els Quatre Gats
From 1897 to 1903, this was the hang-out for avant-garde artists of the day. A young Picasso had his first exhibition here in 1900.

Casa Batlló & Casa Amatller
These two side-by-side buildings show how wildly different the Modernistas ranged in their inspirations. Puig i Cadafalch references Gothic Dutch architecture, while Gaudí's is a shimmering tile-covered fantasy.

Gràcia & Park Güell

Neighbourhood Top Five

1 **Park Güell** (p160) Meandering along the winding paths amid the wild sculptures, mosaics and columns of Gaudí's open-air wonderland high above the city.

2 **Casa Vicens** (p162) Admiring the strange interplay of brick, chequerboard patterns and Moorish elements on this Unesco-listed castle mansion, Gaudí's first commission.

3 **Mercat de la Llibertat** (p162) Shopping for delectable local specialities (and sampling them too) at the neighbourhood's emblematic market, dating from the 19th century.

4 **Soda Acústic** (p168) Hearing Balkan beats, experimental jazz and other eclectic sounds in one of Gràcia's most innovative performance spaces.

5 **Verdi** (p168) Watching an indie film at this neighbourhood icon, followed by tapas on the restaurant-lined lane out the front.

For more detail of this area see Map p296 ➡

Explore Gràcia & Park Güell

Once a separate village north of L'Eixample, and an industrial district famous for its republican and liberal ideas, Gràcia was incorporated into the city of Barcelona in 1897, despite staunch opposition from locals. The neighbourhood retains its distinct character today, with a boho feel – it's home to artists, hip local luminaries and young families.

Start the day in Gràcia by exploring Park Güell (p160) and move down to the centre of the neighbourhood. If you walk from the park, cut across the traffic-choked Travessera de Dalt and go down Carrer de Verdi, into the heart of Gràcia – it's around 1km in total.

Plunge into the atmosphere of its narrow streets and small plazas, and the bars and restaurants on and around them. The liveliest are Carrer de Verdi, where you will find wonderful cafes, bars and shops; Plaça del Sol, a raucous square populated by cool bars; Plaça de la Vila de Gràcia, dotted with cafes and restaurants; family-friendly Plaça de la Revolució de Setembre de 1868; and the tree-lined Plaça de la Virreina, a particularly lovely square with cafes, shops and a chilled-out feel. Gràcia is great during the day or at night – the squares are sunny and relaxed for breakfast or lunch, and lively at night with scenesters enjoying a drink alfresco.

Local Life

→ **Independent shops** Wander up Carrer de Verdi and along Travessera de Gràcia for an insight into what Gràcia does best. One-off boutiques and food shops abound on these people-filled streets.

→ **Markets** The Mercat de la Llibertat (p162) is a neighbourhood jewel but it's not the only historic market here. The Mercat de l'Abaceria Central (p170) dates from the late 19th century and has stalls filled with delicious products as well as ready-to-eat dishes.

→ **Old-time bars** Gràcia still has plenty of tapas bars that have been around forever – Bar Bodega Quimet (p163) is a classic example.

Getting There & Away

→ **Foot** Strolling along Passeig de Gràcia from Plaça de Catalunya is a wonderful way to reach the neighbourhood. The 1.5km walk takes around 25 minutes.

→ **Metro** Línia 3 (Fontana stop) leaves you halfway up Carrer Gran de Gràcia and close to a network of busy squares. To enter Gràcia from the northern side, take Línia 4 to Joanic.

Lonely Planet's Top Tip

A wonderful way to take in Gràcia's atmosphere is from a cafe or restaurant on one of its many squares. Arrive after dusk and watch as the place comes to life in the post-work hours.

 ### Best Places to Eat

→ Chivuo's (p162)
→ Con Gracia (p166)
→ La Panxa del Bisbe (p165)
→ Bar Bodega Quimet (p163)

For reviews, see p162.➡

 ### Best Places to Drink

→ Bobby Gin (p166)
→ Rabipelao (p166)
→ Elephanta (p166)
→ Viblioteca (p167)

For reviews, see p166.➡

 ### Best Places to Shop

→ Colmillo de Morsa (p168)
→ Family Beer (p168)
→ Can Luc (p168)
→ Amalia Vermell (p169)

For reviews, see p168.➡

TOP SIGHT
PARK GÜELL

Park Güell – north of Gràcia and about 4km from Plaça de Catalunya – is where Gaudí turned his hand to landscape gardening. It's a surreal, enchanting place where the iconic Modernista's passion for natural forms really took flight, to the point where the artificial almost seems more natural than the natural.

A City Park

Park Güell originated in 1900, when Count Eusebi Güell bought the tree-covered hillside of El Carmel (then outside Barcelona) and hired Gaudí to create a miniature city of houses for the wealthy, surrounded by landscaped grounds. The project was a commercial flop and was abandoned in 1914 – but not before Gaudí had created, in his inimitable manner, steps, a plaza, two gatehouses and 3km of roads and walks. In 1922 the city bought the estate for use as a public park. The park became a Unesco World Heritage site in 2004. The idea was based on the English 'garden cities', much admired by Güell, hence the spelling of 'Park'.

Just inside the main entrance on Carrer d'Olot, immediately recognisable by the two Hansel-and-Gretel gatehouses, is the park's Centre d'Interpretació, in the Pavelló de Consergeria, which is a typically curvaceous former porter's home that hosts a display on Gaudí's building methods and the history of the park. There are superb views from the top floor.

Much of the park is still wooded, but it's laced with pathways. The best views are from the cross-topped Turó del Calvari in the southwest corner.

DON'T MISS

➡ Learning about Gaudí's building methods at the Centre d'Interpretació

➡ The Sala Hipóstila's stone forest

➡ The life of the artist at Casa-Museu Gaudí

➡ The undulating tiled bench with views across the city

PRACTICALITIES

➡ ☎93 409 18 31
➡ www.parkguell.cat
➡ Carrer d'Olot 7
➡ adult/child €8/5.60
➡ ⏱8am-9.30pm May-Aug, to 8.30pm Apr, Sep & Oct, to 6.30pm Nov-Mar
➡ 🚌24, 92, Ⓜ Lesseps, Vallcarca

EL ASEN/AGE I I ! IMAGES ©

Sala Hipóstila (The Doric Temple)

The steps up from the entrance, guarded by a mosaic dragon/lizard (a copy of which you can buy in many central souvenir shops), lead to the Sala Hipóstila (aka the Doric Temple). This forest of 86 stone columns – some leaning like mighty trees bent by the weight of time – was originally intended as a market. To the left curves a gallery whose twisted stonework columns and roof give the effect of a cloister beneath tree roots – a motif repeated in several places in the park. On top of the Sala Hipóstila is a broad open space. Its centrepiece is the Banc de Trencadís, a tiled bench curving sinuously around its perimeter, which was designed by one of Gaudí's closest colleagues, architect Josep Maria Jujol (1879–1949). With Gaudí, however, there is always more than meets the eye. This giant platform was designed as a kind of catchment area for rainwater washing down the hillside. The water is filtered through a layer of stone and sand, and it drains down through the columns to an underground cistern.

Casa-Museu Gaudí

Above and to the right of the entrance, the spired house you see is the **Casa-Museu Gaudí** (☑93 219 38 11; www.casamuseugaudi.org; Carretera del Carmel 23a; adult/child €5.50/free; ☉9am-8pm Apr-Sep, 10am-6pm Oct-Mar; ☑24, 92, 116, Ⓜ Lesseps), where Gaudí lived for almost the last 20 years of his life (1906–26). Furniture he designed (including items that once lived in La Pedrera, Casa Batlló and Casa Calvet) is displayed along with other memorabilia. The house was built in 1904 by Francesc Berenguer i Mestres as a prototype for the 60 or so houses that were originally planned here.

ADMISSION

With an estimated four million visitors a year, the park is extremely popular and an entrance fee is imposed on the central area containing most of its attractions. Access is limited to a certain number of people every half-hour, and it's wise to book ahead online (which also saves you a euro).

One-hour guided tours in multiple languages including English take place year-round and cost €7 (plus park admission); prebook online.

TAKE A BREAK

Before or after making the trip up to the park, stop off at La Panxa del Bisbe (p165) for deliciously creative tapas and good wines.

The park makes a spectacular setting for a picnic; bring supplies with you as there's nowhere to stock up nearby.

🎯 SIGHTS

PARK GÜELL PARK
See p160.

CASA VICENS MUSEUM
(📞93 348 42 58; www.casavicens.org; Carrer de les Carolines 18-24; adult/child €16/14, guided tour per person additional €3; ⊘10am-8pm, last tour 7.30pm; Ⓜ Fontana) A Unesco-listed masterpiece, Casa Vicens was first opened regularly to the public in 2017. The angular, turreted 1885-completed private house created for stock and currency broker Manuel Vicens i Montaner was Gaudí's inaugural commission, when the architect was aged just 30. Tucked away west of Gràcia's main drag, the richly detailed facade is awash with ceramic colour and shape. You're free to wander through at your own pace but 30-minute guided tours (available in English) bring the building to life.

As was frequently the case, Gaudí sought inspiration from the past, in this case the rich heritage of building in the Mudéjar-style brick, typical in those parts of Spain reconquered from the Moors. Mudéjar architecture was created by those Arabs and Berbers allowed to remain in Spain after the Christian reconquests.

The renovated building is accessible for visitors with limited mobility (including wheelchairs). Temporary exhibitions are mounted alongside permanent displays covering the building's history. Allow time for a drink at the cafe in the garden.

GAUDÍ EXPERIENCE MUSEUM
(📞93 285 44 40; www.gaudiexperiencia.com; Carrer de Larrard 41; adult/child €9/7.50; ⊘10.30am-7pm Apr-Sep, to 5pm Oct-Mar; Ⓜ Lesseps) The Gaudí Experience is a fun-filled Disney-style look at the life and work of Barcelona's favourite son, just a stone's throw from Park Güell. There are models of his buildings and whizz-bang interactive exhibits and touchscreens, but the highlight is the stomach-churning 4D presentation in its tiny screening room. Not recommended for the frail or children aged under six years.

ESGLÉSIA DE SANT JOAN CHURCH
Map p296 (📞93 237 73 58; www.conferencia episcopal.es; Carrer de la Santa Creu 2; ⊘8am-12.45pm & 4-8pm, hours can vary; Ⓜ Fontana, Joanic) Construction on this striking church

began in 1878 and was completed in 1884. Designed by Francesc Berenguer i Mestres, Gaudí's protégé, it's believed that the interior chapel is the work of Gaudí himself, though the jury is still out. What is certain is that Gaudí regularly worshipped here. Much of the church was destroyed by Leftists in 1909 and again in 1938, though the chapel survived unscathed. Rebuilding wrapped up in 1951. Enter via Plaça de la Virriena.

MERCAT DE LA LLIBERTAT MARKET
Map p296 (📞93 217 09 95; www.mercatsbcn. com; Plaça de la Llibertat 27; ⊘8am-8pm Mon-Fri, to 3pm Sat; 🚈 FGC Gràcia) Opened in 1888, the 'Market of Liberty' was covered over in 1893 by Francesc Berenguer i Mestres (1866–1914), Gaudí's long-time assistant, in typically fizzy Modernista style, employing generous whirls of wrought iron. It received a considerable facelift in 2009 but remains emblematic of the Gràcia district: full of life and fabulous fresh produce.

EATING

LA PUBILLA CATALAN €
Map p296 (📞93 218 29 94; Plaça de la Llibertat 23; mains €8-13.50; ⊘8.30am-5pm Mon, to midnight Tue-Sat; Ⓜ Fontana) Hidden away by the Mercat de la Llibertat, La Pubilla specialises in hearty *'esmorzars de forquilla'* ('fork breakfasts') beloved by market workers and nearby residents. There's also a daily three-course *menú del día* for €16, which includes Catalan dishes such as baked cod, or roast pork cheek with chickpeas. Arrive early for a chance of a table.

CHIVUO'S BURGERS €
Map p296 (📞93 218 51 34; www.chivuos.com; Carrer del Torrent de l'Olla 175; burgers €7-9; ⊘1-5pm & 7pm-midnight Mon-Sat; Ⓜ Fontana) Burgers and craft beers make a fine pair at this buzzing den. A mostly local crowd comes for huge burgers (served rare unless you specify otherwise) with house-made sauces – best ordered with fluffy, golden-fried *fritas* (chips). Mostly Catalan and Spanish brews, including excellent offerings from Barcelona-based Edge Brewing, Catalan Brewery, Napar and Garage Beer, rotate on the eight taps.

Sandwiches such as pulled pork or tuna melts are also available.

WORTH A DETOUR

BUNKERS DEL CARMEL

For a magnificent view over the city that's well off the beaten path, head to the neighbourhood of El Carmel and make the ascent up the hill known as **Turó de la Rovira** (Bunkers del Carmel; ☑93 256 21 22; www.museuhistoria.bcn.cat; Carrer de Marià Labèrnia; ⊗museum 10am-2pm Wed, 10am-3pm Sat & Sun; ☐V17, 119) to the Bunkers del Carmel viewpoint. Above the weeds and dusty hillside, you'll find the old concrete platforms that were once part of anti-aircraft battery during the Spanish Civil War (in the postwar, it was a shanty town until the early 1990s, and has lain abandoned since then). There is a small information centre/museum.

Placards at the sight give an overview of what once stood here. These days, those old firing platforms are better used as seating for a mix of students and young travellers who come for the mesmerising 360-degree views over the city. It's a great place to watch the sunset. Before or after visiting here, you can stop for a bite and a drink at the charming, family-run **Las Delicias** (☑93 429 22 02; www.barrestaurantedelicias.com; Carrer de Mühlberg 1; tapas €4-13, mains €9-14; ⊗10am-4pm Tue-Sun & 7-10.30pm Tue-Thu, 8-11pm Fri & Sat; ☑El Carmel, then bus 86).

To get to the park, when you arrive at the neighbourhood of El Carmel, have the bus driver tell you when you're near the bunkers. From the bus stop, it's a further 10-minute walk to the viewpoint.

BAR BODEGA QUIMET   TAPAS €

Map p296 (☑93 218 41 89; Carrer de Vic 23; tapas €3-11.50; ⊗10am-11.30pm Mon-Fri, noon-11.30pm Sat & Sun; ☑Fontana) A remnant from a bygone age, Bar Bodega Quimet is a delightfully atmospheric bar, with old bottles lining the walls, marble tables and a burnished wooden bar. The list of tapas and seafood is almost exhaustive, while another house speciality is *torrades* – huge slabs of toasted white bread topped with cured meats, fresh anchovies and sardines.

In summer you'll be served a refreshing glass of chilled gazpacho.

LA NENA   CAFE €

Map p296 (☑93 285 14 76; www.facebook.com/chocolaterialanena; Carrer de Ramon i Cajal 36; dishes €2-4.50; ⊗8.30am-10.30pm Mon-Fri, 9am-10.30pm Sat & Sun; ⬤; ☑Fontana) At this delightfully chaotic space, indulge in cups of *suïssos* (rich hot chocolate) served with a plate of heavy homemade whipped cream and *melindros* (spongy sweet biscuits), desserts and a few savoury dishes (including crêpes). The place is strewn with books, and you can play with the board games on the shelves.

The area out the back is designed to keep kids busy, with toys, books and a blackboard with chalk, making it an ideal family rest stop.

LA EMPANADERIA DE GRÀCIA   EMPANADAS €

Map p296 (Carrer de Francisco Giner 60; empanadas €1.95; ⊗noon-4pm & 5.30-10pm; ☑FGC Gràcia) For a cheap, filling snack, this corner *empanadería* is a brilliant bet, serving scrumptious stuffed pastries. Each day, 20 different varieties are available: savoury flavours might include pumpkin and mozzarella, pear and goat cheese, hummus, celery and Roquefort or spicy beef and olive, while sweet styles span banana and honey to apple and cinnamon.

.IT   ITALIAN €

Map p296 (☑93 461 92 71; Carrer del Topazi 26; mains €6.50-12; ⊗9.30am-midnight Mon-Fri, noon-4pm & 7pm-midnight Sat, closed Aug; ☺☑; ☑Fontana) Pizza bases at .IT ('Italian Tradition') are made from Caputo flour and fermented for 48 hours before being baked in a 400°C wood-fired oven. Just some of the classic topping combinations include Veneto (gorgonzola, mozzarella, radicchio and walnuts) and Abbruzzo (fresh tomato, scamorza cheese, pistachio mortadella and basil). Huge, fresh salads are a meal in themselves; pastas change daily.

There's a creative range of 'Italian tapas' (fried courgette flowers, meat-stuffed olives and aubergine 'meatballs' with Parmesan) and lush desserts like olive-oil chocolate cake and Limoncello tiramisu.

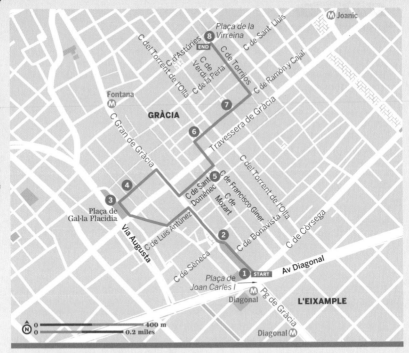

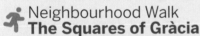

Neighbourhood Walk
The Squares of Gràcia

START PLAÇA DE JOAN CARLES I
END PLAÇA DE LA VIRREINA
LENGTH 1.9KM; 50 MINUTES

The obelisk at **1 Plaça de Joan Carles I** honours Spain's present king for stifling an attempted coup d'état in February 1981, six years after Franco's death.

Where Carrer Gran de Gràcia leads you into Gràcia proper, a grand Modernista edifice now turned hotel, **2 Casa Fuster**, rises in all its glory.

3 Plaça de Gal·la Placidia recalls the brief sojourn of the Roman empress-to-be Galla Placidia, captive and wife of the Visigothic chief Athaulf in the 5th century AD. She hastily returned to her native Italy upon her captor-husband's death.

4 Plaça de la Llibertat (Liberty Sq) is home to the eponymous Modernista produce market. It was designed by one of Gaudí's colleagues, Francesc Berenguer, who was busy in this part of town despite never having been awarded a diploma as an architect.

Popular **5 Plaça de la Vila de Gràcia** was, until a few years ago, named after the mayor under whom Gràcia was absorbed by Barcelona, Francesc Rius i Taulet. It is fronted by the local town hall (designed by Berenguer). At its heart stands the Torre del Rellotge (Clock Tower), long a symbol of Republican agitation.

Possibly the rowdiest of Gràcia's squares, **6 Plaça del Sol** (Sun Sq) is lined with bars and eateries and comes to life on long summer nights. The square was the scene of summary executions after an uprising in 1870. During the 1936–9 civil war, an air-raid shelter was installed.

Busy, elongated **7 Plaça de la Revolució de Setembre de 1868** commemorates the toppling of Queen Isabel II, a cause of much celebration in this working-class stronghold. Today locals gather on benches for a chat or pop into one of the bars or restaurants for refreshment.

Pleasant terraces adorn pedestrianised **8 Plaça de la Virreina**, presided over by the 17th-century Església de Sant Joan. It was largely destroyed by anarchists during the unrest of the Setmana Tràgica (Tragic Week) of 1909. Rebuilt by Berenguer, it was damaged again during the civil war.

CASA PORTUGUESA
BAKERY €

Map p296 (☑93 021 88 03; www.acasaportuguesa. com; Carrer de l'Or 8; dishes €2-8; ☺10.30am-9pm; ⓂFontana) Overlooking Plaça del Diamant, Casa Portuguesa is a delightful bakery and purveyor of delicacies. The *pasteis de belém* (Portuguese-style custard tarts) are magnificent, and you'll also find fruit tarts, daily changing organic salads, good coffee and Portuguese wines. For a kick, have a shot of *ginjinha* (cherry brandy).

CAFÈ CAMÈLIA
VEGETARIAN €

Map p296 (☑93 415 36 86; Carrer de Verdi 79; mains €7.50-11.50; ☺10am-midnight Mon-Sat, to 9pm Sun; 🛜🍽; ⓂFontana) A peaceful spot for coffee, set lunches and desserts, this pretty little vegetarian cafe has a small menu of well-executed dishes – hummus, vegetable curry, open-faced sandwiches, quinoa burgers with roasted vegetables and a risotto of the day.

HIMALI
NEPALI €

Map p296 (☑93 285 15 68; www.restaurante himalibcn.com; Carrer de Milà i Fontanals 60; mains €7.50-13; ☺noon-11.30pm; ⓂJoanic) Strung with Nepalese prayer flags, this simple spot serves dishes such as lamb curry, mixed grills with rice and naan, and lamb and vegetable *momo* (dumplings).

TIMELINE
SANDWICHES €

Map p296 (☑93 217 79 38; Carrer de la Providèn- cia 3; sandwiches €6.50-9; ☺7pm-2am Mon-Thu, 7pm-3am Fri, noon-3am Sat, noon-2am Sun; 🍽; ⓂLesseps, Fontana) Like stepping into an enchanted cuckoo clock, cosy TimeLine is decked with black-and-white tiled floors, curious artwork (roller skates, twisted light sculptures), and a chess-board. A fun, multilingual crowd comes for cocktails, sandwiches (curry chicken, meatballs, veggie barbecue), hummus platters and goat-cheese-drizzled salads. Weekend brunch buffets (€18) include bot-tomless mimosas (made with champagne and orange juice).

LA PANXA DEL BISBE
TAPAS €€

Map p296 (☑93 213 70 49; Carrer del Torrent de les Flors 158; tapas €8.50-15, tasting menus €28-36; ☺1.30-3.30pm & 8.30pm-midnight Tue-Sat; ⓂJoanic) With low lighting and an artfully minimalist interior, the 'Bishop's Belly' serves creative tapas that earn high praise from the mostly local crowd. Feast on prawn-stuffed courgette flowers, grilled octopus with green chilli and watermelon, and slow-roasted lamb with mint couscous. Top off the meal with a bottle of wine such as an Albariño white from Galicia (by-the-glass options are more limited).

PEPA TOMATE
TAPAS €€

Map p296 (☑93 210 46 98; www.pepatomate grup.com; Plaça de la Revolució de Setembre de 1868 17; sharing plates €7-17; ☺8pm-midnight Mon, from 9am Tue-Fri, from 10am Sat, from 11am Sun; 🍽; ⓂFontana) This casual tapas spot on Plaça de la Revolució de Setembre de 1868 is popular at all hours of the day. Fresh produce takes front and centre on the wide-ranging menu in dishes like fried green tomatoes, Andalucian baby squid, tandoori lamb tacos, Iberian pork or mushroom, cro-quettes, and carrot gazpacho in summer.

It's popular with families (crayons are available, and there's a mini playground at the front). Weekday multicourse lunch spe-cials cost €12.50.

CAFÉ GODOT
INTERNATIONAL €€

Map p296 (☑93 368 20 36; www.cafegodot. com; Carrer de Sant Domènec 19; mains €10-18.50; ☺10am-1am Mon-Fri, 11am-2am Sat & Sun; ⓂFontana) A stylish space of exposed brick, timber and tiles, opening to a garden out back, Godot is a relaxing place with an extensive menu, ranging from white-wine-steamed mussels and scallops with Thai-style green curry to duck confit with lentils and spinach. Brunch is an American-style affair with eggs, crispy bacon and fluffy pancakes.

CANTINA MACHITO
MEXICAN €€

Map p296 (☑93 217 34 14; Carrer de Torrijos 47; mains €9.50-16.50; ☺1-4pm & 7pm-1am; ⓂFontana, Joanic) On a leafy street, colour-ful Machito – adorned with Frida Kahlo images – gets busy with locals, and the outside tables are a great place to eat and drink until late. Start with a *miche-lada* (spicy beer cocktail) before dining on Mexican delights like quesadillas, tacos and enchiladas. Refreshing iced waters are flavoured with honey and lime or mint and fruit.

CAL BOTER
CATALAN €€

Map p296 (☑93 458 84 62; www.restaurant calboter.com; Carrer de Tordera 62; mains €8-15; ☺1-4pm & 9pm-midnight Tue-Sat, 1-4pm Sun & Mon; ⓂJoanic) Families and high-spirited groups of pals are drawn to this classic restaurant for *cargols a la llauna* (snails sautéed in a tin), *filet de bou amb salsa de foie* (a thick clump of tender beef drowned in an orange and foie gras sauce), and other Catalan specialities.

BILBAO
SPANISH €€

Map p296 (☑93 458 96 24; www.restaurant bilbao.com; Carrer del Perill 33; mains €16-30; ⊙1-4pm & 9-11pm Mon-Fri, 2-4pm & 9-11pm Sat, closed Aug; ⓜDiagonal) Behind its unassuming exterior, Bilbao is a timeless classic, where reservations for dinner are imperative. The back dining room, with bottle-lined walls, stout timber tables and sepia lighting evocative of a country tavern, sets the stage for feasting on hearty dishes like oxtail in red wine sauce, grilled pork trotters and codfish with garlic mousse, accompanied by good Spanish wines.

BOTAFUMEIRO
SEAFOOD €€€

Map p296 (☑93 218 42 30; www.botafumeiro.es; Carrer Gran de Gràcia 81; mains €22-59; ⊙noon-1am; ⓜFontana) This temple of Galician shellfish has long been a magnet for VIPs visiting Barcelona. You can bring the price down by sharing a few *medias raciones* (large tapas plates) to taste a range of marine offerings followed by mains like spider crab pie, squid ink paella or grilled spiny lobster.

ROIG ROBÍ
CATALAN €€€

Map p296 (☑93 218 92 22; www.roigrobi.com; Carrer de Sèneca 20; mains €21-36; ⊙1.30-4pm & 8.30-11.30pm Mon-Fri, 8.30-11.30pm Sat; ⓟ; ⓜDiagonal) At this altar to refined traditional cooking, the seasonally changing menu serves as a showcase for beautifully presented creations with local and organic ingredients. Start off with tomato crème with Gorgonzola ice cream, before moving on to outstanding seafood rice dishes, salt-baked market-fresh fish or slow-roasted Pyrenees lamb. Call ahead to reserve a table on the vine-draped back patio.

CON GRACIA
FUSION €€€

Map p296 (☑93 238 02 01; www.congracia.es; Carrer de Martínez de la Rosa 8; tasting menus €65, with wine €95; ⊙7-11pm Tue-Sat; ⓜDiagonal) This teeny hideaway (seating about 20 in total) is a hive of originality, producing delicately balanced Mediterranean cuisine with Asian touches. On offer is a regularly changing surprise tasting menu or the set 'traditional' one (both six courses), with

dishes such as squid stuffed with *jamón ibérico* and black truffle, and sake-marinated tuna with walnut pesto. Book ahead.

CAN TRAVI NOU
CATALAN €€€

(☑93 428 03 01; www.gruptravi.com; Carrer de Jorge Manrique 8; mains €15.50-30; ⊙1-4pm & 8-11pm; ⓜMontbau) Dining areas stretch out across two floors of this expansive 18th-century mansion. The warm colours, grandfather clock and rustic air make for a magical setting for dining on Catalan specialities like slow-roasted pork and lamb, and seafood casseroles. Reserve ahead.

DRINKING & NIGHTLIFE

★BOBBY GIN
COCKTAIL BAR

Map p296 (☑93 368 18 92; www.bobbygin.com; Carrer de Francisco Giner 47; ⊙4pm-2am Sun-Wed, to 2.30am Thu, to 3am Fri & Sat; ⓜDiagonal) With over 60 varieties, this whitewashed stone-walled bar is a haven for gin lovers. Try an infusion-based concoction (rose-tea-infused Hendrick's with strawberries and lime; tangerine-infused Tanqueray 10 with agave nectar and bitter chamomile) or a cocktail like the Santa Maria (chardonnay, milk-thistle syrup, thyme, sage and lemon). Fusion tapas choices include G&T-cured salmon. Shrimp coated in green puffed rice and beef and shiitake wontons are other great options.

★RABIPELAO
COCKTAIL BAR

Map p296 (☑93 182 50 35; www.elrabipelao.com; Carrer del Torrent d'En Vidalet 22; ⊙7pm-1.30am Sun-Thu, to 3am Fri & Sat, 1-4.30pm Sun; ⓜJoanic) An anchor of Gràcia's nightlife, Rabipelao is a celebratory space with a shiny disco ball and DJs spinning salsa beats. A silent film plays in one corner beyond the red velvety wallpaper-covered walls and there's a richly hued mural above the bar. Tropical cocktails like mojitos and caipirinhas pair with South American snacks such as *arepas* (meat-filled cornbread patties) and ceviche.

ELEPHANTA
BAR

Map p296 (☑93 237 69 06; www.elephanta. cat; Carrer del Torrent d'en Vidalet 37; ⊙6pm-1.30am Mon-Wed, to 2.30am Thu, to 3am Fri & Sat, to 10pm Sun; ⓡ; ⓜJoanic) Tucked off the main drag, this petite cocktail bar has an old-fashioned vibe, with long plush green banquettes, art-lined walls and a five-seat bar with vintage wood stools. Gin is the drink of choice, with more than 40 varieties on hand, and the cocktails are expertly mixed.

VIBLIOTECA
WINE BAR

Map p296 (☑93 284 42 02; www.viblioteca.com; Carrer de Vallfogona 12; ☉7pm-midnight; ⓂFontana) A glass cabinet piled high with ripe cheese (over 50 varieties) entices you into this small, white, cleverly designed contemporary space. The real speciality at Viblioteca, however, is wine, and you can choose from 150 mostly local labels, many of them available by the glass.

LA VERMUTERIA DEL TANO
BAR

Map p296 (☑93 213 10 58; Carrer Joan Blanques 17; ☉9am-9pm Mon-Fri, noon-4pm Sat & Sun; ⓂJoanic) Scarcely changed in decades, with barrels on the walls, old fridges with wooden doors, vintage clocks and marble-topped tables, this vermouth bar is a local gathering point. Its house-speciality Peruchi is served traditionally with a glass of carbonated water. Tapas is also traditional, with most dishes utilising ingredients from tins (anchovies, smoked clams, cockles and pickled octopus).

EL SABOR
BAR

Map p296 (☑674 993075; Carrer de Francisco Giner 32; ☉9pm-2.30am Sun-Thu, to 3am Fri & Sat; ⓂDiagonal) Ruled since 1992 by the charismatic Havana-born Angelito is this home of *ron y son* (rum and sound). A mixed crowd of Cubans and fans of the Caribbean island come to drink mojitos and shake their stuff in this diminutive, good-humoured hang-out. Stop by on Mondays, Tuesdays and Wednesdays for a free two-hour salsa or bachata lesson (starting at 9.30pm).

BAR CANIGÓ
BAR

Map p296 (☑93 213 30 49; www.barcanigo.com; Carrer de Verdi 2; ☉10am-2am Mon-Thu, 10am-3am Fri, 8pm-3am Sat; ⓂFontana) Now run by the third generation of owners, this corner bar overlooking Plaça de la Revolució de Setembre de 1868 is an animated spot to sip on a house vermouth or an Estrella beer around rickety old marble-top tables, as people have done here since 1922.

Earlier in the day, it's a great spot for a coffee.

RAÏM
BAR

Map p296 (Carrer del Progrés 48; ☉8pm-2am Tue-Thu, to 3am Fri & Sat; ⓂDiagonal) The walls in Raïm are alive with black-and-white photos of Cubans and Cuba. Weathered old wooden chairs of another epoch huddle around marble tables, while grand old wood-framed mirrors hang from the walls. It draws a friendly, garrulous crowd who pile in for first-rate mojitos and an excellent selection of rum.

LA CIGALE
COCKTAIL BAR

Map p296 (☑93 457 58 23; www.facebook.com/la-cigale-barcelona; Carrer de Tordera 50; ☉6pm-2am Sun-Thu, to 3am Fri & Sat; ⓂJoanic) La Cigale is a very civilised place for a cocktail, with oil paintings on the walls, gilded mirrors and leatherbound volumes scattered about. Prop up the zinc bar, sink into a secondhand lounge chair around a teeny table or head upstairs.

EL RINCÓN CUBANO
BAR

Map p296 (☑93 143 77 01; Carrer de l'Or 19; ☉7pm-1am Tue-Thu, 7pm-2am Fri, 6pm-2am Sat, 1pm-midnight Sun; ⓢ; ⓂFontana) Cuban cocktails (including Cuba libres and *el presidentes*) and beers (Mayabe, Tinima and Cacique) are served alongside authentic snacks such as *pasteles* (puff pastry with savoury fillings), Cuban sandwiches and *ropa vieja* (shredded steak in tomato sauce) at this bar with arched brickwork and terracotta-tiled floors. It's in its element on Sundays from 4pm when live acoustic Cuban music plays.

SOL SOLER
BAR

Map p296 (☑93 172 99 75; Plaça del Sol 21; ☉11am-2am; ⓂFontana) With old tile floors, wood panelling and little marble tables, Sol Soler is perfect for a beer, vermouth or Campari overlooking the busy square out front.

CHATELET
COCKTAIL BAR

Map p296 (☑93 284 95 90; Carrer de Torrijos 54; ☉6pm-2.30am Mon-Fri, from noon Sat & Sun; ⓂJoanic) A popular meeting point in the 'hood, Chatelet has big windows for watching the passing people parade, and a buzzing art-filled interior that sees a wide cross-section of Gràcia society. Blues and old-school American soul plays in the background. The cocktails are excellent, and the drink prices fair (with discounts before 10pm).

NOU CANDANCHÚ   BAR

Map p296 (☑93 237 73 62; Plaça de la Vila de Gràcia 9; ◷9.30am-1am; ⓜFontana) Nou Candanchú is a long-time favourite and one of the liveliest spots on Plaça de la Vila de Gràcia. *Barcelonins* flock to its sunny terrace for a few drinks.

LA VERMU   BAR

Map p296 (☑93 171 80 87; Carrer de Sant Domènec 15; ◷6.30pm-midnight Mon-Thu, 12.30-4.30pm & 7.30pm-12.30am Fri-Sun; ⓡFGC Gràcia) House-made *negre* (black) and *blanc* (white) vermouth, served with a slice of orange and an olive, is the speciality of this hip neighbourhood hang-out. The airy space with exposed timber beams and industrial lighting centres on a marble bar with seating and surrounding marble-topped tables. Vermouth aside, it also has a small but stellar wine list and stylishly presented tapas.

 ## ⭐ ENTERTAINMENT

CINE TEXAS   CINEMA

(☑93 348 77 48; www.cinemestexas.cat; Carrer de Bailèn 205; ⓜJoanic) All films at this contemporary four-screen cinema are shown in their original languages (with subtitles in Catalan). Genres span art house through to Hollywood blockbusters. Catalan-language films are subtitled in English.

SODA ACÚSTIC   LIVE MUSIC

Map p296 (☑93 016 55 90; www.soda.cat; Carrer de les Guilleries 6; tickets from €2; ◷8pm-2.30am Wed, Thu & Sun, to 3am Fri & Sat; ⓜFontana) This low-lit modern space stages an eclectic line-up of bands and performing artists. Jazz, world music, Balkan swing, Latin rhythms and plenty of experimental, not easily classifiable musicians all receive their due. The acoustics are excellent. Check the website for upcoming shows.

VERDI   CINEMA

Map p296 (☑93 238 79 90; www.cines-verdi.com; Carrer de Verdi 32; ⓜFontana) In the heart of Gràcia, this five-screen cinema shows art-house and blockbuster films in their original language as well as films in Catalan and Spanish. It's handy to lots of local eateries and bars for pre- and post-film enjoyment.

 # 🛍 SHOPPING

⭐COLMILLO DE MORSA   FASHION & ACCESSORIES

Map p296 (☑645 206365; www.facebook.com/colmillodemorsa; Carrer de Vic 15-17; ◷4.30-8.30pm Mon, 11am-2.30pm & 4.30-8.30pm Tue-Sat; ⓡFGC Gràcia) Design team Javier Blanco and Elisabet Vallecillo have made waves at Madrid's Cibeles Fashion Week and Paris' fashion fair Who's Next, and showcase their Barcelona-made women's fashion here at their flagship boutique. They've also opened the floor to promote other young, up-and-coming local labels. The light-filled space also hosts art, graphic design and photography exhibitions and fashion shows.

Fabrics used by Colmillo de Morsa are all sustainably produced in Europe using non-toxic dyes.

⭐FAMILY BEER   DRINKS

Map p296 (☑93 219 29 88; www.family-beer.com; Carrer de Joan Blanques 55; ◷5-8.30pm Mon, 10am-2pm & 5-8.30pm Tue-Sat; ⓜJoanic) Over 130 varieties of local and international craft beers and ciders are stocked in the fridges here, so you can pick up a cold brew to go. It also has brewing kits and books, and runs regular brewing workshops (three hours €45) and hosts free demonstrations of cheese making and cookery using beer, as well as 'meet the brewer' tastings.

HIBERNIAN   BOOKS

Map p296 (☑93 217 47 96; www.hibernian-books.com; Carrer de Montseny 17; ◷4-8.30pm Mon, 11am-8.30pm Tue-Sat; ⓜFontana) Barcelona's biggest secondhand English bookshop stocks thousands of titles covering all sorts of subjects, from cookery to children's classics. There's a smaller collection of new books in English too.

CAN LUC   CHEESE

Map p296 (☑93 007 47 83; www.canluc.es; Carrer de Berga 4; ◷5-9pm Mon, 10am-2.30pm & 5-8.30pm Tue-Sat; ⓡFGC Gràcia) At any one time, this brightly lit shop has 150 different varieties of cheese. Catalan cheeses are the speciality, but you'll also find a selection from France, Italy, the Netherlands, Switzerland and Britain. Expert staff provide guidance. Wines, condiments, crackers and cheese knives are also available. For a gourmet picnic, pre-order a brimming hamper (€25 to €100).

BODEGA BONAVISTA
WINE

Map p296 (☑93 218 81 99; Carrer de Bonavista 10; ◷10am-2.30pm & 5-9pm Mon-Fri, noon-3pm & 6-9pm Sat, noon-3pm Sun; Ⓜ Fontana) An excellent little neighbourhood bodega, Bonavista endeavours to seek out great wines at reasonable prices. The stock is mostly from Catalonia and elsewhere in Spain, but there's also a well-chosen selection from France. The Bonavista also acts as a deli, and there are some especially good cheeses. You can sample wines by the glass, along with cheeses and charcuterie, at one of the in-store tables.

AMALIA VERMELL
JEWELLERY

Map p296 (☑655 754008; www.amaliavermell. com; Carrer de Francisco Giner 49; ◷11am-2pm & 5-9pm Mon-Sat; Ⓜ Diagonal) Striking geometric jewellery made from high-quality materials such as sterling silver is handcrafted by Amalia Vermell here in her atelier. Browse for pendants and necklaces, bracelets and rings, or sign up for a jewellery-making course (from €65 for two hours; English available).

VINIL VINTAGE
MUSIC

Map p296 (☑93 192 39 99; Carrer de Ramón y Cajal 45-47; ◷10.30am-2pm & 5-8.30pm Tue-Sat; Ⓜ Joanic) Crate diggers will love rummaging through the vinyl collection here. There's a huge range of rock, pop and jazz, including plenty of Spanish music. It also sells turntables and speakers.

REKUP & CO
HOMEWARES

Map p296 (☑694 472297; www.rekupandco.com; Carrer de Verdi 63; ◷11am-2.30pm & 5-9pm; Ⓜ Fontana) Recycled timbers and metals are used by French native Emmanuel Wagnon to create individual works of art that are functional too: chairs, tables, shelves, mirrors, lamps and quirkier items like shutters made from wooden pallets. International shipping can be arranged.

LADY LOQUITA
CLOTHING

Map p296 (☑93 217 82 92; www.ladyloquita. com; Travessera de Gràcia 126; ◷11am-2pm & 5-8.30pm Mon-Sat; Ⓜ Fontana) At this hip little shop you can browse through light, locally made summer dresses by Tiralahilacha, evening wear by Japamala and handmade jewellery by local design label Klimbim. There are also whimsical odds and ends: dinner plates with dog-people portraits and digital prints on wood by About Paola.

AMAPOLA VEGAN SHOP
CLOTHING

Map p296 (☑93 010 62 73; www.amapolavegan shop.com; Travessera de Gràcia 129; ◷11am-2pm & 5-8.30pm Mon-Sat; Ⓜ Fontana) ⌁ A shop with a heart of gold, Amapola proves that you need not toss your ethics aside in the quest for stylish clothing and accessories. You'll find sleek leather-alternatives for wallets, handbags and messenger bags by Matt & Nat, belts by Nae Vic, and elegant scarves by Barts.

TINTIN SHOP
GIFTS & SOUVENIRS

Map p296 (☑93 289 25 24; www.tintinshopbcn. com; Travessera de Gràcia 176; ◷10.30am-2.30pm & 5-8.30pm Mon-Fri, 11am-2.30pm Sat; Ⓜ Fontana) Fans of the Belgian boy wonder should make a beeline to this Gràcia store, where you'll find Tintin T-shirts, posters, action figures, book bags, wristwatches, pencil cases, and even a soft, irresistible Milou (Tintin's wire fox terrier, known as Snowy in English) – plus, of course, the books that made him famous (with titles in Catalan, Spanish and French).

LA FESTIVAL
WINE

Map p296 (☑93 023 22 81; Carrer de Verdi 67; ◷5-9pm Mon, 10.30am-2.30pm & 5-9pm Tue-Thu, 10.30am-2.30pm & 5-9.30pm Fri & Sat, 10.30am-2.30pm & 5-8pm Sun; Ⓜ Fontana) Knowledgeable English-speaking staff can give you a wealth of information about the excellent wines for sale here. Most are from Spanish producers, though there are a few French labels, and some organic and biodynamic wines. You can refill your bottle with wine or vermouth from one of the casks at the front, starting at €3 a bottle.

PICNIC
CLOTHING

Map p296 (☑93 016 69 53; www.picnicstore. es; Carrer de Verdi 17; ◷11am-9pm Mon-Fri, 11am-3pm & 4-9pm Sat; Ⓜ Fontana) This tiny, beautifully curated boutique has many temptations: stylish sneakers by Meyba (a Barcelona brand), striped jerseys from Basque label Loreak Mendian and boldly patterned Mödernaked backpacks. Other finds include animal-print ceramics for the home, small-scale art prints and fashion mags.

SURCO
MUSIC

Map p296 (☑93 218 34 39; www.facebook.com/surcobcn; Travessera de Gràcia 144; ◷10.30am-2pm & 5.30-9pm Mon-Sat; Ⓜ Fontana) Surco is an obligatory stop for music lovers, especially fans of vinyl. You'll find loads of new and used records and CDs here, with a mix of Tom Waits, Mishima (a Catalan indie pop band), Calexico and more.

MUSHI MUSHI FASHION & ACCESSORIES
Map p296 (✍93 292 29 74; www.mushimushi collection.com; Carrer de Bonavista 12; ⊙11am-3pm & 4.30-8.30pm Mon-Sat; Ⓜ Diagonal) A gorgeous little fashion boutique in an area that's not short of them, Mushi Mushi specialises in quirky but elegant women's fashion and accessories. It stocks small labels such as Des Petits Hauts, Sessùn and Orion London, as well as jewellery by Adriana Llorens. The collection changes frequently, so a return visit can pay off.

NOSTÀLGIC PHOTOGRAPHY
Map p296 (✍93 368 57 57; www.nostalgic.es; Carrer de Goya 18; ⊙10.30am-2pm & 5-8pm Mon-Fri, 11am-2.30pm Sat; Ⓜ Fontana) In a beautiful space with exposed brick walls and wooden furniture, Nostàlgic specialises in all kinds of modern and vintage photography equipment. You'll find camera bags and tripods for the digital snappers, rolls of film, and quirky Lomo cameras. There is also a decent collection of photography books to buy or browse.

MERCAT DE L'ABACERIA CENTRAL MARKET
Map p296 (www.mercatsbcn.cat; Travessera de Gràcia 186; ⊙7am-2.30pm & 5.30-8pm Mon-Sat; Ⓜ Fontana, ⒭FGC Gràcia) Dating from 1892, this sprawling iron and brick market is an atmospheric place to browse for fresh produce, cheeses, bakery items and more. There are also several food stalls where you can grab a quick bite on the cheap.

BE GIFTS & SOUVENIRS
Map p296 (✍93 218 89 49; www.bethestore.com; Carrer de Bonavista 7; ⊙10.30am-9pm Mon-Sat; Ⓜ Diagonal) Be is a fun place to browse for accessories and gift ideas. You'll find rugged vintage-looking satchels, leather handbags, stylish (and reflective) Happy Socks, portable record players, sneakers (Vans, Pumas, old-school Nikes) and gadgets (including richly hued Pantone micro speakers and Polaroid digital cameras).

SPORTS & ACTIVITIES

AQUA URBAN SPA SPA
Map p296 (✍93 238 41 60; www.aquaurbanspa. es; Carrer Gran de Gràcia 7; 90min baths session from €51; ⊙9am-9pm Mon-Sat; Ⓜ Diagonal) With treatments for everything from stress to tired legs (merciful for diehard sightseers), this spa offers smallish pool and shower areas, along with steam baths, Roman-style baths and a series of massages and beauty treatment options such as body scrubs (from €39 for 30 minutes).

Camp Nou, Pedralbes & La Zona Alta

Neighbourhood Top Five

1 **Camp Nou** (p173) Reliving the great moments of one of the world's legendary football teams at the multimedia museum – or, better yet, cheering along with their fans during a live game.

2 **Museu-Monestir de Pedralbes** (p174) Walking along the 14th-century cloister and gazing at exquisite murals at this convent turned museum.

3 **CosmoCaixa** (p176) Getting a feel for the Amazon (tropical downpour and all), and travelling through Earth's evolution at warp speed at this excellent science museum.

4 **Bellesguard** (p175) Gazing upon Gaudí's imposing, medieval-like masterpiece with its crenellated walls, stained glass and ornate ironwork.

5 **Tibidabo** (p180) Travelling by tram and funicular railway up to this forested mountain for lovely views and an old-fashioned amusement park.

For more detail of this area see Map p298 and p300 ➡

Lonely Planet's Top Tip

To make the most of the neighbourhood, try to visit on a weekend. Saturday and Sunday are the most reliable days for getting a tour (offered in English) inside the Pavellons Güell, near Palau Reial de Pedralbes. It's also the best time to travel to Tibidabo via the 1901-built *tramvia blau,* which runs daily from June to early September and on weekends year-round.

Best Places to Eat

➡ Acontraluz (p177)

➡ Aspic (p178)

➡ La Balsa (p178)

➡ Via Veneto (p178)

For reviews, see p176.➡

Best Places to Drink

➡ Dō Bar (p181)

➡ El Maravillas (p180)

➡ Mirablau (p180)

For reviews, see p180.➡

Best Parks & Gardens

➡ Parc de Collserola (p180)

➡ Jardins del Laberint d'Horta (p179)

➡ Jardins del Palau de Pedralbes (p175)

➡ Parc de la Creueta del Coll (p175)

Explore Camp Nou, Pedralbes & La Zona Alta

This vast area, which runs north of L'Eixample and west of Gràcia, includes some intriguing attractions. Yet few visitors make the journey here, due to the area's relative remoteness and the longer distances between sights. On the upside, you'll have the chance to explore Barcelona off the tourist path.

Framing the north end of La Zona Alta (the High Zone) are the Collserola hills. Rugged Parc de Collserola (p180) attracts cyclists, runners and walkers, and has a sprinkling of historic sites.

Upmarket Pedralbes has a mix of high-end gated residences and boxy apartment buildings, peaceful streets and manicured gardens hidden off the busy thoroughfares. Standouts include an atmospheric monastery (p174), the elegant Jardins del Palau de Pedralbes (p175) and Gaudí's little-visited Pavellons Güell (p175).

Just south of Pedralbes is Camp Nou (p181), the home of FC Barcelona, one of the world's best football teams.

To the northeast lies Sarrià (p177), a quaint neighbourhood of brick streets, tiny plazas and medieval buildings. Another area well worth exploring is nearby Sant Gervasi; with its handful of upmarket restaurants and bars.

Local Life

➡ **Outdoor pursuits** Head up into the hills to join locals running, mountain biking and picnicking in the sprawling Parc de Collserola (p180).

➡ **Nightlife** Plaça de la Concòrdia is a charming spot for drinks and tapas at bars such as El Maravillas (p180) before a recital or mini-exhibition at Centre Cívic Can Deu (p175).

➡ **Village days** The picturesque narrow lanes of Sarrià are idyllic for a stroll, stopping for cakes at Foix De Sarrià (p177), tapas at Bar Tomàs (p177) and a great meal on the leafy terrace at Vivanda (p178).

Getting There & Away

➡ **Metro** Línia 3 is handy for the Jardins del Laberint d'Horta (Mundet), and Camp Nou and Palau Reial de Pedralbes (Palau Reial).

➡ **Train** FGC trains are handy for getting close to sights in and around Tibidabo and Parc de Collserola.

➡ **Tram** Outside Avinguda Tibidabo station, the *tramvia blau* runs to Plaça del Doctor Andreu, where you can catch an onward funicular up to Tibidabo. Trams T1, T2 and T3 serve the area's southwest, linking Camp Nou and Palau Reial with Plaça de Francesc Macià.

➡ **Funicular** Two funicular railways provide hilltop access: the Funicular del Tibidabo runs between Plaça del Doctor Andreu and Plaça del Doctor Tibidabo. The Funicular de Vallvidrera runs between Peu del Funicular and Vallvidrera Superior.

TOP SIGHT
CAMP NOU

While nothing compares to the excitement of attending a live match, the Camp Nou Experience is a must for football fans. On this self-guided visit of FC Barcelona's home ground, you'll get an in-depth look at the club, starting with a museum filled with multimedia exhibits, trophies and historical displays, followed by a tour of the stadium.

Camp Nou Experience Museum

Camp Nou Experience begins in FC Barcelona's museum, which provides a high-tech view into the club. Massive touchscreens allow visitors to explore arcane aspects of the legendary team. You can also watch videos of particularly artful goals. Displays delve into the club's history, its social commitment and connection to Catalan identity, and in-depth stats of on-field action. Sound installations include the club's anthem (with translations in many languages) and the match-day roar of the amped-up crowds.

The museum's highlights are the photo section, the goal videos and the views out over the stadium. You can admire the golden boots (in at least one case literally) of great goal scorers of the past and learn about the greats who have played for the club over the years, including Maradona, Ronaldinho, Kubala and many others. A special area is devoted to Lionel Messi, considered by many to be the world's greatest footballer playing the game today.

The Stadium

Gazing out across Camp Nou is an experience in itself. The stadium, built in 1957 and enlarged for the 1982 World Cup, is one of the world's biggest, holding almost 100,000 people. The club has a world-record membership of 173,000. After renovations that will last until 2022 (the stadium will remain open throughout), Camp Nou will have a capacity of 105,000.

The self-guided tour of the stadium takes in the team's dressing rooms, heads out through the tunnel, on to the pitch and winds up in the presidential box. You'll also get to visit the television studio, the press room and the commentary boxes. Set aside about 2½ hours for the whole visit.

To make the tour, enter at Gate 9 (Avinguda de Joan XXIII near Carrer de Martí i Franquès).

Getting Tickets

Tickets to FC Barcelona matches are available at Camp Nou, online (through FC Barcelona's official website), and through various city locations. Tourist offices sell them there – the main office at Plaça de Catalunya is a centrally located option – as do FC Botiga stores. Tickets can cost anything from €39 to upwards of €250, depending on the seat and match. On match day the ticket windows open from 9.15am until kick off. Tickets for matches with Real Madrid sell out years in advance.

If you attend a game, go early so you'll have ample time to find your seat (this stadium is massive) and soak up the atmosphere.

You will almost definitely find scalpers lurking near the ticket windows. They are often club members and can sometimes get you in at a significant reduction. Don't pay until you are safely seated.

DON'T MISS

➜ Hearing the rousing anthem sung before FC Barcelona takes the field

➜ The museum's footage of the team's best goals

➜ A self-guided tour of the stadium

PRACTICALITIES

➜ Map p298, C8

➜ ☎902 189900

➜ www.fcbarcelona.com

➜ Gate 9, Avinguda de Joan XXIII

➜ adult/child €25/20

➜ ⏱9.30am-7.30pm Apr-Sep, 10am-6.30pm Mon-Sat, to 2.30pm Sun Oct-Mar

➜ Ⓜ Palau Reial

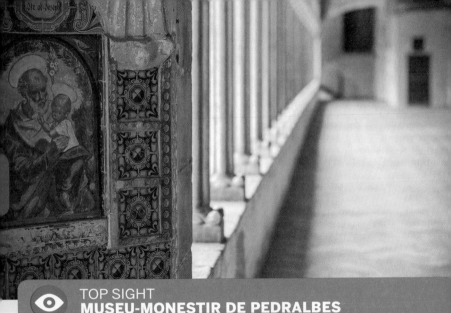

TOP SIGHT
MUSEU-MONESTIR DE PEDRALBES

Dating from medieval times, this atmospheric convent is now a museum of monastic life. Perched at the top of busy Avinguda de Pedralbes in what was once unpeopled countryside, the monastery remains a divinely quiet corner of Barcelona and is full of architectural treasures. Adjoining the monastery is the sober church, an excellent example of Catalan Gothic.

The Cloister & Chapel

The architectural highlight is the large, elegant, three-storey cloister, a jewel of Catalan Gothic, built in the early 14th century. Following its course to the right, stop at the first chapel, the Capella de Sant Miquel, the murals of which were done in 1346 by Ferrer Bassá, one of Catalonia's earliest documented painters. A few steps on is the ornamental grave of Queen Elisenda, who founded the convent. Curiously, it's divided in two: the side in the cloister shows her dressed as a penitent widow, while the other part, an alabaster masterpiece inside the adjacent church, shows her dressed as queen.

The Refectory & Sleeping Quarters

As you head around the ground floor of the cloister, you can peer into the restored refectory, kitchen, stables, stores and a reconstruction of the infirmary – all giving a good idea of convent life. Eating in the refectory must not have been a whole lot of fun, judging by the inscriptions around the walls exhorting *Silentium* (Silence) and *Audi Tacens* (Listen and Keep Quiet).

Upstairs is a grand hall that was once the *dormidor* (sleeping quarters). It was lined by tiny night cells, but they were long ago removed. Today a modest collection of the monastery's art, especially Gothic devotional works, and furniture grace this space.

DON'T MISS

➡ Ferrer Bassá's murals

➡ The three-storey Gothic cloister

➡ The refectory's admonishing inscriptions

PRACTICALITIES

➡ Map p298, B5

➡ ☎93 256 34 34

➡ http://monestir
pedralbes.bcn.cat

➡ Baixada del Monestir 9

➡ adult/child €5/free, after 3pm Sun free

➡ ⊙10am-5pm Tue-Fri, to 7pm Sat, to 8pm Sun Apr-Sep, 10am-2pm Tue-Fri, to 5pm Sat & Sun Oct-Mar

➡ 🚌63, 68, 75, 78, H4, 🚇FGC Reina Elisenda

◉ SIGHTS

CAMP NOU EXPERIENCE MUSEUM
See p173.

**MUSEU-MONESTIR
DE PEDRALBES** MONASTERY
See p174.

JARDINS DEL PALAU DE PEDRALBES PARK
Map p298 (Avinguda Diagonal 686; ☺10am-9pm
Apr-Oct, to 7pm Nov-Mar; Ⓜ Palau Reial) A few
steps from busy Avinguda Diagonal lies this
small enchanting green space. Sculptures,
fountains, citrus trees, bamboo groves, fragrant eucalyptus, towering cypresses and
bougainvillea-covered nooks lie scattered
along the paths criss-crossing these peaceful
gardens. Among the little-known treasures
here are a vine-covered parabolic pergola
and a gurgling fountain of Hercules (buried
in thick vegetation before being rediscovered
in 1984), both designed by Antoni Gaudí.

At the north end of the park is the Palau
Reial de Pedralbes, an early-20th-century
building that belonged to the family of
Eusebi Güell (Gaudí's patron) until they
handed it over to the city in 1926 to serve as
a royal residence. Past guests include King
Alfonso XIII, the president of Catalonia and
General Franco. The *palau* (palace) itself is
closed to the public.

PARC DE LA CREUETA DEL COLL PARK
(Passeig de la Mare de Déu del Coll 77; ☺10am-
9pm Apr-Oct, to 7pm Nov-Mar; 🚌 92, 129, N5,
Ⓜ Penitents) A favourite with families, this
refreshing public park has a meandering,
splashing lake pool, along with swings,
showers and a snack bar. Only the pool closes outside summer. The park is set inside a
deep crater left by long years of stone quar-
rying, with an enormous concrete sculpture, *Elogio del agua* (In Praise of Water) by
Eduardo Chillida, suspended on one side.

Enter from Carrer Mare de Déu del
Coll, a 1km walk east from the Penitents
metro station.

Views of the city and Tibidabo extend
from the hilly trails.

BELLESGUARD ARCHITECTURE
Map p298 (📞93 250 40 93; www.bellesguard
gaudi.com; Carrer de Bellesguard 16; adult/child
€9/free; ☺10am-3pm Tue-Sun; 🚃 FGC Avinguda
Tibidabo) This Gaudí masterpiece was rescued from obscurity and opened to the public in 2013. Built between 1900 and 1909,

this private residence (still owned by the
original Guilera family) has a castle-like
appearance with crenellated walls of stone
and brick, narrow stained-glass windows,
elaborate ironwork and a soaring turret
mounted by a Gaudían cross. It's a fascinating work that combines both Gothic and
Modernista elements.

Guided tours in English (€16 per person)
take place on weekends at 11am. At other
times, you can visit the interior of the building and the grounds with an audioguide
that gives historical background.

The downside: it's a long walk to a train
station, though many buses pass near (including bus 22 and bus 58 from Plaça de
Catalunya). Be sure to call before making
the trek out – Bellesguard sometimes closes
for private events.

PAVELLONS GÜELL ARCHITECTURE
Map p298 (📞93 317 76 52; Avinguda de Pedralbes
7; guided tours adult/child €5/2.50; ☺10am-4pm;
Ⓜ Palau Reial) These stables and porter's
lodge were designed by Gaudí for the Finca
Güell, as the Güell estate here was called.
The structures here were built between
1884 and 1887, when Gaudí was strongly
impressed by Islamic architecture. You can
peer inside on guided visits, with English-
language tours at 10.15am, 11.15pm and
3pm. Unexpected closures can occur, so
confirm opening hours before heading out.

One of the most eye-catching features is
the fantastical wrought-iron dragon gate
near Avinguda de Pedralbes.

CENTRE CÍVIC CAN DEU CULTURAL CENTRE
Map p298 (📞93 410 10 07; www.cccandeu.com;
Plaça de la Concòrdia 13; ☺9am-10pm Mon-Sat,
10am-2pm Sun, closed Aug; Ⓜ Numància) Set in
a late-19th-century neo-Gothic mansion,
this cultural centre stages concerts, exhibitions and workshops throughout the year.
Its cafe opens to a peaceful plaza.

OBSERVATORI FABRA OBSERVATORY
Map p298 (📞93 417 57 36; www.fabra.cat; Carretera del Observatori; tours €2, night observation
€15-25; ☺tours 11am-2pm Sun, night observation
by reservation Fri & Sat Oct-Jun; 🚃 FGC Avinguda
Tibidabo) Inaugurated in 1904, this Modernista observatory 415m above sea level is
still a functioning scientific foundation. On
certain evenings visitors can observe the
stars through its grand old telescope (check
the website for the latest schedule). Visits,
generally in Catalan or Spanish, must be

TOP SIGHT
COSMOCAIXA

One of the city's most popular attractions, this science museum is a favourite with kids (and kids at heart). Its centrepiece is the recreation of over 1 sq km of flooded **Amazon** rainforest *(Bosc Inundat)*, where more than 100 flora and fauna species – including anacondas, colourful poisonous frogs and caimans – thrive. It's even possible to watch a tropical downpour in this unique, living diorama. Another highlight is the Mur Geològic: seven great chunks of rock (90 metric tons in all) that have been assembled to create the **Geological Wall**.

Also worthwhile are the 3D shows in the **Planetari** (Planetarium), which are screened several times a day. Shows typically run for 35 minutes; headsets provide commentary in English and other languages. Various guided tours are also available.

Other displays cover many fascinating areas of science, from fossils to physics, and from the alphabet to outer space.

The bulk of the museum is underground. Outside, there's a nice stroll through the extensive Plaça de la Ciència, whose modest garden flourishes with Mediterranean flora.

DON'T MISS

→ A tropical storm in the Amazon
→ The Geological Wall
→ The Planetarium

PRACTICALITIES

→ Museu de la Ciència
→ Map p298, D2
→ ☑93 212 60 50
→ www.cosmocaixa. com
→ Carrer d'Isaac Newton 26
→ adult/child €4/free, guided tours from €2, planetarium €4
→ ⏰10am-8pm Tue-Sun
→ 🚌60, 196

---

pre-booked. From mid-June to mid-September, Sopars amb Estrelles (p179) offers an evening of high-end dining and astronomy.

COL·LEGI DE LES TERESIANES ARCHITECTURE
Map p298 (Carrer de Ganduxer 85-105; 🚆FGC Les Tres Torres) This striking work by Gaudí has exposed brick pillars and steep catenary arches, each of which is unique. It was built in 1889 for the Order of St Teresa. The interior is closed to the public.

✗ EATING

LA FERMATA DE SARRIÀ PIZZA €
Map p298 (☑93 315 84 02; www.lafermata.es; Carrer Major de Sarrià 2-4; pizza per kg €14-28; ⏰12.30-4pm & 7.30-11pm; 🚌66,130, 🚆FGC Sarrià) Rectangular pizza slices are sold *al taglio* (by weight) at this little pizzeria run by a Rome-trained chef, and come in an array of classic and Catalonian-inspired toppings (150 varieties altogether, though not at the same time). It's perfect for picking up takeaway, but there's also a counter with stool seating and a handful of tables on the pavement.

LA BURG BURGERS €
Map p298 (☑93 205 63 48; www.laburg.com; Passeig de Sant Joan Bosco 55; burgers €7-15.50; ⏰1-4pm & 8-11.30pm Mon-Wed, 1-4pm & 8pm-midnight Thu, 1-4.30pm & 8pm-midnight Fri & Sat, 1.30-4pm & 8-11.30pm Sun; 🚀; 🚌V7, 🚆FGC Sarrià) 🍷 Wines by the glass or bottle at this sleek spot pair with gourmet burgers made from organic, farm-to-table ingredients. Cheese lovers should try La Quesos (alpine-bred beef, Emmental, Gouda and Manchego); other standouts from the 13 choices include La Sarrià (veal, porcini mushrooms, fried egg and black truffle shavings). Buns are handmade; gluten-free options are available.

MITJA VIDA TAPAS €
Map p300 (www.morrofi.cat; Carrer de Brusi 39; tapas €3-7; ⏰6-11pm Mon-Thu, noon-4pm & 6-11pm Fri & Sat, noon-4pm Sun, closed Aug; 🚆FGC Sant Gervasi) A young, fun, mostly local crowd gathers around the stainless-steel tapas bar of tiny Mitja Vida. It's a jovial eating and drinking spot, with good-sized portions of anchovies, calamari, smoked herring, cheeses and *mojama* (salt-cured tuna). The drink of choice is house-made vermouth.

SANTAMASA

CATALAN €

Map p298 (☑93 676 35 74; www.santamasa restaurant.com; Carrer Major de Sarrià 97; dishes €6.50-13; ⊙8am-midnight Mon-Fri, 9am-midnight Sat & Sun; ☒FGC Reina Elisenda) Next door to Sarrià's pretty 18th-century church Sant Vicenç de Sarrià, Santamasa is an enticing spot for a light meal at any time of day. The menu here is wide-ranging, with a mix of creatively topped *pizzetes* (small pizzas), salads, open-faced sandwiches, fondue, burgers, quesadillas and good sharing appetisers like hummus and guacamole.

FLASH FLASH

SPANISH €

Map p300 (☑93 237 09 90; www.flashflash barcelona.com; Carrer de la Granada del Penedès 25; dishes €6.30-13.80; ⊙1pm-1.30am; ☑; ☒FGC Gràcia) Decorated with black-and-white murals and an all-white interior, Flash Flash has a fun and kitschy pop-art aesthetic that harks back to its opening in 1970. Fluffy tortillas are the speciality, with more than 50 varieties, as well as massive bunless hamburgers.

FOIX DE SARRIÀ

BAKERY €

Map p298 (☑93 203 04 73; www.foixdesarria. com; Plaça de Sarrià 12-13; pastries €2-5; ⊙8am-9pm; ☒FGC Reina Elisenda) Since 1886 this exclusive pastry shop has been selling the most exquisite cakes and sweets. You can take them away or head out the back to sip tea, coffee or hot chocolate while sampling little cakes and other baking wizardry.

BAR TOMÀS

TAPAS €

Map p298 (☑93 203 10 77; www.eltomasdesarria. com; Carrer Major de Sarrià 49; tapas €2.50-7; ⊙noon-4pm & 6-10pm Mon-Sat; ☒FGC Sarrià) Many *barcelonins* swear Bar Tomàs is the best place in the city for *patatas bravas* (potato chunks) served with its house-speciality garlic aioli. Despite the fluorescent lights and low-key service, folks from all walks of life pile in, particularly for lunch on weekends. Fried artichokes, anchovies and other snacks also go nicely with an ice-cold beer.

COMAXURROS

CHURROS €

Map p298 (☑93 417 94 05; www.comaxurros.com; Carrer de Muntaner 562; churros from €2; ⊙4.30-8.30pm Tue, 9am-2pm & 4.30-8.30pm Wed-Fri, 9am-2pm & 5-8.30pm Sat & Sun; ☒FGC El Putxet) At this eye-catching little cafe, brought to you by Barcelona's famous *pastelería* Canals, the humble churro receives a dramatic makeover: it's fried in olive oil to crispy (healthier) perfection and served with unique fillings and toppings (pistachio, strawberry sauce, dark chocolate). Savoury churros include cheese, mushrooms and *jamón ibérico* (Iberian ham), among other delicacies.

★ACONTRALUZ

MEDITERRANEAN €€

Map p298 (☑93 203 06 58; www.acontraluz.com; Carrer del Milanesat 19; mains €15-27; ⊙1.30-4pm & 8.30pm-midnight Mon-Sat, 1.30-4pm Sun; ☒FGC Les Tres Torres) The most magical place to dine at this romantic restaurant is in the bougainvillea-draped, tree-filled garden, reached by an arbour. Olive-crusted monkfish with caramelised fennel, black paella with squid and clams, and suckling pig with fig jam are all outstanding choices. Don't miss the rum-soaked carrot cake with cardamom ice cream for dessert.

BANGKOK CAFE

THAI €€

Map p298 (☑93 339 32 69; Carrer d'Evarist Arnús 65; mains €10-14; ⊙8-11pm Mon-Wed, 1-3.45pm & 8-11pm Thu-Sun; Ⓜ Plaça del Centre) If you're

---

A WANDER THROUGH OLD SARRIÀ

Hugging the left flank of busy main road Via Augusta, the old centre of Sarrià is a largely pedestrianised haven of peace. Probably founded in the 13th century and incorporated into Barcelona only in 1921, ancient Sarrià is formed around sinuous **Carrer Major de Sarrià**, today a mix of old and new, with a sprinkling of shops and restaurants.

At the street's top end is pretty **Plaça de Sarrià** (from where Passeig de la Reina Elisenda de Montcada leads west to the medieval Museu-Monestir de Pedralbes), where you'll want to check out **Foix De Sarrià**, an exclusive pastry shop. As you wander downhill, duck off into **Plaça del Consell de la Vila**, **Plaça de Sant Vicenç de Sarrià** and Carrer de Rocaberti, at the end of which is the Monestir de Santa Isabel, with a neo-Gothic cloister. Built in 1886 to house Clarissan nuns, whose order first set up in El Raval in the 16th century, it was abandoned during the civil war and used as an air-raid shelter.

craving Thai cuisine, it's well worth making the trip out to Bangkok Cafe, which serves up spicy green papaya salad, *tam yam kung* (spicy prawn soup), crispy prawns with plum sauce, red curries and other standouts, with more spice than you'll find in most Catalan eateries.

It's a small, buzzing place with an open kitchen, photos of the Thai royals, blackboard specials and an oversized chandelier. Enter from the side lane.

★ASPIC   CAFE, DELI €€

Map p300 (☑93 200 04 35; www.aspic.es; Avinguda de Pau Casals 24; dishes €9-19.50; ⊙cafe 11am-1.30pm & 6-8.30pm Tue-Sat, 11am-4pm Sun, deli 9am-8pm Tue-Sat, to 4pm Sun, bar to midnight Tue-Sat, to 4pm Sun; 🕾☑; ☑T1, T2, T3 Francesc Macià) Luxury ingredients (smoked salmon, premium charcuterie and cheeses, high-grade olive oils and carefully chosen Spanish wines) are utilised at the flagship cafe of this Barcelona caterer in stunning dishes like local carrelet fish with cockle foam and broccoli purée. The attached deli is perfect for picking up items for a gourmet picnic in nearby Jardins del Poeta Eduard Marquina.

VIVANDA   CATALAN €€

Map p298 (☑93 203 19 18; www.vivanda.cat; Carrer Major de Sarrià 134; sharing plates €9-21; ⊙1.30-3.30pm & 8.30-11pm Tue-Sat, 1.30-3.30pm Sun; ☑FGC Reina Elisenda) With a menu designed by acclaimed Catalan chef Jordi Vilà, diners are in for a treat at this Sarrià classic. Changing dishes showcase seasonal fare, such as eggs with truffles, rice with cuttlefish, and artichokes with romesco sauce. Hidden behind the restaurant is the tree-shaded terrace with terracotta tiles and white-clothed tables.

It's open year-round – heat lamps are switched on in winter, and blankets and hot broth are distributed to diners.

5° PINO   CATALAN €€

Map p298 (Quinto Pino; ☑93 252 22 81; www.quinto pino.es; Passeig de la Bonanova 98; sandwiches €8-13, tapas €1.50-7.50; ⊙kitchen 8.30am-midnight Mon-Fri, 10am-midnight Sat, bar to 1.30am; ☑; ☑FGC Sarrià) While exploring Sarrià, it's worth detouring a few blocks east to this charming cafe and restaurant, which is a favourite local spot for tasty sandwiches, salads, tortillas, tapas and drinks. It's on a busy road, though the outdoor pine-shaded terrace is still a pleasant spot for a bite.

EL ASADOR DE ARANDA   SPANISH €€

Map p298 (☑93 417 01 15; www.asadordearanda. net; Avinguda del Tibidabo 31; tapas €6-16.50, mains €15-22.50; ⊙1-4.30pm & 8-11.30pm; 🕾; ☑FGC Avinguda Tibidabo) Set in a striking Modernista building, complete with stained-glass windows, Moorish-style brick arches and elaborate ceilings, El Asador de Aranda's most popular seats are on the landscaped terrace. You'll find a fine assortment of tapas plates for sharing, though the speciality is the meat (roast lamb, spare ribs, beef), prepared in a wood-fired oven.

AJOBLANCO   CATALAN €€

Map p300 (☑93 667 87 66; www.ajoblanco restaurant.com; Carrer de Tuset 20; tapas €7.50-19, mains €14-21; ⊙8pm-1am Mon-Wed, to 3am Thu-Sat, noon-1am Sun; ☑; ☑FGC Gràcia) This beautifully designed, timber-furnished space serves up a mix of classic and creative tapas plates that go nicely with the imaginative cocktail menu. Sip the house vermouth while dining on crispy artichoke hearts with romesco sauce, slow-roasted lamb shoulder, or wild sea bass ceviche with mango and chilli. Live music or DJs play from Wednesday to Saturday.

LA MOLINA   CATALAN €€

Map p298 (☑93 417 11 24; www.restaurante molina.net; Passeig de Sant Gervasi 65; mains €12.50-18; ⊙9am-5pm & 8pm-midnight Mon-Fri, 11am-5pm Sat & Sun; ☑FGC Avinguda Tibidabo) La Molina looks like a typical tapas bar at first glance – pavement tables, nondescript bar in front – but head to the back room and you'll discover one of the great unsung Catalan restaurants in the neighbourhood. Reservations are recommended of an evening.

★LA BALSA   MEDITERRANEAN €€€

Map p298 (☑93 211 50 48; www.labalsarestaurant. com; Carrer de la Infanta Isabel 4; mains €20-28; ⊙1.30-3.30pm & 8.30-10.30pm Tue-Sat, 1.30-3.30pm Sun; 🕾; ☑FGC Avinguda Tibidabo) With its grand ceiling and the scented gardens that surround the main terrace dining area, La Balsa is one of the city's premier dining addresses. The seasonally changing menu is a mix of traditional Catalan and creative expression (suckling pig with melon; cod confit with prune compote). Lounge over a cocktail at the bar before being directed to your table.

★VIA VENETO   GASTRONOMY €€€

Map p300 (☑93 200 72 44; www.viaveneto.es; Carrer de Ganduxer 10; mains €28-52.50; ⊙1-4pm

WORTH A DETOUR

JARDINS DEL LABERINT D'HORTA

Laid out in the late 18th century by Antoni Desvalls, Marquès d'Alfarràs i de Llupià, this carefully manicured **park** (☎93 413 24 00; http://lameva.barcelona.cat; Passeig del Castanyers 1; adult/child €2.23/1.42, free Wed & Sun; ⊙10am-8pm Apr-Oct, to 7pm Dec-Mar; Ⓜ Mundet) remained a private family idyll until the 1970s, when it was opened to the public. The *laberint* ('labyrinth' in Catalan) refers to the central maze; other paths take you past a pleasant artificial lake, waterfalls, a neoclassical pavilion and a false cemetery. The last is inspired by 19th-century romanticism, characterised by an obsession with a swooning vision of death.

The labyrinth, in the middle of these cool gardens (somehow odd in this environment, with modern apartments and ring roads nearby), can be surprisingly frustrating. Aim to reach the centre from the bottom end, and then exit towards the ponds and neoclassical pavilion. This is a good one for kids. Scenes of the film adaptation of Patrick Süskind's novel *Perfume* were shot in the gardens.

To reach the gardens, take the right exit upstairs at Mundet metro station; on emerging, turn right and then left along the main road (with football fields on your left), then the first left uphill to the gardens (about five minutes).

& 8-11.45pm Mon-Fri, 8-11.45pm Sat, closed Aug; ⓇFGC La Bonanova) Dalí was a regular in this high-society restaurant after it opened in 1967, and you can still dine at his favourite table today. The oval mirrors, orange-rose tablecloths, leather chairs and fine cutlery set the stage for intricate dishes such as smoked oysters with minced black bread and red mullet with chargrilled onion leaves.

The cellar has over 1800 wines from Catalonia and throughout Spain.

HISOP MEDITERRANEAN €€€
Map p300 (☎93 241 32 33; www.hisop.com; Passatge de Marimon 9; mains €24-28.50; ⊙1.30-3.30pm & 8.30-11pm Mon-Fri, 8.30-11pm Sat; Ⓜ Diagonal) Black, white and burgundy dominate the dining room decor at this elegant little Michelin-starred eatery just off the beaten path. The seasonal menu is a work of art that might feature elderflower, fennel and grappa-marinated duck, grilled turbot with pistachio-stuffed jalapeño peppers and olive-oil-poached peach with caramelised ginger.

ABAC CATALAN €€€
Map p298 (☎93 319 66 00; www.abacrestaurant. com; Avinguda del Tibidabo 1; tasting menus €140-170, with wine €215-265; ⊙1.30-3pm & 8.30-10pm; ⓇFGC Avinguda Tibidabo) Led by celebrated chef Jordi Cruz, this triple-Michelin-starred restaurant offers one of Barcelona's most memorable dining experiences (and also one of its priciest). Expect creative, mouth-watering perfection in dishes like sherry consommé with

tuna marrow, foie gras tacos, fossilised sea urchins with plankton butter and Bloody Mary macarons. Reservations are essential.

CAN CORTADA CATALAN €€€
(☎93 427 23 15; www.cancortada.com; Avinguda de l'Estatut de Catalunya; mains €21.50-29; ⊙1-4pm & 8-11pm; Ⓜ Mundet) The setting and the hearty welcome make this 11th-century estate (complete with the remains of a defensive tower) worth the excursion. Grilled meats dominate, though you'll also find seasonal dishes like artichokes fired up on the grill and *calçots* (spring onions) in winter. Try for a table in the former cellars or on the garden terrace.

HOFMANN MEDITERRANEAN €€€
Map p300 (☎93 218 71 65; www.hofmann-bcn. com; Carrer de la Granada del Penedès 14; mains €23-37; ⊙1.30-3.45pm Mon-Fri & 9-11pm Mon-Sat; ⓇFGC Gràcia) Trainee chefs run the kitchen here, helped along by their instructors. Dishes are generally elegant renditions of classic Mediterranean food (pork trotters with foie gras and truffled port jus; smoked eel with black garlic consommé), followed by such delicious desserts that some people prefer a starter and two sweets, skipping the main course altogether.

SOPARS AMB ESTRELLES CATALAN €€€
Map p298 (Dinner under the Stars; ☎93 327 01 21; www.sternalia.com; Carretera del Observatori; meal & observatory packages €71-125; ⊙mid-Jun–mid-Sep; ✈👶) Held at the Observatori Fabra (p175), this astronomical evening includes an outdoor meal, a tour of the

WORTH A DETOUR

TIBIDABO: GARDENS OF EARTHLY DELIGHTS

Framing the north end of the city, the forest-covered mountain of Tibidabo, which tops out at 512m, is the highest peak in Serra de Collserola. Aside from the superb views from the top, highlights include an 8000-hectare park, the **Parc de Collserola** (Map p298; ☑93 280 35 52; www.parcnaturalcollserola.cat; Carretera de l'Església 92; ⊙Centre d'Informació 9.30am-3pm, Can Coll 9.30am-2.30pm Sun & holidays, closed late Jun-early Sep); an old-fashioned amusement park, **Parc d'Atraccions** (Map p298; ☑93 211 79 42; www.tibidabo.cat; Plaça de Tibidabo 3-4; adult/child €28.50/10.30; ⊙closed Jan & Feb); the **Torre de Collserola** (Map p298; ☑93 406 93 54; www.torredecollserola.com; Carretera de Vallvidrera al Tibidabo; adult/child €5.60/3.30; ⊙hours vary, closed Jan-Feb) telecommunications tower with viewing platform; and a looming basilica, **Basílica del Sagrat Cor de Jesús** (Basilica of the Sacred Heart of Jesus; Map p298; ☑93 417 56 86; www.templotibidabo.es; Plaça de Tibidabo; lift €3.50; ⊙11am-7pm) FREE, which is visible from many parts of the city. Tibidabo gets its name from the devil, who, trying to tempt Christ, took him to a high place and said, in Latin: *'Haec omnia tibi dabo si cadens adoraberis me'* ('All this I will give you if you fall down and worship me').

To reach the basilica and amusement park, take an FGC train to Avinguda Tibidabo. Outside Avinguda Tibidabo station, hop on the *tramvia blau*, which runs past fancy Modernista mansions to Plaça del Doctor Andreu (one way €5.50, 15 minutes, every 15 or 30 minutes 10am to 7.30pm daily late June to early September, 10am to 6.15pm Saturday, Sunday and holidays early September to late June; hours can vary). Bus 196 runs the same route. From Plaça del Doctor Andreu the Tibidabo funicular railway climbs to the top of the hill (return €7.70, five minutes). Departures start around 10am and run every 15 minutes until shortly after the Parc d'Atraccions' closing time. Start queuing well before the funicular stops running, as places are limited.

An alternative is bus T2A, the 'Tibibús', from Plaça de Catalunya to Plaça de Tibidabo (€3, 30 minutes, every 30 to 50 minutes on Saturday, Sunday and holidays March to December, and hourly from 10.15am Monday to Friday late June to early September).

For Parc de Collserola, take an FGC train to Baixador de Vallvidrera. Alternatively, you can stop one station earlier at Peu del Funicular and ride to the top via the Funicular Vallvidrera.

Bus 111 runs between Tibidabo and Vallvidrera (passing the Torre de Collserola).

observatory, telescope viewing and a lecture on the heavens. The evening starts at 8.30pm and ends at midnight. Prices vary based on type of menu ordered; vegetarian and kids' menus are available. Reservations are essential. The easiest way here is by taxi.

🍷 DRINKING & NIGHTLIFE

EL MARAVILLAS
COCKTAIL BAR

Map p298 (☑93 360 73 78; www.elmaravillas.cat; Plaça de la Concòrdia 15; ⊙noon-midnight Mon & Tue, to 1am Wed, to 2am Thu, to 3am Fri-Sun; Ⓜ Maria Cristina, ⒯T1, T2, T3 Numància) Overlooking the peaceful Plaça de la Concòrdia, El Maravillas feels like a secret hideaway – especially if you've just arrived from the crowded lanes of the *Ciutat Vella* (Old City). The glittering bar has just a few tables, plus outdoor seating on the square in warm weather. Creative cocktails, good Spanish red wines and easy-drinking vermouths are the drinks of choice.

MIRABLAU
BAR

Map p298 (☑93 418 58 79; www.mirablaubcn.com; Plaça del Doctor Andreu; ⊙11am-3.30am Mon-Wed, 11am-4.30am Thu, 10am-5am Fri-Sat, 10am-2.30am Sun; ⒠196, ⒭FGC Avinguda Tibidabo) Gaze out over the entire city from this privileged balcony restaurant at the base of the Funicular del Tibidabo. The bar is renowned for its gin selection, with 30 different varieties. Wander downstairs to join the folk in the tiny dance space, which opens at 11.30pm. In summer you can step out onto the even smaller terrace for a breather.

CAFE TURÓ
CAFE

Map p300 (Carrer del Tenor Viñas 1; ⊙8am-midnight; ⒠68, ⒯T1, T2, T3 Francesc Macià) Framed by red awnings, with vivid crimson walls brightening the low-lit interior, this cafe on the edge of Turó Parc has year-round seating on the footpath at the front – ideal for catching some sun over a morning coffee, afternoon glass of wine or evening cocktail. There's a good selection of bistro plates and tapas.

DÕ BAR
BAR

Map p300 (☎93 209 18 88; www.do-bcn.com; Carrer de Santaló 30; ⊙7pm-midnight Tue-Thu, 8pm-1am Fri & Sat; 🛜; 🚈FGC Muntaner) This neighbourhood charmer has a warm and inviting interior, where locals gather at wooden tables to enjoy excellent gin and tonics, wines by the glass, craft beer and satisfying small plates (anchovies, mussels, tacos, charcuterie). On warm nights, arrive early for one of the terrace tables out the front. Enter via Carrer de l'Avenir.

MARCEL
BAR

Map p300 (☎93 209 89 48; Carrer de Santaló 42; ⊙7.30am-1am Mon-Thu, 7.30am-3am Fri & Sat, 9.30am-midnight Sun; 🚈FGC Muntaner) A classic meeting place, Marcel has a homely, old-world feel, with a wood bar, black-and-white floor tiles and high windows. It offers snacks and tapas as well. Space is somewhat limited and customers inevitably spill out onto the footpath, where there are also a few tables.

BIKINI
CLUB

Map p298 (☎93 322 08 00; www.bikinibcn. com; Avinguda Diagonal 547; cover from €12; ⊙midnight-6am Thu-Sat; 🚌6, 7, 33, 34, 63, 67, L51, L57, 🚈T1, T2, T3 L'Illa) This old star of the Barcelona nightlife scene has been keeping the beat since 1953. Every possible kind of music gets a run, from Latin and Brazilian beats to 1980s disco, depending on the night and the space you choose.

LIZARRAN
BAR

Map p298 (www.lizarran.es; Carrer de Can Bruixa 6; ⊙8am-midnight Sun-Thu, to 2am Fri & Sat; 🚇Les Corts) This is a fine pre- or postgame drinking spot if you're catching an FC Barça match at Camp Nou, 800m to the southwest. The beer and sangría is plentiful and cheap, there's a decent selection of *pintxos* (Basque tapas), and on warm days you can sit on the canopied terrace at the front.

SUTTON CLUB
CLUB

Map p300 (☎667 432759; www.thesuttonclub. com; Carrer de Tuset 13; cover from €15; ⊙11.30pm-5.30am Wed & Thu, to 6am Fri & Sat; 🚈FGC Gràcia)

With mainstream sounds on the dance floor and some hopping house in a side bar, this neon-lit disco inevitably attracts just about everyone pouring in and out of the nearby bars at some stage of the evening. The main dance floor gets packed with a beautiful crowd and, even with reservations, the bouncers can be tough.

BERLIN
BAR

Map p300 (☎93 200 65 42; www.cafeberlin barcelona.com; Carrer de Muntaner 240; ⊙10am-2am Mon-Thu, to 3am Fri & Sat; 🚇Hospital Clínic) This elegant corner bar offers views over Avinguda Diagonal. There is a cluster of tables outside on the ground floor and designer lounges downstairs. Service can be harried, but the location is excellent for starting an uptown night before kicking on to nearby clubs.

 ## ENTERTAINMENT

CAMP NOU
FOOTBALL

Map p298 (☎902 189900; www.fcbarcelona.com; Carrer d'Arístides Maillol; 🚇Palau Reial) The massive stadium of Camp Nou ('New Field' in Catalan) is home to the legendary Futbol Club Barcelona. Attending a game amid the roar of the crowds is an unforgettable experience; the season runs from September to May. Alternatively, get a taste of all the excitement at the interactive Camp Nou Experience (p173), which includes a tour of the stadium.

LUZ DE GAS
LIVE MUSIC

Map p300 (☎93 209 77 11; www.luzdegas.com; Carrer de Muntaner 246; ⊙midnight-6am Thu-Sat; 🚌6, 7, 27, 32, 33, 34, H8, 🚈T1, T2, T3 Francesc Macià) Several nights a week this club, set in a grand former theatre, stages concerts ranging through rock, soul, salsa, jazz and pop. Concerts typically kick off around 1am; from about 2am, the place turns into a club that attracts a well-dressed crowd with varying musical tastes, depending on the night. Check the website for the latest schedule.

 ## SHOPPING

CATALINA HOUSE
HOMEWARES

Map p300 (☎93 140 96 39; www.catalinahouse. net; Carrer d'Amigó 47; ⊙10.30am-2pm & 5-8pm Mon-Fri, 10.30am-2pm Sat; 🚈FGC Muntaner)

✒ After its decade-long success on the Balearic island of Formentera, Catalina House opened its second shop in Barcelona in 2016. Sustainable materials such as linen, cotton, stone, glass, terracotta and oil-treated recycled timbers are used in stylish Mediterranean designs for the home including cushions, tableware, vases, clocks, sculptures and furniture.

L'ILLA DIAGONAL   MALL
Map p298 (⊘93 444 00 00; www.lilla.com; Avinguda Diagonal 557; ⊙9.30am-9pm Mon-Sat; ⓂMaria Cristina) One of Barcelona's best malls, this is a fine place to while away a few hours (or days), with high-end shops and a mesmerising spread of eateries.

FC BOTIGA MEGASTORE   GIFTS & SOUVENIRS
Map p298 (⊘93 409 02 71; www.fcbmegastore. com; Gate 9, off Avinguda Joan de XXIII; ⊙10am-7pm Mon-Sat, 10.30am-3.30pm Sun, until kick-off match days; ⓂPalau Reial) This sprawling three-storey shop at Camp Nou (p181) has footballs, shirts, scarves, socks, wallets, bags, footwear, smartphone covers – pretty much anything you can think of – all featuring the team's famous red-and-blue insignia.

NORMANDIE   CHILDREN'S CLOTHING
Map p300 (⊘93 209 14 11; www.normandie baby.com; Plaça de Sant Gregori Taumaturg; ⊙10.30am-2.30pm & 4.30-8.30pm Mon-Sat; ⓇFGC La Bonanova) Set up by Barcelona-born, Paris-trained designer Graziella Antón de Vez in 2000, this fashion label for babies and children up to six years utilises all-natural materials such as angora, cotton, cashmere and wool. Adorable outfits are inspired by France's Normandy region, with vintage- and retro-style lines.

ORIOL BALAGUER   FOOD
Map p300 (⊘93 201 18 46; www.oriolbalaguer. com; Plaça de Sant Gregori Taumaturg 2; ⊙9am-2.30pm & 4-9pm Mon-Fri, 8.30am-2.30pm & 4-9pm Sat, 8.30am-2.30pm Sun; ⓇFGC La Bonanova) Magnificent cakes, sweets, ice cream, chocolates and other sweet creations tantalise in this museumlike shop.

UKKA   FASHION & ACCESSORIES
Map p300 (⊘661 919710; Carrer de Laforja 122; ⊙10.30am-2pm & 5-8.30pm Mon-Fri, 11am-2pm & 5.30-8.30pm Sat; ⓇFGC Muntaner) Ukka makes its bohemian-inspired women's fashion and accessories (including scarves, hats and some eye-catching jewellery) at its Barcelona factory and sells them exclusively in this chic little terracotta-floored boutique.

LABPERFUM   COSMETICS
Map p300 (⊘93 298 95 12; www.labperfum. com; Carrer de Santaló 45; ⊙10am-2.30pm & 5-8.30pm Mon-Sat; ⓇFGC Muntaner) This tiny shop looks like an old apothecary, with its shelves lined with pretty glass bottles of extraordinary fragrances (for men and women) made in-house and beautifully packaged. Scents diverge from run-of-the-mill Obsession, with varieties like tobacco, black orchid and leather. You can also buy scented candles, soaps and creams.

MERCAT DE GALVANY   MARKET
Map p300 (www.mercatgalvany.es; Carrer de Santaló 65; ⊙7am-2.30pm Mon-Thu & Sat, 7am-2.30pm & 7-8pm Fri; ⓇFGC Muntaner) Opened in 1927, Galvany is one of the city's most beautiful markets, with a brick facade and glass- and cast-iron interior. Over 80 different stalls sell an enticing variety of bakery items, fresh produce and deli goods.

EL CORTE INGLÉS   DEPARTMENT STORE
Map p298 (⊘93 493 48 00; www.elcorteingles.es; Avinguda Diagonal 617; ⊙9.30am-9pm Mon-Sat; ⓂMaria Cristina) On busy Avinguda Diagonal, this massive shopping complex has a supermarket and a handful of eateries.

PASTISSERIA NATCHA   FOOD
Map p300 (⊘93 430 10 70; www.natcha.cat; Avinguda de Sarrià 45; ⊙8am-9pm; ⓂHospital Clínic) Pastisseria Natcha has been tempting *barcelonins* with chocolates and custom-made cakes since 1958.

🏃 SPORTS & ACTIVITIES

RITUELS D'ORIENT   SPA
Map p300 (⊘93 419 14 72; www.rituelsdorient. com; Carrer de Loreto 50; baths per 45min €29, treatments from €21; ⊙11am-9pm Tue, Wed & Sun, to 10pm Thu-Sat; ⓂHospital Clínic) Rituels d'Orient resembles a Moroccan fantasy, with dark woods, window grills, candle lighting and ancient-looking stone walls. It's a wonderfully relaxing setting for luxuriating in a hammam and indulging in a massage, a body scrub, a facial or hand and foot treatments.

Montjuïc, Poble Sec & Sant Antoni

Neighbourhood Top Five

1 Museu Nacional d'Art de Catalunya (p186) Dedicating a day to the world's most important collection of early-medieval art in the Romanesque halls, followed by a masterpiece-filled stroll through six centuries of Catalan art.

2 Fundació Joan Miró (p185) Viewing brilliant works from one of the giants of the art world, all the more captivating inside the light-filled galleries designed by Josep Lluís Sert.

3 CaixaForum (p188) Catching a ground-breaking art exhibition in this Modernista former factory.

4 Museu Etnològic (p190) Going eye-to-eye with *gegants* (giant papier-mâché figures) while learning about the festivals and folklore of Catalonia.

5 Teleférico del Puerto (p192) Gazing out over the sea and city on a high-flying cable-car ride between Barceloneta and Montjuïc.

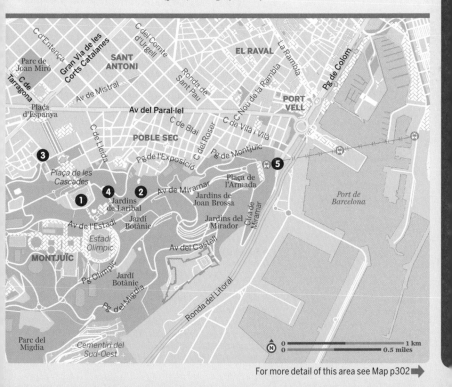

For more detail of this area see Map p302 ➡

Montjuïc, poble sec & sant antoni

Lonely Planet's Top Tip

The Arqueoticket is a special pass, available at tourist offices and participating museums for €14.50, that allows entry into the **Museu d'Arqueologia de Catalunya** (MAC; p190), the **Museu Egipci** (p135), the **Born Centre de Cultura i Memòria** (p97) and the **Museu d'Història de Barcelona** (p65).

Best Places to Eat

➡ Enigma (p196)

➡ Agust Gastrobar (p193)

➡ Tickets (p196)

➡ Quimet i Quimet (p193)

➡ Mano Rota (p193)

For reviews, see p192.➡

Best Places to Drink

➡ Abirradero (p196)

➡ La Caseta del Migdia (p196)

➡ El Rouge (p197)

For reviews, see p196.➡

Best Art Collections

➡ Museu Nacional d'Art de Catalunya (MNAC; p186)

➡ Fundació Joan Miró (p185)

➡ CaixaForum (p188)

Explore Montjuïc, Poble Sec & Sant Antoni

Montjuïc hosts outstanding art collections alongside several lesser museums, replica Spanish buildings at Poble Espanyol (p189), the sinister Castell de Montjuïc (p188) and the beautiful remake of Mies van der Rohe's 1929 German pavilion (p191). The bulk of the 1992 Olympic installations are also here. Come at night and witness the spectacle of the Font Màgica (p188), several busy theatres and a couple of nightclubs. Throw in various parks and gardens and you have the makings of a very full couple of days.

You can approach the hill from Plaça d'Espanya on foot and take advantage of a series of escalators from the west side of the Palau Nacional up to Avingunda de l'Estadi; alternatively, and spectacularly, you can get onto a cable car and take in the beautiful aerial views of the verdant hill. Otherwise, explore on foot along the numerous forest paths that zigzag through gardens and skirt the various sights.

Sloping down the north face of Montjuïc is the tight warren of working-class El Poble Sec. Though short on sights, it hides some of Barcelona's most creative bars and eateries. Cross busy Avinguda del Paral·lel to reach Sant Antoni, a formerly humdrum neighbourhood that's become the epicentre of Barcelona hipsterdom. Vintage-esque cafes, organic eateries and crafty tapas and vermouth joints are in abundance – particularly along Carrer del Parlament.

Local Life

➡ **Hang-outs** Lined with tapas bars, most with outdoor seating, Carrer de Blai draws a student crowd.

➡ **Nightlife** Join the dance party at iconic Sala Apolo (p198), catch a concert at BARTS (p198) or see an avant-garde performing arts piece at Hiroshima (p198).

➡ **Greenery** Stroll through the gardens of Montjuïc (and catch all that art on the way).

Getting There & Away

➡ **Metro** Montjuïc's closest metro stops are Espanya, Poble Sec and Paral·lel.

➡ **Bus** Bus 150 loops from Plaça d'Espanya to Castell de Montjuïc. Bus 55 runs across town via Plaça de Catalunya past the Museu d'Arqueologia de Catalunya to the Estació Parc Montjuïc funicular station.

➡ **Funicular** From the Paral·lel metro station, pick up the funicular (⊙7.30am-10pm Mon-Fri, 9am-10pm Sat & Sun Apr-Oct, 7.30am-8pm Mon-Fri, 9am-8pm Sat & Sun Nov-Mar) railway, part of the metro fare system, to Estació Parc Montjuïc. It departs every 10 minutes; journey time is two minutes.

➡ **Cable car** The Teleférico del Puerto (p192) goes between Torre de Sant Sebastià in Barceloneta and the Miramar stop on Montjuïc. On Montjuïc (1.3km west of the other cable car), the Telefèric de Montjuïc (p192) runs from Estació Parc Montjuïc to the Castell de Montjuïc.

TOP SIGHT
FUNDACIÓ JOAN MIRÓ

Joan Miró, the city's best-known 20th-century artistic progeny, bequeathed this art foundation to his home town in 1971. Its light-filled buildings, designed by close friend and architect Josep Lluís Sert (who also built Miró's Mallorca studios), are crammed with seminal works, from Miró's earliest timid sketches to paintings from his last years.

Sert's Temple to Miró's Art

Sert's shimmering white temple to one of Spain's artistic luminaries is considered one of the world's most outstanding museum buildings. The architect designed it after spending many of Franco's dictatorship years in the USA as the head of the School of Design at Harvard University. The foundation rests amid the greenery of the mountains and holds the greatest single collection of the artist's work, containing around 220 of his paintings, 180 sculptures, some textiles and more than 8000 drawings spanning his entire life. Only a small portion is ever on display.

The Collection

The exhibits give a broad impression of Miró's artistic development. The first couple of rooms (11 and 12) hold various works, including a giant tapestry in his trademark primary colours. Along the way, you'll pass *Mercury Fountain* by Alexander Calder, a rebuilt work that was originally created for the 1937 Paris Fair and represented Spain at the Spanish Republic's Pavilion. Room 13, a basement space called Espai 13, leads you downstairs to a small room for temporary exhibitions.

After visiting Room 13, climb back up the stairs and descend to two other basement rooms (14 and 15). Together labelled Homenatge a Joan Miró (Homage to Joan Miró), this space is dedicated to photos of the artist, a 15-minute video on his life and a series of works from some of his contemporaries, like Henry Moore, Antoni Tàpies, Eduardo Chillida, Yves Tanguy, Fernand Léger and others.

Returning to the main level, you'll find Room 16, the Sala Joan Prats, with works spanning the early years until 1919. Here you can see how the young Miró moved away, under surrealist influence, from his relative realism (for instance his 1917 painting *Ermita de Sant Joan d'Horta,* with obvious Fauvist influences) towards his own unique style that uses primary colours and morphed shapes symbolising the moon, the female form and birds.

This theme is continued upstairs in Room 17, the Sala Pilar Juncosa (named after his wife), which covers the years 1932–55, his surrealist years. Rooms 18 and 19 contain masterworks of the years 1956–83, and Room 20 a series of paintings done on paper. Room 21 hosts a selection of the private Katsuta collection of Miró works from 1914 to 1974. Room 22 rounds off the permanent exhibition with some major paintings and bronzes from the 1960s and 1970s.

The museum library contains Miró's personal book collection.

The Garden

Outside on the eastern flank of the museum is the Jardí de les Esculptures, a small garden with various pieces of modern sculpture. The green areas surrounding the museum, together with the garden, are perfect for a picnic in the shade, after a hard day's sightseeing.

DON'T MISS

→ Sert's architectural design

→ Masterworks in Rooms 18 and 19

→ Miro's move to surrealism, Room 17

→ The sculpture garden

PRACTICALITIES

→ Map p302, E4

→ 93 443 94 70

→ www.fmirobcn.org

→ Parc de Montjuïc

→ adult/child €12/free

→ 10am-8pm Tue, Wed, Fri & Sat, to 9pm Thu, to 3pm Sun

→ 55, 150, Paral·lel

TOP SIGHT
MUSEU NACIONAL D'ART DE CATALUNYA

From across the city, the flamboyant neobaroque silhouette of the Mirador del Palau Nacional can be seen on the slopes of Montjuïc. Built for the 1929 World Exhibition and restored in 2005, it houses a vast collection of mostly Catalan art spanning the early Middle Ages to the early 20th century. The highlight is the collection of extraordinary Romanesque frescoes.

Romanesque Masterpieces

The Romanesque art section is considered the most important concentration of early medieval art in the world. Rescued from neglected country churches across northern Catalonia in the early 20th century, the collection consists of 21 frescoes, woodcarvings and painted altar frontals (low-relief wooden panels that were the forerunners of the elaborate altarpieces that adorned later churches). The insides of several churches have been recreated and the frescoes – in some cases fragmentary, in others extraordinarily complete and alive with colour – have been placed as they were when in situ.

The first of the two most striking frescoes, in Sala 7, is a magnificent image of Christ in Majesty done around 1123. Based on the text of the Apocalypse, we see Christ enthroned with the world at his feet. He holds a book open with the words *Ego Sum Lux Mundi* (I am the Light of the World) and is surrounded by the four Evangelists. The images were taken from the apse of the Església de Sant Climent de Taüll in northwest Catalonia. Nearby in Sala 9 are frescoes done around the same time in the nearby Església de Santa Maria de Taüll. This time the central image taken from the apse is of the Virgin Mary and Christ Child. These images were not mere decoration but tools of instruction

DON'T MISS

➡ Romanesque pieces

➡ Gothic artworks

➡ The paintings of the Cambò Bequest and Thyssen-Bornemisza collections

➡ 1930s Spanish Civil War posters

PRACTICALITIES

➡ MNAC

➡ Map p302, D4

➡ ☑93 622 03 76

➡ www.museunacional. cat

➡ Mirador del Palau Nacional

➡ adult/child €12/free, after 3pm Sat & 1st Sun of month free, rooftop viewpoint only €2

➡ ◷10am-8pm Tue-Sat, to 3pm Sun May-Sep, to 6pm Tue-Sat Oct-Apr

➡ ▯55, Ⓜ Espanya

in the basics of Christian faith for the local population – try to set yourself in the mind of the average medieval citizen: illiterate, ignorant, fearful and in most cases eking out a subsistence living. These images transmitted the basic personalities and tenets of the faith and were accepted at face value by most.

The Gothic Collection

Opposite the Romanesque collection on the ground floor is the museum's Gothic art section. In these halls you can see Catalan Gothic painting and works from other Spanish and Mediterranean regions. Look out especially for the work of Bernat Martorell in Sala 25 and Jaume Huguet in Sala 26. Among Martorell's works figure images of the martyrdom of St Vincent and St Llúcia. Huguet's *Consagració de Sant Agustí,* in which St Augustine is depicted as a bishop, is dazzling in its detail.

The Cambò Bequest & the Thyssen-Bornemisza Collection

As the Gothic collection draws to a close, you pass through two separate and equally eclectic private collections. The Cambò Bequest by Francesc Cambò spans the history of European painting between the 14th century and the beginning of the 19th century, and the Thyssen-Bornemisza collection presents a selection of European painting and sculpture produced between the 13th and the 18th centuries on loan to the MNAC by the Museo Thyssen-Bornemisza in Madrid. The Thyssen-Bornemisza collection's highlight is Fra Angelico's *Madonna of Humility,* whereas the Cambò Bequest holds wonderful works by masters Veronese, Titian and Canaletto, particularly. Cranach, Titian, El Greco, Rubens and even Gainsborough also feature, but the collection's finale is examples of work by Francisco de Goya.

Modern Catalan Art

Up on the next floor, the collection turns to modern art, mainly but not exclusively Catalan. This collection is arranged thematically: Modernisme, Noucentisme, Art and the Civil War and so on. Among the many highlights: an early Salvador Dalí painting *(Portrait of My Father),* Juan Gris' collage-like paintings, the brilliant portraits of Marià Fortuny, and 1930s call-to-arms posters against the Francoist onslaught (nearby you'll find photos of soldiers and bombed-out city centres). There are works by Modernista painters Ramon Casas and Santiago Rusiñol, as well as Catalan luminary Antoni Tàpies.

Also on show are items of Modernista furniture and decoration, which include a mural by Ramon Casas (the artist and Pere Romeu on a tandem bicycle) that once adorned the legendary bar and restaurant Els Quatre Gats.

THE FRESCO STRIPPERS

The Stefanoni brothers, Italian art restorers, brought the secrets of *strappo* (stripping of frescoes from walls) to Catalonia in the early 1900s. The Stefanoni would cover frescoes with a sheet of fabric, stuck on with a glue made of cartilage. When dry, this allowed the image to be stripped off the wall and rolled up. For three years the Stefanoni roamed the Pyrenean countryside, stripping churches and sending the rolls back to Barcelona, where they were eventually put back up on walls to reflect how they had originally appeared.

TOP TIPS

➡ If you're on a museum mission, you can save money by purchasing the Articket, a pass that will give you discounted admission to six museums (including MNAC).

➡ An audioguide costs €4.

➡ Be sure to take in the fine view from the terrace just in front of the museum. It draws crowds around sunset.

➡ Another fine viewpoint is on the museum's roof terrace (included in admission or €2 if you only want to visit the rooftop).

◉ SIGHTS

MONTJUÏC, POBLE SEC & SANT ANTONI SIGHTS

**MUSEU NACIONAL D'ART
DE CATALUNYA**   MUSEUM
See p186.

FUNDACIÓ JOAN MIRÓ   MUSEUM
See p185.

CAIXAFORUM   GALLERY

Map p302 (☑93 476 86 00; www.caixaforum.es;
Avinguda de Francesc Ferrer i Guàrdia 6-8; adult/
child €4/free, 1st Sun of month free; ☺10am-
8pm; ⓂEspanya) The Caixa building society prides itself on its involvement in (and
ownership of) art, in particular all that is
contemporary. Its premier art expo space in
Barcelona hosts part of the bank's extensive
collection from around the globe. The setting is a completely renovated former factory, the Fàbrica Casaramona, an outstanding Modernista brick structure designed
by Puig i Cadafalch. From 1940 to 1993 it
housed the First Squadron of the police cav-
alry unit – 120 horses in all.

On occasion, portions of La Caixa's own
collection of 800 works of modern and contemporary art go on display, but more often
than not major international exhibitions
are the key draw.

In the courtyard where the police horses
used to drink is a steel tree designed by the
Japanese architect Arata Isozaki. Musical
recitals are sometimes held in the museum,
especially in the warmer months.

FONT MÀGICA   FOUNTAIN

Map p302 (☑93 316 10 00; Avinguda de la Reina
Maria Cristina; ☺every 30min 7.30-10.30pm
Wed-Sun Jun-Sep, 9-10pm Thu-Sat Apr, May &
Oct, 8-9pm Thu-Sat Nov-early Jan & mid-Feb–
Mar; ⓂEspanya) FREE A huge fountain that
crowns the long sweep of the Avinguda de
la Reina Maria Cristina to the grand facade of the Palau Nacional, Font Màgica is
a unique performance in which the water
can look like seething fireworks or a mysti-
cal cauldron of colour.

Originally created for the 1929 World
Exposition, it has again been a magnet
since the 1992 Olympics. With a flourish,
the 'Magic Fountain' erupts into a feast of
musical, backlit aquatic life. On hot summer evenings especially, this 15-minute
spectacle (repeated several times throughout the evening) mesmerises onlookers. On
the last evening of the Festes de la Mercè
in September, a particularly spectacular
display includes fireworks. Eco initiatives include the use of groundwater and
LED lights.

JARDÍ BOTÀNIC   GARDENS

Map p302 (www.museuciencies.cat; Carrer del
Doctor Font i Quer 2; adult/child €3.50/free, after
3pm Sun & 1st Sun of month free; ☺10am-7pm
Apr-Sep, to 5pm Oct-Mar; ☐55,150) This botan-
ical garden is dedicated to Mediterranean
flora and has a collection of some 40,000
plants and 1500 species, including many
that thrive in areas with a climate similar
to that of the Mediterranean, such as the
Canary Islands, North Africa, Australia,
California, Chile and South Africa.

CASTELL DE MONTJUÏC   FORTRESS

Map p302 (☑93 256 44 45; http://ajuntament.
barcelona.cat/castelldemontjuic; Carretera de
Montjuïc 66; adult/child €5/3, after 3pm Sun & 1st
Sun of month free; ☺10am-8pm Apr-Oct, to 6pm
Nov-Mar; ☐150, ☐Telefèric de Montjuïc, Castell
de Montjuïc) This forbidding *castell* (castle
or fort) dominates the southeastern heights
of Montjuïc and enjoys commanding views
over the Mediterranean. It dates, in its present form, from the late 17th and 18th centuries. For most of its dark history, it has
been used to watch over the city and as a
political prison and killing ground.

Anarchists were executed here around
the end of the 19th century, fascists during the civil war and Republicans after
it – most notoriously Lluís Companys in
1940. The castle is surrounded by a network of ditches and walls (from which its
strategic position over the city and port becomes clear).

An exhibition space in several of the
rooms of the castle explains the history of
the place, with archaeological finds from
prehistoric days to its role as medieval bea-
con and its later days as a strategic bastion.
Most interesting (and disturbing) is the
exhibition devoted to the imprisonments,
trials and executions that happened here.
Don't miss the tombstones (some dating
from the 11th century) from the one-time
Jewish cemetery on Montjuïc.

The views from the castle and the surrounding area looking over the sea, port
and city below are the best part of making the trip here. Around the seaward foot
of the castle is an airy walking track, the
Camí del Mar, which offers breezy views of
the city and sea.

COLÒNIA GÜELL

Apart from La Sagrada Família, Gaudí's last big project was the creation of a utopian textile workers' complex for his magnate patron Eusebi Güell outside Barcelona at Santa Coloma de Cervelló. Gaudí's main role was to erect the colony's church, **Colònia Güell** (☑93 630 58 07; www.gaudicoloniaguell.org; Carrer Claudi Güell; adult/concession €7/5.50; ⊙10am-7pm Mon-Fri, to 3pm Sat & Sun May-Oct, 10am-5pm Mon-Fri, to 3pm Sat & Sun Nov-Apr; ᵮFGC lines S4, S8, S33 to Colònia Güell). Work began in 1908, but the idea fizzled out eight years later and Gaudí only finished the crypt, which still serves as a working church.

This structure is a key to understanding what the master had in mind for his magnum opus, La Sagrada Família. The mostly brick-clad columns that support the ribbed vaults in the ceiling are inclined at all angles in much the way you might expect trees in a forest to lean. That effect was deliberate, but also grounded in physics. Gaudí worked out the angles so that their load would be transmitted from the ceiling to the earth without the help of extra buttressing. Similar thinking lay behind his plans for La Sagrada Família, whose Gothic-inspired structure would tower above any medieval building, without requiring a single buttress. Gaudí's hand is visible down to the wavy design of the pews. The primary colours in the curvaceous plant-shaped stained-glass windows are another reminder of the era in which the crypt was built.

Near the church spread the cute brick houses designed for the factory workers, which are still inhabited today. A short stroll away, the 23 factory buildings of a Modernista industrial complex, idle since the 1970s, were brought back to life in the early 2000s, with shops and businesses moving into the renovated complex.

In a five-room display with audiovisual and interactive material, the history and life of the industrial colony and the story of Gaudí's church are told in colourful fashion.

From the **Jardins del Mirador** (Map p302; http://ajuntament.barcelona.cat/ecologiaurbana; Carretera de Montjuïc; ⊙10am-sunset; ᵮTelefèric de Montjuïc, Mirador) FREE, opposite the Mirador (Telefèric) station, you have fine views over the port of Barcelona. A little further downhill, the **Jardins de Joan Brossa** (Map p302; Plaça de la Sardana; ⊙10am-sunset) FREE are charming, landscaped gardens on the site of a former amusement park near **Plaça de la Sardana** (Map p302; ᵮ150). These gardens contain many Mediterranean species, from cypresses to pines and a few palms. There are swings and things, thematic walking trails and some good city views.

POBLE ESPANYOL   CULTURAL CENTRE
Map p302 (www.poble-espanyol.com; Avinguda de Francesc Ferrer i Guàrdia 13; adult/child €14/7; ⊙9am-8pm Mon, to midnight Tue-Thu & Sun, to 3am Fri, to 4am Sat; ᵮ13, 23, 150, ⓂEspanya) Welcome to Spain! All of it! This 'Spanish Village' is an intriguing scrapbook of Spanish architecture built for the Spanish crafts section of the 1929 World Exhibition. You can meander from Andalucía to the Balearic Islands in the space of a couple of hours, visiting surprisingly good copies of Spain's characteristic structures. The 117 buildings include 17 restaurants, cafes and bars, and 20 craft shops and workshops (for glass artists and other artisans), as well as souvenir stores.

You enter from beneath a towered medieval gate from Ávila. Inside, to the right, is an information office with free maps and a worthwhile multimedia guide (€3.50; leave a €20 deposit). Straight ahead from the gate is the Plaza Mayor (Town Sq), surrounded with mainly Castilian and Aragonese buildings. It is sometimes the scene of summer concerts. Elsewhere you'll find an Andalucian *barrio* (district), a Basque street, Galician and Catalan quarters, and even a Dominican monastery (at the eastern end).

Spare some time for the **Fundació Fran Daurel** (Map p302; ☑93 423 41 72; www.fundaciofrandaurel.com; incl in Poble Espanyol admission; ⊙11am-8pm Jun-Sep, 10am-6.30pm Mon, 10am-7pm Tue-Sun Oct-May), an eclectic collection of 300 works of art, including sculptures, prints, ceramics and tapestries by modern artists ranging from Picasso and Miró to more contemporary figures, such as Miquel Barceló.

Children's groups can participate in the Joc del Sarró. Accompanied by adults, the kids go around the *poble* seeking the answers to various mysteries outlined in a kit distributed to each group. Languages catered for include English.

MUSEU D'ARQUEOLOGIA
DE CATALUNYA
MUSEUM

Map p302 (MAC; ☑93 423 21 49; www.mac. cat; Passeig de Santa Madrona 39-41; adult/ child €5.50/free; ☺9.30am-7pm Tue-Sat, 10am-2.30pm Sun; ☐55, Ⓜ Poble Sec) This archaeology museum, housed in what was the Graphic Arts Palace during the 1929 World Exhibition, covers Catalonia and cultures from elsewhere in Spain. Items range from copies of pre-Neanderthal skulls to lovely Carthaginian necklaces and jewel-studded Visigothic crosses.

There's good material on the Balearic Islands (Rooms X to XIII) and Empúries (Emporion, the Greek and Roman city on the Costa Brava; Rooms XIV and XVII). The Roman finds upstairs were mostly dug up in and around Barcelona. The most beautiful piece is a mosaic depicting Les Tres Gràcies (The Three Graces), unearthed near Plaça de Sant Jaume in the 18th century. Another is of Bellerophon and the Chimera. In the final room, dedicated to the dying centuries of the Roman world, a beautiful golden disc depicting Medusa stands out.

MUSEU ETNOLÒGIC
MUSEUM

Map p302 (☑93 424 68 07; http://ajuntament. barcelona.cat/museuetnologic; Passeig de Santa Madrona 16-22; adult/child €5/free, 4-8pm Sun & 1st Sun of month free; ☺10am-7pm Tue-Sat, to 8pm Sun; ☐55) Barcelona's ethnology museum presents an intriguing permanent collection that delves into the rich heritage of Catalonia. Exhibits cover origin myths, religious festivals, folklore, and the blending of the sacred and the secular (along those lines, don't miss the Nativity scene with that quirky Catalan character *el caganer,* aka 'the crapper').

The collection also has instruments and archive images of traditional dances from the Catalan Pyrenees, plus accoutrements of bygone days showcasing the region's blacksmiths, winemakers, weavers, apothecaries, shepherds, potters, toymakers and even *saurí* ('diviners'; those tasked with finding water and hidden things). There are also several *gegants* (massive figures made of papier-mâché) depicting King Jaume I and Queen Violant. You can also check out a dragon (though you'll have to imagine the spewing burning embers it emits) and devil costumes used in *correfocs* (fire runs), which still figure prominently in Catalan festivals.

L'ANELLA OLÍMPICA
& ESTADI OLÍMPIC
AREA

Map p302 (www.estadiolimpic.cat; Avinguda de l'Estadi; ☐13, 150) **FREE** L'Anella Olímpica (Olympic Ring) is the group of installations built for the main events of the 1992 Olympics. They include the **Piscines Bernat Picornell**, where the swimming and diving events were held, and the **Estadi Olímpic** (Map p302; ☑93 426 20 89; Passeig Olímpic 15-17; ☺8am-8pm May-Sep, 10am-6pm Oct-Apr) **FREE**, which is open to the public when it's not in use for sporting events or concerts.

PARC DE JOAN MIRÓ
PARK

Map p302 (Carrer de Tarragona; ☺10am-sunset; Ⓜ Tarragona) **FREE** This palm-filled park is worth a look for its massive Miró sculpture, **Dona i Ocell**, which towers above the surrounding concrete. Locals know the park as the Parc de l'Escorxador (Abattoir Park), after the slaughterhouse that once stood here – unsurprisingly given the proximity to the former Les Arenes bullring (now a shopping centre).

JARDINS DE MOSSÈN
CINTO DE VERDAGUER
GARDENS

Map p302 (http://ajuntament.barcelona.cat/ ecologiaurbana; Avinguda Miramar 30; ☺10am-sunset; ☐55, 150) **FREE** Near the Estació Parc Montjuïc funicular/Telefèric station are the ornamental Jardins de Mossèn Cinto de Verdaguer. These sloping, verdant gardens are home to various kinds of bulbs and aquatic plants. Many of the former (some 80,000) have to be replanted each year. They include tulips, narcissus, crocus, varieties of dahlia and more. The aquatic plants include lotus and water lilies.

CEMENTIRI DEL SUD-OEST
CEMETERY

(Cementiri Nou; ☑93 484 19 99; www.cbsa.cat; Carrer de la Mare de Déu de Port 56-58; ☺8am-6pm; ☐21, 107) **FREE** On the hill to the south of the Anella Olímpica, this huge 1883-opened cemetery stretches down the southern slopes, combining elaborate architect-designed tombs for rich families and small niches for the rest. It includes the graves of numerous Catalan artists and politicians, and, at the southern entrance, the Col·lecció de Carrosses Fúnebres hearse collection. On Sundays and public holidays only, bus 107 goes right through the cemetery. From Monday to Saturday, take bus 21 to the main gates.

MUSEU OLÍMPIC I DE L'ESPORT   MUSEUM

Map p302 (☑93 292 53 79; www.museu olimpicbcn.cat; Avinguda de l'Estadi 60; adult/child €5.80/free; ☺10am-8pm Tue-Sat, to 2.30pm Sun Apr-Sep, 10am-6pm Tue-Sat, to 2.30pm Sun Oct-Mar; ☑55, 150) The Museu Olímpic i de l'Esport is an information-packed interactive sporting museum. After picking up tickets, you wander down a ramp that snakes below ground level and is lined with multimedia displays on the history of sport and the Olympic Games, starting with the ancients.

PAVELLÓ MIES
VAN DER ROHE   ARCHITECTURE

Map p302 (☑93 215 10 11; www.miesbcn.com; Avinguda de Francesc Ferrer i Guàrdia 7; adult/child €5/free; ☺10am-8pm Mar-Oct, 10am-6pm Nov-Feb; Ⓜ Espanya) The Pavelló Mies van der Rohe is a work of artful simplicity that is emblematic of the Modernisme movement. The structure has been the subject of many studies and interpretations, and it has inspired several generations of architects. That said, unless you're an avid architecture fan, there isn't much to see inside beyond what you can glean from the building's exterior.

COL·LECCIÓ DE CARROSSES
FÚNEBRES   MUSEUM

(☑93 484 19 99; www.cbsa.cat; Carrer de la Mare de Déu de Port 56-58; ☺10am-2pm Sat & Sun; ☑21, 107) FREE If late-18th-century to mid-20th-century hearses capture your imagination, then this collection at the Cementiri del Sud-Oest (p190) is probably the city's weirdest sight, a place to contemplate the pomp and circumstance of people's last earthly ride. The funeral company claims it is the biggest museum of its kind in the world.

PARC DE L'ESPANYA INDUSTRIAL   PARK

Map p302 (Carrer de Muntadas 37; ☺10am-sunset; Ⓜ Sants Estació) FREE With ponds, little waterfalls, green spaces, trees, a dragon-shaped children's slide, bar, and towers that look like sci-fi prison-camp searchlight towers, this park is playfully postmodern.

GOING UNDERGROUND

Part of the Museu d'Història de Barcelona (MUHBA), **MUHBA Refugi 307** (Map p302; ☑93 256 21 22; http://ajuntament.barcelona.cat/museuhistoria; Carrer Nou de la Rambla 175; adult/child incl tour €3.40/free; ☺tours in English 10.30am Sun; Ⓜ Paral·lel) dates back to the days of the Spanish Civil War. Barcelona was the city most heavily bombed from the air during the war and had more than 1300 air-raid shelters. Local citizens started digging this one under a fold of Montjuïc in March 1937. Compulsory tours are conducted in English at 10.30am, Spanish at 11.30am and Catalan at 12.30pm on Sundays. Reserve ahead as places are limited.

Over the course of the next two years, the web of tunnels was slowly extended to 200m, with a theoretical capacity for 2000 people. People were not allowed to sleep overnight in the shelter – when raids were not being carried out work continued on its extension. Vaulted to displace the weight above the shelter to the clay brick walls (clay is porous, which allowed the bricks to absorb the shock waves of falling bombs without cracking), the tunnels were narrow and winding. Coated in lime to seal out humidity and whitewashed to relieve the sense of claustrophobia, they became a second home for many El Poble Sec folks.

When the civil war ended, Franco had some extensions made because he considered the option of entering WWII on Hitler's side. When he decided not to join the war, this and other shelters were largely abandoned. In the tough years of famine and rationing during the 1940s and 1950s, families from Granada took up residence here rather than in the shacks springing up all over the area, as poor migrants arrived from southern Spain. Later on, an enterprising fellow grew mushrooms here for sale on the black market.

MAR I MUNTANYA (SEA & MOUNTAIN)

The quickest way from the beach to the mountain is via the **cable car** (Map p302; ☑93 430 47 16; www.telefericodebarcelona.com; Avinguda de Miramar; one way/return €11/16.50; ⊙10.30am-8pm Jun–mid-Sep, 10.30am-7pm Mar-May & mid-Sep–Oct, 11am-5.30pm Nov-Feb; ☐150) that runs between Torre de Sant Sebastiá in Barceloneta and the Miramar stop on Montjuïc. From Estació Parc Montjuïc, the separate Telefèric de Montjuïc (Map p302; ☑93 328 90 03; www.telefericde-montjuic.cat; Avinguda de Miramar 30; adult/child one way €8.20/6.50; ⊙10am-9pm Jun-Sep, 10am-7pm Mar-May & Oct, 10am-6pm Nov-Feb; ☐55, 150) cable car carries you to the **Castell de Montjuïc** (p188) via the mirador (lookout point).

It's transformed when illuminated at night and worth a look if you're waiting for a train at Barcelona Sants.

JARDINS DE MOSSÈN COSTA I LLOBERA   GARDENS
Map p302 (http://ajuntament.barcelona.cat/ecologiaurbana; Carretera de Miramar 38; ⊙10am-sunset; ☐Transbordador Aeri, Miramar) **FREE** Above the thundering traffic of the main road to Tarragona, the Jardins de Mossèn Costa i Llobera have a good collection of tropical and desert plants – including a veritable forest of cacti (Europe's largest collection), with some species reaching over 5m in height.

✖ EATING

FEDERAL   CAFE €
Map p302 (☑93 187 36 07; www.federalcafe.es; Carrer del Parlament 39; mains €9-12; ⊙8am-11pm Mon-Thu, 8am-1am Fri, 9am-1am Sat, 9am-5.30pm Sun; ☎☑; ⓂSant Antoni) On a stretch that now teems with cafes, Australian-run Federal was the trailbazer, with its good coffee (including a decent flat white) and superb brunches. Later in the day, healthy, tasty options span snacks (prawn toast, polenta chips with gorgonzola) to larger dishes like veggie burgers or grilled salmon with soba noodles. Head to the small, breezy roof terrace.

ESCRIBÀ   PASTRIES €
Map p302 (☑93 454 75 35; www.escriba.es; Gran Via de les Corts Catalanes 546; pastries €2-6.50; ⊙8.30am-8.30pm; ⓂUrgell) Antoni Escribà carries forward a family tradition (since 1906) of melting *barcelonins'* hearts with remarkable pastries and chocolate creations. Seasonal treats include the Easter *bunyols de xocolata* (little round pastry balls filled with chocolate cream). Escribà has another branch (p276) in a Modernista setting at La Rambla.

HORCHATERIA SIRVENT   ICE CREAM €
Map p302 (☑93 441 27 20; www.turronessirvent.com; Carrer del Parlament 56; ice cream €1.60-3, horchata €2.20-3.90; ⊙9am-10pm; ⓂSant Antoni) Along with ice cream, *granissat* (iced fruit crush) and *turrón* (nougat), this old-school parlour has served *barcelonins'* favourite source of *orxata/horchata* (tiger-nut drink) since 1926 – the best you'll try without having to catch the train down to this drink's spiritual home, Valencia. You can get it by the glass or take it away.

SPICE   CAFE €
Map p302 (☑93 624 33 59; www.spicecafe.es; Carrer de Margarit 13; dishes €3.50-5; ⊙4-9pm Tue-Thu, 11am-9pm Fri-Sun; ☎; ⓂPoble Sec) Run by friendly English-speaking staff, Spice is a delightful cafe that's earned a following for its delicious homemade desserts, such as ricotta and cinnamon cheesecake or a gluten-free orange and cardamom loaf. Along with excellent coffees, there are loose-leaf teas and homemade sodas.

JUICE HOUSE   HEALTH FOOD €
Map p302 (☑93 117 15 15; www.thejuicehouse.es; Carrer del Parlament 12; dishes €5.50-11.50; ⊙11am-4pm & 7-11pm Mon, Tue & Thu, 11am-4pm Wed, 10am-5pm & 7pm-midnight Fri & Sat, 10am-5pm Sun; ☑; ⓂPoble Sec) Whether you're a vegetarian, vegan, flexitarian, raw food fan or simply after a tasty, thoughtfully prepared meal, this cheery cafe should figure high on your itinerary. Oat and chia pancakes, açaí fruit bowls, and oven-baked eggs are fine ways to start the morning.

★QUIMET I QUIMET   TAPAS €€

Map p302 (☑93 442 31 42; Carrer del Poeta Cabanyes 25; tapas €4-10, montaditos €2.80-4; ◷noon-4pm & 7-10.30pm Mon-Fri, noon-4pm Sat, closed Aug; MParal·lel) Quimet i Quimet is a family-run business that has been passed down from generation to generation. There's barely space to swing a *calamar* (squid) in this bottle-lined, standing-room-only place, but it is a treat for the palate, with *montaditos* (tapas on a slice of bread) made to order.

★AGUST GASTROBAR   BISTRO €€

Map p302 (☑93 162 67 33; www.agustbarcelona. com; Carrer del Parlament 54; mains €12.50-24; ◷kitchen 7pm-midnight Mon-Thu, 2pm-midnight Fri-Sun, bar to 2am; MPoble Sec) Set up by two French chefs (one of whom trained under Gordon Ramsay), Agust occupies a fabulous mezzanine space with timber beams, exposed brick and textured metro tiles. Baby scallops with seaweed butter and prawn-stuffed avocado cannelloni are savoury standouts; desserts include the extraordinary 'el cactus' (chocolate-crumble soil, mojito mousse and prickly pear sorbet) served in a terracotta flower pot.

MANO ROTA   BISTRO €€

Map p302 (☑93 164 80 41; www.manorota.com; Carrer de la Creu dels Molers 4; mains €15-22; ◷8-11.30pm Mon, 1-3.30pm & 8-11.30pm Tue-Sat, 1-3.30pm Sun; MPoble Sec) Exposed brick, aluminium pipes, industrial light fittings and recycled timbers create a hip, contemporary setting for inspired bistro cooking at Mano Rota (which literally translates as 'broken hand', but is actually a Spanish idiom for consummate skill). Asian, South American and Mediterranean flavours combine in dishes such as crispy squid with yuzu aioli or dorade (bream) with pak choy pesto.

LASCAR 74   PERUVIAN €€

Map p302 (☑93 017 98 72; www.lascar.es; Carrer del Roser 74; mains €12-15; ◷7-11.30pm Mon-Thu, 2-5pm & 7pm-11.30pm Fri-Sun; MParal·lel) At this self-styled 'ceviche and pisco bar', oyster shooters with leche de tigre (the traditional ceviche marinade) are served alongside exquisite Peruvian ceviches as well as renditions from Thailand, Japan and Mexico. Pisco sours are the real deal, frothy egg white and all.

PALO CORTAO   TAPAS €€

Map p302 (☑93 188 90 67; www.palocortao.es; Carrer de Nou de la Rambla 146; mains €10-15; ◷8pm-1am Tue-Fri, 1-5pm & 8pm-1am Sat & Sun; MParal·lel) Contemporary Palo Cortao is renowned for its beautifully executed seafood and meat dishes, served at fair prices. Highlights include roast oxtail with vermouth jus, octopus with white bean hummus, smoked mackerel with pickled jalapeño and tuna tataki tempura. Its long wooden bar with metal stools is ideal for solo diners.

CASA XICA   FUSION €€

Map p302 (☑93 600 58 58; Carrer de la França Xica 20; sharing plates €5-15; ◷8.30-11pm Mon, 1.30-11pm Tue-Sat; MPoble Sec) On the parlour floor of an old house, Casa Xica is a casual but artfully designed space where elements of the Far East are fused with fresh Catalan ingredients (owners Marc and Raquel lived and travelled in Asia).

CASA DE TAPAS CAÑOTA   TAPAS €€

Map p302 (☑93 325 91 71; www.casadetapas. com; Carrer de Lleida 7; tapas €5-14; ◷1-4pm & 7.30pm-midnight Tue-Sat, 1-4pm Sun; MPoble Sec) Between Poble Sec and Plaça d'Espanya, this friendly, unfussy option serves affordable, nicely turned out tapas plates. Seafood is the speciality, with rich razor clams, garlic-fried prawns and tender octopus. Wash it down with a refreshing bottle of *albariño* (a Galician white).

XEMEI   ITALIAN €€

Map p302 (☑93 553 51 40; www.xemei.es; Passeig de l'Exposició 85; mains €16-26; ◷1.30-3.30pm & 9-11pm Mon-Fri, 2-4.30pm & 9pm-midnight Sat & Sun; MPoble Sec) Xemei ('Twins' in Venetian, for its twin Venetian owners) is a wonderful slice of Venice in Barcelona. To the accompaniment of gentle jazz, you might try a starter of burrata with crispy leeks and potato rosti, followed by *bigoi in salsa veneziana* (thick spaghetti in an anchovy and onion sauce) or *pasta alla seppia nera polpo* (squid-ink pasta with octopus).

BODEGA SEPÚLVEDA   CATALAN €€

Map p302 (☑93 323 59 44; www.bodega sepulveda.net; Carrer de Sepúlveda 173; mains €11-21; ◷1.30-4.30pm & 8pm-1am Mon-Fri, 8pm-1am Sat; MUniversitat) This venerable tavern has been in business since 1952. The dizzying range of dishes mixes traditional (Catalan faves like *cap i pota* – stew made with bits of the calf you don't want to think

MONTJUÏC, POBLE SEC & SANT ANTONI EATING

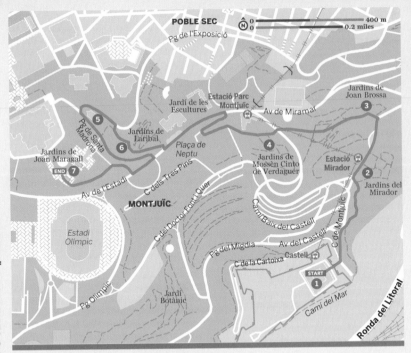

🏃 Neighbourhood Walk
Views & Gardens on Montjuïc

START CASTELL DE MONTJUÏC
END JARDINS DE JOAN MARAGALL
LENGTH 3KM; 1½ HOURS

Long synonymous with oppression, the dark history of **1 Castell de Montjuïc** (p188) is today overshadowed by the stupendous views it commands over the city and sea. (Don't miss the little sea-facing trail behind the fortress.) The ride up on the Telefèric de Montjuïc is the perfect way to get here.

A short stroll down the road or the parallel Camí del Mar pedestrian trail leads to another fine viewpoint overlooking the city and sea, the **2 Jardins del Mirador** (p189). Take the weight off on the park benches or pick up a snack.

Further downhill is the multitiered **3 Jardins de Joan Brossa** (p189). Enter on the left just beyond Plaça de la Sardana, which has a sculpture of people engaged in the classic Catalan folk dance. More fine city views can be had from among the many Mediterranean trees and plants.

Exiting the Jardins de Joan Brossa on the western side, cross Camí Baix del Castell

to the painstakingly laid out **4 Jardins de Mossèn Cinto de Verdaguer** (p190). This is a beautiful setting for a slow meander among tulip beds and water lilies.

Dropping away behind the Fundació Joan Miró, the 1922-established **5 Jardins de Laribal** comprise a combination of terraced gardens linked by paths and stairways. The pretty sculpted watercourses along some of the stairways were inspired by Granada's Alhambra.

While in the gardens, you can take a break for a meal if hunger strikes. **6 La Font del Gat** (p195) has a daily changing menu (no à la carte), and a lovely and spacious terrace dotted with orange trees and surrounded by greenery.

Continue walking west, past the Estadi Olímpic (Olympic Stadium) to reach the lovely, but little visited **7 Jardins de Joan Maragall**. Lush lawns, ornamental fountains, photogenic sculptures and a neoclassical palace (the Spanish royal family's residence in Barcelona) set these gardens apart. The catch: the grounds are only open on weekends (10am to 3pm).

about) with more surprising options like *carpaccio de calabacín con bacalao y parmesán* (thin courgette slices draped in cod and Parmesan).

MALAMÉN
CATALAN €€

Map p302 (☑93 252 77 63; www.malamen.es; Carrer de Blai 53; mains €12-24; ⊗8pm-midnight Tue-Sun; MPoble Sec) Carrer de Blai is lined with bars and restaurants, but Malamén towers above most for its elegant art-deco-inspired design, immaculate service and gourmet versions of Catalan classics. Its shortish menu offers confit tuna, dill and caper salad, juicy steak with creamed mushrooms and blue-cheese croquettes, and the wine list is equally concise.

BODEGA 1900
TAPAS €€

Map p302 (☑93 325 26 59; www.bodega1900. com; Carrer de Tamarit 91; tapas €6-15; ⊗1pm-10.30pm Tue-Sat, closed Aug; MPoble Sec) Bodega 1900 mimics an old-school tapas and vermouth bar, but don't be fooled: this venture from the world-famous Adrià brothers creates gastronomic tapas such as 'spherified' reconstructed olives, or its *mollete de calamars,* probably the best squid sandwich in the world, hot from the pan and served with chipotle mayonnaise, kimchi and lemon zest.

BAR RAMÓN
TAPAS €€

Map p302 (☑93 325 02 83; http://barramon. dudaone.com; Carrer del Comte Borrell 81; tapas €5-12; ⊗8.30-11.30pm Mon-Thu, 9am-4pm & 8.30pm-midnight Fri & Sat; MSant Antoni) A much-loved local haunt in Sant Antoni, Bar Ramón is a lively blues-filled joint near the market. Old photos of American musical R&B legends (and a few guitars) line the walls – a fine backdrop for tapas like tender slices of *jamón ibérico,* grilled prawns and house-speciality *jabuguitos* (chorizo cooked in cider). It fills up fast, so reserve ahead.

FÀBRICA MORITZ
GASTROPUB €€

Map p302 (☑93 426 00 50; www.moritz.com; Ronda de Sant Antoni 41; sandwiches €6.50-11, mains €8-19.50; ⊗9am-3am; MSant Antoni) In a building redesigned by architect Jean Nouvel, with a menu created by chef Jordi Vilà of Michelin-starred Alkímia (p196; also on the premises), this restaurant at the Moritz brewery offers pan-European gastropub fare such as gourmet sandwiches, *moules-frites* (mussels and fries), steak tartare, whole roast chicken, fish and chips, frankfurters with sauerkraut and *flammkuchen* (Alsatian-style pizza).

PIZZA DEL SORTIDOR
PIZZA €€

Map p302 (☑93 173 04 90; www.lapizzadel sortidor.com; Carrer de Blasco de Garay 46; pizza €7-13; ⊗7.30pm-midnight Mon-Fri, 1.30-4pm & 7.30pm-midnight Sat & Sun; MPoble Sec) Dive into this rock-loving pizzeria for delicious thin-crust pizza, served piping hot from the wood-burning oven. It's utterly pretension-free – served without utensils or even plates (cardboard is used instead). Cheap beer is served in plastic cups, but you won't leave dissatisfied, especially after the complimentary shot of limoncello at the meal's end. Cash only.

BASÍLICO
MEDITERRANEAN €€

Map p302 (☑93 423 73 76; www.grupandiliana. com; Avinguda del Paral·lel 142; mains €10-17; ⊗1-3.30pm & 8.30-11.30pm; MPoble Sec) Shelves filled with wine bottles line the walls of this cavernous space, which turns out contemporary Mediterranean cuisine (Iberian pork cheeks with mango salsa; salt-baked lamb with crushed potatoes and fig jus; confit octopus with deep-fried softshell crab). Two-course lunch menus (€11.15) and four- and five-course dinner menus (€25/30) are fantastic value.

LA FONT DEL GAT
MEDITERRANEAN €€

Map p302 (☑93 289 04 04; www.lafontdelgat. com; Passeig de Santa Madrona 28; 3-course menu €16; ⊗10am-6pm Tue-Fri, noon-6pm Sat & Sun; ☐55) Set on the edge of the Jardins de Laribal, La Font del Gat's lovely, spacious terrace is dotted with orange trees and surrounded by greenery. It has a daily changing menu (no à la carte); dishes might include cinnamon- and lemon-marinated chicken or grilled tuna with caper butter. There's always a vegetarian option such as vegetable and goat cheese risotto.

LA BELLA NAPOLI
PIZZA €€

Map p302 (☑93 442 50 56; www.labellanapoli.es; Carrer de Margarit 14; pizza €10-16, mains €12-24; ⊗1.30-4pm & 8.30pm-midnight; MParal·lel) Pizzas here, ranging from the simple margherita to the more complex *tartufo nero* with gorgonzola and black truffles, are made the way they make them in Naples. The waiters are mostly from across the Med and have a cheeky southern Italian approach to food, customers and everything else.

TAVERNA CAN MARGARIT
CATALAN €€

Map p302 (☎93 441 67 23; Carrer de la Concòrdia 21; mains €10-15; ◎8.30pm-midnight Mon-Sat; Ⓜ Poble Sec) For decades this former wine store has been dishing out dinner to often raucous groups. Traditional Catalan cooking is the name of the game. Surrounded by aged wine barrels, take your place at old tables and benches and perhaps order the *conejo a la jumillana* (fried rabbit served with garlic, onion, bay leaves, rosemary, mint, thyme and oregano).

★ENIGMA
GASTRONOMY €€€

Map p302 (☎616 696322; www.enigmaconcept. es; Carrer de Sepúlveda 38-40; tasting menu €220; ◎1-4pm & 4.30-10.30pm Tue-Fri, noon-5.30pm & 6-10.30pm Sat; Ⓜ Espanya) Resembling a 3D art installation, this conceptual offering from the famed Adrià brothers is a 40-course tour de force of cutting-edge gastronomy across six different dining spaces. A meal takes 3½ hours all up and includes customised cocktail pairings (you can order additional drinks). There's a minimum of two diners; reserve months in advance. A €100 deposit is required upon booking.

Once your booking's confirmed, you'll receive the door code by email. Note that it's not suitable for kids, vegetarians or anyone with dietary restrictions. Diners are instructed not to post images on social media to preserve the enigmatic experience.

★TICKETS
TAPAS, GASTRONOMY €€€

Map p302 (☎93 292 42 50; www.ticketsbar. es; Avinguda del Paral·lel 164; tapas €3-26; ◎7-11.30pm Tue-Fri, 1-3.30pm & 7-11.30pm Sat, closed Aug; Ⓜ Paral·lel) A flamboyant affair playing with circus images and theatre lights, this is one of the sizzling tickets in the restaurant world, a Michelin-starred tapas bar opened by Ferran Adrià, of the legendary (since closed) El Bulli, and his brother Albert. Bookings are only taken online two months in advance, but you can try calling for last-minute cancellations.

The food veers towards the deliciously surreal in concoctions like crispy octopus with kimichi mayo or sage-marinated prawns with frozen salt, followed by sweet-potato sorbet with liquorice and tangerine sponge. The seafood bar serves a variety of oysters, with caviar, borscht and other unusual toppings.

ALKÍMIA
CATALAN €€€

Map p302 (☎93 207 61 15; www.alkimia.cat; Ronda de Sant Antoni 41; mains €22-42; ◎1.30-3.30pm & 8-10.30pm Mon-Fri; Ⓜ Universitat) Inside the Fàbrica Moritz (p195) brewery, culinary alchemist Jordi Vilà creates refined Catalan dishes with a twist (oyster-stuffed courgette flowers; roast royal hare with beetroot; candied lemon soufflé with pickled plum ice cream) that have earned him a Michelin star. Set menus range from €98 to €155.

MARTÍNEZ
SPANISH €€€

Map p302 (☎93 106 60 52; www.martinez barcelona.com; Carretera de Miramar 38; mains €21.50-32; ◎1-11pm; ☐21, ☐ Teleférico del Puerto) With a fabulous panorama over the city and port, Martínez is a standout among the lacklustre dining options atop Montjuïc. On warm days, head to the outdoor terrace for its signature rice and paella dishes (€38 to €62 for two). There are also oysters, calamari, fresh market fish and other seafood hits, plus *jamón* and grilled meat dishes.

If you're not up for the pricey main courses, Martínez is also a fine destination for drinks at any time of day; the bar stays open until 1.30am.

🍷 DRINKING & NIGHTLIFE

★ABIRRADERO
BREWERY

Map p302 (☎93 461 94 46; www.abirradero. com; Carrer Vila i Vilà 77; ◎5pm-1am Mon-Thu, noon-2am Fri & Sat, noon-1am Sun; 📶; Ⓜ Paral·lel) Barcelona is spoilt for choice with craft breweries, and this bright, buzzing space has 20 of its own beers rotating on the taps, including IPAral·lel (a double IPA), Excuse Me While I Kiss My Stout, and Tripel du Poble Sec. Tapas, sharing boards and burgers are standouts from the kitchen. You'll occasionally catch live jazz and blues here.

★LA CASETA DEL MIGDIA
BAR

Map p302 (☎617 956572; www.lacaseta.org; Mirador del Migdia; ◎8pm-1am Wed-Fri, noon-1am Sat & Sun Apr-Sep, noon-sunset Sat & Sun Oct-Mar; ☐150) The effort of getting to what is, for all intents and purposes, a simple *chiringuito* (makeshift cafe-bar) is worth it. Gaze out to sea over a beer or coffee by day. As sunset approaches the atmosphere changes, as reggae, samba and funk wafts out over the hillside. Drinks aside, you can also order food fired up on the outdoor grills.

Walk below the walls of the Castell de Montjuïc along the dirt track or follow Passeig del Migdia – look out for signs for the Mirador del Migdia.

PERVERT CLUB @ THE ONE   GAY

Map p302 (📞93 453 05 10; http://pervert-club.negocio.site; Avinguda Francesc Ferrer i Guàrdia 13; cover from €18; ☺midnight-6am Sat; 🚌13, 23, 150, ℳEspanya) This weekly fest takes place at The One club in Poble Espanyol (p189). Electronic music dominates and, in spite of the 6am finish, for many this is only the start of the 'evening'. Expect loads of tanned and buff gym bunnies – and plenty of topless eye candy.

LA TERRRAZZA   CLUB

Map p302 (📞687 969825; www.laterrrazza.com; Avinguda de Francesc Ferrer i Guàrdia; cover from €15; ☺midnight-6.30am Thu-Sat May-Sep; 🚌13, 23, 150, ℳEspanya) Come summer, La Terrrazza attracts squadrons of beautiful people, locals and foreigners alike, for a full-on night of music (mainly house, techno and electronica) and cocktails partly under the stars inside the Poble Espanyol (p189) complex.

BAR OLIMPIA   BAR

Map p302 (📞676 828232; Carrer d'Aldana 11; ☺5pm-1am Mon-Wed, 5pm-2am Thu, 5pm-3am Fri, 1pm-3am Sat, 1pm-1am Sun; ℳParal·lel) This great little neighbourhood bar is a small slice of Barcelona history. It was here (and on the surrounding block), where the popular Olimpia Theatre Circus performed between 1924 and 1947. Today the retro setting draws a diverse crowd, who come for house-made vermouth, snacks (like quesadillas, cheese platters and tuna tartare) and strong gin and tonics.

REDRUM   BAR

Map p302 (📞670 269126; Carrer de Margarit 36; ☺6pm-1am Mon-Thu, 6pm-2am Fri, 2pm-2am Sat, 6pm-12.30am Sun; ℳPoble Sec) Redrum's craft brews and cocktails are complemented by Mexican street food (including excellent tacos and ceviche). It has a brightly coloured interior and friendly service. Happy hour runs from 6pm to 8pm.

EL ROUGE   BAR

Map p302 (📞666 251556; Carrer del Poeta Cabanyes 21; ☺9pm-2am Thu, 10pm-3am Fri & Sat, 11am-2am Sun; 📷; ℳPoble Sec) Decadence is the word that springs to mind in this bordello-red lounge-cocktail bar, with acid jazz, drum and bass and other sounds drifting along in the background. The walls are covered in heavy-framed paintings, dim lamps and mirrors, and no two chairs are alike. You can sometimes catch DJs, risqué poetry soirées, cabaret shows or even nights of tango dancing.

LA CAMBICHA   BAR

Map p302 (📞93 187 25 13; Carrer del Poeta Cabanyes 43; ☺6pm-2am Mon-Wed, 1pm-2am Thu-Sun; ℳParal·lel) This shoebox-sized bar feels a bit like a lost cabin in the woods with its newspaper-covered walls, lanterns and old sporting photos. Once you've wedged yourself alongside a tiny table, you can join the young soul- and blues-loving crowd over inexpensive empanadas and vermouth. Bands also occasionally play.

BAR CALDERS   BAR

Map p302 (📞93 329 93 49; Carrer del Parlament 25; ☺5pm-2am Mon-Fri, 11am-2.30am Sat, 11am-12.30am Sun; ℳSant Antoni) It bills itself as a wine bar, but actually the wine selection at Bar Calders is its weak point. As an all-day cafe and tapas bar, however, it's unbeatable, with outdoor tables on a tiny pedestrian lane, and has become the favoured meeting point for the neighbourhood's boho element.

SALA PLATAFORMA   CLUB

Map p302 (📞93 329 00 29; www.salaplataforma.com; Carrer Nou de la Rambla 145; cover from €6; ☺10pm-6am Thu-Sat, 7pm-2am Sun; ℳParal·lel) With two adjoining if smallish dance spaces, 'Platform' feels like a clandestine location in an otherwise quiet residential street. Inside this friendly, straightforward dance dive, you'll find popular '80s grooves, timeless rock and occasional live bands – plus drum and bass.

TINTA ROJA   BAR

Map p302 (📞93 443 32 43; www.tintaroja.cat; Carrer de la Creu dels Molers 17; ☺8.30pm-12.30am Wed, to 2am Thu, to 3am Fri & Sat, closed Aug; ℳPoble Sec) A succession of nooks and crannies, dotted with flea-market finds and dimly lit in violets, reds and yellows, makes Tinta Roja an intimate spot for a craft beer, cocktail or glass of Argentinean wine – and the occasional show in the back, featuring anything from actors to acrobats.

This was once a *vaqueria* (small dairy farm) that kept cows out the back and sold fresh milk at the front.

METRO
GAY

Map p302 (📝93 323 52 27; www.metrodiscobcn. com; Carrer de Sepúlveda 185; cover before/after 2am from €8/20; ⊙12.15am-5.30am Sun-Thu, to 6.45am Fri & Sat; Ⓜ Universitat) Metro attracts a fun-loving gay crowd with its two dance floors, three bars and very dark room. Keep an eye out for shows and parties, which can range from parades of models to bingo nights (on Thursday nights, with sometimes-interesting prizes), plus the occasional striptease.

To save cash, come before 2am, though you're likely to be drinking all by your lonesome, as Metro doesn't fill up till late.

 ENTERTAINMENT

SALA APOLO
LIVE MUSIC

Map p302 (📝93 441 40 01; www.sala-apolo.com; Carrer Nou de la Rambla 113; club from €15, concerts vary; ⊙concerts from 8pm, club from midnight; Ⓜ Paral·lel) This is a fine old theatre, where red velvet dominates and you feel as though you're in a movie-set dancehall scene. 'Nasty Mondays' and 'Crappy Tuesdays' are aimed at a diehard, never-stop-dancing crowd. Club entry includes a drink. Earlier in the evening, concerts generally take place here and in 'La 2', a smaller auditorium downstairs.

BARTS
CONCERT VENUE

Map p302 (Barcelona Arts on Stage; 📝93 324 84 92; www.barts.cat; Avinguda del Paral·lel 62; Ⓜ Paral·lel) BARTS has a solid reputation for its innovative line-up of urban dance troupes, electro swing, psychedelic pop and other eclectic fare. Its smart design combines a comfortable midsized auditorium with excellent acoustics. Hours and ticket prices vary; check the agenda online.

TEATRE GREC
THEATRE

Map p302 (http://lameva.barcelona.cat/grec; Passeig de Santa Madrona; 🚌55, 150) Built in 1929 by Catalan architect Ramon Revento in ancient Greek style, this lovely stone amphitheatre on Montjuïc stages one of the city's best summer festivals, the Festival Grec de Barcelona, with theatre, dance and music events.

GRAN BODEGA SALTÓ
LIVE MUSIC

Map p302 (📝93 441 37 09; www.bodegasalto.net; Carrer de Blesa 36; ⊙7pm-2am Mon-Thu, noon-3am Fri & Sat, noon-midnight Sun; Ⓜ Paral·lel) The ranks of barrels give away the bar's history as a traditional bodega. Now, after a little homemade psychedelic redecoration with odd lamps, figurines and old Chinese beer ads, it's a magnet for an eclectic barfly crowd. The crowd is mixed and friendly, and gets pretty animated on nights when there's live music.

HIROSHIMA
LIVE PERFORMANCE

Map p302 (📝93 315 54 58; www.hiroshima. cat; Carrer de Vilà i Vilà 67; ⊙7-11pm Wed-Sun; Ⓜ Paral·lel) Hiroshima is a creative lynchpin in Poble Sec. In a former elevator factory, it hosts emerging and avant-garde musicians, dancers and performing artists. There are two stages (seating 130 and 250 people, respectively) and a lively ground-floor bar where you can grab a drink after the show. For unconventional fare, this is a good place to look.

RENOIR FLORIDABLANCA
CINEMA

Map p302 (📝91 542 27 02; www.cinesrenoir. com; Carrer de Floridablanca 135; Ⓜ Sant Antoni) With seven screens, this cinema shows a mix of quality art-house flicks and blockbusters in their original language (with Spanish subtitles). It's handily located just beyond El Raval, so you'll find no shortage of post-film entertainment options nearby.

TEATRE MERCAT DE LES FLORS
DANCE

Map p302 (📝93 256 26 00; www.mercatflors. cat; Carrer de Lleida 59; ⊙box office 11am-2pm & 4-7pm Mon-Fri, plus 1hr before show; 🚌55) Next door to the **Teatre Lliure** (Map p302; 📝93 289 27 70; www.teatrelliure.com; Plaça de Margarida Xirgu 1; ⊙box office 9am-8pm, plus 2hr before performance), and together with it known as the Ciutat de Teatre (Theatre City), this spacious modern stage is Barcelona's top venue for local and international contemporary dance acts.

SHOPPING

POPCORN STORE FASHION & ACCESSORIES

Map p302 (Carrer Viladomat 30-32; ⊙11am-3pm
& 4.30-8.30pm Mon-Sat) Cutting-edge Barcelona labels for women at this 2017-opened
boutique include Sister Dew, with asym-
metrical tops, jackets, dresses and more,
and Ester Gueroa, with bold prints and
lace. Men will find stylish shirts, trousers
and belts from Italian and other European
designers.

10000 RECORDS MUSIC

Map p302 (✍93 292 77 76; www.10000records.
es; Carrer de Floridablanca 70; ⊙5-8pm Mon,
10am-2pm & 5-8pm Tue-Fri, 10am-2pm Sat;
ⓂPoble Sec) As its name suggests, this record shop overflows with vintage and new
vinyl in all genres but especially rock, pop,
metal and jazz. You'll also unearth retro ra-
dios, cassettes and music books.

MERCAT DE SANT ANTONI MARKET

Map p302 (✍93 426 35 21; www.mercatde
santantoni.com; Carrer de Comte d'Urgell 1;
⊙7am-2.30pm & 5-8.30pm Mon-Thu, 7am-
8.30pm Fri & Sat; ⓂSant Antoni) Just beyond
the western edge of El Raval is Mercat de
Sant Antoni, a glorious old iron-and-brick
building constructed between 1872 and
1882. The secondhand book market takes
place alongside on Sunday mornings.

The market recently underwent a nine-
year renovation and reopened in 2018 with
250 stalls.

GI JOE FASHION & ACCESSORIES

Map p302 (✍93 329 96 52; www.gijoebcn.com;
Ronda de Sant Antoni 49; ⊙10am-2pm & 4.30-
8.30pm Mon-Sat; ⓂUniversitat) This is the best
central army-surplus warehouse. Get your
khakis here, along with urban army fashion
T-shirts, boots, and more. You can also find
vintage WWII items.

 # SPORTS & ACTIVITIES

PISCINES BERNAT PICORNELL SWIMMING

Map p302 (✍93 423 40 41; www.picornell.cat; Avinguda de l'Estadi 30-38; adult/child €11.90/7.30,
nudist hours €6.55/4.70; ⊙6.45am-midnight
Mon-Fri, 7am-9pm Sat, 7.30am-4pm Sun; 🚌13,
150) Admission to Barcelona's official Olympic pool on Montjuïc also includes use of
the complex's fitness room, sauna, Jacuzzi,
steam bath and track. On Saturday nights,
between 9pm and 11pm, the pool (with access to sauna and steam bath) is open only
to nudists. On Sundays between October
and May the indoor pool also opens for nudists only from 4.15pm to 6pm.

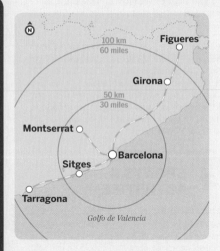

Day Trips from Barcelona

Girona (p201)

A splendid cathedral, a maze of narrow cobbled streets and Catalonia's finest medieval Jewish quarter are part of this riverside town's charms.

Figueres (p204)

The Teatre-Museu Dalí is Spain's most surreal sight, a place of pilgrimage for any fan of Salvador Dalí, and the artist's final resting place.

Montserrat (p206)

Catalonia's most important shrine is in this spectacularly sited mountain monastery, complete with Europe's oldest choir and superb scenic walks.

Sitges (p208)

A classy old town and eating scene, a pretty string of beaches, great nightlife and a hedonistic carnival await visitors at the south coast's premier seaside town.

Tarragona (p210)

This sunny port city has a beautiful medieval core, along with some of Spain's most extensive Roman ruins and studded with tempting eating options.

Girona

Explore

Northern Catalonia's largest city, Girona is a jewellery box of museums, galleries and Gothic churches, strung around a web of cobbled lanes and medieval walls. Reflections of Modernista mansions shimmer in the Riu Onyar, which separates the walkable historic centre on its eastern bank from the gleaming commercial centre on the west.

The Roman town of Gerunda lay on the Via Augusta from Gades (now Cádiz) to the Pyrenees. Taken from the Muslims by the Franks in the late 8th century, Girona became the capital of one of Catalonia's most important counties, falling under the sway of Barcelona in the late 9th century. Girona's wealth in medieval times produced many fine Romanesque and Gothic buildings that have survived repeated attacks, while a Jewish community flourished here until its expulsion in 1492.

With Catalonia's most diverse nightlife and dining scene outside Barcelona, Girona makes a delicious distraction from the coast.

The Best...

➡ **Sight** Catedral de Girona

➡ **Place to Eat** El Celler de Can Roca (p204)

➡ **Place to Drink** Lola Café (p204)

Top Tip

For the best views, take a walk along the top of the city walls, on the Passeig Arquelògic – accessed from the Banys Àrabs or the Plaça de Catalunya.

Getting There & Away

Car Take the AP7 (toll) motorway via Granollers

Train Regular trains run from Barcelona (from €10, up to 90 minutes)

Need to Know

➡ **Location** 95km northeast of Barcelona

➡ **Tourist office** (☑972 22 65 75; www.girona.cat/turisme; Rambla de la Llibertat 1; ◷9am-8pm Mon-Fri, 9am-2pm & 4-8pm Sat Apr-Oct, 9am-7pm Mon-Fri, 9am-2pm & 3-7pm Sat Nov-Mar, 9am-2pm Sun year-round)

◉ SIGHTS

Girona's exquisitely preserved **Call** (Jewish Quarter) – a labyrinth of low-slung stone arches and slender cobbled streets – flourished around narrow Carrer de la Força for six centuries, until relentless Christian persecution forced the Jews out of Spain.

★CATEDRAL DE GIRONA CATHEDRAL

(www.catedraldegirona.org; Plaça de la Catedral; adult/student incl Basílica de Sant Feliu €7/5; ◷10am-7.30pm Jul & Aug, to 6.30pm Apr-Jun, Sep & Oct, to 5.30pm Nov-Mar) Towering over a flight of 86 steps rising from Plaça de la Catedral, Girona's imposing cathedral is far more ancient than its billowing baroque facade suggests. Built over an old Roman forum, parts of its foundations date from the 5th century. Today, 14th-century Gothic styling – added over an 11th-century Romanesque church – dominates, though a beautiful, double-columned Romanesque **cloister** dates from the 12th century. With the world's second-widest Gothic nave, it's a formidable sight to explore, but audio guides are provided.

★MUSEU D'HISTÒRIA DELS JUEUS MUSEUM

(www.girona.cat/call; Carrer de la Força 8; adult/child €4/free; ◷10am-8pm Mon-Sat, 10am-2pm Sun Jul & Aug, 10am-2pm Mon & Sun, 10am-6pm Tue-Sat Sep-Jun) Until 1492, Girona was home to Catalonia's second-most important medieval Jewish community, after Barcelona, and one of the country's finest Jewish quarters. This excellent museum takes pride in Girona's Jewish heritage, without shying away from less salubrious aspects such as Inquisition persecution and forced conversions. You also see a rare 11th-century *miqvé* (ritual bath) and a 13th-century Jewish house.

MUSEU DEL CINEMA MUSEUM

(www.museudelcinema.cat; Carrer de la Sèquia 1; adult/child €5/free; ◷10am-8pm Jul & Aug, 10am-6pm Tue-Fri, 10am-8pm Sat, 11am-3pm Sun Sep-Jun) There's much more to this entrancing museum than the silver screen. Displays examine why humanity longs to indulge its imagination, probing the origins of visual storytelling, such as Chinese and Indian shadow puppets. It's a whistle-stop tour taking in the invention of the camera obscura, the 19th-century debut of the Lumière brothers, and optical illusions using

Girona

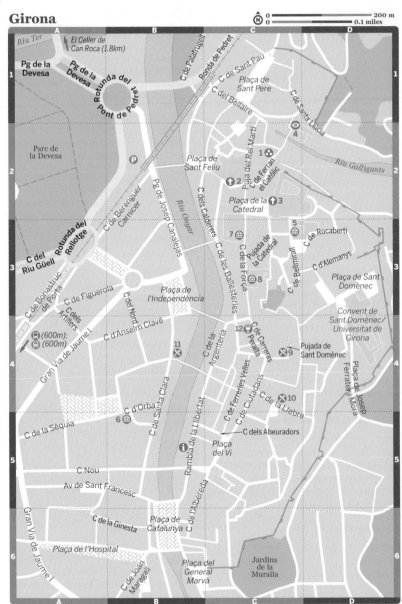

mirrors and trickery of light, including eerie phantasmagoria. Displays are in Catalan, Spanish, English and French.

BANYS ÀRABS
RUINS

(www.banysarabs.org; Carrer de Ferran el Catòlic; adult/child €2/1; ☾10am-7pm Mon-Sat, to 2pm Sun Mar-Oct, 10am-2pm Nov-Feb) Although modelled on earlier Islamic and Roman bathhouses, the Banys Àrabs are a finely preserved, 12th-century Christian affair in Romanesque style (restored in the 13th century). The baths contain an *apodyterium* (changing room), with a small octagonal

Girona

◎ Sights	p201
1 Banys Àrabs	C2
2 Basílica de Sant Feliu	C2
3 Catedral de Girona	C2
4 Monestir de Sant Pere de Galligants	C2
5 Museu d'Art de Girona	C3
6 Museu del Cinema	B5
7 Museu d'Història de Girona	C3
8 Museu d'Història dels Jueus	C3

⊗ Eating	p203
9 Café Le Bistrot	C4
10 La Fábrica	C4
11 Rocambolesc	B4

◎ Drinking	p203
12 Lola Cafè	C4

pool framed by slender pillars, followed by a *frigidarium* and *tepidarium* (with respectively cold and warm water) and a *caldarium* (a kind of sauna) heated by an underfloor furnace.

MONESTIR DE SANT PERE DE GALLIGANTS   MONASTERY

(www.mac.cat; Carrer de Santa Llúcia; adult/child incl Museu d'Arqueologia de Catalunya–Girona €4.50/3.50; ◎10am-6pm Tue-Sat Oct-Apr, 10am-7pm Tue-Sat May-Sep, 10am-2pm Sun year-round) This beautiful 11th- and 12th-century Romanesque Benedictine monastery has a sublime bell tower and a splendid cloister featuring otherworldly animals and mythical creatures on the 60 capitals of its double columns; there are some great ones in the church too.

BASÍLICA DE SANT FELIU   BASILICA

(Plaça de Sant Feliu; adult/student incl Catedral €7/5; ◎10am-5.30pm Mon-Sat, 1-5.30pm Sun) Just downhill from the cathedral stands Girona's second great church, with its landmark truncated bell tower. The nave is majestic with Gothic ribbed vaulting, while St Narcissus, the city's patron, is venerated in an enormous marble-and-jasper, late-baroque side chapel. To the right of the chapel is the saint's Gothic, 1328 sepulchre (which previously held his remains), displaying his reclining form and scenes from his life including the conversion of women, martyrdom and expelling of an evil genie. Audio guides included.

MUSEU D'HISTÒRIA DE GIRONA   MUSEUM

(www.girona.cat/museuhistoria; Carrer de la Força 27; adult/student/child €4/2/free; ◎10.30am-5.30pm Tue-Sat Oct-Apr, 10.30am-6.30pm Tue-Sat May-Sep, 10.30am-1.30pm Sun year-round) Eighteenth-century cloisters lend an appropriately antique feel to this journey from Roman Girona to medieval times to the present day. The museum's highlights include an exhibition illuminating the 3rd- to 4th-century Can Pau Birol mosaic, which depicts a lively circus scene with charioteers, and an explanation of the 1808 to 1809 siege of Girona by Napoleonic troops. Many pieces on display are copies rather than originals. Spanish-, English- and French-language booklets help with the Catalan-only display labels.

MUSEU D'ART DE GIRONA   GALLERY

(www.museuart.com; Pujada de la Catedral 12; admission €4.50, incl Catedral and Basílica de Sant Feliu €10; ◎10am-7pm Tue-Sat May-Sep, to 6pm Oct-Apr, 10am-2pm Sun year-round) Next to the cathedral, in the 12th- to 16th-century Palau Episcopal, this art gallery impresses with the scale and variety of its collection. Around 8500 pieces of art, mostly from this region, fill its displays, which ranges from Romanesque woodcarvings and murals to paintings of the city by 20th-century Polish-French artist Mela Mutter, early-20th-century sculptures by influential Catalan architect Rafael Masó i Valentí, and works by leading Modernista artist Santiago Rusiñol.

✗ EATING & DRINKING

There's extraordinary variety and quality to Girona's dining scene, from casual tapas bars and brunch-tastic cafes to paella specialists and one of the world's best restaurants, El Celler de Can Roca (p204). Unlike in other parts of Catalonia, vegetarians, vegans and diners with food allergies will enjoy plenty of choice here.

★ LA FÁBRICA   CAFE €

(http://lafabrica.cc; Carrer de la Llebre 3; dishes €3-8; ◎9am-3pm; 🛜📶) 🖊 Girona's culinary talents morph into top-quality coffee and Catalan-inspired brunchy favourites starring local ingredients at this energetic German-Canadian–owned cycle-themed cafe. Pillowy artisan *torrades* (toasts) – perhaps topped with avocado, feta and peppers – arrive on wooden sliders, washed down with expertly poured brews made with beans sourced from ecoconscious suppliers.

ROCAMBOLESC
ICE CREAM €

(☑972 41 66 67; www.rocambolesc.com; Carrer de Santa Clara 50; ice cream €2.90-4.50; ⊘11am-10pm Sun-Thu, to midnight Fri & Sat) Savour some of Spain's most lip-smackingly delicious ice cream at Rocambolesc, part of the world-famous El Celler de Can Roca culinary clan. Candy-striped decor sets the magical scene for creatively cool concoctions like baked-apple ice cream or mandarin sorbet sprinkled with passionfruit flakes.

CAFÉ LE BISTROT
CATALAN, FRENCH €€

(☑972 21 88 03; www.lebistrot.cat; Pujada de Sant Domènec 4; mains €7.50-14; ⊘noon-4pm & 7-11pm) Walls are draped in jasmine and tables spill out onto stairs climbing to a 17th-century church at what might just be Girona's most romantically set restaurant. The classic bistro-style menu twins French and Catalan cuisine, with crêpes, pastas, meaty mains, '*pagès*' pizzas and a rainbow of salads served alongside local cheeses. Inside, it's all check-print tiles and an old-world feel.

★EL CELLER DE CAN ROCA
CATALAN €€€

(☑972 22 21 57; www.cellercanroca.com; Carrer Can Sunyer 48; degustation menus €180-205; ⊘12.30-2pm Tue, 12.30-2pm & 8-9.30pm Wed-Sat, closed late Dec–mid-Jan & 10 days late Aug) Ever-changing avant-garde takes on Catalan dishes have catapulted El Celler de Can Roca to global fame. Holding three Michelin stars, it was named the best restaurant in the world in 2015 by The World's 50 Best. Each year brings new innovations, from molecular gastronomy to multi-sensory food-art interplay to sci-fi dessert trolleys, all with mama's home cooking as the core inspiration.

Run by the three Girona-born Roca brothers, El Celler is set in a refurbished country house, 2km northwest of central Girona. Book online 11 months in advance or join the standby list.

LOLA CAFÈ
BAR

(www.facebook.com/LolaCafe; Carrer de la Força 7; ⊘11pm-3am Wed-Sat) Baroque-style gilt mirrors, luscious cocktails and intimate tables for two make this a sultry night among the cobbled lanes of Girona's medieval town. Dance into the night to live rumba or the regular mash-up of 80s and 90s pop, and stay hydrated with caipirinhas, mojitos and more. Check the Facebook page for upcoming events.

Figueres

Explore
You'll want to spend the whole morning at the incomparable Teatre-Museu Dalí, admiring everything from the exterior to the bizarre decorative touches and Dalí's distinctive works. But there's more to Figueres than Dalí and there are several other attractions worth your time, as well as a clutch of good restaurants.

The Best...
➧ **Sight** Teatre-Museu Dalí (p205)
➧ **Place to Eat** El Motel (p206)
➧ **Place to Drink** Sidreria Txot's (p206)

Top Tip
It pays to reserve online in advance for the Teatre-Museu Dalí, and to visit outside weekends and public holidays. Get here for opening time to avoid the worst of the crowds.

Getting There & Away
Car Take the AP7 (toll) motorway via Granollers and Girona

Trains Trains run from Barcelona (€12 to €16, up to 2½ hours)

Need to Know
➧ **Location** 118km northeast of Barcelona
➧ **Tourist office** (☑972 50 31 55; http:// visitfigueres.cat; Plaça de l'Escorxador 2; ⊘9am-8pm Mon-Sat, 10am-3pm Sun Jul-Sep, 9.30am-2pm & 4-6pm Tue-Sat, 10am-2pm Mon & Sun Oct-Jun)

DALÍ'S CASTLE

If you're intrigued by artist Salvador Dalí, the **Castell de Púbol** (www.salvador-dali.org; Plaça de Gala Dalí, Púbol; adult/concession €8/6; ⊙10am-7.15pm mid-Jun–mid-Sep, 10am-5.15pm Tue-Sun mid-Mar–mid-Jun & mid-Sep–Oct, 10am-4.15pm Tue-Sun Nov–early Jan) is an essential piece of the puzzle. Between Girona and Palafrugell (22km northwest of the latter, south off the C66), this 14th-century castle was Dalí's gift to his wife and muse Gala, who is buried here. The Gothic-Renaissance building, with creeper-covered walls, spiral stone staircases and a shady garden, was decorated to Gala's taste, though there are surrealist touches like a grimacing anglerfish fountain and a pouting-lips sofa.

The life of Gala Dalí is fascinating in its own right, due to her entanglement with several pivotal figures in the first half of the 20th century. Gala married French poet Paul Éluard in 1917, had a two-year affair with pioneer of Dadaism Max Ernst, and then met Dalí in 1929. With Dalí's approval she continued to take lovers, though their loyalty to each other remained fierce. Dalí was only permitted to visit the castle with advance written permission, a restriction that held considerable erotic charge for the artist.

Today the Castell de Púbol forms the southernmost point of Catalonia's 'Salvador Dalí triangle'. The sombre castle is almost an antithesis to the flamboyance of Figueres' **Teatre-Museu Dalí** and Dalí's seaside **home** (☎972 25 10 15; www.salvador-dali.org; Port Lligat; adult/child under 8yr €11/free; ⊙9.30am-9pm mid-Jun–mid-Sep, 10.30am-6pm mid-Sep–Jan & mid-Feb–mid-Jun, closed mid-Jan–mid-Feb, closed Mon Nov–mid-Mar) in Port Lligat near Cadaqués.

To get here, catch a bus to Cruïlla de la Pera from Girona (€3, 40 minutes, 10 to 19 daily) or Palafrugell (€3.05, 25 minutes, seven to 13 daily), and alight at the stop on the C66 then walk 2km south to the castle. Alternatively, take a train from Girona to Flaçà (€3.30, 15 minutes, at least 15 daily), then taxi the last 5km.

◉ SIGHTS

★ TEATRE-MUSEU DALÍ   MUSEUM

(www.salvador-dali.org; Plaça de Gala i Salvador Dalí 5; adult/child under 9yr €14/free; ⊙9am-8pm Jul-Sep, 10.30am-6pm Oct-Jun, closed Mon Oct-May, also open 10pm-1am Aug) The first name that pops into your head when you lay eyes on this red castle-like building, topped with giant eggs and stylised Oscar-like statues and studded with plaster-covered croissants, is Salvador Dalí. An entirely appropriate final resting place for the master of surrealism, it has assured his immortality. Exhibits range from enormous, impossible-to-miss installations – like *Taxi Plujós* (Rainy Taxi), an early Cadillac surmounted by statues – to the more discreet, including a tiny, mysterious room with a mirrored flamingo.

MUSEU DEL JOGUET   MUSEUM

(www.mjc.cat; Carrer de Sant Pere 1; adult/child €7/free; ⊙10am-7pm Mon-Sat & 11am-6pm Sun Jun-Sep, 10am-6pm Tue-Sat, 11am-2pm Sun Oct-May) This museum has more than 5000 toys from throughout the ages – from the earliest board games involving coloured stones, to intricate dolls' houses, to 1920s dolls with baleful stares that may haunt your dreams, to choo-chooing train models, to Catalonia- and Valencia-made religious processions of tiny figures. It's a mesmerising display, with plenty to amuse the kids, and a section devoted to Dalí's childhood. Admission is reduced by 30% if you flash a Teatre-Museu Dalí ticket.

CASTELL DE SANT FERRAN   FORT

(www.lesfortalesescatalanes.info; Pujada del Castell; adult/child €3.50/free; ⊙10am-8pm Jul–mid-Sep, 10.30am-6pm mid-Sep–Oct & Apr-Jun, 10.30am-3pm Nov-Mar) Figueres' sturdy 18th-century fortress commands the surrounding plains from a low hill 1km northwest of the centre. The complex is a wonder of military engineering: it sprawls over 32 hectares, with the capacity for 6000 men to march within its walls and snooze in military barracks. Admission fees include clanking audio guides (nearly as old as the castle).

Built in the 1750s to repel French invaders, the fortress nevertheless fell to its Gallic neighbours – both in 1794 and 1808. Spain's Republican government held its final meeting of the civil war (on 1 February, 1939) in the dungeons here.

MUSEU DE L'EMPORDÀ   MUSEUM
(www.museuemporda.org; La Rambla 2; adult/child €4/free; ⊘11am-8pm Tue-Sat May-Oct, 11am-7pm Tue-Sat Nov-Apr, 11am-2pm Sun year-round) Extending over four floors, the local museum time travels from ancient amphorae to 7th-century sculptures to rotating installations of contemporary art. The region's culture and history are presented in a fragmented way, but it's an enjoyable journey. The 17th-century religious art is especially worthy of attention. Don't miss a colour-bursting 1962 *Sant Narcís* by Dalí.

Labels are in Catalan, though there are laminated information cards in Spanish, English and French. Admission is free with a Teatre-Museu Dalí ticket.

 EATING & DRINKING

SIDRERIA TXOT'S   CATALAN, BASQUE €
(☑972 67 85 23; www.sidreriatxots.com; Avinguda Salvador Dalí 114; dishes €5-16; ⊘noon-midnight; 🐾) Watch your Basque cider poured from on high (the way it's supposed to be) at this lively all-day cider bar with a summer garden. Then tuck into hot and cold *pintxos* (Basque tapas), tasty burgers, cured meats, cheeses and salads, as well as potato omelette, chorizo in cider and L'Escala anchovies.

RESTAURANT DURÁN   CATALAN €€
(☑972 50 12 50; www.hotelduran.com; Carrer Lasauca 5; mains €16-25; ⊘12.45-4pm & 8.30-11pm) Dine under the same roof as Salvador Dalí at this top-class, chandelier-lit restaurant, where smart service and plush decor are matched by such expertly prepared delights as smoked-salmon tartare, sole in orange sauce and pineapple carpaccio topped by mango ice cream. There's a €22, three-course set menu, along with a seasonal tasting menu (€49) if you can't decide.

EL MOTEL   CATALAN €€€
(☑972 50 05 62; www.hotelemporda.com; Hotel Empordà, Avinguda Salvador Dalí 170; mains €13-30; ⊘12.45-3.45pm & 8.30-10.30pm; 🅿🐾)

Jaume Subirós, the chef and owner of this smart roadside hotel-restaurant 1km north of Figueres' centre, is a seminal figure of the transition from traditional Catalan home cooking to the polished, innovative affair it is today. Local, seasonal ingredients star on the menu, which may feature highlights like salted Roses shrimp, ricotta-and-parmesan-stuffed courgette flowers, and rice with Cap de Creus lobster.

Montserrat

Explore

Montserrat, 50km northwest of Barcelona, is at the heart of Catalan identity for its mountain, monastery and natural park weaving among distinctive rock formations. Montserrat mountain is instantly recognisable, sculpted over millennia by wind and frost. Its turrets of rock, a coarse conglomerate of limestone and eroded fragments, extend like gnarled fingers from its 1236m-high bulk. More than halfway up the mountain lies the Benedictine Monestir de Montserrat, home to La Moreneta ('Little Brown One', or 'Black Virgin') one of Spain's most revered icons. Extending from this sacred spot is the **Parc Natural de la Muntanya de Montserrat**, superlative hiking terrain where brooks tumble into ravines and lookout points deliver panoramas of rocky pillars.

Montserrat (often used interchangeably for the monastery and mountain) is a hugely popular day trip from Barcelona. The monastery throngs with visitors, but serenity can still be found on the walking trails or by staying overnight.

The Best...
→ **Sight** Monestir de Montserrat (p207)
→ **Place to Eat** Hotel Abat Cisneros (p208)
→ **Walk** Sant Jeroni

Top Tip

Getting to Montserrat is half the fun, including the cog-wheel and funicular railways, and various combination packages are available at www.cremallerademontserrat.cat.

Getting There & Away

Car By car, take the C16 northwest from Barcelona, then the C58 northwest shortly beyond Terrassa, followed by the C55 south to Monistrol de Montserrat. You can leave your vehicle at the free car park and take the cremallera up to the top, or drive up and park (cars €6.50).

Train The R5 line trains operated by FGC (www.fgc.net) run half-hourly to hourly to/from Barcelona's Plaça d'Espanya station (one hour). Services start at 5.16am, but take the 8.36am train to connect with the first AERI cable car to the monastery from the Montserrat Aeri stop. Alternatively, take the R5 to the next stop on (Monistrol de Montserrat), from where cremallera trains run up to the monastery (20 minutes) every 20 to 40 minutes.

Need to Know

➡ **Location** 50km northwest of Barcelona

➡ **Tourist office** (☑938 77 77 77; www.montserratvisita.com; ☉9am-8pm Easter-Sep, to 5.45pm Oct-Easter)

 SIGHTS

★ MONESTIR DE MONTSERRAT   MONASTERY
(www.abadiamontserrat.net) Catalonia's most renowned monastery was established in 1025 to commemorate local shepherds' visions of the Virgin Mary, accompanied by celestial light and a chorus of holy music. Today, a community of 55 monks lives here. The monastery complex encompasses two blocks: on one side, the basilica and mon-

astery buildings, and on the other, tourist and pilgrim facilities. Admirable monastery architecture lining the main **Plaça de Santa Maria** includes elegant 15th-century cloisters and a gleaming late-19th-century facade depicting St George and St Benedict in relief.

MUSEU DE MONTSERRAT   MUSEUM
(www.museudemontserrat.com; Plaça de Santa Maria; adult/child €7/4, incl Espai (space) audiovisual €10/6; ☉10am-5.45pm Mon-Fri, 10am-6.45pm Sat & Sun) This museum has excellent displays, ranging from an archeological section with an Egyptian mummy to Gothic altarpieces to fine canvases by Caravaggio, El Greco, Picasso and several Impressionists (Monet, Degas), as well as a comprehensive collection of 20th-century Catalan art, and some fantastic Orthodox icons.

CAMBRIL DE LA MARE DE DÉU   CHURCH
(☉8-10.30am & noon-6.30pm, plus 7.30-8pm Jul–mid-Sep) Signs to the right of the entrance to Montserrat's main basilica lead into the intimate Cambril de la Mare de Déu, where you can pay homage to the famous **La Moreneta** ('Little Brown One', or 'Black Virgin'), a revered 12th-century Romanesque wood-carved statue of the Virgin Mary with Jesus seated on her knee.

☆ ENTERTAINMENT

ESCOLANIA DE MONTSERRAT   LIVE MUSIC
(www.escolania.cat; ☉performances 1pm Mon-Thu, 11am Sun, 6.45pm Sun-Thu) The clear voices of one of Europe's oldest boys' choirs have echoed through the basilica since the

DAY TRIPS FROM BARCELONA MONTSERRAT

WALKING IN MONTSERRAT

Take the 10-minute **Funicular de Sant Joan** (www.cremallerademontserrat.cat; one-way/return €8.10/13; ☉every 12-20min 10am-4.50pm Nov-Mar, to 5.50pm Sep, Oct, Apr & May, to 6.50pm Jul–mid-Sep, closed 3 weeks Jan) for the first 250m uphill from the monastery; alternatively, it's a 45-minute walk along the road between the funicular's lower and upper stations. From the top, it's a 20-minute stroll (signposted) to the **Ermita de Sant Joan**, with fine westward views.

More exciting is the signposted 7.5km (2½-hour) loop walk from the Funicular de Sant Joan's upper station, northwest to Montserrat's highest peak, **Sant Jeroni** (1236m), then back. The walk takes you across the upper part of the mountain, with a close-up experience of some of the rock pillars.

Wear good walking boots, bring water, and, before setting out, check with the **tourist office** regarding weather and trail conditions.

14th century. The choir performs briefly on most days (except school holidays), singing *Virolai*, written by Catalonia's national poet Jacint Verdaguer, and *Salve Regina*. The 50 *escolanets*, aged between nine and 14, go to boarding school in Montserrat and must endure a two-year selection process to join the choir.

🛏 SLEEPING & EATING

HOTEL ABAT CISNEROS   HOTEL €€

(☎93 877 77 01; www.montserratvisita.com; s/d incl breakfast €66/114; P🛜) The only hotel in the monastery complex has a superb location opposite the basilica. Rooms are comfortable though simple; some make up for the spartan decor with views across Plaça de Santa Maria. There are also inexpensive basic apartments (four people €104). The house restaurant serves imaginative Catalonian dishes (mains €13 to €23).

Sitges

Explore

Sitges has been a resort town since the 19th century, and was a key location for the Modernisme movement, which paved the way for the likes of Picasso. These days it's Spain's most famous gay holiday destination. In July and August, Sitges cranks up the volume to become one big beach party, while **Carnaval** (www.carnavaldesitges. com; ⊙Feb/Mar) unbridles the town's hedonistic side. But despite the bacchanalian nightlife, Sitges remains a classy destination: its array of galleries and museums belie its small size, there's a good choice of upmarket restaurants in its historic centre (which is lined with chic boutiques), and the October **film festival** (Festival Internacional de Cinema Fantàstic de Catalunya; www.sitgesfilmfestival.com; ⊙Oct) draws culture fiends from miles around.

The Best...

→ **Sight** Museu del Cau Ferrat
→ **Place to Eat** El Cable (p209)
→ **Place to Drink** Casablanca (p209)

Top Tip

There is a lovely 8km walk south along the coast to Vilanova, from which there are frequent trains back to Sitges (or Barcelona).

Getting There & Away

Car The best road from Barcelona is the C32 (toll) motorway. More scenic is the C31, which hooks up with the C32 after Castelldefels, but it is often busy and slow.

Train From 5am to 10pm, regular R2 rodalies trains run to Barcelona Passeig de Gràcia and Sants (€4.10, 45 minutes). For Barcelona airport (€4.10, 40 minutes), change at El Prat de Llobregat.

Need to Know

→ **Location** 35km southwest of Barcelona
→ **Tourist Office** (☎938 94 42 51; www.sitgestur.cat; Plaça Eduard Maristany 2; ⊙10am-2pm & 4-8pm Mon-Sat mid-Jun–mid-Oct, 10am-2pm & 4-6.30pm Mon-Sat mid-Oct–mid-Jun, 10am-2pm Sun year-round)

◉ SIGHTS

The most beautiful part of Sitges is the headland area, where noble Modernista palaces and mansions strike poses around the pretty Església de Sant Bartomeu i Santa Tecla (p209), with the sparkling-blue Mediterranean as a backdrop.

★**MUSEU DEL CAU FERRAT**   MUSEUM

(www.museusdesitges.cat; Carrer de Fonollar; incl Museu Maricel del Mar adult/child €10/free; ⊙10am-8pm Tue-Sun Jul-Sep, to 7pm Apr-Jun & Oct, to 5pm Nov-Mar) Built in the 1890s as a house-studio by Catalan artist Santiago Rusiñol, a pioneer of the Modernisme movement, this seaside mansion is crammed with his own art and that of his contemporaries (including his friend Picasso), as well as his extensive private collection of ancient relics and antiques. The visual feast is piled high, from Grecian urns and a 15th-century baptismal font to 18th-century tilework that glitters all the way to the floral-painted wood-beamed ceiling.

SITGES BEACHES

Dotted with *chiringuitos* (beach bars), Sitges' main beach is divided into nine sections (with different names) by a series of breakwaters and flanked by the attractive seafront Passeig Marítim. The most central beaches are lively **La Fragata**, just below Sant Bartomeu church, and **La Ribera**, immediately west. About 500m southwest of the centre, **L'Estanyol** has summer *chiringuitos* with sunbeds; 1.5km further southwest, **Les Anquines** and **Terramar** have paddleboat rental and deck chairs in summer. Northeast of the centre lie easy-access **Sant Sebastià**, sheltered **Balmins** (favoured by nudists; 1km northeast of town) and brown-sand **Aiguadolç** (500m further east). **Bassa Rodona**, immediately west of the centre, is Sitges' famous unofficial 'gay beach', though gay sunbathers are now spread out pretty evenly.

MUSEU MARICEL DEL MAR   MUSEUM
(www.museusdesitges.cat; Carrer de Fonollar; incl Museu del Cau Ferrat adult/child €10/free; ☺10am-8pm Tue-Sun Jul-Sep, to 7pm Apr-Jun & Oct, to 5pm Nov-Mar) This seafront building entered through the adjacent Museu del Cau Ferrat (p208) houses a vast collection of Catalan art spanning the 10th to 20th centuries, including works amassed by the town of Sitges and local collector Jesús Pérez-Rosales. Most spectacular is the downstairs atrium of neoclassical sculptures, framed by arches that overlook the sea.

**ESGLÉSIA DE SANT BARTOMEU
I SANTA TECLA**   CHURCH
(Plaça de l'Ajuntament; ☺Mass 7.30pm Mon-Fri, 8pm Sat, 9am, 11am, 12.30pm & 7.30pm Sun, hours vary) Sitges' most striking landmark is this 17th-century parish church, sitting proudly on a rocky outcrop lapped by the sea, which separates the 2km-long main beach to the southwest from the smaller sandy strands to the northeast.

✕ EATING & DRINKING

★**EL CABLE**   TAPAS €
(☎938 94 87 61; www.facebook.com/elcablebar sitges; Carrer de Barcelona 1; tapas €2-6; ☺7-11.30pm Mon-Fri, 12-3.30pm & 7-11.30pm Sat & Sun) Always packed, down-to-earth El Cable might just be Sitges' most loved tapas bar, rolling out classics like *patatas bravas* (often branded the best in town) alongside divine, inventive bite-sized creations. Try the veggie-stuffed puff-pastry '*saquito*' or the award-winning mushroom-filled squid with risotto and almond praline. Wash it

all down with fine organic Penedès wines, rustled up by welcoming waiters.

EL POU   TAPAS, FUSION €
(☎93 013 47 98; www.elpoudesitges.com; Carrer de Sant Bonaventura 21; dishes €5-10; ☺8-11.30pm Mon, Wed & Thu, 1.30-3.30pm & 8-11.30pm Fri-Sun; ☎) Tiny Wagyu beef burgers, noodle stir-fries, burrata salads, and classics like anchovies, local-cheese boards and honey-fried aubergines crowd tables at this friendly gourmet tapas place, where Catalan and Asian flavours mingle. The presentation is as artful as the creative ingredient combinations.

LADY GREEN   VEGETARIAN, VEGAN €€
(☎931 71 59 14; www.facebook.com/ladygreen sitges; Carrer de Sant Pau 11; 2-/3-course set menu €15/20; ☺7-10pm Mon, 1-4pm & 7-10pm Tue, Wed & Sun, 1-4pm & 7-11pm Thu-Sat, closed Mon & Tue approx Nov-May; ☎☎) Zesty Mexican platters, veggie burgers, falafel with quinoa tabouli, and delectable American-style vegan cheesecake: vegetarian Lady Green will satisfy even the most demanding taste buds with its imaginative meat-free dishes, bold flavours and wonderful desserts. There are also vegan and gluten-free choices, plus invigorating fresh juices and smoothies.

CASABLANCA   BAR
(Carrer de Pau Barrabeig 5; ☺8pm-2am Thu-Sat) This cocktail-driven bar exudes nostalgia with its old-timey soundtrack, vintage furnishings and bygone Hollywood stars crowding its walls. A selection of classy cocktails are stirred by seasoned staff who extend an exuberant welcome to a mainly 30+ clientele.

DAY TRIPS FROM BARCELONA SITGES

Tarragona

....

Explore

In this effervescent port city, Roman history collides with beaches, bars and a food scene that perfumes the air with freshly grilled seafood. The biggest lure is the wealth of ruins in Spain's second-most important Roman site, including a mosaic-packed museum and a seaside amphitheatre. A roll-call of fantastic places to eat gives you good reason to linger in the knot of lanes in the attractive medieval centre, flanked by a towering cathedral with Romanesque and Gothic flourishes.

Tarragona is also a gateway to the Costa Daurada's sparkling beaches and the feast of Modernisme architecture in nearby **Reus** (www.gaudicentre.cat; Plaça del Mercadal 3, Reus; adult/child €9/5; ⊙10am-8pm Mon-Sat Jun-Sep, 10am-2pm & 4-7pm Mon-Sat Oct-May, 10am-2pm Sun year-round).

....

The Best...

➡ **Sight** Museu d'Història de Tarragona

➡ **Place to Eat** Barquet (p211)

....

Top Tip

➡ Don't visit Tarragona on a Sunday or Monday – you'll find your sightseeing options drastically curtailed.

....

Getting There & Away

Train The station is a 10-minute walk south of the old town near the beach, with services to/from Barcelona (from €8.05, one to 1½ hours)

Car Take the C32 toll road along the coast via Castelldefels or the AP7 (toll) motorway

....

Need to Know

➡ **Location** 83km southwest of Barcelona

➡ **Tourist Office** (☑977 25 07 95; www.tarragonaturisme.es; Carrer Major 39; ⊙10am-8pm late Jun-Sep, 10am-2pm & 3-5pm Mon-Fri, 10am-2pm & 3-7pm Sat, 10am-2pm Sun Oct-late Jun)

◉ SIGHTS

MUSEU D'HISTÒRIA DE TARRAGONA   RUINS

(MHT;www.tarragona.cat/patrimoni/museu-historia; adult/child per site €3.30/free, all sites €7.40/free; ⊙sites 9am-9pm Tue-Sat, 9am-3pm Sun Easter-Sep, 9am-7pm Tue-Sat, 9am-3pm Sun Oct-Easter) The Museu d'Història de Tarragona consists of various Unesco World Heritage Roman sites, as well as some other historic buildings around town. A combined ticket covers the Pretori i Circ Romans, Amfiteatre Romà, Passeig Arqueològic Muralles and Fòrum de la Colònia. Get exploring!

★ MUSEU NACIONAL ARQUEOLÒGIC DE TARRAGONA   MUSEUM

(www.mnat.cat; Plaça del Rei 5; adult/child €4.50/free; ⊙9.30am-6pm Tue-Sat Oct-May, to 8.30pm Jun-Sep, 10am-2pm Sun year-round) This excellent museum does justice to the cultural and material wealth of Roman Tarraco. The mosaic collection traces changing trends from simple black-and-white designs to complex full-colour creations; highlights include the fine 2nd- or 3rd-century *Mosaic de la Medusa* and the large, almost complete 3rd-century *Mosaic dels Peixos de la Pineda*, showing fish and sea creatures. Explanations are mostly in Catalan and Spanish, but there are English-language booklets across the galleries.

★ CATEDRAL DE TARRAGONA   CATHEDRAL

(www.catedraldetarragona.com; Plaça de la Seu; adult/child €5/3; ⊙10am-8pm Mon-Sat mid-Jun–mid-Sep, 10am-7pm Mon-Sat mid-Mar–mid-Jun & mid-Sep–Oct, 10am-5pm Mon-Fri, 10am-7pm Sat Nov–mid-Mar) Crowning the town, Tarragona's cathedral incorporates both Romanesque and Gothic features, as typified by the main facade. The flower-filled cloister has Gothic vaulting and Romanesque carved capitals, one of which shows rats conducting a cat's funeral...until the cat comes back to life! Chambers off the cloister display the remains of a Roman temple (unearthed in 2015) and the **Museu Diocesà**, its collection extending from Roman hairpins to 13th- and 14th-century polychrome Virgin woodcarvings. Don't miss the east nave's 14th-century frescoes.

PRETORI I CIRC ROMANS RUINS

(Plaça del Rei; adult/child €3.30/free; ☺9am-9pm Tue-Sat, 9am-3pm Sun Easter-Sep, 9am-7pm Tue-Sat, 9am-3pm Sun Oct-Easter) This sizeable complex with two separate entrances includes part of the vaults of Tarragona's well-preserved, late-1st-century **Roman circus**, where chariot races were once held, as well as the Plaça del Rei's **Pretori tower** (climb it for 360° city views) and part of the **provincial forum**, the political heart of Roman Tarraconensis province. The circus, over 300m long and accommodating 30,000 spectators, stretched from here to beyond Plaça de la Font to the west.

✕ EATING

BARQUET SEAFOOD €€

(☑977 24 00 23; www.restaurantbarquet.com; Carrer del Gasòmetre 16; mains €12-22; ☺12.30-3.30pm Mon, 12.30-3.30pm & 8.30-10pm Tue-Fri, 1-3.30pm & 9-10.30pm Sat) This popular neighbourhood restaurant is a short downhill stroll south from Tarragona centre. It's deservedly famous for its expertly concocted rice dishes bursting with maritime flavour, and also does great seafood *raciones* (large plates). Don't be fooled by the nautical warehouse interior: fish dishes and desserts are executed with finesse.

DEGVSTA FUSION, CATALAN €€

(☑977 25 24 28; www.degvsta.com; Carrer Cavallers 6; mains €15-19; ☺1.30-4pm Mon, 1.30-4pm & 9-10.30pm Tue-Sat) Beyond a stylish lounge/bar hides this rustic-chic restaurant styled in cool creams, adorned with a claw-foot bath tub (!) and specialising in deliciously inventive contemporary Catalan cuisine. Dishes delivered with flair might be avocado gazpacho, citrus-infused sea bass, fancied-up *pa amb tomàquet* or sheep's-cheese salad with zingy strawberry vinaigrette. People pack in for the three-course weekday lunch *menú* (€16).

AQ MEDITERRANEAN, FUSION €€

(☑977 21 59 54; www.aq-restaurant.com; Carrer de les Coques 7; mains €11-24; ☺1.30-3.30pm & 8.30-11pm) The crisp interior design of this palm-patterned restaurant promises fine dining and AQ amply delivers, with its impeccably crafted, playfully executed fusion dishes taking inspiration from Catalan, Italian and Asian cuisines. Treat your taste buds to squid-ink croquettes, chunky strips of *patatas bravas*, grilled Wagyu steak, cod-and-aubergine teriyaki or wok-fried mussels.

ARCS RESTAURANT CATALAN €€€

(☑977 21 80 40; www.restaurantarcs.com; Carrer de Misser Sitges 13; mains €17-22; ☺1-4pm & 8.30-11pm Tue-Sat) Inside a medieval cavern decorated with bright contemporary art and original Gothic arches, dine on Catalan dishes that follow the seasons (some traditional, others updated). Sample duck with hazelnut-and-vermouth sauce, salmon *tataki* with wasabi ice cream, or the always-excellent catch of the day. Desserts please the eye as much as the taste buds.

Sleeping

Barcelona has a wide range of sleeping options, from inexpensive hostels hidden in the old quarter to luxury hotels overlooking the waterfront. The small-scale B&B-style apartment rentals scattered around the city are a good-value choice.

Hotels

Hotels cover a broad range. At the bottom end there is often little to distinguish them from better *pensiones,* and from there they run up the scale to five-star luxury. Some of the better features to look out for include rooftop pools and lounges; views (either of the sea or a cityscape); and of course proximity to the important sights.

For around €100 to €160 there are extensive options for good doubles across a wide range of hotels and areas. The top-end category starts at €250 for a double, and can easily rise to €500 (and beyond for suites).

Pensiones & Hostales

Depending on the season you can pay as little as €15 to €25 for a dorm bed in a youth hostel. If dorm living is not your thing, but you are still looking for a budget deal, check around the many *pensiones* (also known as *hostales* – family-run, small-scale hotels, often housed in sprawling apartments. Some are fleapits, others immaculately maintained gems.)

You're looking at a minimum of around €35/55 for basic *individual/doble* (single/double) rooms, mostly with shared bathrooms. (It is occasionally possible to find cheaper rooms, but they may be unappealing.)

Some places, especially at the lower end, offer triples and quads, which can be good value for groups. If you want a double bed (as opposed to two singles), ask for a *llit/cama matrimonial* (Catalan/Spanish). If your budget is especially tight, look at options outside the centre.

Apartment & Room Rentals

A cosier (and sometimes more cost-effective) alternative to hotels is short-term apartment rental. A plethora of firms organise short lets across town. Typical prices are around €80 to €100 for two people per night. For four people you might be looking at an average of €160 a night.

Travellers with Disabilities

Many hotels claim to be equipped for guests with disabilities but the reality frequently disappoints, although the situation is improving, particularly at the midrange and high-end levels. Check out www.barcelona-access.cat for further information.

Useful Websites

➡ **Lonely Planet** (www.lonelyplanet.com/barcelona) Neighbourhood profiles, plus extensive listings of hotels, hostels, guesthouses and apartments.

➡ **Oh Barcelona** (www.oh-barcelona.com) Hotel and apartment listings, plus tips on deciding where to stay.

➡ **Barcelona Bed and Breakfasts** (www.barcelonabedandbreakfasts.com) Listings of low-key, oft-overlooked lodging options.

Lonely Planet's Top Choices

Casa Gràcia (p219) Style and space on a budget in Gràcia.

Casa Camper (p216) A fun Raval hotel, great for families.

Cotton House (p219) A beautifully designed L'Eixample hotel – you won't want to leave.

Serras Hotel (p215) Luxurious lodging in an ideal Barri Gòtic location.

DO Reial (p215) Magnificent boutique option overlooking the Plaça Reial.

Best by Budget

€

Casa Gràcia (p219) Stylish hostel with colourful rooms, communal dinners, film screenings and other events.

Pensió 2000 (p216) Family-run pensión looking over the Palau de la Música.

Pars Tailor's Hostel (p220) A hip Sant Antoni option with a vintage vibe.

Pars Teatro Hostel (p220) Theatrically decorated space on the edge of Poble Sec.

€€

Five Rooms (p218) Small and charming with beautifully designed rooms.

Barceló Raval (p216) Hotel with design smarts and an appealing rooftop terrace.

Hotel Market (p220) Beautifully designed rooms in the very hot 'hood of Sant Antoni.

Grand Hotel Central (p216) Simply the most stunning pool in town.

€€€

Soho House (p215) Outpost of the London member's club, with every comfort.

Hotel Neri (p215) Beautiful, historic hotel on a tranquil spot in Barri Gòtic.

Hotel Mercer (p215) Peaceful retreat with medieval details and atmospheric rooms.

Hotel Majéstic (p219) A grand dame of L'Eixample.

Best for Style

Chic & Basic Ramblas (p216) Boasts serious design cred – particularly the lobby with its vintage decor.

Margot House (p219) Wes Anderson–inspired hideaway.

Generator Hostel (p219) A head-turner in Gràcia with an artfully designed bar and restaurant.

Best Hotel Pools

Grand Hotel Central (p216) In a great location on Via Laietana, this place has a rooftop infinity pool.

W Barcelona (p217) Splendid poolside fun just a short stroll from the beach.

Hotel Arts Barcelona (p217) Take a swim while admiring the Mediterranean and Frank Gehry's shimmering *Peix* sculpture.

Serras Hotel (p215) Wood-decked bar with a plunge pool and wonderful view over the port.

Best Rooms with a View

W Barcelona (p217) Luxury option with views out to sea.

Ohla Hotel (p215) Staggering views over the old city from the rooftop terrace.

Hotel Continental (p215) Get a room over the Rambla and imagine what Orwell felt when he stayed here in 1937.

NEED TO KNOW

Price Ranges
The following price ranges refer to a double room per night during high season, including tax. Prices include private bathroom unless otherwise stated.

€	less than €75
€€	€75–€200
€€€	more than €200

Room Tax
→ Virtually all accommodation is subject to IVA, a 10% value-added tax.

→ There's also an additional tax of between €0.72 and €2.48 per person per night, depending on the accommodation's level of luxury.

→ These charges are usually included in the quoted rate.

Seasonal Rates
Most hotel rates vary over high, mid and low seasons. Low season is roughly November to Easter, except during the Christmas/New Year period. Whenever there is a major trade fair (they are frequent, but the Mobile World Congress in February/March causes the most problems), high-season prices generally apply. Conversely, business-oriented hotels often consider weekends, holiday periods and other slow business times to be low season.

Reservations
→ Booking ahead is all but essential, especially during peak periods such as Easter, Christmas/New Year, trade fairs and throughout much of summer (although August can be quite a slack month owing to the heat and lack of business visitors).

→ If you arrive without pre-booked lodging, the Plaça de Catalunya tourist office (p253) can help.

Where to Stay

Neighbourhood	For	Against
La Rambla & Barri Gòtic	Great location, close to major sights; perfect area for exploring on foot; good nightlife and dining options	Very touristy; noisy; some rooms are small and lack windows
El Raval	Central option, with good local nightlife and access to sights; bohemian vibe with few tourists	Can be noisy; seedy and run-down in parts; many fleapits best avoided; some streets feel unsafe at night
La Ribera	Great restaurant scene and neighbourhood exploring; central; top sights including the Museu Picasso and the Palau de la Música Catalana	Can be noisy; overly crowded; touristy
Barceloneta & the Waterfront	Excellent seafood restaurants; easygoing local vibe; handy access to the promenade and beaches	Very few sleeping options; beyond Barceloneta can be far from the action and better suited to business travellers
L'Eixample	Wide range of options for all budgets; close to Modernista sights; good restaurants and nightlife; prime LGBTI scene (in 'Gaixample')	Can be very noisy with lots of traffic; not a great area for walking; a little far from the old city
Gràcia	Youthful, local scene with lively restaurants and bars	Far from the old city and beaches; few formal options (but lots of rooms for rent)
Pedralbes & La Zona Alta	Good nightlife and restaurants in parts	Very far from the action; spread-out area requiring frequent metro travel; geared more towards business travellers
Montjuïc, Poble Sec & Sant Antoni	Near the museums, gardens and views of Montjuïc; great bars and restaurants in Sant Antoni; locations in Poble Sec are also convenient to El Raval	Somewhat out of the way; can be a bit charmless up by Sants train station

🛏 La Rambla & Barri Gòtic

ALBERG HOSTEL ITACA
HOSTEL €

Map p276 (☑93 301 97 51; www.itacahostel.com; Carrer de Ripoll 21; dm €15-27, d without bathroom €76; ✳🛜; Ⓜ Jaume I) A bright, quiet hostel near the cathedral, Itaca has spacious dorms (sleeping six to 10 people) with parquet floors and spring colours, as well as two doubles. There's a lively vibe, and the hostel organises activities (pub crawls, flamenco concerts, free daily walking tours), making it a good option for solo travellers.

HOTEL CONTINENTAL
HOTEL €€

Map p276 (☑93 301 25 70; www.hotelcontinental. com; La Rambla 138; s/d from €110/116; ✳🛜; Ⓜ Catalunya) In 1937 George Orwell stayed here on his return from the front during the Spanish Civil War, when Barcelona was tense with factional strife. The Continental's rooms are worn and rather spartan, but have romantic touches like ceiling fans, brass bedsteads and frilly bedclothes. An extra €20 yields a room with a small balcony overlooking La Rambla, and there is a free 24-hour buffet.

VRABAC
B&B €€

Map p276 (☑663 494029; https://vrabacguesthouse.wordpress.com; Carrer de la Portaferrissa 14; s/d incl breakfast €65/85; ✳🛜; Ⓜ Liceu) In a central location just off La Rambla, Vrabac is set in a beautifully restored heritage building complete with original decorative ceilings, exposed sandstone walls and large oil paintings. Rooms vary in size and features – the best have elegant ceramic tile floors, private bathrooms and sizeable balconies. The cheapest are small and basic, lack a bathroom and are not recommended. Cash only.

SERRAS HOTEL
BOUTIQUE HOTEL €€€

Map p276 (☑93 169 18 68; www.hoteltheserras barcelona.com; Passeig de Colom 9; r from €266; ✳🛜🏊; Ⓜ Barceloneta) A fresh and funky five-star that has every comfort – including a rooftop bar with a small dipping pool and a terrific view over the port – but never feels stuffy. Rooms at the front are brighter and have a better view (from the bathtub, in some cases) but rooms at the side are spared the traffic noise.

SOHO HOUSE
BOUTIQUE HOTEL €€€

Map p276 (☑93 220 46 00; www.sohohouse barcelona.com; Plaça del Duc de Medinaceli 4; r from €300; ✳🛜; Ⓜ Drassanes) An elegant outpost of the famous London member's club, with luxuriously appointed rooms, an exclusive bar peopled with celebs, and a rooftop pool with incredible views out to

sea. Cecconi's, the Italian restaurant on the ground floor, is worth a visit in its own right.

HOTEL NERI
DESIGN HOTEL €€€

Map p276 (☑93 304 06 55; www.hotelneri.com; Carrer de Sant Sever 5; d €362; ✳🛜; Ⓜ Liceu) This tranquil hotel occupies a beautifully adapted, centuries-old building backing onto Plaça de Sant Felip Neri. The sandstone walls and timber furnishings lend a sense of history, while the rooms feature cutting-edge technology, including plasma-screen TVs and infrared lights in the stone-clad designer bathrooms. Choose from a menu of sheets and pillows, and sun yourself on the roof deck.

OHLA HOTEL
BOUTIQUE HOTEL €€€

Map p276 (☑93 341 50 50; www.ohlahotel.com; Via Laietana 49; r €265; ℗✳🛜🏊; Ⓜ Urquinaona) This beautifully designed hotel gets almost everything right, from the top-notch service to the lovely rooftop terrace with pool and twinkling views of Montjuïc. The sleek modern rooms have lavish fabrics, long pendular bedside lights, iPod docks and separate shower cubes that face on to the room (take note if you're travelling with someone who needs a touch more privacy).

DO REIAL
BOUTIQUE HOTEL €€€

Map p276 (☑93 481 36 66; www.hoteldoreial.com; Plaça Reial 1; s/d incl breakfast from €288/360; ✳🛜🏊; Ⓜ Liceu) Overlooking the magnificent plaza for which it is named, this 18-room property has handsomely designed rooms with beamed ceilings, hardwood floors and all-important soundproofing. The service is excellent and the facilities extensive, with a roof terrace (bar in summer), dipping pool, solarium and spa. Its excellent market-to-table restaurants draw in visiting foodies.

HOTEL 1898
LUXURY HOTEL €€€

Map p276 (☑93 552 95 52; www.hotel1898.com; La Rambla 109; d €189-221; ✳🛜🏊; Ⓜ Liceu) The former Compañía de Tabacos Filipinas (Philippines Tobacco Company) building has been resurrected as a luxury hotel, complete with an idyllic rooftop bar and pool. Some rooms are smallish, but deluxe rooms and suites have their own terraces. All combine modern comfort and elegance, with hardwood floors and tasteful furniture.

HOTEL MERCER
BOUTIQUE HOTEL €€€

Map p276 (☑93 310 74 80; www.mercerbarcelona. com; Carrer dels Lledó 7; r from €416; ℗✳🛜🏊; Ⓜ Jaume I) Set on a narrow medieval street, Hotel Mercer is one of Barcelona's better boutique hotels. Famed Spanish architect Rafael Moneo stayed true to the building's original Gothic and even Roman elements while creating elegant rooms, some of which overlook an interior garden. There's a lovely rooftop dipping pool, stylish cocktail lounge, tapas bar and restaurant, plus peaceful common areas.

🛏 El Raval

★ BARCELÓ RAVAL   DESIGN HOTEL €€
Map p280 (📞93 320 14 90; www.barceloraval.com; Rambla del Raval 17-21; r from €144; ✳🛱; Ⓜ Liceu) Part of the city's plans to pull the El Raval district up by the bootstraps, this cylindrical designer hotel tower makes a 21st-century splash. The rooftop terrace offers fabulous views and the B-Lounge bar-restaurant is a lively joint for meals and cocktails. Rooms have slick aesthetics (white with lime green or ruby red splashes of colour), Nespresso machines and iPod docks.

CHIC & BASIC RAMBLAS   DESIGN HOTEL €€
Map p280 (📞93 302 71 11; www.chicandbasicramblashotel.com; Passatge Gutenberg 7; r €156-208; ✳🛱; Ⓜ Drassanes) The latest in the Chic & Basic chain is the most riotous to date, with quirky and colourful interiors that hit you from the second you walk in and see a vintage Seat 600 car in the foyer. Note that the name is misleading – the hotel is a couple of blocks into El Raval.

The rooms themselves are solid blocks of colour and each loosely pays homage to an aspect of Barcelona life in the 1960s. All have balconies and very basic kitchens.

HOTEL SANT AGUSTÍ   HOTEL €€
Map p280 (📞93 318 16 58; www.hotelsa.com; Plaça de Sant Agustí 3; r €115-152; ✳🛱; Ⓜ Liceu) This former 18th-century monastery opened as a hotel in 1840, making it the city's oldest. The location is perfect – a quick stroll off La Rambla on a curious square. Rooms sparkle, and are mostly spacious and light filled. Consider the attic room with sloping ceiling and view of the rooftops.

CASA CAMPER   DESIGN HOTEL €€€
Map p280 (📞93 342 62 80; www.casacamper.com; Carrer d'Elisabets 11; s/d €277/297; ✳🛱; Ⓜ Catalunya) The massive foyer looks like a contemporary art museum, but the rooms, decorated in red, black and white, are the real surprise. Most have a sleeping and bathroom area, where you can contemplate the hanging gardens outside your window, with a separate, private sitting room with balcony, TV and hammock located across the corridor.

If you prefer more privacy, the city-view rooms integrate the sleeping and living areas. Get to the rooftop for sweeping cityscapes.

HOTEL ESPAÑA   HOTEL €€€
Map p280 (📞93 550 00 00; www.hotelespanya.com; Carrer de Sant Pau 9-11; r €261-282; ✳🛱🛱; Ⓜ Liceu) Known for its wonderful Modernista interiors in the dining rooms and bar, in which architect Domènech i Montaner, sculptor Eusebi Arnau and painter Ramon Casas had a hand, this hotel offers plush, contemporary rooms in a building that still manages to ooze a little history. There's a plunge pool and sun deck on the roof, along with a bar.

🛏 La Ribera

PENSIÓ 2000   PENSION €
Map p284 (📞93 310 74 66; www.pensio2000.com; Carrer de Sant Pere més Alt 6; d €70-80; ✳🛱; Ⓜ Urquinaona) This 1st-floor, family-run place is opposite the anything-but-simple Palau de la Música Catalana. Seven reasonably spacious doubles have mosaic-tiled floors, and all have private bathrooms. You can eat your breakfast in the little courtyard.

PENSIÓN FRANCIA   PENSION €
Map p284 (📞93 319 03 76; www.milisa.com/P.Francia; Carrer de Rera Palau 4; d €90; 🛱; Ⓜ Barceloneta) The homey smell of laundry pervades this quaint little *pensión* in a great location close to the shore, the Parc de la Ciutadella and the nightlife of El Born. The 11 simple rooms are kept spick and span, with nothing much in the way of frills. Rooms with balconies benefit from plenty of natural light but little noise.

HOTEL BANYS ORIENTALS   BOUTIQUE HOTEL €€
Map p284 (📞93 268 84 60; www.hotelbanysorientals.com; Carrer de l'Argenteria 37; s/d €72/120; ✳🛱; Ⓜ Jaume I) Book well ahead to get into this magnetically popular designer haunt. Cool blues and aquamarines combine with dark-hued floors to lend this clean-lined boutique hotel a quiet charm. All rooms, on the small side, look onto the street or back lanes. There are more spacious suites in two other nearby buildings.

GRAND HOTEL CENTRAL   DESIGN HOTEL €€€
Map p284 (📞93 295 79 00; www.grandhotelcentral.com; Via Laietana 30; d €218; 🅿✳🛱; Ⓜ Jaume I) With supersoundproofed rooms no smaller than 21 sq metres, this design hotel, complete with rooftop infinity pool, is one of the standout hotel offerings along Via Laietana. Rooms are decorated in style, with high ceilings, muted colours (beiges, browns and creams), dark wooden floors and subtle lighting.

🛏 Barceloneta & the Waterfront

POBLENOU BED
& BREAKFAST
GUESTHOUSE €€

Map p288 (☑93 221 26 01; www.hostalpoblenou.com; Carrer del Taulat 30; s/d from €55/88; ✳@🛜; MLlacuna) Just back from the beach and mere steps from the restaurant-lined Rambla del Poblenou, this 1930s house, with high ceilings and beautifully tiled floors, has six appealing rooms named for Spanish artists. Some of its uniquely decorated rooms have little balconies, and all have a fresh feel, light colours and comfortable beds. Minimum stay two nights from May to November.

HOTEL 54
HOTEL €€

Map p286 (☑93 225 00 54; www.hotel54barceloneta.es; Passeig de Joan de Borbó 54; s/d from €135/155; ✳@🛜; MBarceloneta) Hotel 54 is all about location. Modern rooms, with dark tile floors and designer bathrooms, are sought after for the marina and sunset views. Other rooms look out over Barceloneta's lanes. You can also sit on the roof terrace and enjoy the panorama over the city and harbour.

MELIÁ SKY BARCELONA
DESIGN HOTEL €€

Map p288 (☑93 367 20 50; www.melia.com; Carrer de Pere IV 272-286; d/ste from €176/297; P✳@🛜🏊; MPoblenou) This slim tower, designed by Dominique Perrault, is made from two filigree slabs of glass. It overlooks Jean Nouvel's Parc del Centre del Poblenou and offers designer rooms with city or sea views. Extensive amenities include various bars and terraces, and an inviting pool.

⭐HOTEL ARTS BARCELONA
HOTEL €€€

Map p288 (☑93 221 10 00; www.ritzcarlton.com; Carrer de la Marina 19-21; d/ste from €295/445; P✳@🛜🏊; MCiutadella Vila Olímpica) Set in a sky-high tower looming above Port Olímpic, this is one of Barcelona's most fashionable hotels. Its 483 rooms are kitted out with high-end features (Bang & Olufsen entertainment systems, separate shower and soaking tub), plus unbeatable views. Services range from enticing spa facilities to six restaurants including fine dining in celebrated Enoteca, which has two Michelin stars.

W BARCELONA
HOTEL €€€

Map p286 (☑93 295 28 00; www.w-barcelona.com; Plaça de la Rosa del Vents 1; d/ste from €314/554; P✳@🛜🏊; ⛴V15, 39, MBarceloneta) Designed by Barcelona-born architect Ricardo Bofill and opened in 2009, this glinting, spinnaker-shaped glass tower is a coastal landmark. Inside are 473 rooms and 67 suites that epitomise contemporary chic. Guests can flit between the gym, infinity pool (with an adjacent cocktail bar) and spa as well as the gourmet restaurant by star chef Carles Abellán.

PULLMAN BARCELONA
SKIPPER HOTEL
HOTEL €€€

Map p288 (☑93 221 65 65; www.pullmanhotels.com; Avinguda del Litoral 10; d/ste from €212/475; P✳@🛜🏊; MCiutadella Vila Olímpica) Mesmerising views of Frank Gehry's shimmering Peix sculpture unfold from the rooftop infinity pool at this five-star hotel and from some of the 241 rooms, which are decorated in sleek timbers (some open to terraces). There's a second swimming pool at the base of the winged towers in the courtyard. Family-friendly facilities include interconnecting rooms, cots and babysitting services.

H10 PORT VELL
BOUTIQUE HOTEL €€€

Map p286 (☑93 310 30 65; www.h10hotels.com; Pas de Sota Muralla 9; d from €226; ✳@🛜🏊; MBarceloneta) The location is excellent at this 58-room hotel within a short stroll of El Born and Barceloneta. Sleek, modern rooms have a trim, minimalist design with black-and-white bathrooms, and the best rooms (not all) have views over the marina. The rooftop terrace is the best feature, with sunloungers, a tiny plunge pool and evening cocktails.

🛏 L'Eixample

URBANY BARCELONA
HOSTEL €

(☑93 245 84 14; www.urbanyhostels.com; Avinguda Meridiana 97; dm/s/tw from €29.50/118/126; ✳@🛜; MClot, Encants) Near El Poblenou, this massive 400-bed hostel is a good place to meet other travellers, with its own bar and airy lounge set amid graffiti-esque artwork, plus a large terrace with views of Jean Nouvel's glowing Torre Glòries. Single and twin rooms have en suite bathrooms and small fridges. Self-caterers can cook up a storm in the kitchen.

Guests also have access to a pool and gym nearby.

⭐PRAKTIK RAMBLA
BOUTIQUE HOTEL €€

Map p290 (☑93 343 66 90; www.hotelpraktikrambla.com; Rambla de Catalunya 27; s/d/tr from €119/140/165; ✳🛜; MPasseig de Gràcia) This Modernista gem hides a gorgeous little boutique number. While the high ceilings and most of the original tile floors have been maintained, the 43 rooms have bold ceramics, spot lighting and contemporary art. There's a chilled reading area and deck-style lounge terrace. The handy location on a tree-lined boulevard is another plus.

SLEEPING

ANAKENA HOUSE · HOTEL €€

Map p290 (☑93 467 36 15; www.anakenahouse. com; Carrer del Consell de Cent 276; d from €157; ✳ � 🛜 ; Ⓜ Passeig de Gràcia) The 1st floor of this Modernista building designed by Catalan architect Enric Sagnier i Villavecchia has been transformed into an intimate, elegant hotel. Its eight rooms have olive tones, antique furniture and designer lighting. All but one, which overlooks the courtyard, have street views.

CASA BONAY · HOTEL €€

Map p294 (☑93 545 80 70; www.casabonay. com; Gran Via de les Corts Catalanes 700; d/f from €150/234; ✳ 🛜 ; Ⓜ Tetuan) Hip Casa Bonay has sparingly decorated, stylishly tiled rooms, some with glassed-in balconies and others with terraces and outdoor showers. A bar opens on the roof terrace in summer. The hotel's unique selling point is the range of 'guest' shops, bars and restaurants it houses downstairs. These include a specialist coffee bar, a Vietnamese barbecue and a juice bar.

HOTEL CONSTANZA · BOUTIQUE HOTEL €€

Map p294 (☑93 270 19 10; www.hotelconstanza. com; Carrer del Bruc 33; s/d/f from €85/135/190; ✳ 🛜 ; Ⓜ Urquinaona) This 46-room beauty has stolen the hearts of many a visitor to Barcelona. Design elements abound and little details like flowers in the bathroom add charm. Strewn with white sofas, the roof terrace is a stylish spot to relax while looking over L'Eixample's rooftops. Street-facing rooms have balconies.

Family rooms come with fold-out couches; baby cots are available. Several rooms are equipped for wheelchairs.

HOTEL AXEL · HOTEL €€

Map p290 (☑93 323 93 93; www.axelhotels.com; Carrer d'Aribau 33; s/d from €177/188; ✳ 🛜 ⛱ ; Ⓜ Universitat) A sizzling hub of Barcelona's gay scene, all-welcoming Hotel Axel occupies a sleek corner block with a wrought-iron and stained-glass canopied entrance. Its 105 designer rooms have soundproofing and king-sized beds. Take a break in the rooftop pool, in the Finnish sauna or in the spa bath. The rooftop Skybar opens for cocktails from May to September.

CAMI BED & GALLERY · B&B €€

Map p294 (☑93 270 17 48; www.camibedand gallery.com; Carrer de Casp 22; d from €110, without bathroom from €95; ✳ 🛜 ; Ⓜ Catalunya) Footsteps from the Plaça de Catalunya, this handsome Modernista building could not be more central. The seven airy, high-ceilinged rooms are each slightly different in character, though not all have private bathrooms. Guests can use the communal kitchen. It was set up by art lovers and doubles as a gallery, staging exhibitions and cultural events.

FIVE ROOMS · BOUTIQUE HOTEL €€

Map p294 (☑93 342 78 80; www.thefiverooms. com; Carrer de Pau Claris 72; s/d/ste/apt from €137/160/203/230; ✳ 🛜 ; Ⓜ Urquinaona) Nowadays, the Five Rooms has 12 standard rooms and suites in its 1st-floor converted apartment on the border between L'Eixample and Barcelona's old centre. Rooms are all different and features include broad, firm beds, stretches of exposed brick wall, restored mosaic tiles and minimalist decor, as well as minibars.

HOSTAL GOYA · HOSTAL €€

Map p294 (☑93 302 25 65; www.hostalgoya. com; Carrer de Pau Claris 74; s/d/tr from €123/145/167; ✳ 🛜 ; Ⓜ Urquinaona) The Goya is a modestly priced gem on the chi-chi side of L'Eixample. Light-filled rooms are individually decorated, and the original mosaic floors have largely been retained and combined with contemporary design features in the bathrooms. Higher-priced doubles have a balcony.

HOSTAL OLIVA · HOSTAL €€

Map p294 (☑93 488 01 62; www.hostaloliva.com; Passeig de Gràcia 32; s/d from €79/89, without bathroom from €64/74; ✳ @ 🛜 ; Ⓜ Passeig de Gràcia) A picturesque antique lift wheezes its way up to this 4th-floor *hostal*, a terrific, reliable cheapie in one of the city's most expensive neighbourhoods. Some of the single rooms can barely fit a bed but the doubles are big enough, and light and airy (some with tiled floors, others with parquet).

ROOM MATE PAU · HOTEL €€

Map p294 (☑93 343 63 00; www.room-mate hotels.com; Carrer de Fontanella 7; d/ste from €192/252; ✳ 🛜 ; Ⓜ Catalunya) Just off Plaça de Catalunya, Room Mate Pau sits somewhere between an upscale hostel and boutique hotel. Its 66 rooms are cleverly configured with designer furnishings, good mattresses and USB-connected TVs. The striking interior terrace with a bar and vertical garden wall draws a young, hip crowd.

★ EL PALACE · HISTORIC HOTEL €€€

Map p294 (☑93 510 11 30; www.hotelpalace barcelona.com; Gran Via de les Corts Catalanes 668; d/ste from €246/391; 🅿 ✳ @ 🛜 ⛱ ; Ⓜ Passeig de Gràcia) Opened in 1919 as the Ritz (one of four, along with Paris, London and Madrid), Barcelona's first luxury hotel is fresh from extensive renovations that peak in its flowering rooftop garden with a pool, restaurant, bar and solarium with breathtaking 360-degree views of the city. Its 120 exquisite rooms and suites are complemented by state-of-the-art facilities including a Maya-inspired spa.

COTTON HOUSE
HOTEL €€€

Map p294 (☑93 450 50 45; www.hotelcotton house.com; Gran Via de les Corts Catalanes 670; d/tr/ste from €240/340/490; ✴ ☏; Ⓜ Urquinaona) This splendid luxury hotel occupies the former headquarters of the Cottonmakers' Guild, something which is alluded to throughout, from the huge sprays of cotton bolls in the lobby to the room names (damask, taffeta etc). There's even a space off the library where you can select fabric and have a shirt custom made.

All-white rooms are not quite as thrilling as the common areas, but are extremely comfortable, with wide beds, beautifully fragranced Ortiga toiletries and large rain showers.

MANDARIN ORIENTAL
DESIGN HOTEL €€€

Map p294 (☑93 151 88 88; www.mandarinoriental. com/barcelona; Passeig de Gràcia 38-40; d/ste from €625/1350; Ⓟ✴☏⊠; Ⓜ Passeig de Gràcia) At this imposing former bank, the 98 rooms have a contemporary designer style with straight lines, lots of white and muted colours. Many of the standard rooms (no smaller than 32 sq metres) have deep bathtubs, and all overlook either Passeig de Gràcia or an interior sculpted garden. Amenities include a spa with lap pool, fitness area and Michelin-starred restaurant.

MARGOT HOUSE
BOUTIQUE HOTEL €€€

Map p294 (☑93 272 00 76; www.margothouse. es; Passeig de Gràcia 46; d/ste from €202/310; ✴ @ ☏; Ⓜ Passeig de Gràcia) Halfway up Passeig de Gràcia, this elegant boutique hotel with nine rooms (including five suites) is perfect for those who want to be in the thick of it but still need peace, complete with a large, quiet book-filled sitting room with an honesty bar. Splash out for the front rooms, with more natural light. Rates include a fabulous gourmet buffet breakfast.

HOTEL MAJÈSTIC
HOTEL €€€

Map p294 (☑93 488 17 17; www.hotelmajestic. es; Passeig de Gràcia 68; d/apt/ste from €305/413/530; Ⓟ✴☏⊠; Ⓜ Passeig de Gràcia) The rooftop pool at this grand, sprawling hotel is superb for views and relaxing, or you can pamper yourself in the spa after a workout in the gym, a drink in the two bars or meal in one of its four restaurants.

The standard rooms (no singles) are smallish but comfortable and come with marble bathrooms.

SUITES AVENUE
APARTMENT €€€

Map p290 (☑93 487 41 59; www.suitesavenue. com; Passeig de Gràcia 83; apt from €206; Ⓟ✴☏⊠; Ⓜ Diagonal) Apartment-style living is the name of the game here, often at an excellent price given its superb location. Self-contained apartments (41 altogether) with their own kitchen, washing machine and access to a terrace, gym and two pools lie behind the wavy steel facade by Japanese architect Toyo Ito, as does a mini-museum of Hindu and Buddhist art.

🛌 Gràcia

★ CASA GRÀCIA
HOSTEL €

Map p296 (☑93 174 05 28; www.casagraciabcn. com; Passeig de Gràcia 116; dm/s/d/tr/apt from €31/106/120/147/194; ✴ @ ☏; Ⓜ Diagonal) A hostel with a difference, the hip Casa Gràcia has raised the bar for budget accommodation. Enticing common spaces include a terrace, library nook and artistically decorated lounge as well as a fully equipped self-catering kitchen – not to mention a restaurant and DJ-fuelled bar. Dorms aside, there are private rooms and apartments with their own terraces.

GENERATOR HOSTEL
HOSTEL €

Map p296 (☑93 220 03 77; www.generator hostels.com; Carrer de Còrsega 373; dm/d/q/penthouse from €20/109/186/329; Ⓜ Diagonal) Part of the design-forward Generator brand, this stylish hostel has much to recommend it, including a quirky bar made from reclaimed lumber and recycled elevator parts and festooned with an explosion of paper lanterns. The rooms themselves are quite simple if adequately equipped – unless you opt for the penthouse room with a terrace offering panoramic views over the city.

★ HOTEL CASA FUSTER
HISTORIC HOTEL €€€

Map p296 (☑93 255 30 00; www.hotelcasa fuster.com; Passeig de Gràcia 132; d/ste from €287/396; Ⓟ✴@☏⊠; Ⓜ Diagonal) This sumptuous Modernista mansion, built in 1908–11, is one of Barcelona's most luxurious hotels. Standard rooms are plush, if small. Period features have been restored at considerable cost and complemented by hydromassage tubs, plasma TVs and king-size beds. The rooftop terrace (with pool) offers spectacular views.

🛏 Pedralbes & La Zona Alta

ALBERG MARE DE DÉU
DE MONTSERRAT   HOSTEL €
(☎93 210 51 51; www.xanascat.cat; Passeig de la
Mare de Déu del Coll 41-51; dm €24; P⟨⟩; ⟨⟩87,
MVallcarca) The main building of this 197-bed
hostel is a magnificent former mansion with
a Mudéjar-style lobby. Rooms sleep from six
to 12 and the common areas are extensive
and relaxed, though due to the thick walls,
wi-fi can be hit-and-miss. It's 4km north of
Barcelona's city centre, 100m uphill northeast
from the Móra d'Ebre–Sant Eudald bus stop.

★HOTEL POL & GRACE   BOUTIQUE HOTEL €€
Map p300 (☎93 415 40 00; www.polgracehotel.
es; Carrer de Guillem Tell 49; d from €150; P✳⟨⟩;
⟨R⟩FGC Molina, Sant Gervasi) Uniquely designed
rooms revolve around Barcelona themes (images and artefacts that celebrate a Catalan
festival, key architectural icons, gastronomy
etc) at this stylish, ultracontemporary hotel.
There's also a spacious ground-floor lounge
where guests can unwind, and a roof terrace
with sunloungers and an organic garden.

ANITA'S BED & BREAKFAST   B&B €€
Map p298 (☎670 064258; www.anitasbarcelona.
com; Carrer d'August Font 24; d incl breakfast
from €95; @⟨⟩; ⟨⟩124) Spectacular views of
the city and the Mediterranean beyond extend from the three rooms at this hillside
B&B. Rooms are generously sized, with
sitting areas and en suite bathrooms. The
continental buffet breakfast (included in
the rate) can be taken on the communal terrace, which also has sweeping vistas.

WILSON BOUTIQUE HOTEL   BOUTIQUE HOTEL €€
Map p300 (☎93 209 25 11; www.wilsonbcn.com; Avinguda Diagonal 568; d/f/ste from €165/255/264;
✳⟨⟩; ⟨⟩6, 7, 27, 32, 33, 34, H8) At the edge of
L'Eixample, Wilson's 54 rooms over eight
floors are soundproofed, cutting out traffic
noise from busy Avinguda Diagonal. Its ultracontemporary rooms were refurbished and
painted in strong accent colours in 2017; some
open to terraces. It's a good option if you're
travelling with kids: family rooms sleep up
to four people, with cots available on request.

🛏 Montjuïc, Poble
Sec & Sant Antoni

PARS TAILOR'S HOSTEL   HOSTEL €
Map p302 (☎93 250 56 84; www.parshostels.
com; Carrer de Sepúlveda 146; dm €25-33;
✳⟨⟩; MUrgell) Decorated like a mid-20th-

century tailor's shop, with rooms themed
around different fabrics, this popular
hostel's common areas have old sewing
machines, lovingly framed brassieres and
vintage fixtures. You can shoot a round
on the old billiards table, hang out in the
comfy lounge, cook a meal in the well-
equipped kitchen, or join one of the activities on offer.

PARS TEATRO HOSTEL   HOSTEL €
Map p302 (☎93 443 94 66; www.parshostels.
com; Carrer d'Albareda 12; dm €25-35; ⟨⟩;
MDrassanes) True to its name, Teatro Hostel has a theatrically decorated interior:
old photos of actors of yesteryear hang
on the walls of the vintage-filled main
lounge, above an old row of velvety theatre
seats. Rooms are less exciting, but clean
and well maintained, and the hostel organises dinners, beach parties and other
activities.

HOTEL MARKET   BOUTIQUE HOTEL €€
Map p302 (☎93 325 12 05; www.hotelmarket
barcelona.com; Carrer del Comte Borrell 68; d/
ste from €158/186; ✳@⟨⟩; MSant Antoni) At-
tractively located in a renovated building
along a narrow lane just north of the grand
old Sant Antoni market, this chic spot
has 68 black-and-white-toned rooms with
wide-plank floors, oversized armoires, bold
art prints and nicely designed bathrooms
(stone basins, rain showers). Some rooms
have tiny (two-seat) balconies; suites come
with terraces.

★HOTEL BRUMMELL   BOUTIQUE HOTEL €€
Map p302 (☎93 125 86 22; www.hotelbrummell.
com; Carrer Nou de la Rambla 174; d from €160;
✳⟨⟩✲; MParal·lel) Stylish Brummell has
been turning heads since its 2015 opening.
It's a thoughtfully designed hotel with a
creative soul and great atmosphere. The 20
bright rooms have a minimalist design, and
the best of the bunch have sizeable terraces
with views and even outdoor soaking tubs.
The cheapest (the 'poolside classic' rooms)
feel a little tight.

HOSTAL CÈNTRIC   HOSTAL €€
Map p302 (☎93 426 75 73; www.hostalcentric.
com; Carrer de Casanova 13; s/d/f from
€114/124/144; ✳@⟨⟩; MUrgell) Hostal Cèntric has an appealing central location just
beyond the old city. Done out in light timbers and fabrics, the rooms are small but
very well maintained, and some have tiny
balconies overlooking the street. Head to
the higher floors to avoid street noise. Staff
go out of their way to help.

SLEEPING

Understand Barcelona

BARCELONA TODAY 222

Independence is still the hot topic of the day; in the background, the Catalan capital continues to be a leader in innovation and sustainability.

HISTORY 224

Barcelona's 2000-year history has been shaped by Roman rule, an early parliament, a Mediterranean empire and the Spanish Civil War.

CATALAN CULTURE...................... 235

Folk dancing, traditional festivals, towering human *castells* (castels) and one powerhouse football team are essential elements of the Catalan experience.

ARCHITECTURE 237

Barcelona is home to a soaring collection of Gothic treasures, Modernista masterpieces and more recent works by avant-garde architects.

PICASSO, MIRÓ & DALÍ................... 243

Follow in the footsteps of three of Spain's great 20th-century artists, who were all influenced by Barcelona.

MUSIC & DANCE........................ 245

Nova cançó, rumba and old-school guitar rock have shaped the Catalan sound, while flamenco and the *sardana* (Catalonia's national folk dance) still flourish.

Barcelona Today

Take a stroll through the streets of Barcelona, and you'll see more than a few *estelades*, the flag with the lone star (and red and yellow bars) that symbolises Catalonia's drive towards independence. Talk of separatism has reached a fever pitch, and raised deep concerns across Europe. Of course, there's much more brewing than just self-rule. The city's deep commitment to innovation has led to improvements in transport, communications and urban design.

Best on Film

All About My Mother (1999) One of Pedro Almodóvar's best-loved films, complete with transsexual prostitutes and doe-eyed nuns.

Vicky Cristina Barcelona (2008) Woody Allen gives Barcelona the *Manhattan* treatment, showing a city of startling beauty and neuroticism.

L'Auberge espagnole (Cédric Klapisch, 2002) A warmly told coming-of-age story about a mishmash of foreign-exchange students thrown together in Barcelona.

Barcelona (Whit Stillman, 1994) A sharp and witty romantic comedy about two Americans living in Barcelona during the end of the Cold War.

Best in Print

Barcelona (Robert Hughes, 1992) Witty and passionate study of 2000 years of history.

The Shadow of the Wind (Carlos Ruiz Zafón, 2001) Page-turning mystery set in post-civil-war Barcelona.

Homage to Catalonia (George Orwell, 1938) Orwell's classic account of the early days of the Spanish Civil War.

The Time of the Doves (Mercè Rodoreda, 1962) Possibly the best-known novel written in Catalan.

Land of Innovation

The city that gave birth to Gaudí and the ingenious creations of Modernisme continues to break new ground. In particular, Barcelona has become a global model as a Smart City – a place where technology is harnessed to create a more sustainable, efficient, and interconnected environment. Some 120 projects comprise the Smart City initiative, including wide-reaching innovations affecting transport, communications, public and social services, and even tourism.

Making use of the Internet of Things, Barcelona now has sensors to detect parking spaces and pollution levels, and to manage traffic flow. Systems for citizen involvement have been improved, and democratic channels of communication between the municipal government and its people have been opened.

Shrinking the city's carbon footprint is at the forefront of various new technologies. Self-powered lights installed along one stretch of beach use a combination of solar and wind energy. Barcelona has the cleanest fleet of buses in Europe, with a large share of hybrids and natural-gas-powered vehicles (plus antipollution filters on its remaining diesel motors). The city has has launched new bus routes based on the flow of people using the system, creating a new more intuitive grid that moves vertically, horizontally and diagonally across town. It has also been expanding its network for electric cars, with 300 existing charging stations and more in the works.

Barcelona also has a free, and growing, wi-fi network, with over 600 hotspots and plans to add more than 1500 in the coming years – including inside buses and metro stations. Another innovation: smart traffic lights that turn green when emergency vehicles are approaching so they can reach their destination faster.

Fuelling much of the innovation is the 220-hectare district known as 22@ *(vint-i-dos arroba)*. This district in El Poblenou has seen enormous growth since its creation back in 2000. Over 90,000 jobs have been created under the 8000 firms at work, largely in the digital, creative and tech industries.

The State of Catalonia

It's an historic moment in Barcelona. The drive towards independence is under way, with the idea that Catalonia could break away from Spain and become a sovereign republic gaining popularity. With its own language, unique traditions and proud history, Catalonia has always thought of itself as distinct from other parts of the country. But until recently, only a small fringe group sought a permanent and irrevocable break from Madrid.

In the last few years, however, the number of self-proclaimed separatists has skyrocketed. In the regional elections of September 2015, Catalan nationalists won a majority of the 135-seat regional assembly, which they viewed as an implicit endorsement of secession. Catalan leader Artur Mas promised to press ahead, and soon afterwards there was legislation under way to draft a Catalan constitution, create a new treasury and design a social security system.

In September 2017 Mas's successor, Carles Puigdemont, pushed a referendum law through the Catalan parliament, and the vote (deemed illegal and unconstitutional by central government) went ahead on October 1. There was a 42% turnout (relatively few unionists – those against secession – took part in what they saw as an illegitimate referendum) and around 90% voted in favour of secession. The day was marked by the violence doled out by the Guardia Civil (the Spanish police force, shipped in for the occasion) to those attempting to vote. A tense few days followed, in which a political stand-off saw Puigdemont being vague about his intentions while insisting on dialogue with central government in Madrid, and Spanish prime minister Mariano Rajoy refusing to be drawn while making obvious his intention to respond by triggering Article 155 of the constitution, thus imposing direct rule over the region.

Finally independence was declared and immediately quashed by Madrid (in the shape of Article 155), with several high-profile Catalan leaders arrested and charged with crimes including 'rebellion' and 'sedition'. Puigdemont, meanwhile, fled the country, and at the time of writing was in Germany fighting a legal battle against extradition to Spain.

New Catalan elections in December 2017 saw separatist parties win another, albeit narrow, majority in the regional parliament, which finally started functioning again, with regional autonomy restored, in June 2018. The new Catalan president, Quim Torra, was another committed separatist, but it seemed unlikely that his government would go down quite such a confrontational road as its predecessor. A new left-of-centre PSOE (Socialist Workers' Party) national government in Madrid also seemed to present a relatively conciliatory approach. PSOE leader Pedro Sánchez was firmly opposed to Catalan independence, but he seemed ready to talk with Barcelona on other issues.

if Barcelona were 100 people

53 would have Spanish as their first language
39 would have Catalan as their first language
2 would have Arabic as their first language
1 would have English as their first language
5 would have other first languages

belief systems
(% of population)

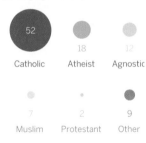

| Catholic | Atheist | Agnostic |
| 52 | 18 | 12 |

| Muslim | Protestant | Other |
| 7 | 2 | 9 |

population per sq km

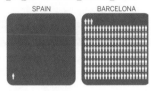

SPAIN   BARCELONA

👤 ≈ 95 people

History

The settlement of Barcelona has seen waves of immigrants and conquerors over its 2000-plus years, including Romans, Visigoths and Franks. Barcelona's fortunes have risen and fallen: from the golden era of princely power in the 14th century to dark days of the Franco era. An independent streak has always run through Barcelona, which has often led to conflict with the Kingdom of Castille – an antagonism that continues today, with a desire for more autonomy (or, increasingly, full independence) from Spain.

In 1991 the remains of 25 corpses, dating from 4000 BC, were found in Carrer de Sant Pau in El Raval. In those days much of El Raval was a bay and the hillock (Mont Tàber) next to Plaça de Sant Jaume may have been home to a Neolithic settlement.

The Romans

Barcelona's recorded history really begins with the Romans when Barcino (much later Barcelona) was founded in the reign of Caesar Augustus. The Romans were attracted to the location for the possibility of building a port here.

Rome's legacy was huge, giving Hispania (as the Iberian Peninsula was known to the Romans) a road system, aqueducts, temples and the religion that still predominates today, Christianity. Before Rome embraced this monotheistic tradition, however, there were waves of persecutions of early Christians. Santa Eulàlia, who may or may not have existed, is one of the great martyrs of this time. She still plays a role in the city's folklore, with a major festival in her name happening in February each year. Her body is believed to be buried under La Catedral. Christian persecution ended a few years after her death, when Emperor Constantine declared Christianity the official religion in 312.

Wilfred the Hairy & the Catalan Golden Age

In the 9th century AD, when much of Spain was ruled by the Moors, Louis the Pious – the son of Charlemagne and the future Frankish ruler – conquered Barcelona and claimed it as part of his empire. Barcelona in those days was a frontier town in what was known as the

TIMELINE	c 4000 BC	218 BC	AD 415
	A Neolithic settlement may have thrived around the present-day Plaça de Sant Jaume at this time, as indicated by jasper implements discovered around Carrer del Paradís.	In a move to block supplies to the Carthaginian general Hannibal, Roman troops under Scipio land at Empúries, found Tarraco (Tarragona) and take control of the Catalan coast.	Visigoths under Ataülf, with captured Roman empress Galla Placidia as his wife, make Barcino their capital. With several interruptions, it remains so until the 6th century.

Frankish or Spanish March – a rough-and-ready buffer zone between the Pyrenees and the Moors who had conquered most of the lands to the south.

The March was under nominal Frankish control but the real power lay with local potentates who ranged across the territory. One of these rulers went by the curious name of Guifré el Pelós (Wilfred the Hairy). This was not a reference to uneven shaving habits: according to legend, old Guifré had hair in parts most people do not (exactly which parts was never specified!). He and his brothers gained control of most of the Catalan counties by 878 and Guifré entered the folk mythology of Catalonia.

Guifré consolidated power over Catalonia and ushered in an era of early building projects. He endowed churches and had a new palace for himself in Barcelona (of which nothing remains). His achievements were later described by medieval monks and Romantic poets, who credit him with transforming a minor town into the future seat of an empire. If Catalonia can be called a nation, then its 'father' was the hirsute Guifré. He founded a dynasty that lasted nearly five centuries, and which developed almost independently from the Reconquista wars that were playing out in the rest of Iberia.

Romanesque Beauties

At the beginning of the second millennium, Catalan culture entered a rich new age. Romanesque churches in the countryside fostered a powerful new style of architecture. Inside lay richly painted frescoes created with the finest pigments and bearing notable Byzantine influences. Some of these works – rescued from churches that later fell into ruin – are beautifully preserved inside the Museu Nacional d'Art de Catalunya (MNAC) on Montjuïc. Commerce was also on the rise, fuelled by a new class of merchants and tradespeople.

A Growing Empire

Shipbuilding, textiles and farming (grain and grapes) helped power expansion. An even bigger catalyst to Catalonia's growth came in 1137 when Ramon Berenguer IV, the Count of Barcelona, became engaged to Petronila, heir to the throne of neighbouring Aragón, thus creating a joint state that set the scene for Catalonia's golden age.

In the following centuries the regime became a flourishing merchant empire, seizing Valencia and the Balearic Islands from the Moors, and later taking territories as far flung as Sardinia, Sicily and parts of Greece.

Barcelona's first patron saint, Santa Eulàlia (290–304), was martyred for her faith during the persecutory reign of Diocletian. Her death involved 13 tortures (one for each year of her life), including being rolled in a glass-filled barrel, having her breasts cut off and crucifixion.

HISTORY ROMANESQUE BEAUTIES

878	985	1060	1137
Wilfred the Hairy consolidates power throughout Catalonia and founds a long-lasting dynasty with his capital in Barcelona.	Al-Mansur (the Victorious) rampages across Catalan territory and devastates Barcelona in a lightning campaign. Much of the population is taken as slaves to Córdoba.	Some 150 years before the Magna Carta, Count Ramon Berenguer I approves the 'Usatges de Barcelona', a bill of rights establishing all free men as equal before the law.	Count Ramon Berenguer IV is betrothed to one-year-old Petronila, daughter of the king of Aragón, creating a new combined state that becomes known as the Corona de Aragón.

Barcelona's Golden Age

The 14th century marked the golden age of Barcelona. Its trading wealth paid for the great Gothic buildings that bejewel the city to this day. La Catedral, the Capella Reial de Santa Àgata (inside the Museu d'Història de Barcelona) and the churches of Santa Maria del Pi and Santa Maria del Mar were all completed during this time. King Pere III (1336–87) later created the breathtaking Drassanes Reials (Royal Shipyards) and also extended the city walls yet again, this time to include El Raval to the west.

According to a medieval legend, Barcelona was founded by Hercules himself. Although versions differ, all tell of nine *barcas* (boats), one of which separates from the others in a storm, and is piloted by Hercules to a beautiful coastal spot where he founds a city, naming it Barca Nona (Ninth Boat).

Black Death & Pogroms

Preserving the empire began to exhaust Catalonia. Sea wars with Genoa, resistance in Sardinia, the rise of the Ottoman Empire and the loss of the gold trade all drained the city's coffers. Commerce collapsed. The Black Death and famines killed about half of Catalonia's population in the 14th century. Barcelona also lost some of its best merchants when bloodthirsty mobs attacked Jewish businesses and homes in 1391.

The Peasants' Revolt

After the last of Guifré el Pelós' dynasty, Martí I, died heirless in 1410, Barcelona saw its star diminish when Catalonia effectively became part of the Castilian state, under the rule of Fernando from the Aragonese throne and Isabel, queen of Castilla. Impoverished and disaffected by ever-growing financial demands from the crown, Catalonia revolted in the 17th century when Catalan peasants gathered on La Rambla outside the walls of the city and began rioting.

Justice in feudal days was a little rough by modern standards. As prescribed in a 1060 bill: 'In regard to women, let the rulers render justice by cutting off their noses, lips, ears and breasts, and by burning them at the stake if necessary.'

They attacked and murdered the Viceroy, Dalmau de Queralt, and sacked and burned his ministers' houses in what was later known as the Guerra dels Segadors (Reapers' War). Under French protection, Catalonia declared itself to be an independent 'republic'. Anarchy ruled over the next few years, until Barcelona was finally besieged into submission by Castilla.

Little was gained from the effort, though the event was later commemorated as the first great Catalan drive towards independence. The song 'Els Segadors', written down in the 19th century (but with an oral tradition dating back to the 1600s), officially became Catalonia's 'national anthem' in 1993.

1225–29	1283	1323	1348
At age 18 Jaume I takes command; four years later he conquers Muslim-held Mallorca, the first of several dazzling conquests that lead him to be called El Conqueridor (the Conqueror).	The Corts Catalanes, a legislative council for Catalonia, meets for the first time and begins to curtail unlimited powers of sovereigns in favour of nobles and the powerful trading class.	Catalan forces land in Sardinia and launch a campaign of conquest that would not end until 1409. Their fiercest enemy was Eleonora de Arborea, a Sardinian Joan of Arc.	Plague devastates Barcelona. Over 25% of the city's population dies. Further waves of the Black Death, a plague of locusts in 1358 and an earthquake in 1373 deal further blows.

War of the Spanish Succession

Although Catalonia had only limited autonomy in the late 1600s, things grew worse at the turn of the 18th century when it supported the wrong side in the War of the Spanish Succession. Barcelona, under the auspices of British-backed archduke Charles of Austria, fell after an 18-month siege on 11 September 1714 to the forces of Bourbon king Felipe V, who established a unitary Castilian state.

Catalonia under a Repressive Regime

Angered at Catalonia's perceived treachery, the new king abolished the Generalitat and levelled a whole district of medieval Barcelona to make way for a huge fort (the Ciutadella) to watch over the city. The excavated ruins beneath El Born Centre de Cultura i Memòria (which opened in 2013) show what life was like for those living in the 1700s on the future site of the Ciutadella. Their lives changed irrevocably as their homes were destroyed and they were relocated to the new soulless geometric grid of Barceloneta. Not surprisingly, the citadel became the city's most hated symbol among most Catalans.

Teaching and writing in Catalan was banned, as Felipe V proceeded with a widespread plan of 'Castilianisation', in hopes of crushing future dissent. What was left of Catalonia's possessions were farmed out to the great powers.

A New Boom

After the initial shock, Barcelona found the Bourbon rulers to be comparatively light-handed in their treatment of the city. The big break came in 1778, when the ban on trade with the Spanish American colonies was lifted. In Barcelona itself, growth was modest but sustained. Small-scale manufacturing provided employment and profit, and wages were rising.

Barcelona's growth was briefly slowed by the French invasion in 1808, but gradually returned after Napoleon's defeat in 1814. The cotton trade with America helped fuel the boom. In the 1830s, the first steam-driven factories opened in Barcelona, heralding a wave of development that would last for most of the century. Wine, cork and iron industries flourished. From the mid-1830s onwards, steamships were launched off the slipways. In the following decade Spain's first railway line was opened between Barcelona and Mataró.

Although 11 September reflects the tragic fall of Barcelona, the day is still commemorated as the Diada, the National Day of Catalonia – often a day of political rallies and demonstrations, with independence very much on the agenda.

History Sites

Museu d'Història de Barcelona

Museu d'Història de Catalunya

Via Sepulcral Romana

Museu Marítim

1383	1387	1469	1478
After 50 or so years of frenzied construction, the massive Santa Maria del Mar rises above La Ribera. It is one of many Gothic architectural gems completed in the 14th century.	During the reign of Juan I, Barcelona hosts its first bullfight (according to the city's historical archive). It isn't until the 19th century, however, that bullfighting gains widespread popularity.	Isabel, heir to the Castilian throne, marries Aragonese heir Fernando, uniting two of Spain's most powerful monarchies and effectively subjugating Catalonia to the Castilian state.	Isabel and Fernando, the Reyes Católicos (Catholic Monarchs), stir up religious bigotry and establish the Spanish Inquisition, which sees thousands killed until it's finally abolished in 1834.

A Dramatic Redesign

Creeping industrialisation and prosperity for the business class did not work out so well down the line. Working-class families lived in increasingly putrid and cramped conditions. Poor nutrition, bad sanitation and disease were the norm in workers' districts, and riots, predictably, resulted. As a rule they were put down with little ceremony – the 1842 rising was bombarded into submission from the Castell de Montjuïc.

In 1869 a plan to expand the city was begun. Ildefons Cerdà designed L'Eixample (the Expansion) as a grid, broken up with gardens and parks and grafted on to the old city, beginning at Plaça de Catalunya. The plan was revolutionary. Until then it had been illegal to build on the plains between Barcelona and Gràcia, as the area was a military zone. As industrialisation got under way this building ban also forced the concentration of factories in Barcelona itself (especially in Barceloneta) and surrounding towns like Gràcia, Sant Martí, Sants and Sant Andreu (all of which were subsequently swallowed up by the burgeoning city).

L'Eixample became the most sought-after chunk of real estate in Barcelona – but the parks were mostly sacrificed to an insatiable demand for housing and undisguised land speculation. The flourishing bourgeoisie paid for lavish, ostentatious buildings, many of them in the unique Modernista style.

Ever at the vanguard, Barcelona had the first daily newspaper printed in Spain, plus its first cinema, public phone and airline (to Mallorca). It also built the world's second metropolitan railway (London was first).

A 19th-Century Renaissance

Barcelona was comparatively peaceful for most of the second half of the 19th century but far from politically inert. The relative calm and growing wealth that came with commercial success helped revive interest in all things Catalan.

The Renaixença (Renaissance) reflected the feeling of renewed self-confidence in Barcelona. Politicians and academics increasingly studied and demanded the return of former Catalan institutions and legal systems. The Catalan language was readopted by the middle and upper classes and new Catalan literature emerged as well.

In 1892, the Unió Catalanista (Catalanist Union) demanded the re-establishment of the Corts in a document known as the *Bases de Manresa*. In 1906 the suppression of Catalan news sheets was greeted by the formation of Solidaritat Catalana (Catalan Solidarity; a nationalist movement). It attracted a broad band of Catalans, not all of them nationalists.

Perhaps the most dynamic expression of the Catalan Renaissance occurred in the world of art. Barcelona was the home of Modernisme, or Catalan art nouveau. While the rest of Spain stagnated, Barcelona was

1640–52	1714	1770	1808
Catalan peasants, angered at having to quarter Castilian troops during the Thirty Years War, declare their independence under French protection. Spain eventually crushes the rebellion.	Barcelona loses all autonomy after surrendering to the Bourbon king, Felipe V, on 11 September at the end of the War of the Spanish Succession.	A freak hurricane strikes Barcelona, causing considerable damage. Among other things, the winds destroy more than 200 of the city's 1500 gaslight street lamps.	In the Battle of Bruc, Catalan militiamen defeat occupying Napoleonic units, yet Barcelona, Figueres and the coast remain under French control until Napoleon's retreat in 1814.

a hotbed of artistic activity – an avant-garde base with close links to Paris. The young Picasso spread his artistic wings here and drank in the artists' hang-out of Els Quatre Gats.

An unpleasant wake-up call came with Spain's short, futile war with the USA in 1898, in which it lost not only its entire navy but also its last colonies (Cuba, Puerto Rico and the Philippines). The blow to Barcelona's trade was enormous.

Working-Class Turmoil

Barcelona's proletariat was growing fast. The total population grew from 115,000 in 1800 to over 500,000 by 1900 and over one million by 1930 – boosted, in the early 19th century, by poor immigrants from rural Catalonia and, later, from other regions of Spain. All this made Barcelona ripe for unrest.

The city became a swirling vortex of poor workers, Republicans, bourgeois regionalists, gangsters, police terrorists and hired *pistoleros* (gunmen). Among the underclasses, who lived in some of the most abysmal conditions in Europe, there was a deep undercurrent of discontent towards the upper classes, the state and the Catholic church (which had long been viewed as an ally to the rich and powerful).

Anarchist Bombings & the Tragic Week

When the political philosophy of anarchism began spreading through Europe, it was embraced by many industrial workers in Barcelona, who embarked on a road to social revolution through violent means.

One anarchist bomb at the Liceu opera house on La Rambla in the 1890s killed 22 people. Anarchists were also blamed for the Setmana Tràgica (Tragic Week) in July 1909 when, following a military call-up for Spanish campaigns in Morocco, rampaging mobs wrecked 70 religious buildings and workers were shot on the street in reprisal.

Class Struggle & the Coming War

In the post-WWI slump, trade unionism took hold. This movement was led by the anarchist Confederación Nacional del Trabajo (CNT; National Labour Confederation), which embraced 80% of the city's workers. During a wave of strikes in 1919 and 1920, employers hired assassins to eliminate union leaders. The 1920s dictator General Miguel Primo de Rivera opposed bourgeois-Catalan nationalism and working-class radicalism, banning the CNT and even closing Barcelona's football club, a potent symbol of Catalanism. But he did support the staging of a second world fair in Barcelona, the Montjuïc World Exhibition of 1929.

Historical Reads

....

Barcelona: The Great Enchantress (Robert Hughes)

....

Barcelona – A Thousand Years of the City's Past (Felipe Fernández Armesto)

....

Homage to Catalonia (George Orwell)

....

Homage to Barcelona (Colm Tóibín)

1869	1873	1888	1895
Ildefons Cerdà designs L'Eixample (the Expansion) district with wide boulevards and a grid pattern. Modernista architects of the day showcase their creations here.	Antoni Gaudí, 21 years old and in Barcelona since 1869, enrols in architecture school, from which he graduates five years later, having already designed the street lamps in Plaça Reial.	Showcasing the grand Modernista touches of recent years (including L'Eixample), Barcelona hosts Spain's first International Exposition, held in the new, manicured Parc de la Ciutadella.	Málaga-born Pablo Picasso, aged 13, arrives in Barcelona with his family. His art-teacher father gets a job in the La Llotja school of fine arts, where Pablo enrols as a pupil.

Rivera's repression succeeded only in uniting, after his fall in 1930, Catalonia's radical elements. Within days of the formation of Spain's Second Republic in 1931, leftist Catalan nationalists of the Esquerra Republicana de Catalunya (ERC; Republican Left of Catalonia), led by Francesc Macià and Lluís Companys, proclaimed Catalonia a republic within an imaginary 'Iberian Federation'. Madrid pressured them into accepting unitary Spanish statehood, but after the leftist Popular Front victory in the February 1936 national elections, Catalonia briefly won genuine autonomy. Companys, its president, carried out land reforms and planned an alternative Barcelona Olympics to the official 1936 games in Nazi Berlin.

But things were racing out of control. The left and the right across Spain were shaping up for a showdown.

Civil War Erupts

On 17 July 1936, an army uprising in Morocco kick-started the Spanish Civil War. The main players in the conflict were the Nationalists and the Republicans. The Nationalists were allied with conservatives (and the Church). Angry at the new leftist direction in which Spain was heading, they staged a coup, led by General Francisco Franco and other rebels, and quickly gained the following of most of the army. On the opposite side was the Republican government, which was supported by those loyal to Spain's democratically elected government. Republican supporters were a loose coalition of workers' parties, socialists, anarchists, communists and other left-wing groups.

Barcelona's army garrison attempted to take the city for General Franco, but was defeated by anarchists and police loyal to the government. Franco's Nationalist forces quickly took hold of most of southern and western Spain; Galicia and Navarra in the north were also his. Most of the east and industrialised north stood with Madrid. Initial rapid advances on Madrid were stifled and the two sides settled in for almost three years of misery.

Life Under the Anarchists

For nearly a year, Barcelona was run by anarchists and the Trotskyist militia of the Partido Obrero de Unificación Marxista (POUM; Workers' Marxist Unification Party), with Companys president only in name. Factory owners and rightists fled the city. Trade unions took over factories and public services, hotels and mansions became hospitals and schools, everyone wore workers' clothes (in something of a foretaste of

Barcelona nearly staged the Olimpíada Popular (People's Olympiad) in 1936, an alternative to the Olympics being held in fascist Germany. Around 6000 athletes from 23 countries registered. However, the civil war erupted just before the start. Some athletes who arrived stayed on and joined militias to help defend the republic.

1898	July 1909	1914	July 1936
Spain loses its entire navy and last remaining colonies (the Philippines, Cuba and Puerto Rico) in two hopeless campaigns against the USA, dealing a heavy blow to Barcelona businesses.	After the call-up of reserve troops to fight a war in Morocco, *barcelonins* riot. Over 100 are reportedly killed in what's later known as Setmana Tràgica (Tragic Week).	The Mancomunitat de Catalonia, a first timid attempt at self-rule (restricted largely to administrative matters) and headed by Catalan nationalist Enric Prat de la Riba, is created in April.	General Franco launches the Spanish Civil War in Morocco. General Goded leads army units to take Barcelona for Franco, but is defeated by left-wing militia, workers and loyalist police.

what would later happen in Mao's China), bars and cafes were collectivised, trams and taxis were painted red and black (the colours of the anarchists), and one-way streets were ignored as they were seen to be part of the old system.

The anarchists were a disparate lot, ranging from gentle idealists to hardliners, who drew up death lists, held kangaroo courts, shot priests, monks and nuns (over 1200 of whom were killed in Barcelona province during the civil war), and also burnt and wrecked churches – which is why so many of Barcelona's churches are today oddly plain inside. They in turn were shunted aside by the communists (directed by Stalin from Moscow) after a bloody internecine battle in Barcelona that left 1500 dead in May 1937.

Barcelona also suffered aerial bombing raids carried out by Italian bombers sympathetic to Franco. The pockmarked walls around Plaça de Sant Felip Neri still bear the scars of one particularly gruesome day of bombardment when dozens of civilians – many of them children – were killed here.

Barcelona became the Republicans' national capital in autumn 1937. The Republican defeat in the Battle of the Ebro in southern Catalonia the following summer left Barcelona undefended. Republican resistance crumbled, in part due to exhaustion, in part due to disunity. In 1938 Catalan nationalists started negotiating separately with the Nationalists. The city fell to Franco's forces in January 1939.

Franco Takes the City

Franco's tanks rolled into a strangely silent and empty city. Almost half a million people had fled to the north. The first few months of occupation were a strange hiatus before the onset of the full machinery of oppression. Within two weeks of the city's fall a dozen cinemas were in operation, and the following month Hollywood comedies were being shown between rounds of Nationalist propaganda. The people were even encouraged to dance the *sardana,* Catalonia's national dance, in public (the Nationalists thought such folkloric generosity might endear them to the people of Barcelona).

On the other hand, the city presented an exhausted picture. The metro was running but there were no buses (they had all been used on the front). Virtually all the animals in the city zoo had died of starvation or wounds. There were frequent blackouts, and would be for years.

March 1938	1939	1940	1957
In just three days of day-and-night air raids on Barcelona carried out by fascist Italian bombers based in Franco-controlled Mallorca, 979 people are killed and 1500 wounded.	The first of Franco's troops, along with Italian tanks, roll into Barcelona and parade down Avinguda Diagonal. Thousands flee the city towards the French border.	Hitler's henchman and chief of the SS, Heinrich Himmler, visits Barcelona, stays at the Ritz, enjoys a folkloric show at Poble Espanyol and has his wallet stolen.	The Francoist Josep Maria de Porcioles becomes mayor of Barcelona and remains in charge until 1973. He presides over a willy-nilly building spree in the city.

Round-Ups & Executions

By 1940, with WWII raging across Europe, Franco had his regime more firmly in place and things turned darker for many. Catalan Francoists led the way in rounding up anarchists and former Republican supporters; up to 35,000 people were shot in purges. At the same time, small bands of resistance fighters continued to harry the Nationalists in the Pyrenees through much of the 1940s. Catalonia's president, Lluís Companys, was arrested in France by the Gestapo in August 1940, handed over to Franco, and shot on 15 October on Montjuïc. He is reputed to have died with the words 'Visca Catalunya!' ('Long live Catalonia!') on his lips.

The executions continued into the 1950s. Most people accepted the situation and tried to get on with living, while some leapt at opportunities, occupying flats abandoned by 'Reds' who had been forced to flee. Speculators and industrialists allied with Franco were able to earn a lucrative income, but the majority of *barcelonins* were affected by nationwide poverty.

Life Under Franco

Franco took a particularly hard line against Barcelona. Catalan monuments in the city were dismantled. He banned public use of Catalan, and had all town, village and street names rendered in Spanish (Castilian). Education, radio, TV and the daily press would henceforth be in Spanish. Independent political activity was banned, as was the celebration of traditional Catalan holidays.

In Barcelona, the Francoist Josep Maria de Porcioles became mayor in 1957, a post he held until 1973. That same year he obtained for the city a 'municipal charter' that expanded the mayor's authority and the city's capacity to raise and spend taxes, manage urban development and, ultimately, widen the city's metropolitan limits to absorb neighbouring territory. He was responsible for such monstrosities as the concrete municipal buildings on Plaça de Sant Miquel in the Barri Gòtic. His rule marked a grey time for Barcelona.

Immigrants Pour into Barcelona

Under Franco a flood of 1.5 million immigrants from poorer parts of Spain – chiefly Andalucía, Extremadura and the northwest – poured into Catalonia (750,000 of them to Barcelona) in the 1950s and '60s looking for work. Many lived in appalling conditions. While some made the effort to learn Catalan and integrate as fully as possible into local

**Films Set
in Franco's
Spain**

Pan's Labyrinth
(2006)

The Spirit of the
Beehive (1973)

¡Bienvenido, Mr
Marshall! (Welcome, Mr Marshall!; 1952)

Las 13 Rosas (The
13 Roses; 2007)

1975	1980	1992	1994
The death of Franco is greeted with mass jubilation, and followed by general elections two years later.	Right-wing Catalan nationalist Jordi Pujol is elected president of the resurrected Catalan regional government at the head of the nationalist CiU coalition; he remains in power until 2003.	Barcelona takes centre stage as it hosts the summer Olympic Games. In preparation the city undergoes a radical renovation program, the momentum of which continues today.	The Gran Teatre del Liceu, Barcelona's opera house, burns to the ground as a spark from a welder's blowtorch sets the stage alight. It is rebuilt and reopens in 1999.

society, the majority came to form Spanish-speaking pockets in the poorer working-class districts of the city and in a ring of satellite towns. Even today, the atmosphere in many of these towns is more Andalucian than Catalan. Catalan nationalists believe it was all part of a Francoist plot to undermine the Catalan identity.

The Road to Democracy

When the death of Franco was announced in 1975, *barcelonins* took to the streets in celebration. The next five years saw the gradual return of democracy. In 1977 Josep Tarradellas, who was head of Catalonia's government in exile, returned to Barcelona and was officially recognised by the Spanish government as head of a new Catalan coalition. *Barcelonins* who lived during that time will likely recall the historic words given from the balcony of the Palau de la Generalitat. Before a huge crowd gathered on Plaça de Sant Jaume, he said, '*Ciutadans de Catalunya, ja sóc aquí!*' (Citizens of Catalonia, I am here!).

Twenty years after his stint in Franco's jails, Jordi Pujol (an early ringleader in protests against the Francoists) was elected president of Catalonia in 1980. These were the first free regional elections since before the civil war. A wily antagonist of the central authorities in Madrid, Pujol waged a quarter-century war of attrition, eking out greater fiscal and policy autonomy and vigorously promoting a re-Catalanisation program, with uneven success.

Barcelona's Olympian Moment

Politics aside, the big event in post-Franco Barcelona was the successful 1992 Olympic Games, planned under the guidance of the popular Socialist mayor, Pasqual Maragall. The games spurred a burst of public works and brought new life to areas such as Montjuïc, where the major events were held. The once-shabby waterfront was transformed with promenades, beaches, marinas, restaurants, leisure attractions and new housing.

Urban Renewal

After the turn of the millennium, Barcelona continued to invest in urban renewal, with ambitious projects such as the 22@ high-tech zone in the once-industrial El Poblenou district, the major development around new trade fairgrounds between the city and the airport, and the Diagonal Mar waterfront development around the Parc del Fòrum at the northeast tip of the city.

2003	2006	2010	2010
Popular former mayor of Barcelona, Pasqual Maragall, becomes the first socialist president of Catalonia in tight elections after Pujol steps aside in favour of CiU's Artur Mas.	The Catalan government negotiates a new autonomy statute with Madrid in a compromise that leaves many unsatisfied and ultimately leads to the fall of Maragall.	Pope Benedict XVI consecrates the basilica of La Sagrada Família before an audience of 6500, including King Juan Carlos I and Queen Sofía.	Hot on the heels of its victory in the European football championship in 2008, Spain defeats the Netherlands in the World Cup held in South Africa, its first-ever World Cup title.

A Move Towards Independence

Since the demise of Franco, Spain has devolved considerable powers to the regions, which are officially known as *comunidades autónomas* (autonomous communities). Catalans approved a new Estatut in a referendum in 2006, but within months the right-wing Partido Popular (warning of the 'Balkanistation' or break-up of Spain) launched an appeal in the Constitutional Court against the Estatut, which it claimed granted too much autonomy.

After four years of wrangling, in 2010 the court delivered a verdict, ruling that 14 of the articles were unconstitutional – including areas of language, taxes, the judiciary and self-recognition as a 'nation'. Catalans converged on the streets en masse to protest the decision, which was widely hailed as one more blow to relations between Barcelona and Madrid.

Separatism on the Rise

The economic crisis that erupted in 2007 has largely shifted the conversation to the realm of economic recovery. Soaring unemployment and painful austerity measures – not to mention Catalonia's heavy tax burden – has led to anger and resentment towards Madrid, and fuelled the drive towards independence.

The fervour to secede has only grown in the last few years. Recent polls and the regional elections held at the end of 2017 indicate that about half of Catalans support the region becoming a new European state. At the close of the year, however, Madrid had imposed direct rule as a result of Catalan leader Carles Puigdemont's declaration of independence, which Spanish judges ruled was in clear violation of the Spanish constitution, and several Catalan politicians found themselves in jail on charges of sedition and rebellion.

The repercussions of Catalan independence would be wide-reaching. It could undermine the financial stability of Spain – and cause economic shock waves across the eurozone. How it all shakes out is anybody's guess, but no one is expecting a smooth ride.

2014	2015	2017	2026
Six months after a human chain stretches 400km scross Catalonia, Spanish judges declare Catalonia's planned referendum on independence unconstitutional.	Following an election, separatists take control of Catalonia's government. They vow to continue the move towards full secession, with a route to achieve Catalan independence within 18 months.	Catalonia's (illegal) referendum goes ahead in October. Independence is declared, Spain imposes direct rule and Catalan leader Carles Puigdemont flees to Belgium, fearing arrest.	Builders aim to finish La Sagrada Família on the centenary of the death of its creator, Gaudí (1852–1926), which is over 140 years after its construction began.

Catalan Culture

The fortunes of Catalonia have risen and fallen over the years, as Barcelona has gone from wealthy mercantile capital to a city of repression under the Franco regime, followed by the boom and bust of more recent years. Despite today's economic challenges, Catalan culture continues to flourish, with a lively festival calendar and abundant civic pride manifested in aspects from the language spoken on the streets to Barcelona's much-loved football team.

Language

In Barcelona, born-and-bred locals proudly speak Catalan, a Romance language related to French, Spanish (Castilian) and Italian. It was only relatively recently, however, that Catalan was deemed 'legitimate'. Since Barcelona was crushed in the War of the Spanish Succession in 1714, the use of Catalan was repeatedly banned or at least frowned upon. Franco was the last of Spain's rulers to clamp down on its public use. All that

Above Traditional Catalan *correfocs* (fire-runners) at a festival.

changed in 1980, when the first autonomous regional parliament was assembled and adopted new laws towards *normalització lingüística* (linguistic normalisation).

Today Catalonia's state school system uses Catalan as the language of instruction, though most Catalan speakers end up bilingual, particularly in urban areas. Around town, Catalan is the lingua franca: advertising and road signs are in Catalan, while newspapers, magazines and other publications can be found in both languages (though you'll find about twice as many options in Catalan as in Spanish). You'll also find a mix of Catalan and Spanish programming on radio and TV stations.

Essential Reading

Barcelona: The Great Enchantress, (Robert Hughes; 2001)

Barcelonas (Manuel Vázquez Montalbán; 1992)

Barça: A People's Passion (Jimmy Burns; 1992)

Folk Dancing

On weekends year-round, devotees of the folk dance *sardana* gather in front of La Catedral, while a 10-piece band puts everyone in motion. Catalans of all ages come out for the dance, which takes place in a circle with dancers holding hands. Together they move right, back and then left, hopping, raising their arms and generally building momentum as the tempo picks up. All are welcome to join in, though you'll have to watch a few rounds to get the hang of it.

Festivals

Catalonia's best celebrations tend to revolve around religious holidays. *Festes* dedicated to Nostra Senyora de la Mercè (Our Lady of Mercy) (p23) and Santa Eulàlia (p22) – Barcelona's two patron saints – are the city's biggest bashes. You'll see plenty of *sardana* and *castell*-building there. You'll also see *gegants* (huge papier-mâché giants: lords, princesses, sultans, fishers and historic and contemporary figures) and *capgrossos* (oversized heads worn by costumed actors).

Another feature of these Catalan fests is the *correfoc* (fire running): horned devils brandishing firework-spouting pitchforks wreak mayhem in the streets. They are sometimes accompanied by firework-spouting dragons, or even wooden carts that are set alight. Full coverings (hats, gloves, goggles) are highly recommended for anyone who wants to get near.

At Christmas some rather unusual Catalan characters appear. The *caganer* (crapper) is a chap with dropped pants who balances over his unsightly offering (a symbol of fertility for the coming year). There's also the *caga tió* (poop log), which on Christmas Day is supposed to *cagar* (crap) out gifts.

Castells

One of the highlights of a traditional Catalan festival is the building of human *castells* (castles), a Catalan tradition that dates back to the 18th century. Teams from across the region compete to build human towers up to 10 storeys tall. These usually involve levels of three to five people standing on each other's shoulders. A crowd of teammates forms a supporting scrum around the thickset lads at the base. To successfully complete the castle, a small child called the *enxaneta* must reach the top and signal with his or her hand.

FC Barcelona

One of the city's best-loved names is FC Barça, which is deeply associated with Catalans and even Catalan nationalism. The team was long a rallying point for Catalans when other aspects of Catalan culture were suppressed. The club openly supported Catalonia's drive towards autonomy in 1918, and in 1921 the club's statutes were drafted in Catalan. The pro-Catalan leanings of the club and its siding with the republic during the Spanish Civil War earned reprisals from the government. Club president Josep Sunyol was murdered by Franco's soldiers in 1936, and the club building was bombed in 1938.

In 1968 club president Narcís de Carreras uttered the now famous words, *El Barça: més que un club* ('more than a club'), which became the team's motto – and emphasised its role as an anti-Franco symbol and catalyst for change in the province and beyond. Today FC Barça is one of the world's most admired teams, with membership at around 170,000 in recent years.

Architecture

Famed for its architectural treasures, Barcelona has striking Gothic cathedrals, fantastical Modernista creations and avant-garde works from more recent days. The city's great building boom first began in the late Middle Ages, when Barcelona was seat of the Catalan empire. The late 19th century was another time of great ferment, when the city began expanding beyond its medieval confines and bold new thinkers transformed the city. The third notable era of design began in the late 1980s and continues today.

The Gothic Period

Barcelona's first big building boom came at the height of the Middle Ages, when its imposing Gothic churches, mansions and shipyards were raised, together creating what survives to this day as one of the most extensive Gothic quarters in Europe. Most of these architectural

Above: A Barri Gòtic street

treasures lie within the boundaries of the Ciutat Vella, but a few examples can be found beyond, notably the Museu-Monestir de Pedralbes (p174) in Pedralbes.

Historical Roots

This soaring style took off in France in the 12th century and spread across Europe. Its emergence coincided with Jaume I's march into Valencia and the annexation of Mallorca and Ibiza, accompanied by the rise of a trading class and a burgeoning mercantile empire. The enormous cost of building the grand new monuments could thus be covered by the steady increase in the city's wealth.

Perhaps the single greatest building spurt came under Pere III (1319–87). This is odd in a sense because, as Dickens might have observed, it was not only the best of times, but also the worst. By the mid-14th century, when Pere III was in command, Barcelona had been pushed to the ropes by a series of disasters: famine, repeated plagues and pogroms.

Maybe he didn't notice. He built, or began to build, much of La Catedral (p65), the Drassanes, the Llotja stock exchange (p99), the **Saló del Tinell**, the Casa de la Ciutat – which now houses the town hall (p64) – and numerous lesser buildings, not to mention part of the city walls. The churches of Santa Maria del Pi (p63) and Santa Maria del Mar (p94) were completed by the end of the 14th century.

Architectural Features

The style of architecture reflected the development of building techniques. The introduction of buttresses, flying buttresses and ribbed vaulting in ceilings allowed engineers to raise edifices that were loftier and seemingly lighter than ever before. The pointed arch became standard and great rose windows were the source of light inside these enormous spaces.

Think about the hovels that labourers on such projects lived in and the primitive nature of building materials available, and you get an idea of the awe such churches, once completed, must have inspired. They were not built in a day. It took more than 160 years, a fairly typical time frame, to finish La Catedral, although its facade was not erected until the 19th century. Its rival, the Basílica de Santa Maria del Mar (p94), was one for the record books, taking only 54 years to build.

Catalan Gothic

Catalan Gothic did not follow the same course as the style typical of northern Europe. Decoration here tends to be more sparing and the most obvious defining characteristic is the triumph of breadth over height. While northern European cathedrals reach for the sky, Catalan Gothic has a tendency to push to the sides, stretching its vaulting design to the limit.

The Saló del Tinell (p65), with a parade of 15m arches (among the largest ever built without reinforcement) holding up the roof, is a perfect example of Catalan Gothic. Another is the present home of the Museu Marítim (p109), the Drassanes, Barcelona's medieval shipyards. In their churches, too, the Catalans opted for a more robust shape and lateral space – step into the Basílica de Santa Maria del Mar or the Basílica de Santa Maria del Pi (p63) and you'll soon get the idea.

Another notable departure from what you might have come to expect of Gothic north of the Pyrenees is the lack of spires and pinnacles. Bell towers tend to terminate in a flat or nearly flat roof. Occasional exceptions prove the rule – the main facade of Barcelona's La Catedral

Catalonia's vast 14th-century mercantile empire fuelled Barcelona's boom. All manner of goods flowed to and from Sardinia, Flanders, North Africa and other places, with Catalan Jews carrying out much of this trade. The later pogroms, Inquisition and expulsion of Jews had devastating financial consequences and helped reduce Barcelona to penury.

Top: Museu del Disseny de Barcelona (p112)

Bottom: Peix (fish) sculpture by Frank Gehry

(p60), with its three gnarled and knobbly spires, does vaguely resemble the outline that confronts you in cathedrals in Chartres or Cologne. But then it was a 19th-century addition, admittedly to a medieval design.

Late Gothic

Gothic had a longer use-by date in Barcelona than in many other European centres. By the early 15th century, the Generalitat still didn't have a home worthy of its name, and architect Marc Safont set to work on the present building on Plaça de Sant Jaume. Even renovations carried out a century later were largely in the Gothic tradition, although some Renaissance elements eventually snuck in – the facade on Plaça de Sant Jaume is a rather disappointing result.

Carrer de Montcada, in La Ribera, was the result of a late-medieval act of town planning. Eventually mansions belonging to the moneyed classes of 15th- and 16th-century Barcelona were erected along it. Many now house museums and art galleries. Although these former mansions appear forbidding on the outside, their interiors often reveal another world of pleasing courtyards and decorated external staircases. They mostly went through a gentle baroque makeover in later years.

Gothic Masterpieces

....
La Catedral
....
Basílica de Santa Maria del Mar
....
Basílica de Santa Maria del Pi
....
Saló del Tinell (in Museu d'Història de Barcelona)
....
The Drassanes (Museu Marítim)

Modernisme

Barcelona's Modernisme buildings arose during the late 19th century, a period of great artistic and political fervour that was deeply connected to Catalan identity, and which transformed early-20th-century Barcelona into a showcase for avant-garde architecture. Aiming to establish a new Catalan archetype, Antoni Gaudí and other visionary architects drew inspiration from the past, using elements from the Spanish vernacular – shapes, details and brickwork reminiscent of Islamic, Gothic and Renaissance designs.

The Modernistas also revived traditional artisan trades, which you can see in the exquisite stonework and stained-glass windows, and in their artful use of wrought iron, ceramics and mosaic tiles. Nature was celebrated and imitated to perfection in Gaudí's organic forms: leaning treelike columns, walls that undulate like the sea, and the use of native plants as decorative elements. Inside these buildings, the artistry and imaginative design continues.

For many, Modernisme is synonymous with Gaudí (1852–1926), but he was by no means alone. Lluís Domènech i Montaner (1850–1923) and Josep Puig i Cadafalch (1867–1956) left a wealth of remarkable buildings across the city. The Rome-trained sculptor Eusebi Arnau (1864–1934) was one of the most popular figures called upon to decorate Barcelona's Modernista piles. The appearance of the Hospital de la Santa Creu i de Sant Pau (p83) is one of his legacies and he also had a hand in the Palau de la Música Catalana (p95) and Casa Amatller (p132).

Modernista Masterpieces

....
Casa Batlló
....
La Sagrada Família
....
Palau de la Música Catalana
....
La Pedrera
....
Palau Güell
....
Casa Amatller
....
Hospital de la Santa Creu i de Sant Pau

Olympic & Contemporary Architecture

Barcelona's latest architectural revolution began in the 1980s. The appointment then of Oriol Bohigas, still regarded as an elder statesman for architecture, as head of urban planning by the ruling Socialist party marked a new beginning. The city set about its biggest phase of renewal since the heady days of L'Eixample.

The Olympic Games Building Boom

The biggest urban makeover in 100 years happened in the run-up to the 1992 Olympics, when more than 150 architects beavered away on almost 300 building and design projects. The city saw dramatic transformations, from the construction of huge arterial highways to the refurbishment of whole neighbourhoods in dire need of repair. In a rather crafty manoeuvre, the city government used national monies to fund urban improvements the capital would never normally have approved. Several kilometres of waterfront wasteland that included Port Vell was beautifully transformed into sparkling new beaches – suddenly Barcelona had prime beachfront real estate. The long road to resurrecting Montjuïc took off with the refurbishment of the Olympic stadium and the creation of landmarks like Santiago Calatrava's **Torre Calatrava**.

Post-1992, landmark buildings still went up in strategic spots, usually with the ulterior motive of trying to pull the surrounding area up by its bootstraps. One of the most emblematic of these projects is the gleaming white Museu d'Art Contemporani de Barcelona, better known as MACBA (p81), which opened in 1995. The museum was designed by Richard Meier and incorporates the characteristic elements for which the American architect is so well known – the geometric minimalism and the pervasive use of all white with glass and steel.

Arousing no little architectural debate, as with so many of architect Ricardo Bofill's projects, the Teatre Nacional de Catalunya (p122), which opened in 1996, is a blend of the neoclassical and the modern. Framed by 26 columns with a single gabled roof and grand entrance steps, the theatre takes the form of a Greek temple, though its all-glass exterior gives it a light and open appearance.

Henry Cobb's **World Trade Center**, at the tip of a quay jutting out into the waters of Port Vell, has been overshadowed by Ricardo Bofill's hotel, W Barcelona (p217), whose spinnaker-like front looks out to sea from the south end of La Barceloneta's beach strip.

The New Millennium

One of the first big projects of the 21st century has occurred around Diagonal Mar. A whole district has been built in the northeast coastal corner of the city, where before there was a void. High-rise apartments, waterfront office towers and five-star hotels – among them the eye-catching Meliá Sky Barcelona (p217) hotel (completed in 2008) by Dominique Perrault – mark this regenerated district. The hovering blue, triangular Edifici Fòrum (p113) by Swiss architects Herzog & de Meuron is the most striking landmark here, along with a gigantic photovoltaic panel that provides some of the area's electricity.

Much of the district was completed in 2004, though the area continues to evolve as new buildings are added to the mix. Among the most notable recent additions is a 24-storey whitewashed trapezoidal prism that serves as the headquarters for the national telephone company, Telefónica. Designed by Enric Massip-Bosch and dubbed the Diagonal 00, it has a deceivingly two-dimensional appearance upon initial approach. Shortly after its completion in 2011, the Torre was awarded the respected Leading European Architects Forum (LEAF) award for commercial building of the year.

Another prominent addition to the skyline came in 2005. The shimmering, cucumber-shaped **Torre Agbar** is a product of French architect Jean Nouvel, emblematic of the city's desire to make the developing high-tech zone of 22@ a reality.

Southwest, on the way to the airport, the **Fira M2** trade fair along Gran Via de les Corts Catalanes is now marked by red twisting twin landmark towers (one the **Hotel Santos Porta Fira**, the other offices) designed by Japanese star architect and self-confessed Gaudí fan Toyo Ito.

The Arabs invented the ancient technique of *trencadís*, but Gaudí was the first architect to revive it. The procedure involves taking ceramic tiles or fragments of broken pottery or glass and creating a mosaic-like sheath on roofs, ceilings, chimneys, benches, sculptures or any other surface.

No one longs for the pre-Olympic days when the waterfront was a dangerous and polluted wasteland. However, some old timers still bemoan the loss of its old rickety restaurant shacks, which sat on stilts over the water and served delectable if utterly unfussy seafood.

ARCHITECTURE OLYMPIC & CONTEMPORARY ARCHITECTURE

The heart of La Ribera got a fresh look with the renovated Mercat de Santa Caterina (p96). The market is quite a sight, with its wavy ceramic roof and tubular skeleton, designed by one of the most promising names in Catalan architecture until his premature death, Enric Miralles. Miralles' **Edifici de Gas Natural** (Map p286; Passeig de Salvat Papasseit; Ⓜ Barceloneta), a 100m glass tower near the waterfront in La Barceloneta, is extraordinary for its mirrorlike surface and weirdly protruding adjunct buildings, which could be giant glass cliffs bursting from the main tower's flank.

The City of Tomorrow

Big projects have slowly taken shape around the city, although the continuing economic crisis has dramatically slowed the pace of construction. The redevelopment of the area near Plaça de les Glòries Catalanes is one of the latest completed projects, with the goal of revitalising the neighbourhood and making it a draw for tourists.

The centrepiece, completed in 2013, is the Museu del Disseny (p112; design museum), which incorporates sustainable features in its cantilevered, metal-sheathed building. Vaguely futuristic (though some say it looks like a stapler), it has a rather imposing, anvil-shaped presence over the neighbourhood.

Nearby stands Els Encants Vells (p122; 'the Old Charms' flea market), which was given a dramatic new look by local architecture firm b720 Fermín Vázquez Arquitectos. Traders now sell their wares beneath a giant, mirrored canopy made up of geometric panels and held aloft with long, slender poles. Work to turn the adjacent traffic-choked roundabout into a park, taking the cars underneath, continues apace.

In a rather thoughtful bit of recycling, British architect Lord Richard Rogers transformed the former **Les Arenes** bullring on Plaça d'Espanya into a singular, circular leisure complex, with shops, cinemas and more, which opened in 2011. He did so while still maintaining its red-brick, 19th-century Moorish-looking facade. Perhaps its best feature is the rooftop with 360-degree views from the open-air promenade and cafes and restaurants.

In the Ciutat Vella (Old City), El Raval has been the latest focal point for urban renewal. The Filmoteca de Catalunya (p88) is a hulking rather brutalist building of concrete and glass, with sharp angles. It was designed by Catalan architect Josep Lluís Mateo and completed in 2011. It sits near the Richard Meier–designed MACBA, which opened in 1995.

Contemporary Buildings

....

Torre Agbar

....

Teatre Nacional de Catalunya

....

Mercat de Santa Caterina

....

Edifici Fòrum

....

W Barcelona

....

Hotel Santos Porta Fira (Llobregat)

....

Les Arenes (Plaça d'Espanya)

Picasso, Miró & Dalí

Three of Spain's greatest 20th-century artists have deep connections to Barcelona. Picasso spent his formative years in the city and maintained lifelong friendships with Catalans. It was Picasso's own idea to create a museum of his works here. Joan Miró is one of Barcelona's most famous native sons. His instantly recognisable style can be seen in public installations throughout the city. Although Salvador Dalí is more commonly associated with Figueres, Barcelona was a great source of inspiration for him, particularly the fantastical architectural works of Antoni Gaudí.

Pablo Picasso

Born in Málaga in Andalucía, Pablo Ruiz Picasso (1881–1973) was already sketching by the age of nine. As a young boy, he lived briefly in A Coruña (in Galicia), before landing in Barcelona in 1895. His father had obtained a post teaching art at the La Llotja school of fine arts (p99), then housed in the stock exchange building, and had his son enrolled there, too. It was in Barcelona and Catalonia that Picasso matured, spending his time ceaselessly drawing and painting.

After a stint at the Real Academia de Bellas Artes de San Fernando in Madrid in 1897, Picasso spent six months with his friend Manuel Pallarès in bucolic Horta de Sant Joan, in western Catalonia – he would later claim that it was there he learned everything he knew. In Barcelona, Picasso lived and worked in the Barri Gòtic and El Raval (where he was introduced to the seamier side of life in the Barri Xinès).

By the time Picasso moved to France in 1904, he had explored his first highly personal style. In this so-called Blue Period, his canvases have a melancholy feel heightened by the trademark dominance of dark blues. Some of his portraits and cityscapes from this period were created in and inspired by what he saw in Barcelona. A number of pieces from this period hang in the Museu Picasso (p92).

By the mid-1920s, he was dabbling with surrealism. His best-known work is *Guernica* (displayed in Madrid's Museo Nacional Centro de Arte Reina Sofia), a complex painting portraying the horror of war, inspired by the German aerial bombing of the Basque town Guernica (Gernika) in 1937.

Picasso worked prolifically during and after WWII and he was still cranking out paintings, sculptures, ceramics and etchings until the day he died in 1973.

Joan Miró

At the time the 13-year-old Picasso arrived in Barcelona, his near contemporary, Joan Miró (1893–1983), was still learning to crawl in the Barri Gòtic, where he was born. He spent a third of his life in Barcelona but later divided his time between France, the Tarragona countryside and the island of Mallorca, where he ended his days.

Like Picasso, Miró attended the Escola de Belles Arts de la Llotja. He was initially uncertain about his artistic vocation – in fact, he studied commerce. In Paris from 1920, he mixed with Picasso, Hemingway, Joyce and friends, and made his own mark, after several years of struggle, with an exhibition in 1925. The masterpiece from this, his so-called realist period, was *La Masia* (The Farm).

With *Les Demoiselles d'Avignon* (The Young Ladies of Avignon; 1907), Picasso broke with all forms of traditional representation, introducing a deformed perspective that would later spill over into cubism. The subject was supposedly taken from the Carrer d'Avinyó in the Barri Gòtic, in those days populated with a series of brothels.

ART ON THE STREETS

Barcelona hosts an array of street sculpture, from Miró's 1983 **Dona i Ocell** (Woman and Bird), in the park dedicated to the artist, to **Peix** (Fish), Frank Gehry's shimmering, bronze-coloured headless fish facing Port Olímpic. Halfway along La Rambla, at Plaça de la Boqueria, you can walk all over Miró's **mosaic** (p57).

Picasso left an open-air mark with his design on the facade of the Col·legi d'Arquitectes de Catalunya opposite La Catedral in the Barri Gòtic. Other works include the **Barcelona Head** (p112) by Roy Lichtenstein at the Port Vell end of Via Laietana and Fernando Botero's rotund El Gat on Rambla del Raval.

Wander down to the Barceloneta seaside for a gander at Rebecca Horn's 1992 tribute to the old shacks that used to line the waterfront. The precarious stack is called **Homenatge a la Barceloneta** (Tribute to La Barceloneta). A little further south is the 2003 **Homenatge a la Natació** (Tribute to Swimming), a complex metallic rendition of swimmers and divers in the water by Alfredo Lanz.

Heading a little further back in time, in 1983 Antoni Tàpies constructed **Homenatge a Picasso** (Tribute to Picasso) on Passeig de Picasso; it's essentially a glass cube set in a pond and filled with, well, junk. Antoni Llena's David i Goliat (David and Goliath), a massive sculpture of tubular and sheet iron, in the Parc de les Cascades near Port Olímpic's two skyscrapers, looks like an untidy kite inspired by Halloween. Beyond this Avinguda d'Icària is lined by architect Enric Miralles' so-called Pergoles – bizarre, twisted metal contraptions.

It was during WWII, while living in seclusion in Normandy, that Miró's definitive leitmotifs emerged. Among the most important images that appear frequently throughout his work are women, birds (the link between Earth and the heavens), stars (the unattainable heavenly world, the source of imagination) and a sort of net entrapping all these levels of the cosmos. The Miró works that most people are acquainted with emerged from this time – arrangements of lines and symbolic figures in primary colours, with shapes reduced to their essence.

He lived in Mallorca, home of his wife Pilar Juncosa, from 1956 until his death in 1983.

Salvador Dalí

The great Catalan artist Salvador Dalí i Domènech (1904–89) was born and died in Figueres, where he left his single greatest artistic legacy, the Teatre-Museu Dalí (p205). Although few of his famed works reside in Barcelona, the city provided a stimulating atmosphere for Dalí, and places like Park Güell, with its surrealist-like aspects, had a powerful effect on him.

Prolific painter, showman, shameless self-promoter or just plain weirdo, Dalí was nothing if not a character – probably a little too much for the conservative small-town folk of Figueres.

Every now and then a key moment arrives that can change the course of one's life. Dalí's came in 1929, when the French poet Paul Éluard visited Cadaqués with his Russian wife, Gala. The rest, as they say, is histrionics. Dalí shot off to Paris to be with Gala and plunged into the world of surrealism.

The Fundació Joan Miró, housed in an extensive gallery atop Montjuïc, has the single largest collection of Miró's work in the world today.

In the 1930s, Salvador and Gala returned to live at Port Lligat on the north Catalan coast, where they played host to a long list of fashionable and art-world guests until the war years – the parties were by all accounts memorable.

They started again in Port Lligat in the 1950s. The stories of sexual romps and Gala's appetite for local young men are legendary. The 1960s saw Dalí painting pictures on a grand scale, including his 1962 reinterpretation of Marià Fortuny's Batalla de Tetuán. On his death in 1989, he was buried (according to his own wishes) in the Teatre-Museu he had created on the site of the old theatre in central Figueres, which also houses an awe-inspiring Dalí collection.

Music & Dance

Barcelona's vibrant music and dance scene has been shaped by artists both traditional and cutting edge. From Nova Cançó, composed during the dark years of the dictatorship, to the hybridised Catalan rumba to hands-in-the air rock ballads of the 1970s and '80s, Barcelona's music evolves constantly. Today's groups continue to push musical boundaries, blending rhythms from all corners of the globe. In the realm of dance, flamenco has a small loyal following, while the old-fashioned folk dance *sardana* continues to attract growing numbers.

Contemporary Music

Nova Cançó

Curiously, it was probably the Francoist repression that most helped foster a vigorous local music scene in Catalan. In the dark 1950s, the Nova Cançó (New Song) movement was born to resist linguistic oppression

Above: A flamenco dancer and guitarist.

with music in Catalan (getting air time on the radio was long close to impossible), throwing up stars that in some cases won huge popularity throughout Spain, such as the Valencia-born Raimon.

More specifically loved in Catalonia as a Bob Dylan–style 1960s protest singer-songwriter was Lluís Llach, much of whose music was more or less antiregime. Joan Manuel Serrat is another legendary figure. His appeal stretches from Barcelona to Buenos Aires. Born in the Poble Sec district, this poet-singer is equally at ease in Catalan and Spanish. He has repeatedly shown that record sales are not everything to him. In 1968 he refused to represent Spain at the Eurovision song contest if he were not allowed to sing in Catalan. Accused of being anti-Spanish, he was long banned from performing in Spain.

Born in Mallorca, the talented singer Maria del Mar Bonet arrived in Barcelona in 1967, and embarked on a long and celebrated singing career. She sang in Catalan, and many of her searing and powerful songs were banned by the dictatorship. On concert tours abroad, she attracted worldwide attention, and she has performed with distinguished groups and soloists across the globe.

> Around the same time Nova Cançó singers were taking aim at the Franco regime, folk singers from Latin America were decrying their own corrupt military dictatorships. Songs by Victor Jara of Chile, Mercedes Sosa of Argentina and Chico Buarque of Brazil helped unite people in the fight against oppression.

Rock, Pop & Beyond

A specifically local strand of rock emerged after the 1980s. (Catalan rock) is not essentially different from rock anywhere else, except that it is sung in Catalan by local bands that appeal to local tastes. Among the most popular groups of years past include Sau, Els Pets, Lax'n Busto and the Valenciano band, Obrint Pas.

Far greater success across Spain has gone to Estopa, a male rock duo from Cornellà, a satellite suburb of Barcelona. The guitar-wielding brothers sing a clean Spanish rock, occasionally with a vaguely flamenco flavour. Along the same vein, the Barcelona hit trio Pastora peddles a successful brand of Spanish pop, mixing electric sounds with a strong acoustic element.

Towards the end of the nineties a very different Barcelona sound emerged, typified by the eclectic sounds of Manu Chao and Ojos de Brujo, both of which had international success. A Barcelona band with similar flavours is Macaco. All three switch between languages – Catalan, Spanish (Castilian), English and Portuguese among others – and blend Latin rhythms with flamenco, ska, electronica and many more. When people talk about the 'Raval sound' (after the name of the still somewhat seedy old-city district), this is the kind of thing they mean.

Born in El Raval, Cabo San Roque is an even more experimental group, incorporating huge soundscapes, powerful rhythms and mechanical accents often using non-traditional John Cage–style instruments in their avant-garde performances. In one show, the five-person group shared the stage with a polyphonic washing machine powered by a bicycle chain.

LONGING FOR CUBA

The oldest musical tradition to have survived to some degree in Catalonia is that of the *havaneres* (from Havana) – nostalgic songs and melancholy sea shanties brought back from Cuba by Catalans who lived, sailed and traded there in the 19th century. Even after Spain lost Cuba in 1898, the *havanera* tradition (a mix of European and Cuban rhythms) continued. A magical opportunity to enjoy these songs is the **Cantada d'Havaneres** (www.havanerescalella.cat), a one-day festival held on the Costa Brava in early July. Otherwise you may stumble across performances elsewhere along the coast or even in Barcelona, but there is no set program.

RETURN OF LA RUMBA

Back in the 1950s, a new sound mixing flamenco with salsa and other Latin sounds emerged in *gitano* (Roma people) circles in the bars of Gràcia and the Barri Gòtic. One of the founders of *rumba catalana* was Antonio González, known as El Pescaílla (married to the flamenco star Lola Flores). Although El Pescaílla was well known in town, the Mataró-born *gitano* Peret later took this eminently Barcelona style to a wider (eventually international) audience.

By the end of the 1970s, however, *rumba catalana* was running out of steam. Peret had turned to religion and El Pescaílla lived in Flores' shadow in Madrid. But Buenos Aires–born Javier Patricio 'Gato' Pérez discovered rumba in 1977 and gave it his own personal spin, bringing out several popular records, such as *Atalaya,* until the early 1980s.

After Pérez, it seemed that rumba was dead. Not so fast! New rumba bands, often highly eclectic, have emerged in recent years. Ai Ai Ai, Barrio Negro, El Tío Carlos and La Pegatina are names to look out for. Others mix rumba with styles as diverse as reggae or ragga.

Another key name on El Raval's scene is 08001 (which is the area's postcode). This ever-evolving collective brings together musicians from all across the globe, fusing unusual sounds from hip-hop, flamenco, reggae and rock to styles from Morocco, West Africa, the Caribbean and beyond. Their last album *No Pain No Gain* came out in 2013, but they continue to work together.

Hailing from Barcelona, Mishima is an indie pop band that has recorded a mix of albums in English and Catalan. They remained largely obscure prior to the release of their 2007 album *Set tota la vida,* which earned accolades across the music industry. The Pinker Tones are a Barcelona duo that attained international success with an eclectic electronic mix of music, ranging from dizzy dance numbers to film soundtracks. Electro group Love of Lesbian is another festival favourite, as is Catalan techno DJ John Talabot.

Classical, Opera & Baroque

Spain's contribution to the world of classical music has been modest, but Catalonia has produced a few exceptional composers. Best known is Camprodon-born Isaac Albéniz (1860–1909), a gifted pianist who later turned his hand to composition. Among his best-remembered works is the *Iberia* cycle.

Montserrat Caballé is Barcelona's most successful voice. Born in Gràcia in 1933, the soprano made her debut in 1956 in Basel (Switzerland). Her home-town launch came four years later in the Gran Teatre del Liceu. In 1965 she performed to wild acclaim at New York's Carnegie Hall and went on to become one of the world's finest 20th-century sopranos. Her daughter, Montserrat Martí, is also a singer and they occasionally appear together. Another fine Catalan soprano was Victoria de los Ángeles (1923–2005), while Catalonia's other world-class opera star is the renowned tenor Josep (José) Carreras.

Jordi Savall has assumed the task of rediscovering a European heritage in music that pre-dates the era of the classical greats. He and his late wife, soprano Montserrat Figueras, have, along with musicians from other countries, been largely responsible for resuscitating the beauties of medieval, Renaissance and baroque music. In 1987 Savall founded La Capella Reial de Catalunya and two years later he formed the baroque orchestra Le Concert des Nations. You can sometimes catch their recitals in locations such as the Gran Teatre del Liceu or the Basílica de Santa Maria del Mar.

Born in Catalonia, Pau Casals (1876–1973) was one of the greatest cellists of the 20th century. Living in exile in southern France, he declared he would not play in public as long as Western democracies continued to tolerate Franco's regime. In 1958 he was a candidate for the Nobel Peace Prize.

Dance

Flamenco

For those who think that the passion of flamenco is the preserve of the south, think again. The *gitanos* (Roma people) get around, and some of the big names of the genre come from Catalonia. They were already in Catalonia long before the massive migrations from the south of the 1960s, but with these waves came an exponential growth in flamenco bars as Andalucians sought to recreate a little bit of home.

First and foremost, one of the greatest *bailaoras* (flamenco dancers) of all time, Carmen Amaya (1913–63) was born in what is now Port Olímpic. She danced to her father's guitar in the streets and bars around La Rambla in the years before the civil war. Much to the bemusement of purists from the south, not a few flamenco stars today have at least trained in flamenco schools in Barcelona – dancers Antonio Canales and Joaquín Cortés are among them.

Other Catalan stars of flamenco include *cantaores* (singers) Juan Cortés Duquende and Miguel Poveda, a boy from Badalona. He took an original step in 2005 by releasing a flamenco album, *Desglaç,* in Catalan. Another interesting flamenco voice in Catalonia is Ginesa Ortega Cortés, actually born in France. She masters traditional genres ably but loves to experiment. In her 2002 album, *Por los espejos del agua* (Through the Water's Mirrors), she does a reggae version of flamenco and she has sung flamenco versions of songs by Joan Manuel Serrat and Billie Holiday.

The seven-man, one-woman group Ojos de Brujo (Wizard's Eyes) melded flamenco and rumba with rap, ragga and electronic music. The band split up in 2013, with lead singer Marina setting off to pursue a reasonably successful solo career as 'Marinah'.

Sardana

The Catalan dance par excellence is the *sardana,* whose roots lie in the far northern Empordà region of Catalonia. Compared with flamenco, it is sober indeed but not unlike a lot of other Mediterranean folk dances.

The dancers hold hands in a circle and wait for the 10 or so musicians to begin. The performance starts with the piping of the *flabiol,* a little wooden flute. When the other musicians join in, the dancers start – a series of steps to the right, one back and then the same to the left. As the music 'heats up' the steps become more complex, the leaps are higher and the dancers lift their arms. Then they return to the initial steps and continue. If newcomers wish to join in, space is made for them as the dance continues and the whole thing proceeds in a more or less seamless fashion.

Top Albums

Barí, Ojos de Brujo

Anells d'aigua, Maria del Mar Bonet

Verges 50, Lluís Llach

Wild animals, Pinker Tones

Set tota la vida, Mishima

Voràgine, 08001

Rey de la rumba, Peret

X anniversarium, Estopa

Survival Guide

TRANSPORT 250

**ARRIVING IN
BARCELONA** **250**
El Prat Airport 250
Girona-Costa
Brava Airport 251
Reus Airport 251

GETTING AROUND **251**
Metro & Train 251
Bus 252
Taxi 252
Tram 252
Cable Car 252
Bicycle 252
Car & Motorcycle 253

TOURS **253**
Walking Tours 253
Bicycle Tours 254
Boat Tours 254

DIRECTORY A–Z 255
Discount Cards 255
Electricity 255
Emergency &
Important Numbers 255
Money 256
Opening Hours 256
Public Holidays 256
Taxes & Refunds 256
Telephone 257
Time 257
Tourist Information 257
Travellers with
Disabilities 257
Visas 258

LANGUAGE 259

Transport

ARRIVING IN BARCELONA

Most travellers enter Barcelona through El Prat airport. Some budget airlines use Girona-Costa Brava airport or Reus airport.

Flights from North America take about eight hours from the east coast (typically 10 to 13 hours, including a stopover); from the west coast count on 13 or more hours including a stopover. Flights from London take around two hours; from Western Europe it's two to three hours.

Travelling by train is a pricier but perhaps more romantic way of reaching Catalonia from other European cities. The TGV takes around seven hours from Paris to Barcelona. Long-distance trains arrive in Estació Sants, about 2.5km west of La Rambla.

Long-haul buses arrive in Estació del Nord.

Flights, cars and tours can be booked online at lonely planet.com/bookings.

El Prat Airport

Barcelona's **El Prat airport** (☎902 404704; www.aena.es) lies 17km southwest of Plaça de Catalunya at El Prat de Llobregat. The airport has two main terminal buildings: the T1 terminal and the older T2, itself divided into three terminal areas (A, B and C).

In T1, the main arrivals area is on the 1st floor (with separate areas for EU Schengen Area arrivals, non-EU international arrivals and the Barcelona–Madrid corridor). Boarding gates are on the 1st and 3rd floors.

The main **tourist office** (www.barcelonaturisme.com; ⏰8.30am-8.30pm) is on the ground floor of Terminal 2B. Others on the ground floor of Terminal 2A and in Terminal 1 operate the same hours.

Lockers come in three sizes; on the 1st floor of T1.

Lost-luggage offices can be found by the arrivals belts in Terminal 1 and on the arrivals floor in Terminals 2A and 2B.

Bus

The **A1 Aerobús** (Map p302; ☎902 100104; www.aerobus-bcn.com; Plaça d'Espanya; one way/return €5.90/10.20; ⏰5.05am-12.35am) runs from Terminal 1 to Plaça de Catalunya (30 to 40 minutes depending on traffic) via Plaça d'Espanya, Gran Via de les Corts Catalanes (corner of Carrer del Comte d'Urgell) and Plaça de la Universitat every five to 10 minutes from 6.10am to 1.05am. Departures from Plaça de Catalunya are from 5.30am to 12.30am and stop at the corner of Carrer de Sepúlveda and Carrer del Comte d'Urgell, and at Plaça d'Espanya.

The **A2 Aerobús** from Terminal 2 (stops outside terminal areas A, B and C) runs from 6am to 1am with a frequency of between 10 and 20 minutes and follows the same route as the A1 Aerobús.

Buy tickets on the bus or from agents at the bus stop. Slower local buses (such as the No 46 to/from Plaça d'Espanya and two night buses, the N17 and N18, to/from Plaça de Catalunya) also serve Terminals 1 and 2.

Mon-Bus (www.monbus. cat) has regular direct buses (which originate in central Barcelona) between Terminal 1 only and Sitges (€7). In Sitges, buses depart from Avinguda de Vilanova 14. The trip takes about 30 minutes and runs half-hourly.

Plana (☎977 553680; www. busplana.com) has services between the airport and Tarragona (one way/return €13/24), along with Reus, Port Aventura and other nearby southwest coastal destinations.

Taxi

A taxi between either terminal and the city centre – about a half-hour ride depending on traffic – costs around €25. Fares and charges are posted inside the passenger side of the taxi; make sure the meter is used.

CLIMATE CHANGE & TRAVEL

Every form of transport that relies on carbon-based fuel generates CO_2, the main cause of human-induced climate change. Modern travel is dependent on aeroplanes, which might use less fuel per kilometre per person than most cars but travel much greater distances. The altitude at which aircraft emit gases (including CO_2) and particles also contributes to their climate change impact. Many websites offer 'carbon calculators' that allow people to estimate the carbon emissions generated by their journey and, for those who wish to do so, to offset the impact of the greenhouse gases emitted with contributions to portfolios of climate-friendly initiatives throughout the world. Lonely Planet offsets the carbon footprint of all staff and author travel.

Train

Train operator Renfe runs the R2 Nord line every half-hour from the airport (from 5.42am to 11.38pm) via several stops to Barcelona's main train station, **Estació Sants** (www.adif.es; Plaça dels Països Catalans; MSants Estació), and Passeig de Gràcia in central Barcelona, after which it heads northwest out of the city. The first service from Passeig de Gràcia leaves at 5.08am and the last at 11.07pm, and about five minutes later from Estació Sants. The trip between the airport and Passeig de Gràcia takes 25 minutes. A one-way ticket costs €2.50.

The airport train station is about a five-minute walk from Terminal 2. Regular shuttle buses run from the station and Terminal 2 to Terminal 1 – allow an extra 15 to 20 minutes.

Girona-Costa Brava Airport

Girona-Costa Brava airport (www.aena.es) is 12km south of Girona and 92km northeast of Barcelona. You'll find a tourist office, ATMs and lost-luggage desks on the ground floor.

Bus

Sagalés (☎902 130014; www.sagales.com) runs hourly bus services from Girona-Costa Brava airport to Girona's main bus/train station (€2.75, 30 minutes) in

connection with flights. The same company runs direct **Barcelona Bus** (Map p294; ☎902 130014; www.sagales airportline.com; MArc de Triomf) services to/from Estació del Nord bus station in Barcelona (one way/return €16/25, 1¼ hours).

Taxi

A taxi ride into Girona from the airport costs €20 to €26. To Barcelona you would pay around €140.

Train

Regular **Renfe** (☎91 232 03 20; www.renfe.es) train services run between Girona and Barcelona (€8.40 to €12.25, around 1¼ hours). Speedier Avant trains get there in 38 minutes (one way €10 to €17).

Reus Airport

Reus airport (☎902 404704; www.aena.es) is 13km west of Tarragona and 108km southwest of Barcelona. The tourist office and lost-luggage desks are in the main terminal building.

Bus

Hispano-Igualadina buses (Map p302; ☎93 339 79 29; www.igualadina.com; Carrer de Viriat; MSants Estació) run between Reus airport and **Estació d'Autobusos de Sants** (Map p302; ☎902 432343; www.adif.es; Carrer de Viriat; MSants Estació) to

meet flights (one way €16, 1½ hours).

Local bus 50 (www.reus transport.cat) serves central Reus (€3, 20 minutes), and other buses run to local coastal destinations.

GETTING AROUND

Metro & Train

The easy-to-use **Transports Metropolitans de Barcelona** (TMB Metro; ☎93 298 70 00; www.tmb.net) system has 11 numbered and colour-coded lines. It runs from 5am to midnight Sunday to Thursday and holidays, from 5am to 2am on Friday and days immediately preceding holidays, and 24 hours on Saturday.

Ongoing work to expand the metro continues on several lines. Línea 9 connects with the airport.

Suburban trains run by the **Ferrocarrils de la Generalitat de Catalunya** (FGC; ☎012; www.fgc.net) include a couple of useful city lines. All lines heading north from Plaça de Catalunya stop at Carrer de Provença and Gràcia. One of these lines (L7) goes to Tibidabo and another (L6 to Reina Elisenda) has a stop near the Monestir de Pedralbes. Most trains from Plaça de Catalunya continue beyond Barcelona to Sant Cugat, Sabadell and Terrassa. Other FGC lines head west from Plaça d'Espanya, including one for Manresa that is handy for the trip to Montserrat.

Depending on the line, these trains run from about 5am (with only one or two services before 6am) to 11pm or midnight Sunday to Thursday, and from 5am to about 1am on Friday and Saturday.

Bus

TMB metro (☑93 298 70 00; www.tmb.net) buses run along most city routes every few minutes from between 5am and 6.30am to around 10pm and 11pm. Many routes pass through Plaça de Catalunya and/or Plaça de la Universitat. After 11pm a reduced network of yellow *nitbusos* (night buses) runs until 3am or 5am. All *nitbus* routes pass through Plaça de Catalunya and most run every 30 to 45 minutes.

Taxi

Taxis charge €2.10 flag fall plus meter charges of €1.10 per kilometre (€1.30 from 8pm to 8am and all day on weekends). A further €3.10 is added for all trips to/from the airport, and €1 for luggage bigger than 55cm x 35cm x 35cm. The trip from Estació Sants to Plaça de Catalunya, about 3km, costs about €11. You can flag a taxi down in the streets or call one:

Fonotaxi (☑93 300 11 00; www.fonotaxi.net)

Radio Taxi 033 (☑93 303 30 33; www.radiotaxi033.com)

The call-out charge is €3.40 (€4.20 at night and on weekends). In many taxis it is possible to pay with a credit card and, if you have a local telephone number, you can join the T033 Ràdio taxi service for booking taxis online (www.radiotaxi033.com, in Spanish). You can also book

online at https://catalunya taxi.com.

Taxi Amic (☑93 420 80 88; www.taxi-amic-adaptat. com) is a special taxi service for people with disabilities or difficult situations (such as transport of big objects). Book at least 24 hours in advance if possible.

Tram

There are a handful of **tram lines** (☑900 701181; www. tram.cat) in the city. All standard transport passes are valid. A scenic option is the *tramvia blau* (blue tram), which runs up to the foot of Tibidabo.

T1, T2 and T3 Run into the suburbs of greater Barcelona from Plaça de Francesc Macià and are of limited interest to visitors.

T4 Runs from behind the zoo (near the Ciutadella Vila Olímpica metro stop) to Sant Adrià via Glòries and the Fòrum.

T5 Runs from Glòries to Badalona (Gorg stop).

T6 Runs between Glòries and Sant Adrià.

Cable Car

Several aerial cable cars operate in Barcelona and provide excellent views over the city. **Teleférico del Puerto** (Map p286; www.teleferico debarcelona.com; Passeig de Joan de Borbó; one way/return €11/16.50; ⊙10.30am-8pm Jun-early Sep, shorter hours early Sep-May; ☐V15, 39, ⓂBarceloneta) travels between the waterfront southwest of Barceloneta and Montjuïc. **Teleféric de Montjuïc** (www.telefericde montjuic.cat; return adult/4-12yr/under 4yr €12.50/9/free; ⊙10am-9pm Jun-Sep, shorter hours rest of the year) runs between Estació Parc Montjuïc and the Castell de Montjuïc.

Bicycle

Over 180km of bike lanes have been laid out across the city, so it's possible to commute on two environmentally friendly wheels. A waterfront path runs northeast from Port Olímpic towards Riu Besòs. Scenic itineraries are mapped for cyclists in the Collserola parkland, and the *ronda verda* is an incomplete 75km cycling path that extends around the city's outskirts. You can cycle a well-signed 22km loop path (part of the *ronda verda*) by following the seaside bike path northeast of Barceloneta.

You can transport your bicycle on the metro on weekdays (except between 7am and 9.30am or 5pm and 8.30pm). At weekends and during holidays and July and August, there are no restrictions. You can use FGC trains to carry your bike at any time and Renfe's *rodalies* trains from 10am to 3pm on weekdays and all day on weekends and holidays.

Countless companies around town offer bicycles (and anything remotely resembling one, from tandems to tricycle carts and more). They include the following:

BarcelonaBiking.com (Map p276; ☑656 356300; www. barcelonabiking.com; Baixada de Sant Miquel 6; bike hire per 1/24hr €5/15, tour €21; ⊙10am-8pm, tour 11am; ⓂJaume I, Liceu)

Biciclot (Map p286; ☑93 221 97 78; www.bikinginbarcelona. net; Passeig Marítim de la Barceloneta 33; bike hire per hour/day €5/17; ⊙10am-8pm; ⓂCiutadella Vila Olímpica)

Fat Tire Bike Tours (Map p276; ☑93 342 92 75; http:// barcelona.fattirebiketours.com; Carrer de Marlet 7; adult/concession/child from €26/24/21; ⊙tours 11am & 4pm; ⓂJaume I, Liceu)

TICKETS & PASSES

The metro, FGC trains, *rodalies/cercanías* (Renfe-run local trains) and buses come under a combined system. Single-ride tickets on all standard transport within Zone 1 cost €2.20.

Targetes are multitrip transport tickets. They are sold at all city-centre metro stations. The prices given here are for travel in Zone 1. Children under four years of age travel free. Options include the following:

➡ Targeta T-10 (€10.20) – 10 rides (each valid for 1¼ hours) on the metro, buses, FGC trains and *rodalies*. You can change between metro, FGC, *rodalies* and buses.

➡ Targeta T-DIA (€8.60) – unlimited travel on all transport for one day.

➡ Two-/three-/four-/five-day tickets (€15/22/28.50/35) – unlimited travel on all transport except the Aerobús; buy them at metro stations and tourist offices.

➡ T-Mes (€54) – 30 days' unlimited use of all public transport.

➡ Targeta T-50/30 (€43.50) – 50 trips within 30 days, valid on all transport.

➡ T-Trimestre (€145.30) – 90 days' unlimited use of all public transport.

For some time the Ajuntament has been studying ways to streamline the various options, under a project named T-Mobilitat. The current transport multi-passes are heavily subsided (54% of the cost of a T-10 is paid by the council) and there is support for a scheme in which visitors pay more than residents, though this is unlikely to come into play before 2019.

My Beautiful Parking (Map p284; ☑93 510 8724; www.mybeautifulparking.com; Carrer de la Bòria 17; bike hire per 2hr/24hr €5/14; ☑10.30am-8pm Mon-Sat, also Sun Apr-Sep; ⓂJaume I)

Rent Electric (☑902 47 44 74; www.rentelectric.com; Plaça del Mar 1; electric bike hire per hour/day from €10/35; ☑10am-7pm; ⓂBarceloneta)

Car & Motorcycle

With the convenience of public transport and the high price of parking in the city, it's unwise to drive in Barcelona. However, if you're planning a road trip outside the city, a car is handy.

Avis, Europcar, National/Atesa and Hertz have desks at El Prat airport, Estació Sants and Estació del Nord. Rental outlets in Barcelona include the following:

Avis (☑902 110275; www.avis.com; Carrer de Còrsega 293-295; ☑8am-9pm Mon-Fri, to 5pm Sat, to 1pm Sun; ⓂDiagonal)

Cooltra (☑93 221 40 70; www.cooltra.com; Via Laietana 6; scooter hire per day €28-35; ☑10am-8pm; ⓂBarceloneta) Rents out scooters and organises scooter tours.

Enterprise (☑93 323 07 01; www.enterprise.es; Carrer de Muntaner 45; ☑8am-8pm Mon-Fri, 9am-1pm Sat; ⓂUniversitat)

Europcar (☑93 302 05 43; www.europcar.es; Gran Via de les Corts Catalanes 680; ☑8am-2pm & 3.30-7.30pm Mon-Fri, 9am-2pm Sat; ⓂGirona)

Hertz (☑902 998707; www.hertz.com; Carrer de Viriat 45; ☑7am-10pm Mon-Fri, to 9pm Sat & Sun; ⓂSants Estació)

MondoRent (☑93 295 32 68; www.mondorent.com; Passeig de Joan de Borbó 80-84; scooter rental per day from €35; ☑10am-8pm; ⓂBarceloneta) Rents out scooters as well as electric bikes.

TOURS

There are many ways to get a more in-depth look at the city, whether on a specialised walking tour through the Ciutat Vella (Old City), on a bicycle excursion around the city centre or on a hop-on, hop-off bus tour all across town.

Walking Tours

The **Oficina d'Informació de Turisme de Barcelona** (☑93 285 38 34; www.barcelonaturisme.com; Plaça de Catalunya 17-S, underground; ☑8.30am-9pm; ⓂCatalunya) organises a series of guided walking tours. One explores the Barri Gòtic (adult/child €16/free); another follows in Picasso's footsteps and winds up at the Museu Picasso, entry to which is included in the price (adult/child €22/7); and a third takes in the main jewels of Modernisme (adult/child €16/free). There's also a 'gourmet' tour of traditional purveyors of fine foodstuffs across the Ciutat Vella (adult/child €22/7). Stop by the tourist office or check online for the latest schedule. Tours typically last two hours and start at the tourist office. There is a 10% discount on all tours if you book online.

More specialised tours are also bookable through the tourist office: themes include running, shopping, literary Barcelona, tapas tours, civil war tours, the Gothic quarter by night, Park Güell and half a dozen other options.

Barcelona Metro Walks

Consists of seven self-guided routes across the city, combining travel on the metro and other public transport as well as stretches on foot. Tourist information points at Plaça de Catalunya and Plaça de Sant Jaume sell the €16 package, which includes a guide, two-day transport pass and map.

My Favourite Things (☑637 265405; www.myft.net; tours from €26) Offers tours for no more than 10 participants based on numerous themes: anything from design to food. Other activities include flamenco and salsa classes, and bicycle rides in and out of Barcelona.

Runner Bean Tours (Map p280;☑636 108776; www.runnerbeantours.com; Carrer del Carme 44; ⊗tours 11am & 4.30pm Apr-Sep, 11am & 3pm Oct-Mar; Ⓜ Liceu) Has several daily thematic tours. Tours are pay-what-you-wish, with a collection taken at the end for the guide. The Gothic Quarter tour explores the Roman and medieval history of Barcelona, visiting highlights in the Ciutat Vella, while the Gaudí tour

takes in the great works of Modernista Barcelona and involves two trips on the metro. There are also ghostly evening tours and a kids and family walking tour; check the website for departure times.

Bicycle Tours

Barcelona is awash with companies offering bicycle tours. Tours typically take two to four hours and generally stick to La Sagrada Família, the Ciutat Vella and the beaches. Operators include the following:

Bike Tours Barcelona (Map p284;☑93 268 21 05; www.biketoursbarcelona.com; Carrer de l'Esparteria 3; per person €25; ⊗10am-7pm; Ⓜ Jaume I)

Barcelona Biking (Map p276;☑656 356300; www.barcelonabiking.com; Baixada de Sant Miquel 6; bike hire per 1/24hr €5/15, tour €21; ⊗10am-8pm, tour 11am; Ⓜ Jaume I, Liceu)

Barcelona By Bike (Map p288;☑671 307 325; www.barcelonabybike.com; Carrer de la Marina 13; tours from €24; Ⓜ Ciutadella Vila Olímpica)

CicloTour (Map p280;☑93 317 19 70; www.barcelonaciclotour.com; Carrer dels Tallers 45; tours €22; ⊗11am, 2pm & 4.30pm daily May-Oct, 11am Mon-Fri, 11am & 4.30pm Sat & Sun Nov, plus 7.30pm Thu-Sun Jun-Sep; Ⓜ Universitat)

Fat Tire Bike Tours (Map p276;☑93 342 92 75; http://barcelona.fattirebiketours.com; Carrer de Marlet 7; adult/concession/child from €26/24/21; ⊗tours 11am & 4pm; Ⓜ Jaume I, Liceu)

Terra BikeTours (Map p294;☑93 416 08 05; www.terrabiketours.com; Carrer de València 337; self-guided tour from €29, 1-day guided tour from €57; Ⓜ Verdaguer) Mostly mountain-bike tours outside the city.

Boat Tours

Several companies take passengers on short jaunts out on the water. These depart several times daily (with many departures in the summer) from Moll de les Drassanes near the southern end of La Rambla. **Las Golondrinas** (Map p286;☑93 442 31 06; www.lasgolondrinas.com; Moll de les Drassanes; adult/child port tour €7.50/2.80, catamaran tour €15/5.50; Ⓜ Drassanes), **BC Naval Tours** (Map p286;☑93 443 60 50; www.barcelonanavaltours.com; Moll de les Drassanes; 40/75min cruise €7.50/20; Ⓜ Drassanes) and other companies offer scenic catamaran trips around the harbour and beyond. Avoid going on a windy day, when the seas can be rough.

Directory A–Z

Discount Cards

The ISIC (International Student Identity Card; www.isic.org) and the European Youth Card (www.euro26.org) are available from most national student organisations and allow discounted access to some sights. Students generally pay a little more than half of adult admission prices, as do children aged under 12 and senior citizens (aged 65 and over) with appropriate ID.

Possession of a **Bus Turístic** (☎93 298 70 00; www.barcelonabusturistic.cat; adult/child 1 day €29/16, 2 days €39/16; ⊙9am-8pm) ticket entitles you to discounts at some museums.

Articket (www.articketbcn.org) gives admission to six sites for €30 and is valid for six months. You can pick up the ticket at the tourist offices at Plaça de Catalunya, Plaça de Sant Jaume and Estació Sants train station and at the museums themselves. The six sights are:

➡ Museu Picasso

➡ Museu Nacional d'Art de Catalunya (MNAC)

➡ Museu d'Art Contemporani de Barcelona (MACBA)

➡ Fundació Antoni Tàpies

➡ Centre de Cultura Contemporània de Barcelona (CCCB)

➡ Fundació Joan Miró

Arqueoticket is for those with an interest in archaeology and ancient history. The ticket (€14.50) is available from participating museums and tourist offices and grants free admission to the following sites:

➡ Museu d'Arqueologia de Catalunya

➡ Museu Egipci

➡ Museu d'Història de Barcelona

➡ Born Centre de Cultura i Memòria

Barcelona Card (www.barcelonacard.com) is handy if you want to see lots in a limited time. It costs €20/45/55/60 for two/three/four/five days. You get free transport, discounted admission (up to 60% off) or free entry to many museums and other sights, and minor discounts on purchases at a small number of shops, restaurants and bars. The card costs about 50% less for children aged four to 12. You can purchase it at tourist offices and online (buying online saves you 5%).

The **Ruta del Modernisme** (www.rutadelmodernisme.com) pack costs €12 and is well worth looking into for visiting Modernista sights at discounted rates.

Electricity

Spain uses 230V/50Hz, like the rest of continental Europe.

Type C
220-230V/50Hz

Emergency & Important Numbers

Ambulance	061
Country code	34
EU standard emergency number	112
International access code	00
Tourist police	93 256 24 30

Money

ATMs

ATMs are widely available (La Rambla has many).

Credit Cards

Major cards such as Visa, MasterCard, Maestro and Cirrus are accepted throughout the city. They can be used in many hotels, restaurants and shops, although there may be a minimum purchase requirement of €5 or €10.

When paying with a credit card, a photo ID is often required, even for chip cards where you're required to enter your PIN (for US travellers without chip cards, just indicate that you'll give a signature).

If your card is lost, stolen or swallowed by an ATM, you can telephone toll-free to immediately stop its use:

Amex (☑900 814500)

Diners Club (☑902 401112)

MasterCard (☑900 971231)

Visa (☑900 991124)

Opening Hours

Standard opening hours are as follows:

Restaurants 1pm to 4pm and 8.30pm to midnight

Shops 9am or 10am to 1.30pm or 2pm and 4pm or 4.30pm to 8pm or 8.30pm Monday to Saturday

Department stores 10am to 10pm Monday to Saturday

Bars 6pm to 2am (to 3am weekends)

Clubs Midnight to 6am Thursday to Saturday

Banks 8.30am to 2pm Monday to Friday; some also 4pm to 7pm Thursday or 9am to 1pm Saturday

Museums & art galleries Vary considerably; generally 10am to 8pm (some shut for lunch around 2pm to 4pm). Many close all day Monday and from 2pm Sunday.

Public Holidays

New Year's Day (Any Nou/Año Nuevo) 1 January

Epiphany/Three Kings' Day (Epifanía or El Dia dels Reis/Día de los Reyes Magos) 6 January

Good Friday (Divendres Sant/Viernes Santo) March/April

Easter Monday (Dilluns de Pasqua Florida) March/April

Labour Day (Dia del Treball/Fiesta del Trabajo) 1 May

Day after Pentecost Sunday (Dilluns de Pasqua Granda) May/June

Feast of St John the Baptist (Dia de Sant Joan/Día de San Juan Bautista) 24 June

Feast of the Assumption (L'Assumpció/La Asunción) 15 August

Catalonia's National Day (Diada Nacional de Catalunya) 11 September

Festes de la Mercè 24 September

Spanish National Day (Festa de la Hispanitat/Día de la Hispanidad) 12 October

All Saints Day (Dia de Tots Sants/Día de Todos los Santos) 1 November

Constitution Day (Día de la Constitución) 6 December

Feast of the Immaculate Conception (La Immaculada Concepció/La Inmaculada Concepción) 8 December

Christmas (Nadal/Navidad) 25 December

Boxing Day/St Stephen's Day (El Dia de Sant Esteve) 26 December

Taxes & Refunds

Value-added tax (VAT) is also known as IVA (*impuesto sobre el valor añadido;* pronounced 'ee-ba'). IVA is 10% on accommodation and restaurant prices and is usually – but not always – included in quoted prices. On most retail goods the IVA is 21%. IVA-free shopping is available in duty-free shops at all airports for people travelling between EU countries.

Non-EU residents are entitled to a refund of the 21% IVA on purchases costing more than €90 from any shop, if the goods are taken out of the EU within three months. Ask the shop for a Cashback (or similar) refund form showing the price and IVA paid for each item and identifying the vendor and purchaser. Then present the form at the customs booth for IVA refunds when you depart from Spain (or elsewhere in the EU). You will need your passport and a boarding card that shows you are leaving the EU, and your luggage (so do this before checking in bags). The officer will stamp the invoice

PRACTICALITIES

→ **Currency** Euro (€)

→ **Smoking** Banned in restaurants and bars.

→ **Newspapers** Major Barcelona newspapers *La Vanguardia* and *El Periódico* are available in Spanish and Catalan. *El País* publishes an online English supplement (elpais.com/elpais/inenglish.html).

and you hand it in at a bank at the departure point to receive a reimbursement.

Telephone

Blue payphones are hard to find but easy to use for international and domestic calls. They accept coins, *tarjetas telefónicas* (phonecards) issued by the national phone company, Telefónica and, in some cases, credit cards. *Tarjetas telefónicas* are sold at post offices and tobacconists.

Various *locutorios* (call centres), which also double as internet centres, are scattered around the Old City, especially El Raval and Sant Pere. Check rates before making calls.

To call Barcelona from outside Spain, dial the international access code, followed by the code for Spain (34) and the full number (including Barcelona's area code, 93, which is an integral part of the number). To make an international call, dial the international access code (00), country code, area code and number.

Mobile Phones

➜ Mobile-phone numbers start with a 6 or 7.

➜ Spain uses GSM 900/1800, compatible with the rest of Europe and Australia but not with the North American GSM 1900 or the system used in Japan. If your phone is tri- or quadriband, you will probably be fine.

➜ You can buy SIM cards and prepaid call time in Spain for your own national mobile phone (provided what you own is a GSM, dual- or tri-band cellular phone and not locked).

➜ You will need your passport to open any kind of mobile-phone account, prepaid or otherwise.

WI-FI ACCESS

Most hotels, hostels, guesthouses and apartment rentals offer their guests wi-fi access (usually for free). A growing array of city bars and restaurants are latching on to the service – look for the black-and-white wi-fi signs.

The city also has dozens of free public wi-fi hotspots, though the signal is generally weak. Look for the small blue signs with the blue 'W' symbol. You can find a complete list of sites at www.bcn.cat/barcelona wifi/en.

Time

➜ Spain is on Central European Time (CET), one hour ahead of GMT/UTC during winter, and two hours ahead during daylight saving (the last Sunday in March to the last Sunday in October).

➜ Most other western European countries are on the same time as Spain year-round. The UK, Ireland and Portugal are one hour behind.

➜ Spaniards use the 24-hour clock for official business (timetables etc) but generally switch to the 12-hour version in daily conversation.

Tourist Information

Several tourist offices operate in Barcelona. A couple of general information telephone numbers worth bearing in mind are 010 and 012. The first is for Barcelona and the other is for all Catalonia (run by the Generalitat). You sometimes strike English speakers, although for the most part operators are Catalan/Spanish bilingual. In addition to tourist offices, information booths operate at Estació del Nord bus station and at Portal de la Pau, at the foot of the Mirador de Colom at the port end of La Rambla. Others set up

at various points in the city centre in summer.

Plaça de Catalunya (☑93 285 38 34; www.barcelonaturisme.com; Plaça de Catalunya 17-S, underground; ⊙8.30am-9pm; Ⓜ Catalunya)

Plaça Sant Jaume (Map p278; ☑93 285 38 34; www.barcelonaturisme.com; Plaça Catalunya 17; ⊙8.30am-8.30pm; Ⓜ Catalunya)

Estació Sants (Map p302; ☑93 285 38 34; www.barcelonaturisme.com; Barcelona Sants; ⊙8.30am-8.30pm; Ⓡ Sants Estació)

El Prat Airport (www.barcelonaturisme.com; ⊙8.30am-8.30pm)

Palau Robert Regional Tourist Office (Map p290; ☑93 238 80 91; www.palaurobert.gencat.cat; Passeig de Gràcia 107; ⊙10am-8pm Mon-Sat, to 2.30pm Sun; Ⓜ Diagonal) Offers a host of material on Catalonia, audiovisual resources, a bookshop and a branch of Turisme Juvenil de Catalunya (for youth travel).

Travellers with Disabilities

Most hotels and public institutions have wheelchair access. All buses in Barcelona are wheelchair accessible and a growing number of metro stations are theoretically wheelchair accessible (generally by lift, although there have been complaints that they are only good for people with prams). Of 156 stations, all but 15 are completely adapted (you can check which ones by looking at a network map at www. tmb.cat/en/transport -accessible). Ticket vending machines in metro stations are adapted for disabled travellers, and have Braille options for those a with visual impairment.

Several taxi companies have adapted vehicles, including **Taxi Amic** (☑93 420 80 88; www.taxi-amic-adaptat.

com) and **Green Taxi** (☑900 827900; www.green taxi.es).

Most street crossings in central Barcelona are wheelchair-friendly.

Visas

Spain is one of 26 member countries of the Schengen Convention, under which 22 EU countries (all but Bulgaria, Cyprus, Ireland, Romania and the UK) plus Iceland, Norway, Liechtenstein and Switzerland have abolished checks at common borders.

The visa situation for entering Spain is as follows:

Citizens or residents of EU & Schengen countries No visa required.

Citizens or residents of Australia, Canada, Israel, Japan, New Zealand & the USA No visa required for tourist visits of up to 90 days out of every 180 days.

Other countries Check with a Spanish embassy or consulate.

To work or study in Spain A special visa may be required – contact a Spanish embassy or consulate before travel.

Language

Catalan (*català*) and Spanish (*español,* more precisely known as *castellano,* or Castilian) both have official-language status in Catalonia. Aranese (*aranés*), which is a dialect of Gascon, is also an official language in the Val d'Aran. In Barcelona, you'll hear as much Spanish as Catalan, so we've provided some Spanish as well as Catalan basics here to get you started.

Most Spanish sounds are pronounced the same as their English counterparts. If you follow our coloured pronunciation guides, you'll be understood. Note that the kh is a throaty sound (like the 'ch' in the Scottish *loch*), ly is pronounced as the 'lli' in 'million', ny as the 'ni' in 'onion', th is pronounced with a lisp, and r is strongly rolled. In our pronunciation guides, the stressed syllables are in italics.

Where necessary, masculine and feminine forms are given for the words and phrases in this chapter, separated by a slash and with the masculine form first, eg *perdido/a* (m/f). Where both polite and informal options are given, they are indicated by the abbreviations 'pol' and 'inf' respectively.

BASICS

Hello.	*Hola.*	o·la
Goodbye.	*Adiós.*	a·dyos
How are you?	*¿Qué tal?*	ke tal
Fine, thanks.	*Bien, gracias.*	byen gra·thyas
Excuse me.	*Perdón.*	per·don
Sorry.	*Lo siento.*	lo see·en·to
Yes./No.	*Sí./No.*	see/no

WANT MORE?

For in-depth language information and handy phrases, check out Lonely Planet's *Spanish phrasebook*. You'll find it at **shop. lonelyplanet.com**, or you can buy Lonely Planet's iPhone phrasebooks at the Apple App Store.

Please.	*Por favor.*	por fa·vor
Thank you.	*Gracias.*	gra·thyas
You're welcome.	*De nada.*	de na·da

My name is ...
Me llamo ... — me lya·mo ...

What's your name?
¿Cómo se llama Usted? ko·mo se lya·ma oo·ste (pol)
¿Cómo te llamas? ko·mo te lya·mas (inf)

Do you speak (English)?
¿Habla (inglés)? a·bla (een·gles) (pol)
¿Hablas (inglés)? a·blas (een·gles) (inf)

I (don't) understand.
Yo (no) entiendo. yo (no) en·tyen·do

ACCOMMODATION

I'd like to book a room.
Quisiera reservar una habitación. kee·sye·ra re·ser·var oo·na a·bee·ta·thyon

How much is it per night/person?
¿Cuánto cuesta por noche/persona? kwan·to kwes·ta por no·che/per·so·na

Does it include breakfast?
¿Incluye el desayuno? een·kloo·ye el de·sa·yoo·no

hotel	*hotel*	o·tel
guesthouse	*pensión*	pen·syon
youth hostel	*albergue juvenil*	al·ber·ge khoo·ve·neel

I'd like a ... room.	*Quisiera una habitación ...*	kee·sye·ra oo·na a·bee·ta·thyon ...
single	*individual*	een·dee·vee·dwal
double	*doble*	do·ble

air-con	*aire acondicionado*	ai·re a·kon·dee·thyo·na·do
bathroom	*baño*	ba·nyo
window	*ventana*	ven·ta·na

KEY PATTERNS

To get by in Spanish, mix and match these simple patterns with words of your choice:

When's (the next flight)?
¿Cuándo sale — kwan·do sa·le
(el próximo vuelo)? — (el prok·see·mo vwe·lo)

Where's (the station)?
¿Dónde está — don·de es·ta
(la estación)? — (la es·ta·thyon)

Where can I (buy a ticket)?
¿Dónde puedo — don·de pwe·do
(comprar — (kom·prar
un billete)? — oon bee·lye·te)

Do you have (a map)?
¿Tiene (un mapa)? — tye·ne (oon ma·pa)

Is there (a toilet)?
¿Hay (servicios)? — ai (ser·vee·thyos)

I'd like (a coffee).
Quisiera (un café). — kee·sye·ra (oon ka·fe)

I'd like (to hire a car).
Quisiera (alquilar — kee·sye·ra (al·kee·lar
un coche). — oon ko·che)

Can I (enter)?
¿Se puede (entrar)? — se pwe·de (en·trar)

Could you please (help me)?
¿Puede (ayudarme), — pwe·de (a·yoo·dar·me)
por favor? — por fa·vor

Do I have to (get a visa)?
¿Necesito — ne·the·see·to
(obtener — (ob·te·ner
un visado)? — oon vee·sa·do)

DIRECTIONS

Where's ...?
¿Dónde está ...? — don·de es·ta ...

What's the address?
¿Cuál es la dirección? — kwal es la dee·rek·thyon

Could you please write it down?
¿Puede escribirlo, — pwe·de es·kree·beer·lo
por favor? — por fa·vor

Can you show me (on the map)?
¿Me lo puede indicar — me lo pwe·de een·dee·kar
(en el mapa)? — (en el ma·pa)

at the corner	en la esquina	en la es·kee·na
at the traffic lights	en el semáforo	en el se·ma·fo·ro
behind	detrás de	de·tras de
far (away)	lejos	le·khos
in front of	enfrente de	en·fren·te de
left	izquierda	eeth·kyer·da
near	cerca	ther·ka
next to	al lado de	al la·do de
opposite	frente a	fren·te a
right	derecha	de·re·cha
straight ahead	todo recto	to·do rek·to

EATING & DRINKING

I'd like to — Quisiera — kee·sye·ra
book a table — reservar una — re·ser·var oo·na
for ... — mesa para ... — me·sa pa·ra ...

  (eight) o'clock — las (ocho) — las (o·cho)
  (two) people — (dos) — (dos)
    personas — per·so·nas

What would you recommend?
¿Qué recomienda? — ke re·ko·myen·da

What's in that dish?
¿Que lleva ese plato? — ke lye·va e·se pla·to

I don't eat ...
No como ... — no ko·mo ...

Cheers!
¡Salud! — sa·loo

That was delicious!
¡Estaba buenísimo! — es·ta·ba bwe·nee·see·mo

Please bring the bill.
Por favor nos trae — por fa·vor nos tra·e
la cuenta. — la kwen·ta

Key Words

appetisers	aperitivos	a·pe·ree·tee·vos
bar	bar	bar
bottle	botella	bo·te·lya
bowl	bol	bol
breakfast	desayuno	de·sa·yoo·no
cafe	café	ka·fe
children's menu	menú infantil	me·noo een·fan·teel
(too/very) cold	(muy) frío	(mooy) free·o
dinner	cena	the·na
food	comida	ko·mee·da
fork	tenedor	te·ne·dor
glass	vaso	va·so
highchair	trona	tro·na
hot (warm)	caliente	ka·lyen·te
knife	cuchillo	koo·chee·lyo
lunch	comida	ko·mee·da
main course	segundo plato	se·goon·do pla·to
market	mercado	mer·ka·do
menu (in English)	menú (en inglés)	oon me·noo (en een·gles)

CATALAN

The recognition of Catalan as an official language in Spain is the end result of a regional government campaign that began when the province gained autonomy at the end of the 1970s. Until the Battle of Muret in 1213, Catalan territory extended across southern France, taking in Roussillon and reaching into the Provence. Catalan was spoken, or at least understood, throughout these territories and in what is now Catalonia and Andorra. In the couple of hundred years that followed, the Catalans spread their language south into Valencia, west into Aragón and east to the Balearic Islands. The language also reached Sicily and Naples, and the Sardinian town of Alghero is still a partly Catalan-speaking outpost today. Catalan is spoken by up to 10 million people in Spain.

In Barcelona you'll hear as much Spanish as Catalan. Your chances of coming across English speakers are also good. Elsewhere in the province, don't be surprised if you get replies in Catalan to your questions in Spanish. However, you'll find that most Catalans will happily speak to you in Spanish, especially once they realise you're a foreigner. This said, the following Catalan phrases might win you a few smiles and perhaps help you make some new friends.

Hello.	*Hola.*	**Monday**	*dilluns*
Goodbye.	*Adéu.*	**Tuesday**	*dimarts*
Yes.	*Sí.*	**Wednesday**	*dimecres*
No.	*No.*	**Thursday**	*dijous*
Please.	*Sisplau./Si us plau.*	**Friday**	*divendres*
Thank you (very much).	*(Moltes) gràcies.*	**Saturday**	*dissabte*
You're welcome.	*De res.*	**Sunday**	*diumenge*
Excuse me.	*Perdoni.*		
May I?/Do you mind?	*Puc?/Em permet?*	1	*un/una (m/f)*
I'm sorry.	*Ho sento./Perdoni.*	2	*dos/dues (m/f)*
		3	*tres*
What's your name?	*Com et dius? (inf)*	4	*quatre*
	Com es diu? (pol)	5	*cinc*
My name is ...	*Em dic ...*	6	*sis*
Where are you from?	*D'on ets?*	7	*set*
Do you speak English?	*Parla anglès?*	8	*vuit*
I understand.	*Ho entenc.*	9	*nou*
I don't understand.	*No ho entenc.*	10	*deu*
Could you speak in	*Pot parlar castellà*	11	*onze*
Castilian, please?	*sisplau?*	12	*dotze*
How do you say ... in	*Com es diu ... en*	13	*tretze*
Catalan?	*català?*	14	*catorze*
		15	*quinze*
I'm looking for ...	*Estic buscant ...*	16	*setze*
How do I get to ...?	*Com puc arribar a ...?*	17	*disset*
Turn left.	*Giri a mà esquerra.*	18	*divuit*
Turn right.	*Giri a mà dreta.*	19	*dinou*
near	*a prop de*	20	*vint*
far	*a lluny de*	100	*cent*

Signs

Abierto	Open
Cerrado	Closed
Entrada	Entrance
Hombres	Men
Mujeres	Women
Prohibido	Prohibited
Salida	Exit
Servicios/Aseos	Toilets

plate	*plato*	*pla*·to
restaurant	*restaurante*	res·tow·*ran*·te
spoon	*cuchara*	koo·*cha*·ra
supermarket	*supermercado*	soo·per·mer·*ka*·do
vegetarian food	*comida vegetariana*	ko·*mee*·da ve·khe·ta·*rya*·na
with/without	*con/sin*	kon/seen

Meat & Fish

beef	*carne de vaca*	*kar*·ne de *va*·ka
chicken	*pollo*	*po*·lyo
duck	*pato*	*pa*·to
lamb	*cordero*	kor·*de*·ro
lobster	*langosta*	lan·*gos*·ta
pork	*cerdo*	*ther*·do
prawns	*camarones*	ka·ma·*ro*·nes
tuna	*atún*	a·*toon*
turkey	*pavo*	*pa*·vo
veal	*ternera*	ter·*ne*·ra

Fruit & Vegetables

apple	*manzana*	man·*tha*·na
apricot	*albaricoque*	al·ba·ree·*ko*·ke
artichoke	*alcachofa*	al·ka·*cho*·fa
asparagus	*espárragos*	es·*pa*·ra·gos
banana	*plátano*	*pla*·ta·no
beans	*judías*	khoo·*dee*·as
beetroot	*remolacha*	re·mo·*la*·cha
cabbage	*col*	kol
carrot	*zanahoria*	tha·na·o·*rya*
celery	*apio*	*a*·pyo
cherry	*cereza*	the·*re*·tha
corn	*maíz*	ma·*eeth*
cucumber	*pepino*	pe·*pee*·no
fruit	*fruta*	*froo*·ta
grape	*uvas*	*oo*·vas

lemon	*limón*	lee·*mon*
lentils	*lentejas*	len·*te*·khas
lettuce	*lechuga*	le·*choo*·ga
mushroom	*champiñón*	cham·pee·*nyon*
nuts	*nueces*	nwe·thes
onion	*cebolla*	the·*bo*·lya
orange	*naranja*	na·*ran*·kha
peach	*melocotón*	me·lo·ko·*ton*
peas	*guisantes*	gee·*san*·tes
(red/green) pepper	*pimiento (rojo/verde)*	pee·*myen*·to (ro·kho/ver·de)
pineapple	*piña*	*pee*·nya
plum	*ciruela*	theer·*we*·la
potato	*patata*	pa·*ta*·ta
pumpkin	*calabaza*	ka·la·*ba*·tha
spinach	*espinacas*	es·pee·*na*·kas
strawberry	*fresa*	*fre*·sa
tomato	*tomate*	to·*ma*·te
vegetable	*verdura*	ver·*doo*·ra
watermelon	*sandía*	san·*dee*·a

Other

bread	*pan*	pan
butter	*mantequilla*	man·te·*kee*·lya
cheese	*queso*	*ke*·so
egg	*huevo*	*we*·vo
honey	*miel*	myel
jam	*mermelada*	mer·me·*la*·da
oil	*aceite*	a·*they*·te
pasta	*pasta*	*pas*·ta
pepper	*pimienta*	pee·*myen*·ta
rice	*arroz*	a·*roth*
salt	*sal*	sal
sugar	*azúcar*	a·*thoo*·kar
vinegar	*vinagre*	vee·*na*·gre

Drinks

beer	*cerveza*	ther·*ve*·tha
coffee	*café*	ka·*fe*
(orange) juice	*zumo (de naranja)*	*thoo*·mo (de na·*ran*·kha)
milk	*leche*	*le*·che
tea	*té*	te
(mineral) water	*agua (mineral)*	*a*·gwa (mee·ne·*ral*)
(red) wine	*vino (tinto)*	*vee*·no (*teen*·to)
(white) wine	*vino (blanco)*	*vee*·no (*blan*·ko)

EMERGENCIES

| Help! | ¡Socorro! | so·ko·ro |
| Go away! | ¡Vete! | ve·te |

Call ...!	¡Llame a ...!	lya·me a ...
a doctor	un médico	oon me·dee·ko
the police	la policía	la po·lee·thee·a

I'm lost.
Estoy perdido/a. es·toy per·dee·do/a (m/f)

I had an accident.
He tenido un e te·nee·do oon
accidente. ak·thee·den·te

I'm ill.
Estoy enfermo/a. es·toy en·fer·mo/a (m/f)

It hurts here.
Me duele aquí. me dwe·le a·kee

I'm allergic to (antibiotics).
Soy alérgico/a a soy a·ler·khee·ko/a a
(los antibióticos). (los an·tee·byo·tee·kos) (m/f)

SHOPPING & SERVICES

I'd like to buy ...
Quisiera comprar ... kee·sye·ra kom·prar ...

I'm just looking.
Sólo estoy mirando. so·lo es·toy mee·ran·do

Can I look at it?
¿Puedo verlo? pwe·do ver·lo

I don't like it.
No me gusta. no me goos·ta

How much is it?
¿Cuánto cuesta? kwan·to kwes·ta

That's too expensive.
Es muy caro. es mooy ka·ro

Can you lower the price?
¿Podría bajar un po·dree·a ba·khar oon
poco el precio? po·ko el pre·thyo

There's a mistake in the bill.
Hay un error en ai oon e·ror en
la cuenta. la kwen·ta

ATM	cajero automático	ka·khe·ro ow·to·ma·tee·ko
internet cafe	cibercafé	thee·ber·ka·fe
post office	correos	ko·re·os
tourist office	oficina de turismo	o·fee·thee·na de too·rees·mo

TIME & DATES

What time is it?
¿Qué hora es? ke o·ra es

It's (10) o'clock.
Son (las diez). son (las dyeth)

Half past (one).
Es (la una) es (la oo·na)
y media. ee me·dya

morning	mañana	ma·nya·na
afternoon	tarde	tar·de
evening	noche	no·che
yesterday	ayer	a·yer
today	hoy	oy
tomorrow	mañana	ma·nya·na

Monday	lunes	loo·nes
Tuesday	martes	mar·tes
Wednesday	miércoles	myer·ko·les
Thursday	jueves	khwe·bes
Friday	viernes	vyer·nes
Saturday	sábado	sa·ba·do
Sunday	domingo	do·meen·go

January	enero	e·ne·ro
February	febrero	fe·bre·ro
March	marzo	mar·tho
April	abril	a·breel
May	mayo	ma·yo
June	junio	khoo·nyo
July	julio	khoo·lyo
August	agosto	a·gos·to
September	septiembre	sep·tyem·bre
October	octubre	ok·too·bre
November	noviembre	no·vyem·bre
December	diciembre	dee·thyem·bre

TRANSPORT

boat	barco	bar·ko
bus	autobús	ow·to·boos
plane	avión	a·vyon
train	tren	tren

first	primer	pree·mer
last	último	ool·tee·mo
next	próximo	prok·see·mo

Question Words		
What?	¿Qué?	ke
When?	¿Cuándo?	kwan·do
Where?	¿Dónde?	don·de
Who?	¿Quién?	kyen
Why?	¿Por qué?	por ke

I want to go to ...
Quisiera ir a ...   kee·*sye*·ra eer a ...

What time does it arrive/leave?
¿A qué hora llega/sale?   a ke o·ra *lye*·ga/*sa*·le

Does it stop at ...?
¿Para en ...?   *pa*·ra en ...

Can you tell me when we get to ...?
¿Puede avisarme   pwe·de a·vee·*sar*·me
cuando lleguemos a ...? *kwan*·do lye·*ge*·mos a ...

What stop is this?
¿Cuál es esta parada?   kwal es es·ta pa·*ra*·da

I want to get off here.
Quiero bajarme aquí.   *kye*·ro ba·*khar*·me a·*kee*

a ... ticket	*un billete de ...*	oon bee·*lye*·te de ...
1st-class	*primera clase*	pree·*me*·ra *kla*·se
2nd-class	*segunda clase*	se·*goon*·da *kla*·se
one-way	*ida*	ee·da
return	*ida y vuelta*	ee·da ee *vwel*·ta
aisle seat	*asiento de pasillo*	a·*syen*·to de pa·*see*·lyo
cancelled	*cancelado*	kan·the·*la*·do
delayed	*retrasado*	re·tra·*sa*·do
platform	*plataforma*	pla·ta·*for*·ma
ticket office	*taquilla*	ta·*kee*·lya
timetable	*horario*	o·*ra*·ryo
train station	*estación de trenes*	es·ta·*thyon* de *tre*·nes
window seat	*asiento junto a la ventana*	a·*syen*·to *khoon*·to a la ven·*ta*·na
I'd like to hire a ...	*Quisiera alquilar ...*	kee·*sye*·ra al·*kee*·lar ...
bicycle	*una bicicleta*	*oo*·na bee·thee·*kle*·ta
car	*un coche*	oon *ko*·che
motorcycle	*una moto*	*oo*·na *mo*·to

Numbers

1	*uno*	*oo*·no
2	*dos*	dos
3	*tres*	tres
4	*cuatro*	*kwa*·tro
5	*cinco*	*theen*·ko
6	*seis*	seys
7	*siete*	*sye*·te
8	*ocho*	*o*·cho
9	*nueve*	*nwe*·ve
10	*diez*	dyeth
20	*veinte*	*veyn*·te
30	*treinta*	*treyn*·ta
40	*cuarenta*	kwa·*ren*·ta
50	*cincuenta*	theen·*kwen*·ta
60	*sesenta*	se·*sen*·ta
70	*setenta*	se·*ten*·ta
80	*ochenta*	o·*chen*·ta
90	*noventa*	no·*ven*·ta
100	*cien*	thyen
1000	*mil*	meel

diesel	*gasóleo*	ga·so·lyo
helmet	*casco*	*kas*·ko
mechanic	*mecánico*	me·*ka*·nee·ko
petrol/gas	*gasolina*	ga·so·*lee*·na
service station	*gasolinera*	ga·so·lee·*ne*·ra

(How long) Can I park here?
¿(Por cuánto tiempo)   (por *kwan*·to *tyem*·po)
Puedo aparcar aquí?   pwe·do a·par·*kar* a·*kee*

The car has broken down.
El coche se ha averiado.   el *ko*·che se a a·ve·*rya*·do

I have a flat tyre.
Tengo un pinchazo.   *ten*·go oon peen·*cha*·tho

I've run out of petrol.
Me he quedado sin gasolina.   me e ke·*da*·do seen ga·so·*lee*·na

GLOSSARY

Items listed below are in Catalan/Spanish (Castilian) where they start with the same letter. Where the two terms start with different letters, or where only the Catalan or the Spanish term is provided, they are listed separately and marked (C) for Catalan or (S) for Spanish. If an entry is not marked at all, it is because it takes the same form in both languages.

ajuntament/ayuntamiento – town hall

artesonado (S) – Mudéjar wooden ceiling with interlaced beams leaving a pattern of spaces for decoration

avinguda (C) – avenue

barcelonin (C) – inhabitant/native of Barcelona

Barcino – Roman name for Barcelona

barri/barrio – neighbourhood, quarter of Barcelona

caganer (C) – the crapper, a character appearing in Catalan nativity scenes

capella/capilla – chapel

carrer/calle – street

casa – house

castellers (C) – human-castle builders

cercanías (S) – local trains serving Barcelona's airport, suburbs and some outlying towns

comte/conde – count

correfoc (C) – appearance of firework-spouting devils at festivals; literally 'fire runs'

El Call (C) – the Jewish quarter in medieval Barcelona

església (C) – church

farmàcia/farmacia – pharmacy

festa/fiesta – festival, public holiday or party

FGC (C) – Ferrocarrils de la Generalitat de Catalunya; local trains operating alongside the Metro in Barcelona

fundació/fundación – foundation

garum – a spicy sauce made from fish entrails, found throughout the Roman Empire

gegants – huge figures paraded at *festes*

Generalitat (C) – Catalan regional government

guiri – foreigner (somewhat pejorative)

hostal – commercial establishment providing one- to three-star accommodation

iglesia (S) – church

IVA – *impost sobre el valor afegit/impuesto sobre el valor añadido*, or value-added tax

masia – Catalan country farmhouse

mercat/mercado – market

Modernisme (C) – the turn-of-the-19th-century artistic style, influenced by art nouveau, whose leading practitioner was Antoni Gaudí

Modernista – an exponent of Modernisme

Mudéjar (S) – a Muslim living under Christian rule in medieval Spain; also refers to their decorative style of architecture

palau (C) – palace

passatge (C) – laneway

pensió/pensión – commercial establishment providing one- to three-star accommodation

plaça/plaza – plaza

platja/playa – beach

Renaixença – rebirth of interest in Catalan literature, culture and language in the second half of the 19th century

rodalies (C) – see *cercanías*

saló (C) – hall

sardana – traditional Catalan folk dance

s/n (S) – *sin número* (without number)

tablao – restaurant where flamenco is performed

teatre – theatre

terrassa/terazza – terrace; often means a cafe or bar's outdoor tables

trencadís – a Modernista style of mosaic, created using broken tiles

turista – second class; economy class

Behind the Scenes

SEND US YOUR FEEDBACK

We love to hear from travellers – your comments keep us on our toes and help make our books better. Our well-travelled team reads every word on what you loved or loathed about this book. Although we cannot reply individually to your submissions, we always guarantee that your feedback goes straight to the appropriate authors, in time for the next edition. Each person who sends us information is thanked in the next edition – the most useful submissions are rewarded with a selection of digital PDF chapters.

Visit **lonelyplanet.com/contact** to submit your updates and suggestions or to ask for help. Our award-winning website also features inspirational travel stories, news and discussions.

Note: We may edit, reproduce and incorporate your comments in Lonely Planet products such as guidebooks, websites and digital products, so let us know if you don't want your comments reproduced or your name acknowledged. For a copy of our privacy policy visit lonelyplanet.com/privacy.

WRITER THANKS

Sally Davies

Thanks to all those on the ground fielding my queries – in no particular order: Maria Parrilla, Dolors Bas, Vera de Frutos, Stefanie Roth, Mónica Homedes, Enrichetta Cardinale, Cristina Rodenas, Gustavo Sánchez and Vanessa Ferrer. Thanks to Mary-Ann Gallagher for suggestions, to Tom Stainer for his patience and, most of all, to my untiring research companion, Tess O'Donovan.

Catherine Le Nevez

Moltes gràcies/muchas gracias/merci beaucoup first and foremost to Julian, and to all of the locals, tourism professionals and fellow travellers who provided insights, inspiration and good times.

Huge thanks too to destination editor Tom Stainer, my co-author Sally Davies and all at LP. As ever, *merci encore* to my parents, brother, *belle-sœur, neveu* and *nièce*.

Isabella Noble

Thanks to Sally, Damien, Javi and Olga in Girona, Josep and Ana in Espot, Llucia in Deltebre and the team who fixed my car brakes in Begur.

ACKNOWLEDGEMENTS

Images of Casa Batlló used with kind permission of CASA BATLLÓ S.L.U.

Cover photograph: Interior of the Basílica de la Sagrada Família. Wendy Rauw Photography/Getty ©

Illustrations pp58–9, 130–1, 156–7 by Javier Zarracina

THIS BOOK

This 11th edition of Lonely Planet's *Barcelona* guidebook was researched and written by Sally Davies, Catherine Le Nevez and Isabella Noble. The previous edition was written by Regis St Louis and Sally Davies. This guidebook was produced by the following:

Destination Editor
Tom Stainer

Senior Product Editor
Genna Patterson

Product Editor Will Allen

Regional Senior Cartographer Anthony Phelan

Cartographers Mark Griffiths, Mick Garrett, Hunor Csutoros

Book Designer Michael Weldon

Assisting Editors Bruce Evans, Samantha Forge, Emma Gibbs, Carly Hall, Jodie Martire, Sarah Reid, Gabrielle Stefanos

Cover Researcher Naomi Parker

Thanks to Joe Bindloss, Josep Maria Braut, Kiko Cisneros, Grace Dobell, Fiona Flores Watson, Nacho Garcia, Gemma Graham, JT Mokko, Virginia Moreno, Jenna Myers, Tanya Parker, Wibowo Rusli

See also separate subindexes for:

🍴 **EATING P270**

🍷 **DRINKING & NIGHTLIFE P271**

☆ **ENTERTAINMENT P272**

🔒 **SHOPPING P272**

🏃 **SPORTS & ACTIVITIES P273**

🛏 **SLEEPING P273**

Index

A

Abellan, Carles 7, 31

accessible travel 257-8

accommodation 15, 49, 212-20, *see also* Sleeping *subindex*

language 259

activities 22-4, *see also* Sports & Activities *subindex*

Adrià, Albert 7, 13, 31

Ajuntament 64

Antic Hospital de la Santa Creu 83

architecture 21, 36, 237-42, *see also* Modernisme

area codes 255

art 21, 243-4

Articket BCN 83

Arxiu Fotogràfic de Barcelona 98-9

ATMs 256

B

Banys Àrabs (Girona) 202-3

Barcelona Head 112

Barceloneta & the Waterfront 53, 107-24, **107**, **117**, **286-7**, **288-9**, **51**, **239**

accommodation 217

cycling 117

drinking & nightlife 108, 119-21

entertainment 121-2

food 108, 114-19

highlights 107-8, 109, 110

shopping 108, 122-3

sights 109-14

sports & activities 117, 124

transport 108

Sights 000

Map Pages **000**

Photo Pages **000**

Barri Gòtic, *see* La Rambla & Barri Gòtic

bars 38, 39, 48, *see also* Drinking & Nightlife *subindex*

Basílica de Santa Maria del Mar 94, **94**

Basílica de Santa Maria del Pi 63

Basílica de Sant Feliu (Girona) 203

Basílica del Sagrat Cor de Jesús 180, **3**

beaches 49, 110, 117, 209, **110**

beer 13, 40

Bellesguard 175

bicycle travel, *see* cycling

boat travel 254

books 222, 236

Born Centre de Cultura i Memòria 97

boutiques 45

budget 14, 29, 31, 35, 213, 255

Bunkers del Carmel 163

bus travel 250, 251, 252

business hours 31, 38, 45, 64, 256

C

cable cars 26, 252

cafes 36, 39, **17**, *see also* Eating *and* Drinking & Nightlife *subindexes*

CaixaForum 188

Cambril de la Mare de Déu (Figueres) 207

Camp Nou 9, 181, **9**

Camp Nou, Pedralbes & La Zona Alta 53, 171-82, **171**, **298-9**, **300**

accommodation 220

drinking & nightlife 172, 180-1

entertainment 181

food 172, 176-80

highlights 171-2, 174, 176

shopping 181-2

sights 174-6

sports & activities 182

transport 172

Capella de Santa Llúcia 64-5

Capella Reial de Santa Àgata 64

car travel 253

Carrer de Montcada 96

Casa Amatller 132, **157**

Casa Batlló 133, **151**, **157**

Casa Bruno Cuadros **58**

Casa de la Seda 98

Casa de l'Ardiaca 67

Casa de les Punxes 135

Casa Golferichs 133

Casa Lleó Morera 132

Casa Llotja de Mar 99

Casa Museu Dalí (Port Lligat) 205

Casa Vicens 13, 162

Casa-Museu Gaudí 161

Castell de Montjuïc 188-9, **12**

Castell de Púbol (La Pera) 205

Castell de Sant Ferran (Figueres) 205-6

castells 24, 236

Catalan culture 235-6

cuisine 7, 31, 32, 34, 36, 7, **30**, **31**, **33**, **35**

independence movement 223, 234

language 235-6, 259, 261

Catedral, *see* La Catedral

Catedral de Girona 201

Catedral de Tarragona 210

cell phones 257

Cementiri del Poblenou 113

Cementiri del Sud-Oest 190-1

Centre Cívic Can Deu 175

Centre d'Art Santa Mònica 57

Centre de Cultura Contemporània de Barcelona 83

Centre de la Imatge 57

children, travel with 25-6

chocolate 36, 72

churches *see individual churches*

cinemas 42, 43

classical music 41, 43, 247

climate 15, 22-4

clubs 39, 48, 49, *see also* Drinking & Nightlife *subindex*

cocktails 40

Col·lecció de Carrosses Fúnebres 191

Col·legi de Arquitectes 68

Col·legi de les Teresianes 176

Colònia Güell 189, **8**

CosmoCaixa 26, 176

costs 14, 213, 255, 256

credit cards 256

crime, *see* safety

culture 222-3, 235-6

currency 14

cycling 42, 117, 252-3, 254

D

Dalí, Salvador 205, 243-4

dance 40, 41, 236, 245-8, **245**, *see also* flamenco, sardana

department stores 45

design 21, 45, 47

disabilities, travellers with 257-8

Domènech i Montaner, Lluís 154

Domus de Sant Honorat 67

drinking & nightlife 21, 37-40, **39**, *see also* Drinking & Nightlife *subindex*, *individual neighbourhoods*

E

economy 222-3

Edge Brewing 112

El Call 68

El Fòrum 113-14
El Fossar de les Moreres 98
El Poblenou Platges 110
El Raval 52, 78-89, **78**, **85**, **280-1**
  accommodation 216
  drinking & nightlife 79, 86-8
  entertainment 88-9
  food 79, 84-6
  highlights 78-9, 80, 81, 82
  shopping 79, 89
  sights 80-3
  sports & activities 89
  transport 79
  walks 85
electricity 255
emergencies 255, 263
entertainment 41-3, *see also individual neighbourhoods, Entertainment subindex*
Església de Betlem 56, **58**
Església de la Mercè 65
Església de la Puríssima Concepció I Assumpció de Nostra Senyora 135
Església de les Saleses 136
Església de Sant Bartomeu i Santa Tecla (Sitges) 209
Església de Sant Joan 162
Església de Sant Pau del Camp 83
Església de Sants Just i Pastor 65-7
etiquette 17
events 22-4, 28, 29, 48, 236, **3**, **24**, **235**

F
fashion 21, 47
Feria d'Artesanía del Palau de Mar 123
Festa Major de Gràcia 23, **24**
Festes de la Mercè 23, **3**
Festes de Santa Eulàlia 22
Festival del Grec 23
festivals 22-4, 28, 29, 48, 236, **3**, **24**, **235**
Figueres 204-6
film 222
flamenco 41, 43, 248, **245**
Font Màgica 26, 188

Sights 000
Map Pages 000
Photo Pages 000

food 27-8, 28, 30-6, **3**, **101**, *see also Eating subindex, individual neighbourhoods*
  Catalan cuisine 7, 31, 32, 34, 36, **7**, **30**, **31**, **33**, **35**
  language 260, 262
  trucks 13
football 28, 42, 236, *see also Camp Nou*
Franco, Francisco 113, 230-3
free attractions 29
Fundació Antoni Tàpies 132
Fundació Foto Colectania 98
Fundació Fran Daurel 189
Fundació Joan Miró 185
Fundació Suñol 135
Funicular de Sant Joan (Montserrat) 207

G
galleries 21, *see also individual galleries*
gardens 20 *see also individual gardens*
Gaudí, Antoni 150-5
Gaudí Experience 162
gay travellers 48-9
Girona 201-4, **202**
Gràcia & Park Güell 53, 158-70, **158**, **164**, **296**
  accommodation 219
  drinking & nightlife 159, 166-8
  entertainment 168
  food 159, 162-6
  highlights 158-9, 160-1
  shopping 159, 168-70
  sights 160-2
  sports & activities 170
  transport 159
  walks 164
Gran Teatre del Liceu 62-3, **58**

H
Hash, Marihuana & Hemp Museum 64
history 224-34
Homenatge a la Barceloneta 112
Homenatge a la Natació 112

I
Institut d'Estudis Catalans 83
itineraries 18-19 *see also walks*

J
Jardí Botànic 188
Jardins de Joan Brossa 189
Jardins de Mossèn Cinto de Verdaguer 190
Jardins de Mossèn Costa i Llobera 192
Jardins del Laberint d'Horta 179, **20**
Jardins del Mirador 188
Jardins del Palau de Pedralbes 175
jazz music 43

L
La Capella 83
La Catedral 11, 60-1, **11**, **60**
La Dreta de L'Eixample
  drinking & nightlife 144-5
  food 139-42
  sights 134-6
La Fura dels Baus 42
La Pedrera 134, **155**, **156**
La Rambla 10, 56-7, 58-9, **58-9**, **11**, **58-9**
La Rambla & Barri Gòtic 52, 54-77, **54**, **66**, **276-7**, **5**, **237**
  accommodation 215-16
  drinking & nightlife 55, 72-4
  entertainment 74-5
  food 55, 69-72
  highlights 54-5, 56-7, 60-1, 63, 65
  shopping 75-7
  sights 56-69
  sports & activities 77
  transport 55
  walks 66
La Ribera 53, 90-106, **90**, **100**, **284-5**
  accommodation 216
  drinking & nightlife 91, 103-4
  entertainment 104
  food 91, 99-103
  highlights 90-1, 92-3, 94, 95
  shopping 104-6
  sights 92-9
  sports & activities 106
  transport 91
  walks 100-1
La Sagrada Família 7, 127-9, 130-1, **6-7**, **127**, **130-1**, **153**, **156**

La Sagrada Família & L'Eixample 53, 125-49, **125**, **140**, **147**, **290-1**, **294-5**
  accommodation 217-19
  drinking & nightlife 126, 142-5
  entertainment 145
  food 126, 136-42
  highlights 125-6, 127-9, 133, 134
  shopping 126, 145-9
  sights 127-36
  sports & activities 149
  transport 126
  walks 140, 146
La Zona Alta, *see Camp Nou, Pedralbes & La Zona Alta*
L'Anella Olímpica & Estadi Olímpic 190
languages 14, 17, 235-6, 259-65
L'Aquàrium 26, 111
L'Eixample, *see La Sagrada Família & L'Eixample*
lesbian travellers 48-9
L'Esquerra de L'Eixample
  drinking & nightlife 142-4
  food 136-9
  sights 132-4
LGBT+ travellers 48-9
local life 27-8
López y López, Antonio 98

M
MACBA 81, **81**
malls 46
markets 20, 34, 46, 47, 123
Mercat de la Boqueria 10, 80, **10**, **34**, **58**, **80**
Mercat de la Llibertat 162
Mercat de Santa Caterina 96-7
metro, *see train travel*
microbreweries 13
Mirador de Colom 112, **58**
Miró, Joan 243-4
mobile phones 257
Modernisme 9, 140, 150-7, 156-7, 240, **156-7**, **8**, **151**, **152-3**, **156-7**, *see also architecture*
Monestir de Montserrat 207
Monestir de Sant Pere de Galligants (Girona) 203
Monestir de Sant Pere de les Puelles 97

money 14, 17, 213, 255, 256
Montjuïc, Poble Sec & Sant
  Antoni 12, 53, 183-99,
  183, **194**, **302-3**
  accommodation 220
  drinking & nightlife 12,
    184, 196-8
  entertainment 198
  food 184, 192-6
  highlights 183-4, 185,
    186-7
  shopping 199
  sights 185-92
  sports & activities 199
  transport 184
  walks 194
Montserrat 206-8
Mosaïc de Miró 57
motorcycle travel 253
MUHBA Refugi 307 191
Museu Blau 114
Museu Can Framis 112
Museu d'Arqueologia de
  Catalunya 190
Museu d'Art de Girona 203
Museu de Cera 69
Museu de Cultures del
  Món 98
Museu de la Música 113
Museu de la Xocolata 26, 97
Museu de l'Empordà
  (Figueres) 206
Museu de l'Eròtica 67
Museu de Montserrat 207
Museu del Cau Ferrat
  (Sitges) 208
Museu del Cinema (Girona)
  201-2
Museu del Disseny de
  Barcelona 112-13, **239**
Museu del Joguet
  (Figueres) 205
Museu del Modernisme
  Barcelona 133
Museu del Perfum 134
Museu d'Història de
  Barcelona 65
Museu d'Història de
  Catalunya 111
Museu d'Història de Girona
  (Girona) 203
Museu d'Història de Tarra-
  gona (Tarragona) 210
Museu d'Història dels
  Jueus (Girona) 201
Museu Diocesà/Gaudí Exhi-
  bition Center 68-9
Museu Egipci 135
Museu Etnològic 190
Museu Europeu d'Art
  Modern 98

Museu Frederic Marès 63
Museu Maricel del Mar
  (Sitges) 209
Museu Marítim 109
Museu-Monestir de Pedral-
  bes 174, **174**
Museu Nacional
  Arqueològic de
  Tarragona 210
Museu Nacional d'Art de
  Catalunya 186-7, **186**
Museu Olímpic i de
  l'Esport 191
Museu Picasso 9, 92-3,
  8, **92**
museums 21, see also
  individual museums
music 41, 43, 245-7

N
newspapers 256
nightlife, see drinking
  & nightlife

O
Observatori Fabra 175-6
opening hours 31, 38, 45,
  64, 256
opera 41, 247
Orwell, George 57

P
paddleboarding 13
Palau Centelles 65
Palau de la Generalitat 62
Palau de la Música
  Catalana 95, 97, **95**,
  151, **157**
Palau de la Virreina 57
Palau del Baró Quadras 135
Palau del Lloctinent 67
Palau Episcopal 67
Palau Güell 82, **82**, **157**
Palau Moja 56
Palau Montaner 136
Palau Robert 133
Parc d'Atraccions 26, 180
Parc de Collserola 26, 180
Parc de Joan Miró 190
Parc de la Ciutadella 26, 96
Parc de la Creueta del Coll
  26, 175
Parc de l'Espanya
  Industrial 191-2
Parc del Centre del
  Poblenou 113
Parc Natural de la Mun-
  tanya de Montserrat
  (Figueres) 206

Park Güell, see Gràcia &
  Park Güell
Park Güell 160-1, **152-3**,
  155, **156**, **160**
parks & gardens 20 see
  also individual parks
  and gardens
Pavelló Mies van der
  Rohe 191
Pavellons Güell 175
Pedralbes, see Camp
  Nou, Pedralbes &
  La Zona Alta
Picasso, Pablo 92-3, 243-4
Plaça de Catalunya 134
Plaça de la Sardana 189
Plaça de Sant Jaume 64
Plaça de Sant Josep
  Oriol 65
Plaça del Rei 62
Plaça Reial 62, **37**, **58**
planning
  Barcelona basics 14-15
  Barcelona's neighbour-
    hoods 52-3
  budgeting 14-15, 29, 255
  children, travel with 25-6
  festivals & events 22-4
  first-time travellers 16-17
  itineraries 18-19
  local life 27-8
  repeat visitors 13
  travel seasons 14-15,
    22-4
  websites 14-15
Platja de la Barceloneta
  111, **110**
Platja de l'Eixample 136
Poble Espanyol 26, 189-
  90, **25**
Poblenou 13 see also
  Barceloneta & the
  Waterfront
Poble Sec, see Montjuïc,
  Poble Sec & Sant
  Antoni
politics 222-3
population 223
Port Antic 123
Port Olímpic, Poblenou & El
  Fòrum see Barceloneta
  & the Waterfront
Port Vell & Barceloneta
  see Barceloneta & the
  Waterfront
Pretori i Circ Romans
  (Tarragona) 211
Primavera Sound 23
public holidays 256
Puig i Cadafalch,
  Josep 154

R
Rambla, see La Rambla
Rambla del Raval 83
Recinte Modernista de
  Sant Pau 134-5
religion 223
Roman walls 67
rumba 247

S
safety 16
Sagrada Família, see La
  Sagrada Família
Sala Fundación
  MAPFRE 132
Sant Antoni, see Montjuïc,
  Poble Sec & Sant Antoni
sardana 28, 41-2, 236, 248
Sarrià 177
shopping 44-7, 49, **44**,
  see also Shopping
  subindex, individual
  neighbourhoods
  language 263
Sinagoga Major 68
Sitges 48, 208-9
smoking 256
soccer, see football
souvenirs 47
Spanish language 259-65
stand-up paddleboarding,
  see paddleboarding
SUP, see paddleboarding

T
tapas 27, 32, 35, **3**
Tarragona 210-11
taxes 17, 256-7
taxis 250, 251, 252
Teatre-Museu Dalí
  (Figueres) 205
Teleférico del Puerto
  111-12, 192
telephone services 257
Temple d'August 62
theatre 41, 43
time 257
tipping 17
Torre de Collserola 180
Torre Glòries 114
tourist information 257
tours 253-4
train travel 251, 251-2
trams 252
travel to/from Barcelona
  15, 250-1
travel within Barcelona 15,
  26, 251-3
Turó de la Rovira 163

U

Universitat de Barcelona 133-4

V

vegetarian travellers 13, 36
Verdi 168
Via Sepulcral Romana 69
vintage fashion 45-6, 47
visas 258

W

walks 29, 253-4
El Raval 85
Gràcia & Park Güell 164
La Rambla & Barri Gòtic 66
La Ribera 100-1
La Sagrada Família & L'Eixample 140, 146
Montjuïc, Poble Sec & Sant Antoni 194
Sarrià 177
waterfront, see Barceloneta & the Waterfront
weather 15, 22-4
websites 14, 28, 38, 49, 212
wi-fi 257
wine 27, 38, 40, 47

Z

Zoo de Barcelona 26, 97-8

✗ EATING

A

5º Pino 178
1881 116
ABaC 179
Acontraluz 177
Aguaribay 118-19
Agust Gastrobar 193
Ajoblanco 178
Alcoba Azul 70
Alkímia 196
Allium 72
Amaltea 137
AQ (Tarragona) 211
Arcs Restaurant (Tarragona) 211

Sights 000
Map Pages **000**
Photo Pages 000

Aspic 178
Auto Rosellon 137

B

Baluard Barceloneta 115
Bangkok Cafe 177-8
Bar Bodega Quimet 163
Bar Cañete 86
Bar del Convent 25
Bar del Pla 102
Bar Kasparo 84
Bar Muy Buenas 84
Bar Pinotxo 84
Bar Ramón 195
Bar Tomàs 177
Barquet (Tarragona) 211
Barraca 115
Basílico 195
Belmonte 70
Benedict 69
Bilbao 166
Bitácora 115
Black Remedy 71
Bodega 1900 195
Bodega Sepúlveda 193-5
Bormuth 99
Botafumeiro 166
Bubó 100

C

Cafè Camèlia 165
Cafè de l'Acadèmia 70
Cafe Emma 141
Café Godot 165
Café Le Bistrot (Girona) 204
Café San Telmo 137
Cal Boter 165-6
Cal Cuc 118
Cal Pep 102
Can Cortada 179
Can Culleretes 70
Can Dendê 118
Can Kenji 141
Can Lluís 84-6
Can Majó 116
Can Maño 114
Can Recasens 119
Can Ros 116-18
Can Solé 116
Can Travi Nou 166
Cantina Machito 165
Cantina Mexicana 139-41
Caravelle 84
Casa Alfonso 141
Casa Amalia 141
Casa Calvet 142
Casa Delfín 101-2

Casa de Tapas Cañota 193
Casa Portuguesa 165
Casa Xica 193
Casablanca (Sitges) 209
Cat Bar 99
Cererìa 71
Cervecería Taller de Tapas 70
Cerveseria Brasseria Gallega 138
Cerveseria Catalana 137
Charlot Cafè 136
Chicha Limoná 141
Chivuo's 162
Cinc Sentits 139
Comaxurros 177
Con Gracia 166
Copasetic 136
Cremeria Toscana 136
Crusto 137
Cu-Cut! 138
Cuines de Santa Caterina 103

D

De Tapa Madre 142
Degvsta (Tarragona) 211
Disfrutar 138

E

El 58 118
El Asador de Aranda 178
El Atril 101
El Cable (Sitges) 209
El Caliu del Poblenou 119
El Casal 99
El Celler de Can Roca (Girona) 204
El Chigre 102
El Colectivo 84
El Foro 103
El Motel (Figueres) 206
El Pou (Sitges) 209
El Quim 84
El Rincón Maya 137
El Tío Ché 118
El Velódromo 138
Elisabets 84
Els Pescadors 119
Els Quatre Gats 72, **157**
Embat 141-2
En Aparté 101
En Ville 86
Enigma 13, 196
Entrepanes Díaz 141
Escribà 192, **157**
Euskal Etxea 99

F

Fàbrica Moritz 195
Farigola 102
Federal 69, 192
Filferro 25, 114-15
Flash Flash 177
Flax & Kale 86
Foix de Sarrià 177
Forneria Tiana 70

G

Gats 86
Ginette 102
Granja la Pallaresa 26
Granja Petitbo 139
Green Spot 115

H

Hawker 45 139
Himali 165
Hisop 179
Hofmann 179
Horchateria Sirvent 192

I

.IT 163

J

Juice House 192

K

Kaiku 115
Koku Kitchen Buns 99
Koy Shunka 72
Koyuki 136

L

La Balsa 178
La Barra de Carles Abellán 116
La Bella Napoli 195
La Bodega La Peninsular 114
La Bodegueta Provença 137
La Burg 84
La Cova Fumada 114
La Empanaderia de Gràcia 163
La Fábrica (Girona) 203-4
La Fermata de Sarrià 176
La Font del Gat 195
La Gavina 116
La Llavor dels Orígens 101
La Molina 178
La Nena 25, 163

La Panxa del Bisbe 165
La Plata 69
La Pubilla 162
La Vinateria del Call 70
Lady Green (Sitges) 209
Lasarte 13, 138
Lascar 74 193
Las Delicias 163
L'Atelier by Amis 118
Le Cucine Mandarosso 102
Levante 71
Lola Cafè (Girona) 204
L'Òstia 115

M
Maians 115
Malanén 195
Mano Rota 193
Martínez 196
Mauri 137
Més De Vi 118
Milk 69
Minyam 119
Mirilla 71
Mitja Vida 176
Mont Bar 138-9
Monvínic 139
Mr Kao 141

N
Nakashita 102
NAP Mar 114

O
Oaxaca 116
Ocaña 70-1
Onofre 71
Opera Samfaina 71

P
Palo Cortao 193
Paradiso/Pastrami Bar 99
Parking Pizza 137
Patagonia Beef & Wine 142
Pepa Tomate 26, 165
Pizza del Sortidor 195
Pla 71

Q
Quimet i Quimet 193, 27

R
Rasoterra 71
Restaurant 7 Portes 116
Restaurant Durán
    (Figueres) 206

Restaurant el Cafetí 86
Rocambolesc (Girona) 204
Rockata 99
Roig Robí 166

S
Santagustina 102-3
Santamasa 177
Sésamo 84
Shibui 138
Sidreria Txot's
    (Figueres) 206
Sopars amb Estrelles
    179-80
Speakeasy 139
Spice 192
Suculent 86
Suquet De L'Almirall 116

T
Taktika Berri 138
Taller de Tapas 69
Tantarantana 101
Tapas 24 139
Taverna Can Margarit 196
Tickets 196
TimeLine 165
Timesburg Poblenou 118

V
Vaso de Oro 114
Via Veneto 178-9
Vivanda 178

X
Xemei 193
Xiringuito Escribà 119
Xurreria 70

DRINKING & NIGHTLIFE

33|45 87

A
Abirradero 196
Absenta 120
Aire 143
Antilla BCN 143
Arena Classic 144
Arena Madre 144
Átame 143

B
Bacon Bear 144
Balius 121

Bar Calders 197, 12
Bar Canigó 167
Bar del Convent 103
Bar La Concha 87
Bar Leo 120
Bar Marsella 87
Bar Olimpia 197
Bar Pastís 86-7
Berlin 181
Betty Ford's 88
Bharma 121
BierCaB 143
Bikini 181
BlackLab 120
Boadas 73
Bobby Gin 166
Bodega Vidrios y
    Cristales 119
Bosc de les Fades 73
Boulevard 74

C
Cactus Bar 104
Caelum 73
Cafè de l'Òpera 73
Cafè del Centre 145
Cafe Turó 180-1
Čaj Chai 74
Can Paixano 120
Casa Almirall 86
Catwalk 120
CDLC 120
Chatelet 167
City Hall 143
Cosmo 143

D
D9 al Poblenou 121
Dô Bar 181
Dry Martini 142

E
El Born Bar 103
El Drapaire 87
El Maravillas 180
El Rincón Cubano 167
El Rouge 197
El Sabor 167
El Viti 144
El Xampanyet 103
Elephanta 166-7
Espai Joliu 121

G
Garage Beer Co 143
Granja La Pallaresa 73
Granja M Viader 87

Guingueta del Bogatell 121
Guzzo 103

K
Karma 73
Kentucky 88

L
La Cambicha 197
La Caseta del Migdia
    196-7
La Cervecita Nuestra de
    Cada Día 121
La Chapelle 144
La Cigale 167
La Clandestina 74
La Confitería 86
La Deliciosa 120
La Fira 144
La Granja 72
La Macarena 74
La Terrrazza 197
La Vermu 168
La Vermuteria del
    Tano 167
La Vinya del Senyor 103
L'Ascensor 72
Les Gens Que
    J'Aime 144
Lizarran 181

M
Madame George 121
Magic 104
Manchester 73
Marcel 181
Marmalade 87
Marula Café 73
Metro 198
Michael Collins Pub 145
Milano 142
Mirablau 180
Miramelindo 103-4
Monkey Factory 143
Monvínic 142
Moog 87
Mudanzas 104

N
Napar BCN 142-3
Negroni 87
New Chaps 145
Nou Candanchú 168

O
Opium 121
Oviso 74

P
Perikete 119
Pervert Club @ The One 197
Plata Bar 143
Polaroid 72-3
Punto BCN 144

Q
Quilombo 144

R
Rabipelao 166
Raïm 167
Redrum 197
Rubí 103

S
Sala Plataforma 197
Salterio 73
Santa Marta 120
Sol Soler 167
Sor Rita 72
Sutton Club 181

T
The Mint 120
Tinta Roja 197-8

V
Viblioteca 167

⭐ **ENTERTAINMENT**

23 Robadors 88

B
BARTS 198

C
Cine Texas 168
City Hall 145

E
El Cangrejo 88-9
El Paraigua 74
Escolania de Montserrat 207-8

Sights 000
Map Pages **000**
Photo Pages **000**

F
Filmoteca de Catalunya 88

G
Gran Bodega Saltó 198
Gran Teatre del Liceu 74

H
Harlem Jazz Club 75
Hiroshima 198

J
Jamboree 75
Jazz Sí Club 88

L
L'Ateneu 75
L'Auditori 122
Luz de Gas 181

M
Mediterráneo 145
Méliès Cinemes 145

P
Palau de Dalmases 104
Palau de la Música Catalana 104

R
Razzmatazz 121-2
Renoir Floridablanca 198

S
Sala Apolo 198
Sala Beckett 122
Sala Monasterio 121
Sala Tarantos 75
Sidecar Factory Club 75
Soda Acústic 168

T
Tablao Nervión 104
Teatre Grec 198
Teatre Llantiol 88
Teatre Lliure 198
Teatre Mercat De Les Flors 198
Teatre Nacional de Catalunya 122
Teatre Romea 88
Teatre Tívoli 145

V
Verdi 168

Y
Yelmo Cines Icària 122

🛍 **SHOPPING**

10000 Records 199

A
Adolfo Domínguez 148
Altaïr 146
Amalia Vermell 169
Amapola Vegan Shop 169
Antinous 149
Arlequí Màscares 105
Art & Crafts Market 77
Artesania Catalunya 76

B
Bagués-Masriera 149
Be 170
Bestiari 123
Bodega Bonavista 169
Bulevard Rosa 149

C
Cacao Sampaka 145
Can Luc 168
Casa Del Llibre 149
Casa Gispert 105
Catalina House 181-2
Centre Comercial de les Glòries 123
Centre Comercial Diagonal Mar 123
Cereria Subirà 76
Chök 89
Coin & Stamp Market 76
Colmillo de Morsa 168
Cómplices 76
Coquette 105
Custo Barcelona 106

D
Drap-Art 76
Dr Bloom 146

E
El Bulevard dels Anti-quaris 148
El Corte Inglés (Barri Gòtic) 75-6, 146, **147**

El Corte Inglés (L'Eixample) 146, 182
El Magnífico 105
El Rei de la Màgia 26, 104
Els Encants Vells 122
Escribà 75

F
Family Beer 168
Fantastik 89
FC Botiga 77
FC Botiga Megastore 182
Fira Alimentació 77
Flores Navarro 145
FNAC 149
Formatgeria La Seu 75

G
GI Joe 199

H
Herboristeria del Rei 76
Hibernian 26, 168
Hofmann Pastisseria 105
Holala! Plaza 89

J
Joan La Llar del Pernil 89
Joan Múrria 145

L
La Basilica Galeria 77
La Bazart 123
La Colmena 76
La Festival 169
La Manual Alpargatera 76-7
La Portorriqueña 89
La Roca Village 148
Labperfum 182
Lady Loquita 169
Laie 148-9
L'Arca 76
Les Topettes 89
L'Illa Diagonal 182
Loewe 148
Loisaida 105
Lurdes Bergada 146

M
Maremàgnum 123
Marsalada 105
Mercat de Galvany 182
Mercat de la Barcelon-eta 123
Mercat de la Concepció 148

Mercat de l'Abaceria Central 170
Mercat de Sant Antoni 199
Mercat del Ninot 148
MI.vintage 105
Mushi Mushi 170

N
Norma Comics 149
Normandie 182
Nostàlgic 170
Nu Sabates 106

O
Obach 77
Oggetto 105
Olisoliva 106
Oriol Balaguer 182

P
Papabubble 26, 77
Pastisseria Natcha 182
Petritxol Xocoa 77
Picnic 169
Popcorn Store 199
Purificación García 146-8

R
Regia 148
Rekup & Co 169

S
Sabater Hermanos 75
Sala Parés 77
Sergio Aranda 146
Surco 169-70
System Action 122-3

T
Taller de Marionetas Travi 76
Teranyina 89
Tintin Shop 26, 169
Torrons Vicens 75

U
Ukka 182
Ultra-Local Records 123

V
Vernita 122
Vila Viniteca 104
Vinil Vintage 169

SPORTS & ACTIVITIES

Aire de Barcelona 106
Aqua Urban Spa 170
Barcelona Biking 77
Barcelona by Bike 124
Barcelona Segway Fun 77
Base Nautica Municipal 124
Bike Tours Barcelona 106
Catalunya Bus Turístic 149
CicloTour 89
Club Natació Atlètic Barcelona 124
Devour 13
Espai Boisà 149
Fat Tire Bike Tours 77
Las Golondrinas 124
Molokai SUP Center 124
Orsom 124
Piscines Bernat Picornell 199
Rituels d'Orient 182
Terra BikeTours 149
Trixi 77

SLEEPING

A
Alberg Hostel Itaca 215
Alberg Mare de Déu de Montserrat 220
Anakena House 218
Anita's Bed & Breakfast 220

B
Barceló Raval 216

C
Cami Bed & Gallery 218
Casa Bonay 218
Casa Camper 216
Casa Gràcia 219
Chic & Basic Ramblas 216
Cotton House 219

D
DO Reial 215

E
El Palace 218-219

F
Five Rooms 218

G
Generator Hostel 219
Grand Hotel Central 216

H
H10 Port Vell 217
Hostal Cèntric 220
Hostal Goya 218
Hostal Oliva 218
Hotel 54 217
Hotel 1898 215
Hotel Abat Cisneros (Montserrat) 208
Hotel Arts Barcelona 217
Hotel Axel 218
Hotel Banys Orientals 216
Hotel Brummell 13, 220
Hotel Casa Fuster 219
Hotel Constanza 218
Hotel Continental 215
Hotel España 216
Hotel Majèstic 219

Hotel Market 220
Hotel Mercer 215-216
Hotel Neri 215
Hotel Pol & Grace 220
Hotel Sant Agustí 216

M
Mandarin Oriental 219
Margot House 219
Meliá Sky Barcelona 217

O
Ohla Hotel 215

P
Pars Tailor's Hostel 220
Pars Teatro Hostel 220
Pensió 2000 216
Pensión Francia 216
Poblenou Bed & Breakfast 217
Praktik Rambla 217
Pullman Barcelona Skipper Hotel 217

R
Room Mate Pau 218

S
Serras Hotel 215
Soho House 215
Suites Avenue 219

U
Urbany Barcelona 217

V
Vrabac 215

W
W Barcelona 217
Wilson Boutique Hotel 220

Barcelona Maps

Sights

- Beach
- Bird Sanctuary
- Buddhist
- Castle/Palace
- Christian
- Confucian
- Hindu
- Islamic
- Jain
- Jewish
- Monument
- Museum/Gallery/Historic Building
- Ruin
- Shinto
- Sikh
- Taoist
- Winery/Vineyard
- Zoo/Wildlife Sanctuary
- Other Sight

Activities, Courses & Tours

- Bodysurfing
- Diving
- Canoeing/Kayaking
- Course/Tour
- Sento Hot Baths/Onsen
- Skiing
- Snorkelling
- Surfing
- Swimming/Pool
- Walking
- Windsurfing
- Other Activity

Sleeping

- Sleeping
- Camping
- Hut/Shelter

Eating

- Eating

Drinking & Nightlife

- Drinking & Nightlife
- Cafe

Entertainment

- Entertainment

Shopping

- Shopping

Information

- Bank
- Embassy/Consulate
- Hospital/Medical
- Internet
- Police
- Post Office
- Telephone
- Toilet
- Tourist Information
- Other Information

Geographic

- Beach
- Gate
- Hut/Shelter
- Lighthouse
- Lookout
- Mountain/Volcano
- Oasis
- Park
- Pass
- Picnic Area
- Waterfall

Population

- Capital (National)
- Capital (State/Province)
- City/Large Town
- Town/Village

Transport

- Airport
- Border crossing
- Bus
- Cable car/Funicular
- Cycling
- Ferry
- Metro station
- Monorail
- Parking
- Petrol station
- S-Bahn/Subway station
- Taxi
- T-bane/Tunnelbana station
- Train station/Railway
- Tram
- Tube station
- U-Bahn/Underground station
- Other Transport

Routes

- Tollway
- Freeway
- Primary
- Secondary
- Tertiary
- Lane
- Unsealed road
- Road under construction
- Plaza/Mall
- Steps
- Tunnel
- Pedestrian overpass
- Walking Tour
- Walking Tour detour
- Path/Walking Trail

Boundaries

- International
- State/Province
- Disputed
- Regional/Suburb
- Marine Park
- Cliff
- Wall

Hydrography

- River, Creek
- Intermittent River
- Canal
- Water
- Dry/Salt/Intermittent Lake
- Reef

Areas

- Airport/Runway
- Beach/Desert
- Cemetery (Christian)
- Cemetery (Other)
- Glacier
- Mudflat
- Park/Forest
- Sight (Building)
- Sportsground
- Swamp/Mangrove

Note: Not all symbols displayed above appear on the maps in this book

MAP INDEX

1 La Rambla &
Barri Gòtic (p276)

2 El Raval (p280)

3 La Ribera (p284)

4 Port Vell &
La Barceloneta (p286)

5 Port Olímpic, El Poblenou
& El Fòrum (p288)

6 L'Esquerra de
L'Eixample (p290)

7 La Dreta de L'Eixample (p294)

8 Gràcia (p296)

9 La Zona Alta (p298)

10 La Zona Alta East (p300)

11 Montjuïc, Poble Sec
& Sant Antoni (p302)

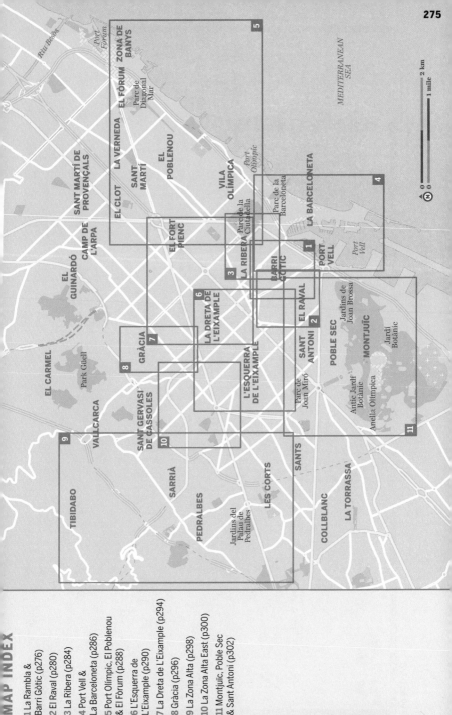

2 km
1 mile

MEDITERRANEAN
SEA

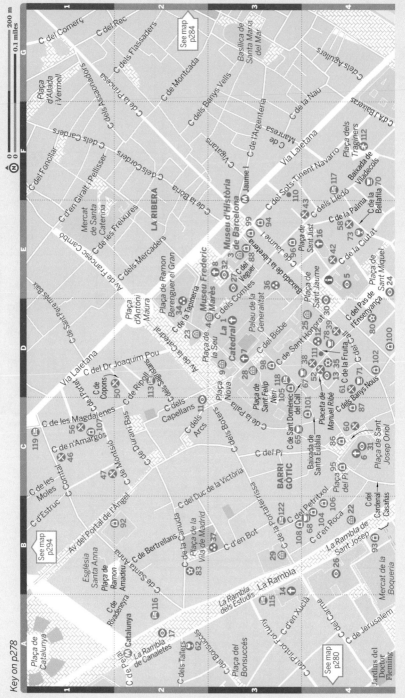

LA RAMBLA & BARRI GÒTIC

Key on p278

200 m
0.1 miles

See map p294

See map p284

See map p280

Plaça de Catalunya

La Rambla de Canaletes

C del Comerç
C del Rec
C dels Flassaders
C de la Princesa
Plaça d'Allada i Vermell
C dels Assaonadors
C dels Carders
C del Fonollar
C d'en Giralt i Pellisser
Mercat de Santa Caterina
C de les Freixures
C dels Mercaders
Av de Francesc Cambó
LA RIBERA
C de la Bòria
C de Montcada
C dels Banys Vells
Basílica de Santa Maria del Mar
C de la Nau
C de l'Argenteria
Via Laietana
C dels Vigatans
C de Manresa
C de Sant
Jaume I
C dels Sots-Tinent Navarro
Plaça dels Traginers
Baixada de Viladecols
C d'Avinyó
C dels Agullers
C dels Lledó
C de la Palma
C de la Bellafila
Museu d'Història de Barcelona
Plaça del Rei
C del Veguer
C de Sant Just
Plaça de Sant Just
C de la Ciutat
Museu Frederic Marès
C dels Comtes
Baixada de la Llibreteria
Plaça de Sant Miquel
Plaça d'Antoni Maura
Plaça de Ramon Berenguer el Gran
C de la Tapineria
La Seu Catedral
Palau de la Generalitat
C del Bisbe
Plaça de Sant Jaume
C del Pas de l'Enseyança
Av de la Catedral
Plaça Nova
Plaça de Sant Felip Neri
C de Sant Honorat
C de Sant Domènec del Call
C de la Fruita
C dels Banys Nous
Via Laietana
C del Dr Joaquim Pou
C de Copons
C de Ripoll
C dels Sagristans
C dels Capellans
C dels Arcs
C dels Boters
C de la Palla
Plaça de Manuel Ribé
Placeta de Manuel Ribé
Baixada de Santa Eulàlia
C de les Magdalenes
C de n'Amargós
C de Montsió
C de Duran i Bas
Plaça de Sant Josep Oriol
C de les Moles
C de n'Arai
C Comtal
C del Pi
BARRI GÒTIC
Plaça del Pi
C d'Estruc
C del Portal de l'Àngel
Plaça de la Vila de Madrid
C del Duc de la Victòria
C de la Portaferrissa
C del Cardenal Casañas
C de Bertrallans
C de la Canuda
C d'en Bot
C d'en Roca
C del Petritxol
La Rambla de Sant Josep
Església Santa Anna
Plaça de Ramon Amadeu
C de Santa Anna
C de Bonsuccés
Mercat de la Boqueria
C de Rivadeneyra
La Rambla dels Estudis
La Rambla
C del Bonsuccés
Plaça del Bonsuccés
C dels Tallers
C del Pintor Fortuny
C d'en Xuclà
C del Carme
C de Jerusalem
Jardins del Doctor Fleming

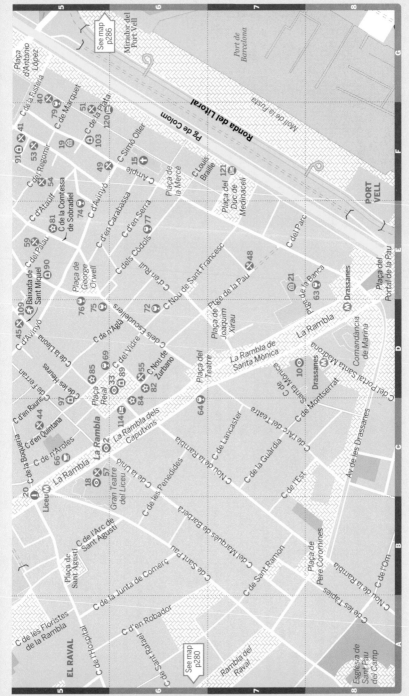

LA RAMBLA & BARRI GÒTIC *Map on p276*

◎ Top Sights (p56)
1 La Catedral.....................................D3
2 La Rambla......................................C5
3 Museu d'Història de Barcelona...........E3
4 Museu Frederic Marès.......................D3

◎ Sights (p62)
5 Ajuntament....................................E4
6 Basílica de Santa Maria del Pi...........C4
7 Capella de Santa Llúcia....................D3
8 Capella Reial de Santa Àgata...........E3
9 Casa de l'Ardiaca............................D3
10 Centre d'Art Santa Mònica...............D7
   Centre de la Imatge.................(see 26)
11 Col·legi de Arquitectes.....................C2
12 Domus de Sant Honorat....................D4
13 El Call..D4
14 Església de Betlem...........................B3
15 Església de la Mercè.........................F6
16 Església de Sants Just i Pastor..........E4
17 Font de Canaletes............................A2
18 Gran Teatre del Liceu.......................C5
19 Hash, Marihuana & Hemp Museum.....F5
20 Mosaic de Miró................................C5

21 Museu de Cera................................E7
22 Museu de l'Eròtica...........................B4
23 Museu Diocesà/Gaudí Exhibition
   Center..D2
24 Palau Centelles...............................E4
25 Palau de la Generalitat....................D4
26 Palau de la Virreina.........................B4
27 Palau del Lloctinent.........................E3
28 Palau Episcopal...............................D3
29 Palau Moja.....................................B3
30 Plaça de Sant Jaume.......................D4
31 Plaça de Sant Josep Oriol................C4
32 Plaça del Rei..................................E3
33 Plaça Reial.....................................D6
34 Roman Walls...................................D2
35 Sinagoga Major...............................D4
36 Temple d'August.............................E3
37 Via Sepulcral Romana......................B3

◎ Eating (p69)
38 Alcoba Azul.....................................D4
39 Allium..D4
40 Belmonte.......................................G5
41 Benedict...F5
42 Black Remedy.................................E4
43 Cafè de l'Acadèmia..........................E4
44 Can Culleretes.................................C5
45 Cereria...D5
46 Cerveceria Taller de
   Tapas...C1
47 Els Quatre Gats...............................C1
48 Federal...E7
49 Forneria Tiana.................................F5
50 Koy Shunka....................................D2
51 La Plata..F5
52 La Vinateria del Call.........................D4
   Levante.....................................(see 52)
53 Milk...F5
54 Mirilla..F5
55 Ocaña...D6
56 Onofre...C1
57 Opera Samfaina...............................C5
58 Pla..E4
59 Rasoterra.......................................E5
60 Taller de Tapas...............................C4
61 Xurreria...D4

⊙ Drinking & Nightlife (p72)
62 Boadas..A2
63 Bosc de les Fades............................E8
64 Boulevard...C6
65 Caelum...C3
66 Cafè de l'Òpera...............................C5
67 Čaj Chai...D4
68 Granja La Pallaresa.........................B4
69 Karma..D5
70 La Clandestina.................................F4
71 La Granja...D4
72 La Macarena....................................D6
73 L'Ascensor.......................................E4
74 Manchester......................................E5
75 Marula Café......................................D5
76 Oviso..D5
77 Polaroid..E6
78 Salterio...D4
79 Sor Rita..F5

⊙ Entertainment (p74)
80 El Paraigua......................................D4
   Gran Teatre del Liceu..............(see 18)
81 Harlem Jazz Club.............................E5

82 Jamboree...D6
83 L'Ateneu..B2
84 Sala Tarantos...................................C6
85 Sidecar Factory Club........................D5

⊙ Shopping (p75)
86 Art & Crafts Market..........................C4
87 Artesania Catalunya.........................C4
88 Cereria Subirà.................................E3
89 Coin & Stamp Market........................D6
90 Cómplices.......................................E5
91 Drap-Art..F5
92 El Corte Inglés.................................B2
93 Escribà..B4
94 FC Botiga...E3
95 Fira Alimentació...............................C4
96 Formatgeria La Seu.........................E3
97 Herboristeria del Rei........................C5
98 La Basílica Galería...........................D3
99 La Colmena......................................E3
100 La Manual Alpargatera....................D4
101 L'Arca...C4
102 Obach...D4
103 Papabubble.....................................F5

104 Petritxol Xocoa................................B4
105 Sabater Hermanos...........................D3
106 Sala Parés.......................................B4
107 Taller de Marionetas Travi...............C1
108 Torrons Vicens................................B3

⊙ Sports & Activities (p77)
109 Barcelona Biking.............................D5
110 Barcelona Segway Fun.....................F3
111 Fat Tire Bike Tours..........................D4
112 Trixi..F4

⊙ Sleeping (p215)
113 Alberg Hostel Itaca.........................D2
114 DO Reial...C6
115 Hotel 1898......................................A3
116 Hotel Continental............................A2
117 Hotel Mercer...................................F4
118 Hotel Neri.......................................D3
119 Ohla Hotel.......................................C1
120 Serras Hotel....................................F5
121 Soho House.....................................F7
122 Vrabac..B3

EL RAVAL

Key on p282

0 200 m
0 0.1 miles

Plaça de la Universitat

M Universitat

C de Gravina

C de Pelai

Plaça de Castella

C dels Tallers

C de Jovellanos

C dels Tallers

C de la Canuda

Av del Portal de l'Angel

C de Montsió

C de la Palla

C dels Boters

Plaça Nova

BARRI GÒTIC

See map p276

C de Ferran

C de n'Aroles

C de la Boqueria

Plaça de St Josep Oriol

C del Pi

C del Petritxol

C del Cardenal Casañas

Plaça de la Boqueria

Liceu M

Plaça de St Josep Oriol

C d'en Bot

C de la Portaferrissa

Plaça de la Vila de Madrid

C d'en Roca

La Rambla de Sant Josep

La Rambla

Plaça de Sant Agustí

C de Santa Anna

M Catalunya

La Rambla de Canaletes

La Rambla dels Estudis

La Rambla dels Estudis

C del Carme

C de Jerusalem

Mercat de la Boqueria

13

47 17

43

8

C de les Floristes de la Rambla

32
21

44

C del Pintor Fortuny

C d'en Xuclà

Plaça de Vicenç Martorell

Plaça del Bonsuccés

Plaça del Pintor Fortuny

31

11

18

54
19

50

48

C d'en Xuclà

C del Notariat

16

C del Doctor Dou

15

Jardins del Doctor Fleming

52

7

4

C de les Egipcíaques

C dels Àngels

C del Pou de la Creu

25

35

12

See map p294

C dels Tallers

51

C de Montalegre

5

Plaça dels Àngels

Plaça de Joan Coromines

MACBA
1

37

C de Joaquín Costa

49
30

C del Lleó

C de la Lluna

C de Sant Vicenç

See map p290

C de Gravina

20

46

Plaça de Terenci Moix

Plaça de Joan Coromines

29

45

C de Valldonzella

C del Tigre

Ronda de Sant Antoni

See map p290

C de Ferlandina

Plaça del Pes de la Palla

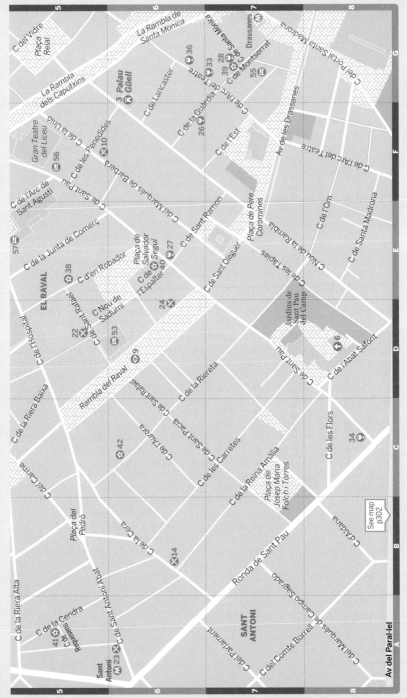

EL RAVAL

EL RAVAL Map on p280

◎ Top Sights (p80)
1 MACBA................................B3
2 Mercat de la Boqueria...............E4
3 Palau Güell.........................G6

◎ Sights (p83)
4 Antic Hospital de la Santa Creu.....D4
5 Centre de Cultura Contemporània de
  Barcelona...........................C2
6 Església de Sant Pau del Camp.......D8
7 Institut d'Estudis Catalans.........D4
8 La Capella..........................E4
9 Rambla del Raval....................D6

✕ Eating (p84)
10 Bar Cañete.........................F5
11 Bar Kasparo........................D2
12 Bar Muy Buenas.....................C4
13 Bar Pinotxo........................E3
14 Can Lluís..........................B6
15 Caravelle..........................D3
16 El Colectivo.......................D3
17 El Quim............................E4
18 Elisabets..........................D2
19 En Ville...........................D3

20 Flax & Kale........................B1
21 Gats...............................E3
22 Restaurant el Cafetí...............D5
23 Sésamo.............................A6
24 Suculent...........................D6

◎ Drinking & Nightlife (p86)
25 33|45..............................C4
26 Bar La Concha......................F6
27 Bar Marsella.......................E6
28 Bar Pastís.........................G7
29 Betty Ford's.......................B2
30 Casa Almirall......................B3
31 El Drapaire........................D2
32 Granja M Viader....................E3
33 Kentucky...........................G7
34 La Confitería......................C8
35 Marmalade..........................C4
36 Moog...............................G6
37 Negroni............................B3

◎ Entertainment (p88)
38 23 Robadors........................E4
39 El Cangrejo........................D2
40 Filmoteca de Catalunya.............D3

41 Jazz Sí Club.......................A5
42 Teatre Llantiol....................C6
43 Teatre Romea.......................E4

◎ Shopping (p89)
44 Chök...............................E3
45 Fantastik..........................B2
46 Holala! Plaza......................B1
47 Joan La Llar del Pernil............E4
48 La Portorriqueña...................D2
49 Les Topettes.......................B3
50 Teranyina..........................D2

◎ Sports & Activities (p89)
51 CicloTour..........................C1
52 Runner Bean Tours..................D4

◎ Sleeping (p216)
53 Barceló Raval......................D6
54 Casa Camper........................D3
55 Chic & Basic Ramblas...............G7
56 Hotel España.......................F5
57 Hotel Sant Agustí..................E5

LA RIBERA *Map on p284*

◎ Top Sights (p92)

1 Basílica de Santa Maria del Mar E6
2 Museu Picasso D5
3 Palau de la Música Catalana A3

◎ Sights (p96)

4 Arc de Triomf D1
5 Arxiu Fotogràfic de Barcelona E4
6 Born Centre de Cultura i Memòria F5
7 Carrer de Montcada E5
8 Casa de la Seda A4
9 Casa Llotja de Mar E7
10 Cascada G2
11 Castell dels Tres Dragons....................... F3
12 El Fossar de les Moreres E6
13 Fundació Foto Colectania........................ E3
14 Homenatge a Picasso G4
15 Mercat de Santa Caterina C4
16 Monestir de Sant Pere de les Puelles C2
17 Museu de Cultures del Món D5
18 Museu de la Xocolata................................ E4
19 Museu Europeu d'Art Modern................. D5
20 Parc de la Ciutadella................................ G3
21 Parlament de Catalunya H3
22 Zoo de Barcelona...................................... H4

◎ Eating (p99)

23 Bar del Pla.. D5
24 Bormuth E5
25 Bubó E7
26 Cal Pep F6
27 Casa Delfín... F5
28 Cat Bar C6
29 Cuines de Santa Caterina........................ C4
30 El Atril.. D4
31 El Casal.. D7
32 El Chigre E5
33 El Foro E4
34 En Aparté C2
35 Euskal Etxea E6
36 Farigola.. D2
37 Ginette... D2
38 Koku Kitchen Buns F5
39 La Llavor dels Orígens.............................. E6
40 Le Cucine Mandarosso B4
41 Nakashita.. D2
42 Paradiso/Pastrami Bar............................ F6
43 Rockata... E3

44 Santagustina.. D3
45 Tantarantana E4

◎ Drinking & Nightlife (p103)

46 Bar del Convent... E4
47 Cactus Bar.. E5
48 El Born Bar E6
49 El Xampanyet... E6
50 Guzzo.. F5
51 La Vinya del Senyor E6
52 Magic... F5
53 Miramelindo E5
54 Mudanzas.. F6
55 Rubí D6

◎ Entertainment (p104)

56 Palau de Dalmases.................................... E6
Palau de la Música Catalana.............(see 3)
57 Tablao Nervión C6

◎ Shopping (p104)

58 Arlequí Màscares C6
59 Casa Gispert E6
60 Coquette... F5
61 Custo Barcelona.. E6
62 El Magnífico... D6
63 El Rei de la Màgia D5
64 Hofmann Pastisseria................................ E5
65 Loisaida.. E5
66 Marsalada... D5
67 Ml.vintage.. E7
68 Nu Sabates... D6
69 Oggetto... E7
Olisoliva ....(see 15)
70 Sans i Sans D6
71 Vila Viniteca E7

◎ Sports & Activities (p106)

72 Aire De Barcelona F4
73 Bike Tours Barcelona E6
74 My Beautiful Parking................................ C6

◎ Sleeping (p216)

75 Grand Hotel Central C5
76 Hotel Banys Orientals.............................. D6
77 Pensió 2000 .... A4
78 Pensión Francia... F6

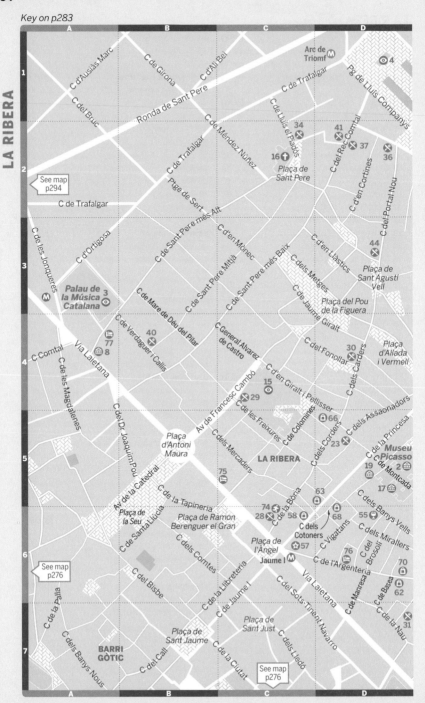

LA RIBERA

See map p294

See map p276

See map p276

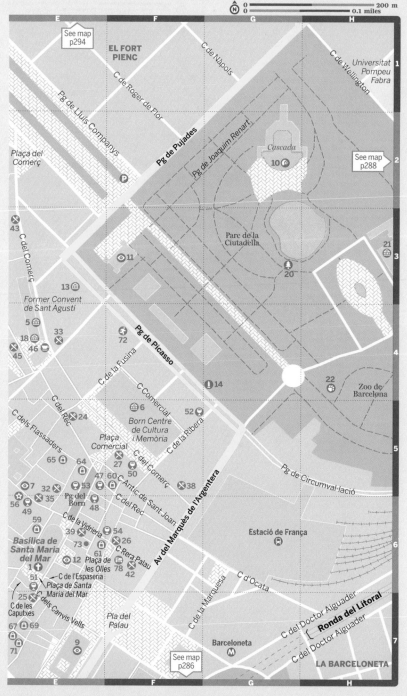

0 ——— 200 m
0 ——— 0.1 miles

See map p294

EL FORT PIENC

C de Nàpols

C de Roger de Flor

C de Wellington

Universitat Pompeu Fabra

Pg de Lluís Companys

Pg de Pujades

Pg de Joaquim Renart

Cascada

10

See map p288

Plaça del Comerç

Parc de la Ciutadella

43

C del Comerç

11

20

21

13

Former Convent de Sant Agustí

5

18   33

46

45   72

Pg de Picasso

C de la Fusina

C Comercial

14

Born Centre de Cultura i Memòria

6

52

C del Comerç

C de la Ribera

22   Zoo de Barcelona

C dels Flassaders

24

C del Rec

Plaça Comercial

27   50

65   64

47 60 C

53   Antic de Sant Joan

7 32   35

56   49

59

39   54

73

61   26

C Rera Palau

78   42

Basílica de Santa Maria del Mar

1

12   Plaça de les Olles

51   C de l'Espaseria

25   Plaça de Santa Maria del Mar

C de les Caputxes

67 69

71   9

38

Av del Marquès de l'Argentera

Pg de Circumval·lació

Estació de França

C d'Ocata

C de la Marquesa

Pla del Palau

Barceloneta

C del Doctor Aiguader

Ronda del Litoral

C del Doctor Aiguader

LA BARCELONETA

See map p286

PORT VELL & LA BARCELONETA

N

0 _____ 500 m
0 _____ 0.25 miles

See map
p284

See map
p288

See map
p276

Zoo de
Barcelona

Pg de Circumval·lació

Ronda del Litoral

C del Gasòmetre

C del Doctor Aiguader

Estació de
França

Parc de la
Barceloneta

C del Comerç

C de la Princesa

LA RIBERA

Av del Marquès
de l'Argentera

C d'Ocata

C Pizarro

C de Balboa

BARRI
GÒTIC

Jaume I

Via Laietana

Barceloneta

13

C de Ginebra

LA BARCELONETA

C de Jaume I

Pg d'Isabel II

30
29
36
20
35 50
38
39

Plaça de
Pau Vila

32

34

25

8

15

C de la Maquinista

18
42

23

C d'Andrea Dòria

C d'Avinyó

C dels Escudellers

C Ample

C de la Mercè

Pg de Colom

Ronda del Litoral

Moll de la Fusta

Mirador del
Port Vell

22

26

11

24
27

C de Sant Carles

19
33

12

17

C de Pepe Rubianes

Platja
de Sant
Sebastià

Plaça del Duc
de Medinaceli

Marina

Pg de Joan de Borbó

Moll de la Barceloneta

C del Mar

16
28
51
C del Almirall
Aixada

14

48

4

La Rambla

Plaça del
Ictínio

Plaça del Portal
de la Pau

PORT VELL

41
6

P

40

Moll d'Espanya

Museu
Marítim

1
7

43
44
49
47

Moll de les Drassanes

Rambla de Mar

C de l'Escar

C del Judici

31
21

Plaça
del Mar

5

Port Vell

Moll de Barcelona

10
46

52

Platja de
Sant Miquel

37

Moll de Sant Beltran

Port de
Barcelona

Moll de Ponent

Moll de Balears

Pg de Joan de Borbó

◎ Top Sights (p109)
1 Museu Marítim A4

◎ Sights (p111)
2 Barcelona Head B2
3 Edifici de Gas Natural...........D2
4 Homenatge a la
    Barceloneta D3
5 Homenatge a la Natació D4
6 L'Aquàrium B4
7 Mirador de Colom..................A4
    Museu d'Història de
    Catalunya...................(see 8)
8 Palau de Mar.........................C2
9 Platja de la Barceloneta E2
10 Teleférico del Puerto C5

✖ Eating (p114)
    1881................................(see 8)
11 Baluard Barceloneta C3
12 Barraca D3
13 Bitácora.................................C2
14 Can Majó................................D3
15 Can Maño................................C2
16 Can Ros D3
17 Can Solé.................................C3
18 El Guindilla D2
19 Filferro...................................D3
20 Green Spot B2
21 Kaiku..................................... D4
22 La Barra de Carles
    Abellán C3
23 La Bodega La Peninsular C2
24 La Cova Fumada D3
25 La Gavina C2
26 L'Òstia C3
27 Maians...................................D3
28 NAP Mar.................................D3
29 Oaxaca B2

30 Restaurant 7 Portes B2
31 Suquet De L'Almirall D4
    Torre d'Alta Mar.......... (see 10)
32 Vaso de Oro...........................C2

◎ Drinking & Nightlife (p119)
33 Absenta..................................D3
    Bar Leo.........................(see 33)
34 BlackLab...............................C2
35 Bodega Vidrios y
    Cristales..............................B2
36 Can Paixano B2
37 La Deliciosa D4
38 Perikete.................................B2
    Santa Marta ....(see 14)
    The Mint......................(see 35)

◎ Shopping (p122)
    Bestiari...........................(see 8)
39 Feria d'Artesanía del
    Palau de Mar B2
40 Maremàgnum B4
41 Mercado de Pintores............B4
42 Mercat de la Barceloneta D2
43 Port Antic..............................A4

◎ Sports & Activities (p124)
44 BC Naval Tours A4
45 Biciclot E1
46 Club Natació Atlètic-
    Barcelona C5
47 Las Golondrinas....................A4
48 Molokai SUP Center D3
49 Orsom....................................A4

◎ Sleeping (p217)
50 H10 Port Vell B2
51 Hotel 54 ....C3
52 W Barcelona..........................D6

PORT VELL & LA BARCELONETA

PORT OLÍMPIC, EL POBLENOU & EL FÒRUM

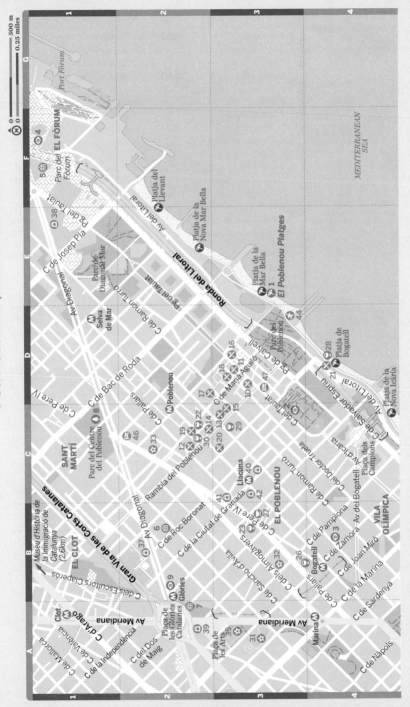

N

0 — 500 m
0 — 0.25 miles

Port Fòrum

EL FÒRUM
Parc del Fòrum

Platja del Llevant

Platja de la Nova Mar Bella

Pg del Taulat

Av del Litoral

Ronda del Litoral

Platja de la Mar Bella

Platja del Poblenou Platges

El Poblenou

Parc del Diagonal-Mar

C de Josep Pla

Av Diagonal

Selva de Mar

C de Ramon Turró

Poblenou

C de Bac de Roda

C de Pere IV

C de Palais

SANT MARTÍ

Parc del Centre del Poblenou

C de Maria Aguiló

C del Taulat

Parc del Poblenou

Platja de Bogatell

Av del Litoral

Platja de la Nova Icària

Av de Salvador Espriu

Pg de Calvell

Rambla del Poblenou

Llacuna

EL POBLENOU

C de la Ciutat de Granada

C de Pere IV

C de Ramon Turró

Av Diagonal

C de Roc Boronat

C de Sancho d'Àvila

C dels Almogàvers

Plaça dels Campions

Av del Bogatell

C del Doctor Trueta

VILA OLÍMPICA

C de Pamplona

C de Zamora

C de Joan Miró

Bogatell

C de la Marina

C de Palais

C de Sardenya

C de Nàpols

Marina

Museu d'Història de la Immigració de Catalunya (2.6km)

EL CLOT

Gran Via de les Corts Catalanes

C dels Escultors Claperós

Clot

C d'Aragó

C de València

C de Mallorca

C de la Independència

C del Dos de Maig

Av Meridiana

Plaça de les Glòries Catalanes

Glòries

Plaça de les Arts

MEDITERRANEAN SEA

PORT OLÍMPIC, EL POBLENOU & EL FÒRUM

Top Sights (p110)
1 El Poblenou Platges................E3

Sights (p112)
2 Cementiri del Poblenou................C3
3 Edge Brewing................B4
4 El Fòrum................F1
5 Museu Blau................F1
6 Museu Can Framis................B2
   Museu de la Música................(see 31)
7 Museu del Disseny de Barcelona................A2
8 Parc del Centre del Poblenou................C1
9 Torre Glòries................B2

Eating (p118)
10 Aguaribay................D3
11 Cal Cuc................D3
   Can Dendé................(see 40)
12 Can Recasens................C2
13 El 58................C2
14 El Caliu del Poblenou................A3
15 El Tío Ché................C3
16 Els Pescadors................D3
17 L'Atelier by Amis................D2
18 Més De Vi................D3
19 Minyam................C2
20 Timesburg Poblenou................C3
21 Xiringuito Escribà................D4

Drinking & Nightlife (p121)
22 Balius................C2
23 Bharma................B3
24 Catwalk................C5
25 CDLC................C5
26 D9 al Poblenou................B3
27 Espai Joliu................B3
28 Guingueta del Bogatell................D4
29 La Cervecita Nuestra de Cada Día................C3
30 Madame George................C2
   Opium................(see 25)

Entertainment (p121)
31 L'Auditori................A3
32 Razzmatazz................B3
33 Sala Beckett................C2
34 Sala Monasterio................C5
35 Teatre Nacional de Catalunya................A3
36 Yelmo Cines Icària................C5

Shopping (p122)
37 Centre Comercial de les Glòries................B2
38 Centre Comercial Diagonal Mar................E1
39 Els Encants Vells................A2
40 La Bazart................C3
41 System Action................C5
42 Ultra-Local Records................C3

Sports & Activities (p124)
43 Barcelona By Bike................C5
44 Base Nautica Municipal................D3

Sleeping (p217)
45 Hotel Arts Barcelona................C5
46 Meliá Sky Barcelona................C2
47 Poblenou Bed & Breakfast................D3
48 Pullman Barcelona Skipper Hotel................B5

See map p286

Key on p292

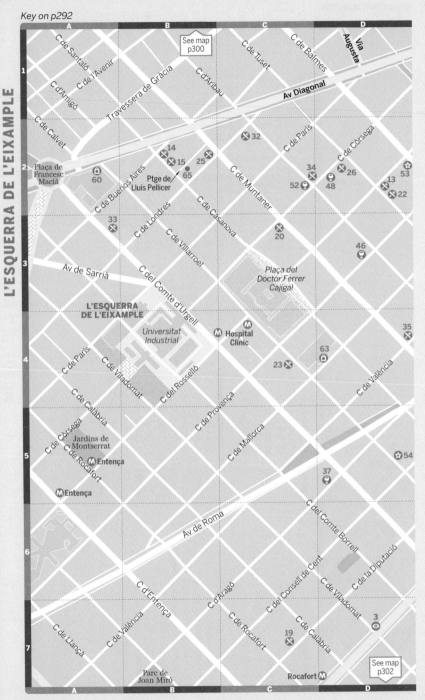

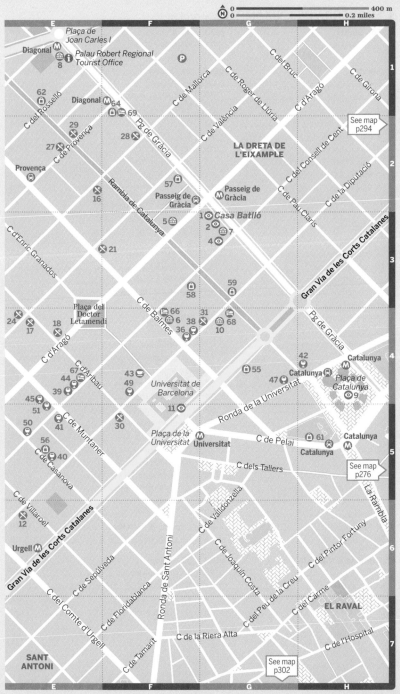

0 400 m
0 0.2 miles

Plaça de Joan Carles I

Diagonal
8 Palau Robert Regional Tourist Office

P

C del Bruc

C de Girona

C d'Aragó

1

62

C del Rosselló

Diagonal 64
69

C de Mallorca

C de Roger de Llúria

C de València

29

C de Provença

27

28

Pg de Gràcia

LA DRETA DE L'EIXAMPLE

See map p294

C del Consell de Cent

C de la Diputació

2

Provença

16

Rambla de Catalunya

57

Passeig de Gràcia

Passeig de Gràcia

C de Pau Claris

C d'Enric Granados

5

1 Casa Batlló
2
4

7

Gran Via de les Corts Catalanes

3

21

58

59

Pg de Gràcia

24
17

18

Plaça del Doctor Letamendi

C de Balmes

66
6 38
36

31

68
10

42

Catalunya

4

C d'Aragó

67
44
39

C d'Aribau

43
49

Universitat de Barcelona

55

47

Catalunya

Plaça de Catalunya
9

45
51

50
41

C de Muntaner

11

Ronda de la Universitat

Catalunya

30

Plaça de la Universitat Universitat

C de Pelai

61

Catalunya

5

56
40

C de Casanova

C dels Tallers

See map p276

La Rambla

12

C de Villarroel

Urgell

Gran Via de les Corts Catalanes

C de Sepúlveda

Ronda de Sant Antoni

C de Valldonzella

C de Joaquín Costa

C del Peu de la Creu

C del Pintor Fortuny

6

C del Comte d'Urgell

C de Floridablanca

C del Carme

EL RAVAL

7

SANT ANTONI

C de Tamarit

C de la Riera Alta

C de l'Hospital

See map p302

L'ESQUERRA DE L'EIXAMPLE *Map on p290*

◎ Top Sights	p133
1 Casa Batlló	G3

◎ Sights	p132
2 Casa Amatller	G3
3 Casa Golferichs	D7
4 Casa Lleó Morera	G3
5 Fundació Antoni Tàpies	F3
6 Museu del Modernisme Barcelona	F4
7 Museu del Perfum	G3
8 Palau Robert	E1
9 Plaça de Catalunya	H4
10 Sala Fundación MAPFRE	G4
11 Universitat de Barcelona	F5

◎ Eating	p136
12 Amaltea	E6
13 Auto Rosellon	D2
14 Café San Telmo	B2
15 Cerveseria Brasseria Gallega	B2
16 Cerveseria Catalana	E2
17 Charlot Cafè	E4
18 Cinc Sentits	E4
19 Copasetic	C7
20 Cremeria Toscana	C3
21 Crusto	F3
22 Cu-Cut!	D2
23 Disfrutar	C4
24 El Rincón Maya	E4
25 El Velódromo	B2
26 Koyuki	D2
27 La Bodegueta Provença	E2
28 Lasarte	F2
29 Mauri	E2
30 Mont Bar	F5
31 Monvínic	G4
32 Parking Pizza	C2
33 Shibui	A3
34 Speakeasy	C2
35 Taktika Berri	D4

◎ Drinking & Nightlife	p142
36 Aire	F4
37 Antilla BCN	D5
38 Arena Classic	F4
Arena Madre	(see 36)

39 Átame	E4
40 Bacon Bear	E5
41 BierCaB	E5
42 City Hall	H4
43 Cosmo	F4
Dry Martini	(see 34)
44 Garage Beer Co	E4
45 La Chapelle	E4
46 La Fira	D3
47 Milano	G4
48 Monkey Factory	D2
Monvínic	(see 31)
49 Napar BCN	F4
50 Plata Bar	E5
51 Punto BCN	E5
52 Quilombo	C2

◎ Entertainment	p145
City Hall	(see 42)
53 Mediterráneo	D2
54 Méliès Cinemes	D5

◎ Shopping	p145
55 Altaïr	G4
56 Antinous	E5
Bagués-Masriera	(see 2)
57 Bulevard Rosa	F2
58 Cacao Sampaka	F3
59 Dr Bloom	G3
El Bulevard dels Antiquaris	(see 57)
60 El Corte Inglés	A2
61 FNAC	H5
Loewe	(see 4)
62 Lurdes Bergada	E1
63 Mercat del Ninot	D4
64 Purificación García	F1
Regia	(see 7)

◎ Sports & Activities	p149
65 Espai Boisà	B2

◎ Sleeping	p217
66 Anakena House	F4
67 Hotel Axel	E4
68 Praktik Rambla	G4
69 Suites Avenue	F1

LA DRETA DE L'EIXAMPLE *See map p294*

◎ Top Sights (p127)
1 La Pedrera A4
2 La Sagrada Família E1

◎ Sights (p134)
3 Casa de les Punxes.......................................B3
4 Església de la Puríssima Concepció i
    Assumpció de Nostra Senyora.............C4
5 Església de les Saleses D3
6 Fundació Suñol...A4
7 Museu Egipci..B5
8 Palau del Baró Quadras A4
9 Palau Montaner..B4
10 Platja de l'Eixample D5

✕ Eating (p139)
11 Cafe Emma...C5
12 Can Kenji...C2
13 Cantina Mexicana E2
14 Casa Alfonso D6
15 Casa Amalia...C4
16 Casa Calvet..D6
17 Chicha Limoná D3
18 De Tapa Madre...C4
19 Embat..C4
20 Entrepanes Díaz...A3
21 Granja Petitbo D3
22 Hawker 45..E5
23 Mr Kao..B4
24 Patagonia Beef & Wine D6
25 Tapas 24 ....C6

◎ Drinking & Nightlife (p144)
26 Cafè del Centre D4
27 El Viti...E4

28 Les Gens Que J'Aime B5
29 Michael Collins Pub....................................D2
30 New Chaps B3

◎ Entertainment (p145)
31 Teatre Tívoli D7

◎ Shopping (p145)
Adolfo Domínguez......................... (see 48)
32 Casa Del Llibre B5
33 El Corte Inglés D7
34 Flores Navarro C4
35 Joan Múrria C4
36 Laie...D6
37 Mercat de la Concepció............................C4
38 Norma Comics...F5
39 Sergio Aranda B4

◎ Sports & Activities (p149)
40 Catalunya Bus Turístic D7
41 Terra BikeTours..C3

◎ Sleeping (p217)
42 Cami Bed & Gallery D6
43 Casa Bonay..E5
44 Cotton House...D6
45 El Palace D6
46 Five Rooms..D6
47 Hostal Goya..D6
48 Hostal Oliva..C6
49 Hotel Constanza D6
50 Hotel Majèstic B5
51 Mandarin Oriental C6
52 Margot House B5
53 Room Mate Pau D7

See key p293

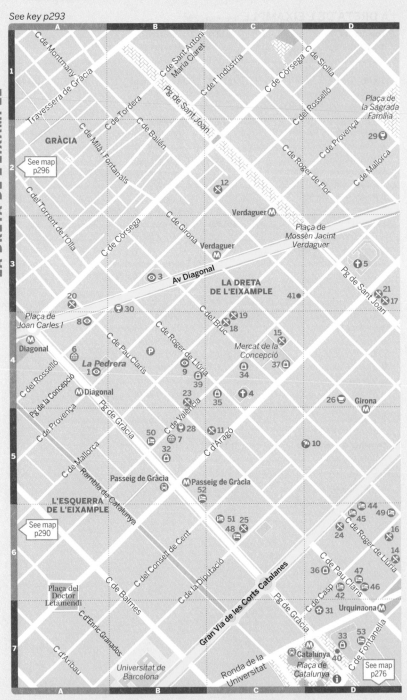

LA DRETA DE L'EIXAMPLE

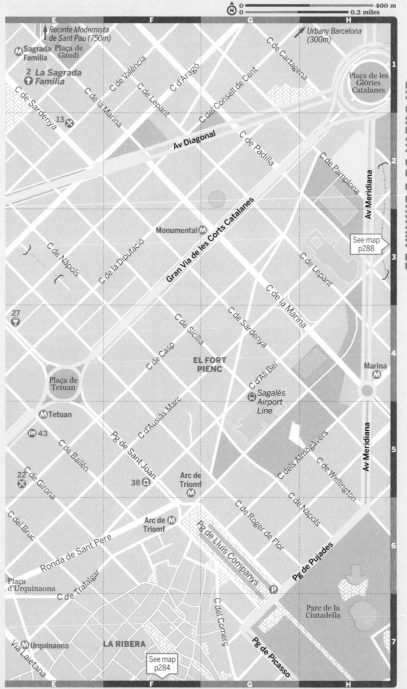

0 400 m
0 0.2 miles

Recinte Modernista
de Sant Pau (750m)

Urbany Barcelona
(300m)

M Sagrada
Família

Plaça de
Gaudí

2 La Sagrada
Família

C de Sardenya

C de València

C d'Aragó

C de la Marina

C de Lepant

C del Consell de Cent

C de Cartagena

Plaça de les
Glòries
Catalanes

13

Av Diagonal

C de Padilla

C de Pamplona

Av Meridiana

Monumental M

C de Nàpols

C de la Diputació

Gran Via de les Corts Catalanes

C de Lepant

See map
p288

C de Sícilia

C de la Marina

C de Sardenya

27

C de Casp

EL FORT
PIENC

C d'Ali Bei

Marina
M

Plaça de
Tetuan

M Tetuan

C d'Ausiàs Marc

Sagalés
Airport
Line

43

C de Bailèn

Pg de Sant Joan

38

Arc de
Triomf
M

C dels Almogàvers

C de Wellington

Av Meridiana

22 C de Girona

C del Bruc

Ronda de Sant Pere

Arc de M
Triomf

Pg de Lluís Companys

C de Roger de Flor

C de Nàpols

Pg de Pujades

P

Parc de la
Ciutadella

Plaça
d'Urquinaona

C de Trafalgar

C del Comerç

Pg de Picasso

M Urquinaona

Via Laietana

LA RIBERA

See map
p284

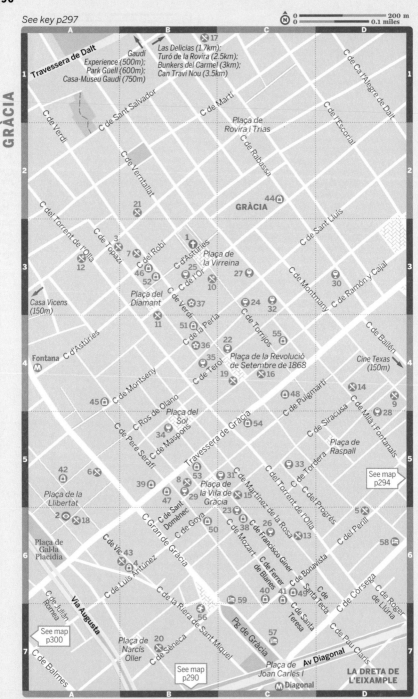

See key p297

GRÀCIA

Travessera de Dalt

Gaudí
Experience (500m);
Park Güell (600m);
Casa-Museu Gaudí (750m)

Las Delicias (1.7km);
Turó de la Rovira (2.5km);
Bunkers del Carmel (3km);
Can Travi Nou (3.5km)

C de Verdi

C de Sant Salvador

C de Vernallat

C de Martí

Plaça de
Rovira i Trias

C de Rabassa

C de l'Escorial

C de Ca l'Alegre de Dalt

C del Torrent de l'Olla

21

GRÀCIA

44

C de Sant Lluís

3

C de Topàzi

7

C del Robí

C d'Astúries

12

25

Plaça de
la Virreina

C de l'Or

27

30

C de Ramón y Cajal

46

52

10

C de Verdi

Plaça del
Diamant

37

24

32

C de Montmany

11

51

C de la Perla

C de Torrijos

55

C de Bailén

36

22

35

Plaça de la Revolució
de Setembre de 1868

Cine Texas
(150m)

Fontana

C d'Astúries

C de Teror

19

16

Casa Vicens
(150m)

45

C de Montseny

C Ros de Olano

Plaça del
Sol

48

C de Puigmartí

14

9

28

C de Milà i Fontanals

34

C de Maspons

Travessera de Gràcia

54

C de Siracusa

Plaça de
Raspall

C de Pere Serafí

33

C de Tordera

See map
p294

42

6

53

31

C de Martínez de la Rosa

C del Torrent de l'Olla

C del Progrés

39

8

C de Sant
Domènec

29

Plaça de
la Vila de
Gràcia

15

23

26

13

5

Plaça de la
Llibertat

2

18

47

50

C de Goya

38

C de Francisco Giner

C de Bonavista

C del Perill

58

Plaça de
Gal·la
Placídia

43

4

C Gran de Gràcia

C de Mozart

C de Ferrer
de Blanes

C de Santa
Teresa

C de Còrsega

C de Roger
de Llúria

C de Vic

C de Luis Antúnez

40

41

49

C de Pau Claris

Via Augusta

59

C de la Riera de Sant Miquel

56

57

Pg de Gràcia

See map
p300

C de Julián
Romea

20

C de Sèneca

Plaça de
Narcís
Oller

See map
p290

Plaça de
Joan Carles I

Diagonal

Av Diagonal

LA DRETA DE
L'EIXAMPLE

C de Balmes

0   200 m
0   0.1 miles

GRÀCIA *See map p296*

⊚ **Sights** (p162)
1 Església de Sant Joan B3
2 Mercat de la Llibertat A6

✖ **Eating** (p162)
3 .IT A3
4 Bar Bodega Quimet B6
5 Bilbao D6
6 Botafumeiro A5
7 Cafè Camèlia B3
8 Café Godot B5
9 Cal Boter D4
10 Cantina Machito B3
11 Casa Portuguesa B4
12 Chivuo's A3
13 Con Gracia C6
14 Himali D4
15 La Empanaderia de Gràcia C5
16 La Nena C4
17 La Panxa del Bisbe B1
18 La Pubilla A6
19 Pepa Tomate C4
20 Roig Robí B7
21 TimeLine B2

◗ **Drinking & Nightlife** (p166)
22 Bar Canigó C4
23 Bobby Gin C6
24 Chatelet C3
25 El Rincón Cubano B3
26 El Sabor C6
27 Elephanta C3
28 La Cigale D5
29 La Vermu B5
30 La Vermuteria del Tano D3
31 Nou Candanchú C5

32 Rabipelao C3
33 Raïm C5
34 Sol Soler B5
35 Viblioteca B4

✪ **Entertainment** (p168)
36 Soda Acústic B4
37 Verdi B3

🛍 **Shopping** (p168)
38 Amalia Vermell C6
39 Amapola Vegan Shop B5
40 Be C6
41 Bodega Bonavista C6
42 Can Luc A5
43 Colmillo de Morsa B6
44 Family Beer C2
45 Hibernian A4
46 La Festival B3
47 Lady Loquita B5
48 Mercat de l'Abaceria Central C4
49 Mushi Mushi C6
50 Nostàlgic B6
51 Picnic B4
52 Rekup & Co B3
53 Surco B5
54 Tintin Shop C5
55 Vinil Vintage C4

✪ **Sports & Activities** (p170)
56 Aqua Urban Spa B7

🛏 **Sleeping** (p219)
57 Casa Gràcia C7
58 Generator Hostel D6
59 Hotel Casa Fuster C6

LA ZONA ALTA

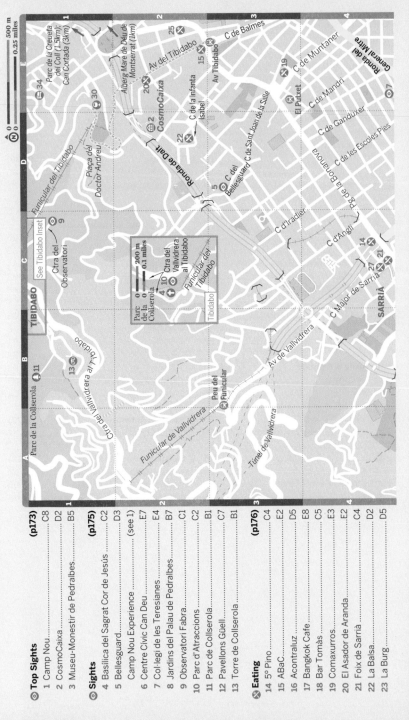

◎ **Top Sights** (p173)
1 Camp Nou................................C8
2 CosmoCaixa...........................D2
3 Museu-Monestir de Pedralbes.....B5

◎ **Sights** (p175)
4 Basílica del Sagrat Cor de Jesús........C2
5 Bellesguard...........................D3
Camp Nou Experience..........(see 1)
6 Centre Cívic Can Deu.............E7
7 Col·legi de les Teresianes.....E4
8 Jardins del Palau de Pedralbes.....B7
9 Observatori Fabra..................C1
10 Parc d'Atraccions.................C2
11 Parc de Collserola...............B1
12 Pavellons Güell....................C7
13 Torre de Collserola..............B1

◎ **Eating** (p176)
14 5° Pino.................................C4
15 ABaC...................................E2
16 Acontraluz..........................D5
17 Bangkok Cafe.....................E8
18 Bar Tomàs...........................C5
19 Comaxurros........................E3
20 El Asador de Aranda...........E2
21 Foix de Sarrià.....................C4
22 La Balsa..............................D2
23 La Burg...............................D5

LA ZONA ALTA

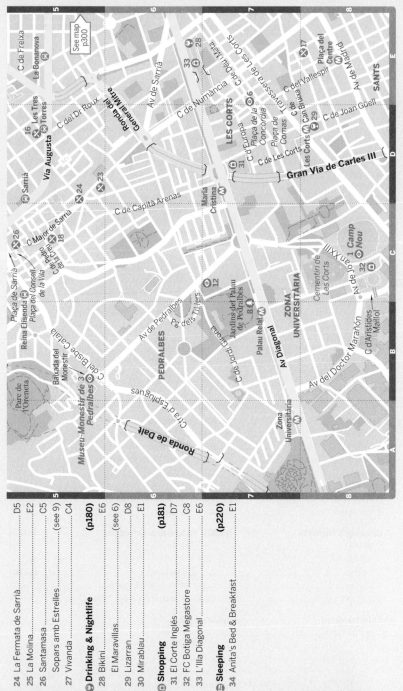

24 La Fermata de Sarrià	D5
25 La Molina	E2
26 Santamasa	C5
Sopars amb Estrelles	(see 9)
27 Vivanda	C4

Drinking & Nightlife (p180)

28 Bikini	E6
El Maravillas	(see 6)
29 Lizarran	D8
30 Mirablau	E1

Shopping (p181)

31 El Corte Inglés	D7
32 FC Botiga Megastore	C8
33 L'Illa Diagonal	E6

Sleeping (p220)

34 Anita's Bed & Breakfast	E1

See map p300

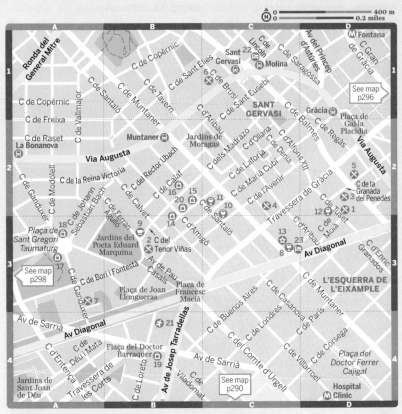

🍽 **Eating**	**(p176)**
1 Ajoblanco	D2
2 Aspic	B3
3 Flash Flash	D2
4 Hisop	C2
5 Hofmann	D2
6 Mitja Vida	C1
7 Via Veneto	A3

🍷 **Drinking & Nightlife**	**(p180)**
8 Berlin	C3
9 Cafe Turó	B3
10 Dô Bar	C2
11 Marcel	C2
12 Sutton Club	D2

⭐ **Entertainment**	**(p181)**
13 Luz de Gas	C3

🛍 **Shopping**	**(p181)**
14 Catalina House	B3
15 Labperfum	B2
16 Mercat de Galvany	B2
17 Normandie	A3
18 Oriol Balaguer	A3
19 Pastisseria Natcha	B4
20 Ukka	B2

🏄 **Sports & Activities**	**(p182)**
21 Rituels d'Orient	B4

🛏 **Sleeping**	**(p220)**
22 Hotel Pol & Grace	C1
23 Wilson Boutique Hotel	C3

MONTJUÏC, POBLE SEC & SANT ANTONI *Map on p302*

◎ **Top Sights**	**(p185)**	
1	Fundació Joan Miró	E4
2	Museu Nacional d'Art de Catalunya	D4
◎ **Sights**	**(p188)**	
3	CaixaForum	C3
4	Castell de Montjuïc	G6
5	Cementiri del Sud-Oest	D7
6	Estadi Olímpic Lluís Companys	D5
7	Font Màgica	C4
8	Fundació Fran Daurel	C4
9	Jardí Botànic	E6
10	Jardins de Joan Brossa	G4
11	Jardins de Mossèn Cinto de Verdaguer	F5
12	Jardins de Mossèn Costa i Llobera	H4
13	Jardins del Mirador	G5
14	L'Anella Olímpica & Estadi Olímpic	D5
15	MUHBA Refugi 307	G4
16	Museu d'Arqueologia de Catalunya	E4
17	Museu Etnològic	D4
18	Museu Olímpic i de l'Esport	E5
19	Parc de Joan Miró	C1
20	Parc de l'Espanya Industrial	A2
21	Pavelló Mies van der Rohe	C4
22	Plaça de la Sardana	G5
23	Poble Espanyol	B4
24	Telefèric de Montjuïc	F4
25	Teleférico del Puerto	H4
❸ **Eating**	**(p192)**	
26	Agust Gastrobar	F2
27	Alkímia	B6
28	Bar Ramón	E1
29	Basílico	E2
30	Bodega 1900	E2
31	Bodega Sepúlveda	B6
32	Casa de Tapas Cañota	D3
33	Casa Xica	E3
34	Enigma	D2
35	Escribà	A6
36	Fàbrica Moritz	B6
37	Federal	F2
38	Horchateria Sirvent	F2
39	Juice House	F2
40	La Bella Napoli	F3
41	La Font del Gat	E5
42	Lascar 74	G3
43	Malamén	F3
44	Mano Rota	F3
45	Martínez	H4
46	Palo Cortao	G3
47	Pizza del Sortidor	F3
48	Quimet i Quimet	G3
49	Spice	F3
50	Taverna Can Margarit	E3
51	Tickets	E2
52	Xemei	E4
❼ **Drinking & Nightlife**	**(p196)**	
53	Abirradero	G3
54	Bar Calders	F2
55	Bar Olimpia	G2
56	El Rouge	G3
57	La Cambicha	F3
58	La Caseta del Migdia	E7
59	La Terrrazza	C4
60	Metro	B5
61	Pervert Club @ The One	C4
62	Redrum	F3
63	Sala Plataforma	G3
64	Tinta Roja	F3
❸ **Entertainment**	**(p198)**	
65	BARTS	G2
66	Gran Bodega Saltó	G3
67	Hiroshima	G3
68	Renoir Floridablanca	B6
69	Sala Apolo	H3
70	Teatre Grec	E4
71	Teatre Lliure	E4
72	Teatre Mercat De Les Flors	E4
❺ **Shopping**	**(p199)**	
73	10000 Records	E1
74	GI Joe	B6
75	Mercat de Sant Antoni	F1
76	Popcorn Store	F2
❸ **Sports & Activities**	**(p199)**	
77	Piscines Bernat Picornell	C5
❺ **Sleeping**	**(p220)**	
78	Hostal Cèntric	B6
79	Hotel Brummell	G3
80	Hotel Market	E1
81	Pars Tailor's Hostel	A6
82	Pars Teatro Hostel	H3

MONTJUÏC, POBLE SEC & SANT ANTONI

Key on p301

SANTS

Sants Estació

Plaça dels Països Catalans

Estació d'Autobusos de Sants

Hispano-Igualadina

Oficina d'Informació de Turisme de Barcelona

Estació Sants

Plaça de Joan Peiró

Parc de l'Espanya Industrial

20

C de Mundadas

C del Rector Triadó

C de Béjar

C de Tarragona

Tarragona

Parc de Joan Miró

19

C de València

C d'Aragó

C de Llança

See map p290

C del Consell de Cent

C de la Diputació

C d'Entença

Rocafort

C de Rocafort

Gran Via de les Corts Catalanes

Les Arenes

34

Av de Mistral

Plaça d'Osca

C de Gavà

C de Sants

Hostafrancs

C de la Creu Coberta

A1 Aerobús

Plaça d'Espanya

Av del Paral·lel

32

C de la Font Honrada

C de la Bordeta

Espanya

Av de la Reina Maria Cristina

Plaça de l'Univers

C de Lleida

C de Mèxic

Av de Rius i Taulet

C de Sant Fructuós

Gran Via de les Corts Catalanes

C de la Dàlia

Av del Marquès de Comillas

3

21

7

Plaça del Marquès de Foronda

Pg de les Cascades

Magòria La Campana

Av de Francesc Ferrer i Guàrdia

C de la Dàlia

23

8

59

61

Av dels Montanyans

Mirador del Palau Nacional

Museu Nacional d'Art de Catalunya

2

17

Plaça de Sant Jordi

Antic Jardí Botànic

Jardins de Joan Maragall

Inset

Av de l'Estadi

Piscines Bernat Picornell

14

Antic Jardí d'Aclimatació

77

Gran Via de les Corts Catalanes

C de Muntaner

60

C de Casanova

C de Sepúlveda

31

74

27

36

78

Ronda de Sant Antoni

35

C de Villarroel

68

81

0 ___ 200 m
0 ___ 0,1 miles

Pg de Minici Natal

Plaça d'Europa

Anella Olímpica

Plaça de Nemesi Ponsatí

6

C de Pierre de Coubertin

Palau Sant Jordi

Pg Olímpic

C dels Jocs de 92

Pg de la Zona Franca

Col·lecció de Carrosses Fúnebres (800m)

Parc del Migdia

Cementiri del Sud-Oest

5